LUTHER'S WORKS

LUTHER'S WORKS

VOLUME 26

LECTURES ON GALATIANS
1535

Chapters 1—4

JAROSLAV PELIKAN
Editor

WALTER A. HANSEN
Associate Editor

CONCORDIA PUBLISHING HOUSE · SAINT LOUIS

Contents

General Introduction

THE first editions of Luther's collected works appeared in the sixteenth century, and so did the first efforts to make him "speak English." In America serious attempts in these directions were made for the first time in the nineteenth century. The Saint Louis edition of Luther was the first endeavor on American soil to publish a collected edition of his works, and the Henkel Press in Newmarket, Virginia, was the first to publish some of Luther's writings in an English translation. During the first decade of the twentieth century, J. N. Lenker produced translations of Luther's sermons and commentaries in thirteen volumes. A few years later the first of the six volumes in the Philadelphia (or Holman) edition of the *Works of Martin Luther* appeared. Miscellaneous other works were published at one time or another. But a growing recognition of the need for more of Luther's works in English has resulted in this American edition of Luther's works.

The edition is intended primarily for the reader whose knowledge of late medieval Latin and sixteenth-century German is too small to permit him to work with Luther in the original languages. Those who can, will continue to read Luther in his original words as these have been assembled in the monumental Weimar edition (*D. Martin Luthers Werke*. Kritische Gesamtausgabe; Weimar, 1883 ff.). Its texts and helps have formed a basis for this edition, though in certain places we have felt constrained to depart from its readings and findings. We have tried throughout to translate Luther as he thought translating should be done. That is, we have striven for faithfulness on the basis of the best lexicographical materials available. But where literal accuracy and clarity have conflicted, it is clarity that we have preferred, so that sometimes paraphrase seemed more faithful than literal fidelity. We have proceeded in a similar way in the matter of Bible versions, translating Luther's translations. Where this could be done by the use of an existing English version — King James, Douay, or Revised Standard — we have done so. Where it could not, we have supplied our own. To indicate this in each specific instance would have been pedantic; to adopt a uniform procedure would have been artificial — especially in view of Luther's own inconsistency in this regard. In each volume the translator will be responsible primarily for matters of text and language, while the responsibility of the editor will extend principally to the historical and theological matters reflected in the introductions and notes.

Although the edition as planned will include fifty-five volumes, Luther's writings are not being translated in their entirety. Nor should they be. As he was the first to insist, much of what he wrote and said was not that important. Thus the edition is a selection of works that have proved their importance for the faith, life, and history of the Christian Church. The first thirty volumes contain Luther's expositions of various Biblical books, while the remaining volumes include what are usually called his "Reformation writings" and other occasional pieces. The final volume of the set will be an index voume; in addition to an index of quotations, proper names, and topics, and a list of corrections and changes, it will contain a glossary of many of the technical terms that recur in Luther's works and that cannot be defined each time they appear. Obviously Luther cannot be forced into any neat set of rubrics. He can provide his reader with bits of autobiography or with political observations as he expounds a psalm, and he can speak tenderly about the meaning of the faith in the midst of polemics against his opponents. It is the hope of publishers, editors, and translators that through this edition the message of Luther's faith will speak more clearly to the modern church.

J. P.
H. L.

Introduction to Volume 26

I F the Epistle of St. Paul to the Galatians is, as it has often been called, the Magna Charta of Christian liberty, then Luther's *Lectures on Galatians* of 1531 (1535) deserves to be called a declaration of Christian independence — of independence from the Law and from anything or anyone else except the God and Father of our Lord Jesus Christ. Characteristically, Luther described his relation to the epistle in more vivid terms. "The Epistle to the Galatians," he once said at table, "is my epistle, to which I am betrothed. It is my Katie von Bora." This volume contains the first four chapters of the *Lectures on Galatians*, which was originally published in 1535 (Weimar, XL-1; St. Louis, IX, 16-601). Luther's six lectures on the first chapter began on July 3, 1531, and ended on July 18. Between July 24 and August 21 he delivered his five lectures on chapter two. Chapter three required eleven lectures for its exposition; these began on August 22 and were concluded on October 10. Six more lectures were devoted to chapter four, from October 17 to November 14.

For the transcription of these lectures and for their expansion into printed form we are indebted to the tireless devotion of George Rörer, one of the first and certainly one of the best of Luther's editors. Veit Dietrich and Caspar Cruciger also helped to prepare the *Lectures*, but the principal effort was Rörer's. His notes have been preserved; they appear in the Weimar edition on the upper half of the page containing the printed version of the same material. Thus we are in the happy position of being able to compare the lectures (i. e., Rörer's *Kollegienheft*) and the book. (We have no such basis of comparison for many of the other commentaries but must rely on bits and pieces of manuscript evidence.) By consulting the notes we have been able to determine in several obscure passages what the intent of the printed text probably is. There are occasional editorial liberties and mollifications of the original language (cf. p. 228, note 42, for example); and Rörer makes complete sentences of individual phrases and even words. But any editor or translator of the *Lectures* who has also worked through the notes will have to agree with the judgment of Karl Drescher, the Weimar editor: "With each new examination, the work of Rörer, who has been so belittled and suspected, must appear ever purer and more selfless in relation to Luther and in the preservation of his intellectual substance." As Luther said in the comments he added to the *Lectures* (which will appear at the end of the *Lectures* in our edition), "I recognize that all the thoughts set down by the brethren with such care in this book are my own."

The *Lectures on Galatians* was one of the works of Luther to be translated into English during the sixteenth century, appearing in 1575 and again in 1578. This translation has been reissued in various printings, revisions, bowdlerizations, and modernizations, perhaps thirty in all; the most recent and the most satisfying was prepared by Philip Watson in 1953. But for the present edition we have executed a new translation, one that is couched in the language of the twentieth century, even though we have felt free to take over felicitous renderings of earlier translators; and we have added the identification of hundreds of citations from the Bible, the fathers, the classics, and medieval thought (although in this last case we have sometimes referred to texts that are readily available rather than to the ones that Luther had presumably consulted). Our translation is based on the first edition of Luther, that of 1535, while the others were based on the revised edition of 1538. The last two chapters of the *Lectures*, Luther's accompanying note, and the entire text of his earlier *Lectures* appear in Volume 27 of *Luther's Works*.   J. P.

LECTURES ON
GALATIANS
1535

Chapters 1–4

Translated by
JAROSLAV PELIKAN

WE have taken it upon ourselves in the Lord's name to lecture on this Epistle of Paul to the Galatians once more. This is not because we want to teach something new or unknown, for by the grace of God Paul is now very well known to you. But it is because, as I often warn you, there is a clear and present danger that the devil may take away from us the pure doctrine of faith and may substitute for it the doctrines of works and of human traditions. It is very necessary, therefore, that this doctrine of faith be continually read and heard in public. No matter how well known it may be or how carefully learned, the devil, our adversary, who prowls around and seeks to devour us (1 Peter 5:8), is not dead. Our flesh also goes on living. Besides, temptations of every sort attack and oppress us on every side. Therefore this doctrine can never be discussed and taught enough. If it is lost and perishes, the whole knowledge of truth, life, and salvation is lost and perishes at the same time. But if it flourishes, everything good flourishes — religion, true worship, the glory of God, and the right knowledge of all things and of all social conditions. To keep from doing nothing, we shall begin again where we broke off, according to the saying (Ecclus. 18:7): "When a man has finished, he is just beginning."

THE ARGUMENT OF ST. PAUL'S EPISTLE
TO THE GALATIANS

FIRST of all, we must speak of the argument, that is, of the issue with which Paul deals in this epistle. The argument is this: Paul wants to establish the doctrine of faith, grace, the forgiveness of sins or Christian righteousness, so that we may have a perfect knowledge and know the difference between Christian righteousness and all other kinds of righteousness. For righteousness is of many kinds. There is a political righteousness, which the emperor, the princes of the world, philosophers, and lawyers consider. There is also a ceremonial righteousness, which human traditions teach, as, for example, the traditions of the pope and other traditions. Parents and teachers may teach this righteousness without danger, because they do not attribute to it any power to make satisfaction for sin, to placate God, and to earn grace; but they teach that these ceremonies are necessary only for moral discipline and for certain observances. There is, in addition to these, yet another righteousness, the righteousness of the Law or of the Decalog, which Moses teaches. We, too, teach this, but after the doctrine of faith.

Over and above all these there is the righteousness of faith or Christian righteousness, which is to be distinguished most carefully from all the others. For they are all contrary to this righteousness, both because they proceed from the laws of emperors, the traditions of the pope, and the commandments of God, and because they consist in our works and can be achieved by us with "purely natural endowments," as the scholastics teach, or from a gift of God.[1] For these kinds of the righteousness of works, too, are gifts of God, as are all the things we have. But this most excellent righteousness, the righteousness of faith, which God imputes to us through Christ without works, is neither political nor ceremonial nor legal nor work-righteousness but is quite the opposite; it is a merely passive righteousness, while all the others, listed above,

---

[1] The Latin phrase is *ex puris naturalibus;* cf. *Luther's Works,* 2, p. 121, note 37. On the meaning of the phrase in high scholasticism cf. Thomas Aquinas, *Summa Theologica,* I—II, Q. 109, Art. 4.

are active. For here we work nothing, render nothing to God; we only receive and permit someone else to work in us, namely, God. Therefore it is appropriate to call the righteousness of faith or Christian righteousness "passive." This is a righteousness hidden in a mystery, which the world does not understand. In fact, Christians themselves do not adequately understand it or grasp it in the midst of their temptations. Therefore it must always be taught and continually exercised. And anyone who does not grasp or take hold of it in afflictions and terrors of conscience cannot stand. For there is no comfort of conscience so solid and certain as is this passive righteousness.

But such is human weakness and misery that in the terrors of conscience and in the danger of death we look at nothing except our own works, our worthiness, and the Law. When the Law shows us our sin, our past life immediately comes to our mind. Then the sinner, in his great anguish of mind, groans and says to himself: "Oh, how damnably I have lived![2] If only I could live longer! Then I would amend my life." Thus human reason cannot refrain from looking at active righteousness, that is, its own righteousness; nor can it shift its gaze to passive, that is, Christian righteousness, but it simply rests in the active righteousness. So deeply is this evil rooted in us, and so completely have we acquired this unhappy habit! Taking advantage of the weakness of our nature, Satan increases and aggravates these thoughts in us. Then it is impossible for the conscience to avoid being more seriously troubled, confounded, and frightened. For it is impossible for the human mind to conceive any comfort of itself, or to look only at grace amid its consciousness and terror of sin, or consistently to reject all discussion of works. To do this is beyond human power and thought. Indeed, it is even beyond the Law of God. For although the Law is the best of all things in the world, it still cannot bring peace to a terrified conscience but makes it even sadder and drives it to despair. For by the Law sin becomes exceedingly sinful (Rom. 7:13).

Therefore the afflicted conscience has no remedy against despair and eternal death except to take hold of the promise of grace offered in Christ, that is, this righteousness of faith, this passive or Christian

[2] A quotation from Bernard of Clairvaux, *Sermones in cantica*, Sermon XX, *Patrologia, Series Latina*, CLXXXIII, 867; cf. also *Luther's Works*, 22, p. 52, note 42.

righteousness, which says with confidence: "I do not seek active righteousness. I ought to have and perform it; but I declare that even if I did have it and perform it, I cannot trust in it or stand up before the judgment of God on the basis of it. Thus I put myself beyond all active righteousness, all righteousness of my own or of the divine Law, and I embrace only that passive righteousness which is the righteousness of grace, mercy, and the forgiveness of sins." In other words, this is the righteousness of Christ and of the Holy Spirit, which we do not perform but receive, which we do not have but accept, when God the Father grants it to us through Jesus Christ.

As the earth itself does not produce rain and is unable to acquire it by its own strength, worship, and power but receives it only by a heavenly gift from above, so this heavenly righteousness is given to us by God without our work or merit. As much as the dry earth of itself is able to accomplish in obtaining the right and blessed rain, that much can we men accomplish by our own strength and works to obtain that divine, heavenly, and eternal righteousness. Thus we can obtain it only through the free imputation and indescribable gift of God. Therefore the highest art and wisdom of Christians is not to know the Law, to ignore works and all active righteousness, just as outside the people of God the highest wisdom is to know and study the Law, works, and active righteousness.

It is a marvelous thing and unknown to the world to teach Christians to ignore the Law and to live before God as though there were no Law whatever. For if you do not ignore the Law and thus direct your thoughts to grace as though there were no Law but as though there were nothing but grace, you cannot be saved. "For through the Law comes knowledge of sin" (Rom. 3:20). On the other hand, works and the performance of the Law must be demanded in the world as though there were no promise or grace. This is because of the stubborn, proud, and hardhearted, before whose eyes nothing must be set except the Law, in order that they may be terrified and humbled. For the Law was given to terrify and kill the stubborn and to exercise the old man.[3] Both words must be correctly divided, according to the apostle (2 Tim. 2:25 ff.).

This calls for a wise and faithful father who can moderate the Law in such a way that it stays within its limits. For if I were to

[3] On the meaning of this term see *Luther's Works*, 24, p. 226.

[W, XL, 44, 45]

teach men the Law in such a way that they suppose themselves to be justified by it before God, I would be going beyond the limit of the Law, confusing these two righteousnesses, the active and the passive, and would be a bad dialectician who does not properly distinguish. But when I go beyond the old man, I also go beyond the Law. For the flesh or the old man, the Law and works, are all joined together. In the same way the spirit or the new man is joined to the promise and to grace. Therefore when I see that a man is sufficiently contrite, oppressed by the Law, terrified by sin, and thirsting for comfort, then it is time for me to take the Law and active righteousness from his sight and to set forth before him, through the Gospel, the passive righteousness which excludes Moses and the Law and shows the promise of Christ, who came for the afflicted and for sinners. Here a man is raised up again and gains hope. Nor is he any longer under the Law; he is under grace, as the apostle says (Rom. 6:14): "You are not under law but under grace." How not under law? According to the new man, to whom the Law does not apply. For the Law had its limits until Christ, as Paul says below (Gal. 3:24): "The Law, until Christ." When He came, Moses and the Law stopped. So did circumcision, sacrifices, and the Sabbath. So did all the prophets.

This is our theology, by which we teach a precise distinction between these two kinds of righteousness, the active and the passive, so that morality and faith, works and grace, secular society and religion may not be confused. Both are necessary, but both must be kept within their limits. Christian righteousness applies to the new man, and the righteousness of the Law applies to the old man, who is born of flesh and blood. Upon this latter, as upon an ass, a burden must be put that will oppress him. He must not enjoy the freedom of the spirit or of grace unless he has first put on the new man by faith in Christ, but this does not happen fully in this life. Then he may enjoy the kingdom and the ineffable gift of grace. I am saying this in order that no one may suppose that we reject or prohibit good works, as the papists falsely accuse us because they understand neither what they themselves are saying nor what we are teaching. They know nothing except the righteousness of the Law; and yet they claim the right to judge a doctrine that is far above and beyond the Law, a doctrine on which the carnal man is unable to pass judgment. Therefore it is inevitable that they be offended, for they cannot see any higher than the Law. Therefore whatever is above the Law is the greatest possible offense to them.

We set forth two worlds, as it were, one of them heavenly and the other earthly. Into these we place these two kinds of righteousness, which are distinct and separated from each other. The righteousness of the Law is earthly and deals with earthly things; by it we perform good works. But as the earth does not bring forth fruit unless it has first been watered and made fruitful from above — for the earth cannot judge, renew, and rule the heavens, but the heavens judge, renew, rule, and fructify the earth, so that it may do what the Lord has commanded — so also by the righteousness of the Law we do nothing even when we do much; we do not fulfill the Law even when we fulfill it. Without any merit or work of our own, we must first be justified by Christian righteousness, which has nothing to do with the righteousness of the Law or with earthly and active righteousness. But this righteousness is heavenly and passive. We do not have it of ourselves; we receive it from heaven. We do not perform it; we accept it by faith, through which we ascend beyond all laws and works. "As, therefore, we have borne the image of the earthly Adam," as Paul says, "let us bear the image of the heavenly one" (1 Cor. 15:49), who is a new man in a new world, where there is no Law, no sin, no conscience, no death, but perfect joy, righteousness, grace, peace, life, salvation, and glory.

Then do we do nothing and work nothing in order to obtain this righteousness? I reply: Nothing at all. For this righteousness means to do nothing, to hear nothing, and to know nothing about the Law or about works but to know and believe only this: that Christ has gone to the Father and is now invisible; that He sits in heaven at the right hand of the Father, not as a Judge but as one who has been made for us wisdom, righteousness, sanctification, and redemption from God (1 Cor. 1:30); in short, that He is our High Priest, interceding for us and reigning over us and in us through grace. Here one notices no sin and feels no terror or remorse of conscience. Sin cannot happen in this Christian righteousness; for where there is no Law, there cannot be any transgression (Rom. 4:15). If, therefore, sin does not have a place here, there is no conscience, no terror, no sadness. Therefore John says: "No one born of God commits sin" (1 John 3:9). But if there is any conscience or fear present, this is a sign that this righteousness has been withdrawn, that grace has been lost sight of, and that Christ is hidden and out of sight. But where Christ is truly seen, there there must be full and perfect joy in the Lord and peace of heart, where the heart declares: "Although I am a sinner according to the Law, judged by the righteousness of the Law, nevertheless I do not despair. I do not die, because Christ lives who is my righteousness and my eternal and heavenly life. In that righteousness and life I have no sin, conscience, and death. I am indeed a sinner according to the present life and its righteousness, as a son of Adam where the Law accuses me, death reigns and devours me. But above this life I have another righteousness, another life, which is Christ, the Son of God, who does not know sin and death but is righteousness and eternal life. For His sake this body of mine will be raised from the dead and delivered from the slavery of the Law and sin, and will be sanctified together with the spirit."

Thus as long as we live here, both remain. The flesh is accused, exercised, saddened, and crushed by the active righteousness of the Law. But the spirit rules, rejoices, and is saved by passive righteousness, because it knows that it has a Lord sitting in heaven at the right hand of the Father, who has abolished the Law, sin, and death, and has trodden all evils underfoot, has led them captive and triumphed over them in Himself (Col. 2:15). In this epistle, therefore, Paul is concerned to instruct, comfort, and sustain us diligently in a perfect knowledge of this most excellent and Christian righteousness. For if the doctrine of justification is lost, the whole of Christian doctrine is lost. And those in the world who do not teach it are either Jews or Turks or papists or sectarians. For between these two kinds of righteousness, the active righteousness of the Law and the passive righteousness of Christ, there is no middle ground. Therefore he who has strayed away from this Christian righteousness will necessarily relapse into the active righteousness; that is, when he has lost Christ, he must fall into a trust in his own works.

We see this today in the fanatical spirits and sectarians, who neither teach nor can teach anything correctly about this righteousness of grace. They have taken the words out of our mouth and out of our writings, and these only they speak and write. But the substance itself they cannot discuss, deal with, and urge, because they neither understand it nor can understand it. They cling only to the righteousness of the Law. Therefore they are and remain disciplinarians of works; nor can they rise beyond the active righteousness. Thus they remain exactly what they were under the pope.

To be sure, they invent new names and new works; but the content remains the same. So it is that the Turks perform different works from the papists, and the papists perform different works from the Jews, and so forth. But although some do works that are more splendid, great, and difficult than others, the content remains the same, and only the quality is different. That is, the works vary only in appearance and in name. For they are still works. And those who do them are not Christians; they are hirelings, whether they are called Jews, Mohammedans, papists, or sectarians.

Therefore we always repeat, urge, and inculcate this doctrine of faith or Christian righteousness, so that it may be observed by continuous use and may be precisely distinguished from the active righteousness of the Law. (For by this doctrine alone and through it alone is the church built, and in this it consists.) Otherwise we shall not be able to observe true theology but shall immediately become lawyers, ceremonialists, legalists, and papists. Christ will be so darkened that no one in the church will be correctly taught or comforted. Therefore if we want to be preachers and teachers of others, we must take great care in these issues and hold to this distinction between the righteousness of the Law and that of Christ. This distinction is easy to speak of; but in experience and practice it is the most difficult of all, even if you exercise and practice it diligently. For in the hour of death or in other conflicts of conscience these two kinds of righteousness come together more closely than you would wish or ask.

Therefore I admonish you, especially those of you who are to become instructors of consciences, as well as each of you individually, that you exercise yourselves by study, by reading, by meditation, and by prayer, so that in temptation you will be able to instruct consciences, both your own and others, console them, and take them from the Law to grace, from active righteousness to passive righteousness, in short, from Moses to Christ. In affliction and in the conflict of conscience it is the devil's habit to frighten us with the Law and to set against us the consciousness [4] of sin, our wicked past, the wrath and judgment of God, hell and eternal death, so that thus he may drive us into despair, subject us to himself, and pluck us from Christ. It is also his habit to set against us those passages in

---

[4] Here, as in some other passages in Luther's writings, the Latin word *conscientia* has the meaning "consciousness" rather than the more specific meaning "conscience."

[W, XL, 50, 51]

the Gospel in which Christ Himself requires works from us and with plain words threatens damnation to those who do not perform them. If here we cannot distinguish between these two kinds of righteousness; if here by faith we do not take hold of Christ, who is sitting at the right hand of God, who is our life and our righteousness, and who makes intercession for us miserable sinners before the Father (Heb. 7:25), then we are under the Law and not under grace, and Christ is no longer a Savior. Then He is a lawgiver. Then there can be no salvation left, but sure despair and eternal death will follow.

Therefore let us learn diligently this art of distinguishing between these two kinds of righteousness, in order that we may know how far we should obey the Law. We have said above that in a Christian the Law must not exceed its limits but should have its dominion only over the flesh, which is subjected to it and remains under it. When this is the case, the Law remains within its limits. But if it wants to ascend into the conscience and exert its rule there, see to it that you are a good dialectician and that you make the correct distinction. Give no more to the Law than it has coming, and say to it: "Law, you want to ascend into the realm of conscience and rule there. You want to denounce its sin and take away the joy of my heart, which I have through faith in Christ. You want to plunge me into despair, in order that I may perish. You are exceeding your jurisdiction. Stay within your limits, and exercise your dominion over the flesh. You shall not touch my conscience. For I am baptized; and through the Gospel I have been called to a fellowship of righteousness and eternal life, to the kingdom of Christ, in which my conscience is at peace, where there is no Law but only the forgiveness of sins, peace, quiet, happiness, salvation, and eternal life. Do not disturb me in these matters. In my conscience not the Law will reign, that hard tyrant and cruel disciplinarian, but Christ, the Son of God, the King of peace and righteousness, the sweet Savior and Mediator. He will preserve my conscience happy and peaceful in the sound and pure doctrine of the Gospel and in the knowledge of this passive righteousness."

When I have this righteousness within me, I descend from heaven like the rain that makes the earth fertile. That is, I come forth into another kingdom, and I perform good works whenever the opportunity arises. If I am a minister of the Word, I preach, I comfort the saddened, I administer the sacraments. If I am a father, I rule my household and family, I train my children in piety and honesty.

[W, XL, 51]

If I am a magistrate, I perform the office which I have received by divine command. If I am a servant, I faithfully tend to my master's affairs. In short, whoever knows for sure that Christ is his righteousness not only cheerfully and gladly works in his calling but also submits himself for the sake of love to magistrates, also to their wicked laws, and to everything else in this present life — even, if need be, to burden and danger. For he knows that God wants this and that this obedience pleases Him.

So far the argument of the epistle, which Paul sets forth because of the false teachers who had obscured this righteousness of faith among the Galatians. Against them he asserts his authority and office.

CHAPTER ONE

1. *Paul an apostle — not from men nor through man, but through Jesus Christ and God the Father, who raised Him from the dead —*

2. *and all the brethren who are with me.*

Now that we have set forth the argument and have shown the summary of this Epistle to the Galatians, it seems appropriate, before we come to the content itself, to indicate the occasion for Paul's composition of this epistle. He had planted the pure doctrine of the Gospel and the righteousness of faith among the Galatians. But immediately after his departure false teachers crept in; they subverted everything that he had planted and taught so well. For the devil cannot do otherwise than attack this doctrine vehemently, with might and with craft; nor does he rest as long as he sees even a spark of it remaining. We, too, merely because we preach the Gospel purely, suffer all sorts of evils both on the right hand and on the left from the world, the devil, and his apostles.

For the Gospel is a doctrine that teaches something far more sublime than the wisdom, righteousness, and religion of the world. It leaves these things at their proper level and commends them as good creatures of God. But the world prefers these creatures to the Creator. Finally, through them it wants to abolish sin, to be delivered from death, and to merit eternal life. This the Gospel condemns. But the world cannot bear the condemnation of that which it regards as best. Therefore it charges the Gospel with being a seditious and erroneous doctrine that subverts commonwealths, principalities, kingdoms, empires, and religions; it accuses the Gospel of sinning against God and Caesar, of abrogating the laws, of subverting morality, and of granting men the license to do with impunity whatever they please. With righteous zeal, therefore, and with the appearance of high service to God (John 16:2), the world persecutes this doctrine and despises its teachers and followers as the greatest plague there can be on earth.

[13]

By the proclamation of this doctrine, moreover, the devil is over-thrown, and his kingdom is cast down. From his hands are torn the Law, sin, and death; through these powerful and invincible tyrants he has subjugated the whole human race. In short, his prisoners are transferred from the kingdom of darkness into the kingdom of light and liberty (Col. 1:13). Is the devil supposed to stand for this? Is it not to be expected that the father of lies (John 8:44) will use all his wiles and power to obscure, corrupt, and eradicate this doctrine of salvation and eternal life? In fact, St. Paul complains in this and in all his other epistles that even in his day Satan was displaying his skill at this business through his apostles.

In our day, too, we complain and lament that Satan has done more damage to our Gospel by his servants, the fanatical spirits, than by all the tyrants, kings, princes, and bishops who have ever persecuted it and who go on persecuting it by force. If we had not been on our guard here in Wittenberg and worked so diligently to plant and teach this doctrine of faith, we would not have remained in harmony for so long; but sects would have arisen even in our midst long ago. But because we continue in this doctrine and never stop stressing it, it preserves us in the most complete unity and peace. Others, however, who either neglect it or seek to teach what they suppose is something more sublime, fall into various vicious errors and endless sects, and so they perish. It seemed good to us to show here in passing why the devil and the world are so spiteful against the Gospel, even though it is the Word of life and eternal salvation.

I have referred earlier in this epistle to the occasion for St. Paul's discussion of Christian righteousness, namely, that right after he had gone away false teachers among the Galatians had destroyed what he had built up so painstakingly. These false apostles, adherents of Judaism and of Pharisaism at that, were men of great prestige and authority. Among the people they boasted that they belonged to the holy and elect race of the Jews, that they were Israelites of the seed of Abraham, that the promises and the patriarchs belonged to them, finally that they were ministers of Christ and pupils of the apostles, whom they had known personally and whose miracles they had witnessed. They may even have performed some signs or miracles themselves, for Christ declares (Matt. 7:22) that the wicked also perform miracles. When men with such authority come into any country or city, the people immediately develop great admiration for them; and they fool even those who are educated and quite steadfast in the faith. They subvert the Galatians by saying: "Who is Paul anyway? After all, was he not the very last of those who were converted to Christ? But we are the pupils of the apostles, and we knew them intimately. We saw Christ perform miracles, and we heard Him preach. But Paul is a latecomer and is our inferior. It is impossible that God should permit us to fall into error, us who are His holy people, who are the ministers of Christ, and who have received the Holy Spirit. Besides, we are many, while Paul is only one. He did not know the apostles, nor has he seen Christ. In fact, he persecuted the church of Christ. Do you imagine that on account of Paul alone God would permit so many churches to be deceived?"

In our time, whenever the pope does not have the authority of the Scriptures on his side, he always uses this same single argument against us: "The church, the church! Do you suppose that God is so offended that for the sake of a few heretical Lutherans He will reject His whole church? Do you suppose that He would leave His church in error for so many centuries?" [5] With might and main he insists that the church can never be destroyed or overthrown. This argument persuades many people. With these and similar arguments these false apostles impressed the Galatians, so that Paul lost his authority among them and his doctrine came under suspicion.

In opposition to this boasting of the false apostles Paul boldly and with great παρρησία pits his apostolic authority, commends his calling, and defends his ministry. Although he does not do this anywhere else, he refuses to yield to anyone, even to the apostles themselves, much less to any of their pupils. To counteract their pharisaical pride and insolence, he refers to the events that took place in Antioch, where he withstood Peter himself. In addition, he pays no attention to the possible offense but says plainly in the text that he took it upon himself to reprove Peter himself, the prince of the apostles, who had seen Christ and had known Him intimately. "I am an apostle," he says, "and one who does not care what others are. Indeed, I did not shrink from reproving the very pillar of the other apostles."

Finally, in these first two chapters he does almost nothing else

<hr>

[5] See Luther's similar remarks in *Luther's Works*, 12, p. 265, and *Luther the Expositor*, p. 78, note 30.

but set forth his calling, his ministry, and his Gospel. He affirms
that it was not from men; that he had not received it from men but
from the revelation of Jesus Christ; and that if he or an angel from
heaven were to bring any gospel other than that which he had
preached, he should be accursed.

But what does Paul intend by this bragging? I reply: This doctrine
has as its purpose that every minister of the Word of God should be
sure of his calling. In the sight of both God and man he should
boldly glory that he preaches the Gospel as one who has been called
and sent. Thus the king's emissary boasts and glories that he does
not come as a private person but as the emissary of the king. Because
of this dignity as the king's emissary he is honored and given the
position of highest honor, which he would never receive if he were
to come as a private person. Therefore let the preacher of the
Gospel be sure that his calling is from God. It is perfectly proper
that he should follow Paul's example and exalt this calling of his,
so that he may gain credence and authority among the people. In
the same way the king's emissary elevates his office and calling.
To glory this way is not vain but necessary; for he does not glory in
himself but in the king who has sent him and whose authority he
seeks to have honored and elevated. When, in the name of the king,
he wants something to be done by his subjects, he does not say,
"We request," but, "We command, we want this to be done." But
as a private person he says, "We request."

In the same way, when Paul commends his calling so highly, he
is not arrogantly seeking his own praise, as some people suppose;
he is elevating his ministry with a necessary and a holy pride. Thus
he says also to the Romans (11:13): "Inasmuch as I am an apostle
to the Gentiles, I magnify my ministry." That is to say: "I want
men to receive me, not as Paul of Tarsus but as Paul the apostle or
ambassador of Jesus Christ." He has to do this to maintain his
authority, so that those who hear this may be more attentive and
more willing to listen to him. For they are not listening to Paul;
but in Paul they are listening to Christ Himself and to God the
Father, who sends him forth. Just as men should devoutly honor
the authority and majesty of God, so they should reverently receive
and listen to His messengers, who bring His Word.

Accordingly, this is a noteworthy passage; for here Paul makes
such a boast of his calling that he despises all the others. If someone

were to follow the normal human pattern and despise all others on his own behalf and attribute everything to himself alone, this would be the height of awkwardness, foolishness, and sin. But this style of boasting is necessary. It has to do, not with the glory of Paul or with our glory but with the glory of God; and by it the sacrifice of praise and thanksgiving is offered up to Him. For by such boasting the name of God is disclosed to the world. Therefore he opens his Epistle to the Galatians as follows:

1. *Paul an apostle — not from men, etc.*

At the very outset Paul deals with those false teachers. They claimed to be the pupils of the apostles, sent by them; and they despised Paul as one who was neither the pupil of the apostles nor sent by them to preach the Gospel but had entered in some other way and had intruded himself upon the ministry on his own initiative. Against them Paul defends his calling and says: "Your preachers look down on my calling. But whoever it is that has come to you, he is sent either from men or through man; that is, he has either entered on his own, without a call, or has been called by someone else. But my calling is not from men or through man; it is superior to any calling that can come after the apostles. For it is 'through Jesus Christ and God the Father.'"

When Paul says "from men," I take this to refer to those who call and intrude themselves, when neither God nor man calls or sends them, but who run and speak on their own. Today the sectarians do this. Either they lurk in corners, look for some place to spew forth their venom, and do not come into public churches; or they go where the Gospel has already been planted. These I call "from men." But when he says "through man," I take this to refer to those who have a divine calling, but one that has come through man.

God calls in two ways, either by means or without means. Today He calls all of us into the ministry of the Word by a mediated call, that is, one that comes through means, namely, through man. But the apostles were called immediately by Christ Himself, as the prophets in the Old Testament had been called by God Himself. Afterwards the apostles called their disciples, as Paul called Timothy, Titus, etc. These men called bishops, as in Titus 1:5 ff.; and the bishops called their successors down to our own time, and so on to the end of the world. This is a mediated calling, since it is done by man. Nevertheless, it is divine.

Thus when someone is called by a prince or a magistrate or me, he has his calling through man. Since the time of the apostles this has been the usual method of calling in the world. It should not be changed; it should be exalted, on account of the sectarians, who despise it and lay claim to another calling, by which they say that the Spirit drives them to teach. But they are liars and impostors, for they are being driven by a spirit who is not good but evil. It is not lawful for me to forsake my assigned station as a preacher, to go to another city where I have no call, and to preach there.[6] (As a doctor of divinity, of course, I could preach throughout the papacy, provided that they let me.)[7] I have no right to do this even if I hear that false doctrine is being taught and that souls are being seduced and condemned which I could rescue from error and condemnation by my sound doctrine. But I should commit the matter to God, who in His own time will find the opportunity to call ministers lawfully and to give the Word. For He is the Lord of the harvest who will send laborers into His harvest; our task is to pray (Matt. 9:38).

Therefore we should not intrude into someone else's harvest, as the devil does through his sectarians. With ardent zeal they claim to be saddened that men are being so miserably led astray, and to want to teach them the truth and rescue them from the devil's clutches. Therefore even when a man seeks, with pious zeal and good intentions, to rescue with his sound doctrine those who have been led astray into error, this is still a bad example, which gives ungodly teachers an excuse to intrude themselves, after which Satan himself occupies the see. This example does a great deal of damage.

But when the prince or some other magistrate calls me, then, with firm confidence, I can boast against the devil and the enemies of the Gospel that I have been called by the command of God through the voice of a man; for the command of God comes through the mouth of the prince, and this is a genuine call. Therefore we, too, have been called by divine authority — not by Christ immediately, as the apostles were, but "through man."

Now this doctrine of the certainty of the call is extremely necessary on account of the pernicious and demonic spirits. Every minister

---

[6] This was Luther's consistent position in opposition to the "sectarians," who claimed the right to preach anywhere; cf. *Luther's Works*, 13, p. 65, note 39.

[7] Luther's theological doctorate was an important support for his work as a Reformer; see *Luther the Expositor*, pp. 46—47.

of the Word may boast with John the Baptist (Luke 3:2): "The Word of the Lord has come upon me." Therefore when I preach, baptize, or administer the sacraments, I do so as one who has a command and a call. For the voice of the Lord has come to me, not in some corner, as the sectarians boast, but through the mouth of a man who is carrying out his lawful right. But if one or two citizens were to ask me to preach, I should not follow such a private call; for this would open the window to the ministers of Satan, who would follow this example and work harm, as we have said above. But when those who are in public office ask me, then I should obey.

Therefore when Paul says "not from men nor through man," he is knocking down the false apostles. It is as though he were saying: "No matter how much these vipers may brag, of what more can they brag than that they have come either 'from men,' that is, on their own, without any call, or 'through man,' that is, being sent by someone else? I am not concerned about any of this; nor should you be. But as for me, I have been called and sent neither from men nor through man but immediately, that is, by Jesus Christ Himself. In every way my call is like that of the apostles, and I am indeed an apostle." Therefore Paul deals thoroughly with this doctrine of the call of the apostles. Elsewhere he distinguishes between apostleship and other ministries, as in 1 Cor. 12:28 ff. and in Eph. 4:11, where he says: "And God has ordained some in the church as apostles, prophets, etc." He puts apostles into first place, so that those may properly be called apostles who have been sent immediately by God Himself without any other person as the means. Thus Matthias was called by God alone; for when the other apostles had chosen two men, they did not dare decide between them but cast lots and prayed God to indicate whom He preferred (Acts 1:23-26). Since he was to be an apostle, it was necessary that he be called by God. Thus Paul was called to be the apostle to the Gentiles (Rom. 11:13). This is why the apostles are called saints; for they are sure of their calling and doctrine and have remained faithful in their ministry, and no one of them has become an apostate except Judas, because their call is a holy one.

This is the first attack Paul makes against the false apostles, who ran when no one sent them. The call, therefore, is not to be despised. For it is not sufficient if a man has the Word and the pure doctrine. He must also have the assurance of his call, and whoever enters without this assurance enters only in order to kill and destroy (John

10:10). For God never prospers the work of those who are not called. Even if they teach something good and useful, it does not edify. Thus in our time the sectarians [8] have the vocabulary of faith in their mouths, but they do not produce any fruit. Their chief aim is to attract men to their false opinions. To remain in their saving task, those who have a sure and holy call must often bear many severe conflicts, as must those whose teaching is pure and sound, against the devil with his constant and endless wiles and against the world with its attacks. In these conflicts what is one to do whose call is unsure and whose doctrine is corrupt?

Therefore we who are in the ministry of the Word have this comfort, that we have a heavenly and holy office; being legitimately called to this, we prevail over all the gates of hell (Matt. 16:18). On the other hand, it is dreadful when the conscience says: "You have done this without a call!" Here a man without a call is shaken by such terror that he wishes he had never heard the Word he preaches. For by his disobedience he sullies all his works, regardless of how good they are, so that even his greatest works and deeds become his greatest sins.

Thus you see how necessary it is to boast and glory in our ministry this way. In the past, when I was only a young theologian and doctor, I thought it was imprudent of Paul in his epistle to boast of his call so often. But I did not understand his purpose, for I did not know that the ministry of the Word of God was so weighty a matter. I did not know anything about the doctrine of faith and a true conscience. In the schools and churches no certainty was being taught, but everything was filled with the sophistic trifles and nursery rhymes of the canonists and commentators on the *Sentences*.[9] Therefore no one could understand how forceful and powerful is this holy and spiritual boasting about a call, which serves first to the glory of God, secondly to the advancement of our own ministry, and also to our own benefit and to that of the people. When we boast this way, we are not looking for prestige in the world or praise from men or money, or for pleasure or the good will of the world. The reason for our proud boasting is that we are in a divine calling and in God's own work, and that the people need

---

[8] Luther's Latinized German word here is *Rottenses*.

[9] The *sententiarii* were the commentators on the *Sentences* of Peter Lombard, of whom Luther himself had been one; cf. *Luther's Works*, 14, p. 286, note 13.

to be assured of our calling, in order that they may know that our word is in fact the Word of God. This, then, is not a vain pride; it is a most holy pride against the devil and the world. And it is a true humility in the sight of God.

And through God the Father, who raised Him from the dead.

So passionate is Paul's zeal here that he cannot restrain himself until he comes to the issue itself, but here in the very title of his epistle he erupts and speaks what he has in his heart. His purpose in this epistle is to discuss and to defend the righteousness that comes by faith,[10] and to refute the Law and the righteousness that comes by works. He is filled with thoughts like these, and out of this marvelous and overflowing abundance of the excellent wisdom and knowledge of Christ in his heart his mouth speaks (Matt. 12:34). This flame, this raging fire in his heart, cannot be hidden; and it will not let him be silent. Therefore he says: "through God the Father, who raised Him from the dead."

The addition of these words, "and through God the Father, etc.," seems to be superfluous. But because, as I have said, he is speaking from the abundance of his heart, his mind is aflame with the yearning to express, even at the very beginning of his epistle, the unsearchable riches of Christ (Eph. 3:8) and to preach the righteousness of God, which is called the resurrection of the dead. Christ, who lives and has been raised from the dead, is speaking through him and prompting him to speak this way. Therefore he calls God "the Father, who raised Jesus Christ from the dead." It is as though he were to say: "I have to contend with Satan and with those vipers, Satan's instruments, who are trying to rob me of the righteousness of Christ, who was raised from the dead by God the Father. By this righteousness alone we are justified, and by it we shall also be raised from death to eternal life on the Last Day. But those who are trying to undermine the righteousness of Christ are resisting the Father as well as the Son and the work of both of Them."

Thus at the very outset Paul explodes with the entire issue he intends to set forth in this epistle. He refers to the resurrection of Christ, who rose again for our justification (Rom. 4:25). His

10 We have translated *iustitia fidei* this way in accordance with Luther's translation of it as *die Gerechtigkeit, die vor Gott gilt.*

victory is a victory over the Law, sin, our flesh, the world, the devil, death, hell, and all evils; and this victory of His He has given to us. Even though these tyrants, our enemies, accuse us and terrify us, they cannot drive us into despair or condemn us. For Christ, whom God the Father raised from the dead, is the Victor over them, and He is our righteousness. Therefore "thanks be to God, who has given us the victory through our Lord Jesus Christ" (1 Cor. 15:57). Amen.

But note how Paul speaks to the point here. He does not say: "Through God, who has made heaven and earth, who is the Lord of angels, who sent Moses to Pharaoh, who brought Israel up out of Egypt," as did the false prophets, who boasted of the God of their fathers, the Creator and Preserver of all things, doing wonders among His people. No, Paul had something else in his heart, namely, the righteousness of Christ, which he taught and defended as Christ's apostle. Therefore he uses words that contribute to this. He says: "I am an apostle — not from men or through man but through Jesus Christ and God the Father, who raised Him from the dead." You see, then, how fervently Paul's spirit is led in this issue, which he proceeds to establish and maintain against the entire kingdom of hell, against the powerful and the wise of the whole world, and against the devil with his apostles.

2. And all the brethren who are with me.

This helps to stop the mouths of these false apostles, for it is the purpose of all his arguments to enhance and exalt his ministry and to discredit theirs. It is as though he were saying: "It is indeed sufficient that by a divine call I have been sent as an apostle through Jesus Christ and God the Father. Yet in order not to stand alone, I add all the brethren — even though I do not have to — who are not apostles but comrades in arms. They are writing this epistle as well as I, and they are bearing witness with me that my doctrine is true and divine. Therefore we are sure that Christ is present in our midst, and that here and in our church He is teaching and speaking. So far as the false apostles are concerned, if they are anything at all, they have only been sent from men or through man; but I have been sent from God the Father and from Jesus Christ, who is our life and resurrection (John 11:25). My other brethren have been sent from God, although by man, that is, by me. There-

[W, XL, 66—68]

fore to avoid the impression that I set myself proudly against so
many all by myself, I have my brethren with me — all of one mind,
as faithful witnesses who think, write, and teach exactly what I do."
So far the signature; now comes the address.

To the churches of Galatia.

Paul had preached throughout Galatia. Although he had not
entirely converted it to Christ, he still had many churches there,
into which the false apostles, the devil's ministers, had sneaked.

Thus in our time the fanatics do not come to those places where
the enemies of the Gospel have the upper hand but to those where
there are Christians and good people, who love the Gospel. They
insinuate themselves among such people, even in the territories of
the tyrants and persecutors of the Gospel. Sneaking into houses
under false pretenses, they spew out their venom and undermine
the faith of the common people. But why do they not rather go
into the cities, countries, and territories of the papists and confess
and support their doctrine there before evil princes, bishops, and
theologians in the universities, as we have done by the grace of
God? These precious martyrs are not willing to take any chances
but move into places where the Gospel has already established itself
and where they can live without danger and in great tranquility.
Thus the false apostles would not run the risk of going to Caiaphas
in Jerusalem or to the emperor in Rome or to some other place
where no one had ever preached before, as Paul and the others did.
Instead, they came to Galatia, which had already been gained and
prepared for Christ by the toil and trouble of Paul, and into Asia,
into Corinth, where there were good men and Christians who were
not persecuting anyone but were suffering everything quietly. There
the enemies of the cross of Christ could live in great smugness,
without undergoing any persecution.

Here you should learn that pious preachers have this lot in life.
In addition to the persecution that they have to endure from the
wicked and ungrateful world and the hard labor that they experience
in planting churches, they are forced to see the quick overthrow of
what they had taught for so long in its purity, at the hands of the
fanatics, who thereupon lord it over them and get the upper hand.
This causes more anguish for godly ministers than any persecution
by tyrants. Therefore let anyone who is reluctant to bear such contempt and reproach not become a minister of the Gospel; or if he

is one, let him turn over his ministry to someone else. As you see, we today are despised and troubled — outwardly by tyrants, inwardly by those whom we have liberated with the Gospel, as well as by false brethren. But this is our comfort and glory: being called by God, we have a promise of eternal life, and we look for that reward which "no eye has seen, nor ear heard, nor the heart of man conceived" (1 Cor. 2:9). For when Christ, the chief Shepherd, is manifested, we shall obtain the unfading crown of glory (1 Peter 5:4); and even in this world He will not let us starve.

Jerome raises an important question here: Why does Paul call "churches" those that were not churches? For Paul, he says, is writing to the Galatians, who had been led astray and turned away from Christ and from grace to Moses and the Law.[11] I reply: When Paul calls them the "churches of Galatia," he is employing synecdoche, a very common practice in the Scriptures.[12] Writing in a similar vein to the Corinthians, he congratulates them that the grace of God was given them in Christ, that is, that they were enriched in Him with all speech and all knowledge (1 Cor. 1:4-5). And yet many of them had been perverted by false apostles and did not believe in the resurrection of the dead, etc. So today we still call the Church of Rome holy and all its sees holy, even though they have been undermined and their ministers are ungodly. For God "rules in the midst of His foes" (Ps. 110:2), Antichrist "takes his seat in the temple of God" (2 Thess. 2:4), and Satan is present among the sons of God (Job 1:6). Even if the church is "in the midst of a crooked and perverse generation," as Paul says to the Philippians (2:15), and even if it is surrounded by wolves and robbers, that is, spiritual tyrants, it is still the church. Although the city of Rome is worse than Sodom and Gomorrah, nevertheless there remain in it Baptism, the Sacrament, the voice and text of the Gospel, the Sacred Scriptures, the ministries, the name of Christ, and the name of God. Whoever has these, has them; whoever does not have them, has no excuse, for the treasure is still there. Therefore the Church of Rome is holy, because it has the holy name of God, the Gospel, Baptism, etc. If these are present among a people, that people is called holy. Thus this Wittenberg of ours is a holy village, and we are truly holy, because we have been baptized, communed, taught, and called

---

[11] Jerome, *Commentarius in Epistolam S. Pauli ad Galatas*, I, *Patrologia, Series Latina*, XXVI, 337.

[12] Cf. *Luther's Works*, 1, p. 195, note 42.

by God; we have the works of God among us, that is, the Word
and the sacraments, and these make us holy.

I say this in order that we may distinguish sharply between
Christian holiness and other kinds of holiness. The monks called
their orders holy, although they did not dare call themselves holy;
but they are not holy, because, as we said above, Christian holiness
is not active but passive.[13] Therefore let no one call himself holy
on the basis of his way of life or of his works — fasting, prayer,
flagellation, almsgiving, or the consolation of the sad and afflicted.
Otherwise the Pharisee in Luke (18:11 ff.) would be holy too. Such
works, of course, are holy, and God strictly demands them of us;
but they do not make us holy. You and I are holy; the church, the
city, and the people are holy — not on the basis of their own holiness
but on the basis of a holiness not their own, not by an active holiness,
but by a passive holiness. They are holy because they possess something that is divine and holy, namely, the calling of the ministry, the
Gospel, Baptism, etc., on the basis of which they are holy.

Therefore even though the Galatians had been led astray, Baptism,
the Word, and the name of Christ still continued among them. Besides,
there were still some good men who had not defected from Paul's
doctrine and who had a proper understanding of the Word and the
sacraments, which could not be defiled by those who did rebel.
For Baptism, the Gospel, etc., do not become unholy because I am
defiled and unholy and have a false understanding of them. On the
contrary, they remain holy and exactly what they were, regardless
of whether they are among the godly or the ungodly; men can neither
defile them nor hallow them. By our good or evil behavior, by our
good or evil life and morals, they are defiled or hallowed in the sight
of the Gentiles (Rom. 2:24) but not in the sight of God. Therefore
the church is holy even where the fanatics are dominant, so long
as they do not deny the Word and the sacraments; if they deny
these, they are no longer the church. Wherever the substance of
the Word and the sacraments abides, therefore, there the holy
church is present, even though Antichrist may reign there; for he
takes his seat not in a stable of fiends or in a pigpen or in a congre-
gation of unbelievers but in the highest and holiest place possible, namely, in the temple of God (2 Thess. 2:4). Thus our brief
answer to this question is this: The church is universal throughout

13 See p. 4.

the world, wherever the Gospel of God and the sacraments are present. The Jews, the Turks, and the fanatics are not the church, because they oppose and deny these things. Now there follows the salutation.

3. *Grace to you and peace from God the Father and our Lord Jesus Christ.*

I hope that you are not ignorant of the meaning of "grace" and "peace," since these terms occur frequently in Paul and are easy to understand. But since we are taking it upon ourselves to expound this epistle — something we are doing, not because it is necessary or because the epistle is very difficult but in order to confirm our consciences against future heresies — it should not bore you if we repeat here what we teach, preach, sing, and write at other times and places. For if we lose the doctrine of justification, we lose simply everything. Hence the most necessary and important thing is that we teach and repeat this doctrine daily, as Moses says about his Law (Deut. 6:7). For it cannot be grasped or held enough or too much. In fact, though we may urge and inculcate it vigorously, no one grasps it perfectly or believes it with all his heart. So frail is our flesh and so disobedient to the Spirit!

The apostle's greeting is new to the world and had never been heard before the proclamation of the Gospel. Grace and peace — these two words embrace the whole of Christianity. Grace forgives sin, and peace stills the conscience. The two devils who plague us are sin and conscience, the power of the Law and the sting of sin (1 Cor. 15:56). But Christ has conquered these two monsters and trodden them underfoot, both in this age and in the age to come. The world does not know this; therefore it cannot teach anything sure about how to overcome sin, conscience, and death. Only Christians have this kind of teaching and are equipped and armed with it, so that they can overcome sin, despair, and eternal death. It is a teaching that is given only by God; it does not proceed from free will, nor was it invented by human reason or wisdom.

These two words, "grace" and "peace," contain a summary of all of Christianity. Grace contains the forgiveness of sins, a joyful peace, and a quiet conscience. But peace is impossible unless sin has first been forgiven, for the Law accuses and terrifies the conscience on account of sin. And the sin that the conscience feels cannot be removed by pilgrimages, vigils, labors, efforts, vows, or any other works; in fact, sin is increased by works. The more we work and sweat to extricate ourselves from sin, the worse off we are. For there is no way to remove sin except by grace. This deserves careful notice. For the words are easy; but in temptation it is the hardest thing possible to be surely persuaded in our hearts that we have the forgiveness of sins and peace with God by grace alone, entirely apart from any other means in heaven or on earth.

Because the world does not understand this doctrine, it neither can nor will tolerate it. It brags about free will, about our powers, about our works — all these as means by which to earn and attain grace and peace, that is, the forgiveness of sins and a joyful conscience. But the conscience cannot be quiet and joyful unless it has peace through this grace, that is, through the forgiveness of sins promised in Christ. Many have worked hard, inventing various religious orders and disciplines, to find peace and a quiet conscience; but instead they have plunged even more deeply into even greater misery, for such tactics are merely ways of multiplying doubt and despair. Therefore your bones and mine will know no rest until we hear the Word of grace and cling to it firmly and faithfully.

The apostle clearly distinguishes this grace and peace from any other kind of grace and peace. He wishes the Galatians grace and peace — not from Caesar or from kings and princes, for these usually persecute the pious and rise up against the Lord and against His Christ (Ps. 2:1); nor from the world, for "in the world," Christ said, "you have tribulation" (John 16:33); but from God our Father. In other words, he wishes them a heavenly peace. So Christ says: "Peace I leave with you; My peace I give to you; not as the world gives do I give to you" (John 14:27).

The world's peace grants nothing except the peace of our property and of our bodies, so that we can live happily and peacefully in the flesh; and the world's grace permits us to enjoy our property and does not deprive us of our possessions. But in trouble and in the hour of death the grace and peace of the world cannot help us or deliver us from trouble, despair, and death. But when the grace and peace of God are present, a man is so strong that he can bear both the cross and peace, both joy and sorrow. He is heartened by the victory that comes from the death of Christ. In his conscience the assurance of this victory begins to prevail over sin and death, for he has the guarantee of the forgiveness of sins. Once he has received this forgiveness, his conscience is gladdened and consoled. Thus when a man is consoled and encouraged by the grace of God — that is, by the forgiveness of sins and the peace of conscience — he can bravely endure and overcome all troubles, including even death itself. This peace of God is given only to those who believe and not to the world, for the world neither desires it nor understands it. And the only way it comes is by the grace of God alone.

But why does the apostle add "and from our Lord Jesus Christ"? Did it not suffice to say "from God the Father"? Why does he link Jesus Christ with the Father? You have often heard from us that it is a rule and principle in the Scriptures, and one that must be scrupulously observed, to refrain from speculation about the majesty of God, which is too much for the human body, and especially for the human mind, to bear. "Man shall not see Me and live," says Scripture (Ex. 33:20).[14] The pope, the Turks, the Jews, and all the sectarians pay no attention to this rule. They put Christ the Mediator out of their sight, speak only of God, pray only to Him, and act only in relation to Him. The monk, for example, imagines this to himself: "The works I am doing are pleasing to God. God will look upon my vows, and on their account He will grant me salvation." The Turk says: "If I live this way and bathe this way, God will accept me and give me eternal life." The Jew thinks to himself: "If I obey the Law of Moses, I shall find God gracious to me, and so I shall be saved." Thus the fanatics of our time boast about the Spirit, visions, and I do not know what other monstrous things; they go around in miracles beyond their comprehension. These new monks[15] invent a new cross and new works, and they imagine that by performing these they will please God. In short, whoever does not know the doctrine of justification takes away Christ the Propitiator.

But true Christian theology, as I often warn you, does not present God to us in His majesty, as Moses and other teachings do, but Christ born of the Virgin as our Mediator and High Priest. Therefore when we are embattled against the Law, sin, and death in the presence of God, nothing is more dangerous than to stray into heaven with our idle speculations, there to investigate God in

[14] On this use of Ex. 33 against speculation see the references in *Luther's Works*, 22, p. 157, note 125.

[15] Luther frequently linked the Anabaptists with the monks of the Middle Ages as wearers of "gray coats"; cf., for example, *Luther's Works*, 22, p. 190, note 150.

[W, XL, 77, 78]

His incomprehensible power, wisdom, and majesty, to ask how He created the world and how He governs it. If you attempt to comprehend God this way and want to make atonement to Him apart from Christ the Mediator, making your works, fasts, cowl, and tonsure the mediation between Him and yourself, you will inevitably fall, as Lucifer did (Is. 14:12), and in horrible despair lose God and everything. For as in His own nature God is immense, incomprehensible, and infinite, so to man's nature He is intolerable. Therefore if you want to be safe and out of danger to your conscience and your salvation, put a check on this speculative spirit. Take hold of God as Scripture instructs you (1 Cor. 1:21, 24): "Since, in wisdom, the world did not know God through wisdom, it pleased God through the folly of what we preach to save those who believe. We preach Christ crucified, a stumbling block to Jews and folly to Gentiles, but to those who are called, both Jews and Greeks, Christ the power of God and the wisdom of God." Therefore begin where Christ began — in the Virgin's womb, in the manger, and at His mother's breasts. For this purpose He came down, was born, lived among men, suffered, was crucified, and died, so that in every possible way He might present Himself to our sight. He wanted us to fix the gaze of our hearts upon Himself and thus to prevent us from clambering into heaven and speculating about the Divine Majesty.

Therefore whenever you consider the doctrine of justification and wonder how or where or in what condition to find a God who justifies or accepts sinners, then you must know that there is no other God than this Man Jesus Christ. Take hold of Him; cling to Him with all your heart, and spurn all speculation about the Divine Majesty; for whoever investigates the majesty of God will be consumed by His glory. I know from experience what I am talking about. But these fanatics, who deal with God apart from this Man, will not believe me. Christ Himself says: "I am the Way, and the Truth, and the Life; no one comes to the Father, but by Me" (John 14:6). Outside Christ, the Way, therefore, you will find no other way to the Father; you will find only wandering, not truth, but hypocrisy and lies, not life, but eternal death. Take note, therefore, in the doctrine of justification or grace that when we all must struggle with the Law, sin, death, and the devil, we must look at no other God than this incarnate and human God.

But when you leave the doctrine of justification and have to engage in controversy with Jews, Turks, or sectarians, etc., about the

power, wisdom, etc., of God, then you must use all your cleverness
and effort and be as profound and subtle a controversialist as possible;
for then you are in another area. But when it comes to the conscience,
to righteousness and life (which I want to be noted carefully here)
against the Law, sin, death, and the devil; or when it comes to satisfaction for sin, the forgiveness of sins, reconciliation, and eternal
salvation, then you must disabuse your mind completely of all
speculation and investigation into the majesty of God, and you
must pay attention only to this Man, who presents Himself to us
as the Mediator and says: "Come to Me, all who labor, etc."
(Matt. 11:28). When you do this, you will see the love, the goodness, and the sweetness of God. You will see His wisdom, His
power, and His majesty sweetened and mitigated to your ability
to stand it. And in this lovely picture you will find everything, as
Paul says to the Colossians: "In Christ are hid all the treasures of
wisdom and knowledge" (2:3); and "In Him the whole fullness
of deity dwells bodily" (2:9). The world does not see this, because
it looks at Him only as a man in His weakness.

This is why Paul makes such a frequent practice of linking
Jesus Christ with God the Father, to teach us what is the true
Christian religion. It does not begin at the top, as all other religions
do; it begins at the bottom. It bids us climb up by Jacob's ladder;
God Himself leans on it, and its feet touch the earth, right by Jacob's
head (Gen. 28:12). Therefore whenever you are concerned to think
and act about your salvation, you must put away all speculations
about the Majesty, all thoughts of works, traditions, and philosophy — indeed, of the Law of God itself. And you must run directly
to the manger and the mother's womb, embrace this Infant and
Virgin's Child in your arms, and look at Him — born, being nursed,
growing up, going about in human society, teaching, dying, rising
again, ascending above all the heavens, and having authority over
all things. In this way you can shake off all terrors and errors, as
the sun dispels the clouds. This vision will keep you on the proper
way, so that you may follow where Christ has gone. When Paul
wishes grace and peace not only from God the Father but also
from Jesus Christ, therefore, this is what should be noted first.

The second thing that Paul teaches us here is a substantiation of
our faith that Christ is true God. Statements like this about the
divinity of Christ should be assembled and carefully noted, not
only against the Arians and other sectarians past or future but also

for the substantiation of our own faith. For until our death Satan will never stop attacking all the doctrines of the Creed in us. He is the implacable enemy of faith, for he knows that it is the victory that overcomes the world (1 John 5:4). Therefore it is our obligation to hold constantly to our faith and to establish it, in order that we may be able to stand up to Satan.

The true deity of Christ is proved by this conclusion: Paul attributes to Him the ability to grant the very same things that the Father does — grace, peace of conscience, the forgiveness of sins, life, and victory over sin, death, the devil, and hell. This would be illegitimate, in fact, sacrilegious, if Christ were not true God. For no one grants peace unless he himself has it in his hands. But since Christ grants it, He must have it in His hands.

Christ gives grace and peace, not as the apostles did, by preaching the Gospel, but as its Author and Creator. The Father creates and gives life, grace, peace, etc.; the Son creates and gives the very same things. To give grace, peace, eternal life, the forgiveness of sins, justification, life, and deliverance from death and the devil — these are the works, not of any creature but only of the Divine Majesty. The angels can neither create these things nor grant them. Therefore these works belong only to the glory of the sovereign Majesty, the Maker of all things. And since Paul attributes the very same power to create and give all this to Christ just as much as to the Father, it follows necessarily that Christ is truly God by nature.

Many such arguments appear in John, where it is proved and concluded from the works ascribed to the Son as well as to the Father that the deity of the Father and of the Son is one. Therefore the gifts we receive from the Father are no other than those we receive from the Son; the same things come both from the Father and the Son. Otherwise Paul would have spoken otherwise and would have said: "Grace from God the Father, and peace from our Lord Jesus Christ." But by knitting them together he attributes them equally to Christ and to the Father.

I am warning you about this matter so earnestly on account of the danger that, amid the many errors and various sects today, some Arians, Eunomians, Macedonians, and other such heretics might arise and damage the churches with their subtlety. The Arians were truly sharp. They conceded that Christ has a double nature and that He is called "God of true God" — but only in name. Christ, they said, is a most noble and perfect creature, higher than the angels; through Him God then created heaven and earth and everything else. Thus Mohammed also speaks of Christ in a laudatory way. But all this is nothing but fallacious reasoning and words that are pleasant and reasonable, by which the fanatics deceive men unless they are careful. But Paul speaks of Christ differently. You, he says, are rooted and grounded in this knowledge, that Christ is not only a perfect creature but true God, who performs the very same works that God the Father performs. He performs divine works, not those of a creature but of the Creator. For He grants grace and peace; and to give these is to condemn sin, to conquer death, and to trample the devil underfoot. No angel can grant any of this; but since it is ascribed to Christ, it necessarily follows that He is God by nature.

4. *Who gave Himself for our sins.*

In a sense Paul treats the argument of this epistle in every word. He has nothing in his mouth but Christ. Therefore in every word there is a fervor of spirit and life. Note how precisely he speaks. He does not say: "Who has received our works from us" or "Who has received the sacrifices required by the Law of Moses — acts of worship, monastic orders, Masses, vows, and pilgrimages." Instead, he says: "Who has given." Has given what? Neither gold nor silver nor cattle nor Passover lambs nor an angel, but "Himself." For what? Neither for a crown nor for a kingdom nor for our holiness or righteousness, but "for our sins." These words are a veritable thunderbolt from heaven against every kind of righteousness, as is the statement (John 1:29): "Behold, the Lamb of God, who takes away the sin of the world!" Therefore we must pay careful attention to every word and not look at it casually or pass over it lightly; for these words are filled with comfort, and they give great encouragement to timid consciences.

But the question is: What are we to do with sins — not only other people's but our own? Paul answers that the man who is called Jesus Christ, the Son of God, has given Himself for them. These are wonderful words of consolation and promises of the old law: that our sins are not removed by any other means than by the Son of God given into death. Such bullets and such artillery must be used to destroy the papacy, all the religions of the heathen, all ceremonies, all works, all merits. For if our sins can be removed by our own satisfactions, why did the Son of God have to be given for them? But since He *was* given for them, it follows that we cannot remove them by works of our own.

In addition, it follows that our sins are so great, so infinite and invincible, that the whole world could not make satisfaction for even one of them. Certainly the greatness of the ransom — namely, the blood of the Son of God — makes it sufficiently clear that we can neither make satisfaction for our sin nor prevail over it. The force and power of sin is amplified by these words: "Who gave Himself for our sins." We are indifferent, and we regard sin as something trivial, a mere nothing. Although it brings with it the sting and remorse of conscience, still we suppose that it has so little weight and force that some little work or merit of ours will remove it. But we should note here the infinite greatness of the price paid for it. Then it will be evident that its power is so great that it could not be removed by any means except that the Son of God be given for it. Anyone who considers this carefully will understand that this one word "sin" includes the eternal wrath of God and the entire kingdom of Satan, and that sin is no trifle.

Therefore this text concludes that all men are the captives and slaves of sin and, as Paul says, are "sold under sin" (Rom. 7:14); and that sin is a very cruel and powerful tyrant over all men throughout the world, a tyrant who cannot be overthrown and expelled by the power of any creatures, whether angels or men, but only by the infinite and sovereign power of Jesus Christ, the Son of God, who was given for it.

If we fortify ourselves with this faith, and if with all our hearts we cling to this man Jesus Christ, we shall get a light and a sound judgment that will enable us to make free and certain judgments about every way of life. For when we hear that sin is such an omnipotent tyrant, we immediately draw the inevitable inference: "Then what are the papists, monks, nuns, priests, Mohammedans, and sectarians doing when they seek to abolish and overcome sin with their own traditions, preparatory works, satisfactions, etc.? From now on we regard all those sects as vain and vicious; for they not only mar the glory of God and of Christ but remove it entirely, and in its place they advance and establish our own glory."

Pay careful attention to Paul's every word, and note particularly this pronoun "our." For we find very often in the Scriptures that their significance consists in the proper application of pronouns, which also convey vigor and force. It is easy for you to say and believe that Christ, the Son of God, was given for the sins of Peter, Paul, and other saints, who seem to us to have been worthy of this grace. But it is very hard for you, who regard yourself as unworthy of this grace, to say and believe from your heart that Christ was given for *your* many great sins. In general, therefore, and without the pronoun, it is easy to praise and exalt the blessing of Christ extravagantly, namely, that Christ was given for sins, but for the sins of other men, who are worthy. But when it comes to applying this pronoun "our," there our weak nature and reason is thrown back; it does not dare approach God or promise itself that it is to receive such a great treasure freely. Therefore it refuses to have anything to do with God unless it is pure and sinless first. Accordingly, even though it reads or hears this sentence, "who gave Himself for our sins," or something similar, it does not apply this pronoun "our" to itself; it applies it to others, who are worthy and holy, and decides to wait until it has been made worthy by its own works.

All this means that human reason would like sin to have no greater force and power than it itself dreams of. Although hypocrites, who do not know Christ, may feel sorry for sin, they still suppose that they can get rid of it easily by their works and merits. And in the privacy of their own hearts they wish that these words, "who gave Himself for our sins," were merely an expression of humility, and that their sins were not serious and real at all but mere trifles and figments. In short, human reason would like to present to God an imitation and counterfeit sinner, who is afraid of nothing and has no sense of sin. It would like to bring one who is well, not one who has need of a physician (Matt. 9:12); and when it has no sense of sin, only then would it like to believe that Christ was given for our sins.

The whole world feels this way, especially those who want a greater reputation for goodness and holiness than others, such as monks and all self-righteous people.[16] With their mouths they confess that they are sinners; they confess also that they sin daily, though not so much that they cannot remove their sins by their own works. Besides all this, they want to bring their righteousness and merit

[16] We have consistently translated *iusticiarius* with "self-righteous," despite the existence of the English word "justiciary," which appears to have been confined to the seventeenth century and has now become obsolete in English usage.

before the judgment seat of Christ and demand that the Judge reward them with eternal life. Meanwhile, since they give the appearance of being very humble friars, they do not claim that they are completely free of sin. Therefore they pretend to be guilty of certain sins, and for the forgiveness of these they pray fervently with the tax collector: "God, be merciful to me a sinner!" (Luke 18:13.) To them these words of St. Paul, "for our sins," seem to be empty and false. Therefore they do not understand them. What is more, in temptation, when they really become conscious of sin, they cannot take any comfort in these words but must fall into utter desperation.

The main knowledge and true wisdom of Christians, then, is this: to regard as very serious and true these words of Paul, that Christ was given over to death, not for our righteousness or holiness but for our sins, which are real sins — great, many, in fact, infinite and invincible. Therefore you must not think of them as minor or suppose that your own works can remove them. Nor must you despair on account of their gravity if you feel them oppressing you either in life or in death. But you must learn from Paul here to believe that Christ was given, not for sham or counterfeit sins, nor yet for small sins, but for great and huge sins; not for one or two sins but for all sins; not for sins that have been overcome — for neither man nor angel is able to overcome even the tiniest sin — but for invincible sins. And unless you are part of the company of those who say "our sins," that is, who have this doctrine of faith and who teach, hear, learn, love, and believe it, there is no salvation for you.

Therefore you must make thorough preparations not only for the time of temptation but also for the time and struggle of death. Then your conscience will be terrified by the recollection of your past sins. The devil will attack you vigorously and will try to swamp you with piles, floods, and whole oceans of sins, in order to frighten you, draw you away from Christ, and plunge you into despair. Then you must be able to say with confident assurance: "Christ, the Son of God, was given, not for righteousness and for saints but for unrighteousness and for sinners. If I were righteous and without sin, I would have no need of Christ as my Propitiator. Satan, you cantankerous saint, why do you try to make me feel holy and look for righteousness in myself, when in fact there is nothing in me but sins, and real and serious sins at that? These are not counterfeit or trivial sins; they are sins against the First Table, namely, infidelity, doubt, despair, contempt for God, hatred, ignorance, blasphemy, ingratitude,

the abuse of the name of God, neglect, loathing, and contempt for
the Word of God, and the like. In addition, there are sins of the flesh
against the Second Table: failure to honor my parents, disobedience
to rulers, coveting another man's property, wife, etc., although these
vices are less grave than those against the First Table. Of course,
I have not been guilty of murder, adultery, theft, and other sins like
those against the Second Table. Nevertheless, I have committed them
in my heart; therefore I have broken every one of God's Commandments,
and the number of my sins is so great that an ox's hide would
not hold them;[17] they are innumerable. "For the sins I have committed
are more in number than the sands of the sea" (Pr. of Man. 9).
The devil is such a clever trickster that he can make great sins out
of my righteousness and good works. Because my sins are so grave,
so real, so great, so infinite, so horrible, and so invincible that my
righteousness does me no good but rather puts me at a disadvantage
before God,[18] therefore Christ, the Son of God, was given into death
for my sins, to abolish them and thus to save all men who believe.

The meaning of eternal salvation, then, consists in taking these
words to be serious and true. I am not speaking empty words.
I have often experienced, and still do every day, how difficult it is
to believe, especially amid struggles of conscience, that Christ was
given, not for the holy, righteous, and deserving, or for those who
were His friends, but for the godless, sinful, and undeserving, for
those who were His enemies, who deserved the wrath of God and
eternal death.

Therefore let us fortify ourselves with these and similar statements
of Paul. When the devil accuses us and says: "You are a sinner;
therefore you are damned," then we can answer him and say: "Because
you say that I am a sinner, therefore I shall be righteous and be saved."
"No," says the devil, "you will be damned." "No," I say, "for I take
refuge in Christ, who has given Himself for my sins. Therefore,
Satan, you will not prevail against me as you try to frighten me
by showing me the magnitude of my sins and to plunge me into
anguish, loss of faith, despair, hatred, contempt of God, and blasphemy.
In fact, when you say that I am a sinner, you provide me

[17] The expression *ut bubalum corium ea complecti non possit* sounds proverbial.

[18] This passage and others like it in Luther's rhetorical denunciation of works
were to figure prominently in the controversies over the necessity of works for
salvation between George Major (1502—74) and Nicholas Amsdorf (1483—1565).

with armor and weapons against yourself, so that I may slit your throat with your own sword and trample you underfoot. You yourself are preaching the glory of God to me; for you are reminding me, a miserable and condemned sinner, of the fatherly love of God, who 'so loved the world that He gave His only Son, etc.' (John 3:16). You are reminding me of the blessing of Christ my Redeemer. On His shoulders, not on mine, lie all my sins. For 'the Lord has laid on Him the iniquity of us all,' and 'for the transgressions of His people He was stricken' (Is. 53:6, 8). Therefore when you say that I am a sinner, you do not frighten me; but you bring me immense consolation."

Anyone who understands this strategy can easily avoid all the tricks of the devil, who kills a man and leads him to hell by reminding him of his sin unless the man resists him with this strategy and Christian wisdom, by which alone sin, death, and the devil are vanquished. But anyone who does not get rid of the memory of his sin but holds on to it and tortures himself with his own thoughts, supposing either that he can help himself by his own strength or that he can wait until his conscience has been pacified, falls into Satan's trap, which Satan has set to ensnare men, destroys himself with sorrow, and is finally overcome completely. For the devil never stops accusing his conscience. This sly serpent really knows how to present Jesus Christ, our Mediator and Savior, as a lawgiver, judge, and condemner.

Against this temptation we must use these words of Paul in which he gives this very good and true definition of Christ: "Christ is the Son of God and of the Virgin; He was delivered and put to death for our sins." If the devil cites any other definition of Christ, you must say: "The definition and the subject are false; therefore I refuse to accept the definition." I am not speaking vainly here, for I know why I define Christ so strictly from the words of Paul. For Christ is not a cruel master; He is the Propitiator for the sins of the whole world. If you are a sinner, therefore – as indeed we all are – do not put Christ on a rainbow as the Judge; for then you will be terrified and will despair of His mercy.[19] No, grasp the true definition of Him, namely, that Christ, the Son of God and of the Virgin, is not One who terrifies, troubles, condemns us sinners or calls us to account

---

[19] On the image of Christ as Judge, sitting at the end of the rainbow, see also *Luther's Works*, 24, p. 24, note 13.

for our evil past but One who has taken away the sins of the whole world, nailing them to the cross (Col. 2:14) and driving them all the way out by Himself.

Learn this definition carefully. Especially practice this pronoun "our" in such a way that this syllable,[20] once believed, may swallow up and absorb all your sins, that is, that you may be certain that Christ has taken away not only the sins of some men but your sins and those of the whole world. The offering was for the sins of the whole world, even though the whole world does not believe. So do not permit your sins to be merely sins; let them be your very own sins. That is, believe that Christ was given not only for the sins of others but also for yours. Hold to this firmly, and do not let anything deprive you of this sweet definition of Christ, which brings joy even to the angels in heaven: that Christ is, in the strictest of terms, not a Moses, a tormentor, or an executioner but the Mediator for sins and the Donor of grace, who gave Himself, not for our merits, holiness, glory, and holy life but for our sins. Christ also interprets the Law, to be sure; but this is not His proper and chief work.[21]

So far as the words are concerned, we know all this very well and can discourse on it. But in the struggle, when the devil tries to mar the image of Christ and to snatch the Word from our hearts, we discover that we do not know them as well as we should. Whoever could define Christ accurately then, exalting Him and looking to Him as his sweet Savior and High Priest and not as a stern Judge, would have overcome all evils and would already be in the kingdom of heaven. But to do this in the midst of struggle is the hardest thing there is. I am speaking from experience, for I am acquainted with the devil's craftiness. Not only does he try to frighten us by inflating the Law and making many logs out of one speck (Matt. 5:3-5), for he is very skillful both at aggravating sin and at inflating the conscience in good works; but he also makes a practice of frightening us by transforming himself into the Person of the Mediator Himself. He cites some passage of Scripture or some saying of Christ and thus strikes our hearts and gives the impression of being Christ

[20] The original has "two syllables" because of the Latin *nostris*.

[21] The distinction between the "proper work" of God and the "alien work" of God, based on Is. 28:21, was basic to Luther's interpretation of the distinction between the Law and the Gospel; cf. *Luther's Works*, 2, p. 134, note 3.

Himself. So strong is this impression that our conscience would be ready to swear that this is the same Christ whose saying he has cited. So crafty is this enemy that he does not present the entire Christ to us; he presents only a part of Him, namely, that He is the Son of God and Man, born of the Virgin. Eventually he attaches something else to this, some saying in which Christ terrifies sinners, like Luke 13:3: "Unless you repent, you will all likewise perish." By adulterating the genuine definition of Christ with his poison he produces this effect, that although we believe that Christ is the Mediator, in fact our troubled conscience feels and judges that He is a tyrant and a tormentor. So Satan deceives us, and we easily lose the pleasant sight of Christ, our High Priest and Mediator. Once this happens, we avoid Christ as though He were Satan.

This is why I am so earnest in my plea to you to learn the true and correct definition of Christ on the basis of these words of Paul: "who gave Himself for our sins." If He gave Himself into death for our sins, then undoubtedly He is not a tormentor. He is not One who will cast down the troubled, but One who will raise up the fallen and bring propitiation and consolation to the terrified. Otherwise Paul would be lying when he says "who gave Himself for our sins." If I define Christ this way, I define Him correctly, grasp the authentic Christ, and truly make Him my own. I avoid all speculations about the Divine Majesty and take my stand in the humanity of Christ. There is no fear here; there is sheer sweetness, joy, and the like. This kindles a light that shows me the true knowledge of God, of myself, of all creatures, and of all the wickedness of the kingdom of the devil.

We are not teaching anything novel; we are repeating and confirming old doctrines. Would that we could teach and confirm them in such a way that we would have them not only in our mouth but in the meditations at the very core of our heart and especially that we might be able to use them in the struggle of death!

To deliver us from the present evil world.

In these words, too, Paul summarizes the argument of this epistle. By "the present world" he means the whole world that has been, is, and will be, in order to differentiate it from the eternal age to come. And he calls it "evil" because whatever is in this age is subject to the evil of the devil, who rules the entire world. Therefore the world is called the kingdom of the devil; for there is nothing in it but ignorance, contempt, blasphemy, hatred of God, and disobedience of all the words and works of God. We exist in this kingdom of the world and under it.

Here you see again that by his own works or his own power no one can abolish sin; for the whole world, as John says, "is in the power of the evil one" (1 John 5:19). All those who are in the world, therefore, are the slaves of sin and the devil, and are members of the devil, who holds all men by his tyranny as captives to his will. Then what was the good of establishing so many religious orders to get rid of sin, of inventing so many great and difficult works, wearing hair shirts, scourging the body to the blood, going on pilgrimages to St. James in armor,[22] and so on? Even if you do all these things, the definition still stands. You are still in the present evil age and not in Christ. If Christ is not present, it is certain that this evil age and the kingdom of Satan are. Therefore all the gifts of body and mind that you enjoy — wisdom, righteousness, holiness, eloquence, power, beauty, or wealth — are only the instruments of the devil's infernal tyranny over you, by which he forces you to serve him and to advance his kingdom.

In the first place, with your wisdom you obscure the wisdom and knowledge of Christ; and with your evil teaching you lead men astray, so that they cannot come to grace and to Christ. You present and preach your own righteousness and holiness; then you hate and condemn as evil and demonic the righteousness of Christ, by which alone we are justified and made alive. In short, you abuse your power to destroy the kingdom of Christ, to extirpate the Gospel, to persecute and kill the ministers of Christ and their hearers. Therefore if you are apart from Christ, this wisdom of yours is foolishness twice over, and your righteousness is sin and wickedness twice over; for it does not know the wisdom and righteousness of Christ but obscures, hinders, blasphemes, and persecutes it. Therefore Paul is correct in calling it the evil world; for when it is at its best, then it is at its worst. The world is at its best in men who are religious, wise, and learned; yet in them it is actually evil twice over. I shall not even speak of the crude vices with which the world is filled, such as adultery, prostitution, covetousness, stealing, murder, slander, and other filth. These are minor compared

[22] On this medieval custom cf. *Luther's Works*, 22, p. 504.

with the other vices. This white devil, who transforms himself into an angel of light (2 Cor. 11:14) — he is the real devil.

Thus by the words "to deliver us, etc.," Paul shows what the argument of this epistle is: that we must have grace and Christ, and that no creature, neither man nor angel, can deliver man from this present evil age. For this is a work that is appropriate only to the Divine Majesty and is not within the power of either man or angel — namely, that Christ has abolished sin and has delivered us from the tyranny and kingdom of the devil, that is, from this evil age, which is an obedient servant and a willing follower of its god, the devil (2 Cor. 4:4). Whatever the murderer and father of lies (John 8:44) does or speaks, that the world, as his most faithful and obedient son, loyally imitates and carries out. Therefore it is filled with ignorance, hatred, blasphemy, contempt for God, deceit, and error, as well as with overt sins like murder, adultery, fornication, theft, robbery, and the like. In short, where the world is at its best, there it is evil twice over. So also, until God enlightened us with the Gospel, we in the papacy were wicked twice over — all this, of course, under the guise of religion and the observance of a holy life.

So let these words of Paul stand just as they are, true and accurate, not painted or counterfeit: this present age is evil. Do not be dissuaded because there are many fine virtues in many men or because hypocrites make a great pretense of sanctity. But pay careful attention to what Paul says. Out of his words you may boldly and freely pronounce this sentence against the world: that the world, with all its wisdom, righteousness, and power, is the devil's kingdom, out of which only God is able to deliver us by His only Son.

Let us praise God the Father, therefore, and give Him thanks for His indescribable mercy, that when we were incapable of doing so by our own strength, He delivered us from the kingdom of the devil, in which we were captives, and did so by His own Son. And with Paul let us confess that all our works and righteousness, with all of which we could not make the devil stoop down one hairbreadth, are nothing but loss and refuse (Phil. 3:8). And let us tread underfoot and utterly abhor, as a polluted garment (Is. 64:6) and the deadly poison of the devil, all the power of free will, all the wisdom and righteousness of the world, all religious orders, all Masses, ceremonies, vows, fasts, hair shirts, and the like. On the other hand, let us praise and magnify the glory of Christ, who has delivered us by His death not only from this world but from this "evil world."

Thus you have two definitions, of "world" and of "Christ," or of the kingdom of the world and of Christ. The kingdom of the world is the kingdom of sin, death, the devil, blasphemy, despair, and eternal death. But the kingdom of Christ is the kingdom of grace, forgiveness of sins, comfort, salvation, and eternal life, into which we have been transferred (Col. 1:13) by our Lord Jesus Christ, to whom be glory forever. Amen.

According to the will of our God and Father.

Paul chooses and arranges his every word here in such a way that each of them does battle against the perverters of the doctrine of justification. Christ, he says, has delivered us from this wicked kingdom of the devil and the world, and has done so according to the will, good pleasure, and command of the Father. Therefore we have not been delivered by our own will or exertion (Rom. 9:16) or by our own wisdom or decision; we have been delivered because God has had mercy on us and has loved us. As it is written in another passage (John 1:13): "Who were born, not of blood nor of the will of the flesh nor of the will of man, but of God." It is by grace, then, and not by our merit that we have been delivered from this present evil world. Paul is so prolix and ardent in his praise of grace that he sharpens and aims every word against the false apostles.

There is another reason why Paul refers to the will of the Father here, a reason cited in many passages in the Gospel of John also, where Christ, in asserting His commission, calls us back to the will of the Father, so that in His words and works we are to look, not at Him but at the Father. For Christ came into the world so that He might take hold of us and so that we, by gazing upon Christ, might be drawn and carried directly to the Father. As we have warned you before, there is no hope that any saving knowledge of God can come by speculating about the majesty of God; this can come only by taking hold of Christ, who, by the will of the Father, has given Himself into death for our sins. When you have grasped this, then all wrath stops, and fear and trembling disappear; and God appears as nothing but the merciful One who did not spare His own Son but gave Him up for us all (Rom. 8:32). It is extremely dangerous to speculate about the majesty of God and His dreadful judgments —

how He destroyed the whole world with the Flood, how He destroyed Sodom, etc.; for this brings men to the brink of despair and plunges them into total destruction, as I have shown before.

Of our God and Father.

This word "our" is to be applied to both, so that the meaning is "of our God and of our Father." Then Christ's Father and our Father are one and the same. Thus Christ says to Mary Magdalene in John 20:17:[23] "Go to My brethren, and say to them: 'I am ascending to My Father and your Father, to My God and your God.'" Therefore God is our Father and our God, but through Christ. This is an apostolic mode of speaking, and Paul's own phrase. He does not speak with such carefully chosen words, but his words are nevertheless very appropriate and ardent in their zeal.

5. *To whom be the glory forever and ever. Amen.*

In their writings the Hebrews make it a custom to mingle praise and thanksgiving, a custom observed both by the Hebrews and by the apostles, as is evident very often in Paul. For the name of the Lord should be held in great reverence and should never be mentioned without praise and thanksgiving, which are a certain kind of worship and divine service. In secular matters, when we speak the name of a king or a prince, we make it a custom to do so with some nice gesture, reverence, and genuflection. Much more should we bow the knee of our heart when we speak about God, and we should mention the name of God with gratitude and the greatest reverence.

6. *I am astonished.*

You see here the art and skill with which Paul treats his Galatians, who had fallen away and had been led astray by the false apostles. He does not attack them with harsh and stern words; he speaks paternally, not only bearing their fall with patience but even excusing it somewhat. He also shows maternal affection toward them; he speaks gently to them, and yet in such a way that he scolds them, though with words that are very appropriate to the purpose. Toward their betrayers, by contrast, he is extremely violent and indignant. He blames everything on them, and so at the very opening of his epistle he erupts into fulminations against them. "If anyone," he

---

23 The original text cites this passage as "John 21"; so does the marginal reference in the Weimar edition.

says, "is preaching to you a gospel contrary to that which you received, let him be accursed" (Gal. 1:9). Later on, in the fifth chapter, he threatens them with condemnation: "He who is troubling you will bear his judgment, whoever he is" (Gal. 5:10). He also invokes a terrible curse upon them: "I wish those who unsettle you would mutilate themselves!" (Gal. 5:12.) These are dreadful words against the righteousness of the flesh or of the Law.

Paul could have treated the Galatians with less courtesy and denounced them more roughly, something like this: "A plague on your apostasy! I am ashamed of you. Your ingratitude wounds me. I am angry with you." Or he could have exclaimed against them tragically: "O what an age! What habits!" [24] But since it is his aim to raise up the fallen and, with fatherly care, to recall them from their error to the Gospel, he refrains from these harsh words, especially at the beginning, and addresses them with great gentleness and mildness. Seeking as he was to heal the wounded, it would not have been right for him to make their wound worse by applying a sharp and painful plaster to it and thus to hurt the wounded instead of healing them. Therefore he could not have found sweeter or gentler words than these: "I am astonished," by which he made clear both that it saddened him and that it displeased him that they had fallen away from him.

Here Paul lives up to his own rule, which he gives later on in the sixth chapter (Gal. 6:1): "Brethren, if a man is overtaken in any trespass, you who are spiritual, etc." We, too, should follow this example. We should show that toward those poor disciples who have been led astray we feel as parents feel toward their children, so that they may see our paternal zeal and maternal feelings toward them and may see that we seek their salvation. But when it comes to the devil and his servants, the originators of perversion and sectarianism, we should follow the example of the apostles. We should be impatient, proud, sharp, and bitter, despising and condemning their sham as sharply and harshly as we can. When a child has been bitten by a dog, the parents chase the dog but console and soothe the weeping child with the sweetest of words.

Paul has wonderful skill in treating the troubled consciences of those who have fallen. By contrast the pope erupts like a tyrant

[24] Luther's exclamation *O secula, o mores!* is an adaptation of the familiar words from Cicero's *First Oration Against Catiline: O tempora, o mores!*

[W, XL, 102, 103]

and hurls his fulminations and curses against those who are miserable and troubled in their consciences, as one can see in his bulls, especially in the bull on the Lord's Supper.[25] The bishops are not a bit better in the performance of their duty. They do not preach the Gospel or concern themselves with saving men's souls. All they try to do with everything they say and do is to establish and maintain their sovereignty over men.

That so quickly.

You see that Paul is complaining about how easy it is to fall from faith. In the same vein he warns Christians in another passage: "Let anyone who thinks that he stands take heed lest he fall" (1 Cor. 10:12). By our own experience we are proving daily how difficult it is for the mind to acquire and keep a steadfast faith, and how difficult it is to present a perfect people before the Lord. A man may labor for a decade before he puts some small church into proper order. And once it is in order, along comes some fanatic who cannot do anything but slander and abuse the sincere preachers of the Word — and in one moment he overthrows everything! Who would not be agitated by such outrageous actions?

By the grace of God we here in Wittenberg have acquired the form of a Christian church. In our midst the Word is taught purely, the sacraments are used properly, there are exhortations and prayers for all social classes; in short, everything is moving along well. But some fanatic could stop this blessed progress of the Gospel in a hurry, and in one moment he could overturn everything that we have built up with the hard work of many years. This is what happened to Paul, the chosen instrument of Christ (Acts 9:15). With great toil and trouble he had gained the churches of Galatia; but in a short time after his departure the false apostles overthrew them, as this and all his other epistles testify. So weak and miserable is this present life, and so beset are we by the snares of Satan, that one fanatic can often destroy and completely undo in a short time what it took faithful ministers the hard labor of many years day and night to build up. We are learning this by bitter experience today, and yet there is nothing we can do about it.

Because the church is so frail and tender, and so easily over-

---

[25] Luther is referring to the bull *Coena Domini,* issued by Pope Leo X on Maundy Thursday, March 28, 1521, and condemned by Luther in a treatise of 1522 (W, VIII, 691—720).

thrown, one must be on constant guard against these fanatics. For
when they have heard two sermons or have read a couple of pages
in the Sacred Scriptures, they suddenly make themselves masters
of all pupils and teachers, contrary to the authority of all men.
You will find many such today among the artisans, those brazen men
who have never been tested by temptation and therefore have not
learned to fear God and have no taste of grace.[26] Lacking the Holy
Spirit, they teach whatever they please and whatever the common
people find plausible. The ignorant mob, eager to hear something
novel, soon attaches itself to them. In fact, even many who think
that they understand the doctrine of faith and have been tested by
temptation are led astray by them.

Thus Paul can teach us from his own experience that churches
gained by great labor can be overthrown quickly and easily. Therefore we should constantly be on our guard against the devil as he
roams everywhere (1 Peter 5:8), so that he does not come while we
are asleep and plant tares among the wheat (Matt. 13:25). Even
though pastors are ever so watchful and diligent, the Christian flock
is threatened by Satan. For, as I said, Paul had established churches
in Galatia with painstaking care. Yet no sooner had he set his foot
out of the door, as the saying goes, than the false apostles overthrew
some of them; and this fall brought on great ruin in the churches
of Galatia. This loss, so sudden and so great, was undoubtedly
bitterer for the apostle than death itself. Therefore we should constantly be on our guard not to enter into temptation (Matt. 26:41) —
first, each for himself, and secondly, the clergy not only for themselves but also for the whole church.

You are removed.

Here again Paul uses a word that is not sharp but is very mild.
He does not say: "I am astonished that you are defecting so quickly,
that you are so disobedient, fickle, inconstant, or ungrateful" but
"that you are removed so soon." It is as though he were saying:
"You are completely passive; for you have not done any harm, but
you have suffered harm." Therefore in order to recall those back-
sliders he accuses those who have removed them rather than those
who were removed. At the same time, however, he shyly puts some

[26] On August 8, 1538, Luther is said to have complained at table about
"the haughty behavior and negligence of the artisans, who took too little care
and too much pay." W, *Tischreden*, IV, No. 3956.

blame on them when he complains that they have been removed. It is as though he were saying: "Yes, I embrace you with fatherly feeling. We know that you have fallen, not by your own fault but by the fault of the false apostles. Still I do wish that you had been a little more mature in the strength of sound doctrine. You did not take hold firmly enough of the Word; you did not sink your roots deeply enough in it. That is why such a light breeze can carry you away so quickly."

Jerome thinks that Paul intended to interpret the name "Galatians" by referring to the Hebrew word גָּלָה, which is tantamount to "fallen or carried away."[27] It is as though he were saying: "You are really Galatians both in name and in fact; that is, you have been removed."

Some people think that we Germans are descended from the Galatians, and there may be some truth in this. For we Germans do resemble them in nature. I myself am obliged to wish that our people were steadier and surer. Whatever we do, we are always very ardent at the beginning; but when the ardor of our initial feelings is spent, we soon lose our enthusiasm. We give up on things and completely reject them as impetuously as we undertake them. When the light of the Gospel first began to appear after the great darkness of human traditions, many listened eagerly to sermons.[28] But now that the teaching of religion has been successfully reformed by the great growth of the Word of God, many are joining the sects, to their destruction. Many despise not only Sacred Scripture but almost all learning.[29] They are certainly worthy of being compared to those ἀνόητοι Galatians.

From Him who called you in the grace of Christ.

This passage is rather ambiguous. Therefore it is capable of two interpretations. The first is "from that Christ who called you in grace." The second is "from Him [that is, from God] who has called you in the grace of Christ." I prefer the former. For it seems right to me that just as a little earlier Paul made Christ the One who snatches us from the present wicked world, as well as the Giver

---

27 Jerome, *Commentarius in Epistolam S. Pauli ad Galatas,* I, *Patrologia, Series Latina,* XXVI, 343—344.

28 By "the light of the Gospel" Luther means the coming of the Reformation; cf. *Luther's Works,* 3, p. 275, note 48.

29 Apparently a reference to the repudiation of both theological and secular learning by Carlstadt; cf. *Luther's Works,* 2, p. 220.

of grace and peace equally with God the Father,[30] so here he makes Him also the Caller. For it is Paul's special purpose to impress Christ on our minds, and through Him the Father.

These words, "from Christ, who called you in grace," also have great force and contain an antithesis, as though he were saying: "Alas, how easily you let yourselves be withdrawn and removed from Christ, who has called you, not as Moses did, to the Law, works, sin, wrath, and damnation but to sheer grace!" So we today complain with Paul that the blindness and perversity of men is so horrible that no one is willing to accept the doctrine of grace and salvation. Or if there are some who accept it, they soon fall away from it. Nevertheless, it brings with it every benefit, both spiritual and physical, namely, the forgiveness of sins, peace of heart, and eternal life. It also brings light and sound judgment about everything. It approves and supports civil government, the home, and every way of life that has been ordained and established by God. It eradicates all doctrines of error, sin, death, sedition, confusion, etc. In short, it uncovers all the works of the devil and opens to us the works of God. What madness is the world up to when it so bitterly hates this Word, this Gospel of eternal comfort, grace, salvation, and eternal life, and when it blasphemes and persecutes it with such satanic rage?

Earlier Paul called this present world "wicked," that is, sheer evil; for otherwise it would acknowledge the blessing and mercy of God, which it spitefully rejects and persecutes. It loves darkness, error, and the kingdom of the devil more than light, truth, and the kingdom of Christ (John 3:19). And it does so not through error but through the devil's extreme spitefulness. By giving Himself into death for the sins of all men, Christ has earned nothing from this world but that it blasphemes Him and persecutes His salutary Word and would like to crucify Him again if it could. Therefore the world not only dwells in darkness but is darkness itself, as is written in John 1:5.

Therefore Paul emphasizes these words, "from Christ, who has called you," and mystically suggests a contrast. It is as though he were saying: "My proclamation was not about the hard laws of Moses; nor did I teach that you should be slaves under the yoke. But I preached sheer grace and freedom to you; that is, that Christ has mercifully called you in grace to make you free men under Christ

[30] See p. 41.

rather than slaves under Moses. But through your false apostles you have now become disciples of Moses; for they have called you by the Law of Moses, not to grace but to wrath, hatred of God, sin, and death. But when Christ calls, this brings grace and salvation. For He transfers them from the Law to the Gospel, from wrath to grace, from sin to righteousness, and from death to life. Will you permit yourselves to be carried — and so quickly and easily at that! — in another direction, away from such a living fountain bubbling over with grace and life?" Now if by the very Law of God Moses calls men to the wrath of God and to sin, where do you suppose the pope calls them by his own traditions?

The other interpretation, according to which it is the Father who calls in the grace of Christ, is also good; but the earlier interpretation, which refers to Christ, is more pleasant and more suitable to comfort afflicted consciences.

To a different gospel.

Here let us learn to recognize the tricks and craft of the devil. A heretic does not come with the label "error" or "devil"; nor does the devil himself come in the form of a devil, especially not that "white devil." [31] In fact, even the black devil, who impels men to overt acts of evil, provides them with a covering for the acts they perpetrate or intend to perpetrate. In his fury the murderer does not see that murder is as great and horrible a sin as it is in fact, because he has a covering for it. Lechers, thieves, covetous men, drunkards, and the like, have the means to flatter themselves and cover up their sins. Thus the black devil always emerges in the disguise and covering of all his works and tricks. But in the spiritual area, where Satan emerges not black but white, in the guise of an angel or even of God Himself, there he puts himself forward with very sly pretense and amazing tricks. He peddles his deadly poison as the doctrine of grace, the Word of God, and the Gospel of Christ. This is why Paul calls the doctrine of the false apostles and ministers of Satan a "gospel," saying, "to a different gospel." But he is speaking ironically, as though he were saying: "Now you Galatians have different evangelists and a different gospel. You despise my Gospel now, and it has lost your respect."

From this it is evident that these false apostles had condemned

31 On the "white devil" see p. 41.

Paul's Gospel among the Galatians, saying: "To be sure, Paul made a good start. But a good start is not enough, for there are more sublime things to follow." As they said in Acts 15:1: "It is not enough for you to believe in Christ or to be baptized. You must also be circumcised; for 'unless you are circumcised according to the custom of Moses, you cannot be saved.'" This is tantamount to saying that Christ is a good workman who has begun a building but has not completed it, and that Moses must complete it.

Nowadays, when the sectarians cannot condemn us overtly, they say instead: "These Lutherans have a cowardly spirit. They do not dare speak the truth frankly and freely and draw the consequences from it. We have to draw these consequences. To be sure, they have laid a foundation, that is, faith in Christ. But the beginning, the middle, and the end must be joined together. God has not assigned to them the task of accomplishing this; He has left it to us." So these perverse and satanic men glorify their wicked proclamation, calling it the Word of God, so that under the guise of the name of God they may work their damage. For in his ministers the devil does not want to be deformed and black but beautiful and white. To put on such an appearance he presents and adorns everything he says and does with the color of truth and with the name of God. This is the source of that familiar German proverb: "All misfortune begins in the name of God." [32]

Therefore let us learn that this is one of the devil's specialties: If he cannot do his damage by persecuting and destroying, he will do it under the guise of correcting and edifying. Thus today he is persecuting us with power and the sword, so that once we are out of the way, he will not only corrupt the Gospel but will obliterate it. So far he has not succeeded. For he has killed many who steadfastly confessed that our doctrine is holy and divine, and by their blood the church was not destroyed but was watered.[33] So since he cannot succeed that way, he is arousing false teachers. At first they accept our teaching and preach it in agreement with us. But later on they say that we have made a good start, but that the more sublime things have been saved until now, etc. In this way the devil impedes the progress of the Gospel, both on the right side

[32] The German text of the proverb is *Inn Gottes namen hebt sich als ungluck an.*

[33] On this proverbial saying and its origin cf. *Luther's Works,* 12, p. 174, note 8.

and on the left — but more on the right, by edifying and correcting, than on the left, by persecuting and destroying. Therefore we must pray constantly (1 Thess. 5:17), read, and hold tightly to Christ and to His Word, so that we may prevail against the tricks with which the devil attacks us on both the right side and the left; "for we are not contending against flesh and blood" (Eph. 6:12).

7. *Not that there is another [or Although there is not another] gospel, but there are some who trouble you.*

Once more Paul makes excuses for the Galatians and bitterly attacks the false apostles. It is as though he were saying: "You Galatians have been persuaded that the Gospel which you received from me is not the true and genuine Gospel. Therefore you suppose that you are doing the right thing when you accept that new gospel which the false apostles are teaching and which seems better than mine. I am not accusing you so much as I am accusing those troublemakers who are disturbing your consciences and snatching you out of my hand."

Here you see again how ardently and vehemently the apostle attacks the seducers and with what harsh words he describes them. He calls them troublers of the churches and of consciences, who do nothing but seduce and deceive an endless number of consciences and cause horrible damage and trouble in the churches. In our own day, too, we are obliged to witness this great evil, much to our sorrow; but we cannot do anything more to remedy it than Paul could in his day.

This passage shows that the false apostles undoubtedly called Paul an imperfect apostle and a weak and erring preacher. For this reason he himself, in turn, calls them troublers of the churches and subverters of the Gospel of Christ. Thus they condemned one another; the false apostles condemned Paul, and Paul, in turn, condemned them. There is always such controversy and condemnation going on in the church, especially when the doctrine of the Gospel is prospering; the wicked teachers persecute, condemn, and oppress the faithful teachers, who, in turn, attack and condemn them. Today the papists and the sectarians hate us violently and condemn us; and we, in turn, detest and condemn their impious and blasphemous doctrine with great hatred. Meanwhile the poor common people are confused. They waver back and forth, wondering and doubting which side to take or whom it is safe to follow. For it is not given to everyone to make Christian judgments about such important issues. The outcome will show which side was right in its teaching and in its condemnation of the other. It is certain that we do not persecute, oppress, or kill anyone; nor does our doctrine trouble consciences, but it delivers them from the endless errors and traps of the devil. In support of this claim we have the testimony of many good men who thank God that our doctrine has given a sure comfort to their consciences. Just as Paul, therefore, was not at fault when the churches were troubled, but the false apostles were, so in our day it is not our fault but that of the Anabaptists, Sacramentarians, and other fanatics that so many great troubles have arisen in the church.

Note carefully here that everyone who teaches works and the righteousness of the Law troubles the church and consciences. Who would believe that the pope, cardinals, bishops, monks and that whole "synagog of Satan" (Rev. 2:9), especially the founders of the holy orders — some of whom God could miraculously save [34] — were troublers of consciences? In fact, they are much worse than those false apostles. The false apostles taught that in addition to faith in Christ, the works of the Law of God were also necessary for salvation. But our opponents skipped faith altogether and taught human traditions and works not commanded by God but invented by them without and against the Word of God; these they have not only put on a par with the Word of God but have raised far above it. But the holier the heretics seem to be in external appearance, the more damage they cause. For if the false apostles had not possessed outstanding gifts, great authority, and the appearance of holiness; and if they had not claimed to be the ministers of Christ, pupils of the apostles, and sincere preachers of the Gospel, they could not so easily have undermined the authority of Paul and made an impression on the Galatians.

The reason Paul takes such a strong stand against them and calls them troublers of the churches is that they taught that in addition to faith in Christ, circumcision and the observance of the Law were necessary for salvation. Paul testifies to this later on in the fifth chapter; and in Acts 15:1 Luke says the same thing: "Some men came down from Judea and were teaching the brethren, 'Unless you are circumcised according to the custom of Moses, you cannot

[34] Luther is probably thinking of Bernard of Clairvaux, perhaps also of Francis of Assisi.

be saved.' " Therefore the false apostles argued seriously and stubbornly that the Law was to be obeyed. The obstinate Jews, who argued for the observance of the Law, immediately allied themselves with them and then easily convinced those who were not well grounded in faith that Paul was not an orthodox teacher, since he neglected the Law. For it seemed incongruous to them that the Law of God should be utterly abolished, and that the Jews should be rejected, those who until that time had always been regarded as the people of God and to whom the promises had been given (Rom. 9:4). And it seemed even more incongruous to them that the Gentiles, those evil idolaters, were to achieve the glory of being the people of God without circumcision and without the works of the Law, solely by grace and faith in Christ.

The false apostles had made a great point of all this in order to bring Paul into disrepute among the Galatians. And to aggravate this they said that he preached to the Gentiles about freedom from the Law, contempt for the Law of God, and even the total abrogation both of the Law and of the entire Jewish kingdom — all this in opposition to the Law of God, the custom of the entire Jewish nation, the example of the apostles, and even his own example. Therefore he was to be avoided as a public blasphemer against God and a rebel against the entire Jewish commonwealth. They maintained that they were the ones to be listened to; for not only did they preach the Gospel correctly, but they were also the very pupils of the apostles, with whom Paul had never been acquainted. By this device they slandered Paul among the Galatians and brought about the defection of the Galatians from him. And to make sure that the truth of the Gospel would abide among the Galatians, Paul was forced with all his strength to oppose the false apostles, whom he confidently attacks and condemns as the troublers of the churches and the subverters of the Gospel of Christ, as follows:

And want to pervert the Gospel of Christ.

That is, they are intent not only on troubling you but also on utterly destroying and extinguishing the Gospel of Christ. Satan is engaged in both of these activities. He is not content to trouble and deceive many people through his false apostles; but through them he is also at work to overthrow and abolish the Gospel completely, and he will not rest until he has accomplished this. Yet such perverters of the Gospel find it intolerable to hear that they

are the devil's apostles. In fact, they are prouder than anyone else
of the name of Christ, and they claim to be the most sincere preachers
of the Gospel. But because they confuse the Law with the Gospel,
it is inevitable that they subvert the Gospel. Either Christ must
abide, and the Law perish; or the Law must abide, and Christ perish.
It is impossible for Christ and the Law to agree and to share the
reign over a conscience. Where the righteousness of the Law reigns,
there the righteousness of grace cannot reign; and, on the other hand,
where the righteousness of grace reigns, there the righteousness of
the Law cannot reign. One of these two will have to yield to the
other. And if you cannot bring yourself to believe that God wants
to forgive your sins for the sake of Christ, how will you be able to
believe that He wants to forgive you for the sake of the works of
the Law or for the sake of your own works? Therefore the doctrine
of grace simply cannot stand with the doctrine of the Law. One of
them must be rejected and abolished, and the other must be confirmed or substantiated.

But just as the Jews were inclined away from this doctrine of
faith and grace, so we also are inclined away from it. I personally
would like to keep both the righteousness of grace as that which
justifies and the righteousness of the Law as the basis for God's
attitude toward me. But, as Paul says here, confusing these means
perverting the Gospel of Christ. Yet in a controversy the stronger
side can defeat the better side. So it happens that the righteousness
of grace and of faith is lost; and the other righteousness, that of the
Law and of works, is advanced and defended. Christ and His side
are weak, and the Gospel is a foolish proclamation. On the other
hand, the kingdom of the world and the devil, its prince, are strong;
in addition, the wisdom of the flesh is very impressive. But this is
our consolation, that the devil with his members cannot accomplish
what he wishes. He may trouble many persons, but he cannot destroy
the Gospel of Christ. The truth may be endangered, but it cannot
perish. It is attacked, but it cannot be conquered; for "the Word
of the Lord abides forever" [35] (1 Peter 1:25).

It seems to be a trivial matter to teach the Law and affirm works,
but this does more damage than human reason can imagine. Not
only does it mar and obscure the knowledge of grace, but it also
removes Christ and all His blessings, and it completely overthrows

[35] In the original this quotation appears completely in capital letters.

the Gospel, as Paul says in this passage. The cause of this great evil is our flesh. Steeped in sins, it sees no way to extricate itself except by works. This is why it wants to live in the righteousnesses of the Law and to rest in trust in its own works. Therefore it knows nothing or nearly nothing about the doctrine of faith and grace, without which the conscience cannot find peace.

From these words of Paul, "and want to pervert the Gospel of Christ," it seems that the false apostles were very bold and brazen in their wholesale opposition to Paul. Therefore he withstands them with zeal and ardor, utterly certain of his calling. He exalts his ministry wonderfully against them and says:

8. *But even if we, or an angel from heaven, should preach to you a gospel contrary to that which we preached to you, let him be accursed.*

Here Paul is breathing fire. His zeal is so fervent that he almost begins to curse the angels themselves. He says: "Even if we ourselves, my brethren, Timothy and Titus, and I, and all who are with me, to say nothing of the others — indeed, even if an angel from heaven should preach to you, etc., I would wish that my brethren and I, yes, even an angel from heaven, be accursed rather than that my Gospel be overthrown." This is a passionate zeal, that he has the courage to curse so boldly not only himself and his brethen but even an angel from heaven. The Greek word ἀνάθεμα, חֵרֶם in Hebrew, means something cursed, execrable, contemptible, something that has no relation, participation, or communication with God. Thus Joshua says (6:17): "Let the city of Jericho be ἀνάθεμα forever, so that it is never reconstructed." And in the last chapter of Leviticus it is written: "If a man or a beast has been devoted or ἀνάθεμα, let him be put to death and not permitted to live" (Lev. 27:28). Thus the divine sentence was that Amalek and some other cities destined for the ἀνάθεμα were to be completely demolished (Ex. 17:14). So this is what Paul means: "I would wish that I, others, yes, even an angel from heaven be accursed rather than that we or others preach any other gospel than the one we or others have preached." Thus Paul curses himself first; for clever debaters usually begin by criticizing themselves, in order that then they may be able to reprove others more freely and more severely.

Therefore Paul concludes that there is no other gospel than the one he himself has been preaching. Nor is any other gospel to be

preached by him or by anyone else, or even by an angel from heaven.
For once the voice of the Gospel has sounded, it will not be revoked
until the Last Day.

9. *As we have said before, so now I say again: If anyone is preaching
to you a gospel contrary to that which you received, let him be
accursed.*

Paul says the same thing over again, but he shifts the persons.
Earlier he had cursed himself, his brethren, and an angel from heaven.
Here he says: "If there is anyone besides us who preached to you
any gospel other than the one you have received from us, let him
also be accursed." Thus he clearly excommunicates and curses all
teachers in general — himself, his brethren, angels, and, in addition,
anyone else at all, that is, his opponents, the false teachers. This
shows great fervor of spirit in the apostle, that he has the courage
to curse all teachers throughout the earth and heaven. For all men
must either yield to that Gospel which Paul had been preaching or
be accursed and damned.

The shift in persons should be noted. Paul speaks one way in his
first anathema and another way in his second. In the first he says:
"If we or an angel from heaven should preach to you a gospel
contrary to that which we preached to you"; in the second he says:
"contrary to that which you received." He does this intentionally,
to keep the Galatians from saying: "Paul, we have not changed the
Gospel that you preached to us. We had misunderstood you, but
the teachers who came after you have set us straight." "I will not
stand for this," he says. "They should neither add anything nor
correct anything. What you heard from me was the pure Word
of God. Let only this stand. I myself do not want to be a different
teacher of the Gospel from what I was, nor do I want you to be
different pupils. Therefore if you hear anyone teaching a gospel
different from the one you heard from me, or bragging that he will
bring you something better than what you received from me, let
him and his disciples be accursed."

In this way the ministers of Satan invade, and insinuate themselves into, the minds of men by promising that they will bring
something better. They admit that those who taught the Gospel
before them made a good start, but they say that this is not enough.
Thus today the fanatics do pay us the compliment that we began
the work of the Gospel correctly. But because we despise and

condemn their blasphemous doctrine, they call us "neopapists," who are twice as bad as the old papists. Thus it is that thieves and robbers invade the Lord's sheepfold "to steal and kill and destroy" (John 10:10). First they confirm our doctrine, but then they correct us and claim to explain more clearly what we have understood incorrectly or only partially. This was how the false apostles gained access to the Galatians. They said: "Yes, Paul has laid the foundation of Christian teaching. But he does not teach the true way of justification, for he teaches men to turn away from the Law. Now what he could not bring you correctly, this you should now receive from us." But Paul refuses to let anything else be taught by anyone or heard and accepted by the Galatians than what he himself had taught them before and what they had heard and accepted from him. "Therefore," he says, "let those who either teach or accept anything else be accursed."

This text contains only examples rather than much instruction. We have not yet come to the main doctrine discussed in this epistle. For the first two chapters contain almost nothing but defenses and refutations. Nevertheless, we are presented here with an example that enables us to know for a certainty that it is an accursed lie that the pope is the arbiter of Scripture or that the church has authority over Scripture. This is what the canonists and commentators on the *Sentences* have wickedly declared, on the following basis: "The church has approved only four gospels, and therefore there are only four. For if it had approved more, there would have been more. Since the church has the right to accept and approve as many gospels as it wishes, it follows that the church is superior to the gospels." [36] What a splendid argument! [37] I approve Scripture. Therefore I am superior to Scripture. John the Baptist acknowledges and confesses Christ. He points to Him with his finger. Therefore he is superior to Christ. The church approves Christian faith and doctrine. Therefore the church is superior to them.

To refute this wicked and blasphemous doctrine of theirs you have here a clear text and a thunderbolt. Here Paul subordinates himself, an angel from heaven, teachers on earth, and any other

[36] See, for example, Ambrosius Catharinus Politus, *Apologia pro veritate catholicae et apostolicae fidei ac doctrinae adversus impia ac valde pestifera Martini Lutheri dogmata* (1520), *Corpus Catholicorum*, 27 (Münster in Westfalen, 1956), I, 27r, p. 74.

[37] The phrase is *a baculo ad angulum;* cf. *Luther's Works,* 2, p. 271, note 29.

masters at all to Sacred Scripture. This queen must rule, and
everyone must obey, and be subject to, her. The pope, Luther,
Augustine, Paul, an angel from heaven — these should not be masters,
judges, or arbiters but only witnesses, disciples, and confessors of
Scripture. Nor should any doctrine be taught or heard in the church
except the pure Word of God. Otherwise, let the teachers and the
hearers be accursed along with their doctrine.

10. *Am I now seeking the favor of men, or of God?*

These words are spoken with the same ardor as the earlier ones;
it is as though he were saying: "Am I, Paul, so unknown among you
after preaching publicly in your churches? Are you still unaware
of my bitter controversies and disputes with the Jews? I should think
it is evident from my preaching and from the many great afflictions
I have endured whether I am serving men or God. Everyone sees
that by my preaching I have not only brought persecution upon
myself everywhere but have also earned the bitter hatred both of
my countrymen and of all others. Thus I make it obvious that by
my preaching I am not seeking the favor or praise of men, but that
I am seeking the grace and glory of God."

We do not seek the favor of men by our teaching either, if we
may be permitted to say this without boasting. For we teach that
all men are wicked; we condemn the free will of man, his natural
powers, wisdom, righteousness, all self-invented religion, and whatever is best in the world. In other words, we say that there is
nothing in us that can deserve grace and the forgiveness of sins.
But we proclaim that we receive this grace solely and altogether
by the free mercy of God. For thus the heavens show forth the
glory of God and His works, universally condemning all men for
their works (Ps. 19:1).[38] This is not preaching that gains favor from
men and from the world. For the world finds nothing more irritating
and intolerable than hearing its wisdom, righteousness, religion, and
power condemned. To denounce these mighty and glorious gifts of
the world is not to curry the world's favor but to go out looking for,
and quickly to find, hatred and misfortune, as it is called. For if
we denounce men and all their efforts, it is inevitable that we
quickly encounter bitter hatred, persecution, excommunication, condemnation, and execution.

[38] See Luther's exegesis of Ps. 19, *Luther's Works*, 12, pp. 140—141.

"If they see other things," Paul says, "why do they not see this too, that what I teach is from God and not from men? That is, I do not seek the favor of any man by my teaching; I seek only the favor of God. For if I were seeking the favor of men, I would not condemn all their works. (Christ speaks the same way in John 3:19: "This is the judgment, that the light has come into the world, and men loved darkness rather than light, because their deeds were evil"; and in John 7:7: "The world cannot hate you, but it hates Me because I testify of it that its works are evil.") Thus I condemn the works of men; that is, I show God's judgment upon all men from His Word, of which I am a minister and an apostle, saying that they are sinners, unrighteous men, children of wrath (Eph. 2:3), captives of Satan, and condemned. I declare that they do not become righteous by works or by circumcision but solely by grace and by faith in Christ. Because this is what I preach, I earn the bitter hatred of men. For they find nothing more intolerable than to be told that this is how they are; instead, they want to be praised as wise, righteous, and holy. Thus this is clear testimony that I am not teaching a human doctrine.

"That I teach divine things is evident enough also from my preaching the grace, mercy, work, and glory of God alone. As Christ says, he who speaks what his Lord and Master has commanded, and who glorifies, not himself but Him whose messenger he is — he brings and teaches the sure Word of God (John 8:28, 50). But I teach only what has been divinely commanded. And I do not glorify myself; I glorify Him who sent me. In addition, I bring upon myself the enmity and indignation both of the Jews and of the Gentiles. Therefore my doctrine is true, pure, sure, and divine. Nor can there be any doctrine that is different from mine, much less better. Therefore any doctrine at all that does not teach as mine does — that all men are sinners and are justified solely by faith in Christ — must be false, uncertain, evil, blasphemous, accursed, and demonic. And so are those who either teach or accept such a doctrine." With Paul, therefore, we boldly and confidently pronounce a curse upon any doctrine that does not agree with ours. We, too, seek by our preaching, not the praise of men or the favor of princes or of bishops but only the favor of God. We preach His grace and gift alone, treading underfoot and condemning whatever is our own. Therefore anyone who teaches something different or something contrary — we confidently declare that he was sent from the devil and is ἀνάθεμα.

Or am I trying to please men?

That is, "Do I serve men or God?" Paul is always looking obliquely at the false apostles. These, he says, always have to try to please and flatter men; for thus they seek to be able to glory in the flesh again. In addition — because they cannot bear the hatred and persecution of men — they teach circumcision, simply to escape the persecution of the cross of Christ, as follows in the eleventh verse of the fifth chapter. Thus today you will find many who try to please men. In order to live in peace and in the smugness of the flesh, they teach human doctrines, that is, impious ones. Or they approve of the blasphemies and wicked judgments of our opponents, contrary to the Word of God and their own consciences, just to be able to retain the favor of princes and bishops and not to lose their property. On the other hand — because we try to please God and not men — we bring upon ourselves the envy of the devil and of hell itself. We bear the slanders and curses of the world, death, and every evil.

Thus Paul says here: "I do not try to please men so that they will praise my doctrine and call me an outstanding teacher. I want to please only God. Whoever tries to please God will have men as his bitter enemies. I experience this too; for they repay me with shame, slander, prison, the sword, etc. By contrast the false apostles teach human doctrine, that is, what is pleasant and reasonable. And they do this so that they can live a life of ease and earn the favor and plaudits of the people. Those who look for this find it, for they are praised and exalted by everyone." Thus Christ says in Matt. 6:2 that hypocrites do everything "that they may be praised by men." And in John 5:44 He severely indicts such men: "How can you believe, who receive glory from one another and do not seek the glory that comes from the only God?" What Paul has been saying so far is almost all examples. Yet he is vigorously urging throughout that his doctrine is true and correct. Therefore he exhorts the Galatians not to forsake it and accept another.

If I were still pleasing men, I should not be a servant of Christ.

All this should be referred to the entire office and ministry of Paul, so that there is an antithesis between his attitude when he was still in Judaism and his present attitude. It is as though he were saying: "Do you think I am still pleasing men?" Thus he says later on in the eleventh verse of the fifth chapter: "If I still preach circumcision, why am I still persecuted?" It is as though he were saying: "Do you not see and hear of my daily battles, great persecutions, and afflictions? After I was converted and called to the apostolate, I never sought the favor of men. I did not try to please men; I tried to please God alone. That is, by my ministry and doctrine I seek the glory and favor of God, not of men."

Here, too, we see how insidiously and slyly the false apostles tried to increase the hostility of the Galatians to Paul by means of such accusations as these: that he was obliged to teach and observe what the apostles commanded about circumcision and the Law; that this was obvious from his having circumcised Timothy, cleansed himself with four other men in the temple at Jerusalem, and shaved his head at Cenchreae.[39] These and similar examples they collected and interpreted to Paul's disadvantage. Then they looked for contradictions and inconsistencies in Paul, as our opponents do nowadays with our books. Thus they tried to convict him of having taught things that were mutually contradictory. "Now," they said, "he is preaching against circumcision, which previously he not only left intact but even observed by circumcising Timothy when the apostles had instructed him and commanded him to do so." From this they concluded that Paul was by no means to be trusted, but that the Law and circumcision were to be observed. But these blind men and leaders of the blind (Matt. 15:14) did not see with what intention Paul and the other apostles refrained from immediately abrogating the Law and circumcision among the Jews but freely observed them for a while.

11. *For I would have you know, brethren, that the Gospel which was preached by me is not man's Gospel.*

12. *For I did not receive it from man, nor was I taught it, but it came through a revelation of Jesus Christ.*

This is the central proposition of this chapter, down to the end of the second chapter; it is a refutation and a defense. Here Paul is reciting a sort of perpetual history. Jerome tortures himself anxiously and labors mightily in an effort to harmonize it.[40] But he does not

39 A reference to Acts 16:3; 21:24; 18:18.

40 Jerome, *Commentarius in Epistolam S. Pauli ad Galatas*, I, *Patrologia, Series Latina*, XXVI, 346—347.

touch the real issue, for he does not consider Paul's purpose or intention.

The histories in the Scriptures are often concise and confused, so that they cannot be easily harmonized, as, for example, the denials of Peter and the history of Christ's Passion, etc.[41] Thus Paul is not reciting the entire history here. Therefore I do not expend any labor or concern on harmonizing these things, but here I pay attention only to Paul's purpose and intention.

The central proposition of this passage is this: "My Gospel is not according to man. Nor did I receive it from man; I received it by a revelation of Jesus Christ." This proposition he sets forth; he will stick by it, and he confirms it with an oath. He bears solemn witness to the Galatians, to make them believe that he did not learn his Gospel from any man but received it by a revelation of Jesus Christ. And they should not pay attention to the false apostles, whom he accuses of being liars, because they said that Paul had accepted and learned his Gospel from the apostles.

When Paul says that his Gospel is "not man's," he does not mean that his Gospel is not human; for that is self-evident, and the false apostles, too, bragged that their doctrine was not human but divine. But he means that he had not learned his Gospel by the ministry of men or received it by any human means, as all of us either learn it by the ministry of men or receive it by some human means — hearing or reading or writing or drawing, etc. But he had simply received it by a revelation of Jesus Christ. If someone else wants to make some other distinction, that is all right with me.[42]

When Paul denies that he received his Gospel from man, he clearly indicates by this that Christ is not a mere man but is true God and man at the same time.

Paul received his Gospel when he was on the way to Damascus, where Christ appeared to him and spoke with him. Later He spoke with him again in the temple at Jerusalem (Acts 22:17-21). But Paul received his Gospel on the road, as Luke tells the story in Acts 9. "Rise," Christ says to him, "and enter the city, and you will be told what you are to do" (Acts 9:6). Christ does not tell him to enter the city in order to learn the Gospel from Ananias. Ananias was

[41] For Luther's attitude toward efforts at harmonization see, for example, *Luther's Works*, 2, p. 242, note 11.

[42] Cf. *Luther's Works*, 14, pp. 284—286.

commanded to go and baptize him, to lay his hands on him, to commit the ministry of the Word to him, and to commend him to the church — but not to teach him the Gospel, which he had already received, as he boasts here, by a revelation of Jesus Christ on the road. Ananias himself acknowledges this when he says (Acts 9:17): "Brother Saul, the Lord who appeared to you on the road has sent me that you may regain your sight." Therefore he did not receive his doctrine from Ananias. But having already been called, enlightened, and taught by Christ on the road, he was sent to Ananias, so that he might have the testimony of men also to his having been called by God to preach the Gospel of Christ.

Paul was forced to recite this to refute the slander of the false apostles, who endeavored to bring the disfavor of the Galatians upon him. They said that Paul was far inferior to the remaining pupils of the apostles, who had received from the apostles what they taught and kept; that they had observed the behavior of the apostles for a long time; and that Paul himself had received the same instruction from them but was now denying it. Why were they listening to an inferior and despising the authority of the apostles, who were the ancestors and teachers not only of the Galatians but of all the churches throughout the world?

This argument, which the false apostles based on the authority of the apostles, was forceful and compelling enough to overwhelm the Galatians suddenly, especially on this issue. If I had not been taught by the examples of the churches in Galatia, Corinth, and elsewhere, I would certainly never have believed that those who initially accepted the Word with such joy, including many outstanding men, could be overwhelmed so quickly. Good God, what dreadful and endless damage can be caused by just one argument, which so pierces a man's conscience when God withdraws His grace that in one moment he loses everything!

By this subtlety the false apostles easily deceived the Galatians, who were not well grounded in faith but were still weak. Besides, the question of justification is an elusive thing — not in itself, for in itself it is firm and sure, but so far as we are concerned. I myself have had considerable experience of this, for I know how I sometimes struggle in the hours of darkness.[43] I know how often I sud-

43 Luther is describing the conflicts of faith and doubt that he usually calls *Anfechtungen*.

denly lose sight of the rays of the Gospel and of grace, which have been obscured for me by thick, dark clouds. In other words, I know how slippery the footing is even for those who are mature and seem to be firmly established in matters of faith. We have an understanding of this, because we are able to teach it; and this is a sure sign that we have it, for no one is able to teach others what he himself does not know. "The sign of the man who knows," it has been said, "is his ability to teach." [44] But when in a struggle we should use the Gospel, which is the Word of grace, consolation, and life, there the Law, the Word of wrath, sadness, and death, precedes the Gospel and begins to raise a tumult. The terrors it arouses in the conscience are no smaller than was the tremendous and horrible spectacle on Mt. Sinai (Ex. 19:16). Thus even one passage in Scripture that presents some of the threats of the Law overwhelms and swamps any other comfort; it shakes our insides in such a way that it makes us forget justification, grace, Christ, and the Gospel.

So far as we are concerned, therefore, this is a very elusive matter, because we are so unstable. In addition, we are opposed by half of our very selves, namely, by reason and all its powers. Moreover, because the flesh cannot believe for sure that the promises of God are true, it resists the spirit. Therefore it contends against the spirit and, as Paul says, holds the spirit captive (Rom. 7:23), to keep it from believing as firmly as it wants to (Gal. 5:17). This is why we continually teach that the knowledge of Christ and of faith is not a human work but utterly a divine gift; as God creates faith, so He preserves us in it. And just as He initially gives us faith through the Word, so later on He exercises, increases, strengthens, and perfects it in us by that Word. Therefore the supreme worship of God that a man can offer, the Sabbath of Sabbaths, is to practice true godliness, to hear and read the Word. On the other hand, nothing is more dangerous than to become tired of the Word. Therefore anyone who is so cold that he thinks he knows enough and gradually begins to loathe the Word has lost Christ and the Gospel. What he thinks he knows, he reaches only by speculation; and, as St. James says, "he is like a man who observes his natural face in a mirror; for he observes himself and goes away and at once forgets what he

---

[44] Perhaps an allusion to Ecclus. 37:22-23.

was like" (James 1:23-24). This is what is finally happening to the frivolous fanatics.

Therefore let every faithful person work and strive with all his might to learn this doctrine and keep it, and for this purpose let him employ humble prayer to God with continual study and meditation on the Word. Even when we have done ever so much, there will still be much to keep us busy. For we are involved, not with minor enemies but with strong and powerful ones, who battle against us continually, namely, our own flesh, all the dangers of the world, the Law, sin, death, the wrath and judgment of God, and the devil himself, who never stops tempting us inwardly with his flaming darts (Eph. 6:16) and outwardly with his false apostles, so as to overcome some if not all of us.

Therefore this argument of the false apostles makes a good impression and seems to be very cogent. Today, too, it convinces many people to say that the apostles, the holy fathers, and their successors have taught thus and so; that the church thinks and believes this way; and that it is impossible for Christ to permit His church to be in error for so many centuries. They say: "Are you, all by yourself, wiser than so many saints, wiser even than the entire church?" [45] Thus the devil, transformed into an angel of light (2 Cor. 11:14), craftily attacks us today through certain evil hypocrites, who say:[46] "We hold no brief for the pope or the bishops, those great despisers and persecutors of the Word; and we abhor the hypocrisy of the monks. But we are concerned that the authority of the holy catholic church stand unimpaired. The church has believed and taught this way for so many centuries; so have all the fathers of the primitive church, who were saints, more ancient and more learned than you are. Who are you, then, to take it upon yourself to dissent from all these and to bring us an opposing doctrine?" When Satan conspires with your flesh and your reason to argue this way, your conscience is

[45] The same idea is developed more fully elsewhere; cf. *Luther's Works,* 2, p. 54, and *Luther the Expositor,* pp. 98—99.

[46] It is not clear whom Luther has in mind specifically; but it may well be Erasmus, who, as one interpreter has put it, "had his criticism of the popes in person, but wished to preserve the institution, be it with a competence limited to moral and arbitral matters, in the expectation that also this human work could be humanly improved, and that respect for a truly human Father could keep mankind morally straight." H. A. Enno van Gelder, *The Two Reformations in the 16th Century* (The Hague, 1961), p. 241.

terrified and despairs completely, unless you continually recover your sense and say: "Whether it is St. Cyprian, Ambrose, or Augustine, St. Peter, Paul, or John, yes, or even an angel from heaven that teaches otherwise — I still know this for certain, that what I teach is not from men but from God. That is, I attribute everything solely to God and nothing at all to men."

I recall that when my movement first began, Dr. Staupitz, a very worthy man and the vicar of the Augustinian Order, said to me: "It pleases me very much that this doctrine of ours gives glory and everything else solely to God and nothing at all to men; for it is as clear as day that it is impossible to ascribe too much glory, goodness, etc., to God." [47] So it was that he consoled me. And it is true that the doctrine of the Gospel takes away all glory, wisdom, righteousness, etc., from men and gives it solely to the Creator, who makes all things out of nothing. Furthermore, it is far safer to ascribe too much to God than to men. For here I can declare boldly: "All right, let the holy church, Augustine and other fathers, also Peter and Apollos, yes, even an angel from heaven, teach an opposing doctrine! Still my doctrine is one that preaches and worships God alone, and it condemns the righteousness and the wisdom of all men. Here I cannot go wrong, for both to God and to man I ascribe what properly and truly belongs to each."

But "the church is holy, the fathers are holy!" Granted. Nevertheless, even though the church is holy, it still has to pray (Matt. 6:12): "Forgive us our debts." Similarly, even though the fathers are holy, they are still obliged to believe in the forgiveness of sins. Therefore if we teach anything contrary to the Word of God, neither I nor the church nor the fathers nor the apostles nor even an angel from heaven should be believed. But let the Word of the Lord abide forever (1 Peter 1:25), for without it this argumentation of the false apostles would have prevailed altogether against Paul's doctrine. For it was really something tremendous to line up the whole church and all the company of the apostles [48] on one side before the Galatians, and on the other side just Paul, a newcomer with very little authority. Thus this was a cogent and nearly conclusive argument. For no one likes to say that the church is in error; and yet, if the church teaches

[47] See also *Luther's Works*, 14, p. 283.

[48] This is a quotation from the *Te Deum:* "the chorus of the apostles praises Thee."

anything in addition or contrary to the Word of God, one must say that it is in error.

Peter, the prince of the apostles, lived and taught contrary to the Word of God. Therefore he was in error. And because he was at fault, Paul "opposed him to the face" (Gal. 2:11), attacking him because he was not in conformity with the truth of the Gospel. Here you see that Peter, the most holy apostle, erred. Thus I will not listen to the church or the fathers or the apostles unless they bring and teach the pure Word of God.

Today, too, this argument makes quite a telling point against us. For if we are to believe neither the pope nor the fathers nor Luther nor anyone else unless they teach us the pure Word of God, whom are we to believe? Who will give our consciences sure information about which party is teaching the pure Word of God, we or our opponents? For they, too, claim to have and to teach the pure Word of God. On the other hand, we do not believe the papists, because they neither teach nor can teach the Word of God. They again hate us bitterly and persecute us as the vilest heretics and seducers of the people. What is to be done here? Is every fanatic to have the right to teach whatever he pleases, since the world refuses to listen to or to tolerate our teaching? With Paul we boast that we teach the pure Gospel of Christ. Not only should the pope, the sectarians, the fathers, and the church submit to this Gospel; they should receive it with open arms, accept it gratefully, embrace it, and propagate it to others. But if anyone teaches otherwise, whether the pope or St. Augustine or an apostle or an angel from heaven, let him and his gospel be accursed. Still we do not make any progress but are forced to hear that our boasting is not only vain, brazen, and arrogant but blasphemous and demonic. And yet, if we lower ourselves and yield to the ravings of our opponents, both the papists and the sectarians will become proud. The sectarians will brag that they are bringing some strange new doctrine never before heard of by the world, and the papists will reestablish their old abominations. Therefore let everyone take care to be most certain of his calling and doctrine, so that he may boldly and surely say with Paul (Gal. 1:8): "Even if we, or an angel from heaven, etc."

So much, then, on the central proposition of this passage, which is: "I have not received my Gospel from a man, but through a revelation of Jesus Christ." Now he will prove this proposition at length by citing many historical events.

13. *For you have heard of my former life in Judaism, how I perse-*
cuted the church of God violently and tried to destroy it;

14. *and I advanced in Judaism beyond many of my own age among*
my people.

Nothing is needed here but word study. Paul is citing his own
example: "I once defended Pharisaism and Judaism more vigorously
and steadfastly than you and your false teachers did. Therefore if
the righteousness of the Law were worth anything, I would have
remained a Pharisee. For I, too, was a Pharisee, and I pursued the
traditions of the fathers with greater zeal than the false apostles do
today. And yet I regarded them and all Judaism as of little worth."
Thus I, too, suffered greater trouble in vigils and fasts when I was
a monk than all those who persecute me today. I was superstitious
to the point of delirium and insanity, and to the jeopardy of my
body and its health. Whatever I did, I did with great zeal and for
the sake of God. I adored the pope sincerely, not out of a desire
for prebends or riches. And yet in comparison with the righteousness
of Christ I threw away these σκύβαλα. But our blind and hardhearted
opponents do not believe that I as well as others have had experience
with such Pharisaism.

So extremely zealous was I for the traditions of my fathers.

Here Paul does not call the traditions of the fathers "pharisaical"
or "human" traditions, as Jerome supposes.[49] For in this passage he
is not discussing the traditions of the Pharisees; he is discussing
a much sublimer issue. Therefore he calls even the holy Law of
Moses "the traditions of my fathers," in the sense that they were
handed down and received as a legacy from the fathers. "For these,"
he says, "I was very zealous when I was a part of Judaism." He
speaks the same way to the Philippians (3:5-6): "As to the Law
I was a Pharisee, as to zeal a persecutor of the church, as to righteousness under the Law blameless." It is as though he were saying:
"Here I may brag openly and put myself against the entire Jewish
people, even the best and holiest of all those who belong to the
circumcision. Let them show me, if they can, a more zealous and
earnest defender of the Law of Moses than I was! I was an outstanding zealot for the traditions of the fathers, a devotee of the

---

[49] Jerome, *Commentarius in Epistolam S. Pauli ad Galatas,* I, *Patrologia,
Series Latina,* XXVI, 349.

righteousness of the Law. This in itself, you Galatians, should have persuaded you not to believe these deceivers, who lay great stress on the righteousness of the Law as an issue of great importance. For if there were any grounds for boasting in the righteousness of the Law, I would have more grounds for boasting than anyone else."

15. *But when He who had set me apart before I was born, and had called me through His grace,*

16. *was pleased to reveal His Son to me, in order that I might preach Him among the Gentiles, I did not confer with flesh and blood,*

17. *nor did I go up to Jerusalem to those who were apostles before me, but I went away into Arabia; and again I returned to Damascus.*

This refers to Paul's first journey. Jerome exerts himself mightily here, saying that in the Book of Acts Luke does not even mention Paul's journey to Arabia — as though it were necessary to record the events and actions of every single day, which would be impossible! [50] Let this suffice, that we have some details and a certain number of accounts from which we can derive teaching and examples.

Here Paul testifies that immediately after he had been called by the grace of God to preach Christ among the Gentiles, he went to Arabia — and that not on the advice of any human being — to perform the task to which he had been called. This text tells you who taught him and by what means he came to the knowledge of grace and to his apostolate. "When God was pleased to," he says. It is as though he were saying: "I did not deserve this; for I was zealous for the Law of God, but without judgment. In fact, my foolish and wicked zeal so blinded me that, with the permission of God, I fell straight into even more abominable and outrageous sins. I persecuted the church of God; I was an enemy of Christ; I blasphemed His Gospel; and finally I was responsible for the shedding of much innocent blood. This was what I had deserved myself. But in the very midst of this cruel rage I was called to such grace. On what grounds? Because of my outrageous cruelty? Of course not! But the abundant grace of God, who calls and shows mercy, pardoned and forgave me all those blasphemies. And in place of these horrible sins of mine, which I then regarded as a service most pleasing to God, He gave me His grace and called me to be an apostle."

[50] Jerome, *Commentarius in Epistolam S. Pauli ad Galatas*, I, *Patrologia, Series Latina*, XXVI, 352—353.

In our own day we have come to the knowledge of grace by the same "merits." I crucified Christ daily in my monastic life, and I blasphemed God through the false trust in which I was constantly living. Outwardly I was not like other men: extortioners, unjust, adulterers (Luke 18:11). I observed chastity, poverty, and obedience.[51] In addition, I was free of the cares of this present life and was devoted only to fasting, vigils, prayers, reading Mass, and things like that. Nevertheless, under the cover of this sanctity and confidence I was nursing incessant mistrust, doubt, fear, hatred, and blasphemy against God. This righteousness of mine was nothing but a cesspool and the delightful kingdom of the devil. For Satan loves such saints and treats as his own beloved those who destroy their own bodies and souls, and who deprive themselves of all the blessings of the gifts of God. Even as they do this, however, malice, blindness, contempt for God, ignorance of the Gospel, profanation of the sacraments, blasphemy and abuse of Christ, and the neglect of all the blessings of God hold full sway in them. In short, such saints are the slaves of Satan. Therefore they are impelled to think, say, and do whatever he wishes, even though outwardly they seem to surpass everyone else in good works, holiness, and austerity of life.

That is how we were under the papacy, truly no less insulting and blasphemous against Christ and His Gospel than Paul was, and perhaps even worse than he. I was especially bad. I had a horror even of the name of John Hus;[52] in fact, I regarded it as a grave offense to think of him. And I would have been willing — so zealously did I obey the pope — to have provided fire and sword to burn and destroy that heretic, if not in deed, then in spirit; and I would have thought that thereby I was offering a high service to God (John 16:2). Therefore if you compare publicans and harlots with these holy hypocrites, they are not evil. For when they offend, such sinners have remorse of conscience, and they do not justify their evil deeds. But these men, far from acknowledging that their abominations, idolatries, and wicked acts of worship are sins, actually declare that they are a sacrifice pleasing to God. In fact, they adore them as a thing of special holiness; and through them they promise

[51] A reference to the threefold monastic vow of poverty, chastity, and obedience.

[52] Luther tells this story at greater length in his preface to the *Confessio Bohemica* (W, L, 379).

salvation to others and even sell them for money as something that
avails for salvation.

This, then, is our great righteousness and valuable merit that
bring us to the knowledge of grace: that we have murderously and
demonically persecuted, blasphemed, abused, and condemned God,
Christ, the Gospel, faith, the sacraments, all pious men, and the true
worship of God, and have taught and established the very opposite.
And the holier we were, the more blinded we were, and the more
sincerely we worshiped the devil. Every single one of us was a blood-
sucker, if not in fact, then in heart.

When God was pleased.

This is as though Paul were saying: "It is only the unspeakable
kindness of God that He has not only spared me — a good-for-nothing,
a criminal, a blasphemer, and a sacrilegious man — but that He has
also given me the knowledge of salvation, His Spirit, Christ His Son,
the apostolic office, and life eternal." Seeing us in similar sins, God
has not only pardoned our wickedness and blasphemies out of His
sheer mercy for the sake of Christ; but He has also showered us
with His great blessings and spiritual gifts. But many among us
not only, as 2 Peter 1:9 says, "have forgotten that they were cleansed
from their old sins"; but, opening a window to the devil again, they
begin to loathe His Word, and many also pervert it and thus become
the founders of new sects. The last state of such men is worse than
the first (Matt. 12:45).

Who had set me apart before I was born.

This is a Hebrew expression. It is as though Paul were saying:
"Who had sanctified, ordained, and prepared me. That is, God had
ordained, even before I was born, that I should rage against His
church this way, and that afterwards He would mercifully call me
back from my cruelty and blasphemy, by His sheer grace, into the
way of truth and salvation. In brief, when I had not yet been born,
I was already an apostle in the sight of God; and when the time had
come, I was declared to be an apostle in the sight of the world."

Thus Paul abolishes all "deserving"; he gives the glory only to
God, but to himself only confusion. It is as though Paul wanted to
say: "Every gift — whether great or small, whether physical or
spiritual — that God intended to give to me, and all the good things
that I was ever to do at any time in all my life — all this God

had predestined even before I was born, when I could not think, wish, or do anything good but was a shapeless embryo. Therefore this gift came to me by the mere predestination and merciful grace of God even before I was born. And then, after I was born, He still supported me, even though I was covered with innumerable and horrible iniquities and evils. To declare the unspeakable and inestimable greatness of His mercy to me even more obviously, He forgave my infinite and horrible sins by His sheer grace. So generously did He shower me with His grace that I not only knew what is given to us in Christ but also preached this to others." This is what all men deserve and merit, and especially those old fools who are busy only in the filth of man's own righteousness.

And had called me through His grace.

Note how diligent the apostle is. "He called me," he says. And how? Was it on the basis of my Pharisaism, my blameless and holy life, or my prayers, fasts, and works? No. Much less was it for my blasphemies, persecutions, and oppressions! How then? By His sheer grace alone.

To reveal His Son to me.

In this passage you hear what sort of doctrine was given and committed to Paul, namely, the doctrine of the Gospel, which is the revelation of the Son of God; as Ps. 2:11 says, "Kiss the Son." This is a doctrine different from all others. Moses does not reveal the Son of God; he discloses the Law, sin, the conscience, death, the wrath and judgment of God, and hell. These things are not the Son of God! Therefore only the Gospel reveals the Son of God. Oh, if only one could distinguish carefully here and not look for the Law in the Gospel but keep it as separate from the Law as heaven is distant from the earth! In itself the difference is easy and clear, but to us it is difficult and well-nigh incomprehensible. For it is easy to say that the Gospel is nothing but the revelation of the Son of God or the knowledge of Jesus Christ and not the revelation or knowledge of the Law. But in the conflict of conscience and in practice it is difficult even for those who have had a lot of experience to hold to this for certain.

Now if the Gospel is the revelation of the Son of God, as it really is, then it certainly does not demand works, threaten death, or terrify the conscience. But it shows the Son of God, who is neither the Law nor a work. But this simply cannot persuade the papists. Therefore they make a "Law of charity" [53] of the Gospel. But Christ is the subject [54] of the Gospel. What the Gospel teaches and shows me is a divine work given to me by sheer grace; neither human reason nor wisdom nor even the Law of God teaches this. And I accept this gift by faith alone.

To reveal His Son to me.

This sort of doctrine, which reveals the Son of God, is not taught, learned, or judged by any human wisdom or by the Law itself; it is revealed by God, first by the external Word and then inwardly through the Spirit. Therefore the Gospel is a divine Word that came down from heaven and is revealed by the Holy Spirit, who was sent for this very purpose. Yet this happens in such a way that the external Word must come first. For Paul himself did not have an inward revelation until he had heard the outward Word from heaven, namely, "Saul, Saul, why do you persecute Me?" (Acts 9:4). Thus he heard the outward Word first; only then did there follow revelations, the knowledge of the Word, faith, and the gifts of the Spirit.

That I might preach Him among the Gentiles.

See how aptly Paul arranges his words! "God was pleased," he says, "to reveal His Son to me." For what purpose? "Not only that I myself might believe in His Son, but also that I might reveal Him among the Gentiles." Why not among the Jews? Here you see that Paul is properly the apostle of the Gentiles, even though he preached Christ among the Jews as well. Here Paul summarizes his whole theology in a few words, as he often does: to preach Christ among the Gentiles. It is as though he were saying: "I refuse to burden the Gentiles with the Law, because I am the apostle and evangelist of the Gentiles, not their lawgiver." Thus he aims all his words against the false apostles. It is as though he were saying: "You Galatians, you have not heard me teach the righteousness of the Law or of works; for this belongs to Moses, not to me,

[53] "The new Law, which derives its preeminence from the spiritual grace instilled into our hearts, is called 'the Law of love.'" Thomas Aquinas, *Summa Theologica*, I—II, Q. 107, Art. 1.

[54] The Latin word *obiectum* here means "subject"; on this development cf. *Luther's Works*, 1, p. 58, note 92.

Paul, who am the apostle to the Gentiles. It is my office and ministry to bring you the Gospel and to show you the same revelation that I myself have had. Therefore you should not listen to any teacher who teaches the Law. For among the Gentiles not the Law but the Gospel should be preached, not Moses but the Son of God, not the righteousness of works but the righteousness of faith. This is the proclamation that is proper for the Gentiles."

I did not confer with flesh and blood.

Here St. Jerome engages in a great controversy with Porphyry and Julian, who accuse Paul of arrogance because he was not willing to confer with the rest of the apostles about his Gospel, as well as because Paul calls the apostles "flesh and blood." [55] But, to answer briefly, when Paul refers to "flesh and blood" here, he is not speaking of the apostles; for later on he adds: "Nor did I go up to Jerusalem, to those who were apostles before me." But what he means is this: Once he had received the revelation of the Gospel from Christ, he did not confer with anyone in Damascus; much less did he ask someone to teach him the Gospel. Nor did he go to Jerusalem, to Peter and the other apostles, to learn the Gospel from them. But immediately upon receiving Baptism from Ananias in Damascus and the laying on of hands — for it was necessary for him to have an outward sign and witness of his calling — he proclaimed Jesus as the Son of God. Luke writes the same thing in the ninth chapter of Acts.

17. *Nor did I go up to Jerusalem, to those who were apostles before me, but I went away into Arabia; and again I returned to Damascus.*

That is: "Before seeing the apostles or conferring with them I went to Arabia, and immediately I took upon myself the ministry of preaching the Gospel among the Gentiles; for I had been called to this and had also received a revelation from God." Therefore it is idle for Jerome to ask what Paul did in Arabia. What else was he to do but preach Christ? For, as he says, the Son of God was revealed to him for this purpose, that he might preach Him among the Gentiles. Therefore he travels from Damascus, a Gentile city, directly to Arabia, where there were Gentiles also; and there he

[55] Jerome, *Commentarius in Epistolam S. Pauli ad Galatas,* I, *Patrologia, Series Latina,* XXVI, 351.

carries out his ministry with vigor. He did not learn his Gospel from any human being or from the apostles themselves, nor did he obtain permission from them; but he was content with his call from heaven and with the revelation of Jesus Christ alone.

Therefore this whole passage is a refutation of the argument that the false apostles were using against Paul. They said that he was only a pupil and hearer of the apostles, who lived according to the Law. They said, moreover, that Paul himself had also lived according to the Law, and that therefore it was necessary for the Gentiles to observe the Law and to be circumcised. To refute them, he narrates this long history: "Before my conversion I did not learn my Gospel from the apostles or from any of the other believers; for I violently persecuted not only this doctrine but the church of God, and ravaged it. Nor did I learn it from them after my conversion; for at Damascus I immediately preached and did not confer with anyone. I had not even seen any of the apostles as yet."

In the same way we can boast that we did not receive our doctrine from the pope. We do indeed have Sacred Scripture and the external symbols from him, but not the doctrine, which came to us solely by the gift of God, to which our own study, reading, and research have been added. Therefore the argument directed against us by our opponents today is vain, when they say: "You Lutherans, why should one believe your doctrine, since you do not occupy a public office? You should take your doctrine from the pope and the bishops, who are properly ordained and occupy a legitimate office."

18. *Then after three years I went up to Jerusalem to visit Cephas, and remained with him fifteen days.*

19. *But I saw none of the other apostles except James, the Lord's brother.*

Paul does not deny that he was with the apostles. Indeed, he concedes that he was with them, but not with all of them. He declares that he went to them in Jerusalem, not under orders but of his own accord, not to learn anything from the apostles but to see Peter. Luke writes the same thing in the ninth chapter of Acts (9:26 ff.): Barnabas brought Paul to the apostles and told them that Paul had seen the Lord on the road, that He had spoken to him, and that Paul had preached boldly in Damascus in the name of Jesus; Barnabas testifies to this about him. All of Paul's words are put in such a way as to prove that his Gospel was not from men. He concedes that he had seen Peter and James, the brother of our Lord, but none of the others except for these two; and from them he did not learn anything.

Thus Paul concedes that he had been at Jerusalem with the apostles, and to this extent the report of the false apostles is correct. He concedes also that he had lived in accordance with the Jewish manner of living, but he had done so only among the Jews. For Paul observed this rule: "When in Rome, do as the Romans do." [56] This is what he says in 1 Cor. 9:19-22: "Though I am free from all men, I have made myself a slave to all, that I might win the more. To the Jews I became as a Jew, etc. I have become all things to all men, that I might save all." Therefore he concedes to the argument of the false apostles that he was at Jerusalem with the apostles; but he denies that he learned his Gospel from the apostles, or that he was obliged to teach the Gospel as the apostles had wished. Thus the whole point lies in the word "see." "I went," he says, "to see Peter, not to learn from him. Therefore Peter is not my master; nor is James." And so far as the other apostles are concerned, he denies completely that he saw any of them.

But why does Paul repeat so often, almost too often, that he did not learn his Gospel from men or even from the apostles themselves? It is his purpose to persuade the churches of Galatia, which had been led astray by the false apostles, and to convince them beyond any doubt that his Gospel was the true Word of God. That is why he repeats it so vigorously. And if he had not made this point, he could never have refuted the false apostles; for they would have raised this objection: "We are just as good as Paul. We are pupils of the apostles as much as he is. Besides, he is only one person, and we are many. Therefore we surpass him both in authority and in number." Here Paul was forced to boast, affirm, and swear that he had not learned his Gospel from anyone or received it from the apostles themselves. Such boasting was extremely necessary and was not empty bragging, as Porphyry and Julian falsely assert; they did not understand Paul's point, and neither did Jerome. For his ministry was in great jeopardy here; so were all the churches that had had him as their teacher. Thus the necessity of Paul's ministry and of all

[56] The origin of this proverb is attributed to Ambrose by Augustine, Epistle XXXVI, *Patrologia, Series Latina*, XXXIII-2, 151.

the churches demanded that with a necessary and holy pride he should boast of his vocation and of the knowledge of the Gospel revealed to him by Christ. Then their consciences would be completely persuaded that Paul's doctrine was the Word of God. Here Paul was dealing with a great and serious issue, namely, that all the churches might be preserved in sound doctrine. In short, the issue in the controversy was a matter of eternal life and death. For once the pure and certain Word is taken away, there remains no consolation, no salvation, no life. Thus the reason Paul recites all this is to keep the churches in true and sound doctrine. He is not battling to defend his own glory, as Porphyry insults him. By this history he seeks to show that he did not receive his Gospel from any man, and that for quite some years — namely, for three or four years — both in Damascus and in Arabia — he had preached by divine revelation the very same Gospel that the apostles had preached, and that before he had seen any of the apostles.

Here Jerome plays around with the mystery of the fifteen days.[57] He says that in those fifteen days Paul was taught by Peter and inducted into the mystery of the Ogdoad and the Hebdoad. But this has nothing to do with the facts. For Paul says in plain words that he came to Jerusalem to see Peter, and that he stayed with him fifteen days. If it had been his purpose to learn the Gospel from Peter, he would have had to stay there several years! In the course of fifteen days he could not have become such a great apostle and teacher of the Gentiles — not to say that in these fifteen days, as Luke testifies in Acts 9:28 ff., he spoke with boldness in the name of the Lord Jesus and disputed with the Greeks, etc.

20. *(In what I am writing to you, before God, I do not lie!)*

Why does Paul add an oath? Because he is narrating a history. He is obliged to swear, in order that the churches may believe him. Otherwise the false apostles might say: "Who knows whether what Paul is saying is true?" Here you see that such a great apostle of Christ was held in such great contempt among his own Galatians, to whom he had preached Christ, that it was necessary for him to swear that he was telling the truth. If this happened to the apostles then — that they had despisers, in fact, big men who dared accuse them of

57 Jerome, *Commentarius in Epistolam S. Pauli ad Galatas*, I, *Patrologia, Series Latina*, XXVI, 354.

lying — it is no wonder that a similar thing happens to us, who are not worthy of comparison with the apostles in any way. He is swearing to what seems to be a trivial matter, namely, that he is telling the truth when he says that he stayed with Peter to see him, not to learn from him. But if you consider the matter more carefully, it is very weighty and grave, as is clear from what has been said earlier. We follow the example of Paul and swear: "God knows that we are not lying!"

21. *Then I went into the regions of Syria and Cilicia.*

Syria and Cilicia are provinces situated close together. Throughout Paul is trying to convince them that before and after he had seen the apostles, he was always a preacher of the Gospel, which he had received by the revelation of Christ, and that he had never been a pupil of any of the apostles.

22. *And I was still not known by sight to the churches of Christ in Judea;*

23. *they only heard it said: He who once persecuted us is now preaching the faith he once tried to destroy.*

24. *And they glorified God because of me.*

Paul adds this to fill in and complete the story, that after seeing Peter he went into Syria and Cilicia and preached there, indeed preached in such a way that he won the testimony of all the churches in Judea. It is as though he were saying: "I appeal to the testimony of all the churches, also of those that are in Judea. For the churches testify — not only those in Damascus, Arabia, Syria, and Cilicia but those in Judea as well — that I preached the same faith I once persecuted and opposed. And they glorified God because of me, not because I taught that circumcision and the Law of Moses were to be observed, but because I preached faith and built up the churches by my ministry of the Gospel. Therefore you have the testimony not only of the people of Damascus and Arabia but also of the whole catholic church in Judea."

CHAPTER TWO

1. *Then after fourteen years I went up again to Jerusalem.*

This was the bitter conflict in which Paul was suddenly so deeply involved. Paul taught that the Gentiles were justified by faith alone, without the works of the Law (Rom. 3:28). When he had broadcast this doctrine among the Gentiles, he came to Antioch and told the disciples what he had been doing. Then those who had been reared according to the old traditions of the Law rose up against Paul and declared that it was intolerable for him to preach to the Gentiles about liberty from the slavery of the Law. This gave rise to an outburst in Antioch. Paul and Barnabas took a strong stand and testified: "Wherever we preached among the Gentiles, the Holy Spirit came down upon those who heard the Word. This happened throughout all the Gentile churches. But we neither preached circumcision nor required observance of the Law of Moses. All we preached was faith in Christ, and upon this proclamation of faith God gave the Holy Spirit to the hearers. Therefore the Holy Spirit gives His approval to the faith of the Gentiles without the Law or circumcision. For if the preaching of the Gospel and the faith of the Gentiles in Christ had not been pleasing to Him, He would not have descended in a visible form upon the uncircumcised who heard the Word. Since He descended upon them merely through the hearing of faith, it is altogether certain that by this sign the Holy Spirit has given His approval to their faith; for this seems never to have happened through the preaching of the Law." This was how Paul and Barnabas argued.

Then many took the opposite position. They said that the Law had to be observed and that if the Gentiles were not circumcised in accordance with the Law of Moses, they could not be saved. Paul fought back vigorously. And this controversy over the observance of the Law continued to plague him for a long time to come. Yet I do not think that this is the same controversy that Luke describes in Acts 15. For that one seems to have arisen right after the beginning of the Gospel; but the history that Paul is reciting here seems to have

[79]

happened much later, because he had already been preaching the Gospel for almost eighteen years.

Then the Jews, who were very zealous for the Law and very contentious, resisted Paul vigorously for preaching that the Gentiles were justified by faith alone, without the works of the Law. And no wonder, for the very name "Law of God" is very forceful and impressive to the human heart. If a pagan who has never known anything about the Law of God hears someone say: "This teaching is the Law of God," he will surely be stirred. Then how could the Jews not be stirred to take a strong stand in support of the Law of God, in which they had been trained since infancy and which they had absorbed deeply into their bones and marrow? In our day we see how obstinately the papists defend their traditions and the doctrines of demons (1 Tim. 4:1). So it is much less surprising that the Jews were so vigorous and zealous in support of their Law, which they had received from God Himself. The force of habit strengthens our nature, which has an inclination of itself to observe the Law; thus a habit of long standing and tradition becomes second nature. Therefore it was impossible for the Jews to give up the Law immediately after being converted to Christ. Although they had accepted faith in Christ, they still thought that it was necessary to observe the Law. God tolerated this weakness of theirs for a while, until there would be a clear distinction between the doctrine of the Gospel and the Law. Thus He tolerated the weakness of Israel during the time of Ahab, when the people were undecided between two sides (1 Kings 16:29 ff.). He tolerated our weakness too while we were under the papacy, for He is patient and merciful. But we must not abuse this goodness of God or persist in our weakness and error, for now the truth is being revealed to us by the light of the Gospel.

Those who opposed Paul and claimed that the Gentiles were to be circumcised had on their side first the Law of the land, then also the example of the apostles, and finally the example of Paul himself, who had circumcised Timothy. Therefore if Paul said that he had done this, not out of compulsion but out of Christian charity and freedom, to keep from offending the weak, who among them would understand him or believe him? The response of all the crowd to this defense would be: "Since it is obvious that you have circumcised Timothy, you may say what you please. The fact remains that you did it." This was a matter that transcended the understanding of the crowd. Besides, when a man has lost favor with the people and has come under such bitter hatred, no defense is of any avail. Seeing that this controversy and this outcry were increasing every day, and having been warned by a divine revelation, Paul went up to Jerusalem to compare his Gospel with that of the other apostles, not indeed on his own account but on account of the people.

With Barnabas, taking Titus along with me.

Paul associates himself with two witnesses, Barnabas and Titus. Barnabas was Paul's companion in preaching to the Gentiles about freedom from the Law. He was also a witness of everything that Paul had done; he had seen that merely through the preaching of faith in Christ the Holy Spirit had been granted to Gentiles who were not circumcised or subject to the Law of Moses. He was the only one to support Paul in the insistence that it was not necessary to burden the Gentiles with the Law, but that it was enough for them to believe in Christ. Therefore he testifies for Paul and against the zealous and legalistic Jews on the basis of his own experience that the Gentiles became children of God and were saved solely by faith in Jesus Christ, without the Law or circumcision.

Titus was not only a Christian. He was an archbishop, to whom Paul had committed the rule of the churches in Crete (Titus 1:5). And this Titus was a Gentile.

2. I went up by revelation.

Otherwise Paul would have been stubborn and would not have gone up. But he went because God warned him by a special revelation and commanded him to go. He did this to restrain, or at least to appease, the Jews who were believers but continued to argue about the observance of the Law. His purpose was to promote and establish the truth of the Gospel.

And I laid before them the Gospel.

Here you are told that finally, after eighteen years, Paul went up to Jerusalem and argued with the apostles regarding his Gospel.

Which I preach among the Gentiles.

Paul means that among the Jews he had permitted the Law and circumcision to stand for a while, as had the other apostles. "I have become all things to all men," he says (1 Cor. 9:22). Yet he always maintained the true doctrine of his Gospel, which he elevated above the Law, above circumcision, above the apostles, yes, even above an angel from heaven (Gal. 1:8). For this is what he says to the Jews in Acts 13:38: "Through this Christ forgiveness of sins is proclaimed to you." And he adds very plainly (v. 39): "And by Him everyone that believes is freed from everything from which you could not be freed by the Law of Moses." This is the reason he teaches and defends the doctrine of the Gospel so diligently everywhere and refuses to let it be endangered. Nevertheless, he did not make a radical break right away; but he took account of those who were weak. In order not to offend the weak he undoubtedly spoke to the Jews as follows: "The observance of the Law of Moses is superfluous and contributes nothing to righteousness. Still, if you like it so well, you may go on observing it for all I care — just so that the Gentiles, who are not bound by this worship, do not have it imposed upon them!"

Thus Paul concedes that he discussed the Gospel with the apostles. "But," he says, "they did not do me any good or teach me anything. Quite the contrary. We were the ones who prevailed on behalf of the freedom of the Gospel. Tell this to your false apostles when they say that it was at the behest of the apostles that I circumcised Timothy, cut my hair at Cenchreae, and went up to Jerusalem; for they are lying.[1] No, I am proud that when I went up to Jerusalem, not at the behest of the apostles but by a divine revelation, and discussed my Gospel with them, I succeeded in obtaining the opposite result, namely, that the apostles approved me rather than them."

The question discussed in this conference about the Gospel was this: whether men could be justified without the Law, and whether observance of the Law was necessary for justification or not. Paul's answer was: "On the basis of the Gospel that I received from God I have proclaimed, not the Law but faith in Christ to the Gentiles. Through this proclamation of faith they have received the Holy Spirit, as Barnabas can attest. From this I conclude that the Gentiles should not be burdened with the Law or be circumcised. Yet I will not stand in the way of those Jews who feel obligated to observe the Law and be circumcised. I have nothing against this, so long as they do so with a free conscience. This is how I have taught and lived among the Jews. 'To the Jews I became as a Jew' (1 Cor. 9:20), but I always kept my Gospel."

[1] See p. 61, note 39.

But privately before those who were of repute.

That is: "I did not confer only with the brethren; I conferred with those among them who had the highest reputation."

Lest somehow I should be running or had run in vain.

This does not mean that Paul was in doubt whether or not he had been, or was, running in vain. For he had been preaching the Gospel for eighteen years now, and the text goes on to say immediately that he had stood firm and sure all this time and had prevailed. It means rather that there were many who supposed that Paul had preached the Gospel for so many years in vain because he had given the Gentiles freedom from the Law. In addition, the idea was continually gaining ground that the Law was necessary for justification. When he went up to Jerusalem by revelation, his purpose was to remedy this condition. This conference was to make it clear to everyone that his Gospel was not contrary in any way to the doctrine of the other apostles, so that in this way he could silence his opponents, who might otherwise be able to say that he was running, or had run, in vain. Note here in passing that man's own righteousness or the righteousness of the Law has this power, that those who teach it run and live in vain.

3. *But even Titus, who was with me, was not compelled to be circumcised, though he was a Greek.*

The term "was not compelled" makes it clear enough what the outcome of the conference was: that the Gentiles should not be forced to be circumcised; but that the Jews should be permitted to keep circumcision for a time, not as something necessary for righteousness but as an act of reverence toward their fathers and as a concession of charity toward the weak, lest they be offended before they matured in their faith. It might have seemed rude suddenly to forsake the Law and the liturgy of the fathers, which God had given to this nation in such a glorious way.

Thus Paul did not reject circumcision as something damnable; nor did he by any word or deed compel the Jews to give it up. For in 1 Cor. 7:18 he says: "Was anyone at the time of his call already circumcised? Let him not seek to remove the marks of circumcision." But he did reject circumcision in the sense of something necessary for righteousness; for the fathers themselves had not been justified by it but had it merely as a sign or a seal of righteousness (Rom.

[W, XL, 157, 158]

4:11), by which they gave witness and expression to their faith. Nevertheless, when Jews who were believers but were still weak and zealous for the Law heard the statement that circumcision was not necessary for righteousness, they could not take it to mean anything else than that for this reason circumcision was altogether useless and damnable. The false apostles aggravated this impression among the weak with the intent of arousing the hearts of the common people against Paul for his attitude and thus thoroughly discrediting his doctrine. In the same way we today do not reject fasting and other pious practices as something damnable, but we do teach that by these practices we do not obtain the forgiveness of sins. When the common people hear this, they immediately conclude that we are condemning good works. And the papists abet this impression of the people through their sermons and books. But this is a lie and a slander, for it has been a long time since anyone taught a more pious and sound doctrine of good works than we do today.

Therefore Paul did not condemn circumcision in the sense that it was sinful to accept or retain it, for this would have been deeply offensive to the Jews. But the decree stated that circumcision was not necessary for justification and that therefore it was not to be forced upon the Gentiles. Thus they found this moderation or ἐπιείκεια,[2] that out of reverence toward the fathers and out of charity toward the weak in faith the Jews were to observe the Law and circumcision for a time but were not to try to be justified by this. In addition, the Gentiles were not to be burdened with the Law, both because it would have been something novel for them and because it would have been an unbearable burden, as Peter says in Acts 15:10. In other words, no one should be forced to be circumcised, and no one should be prevented from being circumcised.

Jerome and Augustine engage in a bitter controversy over this passage.[3] The term "was not compelled" supports Augustine's case. But Jerome did not understand the issue. The issue here is not, as Jerome supposes, what Peter or Paul did about circumcising or not

----

[2] On the notion of ἐπιείκεια see also *Luther's Works*, 3, p. 262, note 31.

[3] For the progress of this controversy cf. Jerome, *Commentarius in Epistolam S. Pauli ad Galatas*, I, *Patrologia, Series Latina*, XXVI, 358—359, and the following letters: Augustine to Jerome, Epistle XL, chs. III—IV, *Patrologia, Series Latina*, XXXIII, 155—157; Jerome to Augustine, Epistle LXXV, ch. III, pars. 4—11, ibid., cols. 252—257; Augustine to Jerome, Epistle LXXXII, ch. II, pars. 4—22, ibid., cols. 277—286.

circumcising. Therefore Jerome is amazed that Paul had the audacity to denounce in Peter what he himself had done; for, he says, Paul circumcised Timothy and lived as a Gentile among Gentiles but as a Jew among Jews. Jerome imagines that what is at issue here is not very important; therefore he concludes that neither Peter nor Paul had sinned, but he imagines that both had covered things up with a "white lie." [4] As a matter of fact, however, this entire controversy of theirs was, and is, serious business; it deals with the gravest of issues. Therefore it was not a matter of covering things up.

The basic issue was this: Is the Law necessary for justification, or is it not? Paul and Peter are in controversy here over this particular theme, on which the whole of Christian doctrine depends. Paul was too responsible a person to launch such a public attack on Peter in the presence of the entire church of Antioch on account of some trivial issue. He is attacking him on account of the basic doctrine of Christianity. For when there were no Jews present, Peter ate with Gentiles; but when the Jews arrived, he withdrew. Paul rebukes him because by his pretense he was compelling the Gentiles to do as the Jews did. The whole emphasis lies on the phrase "you are compelling." But Jerome did not see this.

Therefore Paul did not require that anyone who wanted to be circumcised should remain uncircumcised, but he did want him to know that circumcision was not necessary for justification. Paul wanted to remove this compulsion. Therefore he allowed the Jews to observe the Law as an obligation;[5] but he always taught both Jews and Gentiles that in their conscience they should be free from the Law and circumcision, just as the patriarchs and all the Old Testament saints were free in their conscience and were justified by faith, not by circumcision or the Law.

In fact, Paul might have permitted Titus to be circumcised; but when he saw that they wanted to compel him, Paul refused. For if those who were demanding circumcision had had their way, they would have jumped to the conclusion that circumcision was necessary for righteousness; and thus, because of Paul's permission, they would have prevailed against him. In the same way we grant freedom to everyone to put on a cowl or to take it off, to enter a monastery or to leave it, to eat meat or vegetables. Only let him do these

---

[4] See the discussion, based on Augustine, in *Luther's Works*, 2, pp. 291—292.

[5] The original is *ut legem servarent opere necessariam.*

things freely and without offense to conscience, as an example of charity. And let him know that none of these things avails anything to atone for sins or to win grace. But just as at that time the false apostles refused to leave circumcision and the observance of the Law as matters of indifference but demanded them as something necessary for salvation, so in our day our opponents stubbornly insist that human traditions cannot be dropped without putting salvation in jeopardy. Thus they change a demand of charity into a demand of faith, even though there is only one demand of faith, which is to believe in Jesus Christ. And since this demand is all that is necessary for salvation, it also applies to all men. Yet our opponents would be willing to worship the devil ten times as much as God before admitting this. Day by day they become more obdurate. They use violence and oppression to reestablish and defend their wickedness and blasphemy. They refuse to budge a fingerbreadth. Let us go forth bravely in the name of the Lord of Hosts. Let us set forth the glory of Jesus Christ and do battle against the kingdom of Antichrist with the Word and with prayer, in order that the name of God alone may be hallowed and His kingdom come (Matt. 6:9-10). From the very bottom of our hearts we yearn for this to happen soon. Amen. Amen.

Therefore Paul achieved a glorious victory. Although Titus, the Gentile, was in the midst of the apostles and of all the faithful, where this question was being vehemently debated, he was not compelled to undergo circumcision. Paul obtained this triumph; and he declares that this conference decided, by the consensus of all the apostles and with the approval of the entire church, that Titus was not to be circumcised. This is a powerful argument, one that is very effective against the false apostles. With the argument that "even Titus was not compelled to be circumcised" Paul succeeded in refuting and convincing all his opponents. It is as though he were to say: "Why do these false apostles spread the false rumor about me that I was obligated, at the behest of the apostles, to observe circumcision? For I have the testimony of all the faithful in Jerusalem, indeed of the apostles themselves, that as a result of my efforts the very opposite was decided on. Not only did my position win out there — that Titus was to remain uncircumcised — but the apostles approved and ratified it. Therefore your false apostles are liars; they use the name of the apostles to slander me and to trick you. For I, and not they, have the apostles and all the faithful on my side, and I can prove this from the case of Titus."

At the same time Paul did not condemn circumcision; nor did he compel anyone to undergo it. For it is neither sin nor righteousness to be either uncircumcised or circumcised, just as it is neither sin nor righteousness, but a physical necessity, to eat and drink. For whether you eat or do not eat, you are neither better off nor worse off (1 Cor. 8:8). But if anyone came along and attached either sin or righteousness to it and said: "If you eat, you are sinning; but if you abstain, you are righteous," or vice versa, he would be both foolish and evil. Therefore it is a very wicked thing to attach sin or righteousness to ceremonies. This is what the pope does; in his formula of excommunication he threatens with punishment the soul of anyone who does not obey the laws of the Roman pontiff, and he makes all his laws necessary for salvation.[6] Therefore it is the devil himself who is speaking in the person of the pope and in all such papal decrees. For if salvation consists in the observance of the pope's laws, what need do we have of Christ as our Justifier and Savior?

4. *But because of false brethren secretly brought in, who slipped in to spy out our freedom which we have in Christ Jesus, that they might bring us into bondage –*

5. *to them we did not yield submission even for a moment, that the truth of the Gospel might be preserved for you.*

Here Paul states why he went up to Jerusalem and conferred with the other apostles about his Gospel; he also states why he did not circumcise Titus. It was not to be confirmed by the apostles or to become more certain of his Gospel, for he had no doubts about this. It was rather that the truth of the Gospel might abide among the Galatians and in all the churches of the Gentiles. Thus you see that what was at stake for Paul was no joke and no trifle.

Now when Paul speaks of "the truth of the Gospel," he shows that there are two uses of the Gospel, a true one and a false one, or a true and a false gospel. It is as though he were saying: "The false apostles proclaim a faith and a gospel too, but their gospel is a false gospel. Hence my stubbornness and refusal to yield. I did this in order that the truth of the Gospel might be preserved among you." Thus in our day the pope and the sectarians brag that they proclaim

---

6 In his bull *Unam Sanctam* of November 18, 1302, Boniface VIII had declared: "We declare, say, define, and proclaim to every human creature that they by necessity for salvation are entirely subject to the Roman pontiff."

the Gospel and faith in Christ. Yes, they do, but with the same results that the false apostles once had, those whom Paul (Gal. 1:7) calls troublers of the churches and perverters of the Gospel of Christ. By contrast he says that he is teaching "the truth of the Gospel," the pure and true Gospel, as though he were saying: "Everything else is a lie masquerading as the Gospel." For all the heretics lay claim to the names of God, of Christ, of the church, etc.; and they pretend that they want to teach, not errors but the most certain truth and the purest Gospel.

The truth of the Gospel is this, that our righteousness comes by faith alone, without the works of the Law. The falsification or corruption of the Gospel is this, that we are justified by faith but not without the works of the Law. The false apostles preached the Gospel, but they did so with this condition attached to it. The scholastics do the same thing in our day. They say that we must believe in Christ and that faith is the foundation of salvation, but they say that this faith does not justify unless it is "formed by love." [7] This is not the truth of the Gospel; it is falsehood and pretense. The true Gospel, however, is this: Works or love are not the ornament or perfection of faith; but faith itself is a gift of God, a work of God in our hearts, which justifies us because it takes hold of Christ as the Savior. Human reason has the Law as its object. It says to itself: "This I have done; this I have not done." But faith in its proper function has no other object than Jesus Christ, the Son of God, who was put to death for the sins of the world. It does not look at its love and say: "What have I done? Where have I sinned? What have I deserved?" But it says: "What has Christ done? What has He deserved?" And here the truth of the Gospel gives you the answer: "He has redeemed you from sin, from the devil, and from eternal death." Therefore faith acknowledges that in this one Person, Jesus Christ, it has the forgiveness of sins and eternal life. Whoever diverts his gaze from this object does not have true faith; he has a phantasy and a vain opinion. He looks away from the promise and at the Law, which terrifies him and drives him to despair.

Therefore what the scholastics have taught about justifying faith "formed by love" is an empty dream. For the faith that takes hold of Christ, the Son of God, and is adorned by Him is the faith that

---

[7] On the meaning of *fides charitate formata* cf. Thomas Aquinas, *Summa Theologica*, II—II, Qu. 4, Art. 3.

justifies, not a faith that includes love. For if faith is to be sure and firm, it must take hold of nothing but Christ alone; and in the agony and terror of conscience it has nothing else to lean on than this pearl of great value (Matt. 13:45-46). Therefore whoever takes hold of Christ by faith, no matter how terrified by the Law and oppressed by the burden of his sins he may be, has the right to boast that he is righteous. How has he this right? By that jewel, Christ, whom he possesses by faith. Our opponents fail to understand this. Therefore they reject Christ, this jewel; and in His place they put their love, which they say is a jewel. But if they do not know what faith is, it is impossible for them to have faith, much less to teach it to others. And as for what they claim to have, this is nothing but a dream, an opinion, and natural reason, but not faith.

I am saying all this in order that you may recognize that when Paul speaks emphatically of "the truth of the Gospel," he is vehemently attacking the opposite. He wanted to show that they were abusing the Gospel. By these words he is condemning the false apostles for teaching a false gospel when they required that circumcision be observed. In addition, they used subtle tricks and devices to trap Paul. They watched him closely to see whether he would circumcise Titus and whether he would dare oppose them in the presence of the apostles. On this account he severely condemns them. "They slipped in," he says, "to spy out our freedom which we have in Christ Jesus, that they might bring us into bondage." The false apostles equipped and trained themselves in every possible way to attack and convict Paul in the presence of the church. They also tried to abuse the authority of the apostles, saying: "Paul has brought this uncircumcised Titus into the sight of the whole church. He is denying and condemning the Law in the very presence of you who are apostles. If he has the audacity to try this here in your presence, what would he be willing to try among the Gentiles in your absence?"

When Paul saw that he was being attacked with such tricks, he resisted the false apostles vigorously and said: "We did not permit the liberty we have in Christ Jesus to be imperiled, even though the false brethren tried in every way to trap us and caused us a great deal of trouble. But we overcame them by the very judgment of the apostles themselves, and we did not yield submission to them even for a moment. (For undoubtedly they said: 'Paul, surrender this liberty at least for a while!') For we saw that they wanted to require the observance of the Law as necessary for salvation." If all they had urged was charitable patience with the brethren, Paul would have yielded to them. But they were after something quite different, namely, to bring Paul and all the adherents of his doctrine into bondage. And this was why he refused to yield submission to them even for a moment.

In the same way we are willing to concede everything possible to the papists, in fact, more than we should; but we will not give up the freedom of conscience that we have in Christ Jesus. We will not be forced, or let our conscience be forced, into any work, as though we could be righteous by doing this or that, or as though we could be damned for failing to do it. We are willing to eat the same foods that they eat and to keep the same feasts and fasts, provided that they permit us to do so with a free will and refrain from the threats by which they have terrified and subjugated the whole world, as when they say: "We command, we require, we require once more, we excommunicate, etc." But we cannot obtain the concession of this freedom any more than Paul could. Therefore we do what he did. When he could not obtain this freedom, he refused to yield submission to the false apostles even for a moment.

Just as our opponents refuse to concede to us the freedom that faith in Christ alone justifies, so we refuse to concede to them, in turn, that faith formed by love justifies. Here we intend and are obliged to be rebellious and stubborn with them, for otherwise we would lose the truth of the Gospel. We would lose that freedom which we have, not in the emperor or in kings and princes or in the pope or in the world or in the flesh, but in Christ Jesus. We would lose faith in Christ, which, as I have said, takes hold of nothing but Christ, the Jewel. If our opponents will let us keep intact this faith by which we are born again, justified, and incorporated into Christ, we are willing to do anything for them that is not contrary to this faith. But because we cannot obtain this concession from them, we for our part will not budge the least little bit. For the issue before us is grave and vital; it involves the death of the Son of God, who, by the will and commandment of the Father, became flesh, was crucified, and died for the sins of the world. If faith yields on this point, the death of the Son of God will be in vain. Then it is only a fable that Christ is the Savior of the world. Then God is a liar, for He has not lived up to His promises. Therefore our stubbornness on this issue is pious and holy; for by it we are striving to preserve the freedom we have in Christ Jesus and to keep the truth of the Gospel. If we lose this, we lose God, Christ, all the promises, faith, righteousness, and eternal life.

But here someone will say: "But the Law is divine and holy." Let the Law have its glory. But no Law, no matter how divine or holy, has the right to tell me that I obtain justification and life through it. I will grant that it can teach me that I should love God and my neighbor, and live in chastity, patience, etc.; but it is in no position to show me how to be delivered from sin, the devil, death, and hell. For this I must consult the Gospel and listen to the Gospel, which does not teach me what I should do — for that is the proper function of the Law — but what someone else has done for me, namely, that Jesus Christ, the Son of God, has suffered and died to deliver me from sin and death. The Gospel commands me to accept and believe this, and this is what is called "the truth of the Gospel." It is also the main doctrine of Christianity, in which the knowledge of all godliness is comprehended. It is, therefore, extremely necessary that we come to know this doctrine well and constantly inculcate it. For it is delicate and is easily bruised, as Paul had learned and as all the saints have often experienced.

In short, Paul was not willing to circumcise Titus, and this, as he says, for no other reason than that certain false brethren had slipped in to spy out their liberty and wanted to force Paul to circumcise Titus. When Paul saw this force and compulsion, he would not yield submission to them even for a moment but vigorously resisted them. Therefore he says (Gal. 2:3): "But even Titus, who was with me, was not compelled to be circumcised, though he was a Gentile." If they had demanded this as an act of charity or fraternal deference, he would not have refused. But they demanded it as something necessary, and they did so by compulsion; thus they set a bad example for others and threatened to bring the consciences of men into bondage and to overthrow the Gospel. Therefore Paul took a firm stand against them and won out, so that Titus was not circumcised.

It may seem a trifle whether or not one is circumcised. But if the condition is attached that we are to be afraid or confident on the basis of it, then hell and death are brought in; then God, Christ, grace, and all the promises of God are being refused. If circumcision were by itself, without this condition attached to it, there would be no danger. Thus if the pope simply required that we observe his traditions as mere ceremonies, there would be no danger either. For how hard is it to wear a cowl or a tonsure, since we do observe other ceremonies?[8] But it is satanic and blasphemous to add this wicked condition, that in this trifle, this mere nothing, life or everlasting death is involved. If you keep silence about this issue, whoever you are, may you be accursed! I am willing to eat or drink or wear a cowl or do anything the pope wishes, so long as he leaves all this free. But since he requires these as something necessary for salvation, binding consciences to them and counting them as an act of worship, we must refuse at any cost. There would be no harm in carving a statue of wood or stone; but to set it up for worship and to attribute divinity to the wood, stone, or statue is to worship an idol instead of God. Therefore we must consider carefully what Paul has in mind, lest we speak foolishly, as Jerome did when he imagined that the issue under debate was the practice itself.[9] In this he was wrong. For the issue is not whether wood is wood or stone is stone, but what is attached to them, that is, how these things are used: whether this wood is God, whether divinity resides in this stone. To this we answer that wood is wood, as Paul says that "neither circumcision counts for anything nor uncircumcision" (1 Cor. 7:19). But to attach righteousness, reverence, confidence in salvation, and the fear of death to such things is to attribute divinity to ceremonies. Therefore we must not yield one bit of submission to our opponents, just as Paul did not yield submission to the false apostles. For neither circumcision nor uncircumcision nor a tonsure nor a cowl has anything to do with righteousness; only grace, and grace alone, does. This is "the truth of the Gospel."

6. *And from those who were reputed to be something (what they were makes no difference to me).*

Paul uses an elliptical form of speech, for the words "I did not receive anything" are missing. But it is forgivable when the Holy Spirit, speaking through Paul, sins a little against the rules of grammar. He speaks with great fervor, and anyone who is fervent when he speaks cannot be very precise about following the rules of grammar and the principles of rhetoric. Augustine testifies to this in his *On Christian Doctrine.* "I suppose," he says, "that the orators themselves were unable to live up to their own rules."[10]

[8] See the more extensive discussion of this on p. 411.

[9] Jerome, *Commentarius in Epistolam S. Pauli ad Galatas,* I, *Patrologia, Series Latina,* XXVI, 358—360.

[10] Augustine, *De doctrina Christiana,* Book IV, ch. 3, par. 4.

This is a vehement and proud refutation. For Paul does not call the true apostles themselves by any honorific title. Almost as though he wanted to minimize their position, he speaks of "those who were reputed to be something," that is, those who were in authority and on whose nod or refusal everything depended. Nevertheless, the authority of the apostles was actually very great in all the churches, and Paul does not take any honor away from them. But this is his way of giving a contemptuous answer to the false apostles, who sought to weaken Paul's authority and to cast suspicion upon his whole ministry by pitting the authority of the apostles and of their pupils against Paul in all the churches. This Paul would not stand for. In order to assure the continuance of the truth of the Gospel and the freedom of conscience in Christ among the Galatians and in all the Gentile churches, Paul gives a very proud answer to the false apostles. He did not care how great the apostles were or what they had once been; and if the false apostles cited the authority of the apostolic name against him, this did not impress him. He acknowledges that the apostles are indeed "something" and that their authority deserves respect. Nevertheless, his Gospel and ministry are not to be jeopardized on the basis of anybody's name or title, regardless of how great he may be, even if he were an apostle or an angel from heaven (Gal. 1:8).

This was one of the strongest arguments that the false apostles used. The apostles, they said, had close association with Christ for three years. They heard all His sermons and saw all His miracles. Besides, they themselves preached and performed miracles while Christ was still living in the world, long before Paul, who never saw Christ and was not converted until several years later. Therefore the Galatians should now consider whom of these they should believe more—Paul, who was all by himself, a disciple, to be sure, but only one and one of the last, or the most important and most excellent apostles, who had been sent out and confirmed by Christ Himself long before Paul. Paul replies: "So what? This argument does not prove anything. Let the apostles be ever so great; let them even be angels from heaven — that makes no difference to me. The issue in this controversy is the Word of God and the truth of the Gospel. This must be preserved at all costs; this must prevail. Therefore it makes no difference to me how great Peter and the other apostles have been or how many miracles they have performed. What I am contending for is that the truth of the Gospel be preserved among you." It seems to be a rather weak rebuttal when Paul disparages the apostles and their deeds, which the false apostles were citing against him, and counters their powerful argument with nothing more than the statement: "It makes no difference to me." Still he gives a reason in support of his rebuttal.

God shows no partiality.

Paul cites this passage from Moses, who says this very thing, not once but many times: "You shall do no injustice in judgment; you shall not be partial to the poor or defer to the great" (Lev. 19:15).[11] And this is a γνώμη or principle of theology: "God shows no partiality." With this statement he silences the false teachers. It is as though he were saying: "You pit against me those who are reputed to be something, but God does not care about such things. He is not swayed by the office of an apostle, a bishop, or a prince. He does not look at the honor or the authority of men." As a sign of this, God permitted the apostasy and the damnation of Judas, one of the most important of the apostles, and of Saul, one of the greatest of the kings and the first among them. He rejected both Ishmael and Esau, though both of them were the first-born. Thus you will find throughout the Scriptures that God often rejected the very men who, according to external appearances, were the best and the saintliest. In these instances God sometimes seems cruel, but these dreadful deeds had to be manifested and described. For we are inclined by nature to προσωπολημψία; we have the innate fault that we show great respect for the position [12] of men and pay more attention to it than to the Word. God, however, wants us to cling and be attached only to the Word itself. He wants us to choose the kernel rather than the shell, to care for the householder more than for the house.[13] He does not want us to admire and adore the apostolate in the persons of Peter and Paul, but the Christ who speaks in them and the Word of God itself that proceeds from their mouth.

It is not given to the secular and unregenerate man to see this,

[11] Luther seems to be thinking of passages like Lev. 19:15; Deut. 16:19; etc.

[12] The Latin word here is *persona*, which usually means "person"; but it refers to a "person," not in the psychological sense in which we use the word but in the social sense in which, for example, the language of civil law still uses it. Therefore we have translated it as "position" in several passages, for this seems to come closer to the intent of *persona* than "person" would.

[13] Here Luther appears to be citing a proverbial expression.

but only to the spiritual man. He alone can distinguish the position from the Word, the divine mask [14] from God Himself and the work of God. Until now we have dealt only with the veiled God, for in this life we cannot deal with God face to face. Now the whole creation is a face or mask of God. But here we need the wisdom that distinguishes God from His mask. The world does not have this wisdom. Therefore it cannot distinguish God from His mask. When a greedy man, who worships his belly, hears that "man does not live by bread alone, but by every Word that proceeds from the mouth of God" (Matt. 4:4), he eats the bread but fails to see God in the bread; for he sees, admires, and adores only the mask. He does the same with gold and with other creatures. He puts his trust in them as long as he has them; but when they forsake him, he despairs.

I am saying this to keep anyone from supposing that Paul simply condemns these external masks or social positions. He does not say that there should not be such social position, but that God shows no partiality to certain positions. There must be masks or social positions; for God has given them, and they are His creatures. The point is that we are not to worship and adore them. The emphasis is not on the things themselves but on our use of them, as I said before. There is nothing wrong with circumcision or uncircumcision — "for neither circumcision counts for anything nor uncircumcision" (1 Cor. 7:19) — but with the way it is used. To worship and adore circumcision, to ascribe righteousness to it, and to ascribe sin to uncircumcision — this is a damnable use of it and must be eliminated. Once this has been eliminated, both circumcision and uncircumcision are something good again.

Thus the magistrate, the emperor, the king, the prince, the consul, the teacher, the preacher, the pupil, the father, the mother, the children, the master, the servant — all these are social positions or external masks. God wants us to respect and acknowledge them as His creatures, which are a necessity for this life. But He does not want us to attribute divinity to them, that is, to fear and respect them in such a way that we trust them and forget Him. And therefore God has persons in the positions keep certain offenses and sins, in fact, huge ones, which are intended to warn us to note the difference between this position and God Himself. To avoid the appearance of being a person in whom men should put their trust, David, that very good

14 On the notion of the *larvae* or "masks" of God see also *Luther's Works,* 14, p. 114, note 9; 24, p. 67, note 37.

king, fell into the horrible sins of adultery and murder. So it was that
Peter denied Christ. These and similar examples, with which Scripture is filled, warn us not to put our trust in the social position and
not to suppose that when we have the position, we have everything.
This is the attitude under the papacy, where everything is judged
on the basis of the external appearance. Therefore the entire papacy
is nothing but utter προσωπολημψία. Thus God has given all His
creatures that they may serve us and we may use them, not that we
may serve and worship them. Therefore let us make use of bread,
wine, clothing, possessions, gold, etc.; but let us not trust or glory
in them. For we are to glory and trust in God alone; He alone is to
be loved, feared, and honored.

Paul uses the term "position" of a man here to designate apostleship, the office of the apostles, who performed many great miracles,
taught and converted many to faith, and knew Christ personally.
In other words, this term "position" covers the whole outward conduct of the apostles, which was holy, as well as their authority, which
was great. Nevertheless, Paul says, God does not show partiality to
these things — not that He has no regard for them at all, but that
where justification is involved, He has no regard for them. We must
pay careful attention to this distinction, that about theological issues
we must speak in a way that is vastly different from the way we speak
about social issues. Where social issues are involved, as I have said,
God wants us to honor and respect these "positions" as His masks or
instruments through which He preserves and governs the world. But
when the issue is one involving religion, conscience, the fear of God,
faith, and the worship of God, then we must not fear or trust any
social position or look to it for consolation and rescue, either physical
or spiritual. This is why God wants no partiality "in judgment," [15]
for judgment is something divine. I am not to fear the judge or love
the judge; but my fear and my trust are to be in someone else beyond
the judge, namely, in God, who is the real Judge. I ought to respect
and honor the civil judge, who is the mask of God, for the sake of
God. But my conscience dare not repose its trust in his justice; nor
dare it be intimidated by his tyranny. For if this happened, I could
sin against God and offend Him by lying, false witness, or a denial
of the truth. Otherwise, where God is not involved, I should, of course,
honor the judge.

[15] See the passages referred to on p. 94, note 11.

Thus I shall honor the pope and love his position, provided that he leaves my conscience free and does not require me to offend against God. But he wants to be adored and feared in a way that must offend the Divine Majesty, wound the conscience, and return me to the bondage of sin. Since we have to give up one or the other here, let us give up the social position and cling to God. We could be satisfied to bear the dominion of the pope, but he abuses this authority and dominion. He tries to make us deny God and blaspheme Him, and to acknowledge only the pope as our lord. He seeks to bind and constrain our consciences and take away the fear and trust that we should repose in God alone. Therefore we are required against our will to resist the pope; for it is written (Acts 5:29): "We must obey God rather than men." With a good conscience, therefore, we reject the authority of the pope; and this is a special consolation to us. Otherwise it would surely be oppressive for our consciences that we are guilty of sedition according to the pope, and especially according to His Imperial Majesty the Emperor, whom God has commanded us to revere.[16] Münzer and other sects have been resisting the pope, but for the sake of his social position, not for the sake of God.[17] We would be happy to pay our respects to Behemoth and his scales, that is, the pope and the bishops,[18] with all the station and position they have, if they let us keep Christ. But because we cannot get this concession from them, we reject their social position and say boldly with Paul: "God shows no partiality."

Accordingly, there is a strong emphasis on the word "God." Where religion and the Word of God are the issue, there must be no partiality. But apart from religion, apart from God, there must be προσωπολημψία and partiality; for otherwise confusion would result, and all respect and order would disappear. In this world God wants the observance of order, respect, and a distinction among social positions. Otherwise the child or the pupil or the subject or the servant would say: "I am just as much a Christian as my father or teacher or prince or master! So why should I respect him?" Therefore God wants the difference

---

[16] A reference to the edict issued at the close of the Diet of Worms, May 26, 1521, by Emperor Charles V, placing Luther under the ban of the Holy Roman Empire.

[17] The phrase is *propter personam, non propter Deum;* see also *Luther's Works,* 3, p. 31, note 25.

[18] On the meaning of this metaphor of "scales" cf. *Luther's Works,* 13, p. 280, note 47.

of social position to be observed among us — not in the sight of God, where the distinction ceases. There is neither Greek nor Jew, but they are all one in Christ (Gal. 3:28).

Thus Paul refutes the argument which the false apostles based on the authority of the apostles. He says that it is out of order, beside the point, and therefore irrelevant to the issue. For the issue here is not the distinction among social positions; it is something far more important. It is a divine matter involving God and His Word, the question whether this Word is to have priority over the office of an apostle or vice versa. To this question Paul answers: "To preserve the truth of the Gospel and to keep the Word of God and the righteousness of faith pure and undefiled, let apostleship go! An angel from heaven or Peter or Paul — let them all perish!"

Those, I say, who were of repute added nothing to me.

This is what he means: "I did not confer or converse with the apostles in such a way that they taught me anything. For what were they to teach me when Christ by His revelation had already taught me everything very well, when I had been preaching the Gospel among the Gentiles for a period of eighteen years, and when Christ had performed so many miracles through me to validate my teaching? Therefore it was merely a conference, not a debate, in which I reported on what I had done. To the Gentiles I had proclaimed faith in Christ alone, without the Law; and through this proclamation of faith the Holy Spirit descended upon the Gentiles, and they immediately began to speak in tongues. Therefore it is pointless for the false apostles to cite the authority of the apostles, as though these had instructed me. For I neither learned anything from them nor defended myself to them, but I simply reported how I had been preaching the Gospel among the Gentiles. When the apostles heard this, they attested that I had been preaching correctly."

Now when Paul says that the other apostles did not teach him anything, this pride is not a fault but something very necessary; for if he had yielded submission here, the truth of the Gospel would have perished. But if Paul refused to yield to the false apostles, who boastfully cited the authority of the true apostles against him, much less should we yield to the wicked papists, who brag about the authority of their idol, the pope. I know that the pious should be humble; but in opposition to the pope I am willing and obliged to be proud with a holy pride and to say: "I refuse to be subject to you, pope. I refuse to accept you as my master, for I am certain that my doctrine is true and godly. And I can prove it with sound arguments!" But the pope is not willing to hear this. In fact, he tries to force me to listen to him. If I refuse, he excommunicates and condemns me as a heretic and an apostate from the church. Therefore this pride of ours is extremely necessary in opposition to the pope. If we were not so firm and proud, and if, by the Holy Spirit, we did not utterly condemn him with his teaching as well as the devil, his father, we would never be able to defend the doctrine of the righteousness of faith. It is not because we want to assert sovereignty over the pope; nor are we intent on exalting ourselves above all constituted authority, for it is evident that we teach all men to subject themselves humbly to the governing authorities. All we aim for is that the glory of God be preserved and that the righteousness of faith remain pure and sound. Once this has been established, namely that God alone justifies us solely by His grace through Christ, we are willing not only to bear the pope aloft on our hands but also to kiss his feet. But since we cannot obtain such a concession, we, in turn, become immensely proud in God. And we refuse to yield the least little bit, either to all the heavenly angels or to Peter or to Paul or to a hundred emperors or to a thousand popes or to the whole world! On no account should we humble ourselves here; for they want to deprive us of our glory, namely, the God who has created us and given us everything, and the Christ who has redeemed us with His blood. In short, we can stand the loss of our possessions, our name, our life, and everything else; but we will not let ourselves be deprived of the Gospel, our faith, and Jesus Christ. And that is that. Accursed be any humility that yields or submits at this point! Rather let everyone be proud and unremitting here, unless he wants to deny Christ. With the help of God, therefore, I will be more hardheaded than anyone else. I want to be stubborn and to be known as someone who is stubborn. Here I bear the inscription "I yield to no one." And I am overjoyed if here I am called rebellious and unyielding. Here I admit openly that I am and will be unmovable and that I will not yield a hairbreadth to anyone. Love "bears all things, believes all things, hopes all things, endures all things" (1 Cor. 13:7); therefore it yields. But not faith; it will not stand for anything. As the common saying has it, "A man's reputation, faith, and eye cannot stand being played with." [19] So far as his

---

[19] The proverbial saying reads: *Non patitur ludum fama, fides, oculus.*

faith is concerned, therefore, a Christian is as proud and firm as he can be; and he must not relax or yield the least bit. For at this point faith makes a man God (2 Peter 1:4). But God does not stand for anything or yield to anyone, for He is unchanging. Thus faith is unchanging. Therefore it should not stand for anything or yield to anyone. But so far as love is concerned, a Christian should yield and stand for everything; for here he is only a human being.

7. *But on the contrary, when they saw that I had been entrusted with the Gospel to the uncircumcised, just as Peter had been entrusted with the Gospel to the circumcised*

8. *(for He who worked through Peter for the mission to the circumcised worked through me also to the Gentiles),*

9. *and when they perceived the grace that was given to me, James and Cephas and John, who were reputed to be pillars, gave to me and Barnabas the right hand of fellowship, that we should go to the Gentiles and they to the circumcised.*

This is very powerful confuting evidence against the false apostles. Here Paul claims and adopts for himself the same authority that the false apostles bandied about concerning the true apostles. The tactic he uses here is called a rhetorical inversion. "The false apostles," he says, "cite the authority of the great apostles against me to support their case. But I cite the same authority against them and in my own defense, for the apostles are on my side. Therefore, my dear Galatians, do not believe those who make such a boast of the authority of the apostles against me. For when the apostles saw that the Gospel to the uncircumcised had been entrusted to me and knew of the grace given to me, they extended the hand of fellowship to Barnabas and to me; they approved my ministry and gave thanks to God for the gifts I had received." In this unusual way he turns the arguments of his opponents back upon them. These words are filled with sheer ardor, and there is more passion here than mere words can express. This is also why Paul has forgotten his grammar and confused the sentence structure.

When Paul says (v. 9) that James and Cephas and John "were reputed to be pillars," this is not idle talk; for they really were reputed to be pillars. The apostles were revered and honored throughout the church. They had the authority to approve and declare the true doctrine and to condemn its opposite.

This is a wonderful text. Paul says that the Gospel to the uncircumcised had been entrusted to him, but that the Gospel to the circumcised had been entrusted to Peter; for, after all, the situation on both sides was that Paul preached to the Jews in their synagogs almost everywhere and that Peter also preached to the Gentiles. There are evidences and examples of both in the Book of Acts. Peter converted the centurion and his family, and they were Gentiles (Acts 10:1 ff.). He also wrote to Gentiles, as his epistles testify (1 Peter 2:10). Although Paul preached Christ among the Gentiles, he still went into Jewish synagogs and preached the Gospel there. And in Mark (16:15) and Matthew (28:19) Christ commands all the apostles: "Go throughout the world, and preach the Gospel to every creature." Paul also says in Col. 1:2 that the Gospel "has been preached to every creature under heaven." Then why does he call himself only the apostle to the Gentiles, but Peter and the others the apostles to the circumcised?

This is not a difficult question to answer. What Paul has in mind is that the other apostles had remained in Judea and Jerusalem until God called them elsewhere. For some time, as long as the Jewish state and priesthood continued, the apostles stayed in Judea; but when destruction was imminent, they were scattered through the whole world. But as Acts 13:2 writes, Paul was set aside by a special call as the apostle to the Gentiles and was sent out from Judea to journey through the Gentile lands. And although he also went into Jewish synagogs, he preached elsewhere to the Gentiles — in the public forum, in private homes, on the riverbank. Then the Gentiles came into the Jewish synagogs to hear Paul's proclamation. Thus it is true that Paul was chiefly the apostle to the Gentiles. Hence these words contain a chronological synecdoche,[20] for after the destruction of Judaism there came into being one church made up of both Jews and Gentiles.

Paul is using a Hebrew figure of speech when he speaks of "the Gospel of uncircumcision" and "the Gospel of circumcision." For in Hebrew the genitive case is used in various ways, sometimes in an active sense and sometimes in a passive sense; and this frequently tends to obscure the meaning.[21] There are examples of

[20] See also p. 24, note 12.

[21] This had been the content of Luther's discovery of the Gospel; see his brief autobiography of 1545, *Luther's Works*, 34, p. 337.

this throughout Paul; indeed, throughout Scripture. There is, for example, the phrase "the glory of God," which is rather obscure, since it can be interpreted either in an active or in a passive sense. In an active sense the glory of God is the glory that God has in Himself; in a passive sense it is that glory by which we glory in God. Another instance is "the faith of Christ." We usually interpret such phrases in the passive sense;[22] thus "the faith of Christ" is that by which Christ is believed. In the same way "the Gospel of God" is also to be understood in the active sense, as that which only God gives and sends into the world; but "the Gospel of the circumcision or of the uncircumcision" is to be understood in the passive sense, as that which is sent to the Gentiles or the Jews and is accepted by them. Now by synecdoche, a very common figure of speech in Sacred Scripture, where the part is put for the whole, Paul says "uncircumcision" to mean Gentiles and "circumcision" to mean Jews. He means, then, that "the Gospel of the uncircumcision," namely, that which was to be sent to the Gentiles, was entrusted to him, just as "the Gospel of the circumcision" had been entrusted to Peter.

From this it is sufficiently certain that Peter, James, and John, who seemed to be pillars, did not teach Paul anything and did not entrust to him the ministry of the Gospel, as though they were his superiors and ordainers. For they had no authority to teach, command, or send him. Therefore he does not acknowledge them as superiors and ordainers. "But they themselves," he says, "saw that I had surely been entrusted with the Gospel, but not by Peter. For just as I did not receive or learn the Gospel from any man, so I did not receive the commandment to preach from any man. It was directly from God that I received both the knowledge of the Gospel and the commandment to preach it among the Gentiles, just as Peter was entrusted by God with the Gospel and with the commission to preach it among the Jews."

This is clear proof that all the apostles had the same calling, the same commission, and the same Gospel. Peter did not proclaim a Gospel different from that of the others; nor did he commission the others with their office. But there was parity among them throughout; for they had all been taught and called by God, that is, both the call and the commission of all the apostles had come wholly and immediately from God. Therefore none of the apostles was

---

[22] See the discussion of this phrase on p. 138.

greater than any of the others, and none had any prerogative above the others. And so, when the pope seeks to support and maintain his own primacy by claiming that Peter was the chief of the apostles, this is a brazen lie.

For He who worked through Peter, etc.

Here Paul refutes yet another argument. "Why do the false apostles brag," he says, "that the Gospel was powerful in Peter, that he converted many, that he performed many great miracles, that he raised the dead and healed the sick with his very shadow (Acts 5:15)? I grant that all this is true. But Peter received this power from heaven. God endowed the voice of Peter with a force that caused many to believe him and many miracles to be performed through him. I have the same power. I did not receive it from Peter, but the same God and the same Spirit who worked through Peter worked through me also. I had the same grace; I taught many; I performed many miracles; with my shadow I, too, healed the sick." Luke bears witness to this in Acts 19:11-12 when he says: "And God did extraordinary miracles by the hands of Paul, so that handkerchiefs or aprons were carried away from his body to the sick, and diseases left them, and the evil spirits came out of them." Read the thirteenth, sixteenth, twentieth, and twenty-eighth chapters of the Book of Acts.

In short, Paul refuses to be regarded as inferior to the rest of the apostles in any way, and he takes a pious and holy pride in this. It is useless for Julian and Porphyry to accuse Paul of insolence toward the prince of the apostles.[23] He was obliged by a necessity, and a divine one, to be conceited and proud against Peter; for his passionate zeal for the glory of God motivated him to do so. His detractors did not see this; therefore they supposed that Paul was motivated by an unspiritual pride, as the pope and his bishops are in our own day. But here Paul is not dealing with a personal issue; he is dealing with an issue of faith. Where faith is involved, there we should be invincible, inflexible, stubborn, and harder than adamant, if this were possible; but where love is involved, we should be softer and more flexible than every kind of reed or leaf and ready to yield anything. Thus the controversy here dealt not with pride, glory, or prerogative, as we see among the papists. But the struggle

[23] Jerome, *Commentarius in Epistolam S. Pauli ad Galatas*, I, *Patrologia, Series Latina*, XXVI, 366.

is over the glory of God, the Word of God, the true worship of God, true religion, and the righteousness of faith — these things had to be and remain pure.

9. *And when they perceived the grace.*

That is to say: "When they heard that I had received from God my call and commission to preach the Gospel among the Gentiles, that God had performed so many miracles through me, that so many Gentiles had come to the knowledge of Christ through my ministry, and that the Gentiles had received the Holy Spirit without the Law or circumcision but solely through the hearing of faith — when they heard all this, they glorified God for the grace that had been given to me." The word "grace" here includes whatever Paul had received from God. Here Paul points out that Peter testified to his being a true apostle, who had been taught and sent neither by Peter nor by other apostles but by God alone. Thus did Peter humbly acknowledge and approve Paul's ministry, not as a superior authority but as a witness who confirmed Paul's ministry, his authority, and all his other gifts. Now Peter stands together with him as one man.

The right hand of fellowship.

That is, the hand of communion, the social handshake. They said: "Paul, we preach the Gospel in unanimous consensus with you. There we are companions in doctrine and have fellowship in it; that is, we have the same doctrine. For we preach one Gospel, one Baptism, one Christ, and one faith. Therefore we cannot teach or command anything so far as you are concerned, for we are completely agreed in everything. For we do not teach anything different from what you teach; nor is it better or sublimer. We see that the same gift we have is present in you as well, except that the Gospel to the uncircumcised has been entrusted to you, as the Gospel to the circumcised has been entrusted to us. But we conclude that neither circumcision nor uncircumcision should stand in the way of our fellowship, for your Gospel and ours are the same."

This is clear proof that there is only one and the same Gospel for Gentiles and Jews, monks and laymen, young and old, men and women, etc. There is no partiality; but the Word and its teaching are one and the same for all men, no matter how diverse the mask or social position may be. The apostles circumcised; Paul did not. But both he and the apostles left circumcision free for those who had been born in it, for the apostles could distinguish the Gospel from the Law in a way that was both wise and correct. I also believe that if the believing Jews at that time had observed the Law and circumcision under the condition permitted by the apostles, Judaism would have remained standing until now, and the whole world would have accepted the ceremonies of the Jews. But because they insisted on the Law and circumcision as something necessary for salvation and constructed an act of worship and some sort of god out of it, God could not stand for it. Therefore He threw over the temple, the Law, the worship, and the holy city of Jerusalem, so that not one stone was left on another (Matt. 24:2).

So far Paul has proved that he preached the Gospel correctly and devoutly, and that he had the true and genuine Gospel. This he did not only on the basis of divine testimony but on the basis of human testimony as well, namely, that of the apostles themselves, on whom the false apostles were depending most of all. Thus everything they cited against Paul is found to support him instead. But because Paul is the only one telling the story, he took an oath and called upon God as witness that what he was saying was not a lie.

10. *Only they would have us remember the poor, which very thing I was eager to do.*

Next to the proclamation of the Gospel it is the task of a good pastor to be mindful of the poor. For wherever the church is, there must be poor people. Most of the time they are the only true disciples of the Gospel, as Christ says (Matt. 11:5): "The poor have the Gospel preached to them." For both human beings and the devil persecute the church and bring poverty upon many, who are then forsaken and to whom no one wants to give anything. In addition, no one provides for the preservation of the Gospel, and no one now will take any care for the support of ministers and the construction of schools. For the construction and establishment of false forms of worship and superstition, by contrast, no price was too high; but everyone contributed generously. That was how so many monasteries, cathedrals, and episcopal sees were erected under the papacy, where wickedness itself ruled, and how endowments were provided to support them. But nowadays an entire city thinks that it is too much to support one or two ministers of the Gospel, even though formerly, when wickedness ruled, it easily supported various monasteries and endless numbers of priests who read Mass, to say nothing of "terminaries" and "stationaries." [24] In other words, everywhere true religion is in need, and Christ complains that He is hungry, thirsty, without shelter, naked, and sick (Matt. 25:35). On the other hand, false religion and wickedness flourish and abound with all sorts of possessions. Therefore a true bishop must be concerned also about the poor, and Paul here admits that he was.

11. *But when Cephas came to Antioch I opposed him to his face, because he stood condemned.*

Paul continues his refutation and says not only that he has the testimony of Peter and the other apostles at Jerusalem on his side, but also that he opposed Peter on this issue before the entire church at Antioch. He tells that this took place in the presence of the entire church, not in a corner. This is a marvelous account, and it has provided many — such as Porphyry, Celsus, Julian, and others — with an opportunity to accuse Paul of pride because he attacked the chief of the apostles and did so in the presence of the entire church.[25] By this, they say, he exceeded the bounds of Christian modesty and humility. It is not surprising that these men, who do not get the point of Paul's argument, think and speak as they do.

For the issue here is nothing trivial for Paul;[26] it is the principal doctrine of Christianity. When this is recognized and held before one's eyes, everything else seems vile and worthless. For what is Peter? What is Paul? What is an angel from heaven? What is all creation in comparison with the doctrine of justification? Therefore if you see this threatened or endangered, do not be afraid to stand up against Peter or an angel from heaven. For this cannot be praised highly enough. But those men look at Peter's high prestige; they admire his social position and forget the majesty of this doctrine. Paul does the opposite. He does not attack Peter sharply; he treats him with due respect. But because he sees that the prestige of Peter is endangering the majesty of the doctrine of justification, he ignores the prestige, in order to keep this doctrine pure and undefiled. And we do the same thing, for it is written (Matt. 10:37): "He who loves father or mother or his own soul more than Me is not worthy of Me."

[24] Here Luther seems to be referring to special clergy who officiated at certain seasons and at special "stations," that is, churches where special indulgences were available on stated days of the church year.

[25] See p. 103, note 23.

[26] The phrase *de lana caprina* had become proverbial; cf. Horace, *Epistles,* I, 18, 15.

When it comes to the defense of the truth of the Gospel, therefore, we are not embarrassed to have the hypocrites accuse us of being proud and stubborn, the ones who think that they alone have the truth, those who refuse to listen or to yield to anyone. Here we have to be stubborn and unbending. The cause for whose sake we sin against men, that is, trample underfoot the majesty of someone's social position or of the world, is so great that the sins that are the worst in the eyes of the world are the highest virtues in the eyes of God. It is good for us to love our parents, to honor the magistrates, to show respect for Peter and for other ministers of the Word. But what is involved here is not the cause of Peter or our parents or the emperor or the world or of any other creature; it is the cause of God Himself. If I refuse to yield to my parents, to the emperor, or to an angel from heaven on this issue, I act properly. Why? Just compare a creature with the Creator! In fact, what are all the creatures in comparison with Him? Like a drop of water in comparison with the entire ocean! Then why should I defer to Peter, who is only a little drop, and ignore God, who is the entire ocean? Therefore let the drop yield submission to the ocean, and let Peter yield to God.

I am saying this in order that you may carefully consider the issue with which Paul is dealing; for he is dealing with the Word of God, which no one can praise worthily enough. Augustine has considered this issue more carefully than Jerome, who looked only at the dignity and authority of Peter and argued this way: Peter was the chief apostle. Therefore it was not proper that he should be called to account by Paul; and if Paul did call him to account, it was all a pretense.[27] Thus he ascribes pretense to Paul; but to Peter he ascribes the truth, and he excuses him in every way. This is an uncalled-for distortion of the text, to say that Paul only pretended that Peter was deserving of attack so that he could promote his own apostleship and defend his Gentiles. On the contrary, the text clearly states that Peter was deserving of attack and had erred from the truth, and that other Jews carried on the same pretense that he did, with the result that even Barnabas was led astray into this pretense by them. These clear words Jerome does not see, for he sticks only to this: Peter was an apostle; therefore he was beyond attack and could not sin. To this sentence Augustine correctly replies:

---

[27] Jerome, *Commentarius in Epistolam S. Pauli ad Galatas,* I, *Patrologia, Series Latina,* XXVI, 367.

"It is intolerable to suppose that there was pretense in Paul, for he confirms with an oath that he is speaking the truth." [28]

Therefore Jerome and Erasmus [29] do Paul an injustice when they take the words "to his face" to mean "only according to the outward appearance"; they maintain that Paul did not oppose Peter sincerely, but that he did so with complaisant pretense, since others would have been offended if he had remained completely silent. But "to his face" means "in his presence"; for he opposed Peter openly, not in a corner but in the very presence of Peter and with the entire church standing by. When he says "to his face," this is aimed especially against those poisonous spirits who slander those who are absent but do not dare open their mouths in the presence of these people. That is what the false apostles did; he touches them obliquely here, because they did not dare slander him in his presence; they did so only in his absence. "I did not," he says, "speak evil of Peter this way; but I opposed him candidly and openly, not because of any pretense, ambition, or other human affection or mental disease, but because he himself was deserving of attack."

Here let others argue whether an apostle can sin. We should not extenuate the sin of Peter. The prophets themselves sometimes err and are mistaken. Thus Nathan said on his own that David should build the house of the Lord (2 Sam. 7:3). But this prophecy was soon corrected by a revelation from God that the house of the Lord should be built, not by David, who was a warlike man and had shed much blood, but by his son Solomon. Thus even an apostle can err. Here, however, Peter did not err; but he did sin gravely. Therefore we are not to ascribe to the apostles such perfection that it was impossible for them to sin.

Luke testifies in Acts 15:39 that there was such sharp disagreement between Paul and Barnabas, who had been set aside for the ministry of the Gospel among the Gentiles and had traveled through many areas and announced the Gospel to them, that they parted company. Here there was a fault either in Paul or in Barnabas; it must have been a very sharp disagreement to separate such close companions, and this is what the text suggests. Such examples are written for our comfort. For it is a great comfort for us to hear that even such

[28] Augustine, *Expositio Epistolae ad Galatas*, 15, *Patrologia, Series Latina*, XXXV, 2113—2114.

[29] Erasmus, *Paraphrasis in Epistolam Pauli ad Galatas*, *Desiderii Erasmi Roterodami Opera Omnia*, VII (Hildesheim, 1962), 949—950.

great saints sin — a comfort which those who say that saints cannot sin would take away from us.

Samson, David, and many other celebrated men who were full of the Holy Spirit fell into huge sins. Job (3:3 ff.) and Jeremiah (20:14) curse the day of their birth; Elijah (1 Kings 19:4) and Jonah (4:8) are tired of life and pray for death. Such errors and sins of the saints are set forth in order that those who are troubled and desperate may find comfort and that those who are proud may be afraid. No man has ever fallen so grievously that he could not have stood up again. On the other hand, no one has such a sure footing that he cannot fall. If Peter fell, I, too, may fall; if he stood up again, so can I.

Those whose consciences are weak and tender should set great store by such examples, in order that they may understand better what they are praying when they say: "Forgive us, etc.," or "I believe in the forgiveness of sins," in which the apostles and all the saints believed. They prayed the Our Father just as we do. The apostles were not superior to us in anything except in their apostolic office. We have the same gifts that they had, namely, the same Christ, Baptism, Word, and forgiveness of sins. They needed all this no less than we do; they were sanctified and saved by all this just as we are.

This I say in opposition to the monstrous flattery and praise with which the foolish scholastics and monks have adorned the saints. They said that the church is holy in the sense that it is completely without sin. The church is indeed holy, but it is a sinner at the same time. Therefore it believes in the forgiveness of sins and prays: "Forgive us our debts" (Matt. 6:12) and "For this every saint will pray to Thee" (Ps. 32:6). Therefore we are not said to be holy formally, as a wall is said to be white because of its inherent whiteness.[30] Our inherent holiness is not enough. Therefore Christ is our entire holiness; where this inherent holiness is not enough, Christ is. Therefore I have no doubt that Peter took a great fall here. If Paul had not opposed him, all those, both Jews and Gentiles, who had come to faith would have been forced to return to Judaism and would have perished. And the provocation for this came from Peter and from his pretense.

[30] "Formally," that is, holy in perfect actuality rather than in the process of becoming so.

12. *For before certain men came from James, he ate with the Gentiles.*

The Gentiles who had been converted to the faith ate foods prohibited by the Law. When Peter associated with Gentile converts, he, too, ate these foods and drank forbidden wine. He knew that he was doing right when he did this, and he boldly broke the Law along with the Gentiles. Paul says that he did the same thing (1 Cor. 9:20-22): "To the Jews I became as a Jew; to those outside the Law I became as one outside the Law. That is, with the Gentiles I ate and drank like a Gentile and did not keep the Law at all; but with the Jews I lived according to the Law, abstained from pork, etc. For I made an effort to serve and please all men, that I might gain them all." When Peter acted in this same manner, therefore, he did not sin but did well; and he knew that this was permitted. For by this transgression of his he showed, on the one hand, that the Law was not necessary for righteousness; and, on the other hand, he delivered the Gentiles from the observance of the Law. For if it was permissible for Peter to violate the Law in one particular, it was permissible to violate it in all particulars. Paul does not attack Peter for this violation of the Law; he attacks him for his pretense, as now follows.

> *But when they came, he drew back and separated himself, fearing the circumcision party.*

Here you see Peter's sin. Paul describes it carefully. He accuses Peter of weakness, not of malice or ignorance. Peter was afraid of the Jews who had come from James, and he fell on account of his fear of them; for he did not want to scandalize them in this way. Thus he was more concerned about the Jews than about the Gentiles and was responsible for endangering Christian freedom and the truth of the Gospel. By drawing back, separating himself, and avoiding foods prohibited by the Law — foods which he had previously eaten — he injected a scruple into the consciences of the faithful, who could draw this conclusion from his actions: "Peter abstains from foods prohibited by the Law. Therefore whoever eats foods prohibited by the Law sins and transgresses the Law, but whoever abstains is righteous and keeps the Law. Otherwise Peter would not have drawn back. But because he does so and deliberately avoids the food he ate before, this is a most certain sign that those who eat contrary to the Law sin, but that those who abstain from the foods prohibited in the Law are justified."

This is the topic being discussed here, but Jerome did not see it. He saw only the deed, not the purpose of the deed. The deed in itself was not evil; for to eat and drink, or not to eat and drink, is nothing. But the purpose of the deed — "If you eat, you sin; if you abstain, you are righteous" — this is evil. Thus circumcision in itself is a good thing, but this purpose is evil: "If you are not circumcised in accordance with the Law of Moses, you cannot be saved." This was precisely the direction of the example Peter was setting: "Unless you avoid the food prohibited by the Law, you cannot be saved." Here Paul simply could not pretend, for the truth of the Gospel was being endangered. In order to keep this truth sound, he withstood Peter to his face. Paul makes a distinction here. It is possible to avoid certain foods for one reason, namely, out of a concern for charity. There is no danger in this, for it is good to render such a service to a weak brother. This is what Paul himself both did and taught. A second reason, however, is that you avoid them in order to be righteous and to be saved, supposing that if you do not avoid them, you are sinning and will be damned. A curse on such charity and on all the duties and acts of charity! For to avoid foods this way is to deny Christ, to tread His blood underfoot, to blaspheme against the Holy Spirit, against God, and against everything holy. Therefore if one has to lose one or the other, it is better to lose a friend and a brother than to lose God the Father. For if God the Father is lost, man the brother will not remain very long.

Because he did not see this, Jerome was unable to understand either this passage or the entire epistle. He supposes that Paul is quibbling over something trivial; therefore he extenuates and excuses Peter's sin and says that he sinned in ignorance. But Peter did not sin in ignorance — for he knew that he was permitted to eat anything — but through a pretense that would have established the necessity of the Law. Thus he would have forced both Gentiles and Jews to depart from the truth of the Gospel and would have contributed greatly to their deserting Christ, denying grace, returning to Judaism, and taking upon themselves all the burdens of the Law. All this would have resulted if Paul had not rebuked him and thus called the Gentiles and Jews who had been offended by Peter's example back to freedom in Christ and to the truth of the Gospel. Therefore if someone wanted to criticize and magnify Peter's sin, it would appear very great; and yet he did not sin in malice or ignorance but only because of the situation and out of fear. The fall or error of one man can so easily bring on enormous ruin if it is not corrected. Therefore the doctrine of justification is nothing to be trifled with, and it is not without reason that we inculcate it and insist on it with such diligence.

It is astonishing that Peter, such an outstanding apostle, should do this. Previously, at the council of Jerusalem, he had stood almost alone in obtaining the adoption of his position that righteousness comes to believers by faith, without the Law (Acts 15:7-11). He who had so steadfastly defended the truth and freedom of the Gospel now avoids foods prohibited by the Law, and thus he falls, not only is he the cause of great offense, but he offends against his own decree. "Therefore let anyone who thinks that he stands take heed lest he fall" (1 Cor. 10:12). No one believes how dangerous traditions and ceremonies are, and yet we cannot do without them. What is more necessary in the world than the Law and its works? Yet there is always the danger that from these will come a denial of Christ. For the Law often produces trust in works; and where this is present, there cannot be trust in Christ. Thus Christ is soon denied and lost, as we can see in the case of Peter. He knew the doctrine of justification better than we do. And yet how easily he could have been responsible for such a terrible ruin by his deed and example if Paul had not opposed him! All the Gentiles would have fallen away from the preaching of Paul and would thus have lost the Gospel and Christ Himself. And this would all have happened with the appearance of holiness. For they could have said: "Paul, until now you have been teaching us that we must be justified by grace alone, without the Law. Now you see Peter doing the very opposite, for he abstains from foods prohibited by the Law. Thus he teaches us that we cannot be saved unless we undergo circumcision and observe the Law."

13. *And with him the rest of the Jews acted insincerely, so that even Barnabas was carried away by their insincerity.*

Here you see clearly that Paul accuses Peter of insincerity, of which, by contrast, Jerome accuses Paul. If Peter was pretending, then he surely knew what was the truth and what was not. He who pretends does not sin out of ignorance but deceives by putting on an appearance that he himself knows is false. "And the rest," he says, "acted insincerely along with Peter, so that even Barnabas (who was Paul's colleague and who had been associated with Paul for a long time in preaching faith in Christ, without the Law, to the Gentiles) was carried away by their insincerity." Here you have a clear description of Peter's sin as insincerity, which could have been the cause for the ruin of the Gospel as it had been received if Paul had not opposed him.

It is wonderful that God preserved the church, which had just been established, and the Gospel itself through just one person. Paul alone stands for the truth; for he had lost Barnabas, his associate, and Peter was against him. Sometimes one man can do more in a council than the entire council itself, as the papists themselves testify. They cite the example of Paphnutius, who opposed the entire council of Nicea (the best of those that there have been since the apostolic council at Jerusalem) and prevailed.[31]

I am saying this in order that we may learn the doctrine of justification with the greatest diligence and distinguish most clearly between the Law and the Gospel. On this issue we must not do anything out of insincerity or yield submission to anyone if we want to keep the truth of the Gospel and the faith sound and inviolate; for, as I have said, these are easily bruised. Here let reason be far away, that enemy of faith, which, in the temptations of sin and death, relies not on the righteousness of faith or Christian righteousness, of which it is completely ignorant, but on its own righteousness or, at most, on the righteousness of the Law. As soon as reason and the Law are joined, faith immediately loses its virginity. For nothing is more hostile to faith than the Law and reason; nor can these two enemies be overcome without great effort and work, and you must overcome them if you are to be saved. Therefore when your conscience is terrified by the Law and is wrestling with the judgment of God, do not consult either reason or the Law, but rely only on grace and the Word of comfort. Here take your stand as though you had never heard of the Law. Ascend into the darkness, where neither the Law nor reason shines, but only the dimness of faith (1 Cor. 13:12), which assures us that we are saved by Christ alone, without any Law.[32] Thus the Gospel leads us above and beyond the light of the Law and reason into the darkness of faith, where the Law and reason

[31] The story of Paphnutius is set down in Socrates, *Ecclesiastical History*, Book I, ch. XI.

[32] Both the affinities and the contrasts of Luther's thought with traditional mysticism are evident in his use of "darkness" in passages like this; see also p. 130, note 49.

have no business. The Law, too, deserves a hearing, but in its proper place and time. When Moses was on the mountain speaking with God face to face, he neither had nor established nor administered the Law. But now that he has come down from the mountain, he is a lawgiver and rules the people by the Law. So the conscience must be free from the Law, but the body must obey the Law.

From this it is abundantly clear that Paul did not rebuke Peter for some trivial reason, but that he rebuked him for the sake of the most important doctrine of Christianity, which was being threatened by Peter's pretense. For the rest of the Jews and Barnabas himself acted insincerely along with him. Certainly they all sinned, not through ignorance or malice but because of fear of the Jews, which so blinded their hearts that they did not recognize their sin. It is truly amazing that such great men as Peter, Barnabas, and the others fell so quickly and easily, especially in the matter of a work which they knew to be good and they themselves had previously taught to others. Therefore it is dangerous, as Dr. Staupitz used to warn us, to trust in our own strength, no matter how holy, erudite, or confident of our own knowledge we may be.[33] For in that which we know best we can err and fall, bringing not only ourselves but others as well into danger, as Peter did here.

Therefore we are nothing, even with all our great gifts, unless God is present. When He deserts us and leaves us to our own resources, our wisdom and knowledge are nothing. Unless He sustains us continually, the highest learning and even theology are useless. For in the hour of temptation it can suddenly happen that by a trick of the devil all the comforting texts disappear from our sight and only the threatening ones appear to overwhelm us. Therefore let us learn that if God withdraws His hand, we can easily fall and be overthrown. Therefore let no one boast or glory in his own righteousness, wisdom, and other gifts; but let him humble himself and pray with the apostles (Luke 17:5): "Lord, increase our faith!"

I am making such a point of all this to keep anyone from supposing that the doctrine of faith is an easy matter. It is indeed easy to talk about, but it is hard to grasp; and it is easily obscured and lost. Therefore let us with all diligence and humility devote ourselves to the study of Sacred Scripture and to serious prayer, lest we lose the truth of the Gospel.

[33] See p. 66, note 47.

14. *But when I saw that they were not straightforward about the truth of the Gospel.*

This is a wonderful story to tell about very great men and pillars of the churches. Paul is the only one who has his eyes open and sees the sin of Peter, Barnabas, and the other Jews, who were acting insincerely along with Peter. At the same time they do not see their own sin; in fact, they think they are doing well and are charitably deferring to the Jews who were weak in faith. And Paul does not cover up their sin; but he accuses Peter, Barnabas, and the others in no uncertain terms of failing to walk the proper way according to the truth of the Gospel, that is, of having swerved from the truth of the Gospel. It was a serious matter for Peter to be accused by Paul of falling and of swerving from the truth of the Gospel; there could be no graver reproach. Yet he bears it patiently and undoubtedly accepted it with real gratitude. I warned earlier that many have the Gospel but not the truth of the Gospel. Thus Paul says here that Peter, Barnabas, and the rest of the Jews did not walk properly according to the truth of the Gospel; that is, they had had the Gospel but had not walked in it properly. For although they were preaching the Gospel, still by their pretense, which could not stand with the truth of the Gospel, they were establishing the Law. But the establishment of the Law is the abrogation and overthrow of the Gospel.

Therefore whoever knows well how to distinguish the Gospel from the Law should give thanks to God and know that he is a real theologian. I admit that in the time of temptation I myself do not know how to do this as I should. The way to distinguish the one from the other is to locate the Gospel in heaven and the Law on earth, to call the righteousness of the Gospel heavenly and divine and the righteousness of the Law earthly and human, and to distinguish as sharply between the righteousness of the Gospel and that of the Law as God distinguishes between heaven and earth or between light and darkness or between day and night. Let the one be like the light and the day, and the other like the darkness and the night. If we could only put an even greater distance between them! Therefore if the issue is faith, heavenly righteousness, or conscience, let us leave the Law out of consideration altogether and let it remain on the earth. But if the issue is works, then let us light the lamp of works and of the righteousness of the Law in the night. So let the sun and the immense light of the Gospel and of grace shine in the day, and let the lamp of the Law shine in the night. These two must be distinguished in your mind in such a way that when your conscience is completely terrified by a sense of sin, you will think of yourself: "At the moment you are busy on earth. Here let the ass work, let him serve and carry the burden that has been laid upon him; that is, let the body and its members be subject to the Law.[34] But when you ascend into heaven, leave the ass with his burdens on earth; for the conscience has no relation to the Law or to works or to earthly righteousness. Thus the ass remains in the valley; but the conscience ascends the mountain with Isaac, knowing absolutely nothing about the Law or its works but looking only to the forgiveness of sins and the pure righteousness offered and given in Christ."

In society,[35] on the other hand, obedience to the Law must be strictly required. There let nothing be known about the Gospel, conscience, grace, the forgiveness of sins, heavenly righteousness, or Christ Himself; but let there be knowledge only of Moses, of the Law and its works. When these two topics, the Law and the Gospel, are separated this way, both will remain within their limits. The Law will remain outside heaven, that is, outside the heart and the conscience; and, on the other hand, the freedom of the Gospel will remain outside the earth, that is, outside the body and its members. And just as soon as the Law and sin come into heaven, that is, into the conscience, they should be promptly ejected. For then the conscience should know nothing about the Law and sin but should know only about Christ. On the other hand, when grace and freedom come into the earth, that is, into the body, you must say: "You have no business here among the dirt and filth of this physical life. You belong in heaven!"

Peter had confused this distinction between the Law and the Gospel, and thus he had persuaded the believers that they had to be justified by the Gospel and the Law together. This Paul refused to tolerate. Therefore he rebuked Peter. He did not want to put him to shame, but he wanted to separate these two very sharply again,

[34] On this tropological use of Gen. 22:5 see also *Luther's Works*, 23, p. 169, note 123.

[35] The Latin word here is *politia;* like the German term *regiment* in Luther (cf. *Luther's Works*, 13, p. 147, note 4), *politia* cannot always be reproduced by the same English word but must be translated with "society," "government," "realm," etc.

namely, that the Law justifies on earth and the Gospel in heaven. But the pope has not only confused the Law with the Gospel; but he has changed the Gospel into mere laws, and ceremonial laws at that. He has also confused secular matters and church matters, which is really a satanic and infernal confusion.

The knowledge of this topic, the distinction between the Law and the Gospel, is necessary to the highest degree; for it contains a summary of all Christian doctrine. Therefore let everyone learn diligently how to distinguish the Law from the Gospel, not only in words but in feeling and in experience; that is, let him distinguish well between these two in his heart and in his conscience. For so far as the words are concerned, the distinction is easy. But when it comes to experience, you will find the Gospel a rare guest but the Law a constant guest in your conscience, which is habituated to the Law and the sense of sin; reason, too, supports this sense.

Therefore when the Law terrifies you, sin accuses you, and your conscience is crushed, you must say: "There is a time to die and a time to live (Eccl. 3:2). There is a time to hear the Law and a time to despise the Law. There is a time to hear the Gospel and a time to know nothing about the Gospel. Let the Law go away now, and let the Gospel come; for this is the time to hear the Gospel, not the Law. But you have nothing good; in fact, you have sinned gravely. Granted. Nevertheless, I have the forgiveness of sins through Christ, on whose account all my sins are forgiven." But in a matter apart from conscience, when outward duties must be performed, then, whether you are a preacher, a magistrate, a husband, a teacher, a pupil, etc., this is no time to listen to the Gospel. You must listen to the Law and follow your vocation. Thus the Law remains in the valley with the ass, and the Gospel remains with Isaac on the mountain.

I said to Cephas before them all: If you, though a Jew, live like a Gentile and not like a Jew, how can you compel the Gentiles to live like Jews?

This means: "You are a Jew and one who is bound to live like a Jew, that is, to abstain from foods prohibited by the Law. Nevertheless, you, a Jew, live like a Gentile; that is, you freely act contrary to the Law, transgress it, and trample it underfoot. For you eat common and unclean foods, as does any other Gentile who is free from the Law; and you do right. But when you keep the Law, you compel the Gentiles to act like Jews, that is, to observe the Law by necessity. For by your example of abstaining from profane foods you cause the Gentiles to think as follows: 'Peter now avoids the Gentile foods he used to eat. Therefore we, too, should avoid them and live in a Jewish manner. Otherwise we shall not be righteous and shall not be saved.'" You see, then, that Paul does not rebuke ignorance in Peter — for he knew that he was free to eat any foods at all with the Gentiles — but pretense, by which Peter compelled the Gentiles to live like Jews.

Here I remind you again that in itself there is nothing wrong with living like a Jew, for it is a matter of indifference whether you eat pork or any other meat. But to live like a Jew in the sense that you abstain from certain foods for the sake of conscience is a denial of Christ and the destruction of the Gospel. Therefore when Paul saw that Peter's behavior had this tendency, he opposed him and said: "You know that the observance of the Law is not necessary for righteousness, but that this comes solely through Christ. Therefore you do not observe the Law, but you transgress it and eat all sorts of food. Nevertheless, by your example you are forcing the Gentiles to forsake Christ and to return to the Law. For you lead them to think this way: 'Faith alone is not enough for righteousness, but the Law and works are also required. Peter shows us this by his own example. Therefore if we want to be justified, the observance of the Law is necessary, not only faith in Christ.'" Thus with his behavior Peter offends not only against purity of doctrine but also against the truth of faith and Christian righteousness. For the Gentiles received the impression from it that the Law was necessary for righteousness. If this error is permitted to stand, Christ becomes useless.

From this the full scope of this discord and controversy between Peter and Paul becomes evident. Paul is acting with a serious and sincere heart and is not pretending to rebuke Peter. But the text makes it obvious that Peter was pretending, and that it was for this that Paul rebuked him. In Paul there is no pretense, but there is pure and Christian severity and a holy pride, which would have been a fault if Peter had committed some trivial sin and had not sinned against the chief doctrine of Christianity. But because the truth of the Gospel is endangered by Peter's offense, Paul is neither willing nor able to stop his defense of it. To keep this inviolate, he does not spare Peter, and he cares nothing about Barnabas and all the rest.

Therefore Paul did right when he rebuked Peter. And Porphyry and Julian do him wrong when they accuse him of having rebuked Peter out of sheer arrogance. Indeed, if even reason looks at the scope of the issue with which Paul is dealing, it will be forced to admit that it was better for Peter to be put aside than for the Divine Majesty to yield or for faith to be jeopardized. For this is the issue at stake here: Either Peter must be severely rebuked, or Christ must be removed entirely. Rather let Peter perish and go to hell, if need be, than that Christ be lost. Porphyry and everyone else must assent to this proposition, and no one can deny that Paul acted in a good and pious way in this case.

If it had been a conflict over some matter of indifference — as, by comparison, the disagreement between Paul and Barnabas in Acts 15:39 is nothing but a joke and a trifle — Paul might have yielded. But in this, the most important of causes, he must not yield at all. Therefore let every Christian follow the example of Paul's pride here. Let love bear all things, believe all things, hope all things (1 Cor. 13:7). Let faith, by contrast, bear absolutely nothing; but let it rule, command, triumph, and do everything. For love and faith are exact opposites in their intentions, their tasks, and their values.[36] Love yields even in trifles and says: "I bear everything and yield to everyone." But faith says: "I yield to no one; but everything must yield to me — people, nations, kings, princes, and judges of the earth." As Ps. 2:10-11 says, "Now, therefore, O kings, be wise; be warned, O rulers of the earth. Serve the Lord with fear, etc. If you do not, you will perish in the way."

Therefore the whole emphasis is on the clause "you compel the Gentiles to live like Jews"; that is: "You compel them to fall from grace and faith to the Law and works, and to deny Christ, as though He had suffered and died in vain." This word, "you compel," summarizes all the perils and sins that Paul stresses and discusses throughout this epistle. For if that compulsion or necessity is granted, then faith must be abolished; and where this is abolished and overthrown, there all the promises of God are invalidated, all the gifts of the Holy Spirit are trampled underfoot, and everyone simply has to perish and be damned. Throughout this epistle Paul attributes many such qualities to the righteousness of the Law.

Now if it is so dangerous to deal with the Law, and if this fall

---

[36] We have translated *virtutes* with "values."

was so easy and so great, as though it had been all the way from heaven to hell, let every Christian learn diligently to distinguish between the Law and the Gospel. Let him permit the Law to rule his body and its members but not his conscience. For that queen and bride must not be polluted by the Law but must be kept pure for Christ, her one and only husband; as Paul says elsewhere (2 Cor. 11:2): "I betrothed you to one husband." Therefore let the conscience have its bridal chamber, not deep in the valley but high on the mountain. Here let only Christ lie and reign, Christ, who does not terrify sinners and afflict them, but who comforts them, forgives their sins, and saves them. Therefore let the afflicted conscience think nothing, know nothing, and pit nothing against the wrath and judgment of God except the Word of Christ, which is a Word of grace, forgiveness of sins, salvation, and life everlasting. But it is really hard to do this. For human nature and reason does not hold Christ firmly in its embrace but is quickly drawn down into thoughts about the Law and sin. Thus it always tries to be free according to the flesh but a slave and a captive according to the conscience.

In short, Paul summarized the doctrine of justification for Peter in the words: "If you, though a Jew, etc.," up to the passage (v. 16), "because, etc.," where he addresses the Galatians again. But he said these words to Peter, not in order to instruct him but in order to strengthen him, with the entire church standing by and listening. Therefore he says to Peter:

15. *We ourselves, who are Jews by birth and not Gentile sinners.*

That is: "We are Jews by nature, namely, by being born into the righteousness of the Law, into Moses, and into circumcision; we bring the Law along with our very birth. Not by choice, as the Gentiles do, but by our very nature we have the righteousness of the Law. (As Paul says of himself in the first chapter [Gal. 1:14], 'extremely zealous for the traditions of my fathers.') By comparison with the Gentiles, therefore, we are not sinners, without the Law and without works, as the Gentiles are. But we were born Jewish, born righteous, and reared in righteousness. That is, our righteousness begins with our very birth; for Judaism is something native to us. For in the seventeenth chapter of Genesis God commanded Abraham to circumcise every male child on the eighth day (Gen. 17:10 ff.). Afterwards Moses confirmed that Law of circumcision, which had come down from the patriarchs. Therefore it is something great that we are Jews by nature. Nevertheless, although we do have this prerogative, that we are righteous by nature, are born to the Law and its works, and are not sinners as the Gentiles are — still none of this makes us righteous in the sight of God.

"And so, even if you present me with some very good man who is a Jew, born righteous, and an absolute observer of the Law from his very birth, he still is not righteous on that account. We are indeed circumcised, but we are not justified by circumcision; for it is a 'sign of righteousness' (Rom. 4:11). Boys circumcised in the faith of Abraham are saved, not on account of their circumcision but on account of their faith. No matter how Jewish we are by birth, or how holy, or how able to boast over against the Gentiles that we have the justification of the Law, worship, the promises, and the fathers — all of which is certainly very glorious — still this does not make us righteous in the sight of God or give us any advantage over the Gentiles."

Paul makes it abundantly clear in these words that he is not speaking about ceremonies here and saying that since the revelation of Christ they have become fatal, as Origen and Jerome think.[37] He is speaking about something far more important, namely, the birthright of the Jews. He denies that they are righteous, even though they have been born holy, are circumcised, observe the Law, have the adoption, the glory, the covenants, the fathers, worship, God, and Christ, even though they have the promises, live in them, and boast of them; as they say in John 8:33: "We are descendants of Abraham"; and again (v. 41): "We have one Father, even God"; and in Rom. 2:17: "You call yourself a Jew and rely upon the Law and boast of your relation to God." Therefore although Peter, Paul, and the other apostles were indeed children of God, righteous according to the Law, and, finally, even ministers of Christ, they were not declared righteous in the sight of God on this account. For if you bind all these together into one bundle — the Law, its works and righteousness, circumcision, adoption, the covenants, the promises, the apostolate, etc. — still Christian righteousness does not come through these; for none of these is Christ.

This means that Paul wants to discuss, praise, and defend faith,

---

[37] Actually the object of Luther's polemic here would seem to be the scholastic understanding of the relation between the Ceremonial Law and the Decalog; cf. Thomas Aquinas, *Summa Theologica*, I—II, Q. 103, Art. 4.

because it alone, and not the Law, justifies. Not that the Law is
wicked or damnable; for the Law, circumcision, worship, etc., are
not condemned for their inability to justify. But Paul inveighs against
them because the false apostles maintained that by the sheer performance of these acts,[38] without faith, men are justified and saved.
This Paul would not tolerate; for without faith all these things are
fatal — the Law, circumcision, the adoption, the temple, worship, the
promises, even God and Christ, are of no avail without faith. Therefore Paul speaks in broad and universal terms against anything that
opposes faith, not only against ceremonies.

16. *Yet who know that a man is not justified by works of the Law
but through faith in Jesus Christ.*

These words, "works of the Law," are to be taken in the broadest
possible sense and are very emphatic. I am saying this because of
the smug and idle scholastics and monks, who obscure such words
in Paul — in fact, everything in Paul — with their foolish and wicked
glosses, which even they themselves do not understand. Therefore
take "works of the Law" generally, to mean whatever is opposed to
grace: Whatever is not grace is Law, whether it be the Civil Law,
the Ceremonial Law, or the Decalog. Therefore even if you were
to do the work of the Law, according to the commandment, "You
shall love the Lord your God with all your heart, etc." (Matt. 22:37),
you still would not be justified in the sight of God; for a man is not
justified by works of the Law. But more detail on this later on.

Thus for Paul "works of the Law" means the works of the entire
Law. Therefore one should not make a distinction between the
Decalog and ceremonial laws. Now if the work of the Decalog
does not justify, much less will circumcision, which is a work of the
Ceremonial Law. When Paul says, as he often does, that a man
is not justified by the Law or by the works of the Law, which
means the same thing in Paul, he is speaking in general about the
entire Law; he is contrasting the righteousness of faith with the
righteousness of the entire Law, with everything that can be done
on the basis of the Law, whether by divine power or by human.

[38] The phrase *ex opere operato* may simply mean that the validity of a sacrament depends on its proper administration in accordance with the institution
of Christ rather than on the holiness of the officiant; in this sense Luther followed
and accepted the Augustinian tradition. But in the later Middle Ages it had
come to mean an almost automatic or even magical quality in the sacramental act,
and it is against this interpretation that Luther is speaking here.

[W, XL, 218, 219]

For by the righteousness of the Law, he says, a man is not pronounced righteous in the sight of God; but God imputes the righteousness of faith freely through His mercy, for the sake of Christ. It is, therefore, with a certain emphasis and vehemence that he said "by works of the Law." For there is no doubt that the Law is holy, righteous, and good; therefore the works of the Law are holy, righteous, and good. Nevertheless, a man is not justified in the sight of God through them.

Hence the opinion of Jerome and others is to be rejected when they imagine that here Paul is speaking about the works of the Ceremonial Law, not about those of the Decalog.[39] If I concede this, I am forced to concede also that the Ceremonial Law was good and holy. Surely circumcision and other laws about rites and about the temple were righteous and holy, for they were commanded by God as much as the moral laws were. But then they say: "But after Christ the ceremonial laws were fatal." They invent this out of their own heads, for it does not appear anywhere in Scripture. Besides, Paul is not speaking here about the Gentiles, for whom the ceremonies would be fatal, but about the Jews, for whom they were good; indeed, he himself observed them. Thus even at the time when the ceremonial laws were holy, righteous, and good, they were not able to justify.

Therefore Paul is speaking not only about a part of the Law, which is also good and holy, but about the entire Law. He means that a work done in accordance with the entire Law does not justify. Nor is he speaking about a sin against the Law or a deed of the flesh, but about "the work of the Law," that is, a work performed in accordance with the Law. Therefore refraining from murder or adultery — whether this is done by natural powers or by human strength or by free will or by the gift and power of God — still does not justify.

But the works of the Law can be performed either before justification or after justification. Before justification many good men even among the pagans — such as Xenophon, Aristides, Fabius, Cicero, Pomponius Atticus, etc. — performed the works of the Law and accomplished great things.[40] Cicero suffered death courageously in a righteous and good cause. Pomponius was a man of integrity and

---

39 See p.121, note 37, on these "others."

40 Cf. *Luther's Works*, 2, p. 160.

veracity; for he himself never lied, and he could not bear it if others did. Integrity and veracity are, of course, very fine virtues and very beautiful works of the Law; but these men were not justified by these works. After justification, moreover, Peter, Paul, and all other Christians have done and still do the works of the Law; but they are not justified by them either. "I am not aware of anything against myself," says Paul; that is, "No man can accuse me, but I am not thereby justified" (1 Cor. 4:4). Thus we see that Paul is speaking about the entire Law and all its works, not about sins against the Law.

Therefore the dangerous and wicked opinion of the papists is to be condemned. They attribute the merit of grace and the forgiveness of sins to the mere performance of the work. For they say that a good work performed before grace can earn a "merit of congruity"; but once grace has been obtained, the work that follows deserves eternal life by the "merit of condignity." [41] If a man outside a state of grace and in mortal sin performs a good work by his own natural inclination — such as reading or hearing Mass, giving alms, etc. — this man deserves grace "by congruity." Once he has obtained grace this way, he goes on to perform a work that merits eternal life "by condignity." Now in the first case God is not indebted to anyone. But because He is good and righteous, it is proper for Him to approve such a good work, even though it is performed in mortal sin, and to grant grace for such a deed. But once grace has been obtained, God has become a debtor and is obliged by right to grant eternal life. For now this is not only a work of the free will, carried out externally; but it is performed in the grace that makes a man pleasing before God, that is, in love.

Such is the theology of the antichristian kingdom. I am recounting it here to make Paul's argument more intelligible; for when two opposites are placed side by side, they become more evident. In addition, I want everyone to see how far these "blind guides of the blind" (Matt. 15:14) have strayed. By this wicked and blasphemous teaching they have not only obscured the Gospel but have removed it altogether and have buried Christ completely. For if in a state of mortal sin I can do any tiny work that is not only pleasing before God externally and of itself but can even deserve grace "by congruity"; and if, once I have received grace, I am able to perform works according to grace, that is, according to love, and receive

---

[41] See, among other places, *Luther's Works*, 2, p. 123.

eternal life by a right – then what need do I have of the grace of God, the forgiveness of sins, the promise, and the death and victory of Christ? Then Christ has become altogether useless to me; for I have free will and the power to perform good works, and through this I merit grace "by congruity" and eventually eternal life "by condignity."

Such dreadful monstrosities and horrible blasphemies ought to be propounded to Turks and Jews, not to the church of Christ. This whole business clearly shows that the pope with his bishops, theologians, monks, and all the rest has neither knowledge nor concern about sacred things; nor do they care anything about the health of the flock, which is so deserted and so miserably scattered. For if they had seen, though only through a cloud, what Paul calls sin and what he calls grace, they would not have imposed such abominations and wicked lies on Christian people. They take mortal sin to be only the external work committed against the Law, such as murder, adultery, theft, etc. They did not see that ignorance, hatred, and contempt of God in the heart, ingratitude, murmuring against God, and resistance to the will of God are also mortal sin, and that the flesh cannot think, say, or do anything except what is diabolical and opposed to God. If they had seen that these huge plagues are rooted in the nature of man, they would not have dreamt so wickedly about the "merit of congruity" and the "merit of condignity."

Therefore there must be a proper and clear definition of what a wicked man or mortal sinner is. He is a holy hypocrite and murderer, as Paul was when he went to Damascus to persecute Jesus of Nazareth, to abolish the doctrine of Christ, to murder the faithful, and to overthrow the church of Christ altogether. Those were certainly extremely great and horrible sins against God, but Paul was unable to recognize them as such. For he was so completely blinded by a wicked zeal for God that he regarded these unspeakable crimes of his as the height of righteousness and an act of worship and obedience most pleasing to God. Can such saints, who defend such horrible sins as the height of righteousness, be supposed to merit grace?

With Paul, therefore, we totally deny the "merit of congruity" and the "merit of condignity"; and with complete confidence we declare that these speculations are merely the tricks of Satan, which have never been performed or demonstrated by any examples. For

God has never given anyone grace and eternal life for the merit of congruity or the merit of condignity. Therefore these disputations of the scholastics about merit of congruity and of condignity are nothing but empty fictions, the dreams of idle men; and yet the entire papacy is founded on these nonexistent things and depends on them to this day. For every monk imagines as follows to himself: "By the observance of my holy rule I am able to merit grace 'by congruity.' And by the works I perform after receiving this grace I am able to accumulate such a treasure of merit that it will not only be enough for me to obtain eternal life but can also be given or sold to others." This is how all the monks have taught and lived. In defense of this horrible blasphemy against Christ there is nothing that the papists will not attempt against us today. Among them all, the more holy and self-righteous a hypocrite is, the more vicious an enemy he is of the Gospel of Christ.

Now the true meaning of Christianity is this: that a man first acknowledge, through the Law, that he is a sinner, for whom it is impossible to perform any good work. For the Law says: "You are an evil tree. Therefore everything you think, speak, or do is opposed to God. Hence you cannot deserve grace by your works. But if you try to do so, you make the bad even worse; for since you are an evil tree, you cannot produce anything except evil fruits, that is, sins. 'For whatever does not proceed from faith is sin' (Rom. 14:23)." Trying to merit grace by preceding works, therefore, is trying to placate God with sins, which is nothing but heaping sins upon sins, making fun of God, and provoking His wrath. When a man is taught this way by the Law, he is frightened and humbled. Then he really sees the greatness of his sin and finds in himself not one spark of the love of God; thus he justifies God in His Word and confesses that he deserves death and eternal damnation. Thus the first step in Christianity is the preaching of repentance and the knowledge of oneself.

The second step is this: If you want to be saved, your salvation does not come by works; but God has sent His only Son into the world that we might live through Him. He was crucified and died for you and bore your sins in His own body (1 Peter 2:24). Here there is no "congruity" or work performed before grace, but only wrath, sin, terror, and death. Therefore the Law only shows sin, terrifies, and humbles; thus it prepares us for justification and drives us to Christ. For by His Word God has revealed to us that He wants to be a merciful Father to us. Without our merit – since, after all, we cannot merit anything – He wants to give us forgiveness of sins, righteousness, and eternal life for the sake of Christ. For God is He who dispenses His gifts freely to all,[42] and this is the praise of His deity. But He cannot defend this deity of His against the self-righteous people who are unwilling to accept grace and eternal life from Him freely but want to earn it by their own works. They simply want to rob Him of the glory of His deity. In order to retain it, He is compelled to send forth His Law, to terrify and crush those very hard rocks as though it were thunder and lightning.

This, in summary, is our theology about Christian righteousness, in opposition to the abominations and monstrosities of the sophists about "merit of congruity and of condignity" or about works before grace and after grace. Smug people, who have never struggled with any temptations or true terrors of sin and death, were the ones who made up these empty dreams out of their own heads; therefore they do not understand what they are saying or what they are talking about, for they cannot supply any examples of such works done either before grace or after grace. Therefore these are useless fables, with which the papists delude both themselves and others.

The reason is that Paul expressly states here that a man is not justified by the deeds of the Law, whether they are those that precede (of which he is speaking here) or those that follow justification. Thus you see that Christian righteousness is not an "inherent form," as they call it.[43] For they say: When a man does a good work, God accepts it; and for this work He infuses charity into him. This infused charity, they say, is a quality that is attached to the heart; they call it "formal righteousness." (It is a good idea for you to know this manner of speaking.) Nothing is more intolerable to them than to be told that this quality, which informs the heart as whiteness does a wall, is not righteousness. They cannot climb any higher than this cogitation of human reason: Man is righteous by means of his formal righteousness, which is grace making him pleasing before God, that is, love.[44] Thus they attribute formal righteousness to an attitude and "form" inherent in the soul, namely, to love,

---

[42] Cf. *Luther's Works*, 13, p. 6, note 4.

[43] "Habits are qualities or forms adhering to a power *[formae inhaerentes potentiae].*" Thomas Aquinas, *Summa Theologica*, I—II, Q. 54, Art. 1.

[44] Cf. Thomas Aquinas, *Summa Theologica*, I—II, Q. 111, Art. 1.

which is a work and gift according to the Law; for the Law says: "You shall love the Lord" (Matt. 22:37). And they say that this righteousness is worthy of eternal life; that he who has it is "formally righteous"; and, finally, that he is righteous in fact, because he is now performing good works, for which eternal life is due him. This is the opinion of the sophists — and of the best among them at that.

Others are not even that good, such as Scotus and Occam.[45] They said that this love which is given by God is not necessary to obtain the grace of God, but that even by his own natural powers a man is able to produce a love for God above all things. Scotus disputes this way: "If a man can love a creature, a young man love a girl, or a covetous man love money — all of which are a lesser good — he can also love God, who is a greater good. If by his natural powers he has a love for the creature, much more does he have a love for the Creator." This argument left all the sophists confounded, and none of them could refute it. Nevertheless, this is what they said:[46]

"Scripture requires us to say that in addition to our natural love, with which He is not satisfied, God also demands a love that He Himself grants." Thus they accuse God of being a severe tyrant and a cruel taskmaster, who is not content that I observe and fulfill His Law but demands also that beyond the Law, which I can easily fulfill, I dress up my obedience with additional qualities and adornments. It is as though the lady of the house were not content that her cook had prepared the food very well but scolded her for not wearing precious garments and adorning herself with a golden crown while she prepared the food. What sort of housewife would that be who, after her cook has done everything she is required to do and has done it superbly, would demand that she should also wear a golden crown, which it is impossible for her to have? Likewise, what sort of God would that be who would demand that we fulfill His Law, which we otherwise observe by our natural powers, with an ornamentation that we cannot possess?

To avoid the impression of contradicting themselves, they make a distinction at this point and say that the Law can be fulfilled in two ways: first, according to the content of the act; secondly, accord-

[45] See the passages from Duns Scotus quoted by Parthenius Minges, *Ioannis Duns Scoti doctrina philosophica et theologica* (Quaracchi, 1930), I, 506, and II, 444—445.

[46] Cf. Thomas Aquinas, *Summa Theologica*, I—II, Q. 109, Arts. 3—4.

ing to the intention of Him who gave the commandment.[47] According to the content of the act, that is, so far as the deed itself is concerned, we can simply fulfill everything that the Law commands. But we cannot do so according to the intention of Him who gave the commandment; for this means that God is not content that you have performed and fulfilled everything commanded in the Law (although He has no more than this to demand of you), but He requires in addition that you keep the Law in love — not the natural love that you have but a supernatural and divine love that He Himself confers. What is this but to make God a tyrant and a tormentor who demands of us what we cannot produce? In a sense it is as though they were saying that if we are damned, the fault is not so much in us as in God, who requires us to keep His Law in this fashion.

I am reciting all this to make you see how far they have strayed from the meaning of Scripture with their declaration that by our own natural powers we are able to love God above all things, or at least that by the mere performance of the deed we are able to merit grace and eternal life. And because God is not content if we fulfill the Law according to the content of the act but also wants us to fulfill it according to the intention of Him who gave the commandment, therefore Sacred Scripture requires us to have a supernatural quality infused into us from heaven, namely, love, which they call the formal righteousness that informs and adorns faith and makes it justify us. Thus faith is the body, the shell, or the color; but love is the life, the kernel, or the form.

Such are the dreams of the scholastics. But where they speak of love, we speak of faith. And while they say that faith is the mere outline [48] but love is its living colors and completion, we say in opposition that faith takes hold of Christ and that He is the form that adorns and informs faith as color does the wall. Therefore Christian faith is not an idle quality or an empty husk in the heart, which may exist in a state of mortal sin until love comes along to make it alive. But if it is true faith, it is a sure trust and firm acceptance in the heart. It takes hold of Christ in such a way that Christ is the object of faith, or rather not the object but, so to speak, the One who is present in the faith itself. Thus faith is a sort of

47 Where the Weimar text has *praecipientes,* we have read *praecipientis.*

48 Luther uses the Greek word μονόγραμμα here.

knowledge or darkness that nothing can see. Yet the Christ of whom faith takes hold is sitting in this darkness as God sat in the midst of darkness on Sinai and in the temple.[49] Therefore our "formal righteousness" is not a love that informs faith; but it is faith itself, a cloud in our hearts, that is, trust in a thing we do not see, in Christ, who is present especially when He cannot be seen.

Therefore faith justifies because it takes hold of and possesses this treasure, the present Christ. But how He is present — this is beyond our thought; for there is darkness, as I have said. Where the confidence of the heart is present, therefore, there Christ is present, in that very cloud and faith. This is the formal righteousness on account of which a man is justified; it is not on account of love, as the sophists say. In short, just as the sophists say that love forms and trains faith, so we say that it is Christ who forms and trains faith or who is the form of faith. Therefore the Christ who is grasped by faith and who lives in the heart is the true Christian righteousness, on account of which God counts us righteous and grants us eternal life. Here there is no work of the Law, no love; but there is an entirely different kind of righteousness, a new world above and beyond the Law. For Christ or faith is neither the Law nor the work of the Law. But we intend later on to go into more detail on this issue, which the sophists have neither understood nor written about. For the present let it be enough for us to have shown that Paul is speaking here not only about the Ceremonial Law but about the entire Law.

I have warned in passing of the dangerous error of the scholastic theologians, who taught that a man obtains forgiveness of sins and justification in the following manner: By his works that precede grace, which they call a "merit of congruity," he merits grace, which, according to them, is a quality that inheres in the will, granted by God over and above the love we have by our natural powers. They say that when a man has this quality, he is formally righteous and a true Christian. I say that this is a wicked and dangerous notion, which does not make a man a Christian but makes him a Turk, a Jew, an Anabaptist, or a fanatic. For who cannot perform a good work by his own powers without grace and thus merit grace? In this way these dreamers have made faith an empty quality in the soul, which is of no use alone, without love, but becomes effective and justifies when love is added to it.

[49] See p. 113, note 32.

They go on to say that the works that follow have the power to merit eternal life "by condignity," because God accepts the work that follows and applies it to eternal life, on account of the love that He has infused into man's will. Thus they say that God "accepts" a good work for eternal life but "disaccepts" an evil work for damnation and eternal punishment.[50] They have heard something in a dream about "acceptance" and have ascribed this relation to works. All this is false and blasphemous against Christ. Nevertheless, they do not all speak even this well; but some, as we have said, have taught that by our purely natural powers [51] we are able to love God above all things. These things are useful to know, to make Paul's argument clearer.

In opposition to these trifles and empty dreams, as we have noted briefly above, we teach faith and the true meaning of Christianity. First, a man must be taught by the Law to know himself, so that he may learn to sing: "All have sinned and fall short of the glory of God" (Rom. 3:23); again: "None is righteous, no, not one; no one understands, no one seeks for God. All have turned aside" (Rom. 3:10-12); again: "Against Thee only have I sinned" (Ps. 51:4). By this opposition of ours we drive men away from the merit of congruity and of condignity. Now once a man has thus been humbled by the Law and brought to the knowledge of himself, then he becomes truly repentant; for true repentance begins with fear and with the judgment of God. He sees that he is such a great sinner that he cannot find any means to be delivered from his sin by his own strength, effort, or works. Then he understands correctly what Paul means when he says that man is the slave and captive of sin, that God has consigned all men to sin, and that the whole world is guilty in the sight of God.[52] Then he sees that the doctrine of the sophists about the merit of congruity and of condignity is mere ματαιολογία (1 Tim. 1:6) and that the entire papacy is undermined.

Now he begins to sigh: "Then who can come to my aid?" Terrified by the Law, he despairs of his own strength; he looks about and sighs for the help of the Mediator and Savior. Then there comes, at the appropriate time, the saving Word of the Gospel, which says:

[50] For the Latin *deacceptare* we have used the rare and obsolete English word "disaccept," to retain the contrast with *acceptare* in the original.

[51] See p. 4, note 1.

[52] Luther is referring to the following passages: Rom. 6:16; Gal. 3:22; Rom. 3:23.

"Take heart, my son; your sins are forgiven (Matt. 9:2). Believe in Jesus Christ, who was crucified for your sins. If you feel your sins, do not consider them in yourself but remember that they have been transferred to Christ, 'with whose stripes you are healed' (Is. 53:3)."

This is the beginning of salvation. By this means we are delivered from sin and justified, and eternal life is granted to us, not for our own merits and works but for our faith, by which we take hold of Christ. Therefore we, too, acknowledge a quality and a formal righteousness in the heart; but we do not mean love, as the sophists do, but faith, because the heart must behold and grasp nothing but Christ the Savior. Here it is necessary to know the true definition of Christ. Ignoring this altogether, the sophists have made Him a judge and a torturer, and have invented this stupid notion about the merit of congruity and of condignity.

But by the true definition Christ is not a lawgiver; He is a Propitiator and a Savior. Faith takes hold of this and believes without doubting that He has performed a superabundance of works and merits of congruity and condignity. He might have made satisfaction for all the sins of the world with only one drop of His blood,[53] but now He has made abundant satisfaction. Heb. 9:12: "With His own blood He entered once for all into the Holy Place." And Rom. 3:24-25: "Justified by His grace as a gift, through the redemption which is in Christ Jesus, whom God put forward as an expiation by His blood." Therefore it is something great to take hold, by faith, of Christ, who bears the sins of the world (John 1:29). And this faith alone is counted for righteousness (Rom. 3–4).

Here it is to be noted that these three things are joined together: faith, Christ, and acceptance or imputation. Faith takes hold of Christ and has Him present, enclosing Him as the ring encloses the gem. And whoever is found having this faith in the Christ who is grasped in the heart, him God accounts as righteous. This is the means and the merit by which we obtain the forgiveness of sins and righteousness. "Because you believe in Me," God says, "and your faith takes hold of Christ, whom I have freely given to you as your Justifier and Savior, therefore be righteous." Thus God accepts you or accounts you righteous only on account of Christ, in whom you believe.

Now acceptance or imputation is extremely necessary, first, because we are not yet purely righteous, but sin is still clinging to our

[53] See *Luther's Works*, 22, p. 459, note 156, on this idea.

flesh during this life. God cleanses this remnant of sin in our flesh. In addition, we are sometimes forsaken by the Holy Spirit, and we fall into sins, as did Peter, David, and other saints. Nevertheless, we always have recourse to this doctrine, that our sins are covered and that God does not want to hold us accountable for them (Rom. 4). This does not mean that there is no sin in us, as the sophists have taught when they said that we must go on doing good until we are no longer conscious of any sin; but sin is always present, and the godly feel it. But it is ignored and hidden in the sight of God, because Christ the Mediator stands between; because we take hold of Him by faith, all our sins are sins no longer. But where Christ and faith are not present, here there is no forgiveness of sins or hiding of sins. On the contrary, here there is the sheer imputation and condemnation of sins. Thus God wants to glorify His Son, and He Himself wants to be glorified in us through Him.

When we have taught faith in Christ this way, then we also teach about good works. Because you have taken hold of Christ by faith, through whom you are righteous, you should now go and love God and your neighbor. Call upon God, give thanks to Him, preach Him, praise Him, confess Him. Do good to your neighbor, and serve him; do your duty. These are truly good works, which flow from this faith and joy conceived in the heart because we have the forgiveness of sins freely through Christ.

Then whatever there is of cross or suffering to be borne later on is easily sustained. For the yoke that Christ lays upon us is sweet, and His burden is light (Matt. 11:30). When sin has been forgiven and the conscience has been liberated from the burden and the sting of sin, then a Christian can bear everything easily. Because everything within is sweet and pleasant, he willingly does and suffers everything. But when a man goes along in his own righteousness, then whatever he does and suffers is painful and tedious for him, because he is doing it unwillingly.

Therefore we define a Christian as follows: A Christian is not someone who has no sin or feels no sin; he is someone to whom, because of his faith in Christ, God does not impute his sin. This doctrine brings firm consolation to troubled consciences amid genuine terrors. It is not in vain, therefore, that so often and so diligently we inculcate the doctrine of the forgiveness of sins and of the imputation of righteousness for the sake of Christ, as well as the doctrine that a Christian does not have anything to do with the Law and sin, especially in a time of temptation. For to the extent that he is a Christian, he is above the Law and sin, because in his heart he has Christ, the Lord of the Law, as a ring has a gem. Therefore when the Law accuses and sin troubles, he looks to Christ; and when he has taken hold of Him by faith, he has present with him the Victor over the Law, sin, death, and the devil — the Victor whose rule over all these prevents them from harming him.

Therefore a Christian, properly defined, is free of all laws and is subject to nothing, internally or externally. But I purposely said, "to the extent that he is a Christian" (not "to the extent that he is a man or a woman"); that is, to the extent that he has his conscience trained, adorned, and enriched by this faith, this great and inestimable treasure, or, as Paul calls it, "this inexpressible gift" (2 Cor. 9:15), which cannot be exalted and praised enough, since it makes men sons and heirs of God. Thus a Christian is greater than the entire world. For in his heart he has this seemingly small gift; yet the smallness of this gift and treasure, which he holds in faith, is greater than heaven and earth, because Christ, who is this gift, is greater.

When this doctrine, which pacifies consciences, remains pure and intact, Christians are constituted as judges over all kinds of doctrine and become lords over all the laws of the entire world. Then they can freely judge that the Turk with his Koran is damned, because he does not follow the right way; that is, he does not acknowledge that he is a miserable and damned sinner, and he does not take hold of Christ by faith, for whose sake he could believe that his sins are forgiven. With similar confidence they can pronounce sentence against the pope. He is damned with all his kingdom, because he, with all his monks and universities, acts as though we came to grace through the merit of congruity and as though we were then received into heaven by the merit of condignity. Here the Christian says: "That is not the right way to justify. This is not the road to the stars.[54] For through my works preceding grace I cannot merit grace by congruity, nor can I deserve eternal life by condignity through my merits following grace; but sin is forgiven and righteousness is imputed to him who believes in Christ. This confidence makes him a son and heir of God, who in hope possesses the promise of eternal life. Through faith in Christ, therefore, and not through the merit of congruity and

[54] The phrase *sic itur ad astra,* from Vergil, *Aeneid,* IX, 641, had become a common saying.

of condignity, everything is granted to us — grace, peace, the forgiveness of sins, salvation, and eternal life."

Therefore this doctrine of the sententiaries about the merit of congruity and condignity — with all their ceremonies, Masses, and innumerable foundations of the papal kingdom — is an abominable blasphemy against God, a sacrilege, and a denial of Christ. Peter predicted it in these words from 2 Peter 2:1: "There will be false teachers among you, who will secretly bring in destructive heresies, even denying the Master who bought them." It is as though he were saying: "The Master has redeemed and bought us with His blood, to justify and save us; this is the way of righteousness and salvation. But false teachers will come; they will deny the Master and will blaspheme the way of truth, righteousness, and salvation. They will invent new ways of falsehood and perdition, and many will follow their perdition." Throughout this chapter Peter draws an outstanding portrait of the papacy, which has neglected the Gospel and faith in Christ and has taught human works and traditions, like the merit of congruity and of condignity, special days, foods, as well as persons, vows, the invocation of saints, pilgrimages, purgatory, etc. The papists have imbibed these fanatical opinions about traditions and works to such an extent that it is impossible for them to understand a single syllable about the Gospel, about faith, or about Christ.

This is sufficiently evident from the matter at hand. For they usurp for themselves the right that belongs to Christ alone. Only He delivers from sin and grants righteousness and eternal life; yet they claim that they are able to obtain these things by their own merits of congruity and of condignity, to the exclusion of Christ. Peter and the other apostles call this bringing in "destructive heresies," denying Christ, treading His blood underfoot, and blaspheming the Holy Spirit and the grace of God. Therefore no one sees sufficiently how horrible the idolatry of the papists is. As inestimable as the gift offered to us in Christ is, that is how abominable these papistic profanations are. Therefore they should not be lightly dismissed or consigned to oblivion but should be diligently considered. And this, by contrast, serves to magnify the grace of God and the blessings of Christ. For the more I recognize the profanation of the papistic Mass, the more I abhor and detest it. The pope has taken away the true use of the Mass and has simply turned it into merchandise that one may buy for the benefit of another person. There stood the Mass priest at the altar, an apostate who denied Christ and blasphemed the Holy Spirit; and he was doing a work not only for himself but for others, both living and dead, even for the entire church, and that simply by the mere performance of the act.

Even from this, therefore, it is evident that the patience of God is inestimable, since He did not destroy the whole papacy long ago and consume it with fire and brimstone, as he did Sodom and Gomorrah. But now these fine people want to cover and adorn their wickedness and infamy. For us this is intolerable. From the darkness and night of their hypocrisy we must drag them into the light, in order that the doctrine of justification, like the sun, may reveal their infamy and shame. This is why we gladly give sharp expression to the righteousness of faith — in order that the papists and all the sectarians may be confounded and this doctrine may be established and made certain in our hearts. And this is extremely necessary; for once we have lost this sun, we relapse into our former darkness. And it is horrendous to the highest degree that the pope should have managed to accomplish this in the church, that Christ should be denied, trodden underfoot, spit upon, and blasphemed — and all this by means of the Gospel and the sacraments, which the pope has so obscured and distorted that he has made them serve him against Christ in establishing and supporting his diabolical abominations. What darkness! And how infinite is the wrath of God!

Even we have believed in Christ Jesus, in order to be justified by faith in Christ, and not by works of the Law.

This is the true meaning of Christianity, that we are justified by faith in Christ, not by the works of the Law. Do not let yourself be swayed here by the wicked gloss of the sophists, who say that faith justifies only when love and good works are added to it. With this pernicious gloss they have darkened and distorted some of the finest texts of this sort. When a man hears that he should believe in Christ, but that faith does not justify unless this "form," that is, love, is added, then he quickly falls from faith and thinks to himself: "If faith does not justify without love, then faith is vain and useless, and love alone justifies; or unless faith is formed and adorned by love, it is nothing."

In support of this wicked and destructive gloss the opponents cite this passage from 1 Cor. 13:1-2: "If I speak in the tongues of men and of angels, and if I have prophetic powers and understand all mysteries and all knowledge, and if I have all faith, so as to remove mountains, but have not love, I am nothing." [55] They suppose that this passage is their wall of bronze. But they are men without understanding, and therefore they cannot grasp or see anything in Paul. With this false interpretation they have not only done injury to Paul's words but have also denied Christ and buried all His blessings. Therefore this gloss is to be avoided as a hellish poison, and we must conclude with Paul: By faith alone, not by faith formed by love, are we justified. We must not attribute the power of justifying to a "form" that makes a man pleasing to God; we must attribute it to faith, which takes hold of Christ the Savior Himself and possesses Him in the heart. This faith justifies without love and before love.

We concede that good works and love must also be taught; but this must be in its proper time and place, that is, when the question has to do with works, apart from this chief doctrine. But here the point at issue is how we are justified and attain eternal life. To this we answer with Paul: We are pronounced righteous solely by faith in Christ, not by the works of the Law or by love. This is not because we reject works or love, as our adversaries accuse us of doing, but because we refuse to let ourselves be distracted from the principal point at issue here, as Satan is trying to do. So since we are now dealing with the topic of justification, we reject and condemn works; for this topic will not allow of any discussion of good works. On this issue, therefore, we simply cut off all laws and all works of the Law.

"But the Law is good, righteous, and holy." Very well! But when we are involved in a discussion of justification, there is no room for speaking about the Law. The question is what Christ is and what blessing He has brought us. Christ is not the Law; He is not my work or that of the Law; He is not my love or that of the Law; He is not my chastity, obedience, or poverty. But He is the Lord of life and death, the Mediator and Savior of sinners, the Redeemer of those who are under the Law. By faith we are in Him, and He is in us (John 6:56). This Bridegroom, Christ, must be alone with His bride in His private chamber, and all the family and household must be shunted away. But later on, when the Bridegroom opens the door and comes out, then let the servants return to take

[55] See the Confutation of the Augsburg Confession in M. Reu, *The Augsburg Confession* (Chicago, 1930), II, 352.

care of them and serve them food and drink. Then let works and love begin.

Thus we must learn to distinguish all laws, even those of God, and all works from faith and from Christ, if we are to define Christ accurately. Christ is not the Law, and therefore He is not a taskmaster for the Law and for works; but He is the Lamb of God, who takes away the sin of the world (John 1:29). This is grasped by faith alone, not by love, which nevertheless must follow faith as a kind of gratitude. Therefore victory over sin and death, salvation, and eternal life do not come by the Law or by the deeds of the Law or by our will but by Jesus Christ alone. Hence faith alone justifies when it takes hold of this, as becomes evident from a sufficient division and induction:[56] Victory over sin and death does not come by the works of the Law or by our will; therefore it comes by Jesus Christ alone. Here we are perfectly willing to have ourselves called "solafideists"[57] by our opponents, who do not understand anything of Paul's argument. You who are to be the consolers of consciences that are afflicted, should teach this doctrine diligently, study it continually, and defend it vigorously against the abominations of the papists, Jews, Turks, and all the rest.[58]

In order to be justified by faith in Christ, and not by works of the Law.

All these words are to be read with feeling and emphasis. As I have warned before, Paul is speaking here not about the Ceremonial Law alone but about the entire Law. For the Ceremonial Law was as much the divine Law as the moral laws were. Thus circumcision, the institution of the priesthood, the service of worship, and the rituals were commanded by God as much as the Decalog was. In addition, it was the Law when Abraham was commanded to sacrifice his son Isaac. This work of Abraham pleased God as much as other ceremonial works did. And yet he was not justified by this work; he was justified by faith. For Scripture says (Rom. 4:3): "Abraham believed God, and it was reckoned to him as righteousness."

"But after Christ was revealed," they say, "the ceremonial laws

[56] Cf. Aristotle, *Prior Analytics*, Book II, ch. 23.

[57] For the Latin *solarii*, used by Luther's detractors, we have borrowed the Wesleyan term "solafideists."

[58] This is one of the passages in the commentary where we may still hear an echo of Luther's lectures.

are fatal." Yes, the entire Law, including the Law of the Decalog, is also fatal without faith in Christ. Moreover, no Law should reign in the conscience except that of the Spirit of life, by which we are delivered in Christ from the Law of the letter and of death, from its works, and from sins. This does not mean that the Law is evil; it means that it cannot contribute anything to justification. It is something sublime and great to have a gracious God; and for this we need quite another Mediator than Moses or the Law, other than our own will, indeed, other even than that grace which they call "the love of God." Here we are not obliged to do anything at all. The only thing necessary is that we accept the treasure that is Christ, grasped by faith in our hearts, even though we feel that we are completely filled with sins. Thus these words, "by faith in Christ," are very emphatic, not empty and vain, as the sophists think when they leap over them so boldly.

Because by works of the Law shall no one be justified.

Thus far the words have been those that Paul spoke to Peter. In them he has summarized the chief doctrine of Christianity, which makes true Christians. Now he shifts the address to the Galatians, to whom he is writing, and he concludes: "Since the situation is that we are justified by faith in Christ, it follows that 'by works of the Law shall no one be justified.'"

"Not all flesh" [59] is a Hebraism that sins against grammar. Thus Gen. 4:15 says: "Lest any who came upon him should kill him." The Greeks and the Latins do not speak this way. "Not everyone" means "no one," and "not all flesh" means "no flesh." But in Latin "not all flesh" sounds as though it meant "some flesh." But the Holy Spirit does not observe this strict rule of grammar.

Now in Paul "flesh" does not, as the sophists suppose, mean crass sins;[60] for these he usually calls by their explicit names, like adultery, fornication, uncleanness, etc. (Gal. 5:19 ff.). But by "flesh" Paul means here what Christ means in John 3:6: "That which is born of the flesh is flesh." Therefore "flesh" means the entire nature of man, with reason and all his powers. This flesh, he says, is not justified by works, not even by those of the Law. He is not saying: "The flesh is not justified by works against the Law, such as de-

---

[59] The unusual Latin phrase was *non omnis caro.*

[60] Cf. *Luther the Expositor,* p. 150.

bauchery, drunkenness, etc." But he is saying: "It is not justified by works done in accordance with the Law, works that are good." For Paul, therefore, "flesh" means the highest righteousness, wisdom, worship, religion, understanding, and will of which the world is capable. Therefore the monk is not justified by his order, nor the priest by the Mass and the canonical hours, nor the philosopher by wisdom, nor the theologian by theology, nor the Turk by the Koran, nor the Jew by Moses. In other words, no matter how wise and righteous men may be according to reason and the divine Law, yet with all their works, merits, Masses, righteousnesses, and acts of worship they are not justified.

The papists do not believe this. In their blindness and stubbornness, they defend their abominations against their own consciences. They persist in this blasphemy of theirs and still boast in these sacrilegious words: "Whoever does this or that merits the forgiveness of sins; whoever serves this or that holy order, to him we give a sure promise of eternal life." To take what Paul, the apostle of Christ, refuses to ascribe to the divine Law and its works, and to attribute this to the doctrines of demons (1 Tim. 4:1), to the statutes and rules of men, to the wicked traditions of the pope, and to the works of monks — this is an unspeakable and horrible blasphemy! For if, according to the testimony of the apostle, no one is justified by the works of the divine Law, much less will anyone be justified by the rule of Benedict, Francis, etc., in which there is not a syllable about faith in Christ but only the insistence that whoever observes these things has eternal life.

Therefore I have wondered a great deal that with these destructive heresies persisting for so many centuries the church could still endure amid such great darkness and error. There were some whom God called simply by the text of the Gospel, which nevertheless continued in the pulpit, and by Baptism. They walked in simplicity and humility of heart; they thought that the monks and those whom the bishops had ordained were the only ones who were religious and holy, while they themselves were profane and secular and therefore not to be compared with them. Since they found in themselves no good works or merits to pit against the wrath and judgment of God, they took refuge in the suffering and death of Christ; and in that simplicity they were saved.

The wrath of God is horrible and infinite, that for so many centuries He has been punishing the ingratitude and contempt of the

Gospel and of Christ in the papists by giving them up to a reprobate mind (Rom. 1:24 ff.). Denying Christ completely and blaspheming Him in His saving work, they received, in place of the Gospel, the abomination of these rules and human traditions. These they treated with special reverence and preferred to the Word of God, until finally matrimony was forbidden them, and they were forced into an incestuous celibacy, in which they were outwardly polluted with all sorts of horrible vices — adultery, prostitution, impurity, sodomy, etc. This was the fruit of that impure celibacy. In His righteousness God gave them up to a reprobate mind inwardly, and outwardly He permitted them to fall into such great crimes because they had blasphemed the only Son of God, in whom the Father wants to be glorified and whom He gave into death in order that all who believe in the Son might be saved by Him, and not by their orders. "Those who honor Me," He says (1 Sam. 2:30), "I will honor." Now God is honored in the Son (John 5:23). Therefore whoever believes that the Son is our Mediator and Savior, honors the Father; and God honors Him in turn, that is, adorns him with His gifts of the forgiveness of sins, righteousness, the Holy Spirit, and eternal life. But, on the other hand, "those who despise Me shall be lightly esteemed" (1 Sam. 2:30).

Therefore this is a universal principle: "By works of the Law shall no one be justified." Enlarge on this by running through all the stations of life as follows: "Therefore a monk shall not be justified by his order, a nun by her chastity, a citizen by his uprightness, a prince by his generosity, etc." The Law of God is greater than the entire world, since it includes all men; and the works of the Law are far more excellent than the works chosen by self-righteous people. And yet Paul says that neither the Law nor the works of the Law justify. Therefore faith alone justifies. Once this proposition is established, he proceeds to confirm it with further arguments. The first argument is "from a denial of the conclusion": [61]

17. *But if, in our endeavor to be justified in Christ, we ourselves were found to be sinners, is Christ then an agent of sin? Certainly not!*

These are not Latin phrases; they are Hebrew and theological. "If it is true," he says, "that we are justified in Christ, then it is impossible for us to be sinners or to be justified through the Law.

---

[61] Cf. Aristotle, *Prior Analytics*, Book II, ch. 17.

On the other hand, if this is not true and we must be justified through the Law and its works, then it is impossible for us to be justified through Christ. One of these two has to be false: Either we are not justified in Christ, or we are not justified in the Law. But we are justified in Christ. Therefore we are not justified in the Law." Thus he is arguing in this way: "If, in our endeavor, etc." That is: "If we try to be justified through faith in Christ, and, being justified in this way, are still found to be sinners who need the Law to justify us because we are sinners; if, I say, we need the observance of the Law for justification, so that those who are righteous in Christ are not really righteous but need the Law to justify them; or if he who is justified through Christ still has to be justified through the Law — then Christ is nothing but a lawgiver and an agent of sin. Then he who is justified and holy in Christ is not justified or holy but is still in need of the righteousness and holiness of the Law.

"But we are surely justified and righteous in Christ, because the truth of the Gospel teaches that a man is not justified in the Law but is justified in Christ. But if those who are justified in Christ are still found to be sinners, that is, if they still belong to the Law and are under the Law, as the false apostles teach, then they are not yet justified. For the Law accuses them, shows that they are still sinners, and demands that they do the works of the Law to be justified. Therefore those who are justified in Christ are not justified; and so it necessarily follows that Christ is not a justifier, but an agent of sin."

Here he accuses the false apostles and all self-righteous people most gravely of perverting everything: They change Law into grace and grace into Law, Moses into Christ and Christ into Moses. For they teach that after Christ and all the righteousness of Christ the observance of the Law is necessary for one to be justified. By this intolerable perversity the Law becomes Christ; for they attribute to the Law what properly belongs to Christ. "If you do the works of the Law," they say, "you will be justified. But if you do not do them, you will not be justified, regardless of how much you believe in Christ." Now if it is true that Christ does not justify but is an agent of sin, as must necessarily follow from their teaching, then Christ is the Law; for since He teaches that we are sinners, we have nothing else from Him than what we have from the Law. Thus Christ, the teacher of sin, sends us to the Law and to Moses, the justifier!

Therefore it is inevitable that the papists, the Zwinglians, the Anabaptists, and all those who either do not know about the righteousness of Christ or who do not believe correctly about it should change Christ into Moses and the Law and change the Law into Christ. For this is what they teach: "Faith in Christ does indeed justify, but at the same time observance of the Commandments of God is necessary; for it is written (Matt. 19:17): 'If you would enter life, keep the Commandments.'" Here immediately Christ is denied and faith is abolished, because what belongs to Christ alone is attributed to the Commandments of God or to the Law. For Christ is, by definition, the Justifier and the Redeemer from sins. If I attribute this to the Law, then the Law is my justifier, which delivers me from my sins before I do its works. And so the Law has now become Christ; and Christ completely loses His name, His work, and His glory, and is nothing else than an agent of the Law, who accuses, terrifies, directs, and sends the sinner to someone else to be justified. This is really the work of the Law.

But the work of Christ, properly speaking, is this: to embrace the one whom the Law has made a sinner and pronounced guilty, and to absolve him from his sins if he believes the Gospel. "For Christ is the end of the Law, that everyone who has faith may be justified" (Rom. 10:4); He is "the Lamb of God, who takes away the sin of the world" (John 1:29). But the papists and the fanatics turn this upside down; and it is inevitable that they should, since they do not believe correctly about the doctrine of justification and teach the very opposite, namely, that Moses is Christ and Christ is Moses. This is their main proposition. Then they ridicule us for inculcating and emphasizing faith with such diligence: "Ha, ha! Faith, faith! Just wait until you get to heaven by faith! No, you must strive for something more sublime. You must fulfill the Law of God, according to the statement (Luke 10:28): 'Do this, and you will live.' You must suffer many things, shed your blood, forsake your house, wife, and children, and imitate the example of Christ. This faith of yours makes men smug, lazy, and sleepy." So they have become nothing but legalists and Mosaists, defecting from Christ to Moses and calling the people back from Baptism, faith, and the promises of Christ to the Law and works, changing grace into the Law and the Law into grace.

Who would ever believe that these things could be mixed up so easily? There is no one so stupid that he does not recognize how

[W, XL, 250—252]

definite this distinction between Law and grace is. Both the facts and the words require this distinction, for everyone understands that these words "Law" and "grace" are different as to both denotation and connotation.[62] Therefore it is a monstrosity, when this distinction stands there so clearly, for the papists and the fanatics to fall into the satanic perversity of confusing the Law and grace and of changing Christ into Moses. This is why I often say that so far as the words are concerned, this doctrine of faith is very easy, and everyone can easily understand the distinction between the Law and grace; but so far as practice, life, and application are concerned, it is the most difficult thing there is.

The pope and his scholastic theologians say clearly that the Law and grace are distinct things, but in his practice he teaches the very opposite. "Faith in Christ," he says, "whether it is acquired by man's natural powers, actions, and qualities or whether it is infused by God, is still dead if love does not follow." What has happened to the distinction between the Law and grace? He distinguishes them in name, but in practice he calls grace love. Thus the sectarians demand works in addition to faith. Therefore anyone who does not believe correctly about the doctrine of justification must necessarily confuse Law and grace.

Let everyone who is godly, therefore, learn to distinguish carefully between Law and grace, both in feeling and in practice, not only in words, as the pope and the fanatics do. So far as the words are concerned, they admit that the two are distinct things; but in fact, as I have said, they confuse them, because they do not concede that faith justifies without works. If this is true, then Christ is of no use to me. For though I may have as true a faith as possible, yet, according to their opinion, I am not justified if this faith of mine is without love; and however much of this love I may have, it is never enough. Thus the Christ whom faith grasps is not the Justifier; grace is useless; and faith cannot be true without love — or, as the Anabaptists say, without the cross, suffering, and bloodshed.[63] But if love, works, and the cross are present, then faith is true, and it justifies.

With this doctrine the fanatics obscure the blessings of Christ

[62] The Latin words which we have rendered as "denotation" and "connotation" are *res* and *nomen*.

[63] Cf. *Luther's Works*, 23, pp. 202—203.

today; they deprive Him of His honor as the Justifier and set Him up as an agent of sin. They have learned nothing from us except to recite the words; they do not accept the content. They want to give the impression that they, too, teach the Gospel and faith in Christ as purely as we do; but when it comes to the practice, they are teachers of the Law, just like the false apostles. Throughout all the churches the false apostles required, in addition to faith in Christ, that there be circumcision and the observance of the Law, without which they denied that faith could justify. "Unless you are circumcised according to the custom of Moses," they said, "you cannot be saved" (Acts 15:1). In the same way today the sectarians require, in addition to the righteousness of faith, the observance of the Commandments of God. They cite these passages: "Do this, and you will live" (Luke 10:28) and "If you would enter life, keep the Commandments" (Matt. 19:17).[64] Therefore there is no one among them, though he seem ever so wise, who understands the distinction between Law and grace; for they are convicted by their own practice and by the evidence of the facts.

But we do make a distinction here; and we say that we are not disputing now whether good works ought to be done. Nor are we inquiring whether the Law is good, holy, and righteous, or whether it ought to be observed; for that is another topic. But our argument and question concerns justification and whether the Law justifies. Our opponents do not listen to this. They do not answer this question, nor do they distinguish as we do. All they do is to scream that good works ought to be done and that the Law ought to be observed. All right, we know that. But because these are distinct topics, we will not permit them to be confused. In due time we shall discuss the teaching that the Law and good works ought to be done. But since we are now dealing with the subject of justification, we reject works, on which our opponents insist so tenaciously that they ascribe justification to them, which is to take Christ's glory away from Him and to assign it to works instead.

Therefore this is a powerful argument, which I have often used to console myself: "If in our endeavor, etc." It is as though Paul were saying: "If we who are justified in Christ are still regarded as not justified but as sinners who still need to be justified by the Law,

[64] Luther frequently links Luke 10:28 with Matt. 19:17; for example, in *Luther's Works,* 22, p. 425.

then we cannot look for justification in Christ; then we look for it in the Law. But if justification happens through the Law, then it does not happen through grace. This is proved by sufficient division.[65] Now if justification does not happen through grace but happens through the Law, what did Christ accomplish with His suffering, His preaching, His victory over sin and death, and the sending of the Holy Spirit? Either we are justified through Christ, or we are made sinful and guilty through Him. But if the Law justifies, then it follows inevitably that we become sinners through Christ; and so Christ is an agent of sin. So let us establish the proposition: Everyone who believes in the Lord Jesus Christ is a sinner and is worthy of eternal death; and if he does not have recourse to the Law and do its works, he will not be saved."

Holy Scripture, especially the New Testament, always inculcates faith in Christ and magnificently proclaims Him. It says that "whoever believes in Him is saved, does not perish, is not judged, is not put to shame, and has eternal life" (John 3:16). But they say, on the contrary: "Whoever believes in Him is damned, etc., because he has faith without works, which damns." This is how they pervert everything, making Christ the condemner and Moses the savior. Is it not an unspeakable blasphemy to teach this way: "By performing the Law and works you will become worthy of eternal life, but by believing in Christ you will become worthy of eternal death. When the Law is kept, it saves; and faith in Christ damns"?

Of course, our opponents do not use these very words; but this is actually what they teach. For they say that "infused faith," which they properly call faith in Christ, does not free from sin, but that only "faith formed by love" does so. From this it follows that faith in Christ by itself, without the Law and works, does not save. Surely this is to declare that Christ leaves us in our sins and in the wrath of God and makes us worthy of eternal death. On the other hand, if you perform the Law and works, then faith justifies, because it has works, without which faith is useless. Therefore works justify, not faith. That because of which something is what it is, is itself more so. For if faith justifies because of works, then works justify more than faith. How deep the abominable blasphemy of this doctrine is!

Therefore Paul is arguing from the impossible and from a suffi-

[65] See p. 138, note 56.

cient division.[66] If we who are justified in Christ are still sinners who must be justified otherwise than through Christ, namely, through the Law, then Christ cannot justify us but only accuses and condemns us. Then Christ died in vain, and these and similar passages are false: "Behold, the Lamb of God, etc." (John 1:29); "He who believes in the Son has eternal life" (John 3:36). Then all Scripture is false when it testifies that Christ is the Justifier and the Savior. For if we are still sinners after being justified in Christ, then it necessarily follows that those who do the Law without Christ are justified. If this is true, then we are Turks or Jews or Tartars, who keep the Word and name of Christ for the sake of external appearances, but who, in practice and in fact, completely deny Christ and His Word. But Paul wants faith to be ἀνυπόκριτον (1 Tim. 1:5). Therefore it is wrong and wicked to assert that infused faith does not justify unless it is adorned with works of love. But if our opponents feel obliged to defend this doctrine, then why do they not reject faith in Christ completely, especially since they make it nothing but an empty quality in the soul, which is worthless without love? Why do they not call a spade a spade?[67] In other words, why do they not say in clear words that works, not faith, justify? Why do they not publicly deny the entire Gospel and Paul — as they do in fact — who attribute righteousness to faith alone and not to works? For if faith justifies only with love, then Paul's argument is completely false; for he says clearly that a man is not justified by works of the Law, but alone by faith in Jesus Christ.

Is Christ then an agent of sin?

"Minister of sin"[68] is once more a Hebrew phrase, which Paul uses also in 2 Cor. 3:7 ff., where he discusses these two ministries so magnificently and clearly, namely, the ministry of the letter and of the spirit, of the Law and of grace, of death and of life. And he says that Moses, the minister of the Law, has the ministry of the Law, which he calls a ministry of sin, wrath, death, and damnation.

---

[66] See p. 141, note 61.

[67] The saying, *appellant Scapham scapham*, appears also in *Luther's Works*, 1, p. 5, note 10.

[68] Luther's Latin had *minister peccati*, which is reflected in the translation of the Authorized Version, "minister of sin"; but the translation "agent of sin" in the Revised Standard Version renders both the Greek New Testament and Luther's Latin more accurately.

For Paul usually employs terms of reproach for the Law of God. He is the only one of the apostles to use this phrase; the others do not speak this way. It is important for those who are students of Sacred Scripture to understand this phrase of Paul.

Now a "minister of sin" is nothing else but a lawgiver, a teacher of the Law, or a taskmaster, who teaches good works and love; he teaches that one should bear the cross and suffering, and that one should imitate Christ and the saints. Anyone who teaches and demands this is a minister of the Law as well as of sin, wrath, and death, because all he does by his doctrine is to terrify and trouble consciences and to shut them up under sin. For it is impossible for human nature to fulfill the Law. In fact, in those who are justified and who have the Holy Spirit the law in their members is at war with the law of their mind (Rom. 7:23). Then what would it not do in the wicked, who do not have the Holy Spirit? Therefore anyone who teaches that righteousness comes through the Law does not understand what he is saying or what he is propounding; much less does he observe the Law. Instead, he is fooling himself and others, imposing an unbearable burden upon them, prescribing and demanding something impossible, and ultimately bringing himself and his followers to the point of despair.

Therefore the proper use and aim of the Law is to make guilty those who are smug and at peace, so that they may see that they are in danger of sin, wrath, and death, so that they may be terrified and despairing, blanching and quaking at the rustling of a leaf (Lev. 26:36).[69] To the extent that they are such, they are under the Law. For the Law requires perfect obedience toward God, and it damns those who do not yield such obedience. Now it is certain that no one yields this obedience or even can; nevertheless, this is what God wants. Therefore the Law does not justify; it condemns. For it says (Gal. 3:10): "Cursed be everyone who does not abide, etc." Therefore one who teaches the Law is a "minister of sin."

In 2 Cor. 3:7, therefore, Paul correctly calls the ministry of the Law a "ministry of sin." For the Law does nothing but accuse consciences and manifest sin, which is dead without the Law. The knowledge of sin — I am not speaking about the speculative knowledge that hypocrites have; but I am speaking about true knowledge, in which the wrath of God against sin is perceived and a true taste

---

[69] On this idea see also *Luther's Works*, 3, p. 8, note 7.

of death is sensed – this knowledge terrifies hearts, drives them to despair, and kills them (Rom. 7:11). Scripture calls these teachers of the Law and works taskmasters and tyrants. The taskmasters in Egypt oppressed the Children of Israel with physical slavery. Thus with their doctrine of the Law and works these men drive souls into a miserable spiritual slavery, and eventually they push them into despair and destroy them. Nor is it possible for them to attain peace of conscience amid their genuine terrors and in the agony of death, although they have observed their monastic rule, loved others, performed many good works, and suffered evils; for the Law always terrifies and accuses, saying: "But you have not done enough!" Therefore these terrors still remain and become worse and worse. If these teachers of the Law are not raised up by faith and the righteousness of Christ, they are forced to despair.

There is an outstanding example of this in *The Lives of the Fathers*.[70] Shortly before he died, a certain hermit stood sad and motionless for three days, with his eyes fixed on heaven. When he was asked why he was doing this, he replied that he was afraid of death. Although his pupils tried to comfort him by saying that he had no reason to be afraid of death, since he had lived a very holy life, he responded: "I have indeed lived a holy life and observed the Commandments of God, but the judgments of God are quite different from those of men!" When this man saw that death was present, he was not able to be of a tranquil mind, even though he had lived blamelessly and had observed the Law of God; for it came to his mind that God judges much differently from men. Thus he lost confidence in all his good works and merits; and unless he was raised up by the promise of Christ, he despaired. So all the Law can do is to render us naked and guilty. Then there is no aid or counsel, but everything is lost. Here the lives and martyrdoms of all the saints cannot give us any help.

This was also beautifully foreshadowed in the story of the giving of the Law (Ex. 19—20). Moses led the people out of the camp to meet with the Lord and to hear Him speak from the darkness of the cloud. A little earlier the people had promised to do everything that the Lord commanded. Now they were afraid and trembled, and they ran back. Standing afar off, they said to Moses (Ex. 20:19): "Who can stand seeing the fire and hearing the thunder

[70] This story appears in the *Vitae patrum*, Book III, par. 161, *Patrologia, Series Latina*, LXXIII, 793.

and the blare of the trumpet? You speak to us, and we will hear; but let not God speak to us, lest we die." Thus the proper task of the Law is to lead us forth from our tabernacles, that is, from our peace and self-confidence, to set us into the sight of God, and to reveal the wrath of God to us. Then the conscience senses that it has not satisfied the Law; it cannot satisfy the Law or bear the wrath of God, which the Law reveals when it sets us into the sight of God this way, that is, when it terrifies us, accuses us, and shows us our sins. Here it is impossible for us to stand. Thoroughly frightened, we run away and exclaim with Israel: "We are going to die, we are going to die! Let not the Lord speak, but you speak to us."

Therefore anyone who teaches that faith in Christ does not justify unless the Law is observed makes Christ a minister of sin, that is, a teacher of the Law, who teaches the same thing that Moses did. Then Christ is not the Savior and Dispenser of grace; but He is a cruel tyrant, who, like Moses, demands the impossible, which no man can produce. Thus Erasmus and the papists suppose that Christ is only a new lawgiver; and the fanatics accept nothing of the Gospel, except that they imagine it to be a book containing new laws about works, as the Turks imagine about their Koran.[71] But there are plenty of laws in Moses. The Gospel, however, is a proclamation about Christ: that He forgives sins, grants grace, justifies, and saves sinners. Although there are commandments in the Gospel, they are not the Gospel; they are expositions of the Law and appendices to the Gospel.

Thus if the Law is a ministry of sin, it follows that it is also a ministry of wrath and death. For just as the Law reveals sin, so it strikes the wrath of God into a man and threatens him with death. Immediately his conscience draws the inference: "You have not observed the Commandments; therefore God is offended and is angry with you." This logic is irrefutable: "I have sinned; therefore I shall die." Thus the ministry of sin is necessarily the ministry of the wrath of God and death. For where there is sin, there the conscience soon declares: "You have sinned; therefore God is angry with you. If He is angry, He will kill you and damn you eternally." And this is why many who cannot endure the wrath and judgment of God commit suicide by hanging or drowning.

[71] Cf. p. 73, note 53.

Certainly Not!

It is as though Paul were saying: "Christ is not the minister of sin; He is the Dispenser of righteousness and of eternal life." Therefore Paul separates Christ from Moses just as far as he can. Let Moses remain on earth; let him be the teacher of the letter, the taskmaster of the Law; let him crucify sinners. But the believers, he says, have another teacher in their conscience, not Moses but Christ, who has abrogated the Law, overcome and endured sin, wrath, and death. He commands us to look to Him and believe. Then it is time for the Law to go away and for Moses to die in such a way that no one knows where he is buried (Deut. 34:6).[72] Neither sin nor death can harm us anymore. For Christ, our Teacher, is the Lord of the Law, sin, and death; therefore he who believes in Him is liberated from all these things. Therefore the proper task of Christ is to liberate from death and sin, as Paul teaches and inculcates continually.

Through the Law, therefore, we are condemned and killed; but through Christ we are justified and made alive. The Law terrifies us and drives us away from God. But Christ reconciles us to God and makes it possible for us to have access to Him. For Christ is the Lamb of God, who takes away the sin of the world (John 1:29). Thus the believer in Christ has the One who took away the sins of the world. If the sin of the world is taken away, then it is taken away also from me, as one who believes in Him. And if sin is taken away, then wrath is taken away; and if wrath is taken away, so are death and damnation. Righteousness replaces sin; reconciliation and grace replace wrath; life replaces death; and eternal salvation replaces damnation. Let us learn to practice this distinction, not only in words but in its application to our life and in our feelings. For where Christ is, there must be a good conscience and joy; Christ Himself is our Reconciliation, Righteousness, Peace, Life, and Salvation. Whatever the miserable and afflicted conscience seeks, that it finds in Christ. Now Paul develops this argument persuasively:

18. *But if I build up again those things which I tore down, then I prove myself a transgressor.*

It is as though Paul were to say: "I have not preached in such a way that I would now rebuild what has been destroyed. For if

---

[72] On the allegorical interpretation of the burial of Moses see *Luther's Works,* 9, pp. 310—311.

[W, XL, 262, 263]

I did this, I would not only labor in vain but would make myself a transgressor and overthrow everything, after the style of the false apostles. That is, I would change grace and Christ back into the Law and Moses, and, vice versa, change the Law and Moses into grace and Christ. By the Gospel I have destroyed sin, sadness, wrath, and death. For this is what I have been teaching: 'Your conscience, O man, is liable to the Law and to sin and death. But here comes the Gospel, which preaches the forgiveness of sins to you through Christ, who has abrogated the Law and has destroyed sin and death. Believe in Him, and you will be free of the curse of the Law. You will be righteous and will have eternal life.'

"Thus by the preaching of the Gospel I have destroyed the Law, lest it continue to rule in the conscience. For Moses, the old settler, has to yield and emigrate somewhere else when Christ, the new guest, comes into the new house to live there alone. And where He is, there the Law, sin, wrath, and death have no place. In their stead there is present now nothing but grace, righteousness, joy, life, and a filial confidence in the Father, who is now placated, gracious, and reconciled. Am I now to expel Christ and destroy His kingdom, which I planted through the Gospel, and set up the Law once more? What would happen if, after the fashion of the false apostles, I were to teach that circumcision and the observance of the Law are necessary for salvation? In this way I would restore sin and death in place of righteousness and life. For all that the Law does is to manifest sin, cause wrath, and kill."

What, I ask you, are the papists, even at their best, but destroyers of the kingdom of Christ and builders of the devil's kingdom, of sin, of the wrath of God, and of eternal death? They destroy the church, which is the building of God, not through the Law of Moses, as the false apostles did, but through human traditions and the doctrines of demons (1 Tim. 4:1). Thus the fanatical spirits of our own time and those who will follow us are destroying and will destroy what we have built up, and they are building up and will build up what we have destroyed.

But we who, by the grace of God, accept the doctrine of justification know for certain that we are justified solely by faith in Christ. Therefore we do not confuse the Law and grace, or faith and works; but we separate them as far as possible. Let everyone who is concerned for godliness observe this distinction of Law and grace diligently. Let him permit it to prevail, not in letters and syllables but in practical application. Then when he hears that good works should be performed or that Christ should be imitated, he will be able to judge correctly and say: "Fine. I shall gladly do this. What else is there?" "Then you will be saved!" "No! I grant that everything good should be done, that evil should be endured, and that one's blood should be shed, if necessary, for the sake of Christ. But I am not justified or saved through any of this."

Therefore exercises of devotion and afflictions of the body are not to be dragged into the question of justification. This is what the monks did. When they were supposed to comfort someone about to be executed for his crimes, they said: "You must suffer this ignominious death willingly. And if you do, you will merit the forgiveness of your sins and eternal life." What a horrible thing this is, that a wretched thief, murderer, or robber in his supreme anguish is seduced this way! In the very moment of death, when he is about to be hanged or beheaded, he is robbed of the Gospel about Christ, who is the only One able to bring him comfort and salvation then; and he is told to hope for pardon and the forgiveness of sins if he willingly endures that ignominious death which is being inflicted on him for his crimes. This is adding extreme perdition to someone who is already most afflicted, and showing him the way to hell through a false notion about and confidence in his own death.

Thus these hypocrites showed clearly that they neither taught nor understood a single letter about grace, the Gospel, or Christ. They kept the name of the Gospel and of Christ only for the sake of external appearances, so that they might more easily make an impression on simple people. In fact, by denying Christ and treading Him underfoot they ascribed more to human traditions than to the Gospel of Christ. Evidence for this can be found in the many forms of worship, the many kinds of orders, the many ceremonies, and the many works, all instituted with the idea that they would merit grace, etc. In their confession they made no mention of faith or of the merit of Christ. All they inculcated was human satisfactions and merits, as one can judge from this form of absolution (not to speak of anything else), which the monks — in fact, the more religious ones among them — used among themselves. It is useful to write it down so that posterity may understand how infinite and unspeakable the abomination of the papal kingdom was.

A Form of Monastic Absolution

"MAY GOD SPARE YOU, BROTHER"

"May the merit of the suffering of our Lord Jesus Christ, of Blessed and Ever Virgin Mary, and of all the saints; the merit of your order; the burden of your order; the humility of your confession; the contrition of your heart; the good works that you have done and will do for the love of our Lord Jesus Christ — may all this be granted to you for the forgiveness of your sins, for the growth of merit and grace, and for the reward of eternal life. Amen." [73]

You hear "the merit of Christ" here. But if you weigh these words more carefully, you will understand that Christ is completely idle here, and that the glory and the name of Justifier and Savior are taken away from Him and attributed to monastic works. Is this not taking the name of God in vain? Is this not confessing Christ in words but denying His power and blaspheming Him? I myself was once stuck in this mire too. Although I confessed with my mouth that Christ had suffered and died for the redemption of the human race, I thought that He was a judge,[74] who had to be placated by the observance of my monastic rule. Therefore whenever I prayed or celebrated Mass, I always used to add this at the end: "Lord Jesus, I come to Thee and pray that the burdens of my order may be a recompense for my sins." But now I thank the Father of mercies, who has called me out of the darkness into the light of the Gospel and has endowed me with an abundant knowledge of Christ Jesus my Lord. For His sake, as Paul says (Phil. 3:8-9), "I count everything as loss, yes, count it as σκύβαλα, that I may gain Christ and be found in Him, not having a righteousness of my own, based on the rule of Augustine, but that which is through faith in Christ," to whom, with the Father and the Holy Spirit, be praise and glory forever and ever. Amen.

Therefore we conclude with Paul that we are justified solely by faith in Christ, without the Law and works. But after a man is justi-

[73] The full text in Latin reads: *Parcat tibi Deus, frater. Meritum passionis Domini nostri Iesu Christi et Beatae Mariae semper virginis et omnium Sanctorum, Meritum ordinis, gravamen religionis, humilitas confessionis, contritio cordis, Bona opera quae fecisti et facies pro amore domini nostri Iesu Christi, cedant tibi in remissionem peccatorum tuorum, in augmentum meriti et gratiae et in praemium vitae aeternae, Amen.*

[74] Cf. *Luther's Works*, 13, pp. 86—87.

fied by faith, now possesses Christ by faith, and knows that He is his righteousness and life, he will certainly not be idle but, like a sound tree, will bear good fruit (Matt. 7:17). For the believer has the Holy Spirit; and where He is, He does not permit a man to be idle but drives him to all the exercises of devotion, to the love of God, to patience in affliction, to prayer, to thanksgiving, and to the practice of love toward all men.

Therefore we, too, say that faith without works is worthless and useless. The papists and the fanatics take this to mean that faith without works does not justify, or that if faith does not have works, it is of no avail, no matter how true it is. That is false. But faith without works — that is, a fantastic idea and mere vanity and a dream of the heart — is a false faith and does not justify.

Thus far we have discussed the first argument, in which Paul maintains: "Either we cannot be justified by the Law, or Christ is necessarily an agent of sin." But this latter is impossible. Therefore it must not be conceded on any score that we are justified by the Law. We have discussed this topic carefully and at length, as it deserves, although it cannot be inculcated and believed too much.

19. *For I through the Law died to the Law, that I might live to God.*

This is amazing language and unheard-of speech which human reason simply cannot understand. It is spoken briefly but very emphatically. Paul seems to be speaking from a fervent and ardent spirit, with great zeal, as though he were indignant. It is as though he were saying: "Why do you boast so much about the Law, about which I do not want to know anything? Why do you din this into me so often? But if there must be a Law, I have a Law of my own." As though he were speaking by the indignation of the Holy Spirit, he calls grace itself "Law." He stamps the content of grace with a new name, as an expression of contempt for the Law of Moses and for the false apostles, who claimed that it was necessary for justification. Thus he opposes the Law to the Law. This is most delicious language. In Scripture, especially in Paul, Law is often opposed to Law, sin to sin, death to death, captivity to captivity, the devil to the devil, hell to hell, altar to altar, lamb to lamb, Passover to Passover.

Rom. 8:3: "For sin He condemned sin"; Ps. 68:18 and Eph. 4:8: "He led captivity captive"; Hos. 14:14: "O death, I will be your death. O hell, I will be your destruction." Thus he says here that through the Law he has died to the Law. It is as though he were say-

[W, XL, 267, 268]

ing: "The Law of Moses accuses and damns me. But against that accusing and damning Law I have another Law, which is grace and freedom. This Law accuses the accusing Law and damns the damning Law." Thus death killed death, but this death which kills death is life itself. But it is called the death of death, by an exuberant indignation of the spirit against death. So also righteousness takes the name "sin," because it damns sin; and this damning sin is true righteousness.

Here Paul is the most heretical of heretics; and his heresy is unheard-of, because he says that, having died to the Law, he lives to God. The false apostles taught: "Unless you live to the Law, you do not live to God. That is, unless you live according to the Law, you are dead in the sight of God." But Paul teaches the opposite: "Unless you are dead to the Law, you do not live to God." The doctrine of the fanatics today is the same as that of the false apostles at that time. "If you want to live to God," they say, "that is, to be alive in the sight of God, then live to the Law, or according to the Law." But we say in opposition: "If you want to live to God, you must completely die to the Law." Human reason and wisdom do not understand this doctrine. Therefore they always teach the opposite: "If you want to live to God, you must observe the Law; for it is written (Matt. 19:17): 'If you would enter life, keep the Commandments.'" This is a principle and maxim of all the theologians: "He who lives according to the Law lives to God." Paul says the exact opposite, namely, that we cannot live to God unless we have died to the Law. Therefore we must climb up to this heavenly altitude, in order that we may establish for certain that we are far above the Law, in fact, that we are completely dead to the Law. Now if we are dead to the Law, then the Law has no jurisdiction over us, just as it has no jurisdiction over Christ, who has liberated us from the Law in order that in this way we may live to God. This supports the declaration that the Law does not justify, but that only faith in Christ justifies.

Paul is not speaking about the Ceremonial Law here. He sacrificed in the temple, circumcised Timothy, and cut his hair at Cenchreae.[75] He would not have done these things if he had died to the Ceremonial Law. But he is speaking about the entire Law. For the Christian, therefore, the entire Law has been completely abrogated — whether it be the Ceremonial Law or the Decalog — because he has

---

[75] See the passages cited on p. 61, note 39.

died to it. This does not mean that the Law is destroyed; for it remains, lives, and rules in the wicked. But the godly man is dead to the Law as he is dead to sin, the devil, death, and hell, all of which still remain, and all of which the world and the wicked will inherit. Therefore when the sophist takes Paul to mean that only the Ceremonial Law is abrograted, you understand that for Paul and for every Christian the entire Law is abrogated, and yet that the Law still remains.

For example, when Christ arises from the dead, He is free from the grave; and yet the grave remains. Peter is liberated from prison, the paralytic from his bed, the young man from his coffin, the girl from her couch; nevertheless, the prison, the bed, the coffin, and the couch remain. So also the Law is abrogated when I am freed from it, and the Law dies when I have died to it; and yet the Law still remains. But because I die to it, it also dies to me. Thus Christ's grave, Peter's prison, the girl's couch — all remain. But by His resurrection Christ dies to the grave; by his deliverance Peter is freed from the prison; by her restoration to life the girl is delivered from the couch.

Therefore the words "I have died to the Law" are very emphatic. He does not say: "I am free of, or liberated from, the Law for a while" or "I am the lord of the Law." All he says is: "I have died to the Law," that is, "I have no business with the Law." No one could have said anything more forceful against justification by the Law than what Paul says: "I have died to the Law," that is, "I do not care anything about the Law at all; therefore I am not justified by it."

To die to the Law means not to be bound by the Law but to be free from the Law and not to know the Law. Therefore let anyone who wants to be alive in the sight of God strive to be found outside the Law, and let him come out of the grave with Christ. The soldiers were astounded when Christ had arisen from the grave. Similarly, those who saw the girl raised from the dead were astounded. Thus human reason and wisdom are astounded and dazed when they hear that we are not justified unless we are dead to the Law, for reason cannot grasp this.

But let us teach that when by faith we consciously [76] take hold of Christ Himself, we enter into a kind of new Law which devours the other Law that held us captive. Just as the grave in which Christ

---

[76] As on p. 10, we have translated *secundum conscientiam* as "consciously."

lay dead opened and was seen to be empty after He had risen, and Christ disappeared, so when I believe in Christ, I rise with Him and die to my grave, that is, to the Law that held me captive. Hence the Law is now empty; and I have escaped from my prison and grave, that is, from the Law. Therefore the Law has no further right to accuse me or to hold me, for I have risen again.

Consciences should be carefully taught to understand the doctrine of the distinction between the righteousness of the Law and that of grace. The righteousness of grace simply does not pertain to the flesh. For the flesh must not be free but must stay in the grave, in the prison, and on the couch. It must be subjected to the Law and be disciplined by the Egyptians. But the Christian conscience must be dead to the Law, that is, free from the Law, and must have no business with it. This important and basic doctrine does much to comfort afflicted consciences. Therefore when you see a man terrified and saddened by a consciousness [77] of sin, say: "Brother, you are not distinguishing properly. Into your conscience you are putting the Law, which belongs in the flesh. Wake up, get up, and remember that you believe in Christ, the Victor over the Law and sin. With this faith you will transcend the Law and enter into grace, where there is neither Law nor sin. And although the Law and sins still exist, they have nothing to do with you; for you are dead to the Law and to sins."

This is easy enough to say. But blessed is the man who knows this properly amid a conflict of conscience, who, when sin attacks him and the Law accuses and terrifies him, can say: "Law, what is it to me if you make me guilty and convict me of having committed many sins? In fact, I am still committing many sins every day. This does not affect me; I am deaf and do not hear you. Therefore you are telling your story to a deaf man,[78] for I am deaf to you. But if you really want to argue with me about sins, then go over to my flesh and my limbs, which are my servants. Teach them; discipline and crucify them. But do not trouble my conscience, which is lord and king; for I have nothing to do with you. For I am dead to you; I now live to Christ, where I am under another Law, namely, the Law of grace, which rules over sin and the Law." By what means? Through faith in Christ, as Paul will explain below.

[77] See p. 157, note 76.

[78] Horace, *Epistles*, Book II, I, lines 199—200; cf. *Luther's Works*, 2, p. 22, note 34.

But this is a strange and unheard-of definition, that to live to the Law is to die to God and that to die to the Law is to live to God. These two propositions are utterly contrary to reason; therefore no sophist or legalist understands them. But you must learn to understand them correctly. Anyone who strives to live to the Law, that is, wants to act in such a way that he is justified through the Law, is a sinner and remains a sinner; therefore he is dead and damned. For the law cannot justify and save him; but because it rightly accuses him, it kills him. To live to the Law, therefore, is to die to God; on the other hand, to die to the Law is to live to God. And to live to God is to be justified through grace or through faith for the sake of Christ, without the Law and works. Therefore if you want to live to God, you must die to the Law. But if you live to the Law, then you are dead to God.

If a Christian is defined properly and accurately, therefore, he is a child of grace and of the forgiveness of sins. He has no Law at all, but he is above the Law, sin, death, and hell. Just as Christ is free of the grave and as Peter is free of the prison, so the Christian is free of the Law. The relation between Christ raised from the grave and the grave, or the relation between Peter delivered from prison and the prison — such is the relation between the justified conscience and the Law. And just as Christ by His death and resurrection dies to the grave, so that it has no jurisdiction over Him and cannot hold Him, and He rises and goes away freely, now that the stone and the seals have been broken, and the guards have been terrified; and just as Peter dies to his prison through his deliverance and goes where he pleases — so by grace the conscience is liberated from the Law. "So it is with everyone who is born of the Spirit" (John 3:8). But the flesh does not know whence this comes or whither it goes, for it cannot judge except according to the Law. But the spirit says: "Let the Law accuse me; let sin and death terrify me. I do not despair on their account; for I have a law against the Law, sin against sin, and death against death."

Whenever I feel remorse in my conscience on account of sin, therefore, I look at the bronze serpent, Christ on the cross (John 3:14-15). Against my sin, which accuses and devours me, I find there another sin. But this other sin, namely, that which is in the flesh of Christ, takes away the sin of the world. It is omnipotent, and it damns and devours my sin. Lest my sin accuse and damn me, it is itself damned by sin, that is, by Christ the crucified, "who for our sake was made to be sin, so that in Him we might become the righteousness of God" (2 Cor. 5:21). Thus in my flesh I find a death that afflicts and kills me; but I also have a contrary death, which is the death of my death and which crucifies and devours my death.

All these things happen, not through the Law or works but through Christ the crucified, on whose shoulders lie all the evils of the human race — the Law, sin, death, the devil, and hell — all of which die in Him, because by His death He kills them. But we must accept this blessing of Christ with a firm faith. For just as what is offered to us is neither the Law nor any of its works but Christ alone, so what is required of us is nothing but faith, which takes hold of Christ and believes that my sin and death are damned and abolished in the sin and death of Christ.

Thus we always have the surest kinds of argument from which to draw the necessary conclusion that faith alone justifies. How could the Law and works contribute to justification, since Paul contends against the Law and works and says expressly that we must be dead to the Law if we want to live to God? But if we are dead to the Law and it is dead to us, then it surely has no business with us. Then how could it contribute to justification? Therefore it is necessary to say that we are pronounced righteous solely by grace or by faith in Christ, without the Law and works.

The blind sophists do not understand this. Therefore they dream that faith does not justify unless it does the works of love. In this way the faith that believes in Christ becomes idle and useless, for it is deprived of the power to justify unless it has been "formed by love." [79] But you set the Law and love aside until another place and time; and you direct your attention to the point at issue here, namely, that Jesus Christ, the Son of God, dies on the cross and bears my sin, the Law, death, the devil, and hell in His body. These enemies and unconquerable tyrants press in upon me and now create trouble for me; therefore I am anxious to be delivered from them, justified, and saved. Here I find neither Law nor work nor any love that can deliver me from them. Only Christ takes away the Law, kills my sin, destroys my death in His body, and in this way empties hell, judges the devil, crucifies him, and throws him down into hell. In other words, everything that once used to torment and oppress me Christ has set aside; He has disarmed it and made a public example of it,

[79] See p. 88, note 7.

triumphing over it in Himself (Col. 2:14-15), so that it cannot dominate any longer but is compelled to serve me.

From this it can be sufficiently understood that there is nothing to be done here but to hear that this has been done in this way, and to take hold of it with an undoubted faith. This really is a "formed faith." Afterwards, when Christ has thus been grasped by faith and I am dead to the Law, justified from sin, and delivered from death, the devil, and hell through Christ – then I do good works, love God, give thanks, and practice love toward my neighbor. But this love or the works that follow faith do not form or adorn my faith, but my faith forms and adorns love.

This is our theology; and when it is said that I am not only blind and deaf to the Law and free from it but completely dead to it, these are paradoxes strange to reason and absurd. And this statement of Paul's, "I through the Law died to the Law," is full of comfort. If it could come to a person's mind at the opportune time and cling firmly to his mind with genuine understanding, he would stand bravely against all the dangers of death and the terrors of conscience and of sin, no matter how much they attacked him, accused him, and wanted to drive him to despair. Of course, everyone is tempted, if not during his life, then at his death. Then, when the Law accuses and manifests his sin, his conscience immediately says: "You have sinned." If now you hold to what Paul, the apostle of Christ, teaches here, you will reply: "It is true. I have sinned." "Then God will punish and damn you." "No." "But that is what the Law of God says." "I have nothing to do with this Law." "Why is that?" "Because I have another Law, one that strikes this Law dumb. I am referring to liberty." "What liberty?" "That of Christ, for through Christ I am liberated from the Law." Therefore the Law which is and remains a Law for the wicked is liberty for me, and it binds the Law that damns me. Thus the Law that once bound me and held me captive is now bound and held captive by grace or liberty, which is now my Law. The accusing Law now hears this Law say: "You shall not bind this man, hold him captive, or make him guilty. But I will hold you captive and tie your hands, lest you hurt him who now lives to Christ and is dead to you."

This knocks out the teeth of the Law, blunts its sting and all its weapons, and utterly disables it. Yet it remains a Law for the wicked and unbelieving; it remains also for us who are weak, to the extent that we do not believe. Here it still has its sharpness and its teeth. But if I believe in Christ, regardless of how sin may trouble me to the point of despair, I shall rely on the liberty I have in Christ and say: "I admit that I have sinned. But my sin (which is a sin that is damned) is in Christ (who is a sin that damns). This sin that damns is stronger than the sin that is damned; for it is justifying grace, righteousness, life, and salvation." And so when I feel the terrors of death, I say: "Death, you have nothing on me. For I have another death, one that kills you, my death. And the death that kills is stronger than the death that is killed."

Thus the believer can raise himself up through faith alone and gain a comfort that is sure and firm; and he need not grow pale at the sight of sin, death, the devil, or any evil. The more the devil attacks him with all his force and tries to overwhelm him with all the terrors of the world, the more hope he acquires in the very midst of all these terrors and says: "Mr. Devil,[80] do not rage so. Just take it easy! For there is One who is called Christ. In Him I believe. He has abrogated the Law, damned sin, abolished death, and destroyed hell. And He is your devil, you devil, because He has captured and conquered you, so that you cannot harm me any longer or anyone else who believes in Him." The devil cannot overcome this faith, but he is overcome by it. For "this," says John (1 John 5:4-5), "is the victory that overcomes the world, our faith. Who is it that overcomes the world but he who believes that Jesus is the Son of God?"

With exceeding zeal and indignation of spirit, therefore, Paul calls grace itself "Law," even though in reality it is nothing else than the very great and boundless liberty of the grace that we have in Christ Jesus. Then he also assigns this most shameful name to the Law for our comfort, to let us know that it has now been baptized with a new name, because it is no longer alive but is dead and damned. It is a very pleasing sight as he sets forth and produces the Law as a thief or a robber who has already been condemned and sentenced to death. For by personification [81] he represents the Law as being held captive, with its hands and its feet bound and shorn of all power, so that it cannot exert its tyranny, that is, accuse and condemn. With this most pleasing picture he makes it contemptible to the conscience, so that the believer in Christ now has the courage to insult the Law with

[80] Cf. *Luther's Works*, 13, pp. 262—263.

[81] The original has the Greek word προσωποποιία; cf. also *Luther's Works*, 24, p. 193, note 1.

a certain holy pride and to say: "I am a sinner. If you can do anything against me, Law, go ahead and do it!" That is how far the Law now is from frightening the believer.

Now that Christ has risen from death, why should He be afraid of the grave? Now that Peter has been liberated from prison, why should he still be afraid of it? When the girl was about to die, the couch could frighten her. But now that she has been raised, why should she be afraid of it? Thus why should the Christian, who truly possesses Christ by faith, be afraid of the Law? To be sure, he feels the terrors of the Law; but he is not conquered by them. Relying on the liberty that he has in Christ, he says: "Law, I hear you muttering that you want to accuse and condemn me. But this does not move me at all. To me you are as the empty tomb was to Christ. For I see that you are captive and bound, hand and foot; and this is what my Law has done to you." "What Law is that?" "Liberty, which is called Law, not because it binds me, but because it binds my Law." The Law of the Decalog used to bind me; but against it I now have another Law, that of grace. This is not a Law to me. Nor does it bind me; it liberates me. It is a Law in opposition to the Law that damns. It binds this Law in such a way that it can no longer bind me. Thus against my death, which binds me, I have another death, that is, life, which makes me alive in Christ. It releases and frees me from the bonds of my death, and it ties up my death with the same bonds. Thus death, which bound me, is now bound itself; death, which killed me, is now killed itself through death, that is, through life itself.

Thus with the sweetest names Christ is called my Law, my sin, and my death, in opposition to the Law, sin, and death, even though in fact He is nothing but sheer liberty, righteousness, life, and eternal salvation. Therefore He became Law to the Law, sin to sin, and death to death, in order that He might redeem me from the curse of the Law, justify me, and make me alive. And so Christ is both: While He is the Law, He is liberty; while He is sin, He is righteousness; and while He is death, He is life. For by the very fact that He permitted the Law to accuse Him, sin to damn Him, and death to devour Him He abrogated the Law, damned sin, destroyed death, and justified and saved me. Thus Christ is a poison against the Law, sin, and death, and simultaneously a remedy to regain liberty, righteousness, and eternal life.

This particulary Pauline way of thinking and speaking is very pleasing and comforting. Similarly in Romans (7:23) he opposes the Law of the Spirit to the law in his members. Because this way of speaking is so new and strange, it enters more easily into the heart and remains more firmly in the memory. Besides, it sounds sweeter when he says: "I through the Law died to the Law" than if he were to say: "I through liberty died to the Law." For he is drawing a picture, as though Law were battling against Law. It is as though he were saying: "Law, if you are able to bite me, bind me, and plague me, I will put another Law above you, that is, another tyrant and tormentor, who will accuse you, bind you, and oppress you in turn. You are indeed my tormentor. But I have another tormentor, namely, Christ. He will torment you all the way. When you have been tormented all the way by Him, then I am free." Likewise, if the devil whips me, I have a stronger devil, who will whip him in turn. And when the more powerful devil battles and conquers the powerful one, I am set free. Thus grace is a Law — not to me, because it does not bind me, but to my Law; this it binds in such a way that it cannot bind me any longer.

Therefore Paul would like to draw us away completely from looking at the Law, sin, death, and other evil things, and to transfer us to Christ, in order that there we might see this very joyous duel:[82] the Law battling against the Law, in order to become liberty to me; sin battling against sin, in order to become righteousness to me; death battling against death, in order that I might have life. For Christ is my devil against the devil, that I might be a son of God; He destroys hell, that I might have the kingdom of heaven.

That I might live to God.

That is, "that I might be alive in the sight of God." You see, then, that there is no life unless you are without the Law, indeed, unless you are completely dead to the Law, namely, in your conscience. Meanwhile, as long as the body is alive, the flesh must be disciplined by laws and vexed by the requirements and punishments of laws, as I have often admonished. But the inner man, who owes nothing to the Law but is free of it, is a living, righteous, and holy person — not of himself or in his own substance but in Christ, because he believes in Him, as now follows:

[82] For other discussions of the idea of Christ's conflict with the devil as a *iucundissimum duellum* cf. *Luther's Works,* 22, pp. 355—356.

20. *I have been crucified with Christ.*

Paul adds this because he wants to declare that the Law is the devourer of the Law. "Not only am I dead to the Law through the Law so that I might live to God," he says, "but I am also crucified with Christ. But Christ is the Lord of the Law, because He has been crucified and has died to the Law. Therefore I, too, am lord of the Law. For I, too, have been crucified and have died to the Law, since I have been crucified and have died with Christ." How? Through grace and faith. When by this faith I am crucified and die to the Law, then the Law loses all its jurisdiction over me, as it lost it over Christ. Thus, just as Christ Himself was crucified to the Law, sin, death, and the devil, so that they have no further jurisdiction over Him, so through faith I, having been crucified with Christ in spirit, am crucified and die to the Law, sin, etc., so that they have no further jurisdiction over me but are now crucified and dead to me.

But here Paul is not speaking about being crucified with Christ by imitation or example — for imitating the example of Christ is also being crucified with Him — which is a crucifixion that pertains to the flesh. 1 Peter 2:21 deals with this: "Christ suffered for you, leaving you an example, that you should follow in His steps." But he is speaking here about that sublime crucifixion by which sin, the devil, and death are crucified in Christ, not in me. Here Christ does everything alone. But I, as a believer, am crucified with Christ through faith, so that all these things are dead and crucified to me as well.

Nevertheless, I live.

Paul is speaking clearly and precisely. He says: "I am not speaking about my death and crucifixion as though I were not alive now. I am alive indeed, for I am made alive by the very death and crucifixion by which I die. That is, since I am liberated from the Law, sin, and death by grace and by faith, I am truly alive. Therefore the crucifixion and death by which I am crucified and die to the Law, sin, death, and all evils is resurrection and life to me. For Christ crucifies the devil, kills death, damns sin, and binds the Law. As one who believes this, I am liberated from the Law, etc. Therefore the Law is deaf, bound, dead, and crucified to me; and I, in turn, am deaf, bound, dead, and crucified to it. Thus I live by this very death and crucifixion, that is, by this grace or liberty." Here, as I have warned before, Paul's phraseology must be observed. He says that we die and are crucified to the Law, even though it is rather the Law itself that dies and is crucified to us. But he deliberately uses this phraseology and says that we are crucified and dead to the Law; he does so to make his language more pleasant. For although the Law still remains, lives, and rules in the whole world and accuses and condemns all men, it is crucified and dies only to believers in Christ. Therefore only they have the glory of being crucified and dead to the Law, sin, etc.

Yet not I.

That is, "not in my own person or substance." Here Paul clearly shows how he is alive; and he states what Christian righteousness is, namely, that righteousness by which Christ lives in us, not the righteousness that is in our own person. Therefore when it is necessary to discuss Christian righteousness, the person must be completely rejected. For if I pay attention to the person or speak of the person, then, whether intentionally or unintentionally on my part, the person becomes a doer of works who is subject to the Law. But here Christ and my conscience must become one body, so that nothing remains in my sight but Christ, crucified and risen. But if Christ is put aside and I look only at myself, then I am done for. For then this thought immediately comes to my mind: "Christ is in heaven, and you are on earth. How are you now going to reach Him?" "I will live a holy life and do what the Law requires; and in this way I shall enter life." By paying attention to myself and considering what my condition is or should be, and what I am supposed to be doing, I lose sight of Christ, who alone is my Righteousness and Life. Once He is lost, there is no aid or counsel; but certain despair and perdition must follow.

This is an extremely common evil; for such is human misery that in temptation or death we immediately put Christ aside and pay attention to our own life and our own deeds. Unless we are raised up here by faith, we must perish. In such conflicts of conscience, therefore, we must form the habit of leaving ourselves behind as well as the Law and all our works, which force us to pay attention to ourselves. We must turn our eyes completely to that bronze serpent, Christ nailed to the cross (John 3:14). With our gaze fastened firmly to Him we must declare with assurance that He is our Righteousness and Life and care nothing about the threats and terrors of the Law, sin, death, wrath, and the judgment of God. For the Christ on whom

our gaze is fixed, in whom we exist, and who also lives in us, is the
Victor and the Lord over the Law, sin, death, and every evil. In Him
a sure comfort has been set forth for us, and victory has been granted.

Nevertheless, I live; yet not I, but Christ lives in me.

When he says: "Nevertheless, I live," this sounds rather personal,
as though Paul were speaking of his own person. Therefore he quickly
corrects it and says: "Yet not I." That is, "I do not live in my own
person now, but Christ lives in me." The person does indeed live,
but not in itself or for its own person. But who is this "I" of whom
he says: "Yet not I"? It is the one that has the Law and is obliged
to do works, the one that is a person separate from Christ. This
"I" Paul rejects; for "I," as a person distinct from Christ, belongs to
death and hell. This is why he says: "Not I, but Christ lives in me."
Christ is my "form," [83] which adorns my faith as color or light adorns
a wall. (This fact has to be expounded in this crude way, for there
is no spiritual way for us to grasp the idea that Christ clings and
dwells in us as closely and intimately as light or whiteness clings to
a wall.) "Christ," he says, "is fixed and cemented to me and abides
in me. The life that I now live, He lives in me. Indeed, Christ Himself is the life that I now live. In this way, therefore, Christ and
I are one."

Living in me as He does, Christ abolishes the Law, damns sin,
and kills death; for at His presence all these cannot help disappear-
ing. Christ is eternal Peace, Comfort, Righteousness, and Life, to
which the terror of the Law, sadness of mind, sin, hell, and death
have to yield. Abiding and living in me, Christ removes and absorbs
all the evils that torment and afflict me. This attachment to Him
causes me to be liberated from the terror of the Law and of sin, pulled
out of my own skin, and transferred into Christ and into His kingdom,
which is a kingdom of grace, righteousness, peace, joy, life, salvation,
and eternal glory. Since I am in Him, no evil can harm me.

Meanwhile my old man (Eph. 4:22) remains outside and is subject to the Law. But so far as justification is concerned, Christ and
I must be so closely attached that He lives in me and I in Him. What
a marvelous way of speaking! Because He lives in me, whatever grace,
righteousness, life, peace, and salvation there is in me is all Christ's;
nevertheless, it is mine as well, by the cementing and attachment that

---

[83] That is, Christ, not charity, is the *forma* of faith; cf. p. 88, note 7.

are through faith, by which we become as one body in the Spirit. Since Christ lives in me, grace, righteousness, life, and eternal salvation must be present with Him; and the Law, sin, and death must be absent. Indeed, the Law must be crucified, devoured, and abolished by the Law — and sin by sin, death by death, the devil by the devil. In this way Paul seeks to withdraw us completely from ourselves, from the Law, and from works, and to transplant us into Christ and faith in Christ, so that in the area of justification we look only at grace, and separate it far from the Law and from works, which belong far away.

Paul has a peculiar phraseology — not human, but divine and heavenly. The evangelists and the other apostles do not use it, except for John, who speaks this way from time to time. If Paul had not used this way of speaking first and prescribed it for us in explicit terms, no one even among the saints would have dared [84] use it. It is unprecedented and insolent to say: "I live, I do not live; I am dead, I am not dead; I am a sinner, I am not a sinner; I have the Law, I do not have the Law." But this phraseology is true in Christ and through Christ. When it comes to justification, therefore, if you divide Christ's Person from your own, you are in the Law; you remain in it and live in yourself, which means that you are dead in the sight of God and damned by the Law. For you have a faith that is, as the sophists imagine, "formed by love." I am speaking this way for the sake of illustration. For there is no one who has such a faith; therefore what the sophists have taught about "faith formed by love" is merely a trick of Satan. But let us concede that a man could be found who had such a faith. Even if he had it, he would actually be dead, because he would have only a historical faith about Christ, something that even the devil and all the wicked have (James 2:19).

But faith must be taught correctly, namely, that by it you are so cemented to Christ that He and you are as one person, which cannot be separated but remains attached to Him forever and declares: "I am as Christ." And Christ, in turn, says: "I am as that sinner who is attached to Me, and I to him. For by faith we are joined together into one flesh and one bone." Thus Eph. 5:30 says: "We are members of the body of Christ, of His flesh and of His bones," in such a way that this faith couples Christ and me more intimately than a husband is coupled to his wife. Therefore this faith is no idle quality; but it is

---

[84] The Weimar text has *fuisses* here, but we have read *fuisset*.

a thing of such magnitude that it obscures and completely removes those foolish dreams of the sophists' doctrine — the fiction of a "formed faith" and of love, of merits, our worthiness, our quality, etc. I would like to treat this at greater length if I could.

Thus far we have shown that Paul's first argument is this: Either Christ must be an agent of sin, or the Law does not justify. When this argument was concluded, he proposed himself as an example to develop a personification:[85] He said that he was dead to the old Law, on the basis of some sort of new Law. Now he attaches two replies to objections, or anticipations of his opponents' objections.[86] The first deals with slanders by proud men and with offense to weak men. When the free forgiveness of sins is preached, those who are malicious soon slander this preaching, as in Rom. 3:8: "Why not do evil that good may come?" For as soon as such men hear that we are not justified by the Law, they immediately infer slanderously: "Then let us forget about the Law." Or they say: "If grace is superabundant where sin was abundant, then let us be abundant in sin, so that we may be justified and grace may be superabundant." These are the spiteful and arrogant men who willfully distort Scripture and the sayings of the Holy Spirit, as they distorted Paul during the lifetime of the apostles, "to their own destruction," as 2 Peter 3:16 says.

On the other hand, the weak, who are not malicious or slanderous but good, are offended when they hear that the Law and good works do not have to be done for justification. One must go to their aid and explain to them how it is that works do not justify, how works should be done, and how they should not be done. They should be done as fruits of righteousness, not in order to bring righteousness into being. Having been made righteous, we must do them; but it is not the other way around: that when we are unrighteous, we become righteous by doing them. The tree produces fruit; the fruit does not produce the tree.

Paul had said above: "I have died, etc." Here a malicious person could easily cavil and say: "What are you saying, Paul? Are you dead? Then how is it that you are speaking and writing?" A weak person might also be easily offended and say: "Who are you anyway? Do I not see you alive and doing things?" He replies: "I do indeed live;

[85] See p. 162, note 81.

[86] The original text has the meaningless word *antipophoras;* we have followed the suggestion of the St. Louis edition and read *anthypophora,* a technical term from rhetoric; see, for example, Quintilian, *Institutiones rhetoricae,* IX, 2, 106.

and yet not I live, but Christ lives in me. There is a double life: my own, which is natural or animate; and an alien life, that of Christ in me.[87] So far as my animate life is concerned, I am dead and am now living an alien life. I am not living as Paul now, for Paul is dead." "Who, then, is living? "The Christian." Paul, living in himself, is utterly dead through the Law but living in Christ, or rather with Christ living in him, he lives an alien life. Christ is speaking, acting, and performing all actions in him; these belong not to the Paul-life, but to the Christ-life. "You malicious person, do not slander me for saying that I am dead. And you weak person, do not be offended, but make the proper distinction. There is a double life, my life and an alien life. By my own life I am not living; for if I were, the Law would have dominion over me and would hold me captive. To keep it from holding me, I am dead to it by another Law. And this death acquires an alien life for me, namely, the life of Christ, which is not inborn in me but is granted to me in faith through Christ."

The second reply to objections. This objection, too, could have been raised against Paul: "What are you saying? You do not live by your own life or in the flesh; you live in Christ? To be sure, I see your flesh; but I do not see Christ. Are you trying to deceive us by some trick into not seeing that you are present in the flesh, living your familiar life, having five senses, and doing everything in this physical life that any other man does?" He replies:

And the life I now live in the flesh I live by faith in the Son of God.

That is to say: "I do indeed live in the flesh; but this life that is being led within me, whatever it is, I do not regard as a life. For actually it is not a true life but only a mask of life, under which there lives another One, namely, Christ, who is truly my Life. This life you do not see; you only hear it as 'you hear the sound of the wind, but you do not know whence it comes or whither it goes' (John 3:8). Thus you see me talking, eating, working, sleeping, etc.; and yet you do not see my life. For the time of life that I am living I do indeed live in the flesh, but not on the basis of the flesh and according to the flesh, but in faith, on the basis of faith, and according to faith." He does not deny that he lives in the flesh, for he is doing all the works of an animate man. Besides, he is also using physical things — food, clothing, etc. — which is surely living in the flesh. But he says that this is not his life, and that he does not live according to these

---

[87] The terms are *naturalis vel animalis* and *aliena*, scil. *vita*.

things. He does indeed use physical things; but he does not live by them, as the world lives on the basis of the flesh and according to the flesh, because it neither knows nor hopes for any life besides this physical life.

"Therefore," says Paul, "whatever this life is that I now live in the flesh, I live by faith in the Son of God." That is, the Word I speak physically is not the word of the flesh; it is the Word of the Holy Spirit and of Christ. The vision that enters or leaves my eyes does not come from the flesh; that is, my flesh does not direct it, but the Holy Spirit does. Thus hearing does not come from the flesh, even though it is in the flesh; but it is in and from the Holy Spirit. A Christian speaks nothing but chaste, sober, holy, and divine things — things that pertain to Christ, the glory of God, and the salvation of his neighbor. These things do not come from the flesh, nor are they done according to the flesh; nevertheless, they are in the flesh. I cannot teach, preach, write, pray, or give thanks except by these physical instruments, which are required for the performance of these activities. Nevertheless, these activities do not come from the flesh and do not originate there; they are given and revealed divinely from heaven. Thus also I look at a woman with my eyes, yet with a chaste vision and not in desire for her. Such vision does not come from the flesh, even though it is in the flesh; the eyes are the physical instrument of the vision, but the chastity of the vision comes from heaven.

Thus a Christian uses the world and all its creatures in such a way that there is no difference between him and an ungodly man. Their food and clothing are the same; their hearing, vision, and speaking are the same; their gestures, appearance, and shape are the same. Thus Paul also says about Christ: "being found in human form" (Phil. 2:8). Nevertheless, there is the greatest possible difference. I do indeed live in the flesh, but I do not live on the basis of my own self. The life I now live in the flesh I live by faith in the Son of God. What you now hear me speak proceeds from another source than what you heard me speak before. Before his conversion Paul spoke with the same voice and tongue. But his voice and his tongue were blasphemous then; therefore he could not speak anything but blasphemies and abominations against God. After his conversion his flesh, tongue, and voice were the same as they had been before; nothing at all was changed. But now the voice and tongue did not speak blasphemies; now it spoke spiritual words of thanksgiving and praise for God, which came from faith and from the Holy Spirit.

Thus I do live in the flesh, yet not on the basis of the flesh or according to the flesh but by faith in the Son of God.

From all this it is evident whence this alien and spiritual life comes. The unspiritual man does not perceive this, because he does not know what sort of life this is. He "hears the sound of the wind, but he does not know whence it comes or whither it goes" (John 3:8). He hears the voice of the spiritual man; he recognizes his face, his habits, and his gestures. But whence these words come, which are not sacrilegious or blasphemous now but holy and divine, and whence these motives and actions come — this he does not see. For this life is in the heart through faith. There the flesh is extinguished; and there Christ rules with His Holy Spirit, who now sees, hears, speaks, works, suffers, and does simply everything in him, even though the flesh is still reluctant. In short, this life is not the life of the flesh, although it is a life in the flesh; but it is the life of Christ, the Son of God, whom the Christian possesses by faith.

Who loved me and gave Himself for me.

Here you have the true meaning of justification described, together with an example of the certainty of faith. "I live by faith in the Son of God, who loved me and gave Himself for me" — anyone who could say these words with Paul in a certain and constant faith would be truly blessed. With these very words Paul completely abrogates and removes the righteousness of the Law and of works, as we shall point out later. Therefore these words must be diligently pondered: "The Son of God loved me and gave Himself for me." It was not I who loved the Son of God and gave myself for Him, as the sophists pretend that they love the Son of God and give themselves for Him. For they teach that purely by his natural endowments [88] a man is able to perform the "merit of congruity" and to love God and Christ above all things. They anticipate the love of God and of Christ by doing what lies within them; they become monks and observe poverty, chastity, and obedience. Thus they dream that they give themselves for Christ. They turn the words of Paul upside down and read them this way: "We have loved Christ and have given ourselves for Him." But while these wicked men, inflated with the mind of their own flesh, dream and imagine that they are doing what lies within them, loving God and

[88] See the discussion on p. 174 and on p. 4, note 1.

giving themselves for Christ, they actually abolish the Gospel, ridicule, deny, blaspheme, spit upon, and tread Christ underfoot. In words they confess that He is the Justifier and the Savior; but in fact they deprive Him of the power either to justify or to save, and they attribute this to their self-chosen acts of worship. This is not living by faith in the Son of God; it is living by one's own righteousness and works.

Therefore the true way of being justified is not that you begin "to do what lies within you"; that is the phraseology they use. "If a man," they say, "does what lies within him, God infallibly gives him grace." [89] That proposition is extremely important. In fact, it is an article of faith among the sophists. They do, however, tone down the statement "to do what lies within one" by saying that this is not to be taken as an indivisible or mathematical point but as a physical one. That is, it is enough if a man does what can be approved by the judgment of a good man. This need not be judged by an indivisible point, since it is impossible for any such to exist; but it is enough for the point to be approximate. In other words, it is enough that someone acts, fasts, etc., in a way that would be said to be good according to the judgment of a good man. Then grace would certainly follow, not by the merit of congruity itself but by the infallibility of God, who is so good and just that He cannot help granting grace in exchange for something good. And this was the origin of the little verse:

> God does not require of any man
> That he do more than he really can.[90]

This is actually a good statement, but in its proper place, that is, in political, domestic, and natural affairs. For example, if I, who exist in the realm of reason, rule a family, build a house, or carry on a governmental office, and I do as much as I can or what lies within me, I am excused. For this realm has boundaries, and to this realm these statements like "to do what lies within one" or

[89] On this statement cf. Heiko A. Oberman, *Facientibus quod in se est Deus non denegat gratiam, The Harvard Theological Review*, LV (1962), pp. 317—342.

[90] In Latin the verse reads:
> *Ultra posse viri*
> *Non vult Deus ulla requiri.*

The German text reads:
> *Gott fordert nicht von einem Man,*
> *Das er mehr thun soll denn er kan.*

"to do as much as I can" properly apply. But the sophists drag these statements into the spiritual realm, where a man cannot do anything but sin, because he is "sold under sin" (Rom. 7:14). But in external matters, that is, in political and domestic affairs, man is not a slave but a lord of these physical matters. Therefore it was wicked of the sophists to drag these political and domestic statements into the church. For the realm of human reason must be separated as far as possible from the spiritual realm.

They have also handed down the statement that human nature has been corrupted, but that its natural endowments are sound; these latter they attributed also to the demons. But since the natural endowments are sound, the intellect is pure, and the will is good and sound; and thus, by logical consistency, everything is perfect. It is necessary to know these things if the purity of the doctrine of faith is to be preserved. When the sophists say that the natural endowments are sound, I concede this. But if they draw the inference: "Therefore a man is able to fulfill the Law, to love God, etc.," then I deny the conclusion. I distinguish the natural endowments from the spiritual; and I say that the spiritual endowments are not sound but corrupt, in fact, totally extinguished through sin in man and in the devil. Thus there is nothing there but a depraved intellect and a will that is hostile and opposed to God's will — a will that thinks nothing except what is against God. The natural endowments are indeed sound, but which natural endowments? Those by which a man who is drowned in wickedness and is a slave of the devil has a will, reason, free choice, and power to build a house, to carry on a governmental office, to steer a ship, and to do other tasks that have been made subject to man according to Gen. 1:28; these have not been taken away from man. Procreation, government, and the home have not been abolished by such statements; they have been confirmed. But the sophists twisted them into the spiritual realm. Perhaps they received them from the fathers. But because they understood them poorly, they distorted them to apply to spiritual affairs; thus they confused civil and ecclesiastical matters. It is up to us to clean this up and to remove these scandals from the church. We concede that these statements are true, but in their proper place, that is, in the physical realm. But if you drag them into the spiritual realm before the sight of God, we completely deny them. For there we are completely drowned in sins. Whatever is in our will is evil; whatever is in our intellect is error. In divine matters, therefore, man has nothing but darkness, error, malice, and perversity of will and of intellect. Then how could he do good works, love God, etc.?

Therefore Paul says here that not we but Christ took the initiative. "He loved me," he says, "and gave Himself for me." It is as though he were saying: "He did not find a good will or a correct intellect in me, but He Himself took pity on me. He saw that I was ungodly, erring, turned away from God, drawing back and fighting against God; and that I had been captured, directed, and steered by the devil. By a mercy that preceded my reason, will, and intellect He loved me, and loved me so much that He gave Himself for me, that I might be delivered from the Law, sin, the devil, and death."

These words, "the Son of God," "He loved me," and "He gave Himself for me," are sheer thunder and heavenly fire against the righteousness of the Law and the doctrine of works. There was such great evil, such great error, and such darkness and ignorance in my will and intellect that I could be liberated only by such an inestimable price. Then why do we boast about the rule of reason, about our sound natural endowments, about reason's preference for the best things, and about doing what lies within one? Why do I offer to a wrathful God, who is, as Moses says, "a devouring fire" (Deut. 4:24), some straw, in fact, my horrible sins, and want to demand of Him that in exchange for them He grant me grace and eternal life? For I hear in this passage that there is so much evil in my nature that the world and all creation would not suffice to placate God, but that the Son of God Himself had to be given up for it.

But consider this price carefully, and look at this captive, the Son of God. You will see then that He is greater [91] and more excellent than all creation. What will you do when you hear Paul say that such an inestimable price was given for your sins? Will you bring your cowl or tonsure or chastity or obedience or poverty? What are all these? Indeed, what is the Law of Moses and the works of the Law? What are all the works of all men and the sufferings of the martyrs? What is all the obedience of the holy angels compared with the Son of God "given," and given in the most shameful way, into death, even death on a cross (Phil. 2:8), so that all His most precious blood was shed — and for your sins? If you looked at this price, you would take all your cowls, tonsures, vows, works, merits of congruity, and merits of condignity, and you would curse, defile, spit upon,

[91] For *maiorum* in the original we have read *maiorem*.

and damn them, and consign them to hell! Therefore it is an intolerable and horrible blasphemy to think up some work by which you presume to placate God, when you see that He cannot be placated except by this immense, infinite price, the death and the blood of the Son of God, one drop of which is more precious than all creation.[92]

For me.

Who is this "me"? It is I,[93] an accursed and damned sinner, who was so beloved by the Son of God that He gave Himself for me. Therefore if I could have loved the Son of God and come to Him by works or by merits of congruity and condignity, what need would there have been for Him to give Himself for me? From this it is evident how coldly the papists treated the Holy Scriptures and the teaching of faith, in fact, how they completely neglected them. For if they had only looked at these words, that the Son of God had to be given for me, it would have been impossible for any order or sect to arise, because faith would have replied immediately: "Why are you choosing this way of life, this order, this work? Is it so that God may be placated or that you may be justified? You scoundrel, do you not hear that the Son of God was given and that He shed His blood for you?" Thus faith in Christ would have been able very easily to resist all sects.

Therefore I say that there is no force that can resist the sects, and no remedy against them except this one doctrine of Christian righteousness. If this doctrine is lost, it is impossible for us to be able to resist any errors or sects. We can see this today in the fanatics, Anabaptists, and Sacramentarians. Now that they have fallen away from this doctrine, they will never stop falling, erring, and seducing others ad infinitum. Undoubtedly they will arouse innumerable sects and think up new works. Although in outward appearance all these things may be very good and saintly, what are they in comparison with the death and the blood of the Son of God, who gave Himself for me? Who is this Son of God? What are heaven and earth in comparison with Him? Rather than that the truth of the Gospel should be obscured and the glory of Christ perish, let all the fanatics and papists go to hell, with all their righteousnesses, works, and merits — even if the whole world should be on

[92] See p. 132, note 53.

[93] Although the original reads *Ergo peccator*, etc., the reading *Ego* seems preferable.

their side! Then why is it that they brag about works and merits? If I, an accursed and damned sinner, could be redeemed by some other price, what need was there that the Son of God should be given for me? But because there was no price in heaven or on earth except Christ, the Son of God, therefore it was extremely necessary that He be given for me. He also did this because of His great love; for Paul says: "who loved me."

Now these words, "who loved me," are filled with faith. Anyone who can speak this brief pronoun "me" in faith and apply it to himself as Paul did, will, like Paul, be the best of debaters against the Law. For He did not give a sheep or an ox or gold or silver for me. But He who was completely God gave everything He was, gave Himself for me — for me, I say, a miserable and accursed sinner. I am revived by this "giving" of the Son of God into death, and I apply it to myself. This applying is the true power of faith. One who performs works does not say: "Christ loved me, etc."

Paul opposes these words, which are the purest proclamation of grace and of Christian righteousness, to the righteousness of the Law. It is as though he were saying: "All right, let the Law be a divine teaching and let it have its glory. It still did not love me or give itself for me, but it accuses and frightens me. Now I have Another, who has freed me from the terrors of the Law, from sin, and from death, and who has transferred me into freedom, the righteousness of God, and eternal life. He is called the Son of God, who loved me and gave Himself for me."

As I have said, faith grasps and embraces Christ, the Son of God, who was given for us, as Paul teaches here. When He has been grasped by faith, we have righteousness and life. For Christ is the Son of God, who gave Himself out of sheer love to redeem me. In these words Paul gives a beautiful description of the priesthood and the work of Christ, which is to placate God, to intercede and pray for sinners, to offer Himself as a sacrifice for their sins, and to redeem them. Therefore you should learn to define Christ properly, not as the sophists and fanatics do; they make of Him a new lawgiver who, after abrogating the old Law, established a new Law. For them Christ is a taskmaster and a tyrant. But you should define Him as Paul does here, as the Son of God, who, not because of merit or any righteousness of ours, but because of His sheer mercy and love, gave and offered Himself to God as a sacrifice for us miserable sinners, to sanctify us forever.

Therefore Christ is not Moses, not a taskmaster or a lawgiver; He is the Dispenser of grace, the Savior, and the Pitier. In other words, He is nothing but sheer, infinite mercy, which gives and is given. Then you will depict Christ correctly. If you let Him be depicted to you any other way, you will soon be overthrown in the hour of temptation. The highest art among Christians is to be able to define Christ this way; it is also the most difficult of arts. For it is very hard for me, even in the great light of the Gospel and after my extensive experience and practice in this study, to define Christ as Paul does here. That is how much this teaching and noxious idea of Christ as the lawgiver has penetrated into my bones like oil. On this score you younger men are much more fortunate than we older ones.[94] You have not been imbued with these noxious ideas with which I was imbued from boyhood, so that even at the mention of the name of Christ I would be terrified and grow pale, because I was persuaded that He was a judge. Therefore I have to make a double effort: first, to unlearn, condemn, and resist this ingrown opinion of Christ as a lawgiver and a judge, which constantly returns and drags me back; secondly, to acquire a new idea, namely, trust in Christ as the Justifier and the Savior. If you are willing, you can have much less difficulty learning to know Christ purely. Therefore if any sadness or tribulation afflicts one's heart, this should not be ascribed to Christ, even though it may come under the name of Christ, but to the devil, who makes a practice of coming under the name of Christ and of disguising himself as an angel of light (2 Cor. 11:14).

Therefore let us learn to distinguish carefully between Christ and a lawgiver, not only in word but also in fact and in practice. Then, when the devil comes, disguised as Christ and harassing us under His name, we will know that he is not Christ, but that he is really the devil. For Christ is the joy and sweetness of a trembling and troubled heart. We have this on the authority of Paul, who adorns Him with the sweetest of titles here, calling Him the One "who loved *me*[95] and gave Himself for me." Therefore Christ is the Lover of those who are in anguish, sin, and death, and the kind of Lover who gives Himself for us and becomes our High Priest, that is, the One who interposes Himself as the Mediator between

[94] As on p. 138, note 58, this is an echo of Luther's lecture hall.

[95] In the original text the words we have printed in italics appear in capitals.

God and us miserable sinners. I ask you what could be said that would be more joyful and happy than this? If all this is true — and it must be true, or otherwise the whole Gospel is false — then surely we are not justified by the righteousness of the Law, much less by our own righteousness.

Therefore read these words *"me"* and *"for me"* with great emphasis, and accustom yourself to accepting this *"me"* with a sure faith and applying it to yourself. Do not doubt that you belong to the number of those who speak this *"me."* Christ did not love only Peter and Paul and give Himself for them, but the same grace belongs and comes to us as to them; therefore we are included in this *"me."* For just as we cannot deny that we are all sinners, and just as we are obliged to say that through his sin Adam destroyed us and made us enemies of God who are liable to God's wrath and judgment and worthy of eternal death — for all terrified hearts feel and confess this, in fact, more than is proper — so we cannot deny that Christ died for our sins in order that we might be justified. For He did not die to make the righteous righteous; He died to make sinners into righteous men, the friends and sons of God, and heirs of all heavenly gifts. Therefore since I feel and confess that I am a sinner on account of the transgression of Adam, why should I not say that I am righteous on account of the righteousness of Christ, especially when I hear that He loved me and gave Himself for me? Paul believed this most firmly, and therefore he speaks with such πληροφορία.[96]

21. *I do not nullify the grace of God.*

This is the second argument of this epistle. Consider carefully here that to want to be justified by the works of the Law is to nullify the grace of God. I ask you what can be more wicked or a more horrible sin than to nullify the grace of God and to refuse to be justified by faith in Christ? It is bad enough, and more than bad enough, that we are wicked and are transgressors against all the Commandments of God. Yet over and above this we add the sin of sins when we smugly reject the grace of God and the forgiveness of sins being offered to us through Christ. Believe me, this blasphemy is greater and more horrible than anyone can express. Paul and the other apostles did not dwell on and denounce any sin more vehe-

96 Luther uses the Greek word πληροφορία here, perhaps in an allusion to 1 Thess. 1:5.

mently than the contempt of grace and the denial of Christ. Yet we commit this sin so very easily. This is why especially Paul inveighs so severely against Antichrist, because he abolishes grace and denies the blessing of Christ, our High Priest, who gave Himself as a sacrifice for our sins. To deny Christ this way is to spit at Him, to tread Him underfoot, to put oneself in His place, and to say: "I will justify you and save you." "How?" "Through Masses, pilgrimages, indulgences, observance of the rule, etc." Therefore Antichrist exalted himself against and above God (2 Thess. 2:4), put himself in the place of Christ, rejected grace, and denied faith. For he has taught as follows: "Faith does no good unless it has works." With this false idea he has completely obscured and buried the blessing of Christ. And in place of grace, Christ, and His kingdom he has established the doctrine of works and the kingdom of ceremonies, and has confirmed this with his trifles. Thus he has torn the whole world out of the hands of Christ, who is the only One who ought to rule in the conscience, and has thrown it forcibly into hell.

From this it is evident what it means to nullify the grace of God, namely, to want to be justified by the Law. But who has ever heard of this, that by performing the Law we nullify grace? Do we sin by performing the Law? No. But we nullify grace when we perform the Law with the idea of being justified through it. The Law is good (1 Tim. 1:8), holy, and useful; but it does not justify. Therefore he who performs the Law with the intention of being justified by it nullifies grace, rejects Christ and His sacrifice, and refuses to be saved by this inestimable price; instead, he wants to make satisfaction for his sins through the righteousness of the Law or to merit grace by his own righteousness. Such a person is surely blaspheming and nullifying the grace of God. Now it is horrible to say that a man can be so perversely evil as to nullify the mercy and grace of God. Nevertheless, the whole world acts this way, although it does not want to seem to be doing so but claims to be doing God the highest honor. Now there follows the second argument.

For if justification were through the Law, then Christ died to no purpose.

Here again I warn that Paul is not speaking about the Ceremonial Law, as the sophists continually imagine. Origen and Jerome were the originators of this error. They were extremely dangerous teachers on this point; all the scholastics followed them, and in our day Erasmus approves and confirms their error.[97] But the godly should simply avoid the foolishness of these men, who so distorted Paul with their stupid glosses. They are speaking of something they have neither known nor experienced. As though the ceremonies were not good and holy also! Surely the ordinance of the priesthood, circumcision, sacrifices, worship, divine service, and similar holy works were all ceremonies. Therefore he is speaking about the entire Law.

These words of Paul should be pondered carefully, as follows. Is it true or is it not that Christ died? Again, did He die to no purpose? Unless we are obviously insane, we are forced to answer here that He did die, that He did not die to no purpose, and that He died for us, not for Himself. Therefore if He did not die to no purpose, then righteousness is not through the Law.

Now take both Laws, the Ceremonial Law and the Moral Law or the Decalog. Imagine that by the merit of congruity you have made so much progress that the Spirit has been granted to you and that you have love. Of course, all this would be a monstrosity and cannot be found anywhere in the nature of things. But imagine, I say, that, by doing what lies within you, you acquire grace, are righteous, and have the Spirit. On what basis? On the basis of the merit of congruity? Then you do not need Christ, but He has become useless to you and died to no purpose.

Then take even the Decalog itself. It commands the supreme worship, namely, fear of God, faith, love toward God, and love toward one's neighbor. If you can show me anyone who has been justified on the basis of the Law of the Decalog, it is still true that Christ died to no purpose. For anyone who is justified on the basis of the Law of the Decalog has within himself the power to acquire righteousness. For by not standing in the way and by doing what lies within him he infallibly merits grace, and the Holy Spirit is infused into him; thus he is able to love God and his neighbor. If this is true, then it necessarily follows that Christ died to no purpose. For what need would a man have of a Christ who loves him and gives Himself for him when without Christ, by the merit of congruity, he is able to obtain grace and eventually to do good works and to merit eternal life by the merit of condignity, or surely to be justified by performing the Law? Therefore let Christ be removed together

[97] See p. 121, note 37.

with all His blessings, because He is completely useless. But why is Christ born, crucified, and dead? Why does He become my High Priest, who loves me and gives an inestimable sacrifice, Himself, for me? Why does He do all this? Simply to no purpose at all if the meaning of justification which the sophists set forth is true, because I find righteousness in the Law or in myself, outside grace and outside Christ.

But is this blasphemy something to be tolerated and covered up, that when the Divine Majesty did not spare His own Son but gave Him up for us all (Rom. 8:32), He was not doing this seriously but was merely playing? Before I would grant this, I would rather that the holiness not only of the papists and fanatics but even of the angels be eternally rejected and condemned, along with the devil! I refuse to look at anything except this Christ. He should be such a treasure to me that in comparison with Him everything else is filthy. He should be such a light to me that when I have taken hold of Him by faith, I do not know whether there is such a thing as Law, sin, or unrighteousness in the world. For what is everything there is in heaven and on earth in comparison with the Son of God?

Nullifying the grace of God is, therefore, a very great and very common sin, and one that all the self-righteous commit; for as long as they seek to be justified through the merit of congruity or through their own works and afflictions or through the Law, they nullify the grace of God and Christ, as we have said. And the pope has been the founder of all these abominations. Having darkened — in fact, completely buried — the Gospel of Christ, he has filled and burdened the world with his wicked traditions. Evidence for this comes from, among other things, his indulgences and bulls, in which he absolves, not those who believe but those who are contrite, who confess, and who stretch out a helping hand.[98] This is ample testimony that Christ has died to no purpose, and that grace is vain and useless. Therefore the abominations and blasphemies of the papal regime are inestimable. And yet even now, in the bright light of the truth, the sophists persist in their wicked and vain opinions. They still say that man's natural endowments are sound, and that by their own good works and merits men are able to prepare themselves for grace. They are so far from recognizing their wickedness and error that they defend it even against their conscience.

[98] Apparently an allusion to the three steps of penance: contrition, confession, and satisfaction.

But we constantly affirm with Paul — for we do not want to nullify the grace of God — that either Christ died to no purpose or the Law does not justify. But Christ did not die to no purpose; therefore the Law does not justify. Christ, the Son of God, has justified us by His sheer grace and mercy. Therefore the Law could not have accomplished this. For if it could have done so, then Christ acted foolishly when He gave Himself for our sins that we might be justified. Therefore we conclude that we are justified neither by the merit of congruity nor by the merit of condignity nor by our cross and afflictions nor by the Law itself, but solely by faith in Christ.

But if my salvation was worth so much to Christ that He had to die for my sins, then my works and the righteousness of the Law are vile — in fact, nonexistent — in comparison with such an inestimable price. For I cannot buy with a pittance something that cost many thousands of golden talents.[99] Now the Law — not to mention far lesser things — with all its works and righteousness is only a pittance in comparison with Christ, by whose death and resurrection my death has been conquered, and righteousness and eternal life have been granted to me. Shall I despise and nullify this incomparable price or seek through the Law and works of congruity and condignity — this filth and ordure, as Paul calls it, especially if you compare it with Christ — to gain a righteousness which, as Paul testifies here, Christ has already granted to me freely and out of sheer love, at such a cost that He had to give Himself for me? As I have said, the world does this, and especially those who want to appear the best and the saintliest in the world. Thus they clearly testify, regardless of what they may confess with their mouths, that Christ died to no purpose; this is to blaspheme Christ in the extreme, to spit in His face, to tread the Son of God underfoot, to profane the blood of the covenant, etc.

It should be noted carefully that when Paul refers to righteousness here, he is dealing with a sublime doctrine, not with a political or domestic one. That is, he is not discussing civil righteousness; God does indeed approve this, require that it be performed, and offer rewards to it, and to some extent reason is able to perform it. But he is discussing righteousness in the sight of God, by which we are freed from the Law, sin, death, and every evil, become partakers of

[99] From the notes on Luther's lecture it appears that he quoted this proverb in German.

grace, righteousness, and life, and eventually are established as the lords of heaven and earth and of all creatures. This righteousness neither human nor divine Law is able to produce.

The Law is added to reason, to illumine and help man and to show him what he should do and what he should avoid. Nevertheless, with all his strength and reason, and even with the addition of the great light and divine blessing of the Law, man still cannot be justified. Now if the best thing that the world has on this earth — the Law, which, like a sun, is added to feeble reason, the earthly light or human flame, to illumine and direct it — is not able to justify, what, I ask you, would reason do without the Law? What? The same thing that the pope with his universities and his monks has done; with their human traditions they have obscured even the light of the First Commandment. None of them can correctly understand even one letter of the Law, but they all walk in the darkness of reason. This is a much more dangerous error than the one that originated in the doctrine of the works of the Law.

Therefore the words are very powerful when he says: "If justification were through the Law, etc." He is silent about human power, reason, and wisdom, regardless of how great they may be; for the greater they are, the more easily and quickly they deceive a person. He simply says: "If justification were through the Law, etc." Therefore human reason with the assistance of laws, even of divine ones, cannot achieve righteousness but snatches a man away from righteousness and rejects Christ. But if it could achieve righteousness, then Christ would have died to no purpose. Therefore you oppose the death of Christ to every single Law; and, with Paul, you know nothing except Jesus Christ and Him crucified (1 Cor. 2:2), so that nothing except Him may shine. Then you will be learned, righteous, and holy; and you will receive the Holy Spirit, who will preserve you in the purity of the Word and of faith. But once Christ is lost sight of, everything is pointless.

Here again we see an encomium of the righteousness of the Law, or of one's own righteousness, namely, that according to Paul it is contempt and nullification of the grace of God and negation and frustration of the death of Christ. Paul is not a great orator, but look at the great arguments he supplies for oratory. Where, I ask you, is the eloquence that can match words like "to nullify grace" or "the grace of Christ" or "Christ died to no purpose"? The indignation

here is so great that the eloquence of the entire world is inadequate
to express it. It is not much to say "to die to no purpose." But to
say that Christ died to no purpose is to get rid of Him entirely.
Anyone who wants to practice oratory has material enough here to
develop and amplify what horrible blasphemy the doctrine of the
righteousness of the Law and of works is. What can be more
horrible or more blasphemous than to say that I make the death
of Christ useless, if I want to observe the Law in such a way that
I will be justified by it? But to make the death of Christ useless is
to make His resurrection, His victory, His glory, His kingdom, heaven,
earth, God Himself, the majesty of God, in short, everything, useless.
Is this a trivial matter? If you were to say that the realm of the
King of France or the Roman Empire had been established to no
purpose, you would be regarded as utterly insane. But this cannot
even be compared with saying that Christ died to no purpose.

This thunder and lightning from heaven against the righteousness
of the Law and one's own righteousness ought to frighten us away
from it. This thunder has knocked down and condemned whatever
monasticism or religion or righteousness there is in acts of worship
commanded by the Law or in those that have been self-chosen. For
who would not spit upon his vows, his tonsure, his cowl, human
traditions, and even upon the Law of Moses if he heard that for the
sake of these things he is nullifying the grace of God and making the
death of Christ pointless? When the world hears this, it does not
believe that it is true; for it does not think that such wickedness can
enter the human heart that it should discard the grace of God and
regard the death of Christ as pointless. And yet this horrible sin is
extremely common. For whoever seeks righteousness apart from faith
in Christ — whether it be through works or satisfactions or afflictions
or the Law of God — is nullifying the grace of God and despising the
death of Christ, even though he may speak otherwise with his mouth.

CHAPTER THREE

1. *O foolish Galatians!*

PAUL is aflame with a solicitude that is both apostolic and very spiritual in its zeal and emotion. Into his debate and refutation he inserts exhortations and reproofs, on the basis of his rule in 2 Tim. 4:2: "Preach the Word, be urgent in season and out of season, convince, rebuke, and exhort." This deceives an unwary reader. As a result, he supposes that Paul does not observe any method or order at all in his teaching. But although he does not observe any method according to the style of orators, he is following a splendid order in the Spirit.

After debating and substantiating with two powerful arguments that Christian righteousness does not come from the Law but comes from faith in Christ, and at the same time refuting the teaching of the false apostles, now, in the middle of the proceeding, he shifts the address to the Galatians and chides them: "O foolish [or insane] Galatians!" It is as though he were saying: "Alas, to what level have you fallen, you miserable Galatians? I taught you the truth of the Gospel diligently, and you also accepted it from me with great zeal and diligence. Then how does it happen that you have defected from it so quickly? Who has bewitched you?"

Paul seems to be chiding the Galatians very harshly when he calls them fools, bewitched, and disobedient to the truth. I will not argue here whether he did this out of zeal or out of pity; both may be true. An unspiritual man would interpret this as abuse rather than as pious chiding. Then was Paul giving a bad example, or was he abusive toward the churches of Galatia when he called them foolish and bewitched? No. For it is legitimate for an apostle, a pastor, or a preacher to reprove those under him sharply in Christian zeal; and such scolding is both fatherly and holy. Thus parents, in fatherly or motherly feeling, will call their son a foolish or worthless fellow, or their daughter a slattern — something they would not stand for if someone else did it. Sometimes a teacher

[186]

will scold a pupil bitterly, call him a jackass, and beat him with sticks — which the pupil accepts with equanimity, though he would not accept it from a peer or a fellow student. Thus also a magistrate will scold, be angry, and punish. Without severe discipline nothing can be done properly in peace or in war. Therefore unless a magistrate, a clergyman, a public official, or a head of a household is angry and scolds when the situation demands, he is lazy and useless and will never administer his office properly.

Therefore denunciation and anger are as necessary in every kind of life as any other virtue is. Nevertheless, this anger must be moderated and must not proceed from envy; it must proceed only from fatherly concern and Christian zeal. That is, it must not be a childish or womanly show of temper that is out for revenge; its only desire should be to correct the fault, as a father disciplines his son, not to set his own mind at rest with a desire for revenge [1] but to improve the son by such discipline. These forms of anger are good and are called "zeal" in the Scriptures.[2] For when I discipline a brother or a subject in this way, I am not seeking his destruction; I am seeking his welfare. Therefore this anger is necessary and good; without it nothing constructive could exist either in the realm of the world or in that of the church.

It is possible, therefore, that Paul is denouncing the Galatians here out of sheer zeal, not in order to destroy them but by this means to call them back to the right way and rescue them. Or he may be acting out of pity and a feeling of sympathy, behaving like someone who complains out of disappointment that the Galatians have been so miserably seduced. It is as though he were saying: "I am saddened by your unfortunate lot." We scold miserable people in the same way, not in order to insult them or reproach them for their misery but to sympathize with them and to try to take care of them. I am saying this to prevent anyone from accusing Paul of having reviled the churches of God, in violation of the rule of the Gospel.[3]

[1] Luther's Latin phrase, *animum expleat libidine vindictae,* may be an allusion to the words of Vergil:
. . . *animumque explesse iuvabit*
Ultricis flammae. Aeneid, II, 586—7.

[2] Presumably John 2:17 and its source, Ps. 69:9, are the passages Luther has in mind.

[3] By "the rule of the Gospel" Luther appears to mean the rule of the apostle in 1 Cor. 11:22.

Christ reviles the Pharisees in a similar way when He calls them serpents, a brood of vipers (Matt. 23:33), and children of the devil (John 8:44). But these are revilings from the Holy Spirit. They are fatherly and motherly, the rebukes of a faithful friend, as is stated also in Prov. 27:6: "The wounds of a friend are better than the kisses of an enemy." Thus it happens that the same denunciation can be [4] the greatest benefit if it comes from the mouth of a father, but the worst sort of injury if it comes from the mouth of a peer or an enemy. When two men do the same thing, it is praised in the one and denounced in the other.[5] Christ or Paul can revile in a very virtuous and praiseworthy way, but in a philosopher or a private person this would be extremely vicious and slanderous. Therefore the same deed and word is a blessing in the mouth of Paul, but in the mouth of another it is a curse.

There is emphasis on the word "Galatians." Paul does not call them brethren, as he is otherwise wont to do; but he calls them by their national name. And it seems that it was the peculiar national vice of that people to be ἀνόητοι, just as the Cretans were liars (Titus 1:12). It is as though he were saying: "As you are called and as you are said to be, so you are, and so you remain, namely, ἀνόητοι Galatians. You are proving this now in the very matter of the Gospel, where you really should have been very wise. But that nature of yours persists!" In a similar way we also distinguish among nations on the basis of their vices. For every nation has its own peculiar vices. The Germans are eager for novelty; the Italians are arrogant, etc.[6] By this method of rebuke, therefore, Paul reminds the Galatians of their nature.

We are also being admonished here that in churches and in Christians there still remain natural vices according to the flesh. Grace does not so transform the godly as to make them completely new and perfect, but there still remain in the godly certain dregs of their old natural vices. Suppose, for example, that a man with a bad temper is converted to Christ; although he is softened by grace and the Holy Spirit so imbues his heart that he now becomes gentler, still this natural vice is not completely extinguished in his

---

[4] The Weimar text reads *si*, but we have read *sit*.

[5] A paraphrase of the epigram, which was also a maxim of jurisprudence: *Duo cum faciunt idem, non est idem.*

[6] Elsewhere Luther suggests that "Guzzle" is the national devil of the Germans; cf. *Luther's Works*, 13, p. 216.

flesh. Similarly, if harsh men are converted to faith, they still do not get rid of their harshness completely; but a shred of this harshness still clings to them. This is why the Gospels and the Holy Scriptures, whose truth is all of a piece, are treated in differing ways by men of differing dispositions. One is milder and gentler in his teaching; another is harsher. Thus when the Spirit is poured into diverse instruments, He does not immediately extinguish the vices of nature; but throughout life he goes on purging the sin that inheres, not only in the Galatians but in all men of all nations.

Although the Galatians had been illumined, were believers, and had received the Holy Spirit through the preaching of faith, there still remained in them this shred of their old vice, this tinder [7] that so easily caught the flame of false teaching. Therefore let no one be so confident of himself as to suppose that when he has received grace, he is completely cleansed of his old vices. Many things are indeed cleansed, especially the head of the serpent — that is, unbelief and ignorance of God are cut off and crushed (Gen. 3:15) — but the scaly body and the remnants of sin still remain in us. Therefore let no one presume that once faith has been accepted, he can immediately undergo a metamorphosis into a new man. But he will still keep some of his old vices even in Christianity. For we are not dead yet; but we still live in the flesh, which, because it is not yet pure, has desires against the Spirit (Gal. 5:17). And in Rom. 7:14 Paul says: "I am carnal, sold under sin"; and again (Rom. 7:23): "I see in my members another law." Therefore the natural vices that existed before faith remain also after faith has been accepted. But now they are being forced to serve the Spirit, who dominates them so that they do not rule; yet this does not happen without a struggle. Christ alone has the glory and the title of being altogether pure. 1 Peter 2:22 says: "He committed no sin; no guile was found on His lips."

Who has bewitched you so that you do not obey the truth?

Here again you have another encomium for that wonderful righteousness — the righteousness of the Law and the righteousness that is in oneself, namely, that it causes us to despise the truth, that it bewitches us so that we do not obey the truth but rebel against it.

The reason Paul calls the Galatians foolish and bewitched is that

[7] On the scholastic notion of *fomes*, which Luther accepts here, see also *Luther's Works*, 13, p. 81, note 12.

he compares them to children, to whom witchcraft does a great deal of harm. It is as though he were saying: "What is happening to you is precisely what happens to children, whom witches, sorceresses, and hags usually charm quickly and easily with their bewitchment, a trick of Satan." Paul does not deny that witchcraft exists and is possible; for later on, in the fifth chapter (v. 20), he also lists "sorcery," which is the same as witchcraft, among the works of the flesh. Thereby he proves that witchcraft and sorcery exist and are possible. For it is undeniable that the devil lives, yes, rules, in all the world. Therefore witchcraft and sorcery are works of the devil, by which he not only injures people but sometimes, with God's permission, destroys them. But we are all subject to the devil, both according to our bodies and according to our material possessions. We are guests in the world, of which he is the ruler (John 16:11) and the god (2 Cor. 4:4). Therefore the bread we eat, the drinks we drink, the clothes we wear — in fact, the air and everything we live on in the flesh — are under his reign. Through his witches, therefore, he is able to do harm to children, to give them heart trouble, to blind them, to steal them, or even to remove a child completely and put himself into the cradle in place of the stolen child. I have heard that in Saxony there was such a boy. He was suckled by five women and still could not be satisfied.[8] There are many similar instances.

Therefore witchcraft is nothing but an artifice and illusion of the devil, whether he cripples a part of the body or touches the body or takes it away altogether. He can do this uncommonly well, even in the case of old people. No wonder, then, that he bewitches children this way. Nevertheless, this is nothing but some sort of illusion; for they say that he is able to heal what he has crippled with his wiles. But he heals by restoring an eye or some other injured part of the body — not that it had really been injured; but the senses of those whom he has bewitched, as well as of others who looked at the bewitched, were so deluded that they did not regard it as an illusion but supposed that it was a genuine injury. But since he removes the injury in due time, it is evident that it was merely an illusion, not a genuine injury; for a genuine injury cannot be healed or restored.

You have an outstanding example of this thing in *The Lives of*

[8] For a similar story of bewitchment cf. *Luther's Works*, 24, pp. 74—75.

the Fathers, likewise the well-known *Metamorphoses* of the poets.[9] To St. Macarius, in the desert where he was living, there came the parents of a certain maiden. They had lost her because they believed that she had been turned into a cow, since they could not see any form but that of a cow. Bringing their daughter to St. Macarius, therefore, they asked that a prayer be said for her by him, in order that her human form might be restored to her. But when he heard this, he declared: "I see a maiden, not a cow." For he had spiritual eyes; therefore Satan could not deceive him with his tricks as he had deceived the parents and the daughter, whose eyes that evil spirit had so beguiled that they would have sworn that what presented itself to their eyes in their spell was actually happening. But when St. Macarius prayed for the maiden, not that she should regain the human form which she had never lost but that God should remove this illusion of the devil from her, then the eyes of the parents and of the daughter were opened, and they recognized that what had seemed to them to be actually happening was merely a trick of Satan.

So great is the astuteness and the power of Satan to deceive the senses. And no wonder, since a change of sense and of color can take place through glass. Therefore he can easily deceive a man with his wiles, so that the man supposes that he is seeing something that he really does not see, or hearing a voice, thunder, a flute, or a trumpet that he really does not hear. Thus the soldiers of Julius Caesar thought that they were hearing someone playing a shepherd's pipe and a trumpet. Suetonius tells about this in *The Life of Caesar.*[10] Someone of unusual size and shape, he says, suddenly appeared to be sitting nearby and playing a shepherd's pipe. When not only shepherds but also very many soldiers and a few trumpeters had come running from their stations to listen to him, he snatched a trumpet from someone, leaped to the river, blew a blast with a mighty sound, and made for the opposite bank. Thus Satan has uncommon ability to touch all the senses in such a way that you swear you see, hear, or feel something which you nevertheless do not see, etc.

But Satan does not dement men in this crude way only; he also

9 This story is told by Rufinus in *Vitae patrum,* ch. 28, *Patrologia, Series Latina,* XXI, 451; cf. *Luther's Works,* 24, p. 75, note 46. Luther is, of course, thinking also of the *Metamorphoses* of Ovid.

10 Suetonius, *Lives of the Twelve Caesars,* I, 32 (Julius).

does so in a way that is subtler and all the more dangerous. In this he is an especially clever trickster. This is why Paul applies the bewitchment of the senses to the bewitchment of the spirit. But with this spiritual witchcraft that ancient serpent (Rev. 12:9) captures, not men's senses but their minds, and deceives them with false and wicked opinions; those who are bewitched in this way suppose that these opinions are true and godly. Nowadays he is showing his ability to do this in the fanatics, the Anabaptists, and the Sacramentarians. With his tricks he has so bewitched their minds that they are embracing lies, errors, and horrible darkness as the most certain truth and the clearest light. They will not permit themselves to be dissuaded from these dreams of theirs by any admonitions or Scripture passages; for they are altogether persuaded that they alone are wise and have a pious attitude toward sacred things, and that everyone else is blind. Therefore they are acting precisely like the parents of that maiden, who were taken in by the tricks of Satan and were so firmly persuaded that they would have sworn that their daughter was not a human being but a cow; there was nothing more incredible to them than that all this was a trick and illusion of the devil. For on their side they had the testimony of all the senses: their eyes saw the shape of a cow, their ears heard the lowing of a cow, etc. And they thought that one should not fight against common sense.

But the example of Macarius shows that one must fight against common sense in the case of physical witchcraft; much more must one do so in the case of spiritual witchcraft. In the former case the devil deceives with shapes and colors in the senses, externally; but in the latter case he works internally, with plausible opinions and ideas about doctrine, by which, as I have said, he so dements the hearts of men that they would swear that their most vain and wicked dreams are the most certain truth. Thus in our time he has bewitched Münzer, Zwingli, and others; and through these he has bewitched others too many to count.[11]

Finally, so great is this sorcerer's desire to work harm that he not only deceives those smug and proud spirits with his tricks but with his wiles even tries to dement those who have pious and proper thoughts about the Word of God and the Christian religion. Again and again he attacks even me so boldly and overwhelms me with

[11] See p. 97, note 17.

such sorrowful thoughts that he completely obscures Christ for me and almost takes Him away. In other words, there is no one of us who is not bewitched rather often by false opinions, that is, who is not afraid, confident, or joyful where one should not be afraid, confident, or joyful, or who does not sometimes think otherwise than he should about God, Christ, faith, his calling, and the Christian way of life.

Therefore let us learn to recognize the illusions and crafts of this sorcerer, lest he find us smug and snoring, and deceive us with his tricks. Of course, he cannot harm our ministry with his bewitchment. Nevertheless, he is with us in spirit; day and night he prowls around, seeking to devour everyone individually. And unless he finds us sober and equipped with spiritual weapons, that is, with the Word of God and faith, he devours us (1 Peter 5:8).

Therefore Satan continually mounts a new battle against us. It is a real advantage to us that with his plots he attacks and exercises us this way, for by this means he confirms our doctrine and increases faith in us. We have often been struck down in this battle, and we are still being struck down; but we are not destroyed (2 Cor. 4:9). For Christ has always led us in triumph, and He is still triumphing through us (2 Cor. 2:14). From this we gain the firm hope that through Christ we shall eventually emerge as victors over the devil. This hope gives us firm comfort, so that we can take courage this way in all our temptations: "Look, Satan has tempted us before and has urged us with his plots to lose faith, despise God, and despair. Yet he has not accomplished anything, and he will not accomplish anything. He who is in us is greater than he who is in the world (1 John 4:4). Christ is stronger; He has overcome, is overcoming, and will overcome that strong man in us (Luke 11:21-22)." Still the devil does sometimes overcome us in the flesh, in order that even in this way we may experience the power of the Stronger against that strong man and say with Paul (2 Cor. 12:10): "When I am weak, then I am strong."

Therefore let no one think that the Galatians were the only ones to be bewitched by Satan, but let everyone think that he himself could have been bewitched and still can be. No one of us is so vigorous that he can resist Satan, especially if he tries to do so with his own strength. Job was a blameless and upright man, and there was no one like him on earth (Job 1:8). But what could he do against the devil when God withdrew His hand? Did not that holy man fall horribly? Therefore this bewitcher not only was powerful in the Galatians; but he is always making an effort to deceive, if not everyone, then as many as he can, with his false persuasions. "For he is a liar and the father of lies" (John 8:44). With his skill he is surely dementing the fanatical spirits today, as I have said. He rules in them and makes them so inflexible and hard that no anvil could be as hard. They do not permit themselves to be instructed; they do not listen to reason; they do not admit Scripture. All they are concerned about is how, by inventing and making up glosses out of their own heads, to elude the passages of Scripture quoted against them, and how to defend their own dreams that have been smuggled into Scripture. This is an obvious sign that they have been captured by the bewitchment of the devil.

Who has bewitched you?

Here Paul is excusing the Galatians and shifting the blame to the false apostles. It is as though he were saying: "I see [12] that it was not of your own accord or malice that you fell. But the devil has sent those bewitchers, the false apostles, into your midst, my children; and they so bewitched you with the doctrine of the Law that now you believe otherwise about Christ than you used to, when you heard the Gospel being preached by me. But we are laboring both by exhortation and by writing to break the spell with which the false apostles have bound you, so that those among you who have been taken captive by this bewitchment may be set free by us." Thus in our day we, too, must labor with the Word of God against the fanatical opinions of the Anabaptists and the Sacramentarians, to set free those who have been taken captive by them, to recall them to the pure doctrine of faith, and to keep them in it. Nor is this labor of ours useless. For we have recalled many whom they had bewitched, and we have set them free from their bewitchment, from which they could never have been untangled by their own powers if they had not been admonished by us and recalled through the Word of God.

For just as it is impossible for a man to set himself free from the bewitchment of his senses — for the parents could not see any shape but that of a cow before Macarius had prayed, as I have said —

[12] The Weimar text has *Vidos,* but we have read *Video.*

so it is impossible for those who have been bewitched in spirit to set themselves free by their own powers, unless they are set free by those whose minds have not been taken captive by this bewitchment. So great is the efficacy of this satanic illusion in those who have been deluded this way that they would boast and swear that they have the most certain truth. This is how far they are from admitting that they are in the wrong. And though we overcome and convince some, particularly the founders of the sects, on the basis of the Scriptures, we accomplish nothing; for they immediately produce their glosses, with which they evade the Scriptures. Therefore they are not corrected by our admonitions; they are hardened to a greater extent. If I were not learning it today from experience, I would never have believed that the power of the devil is great enough to make a lie so plausible. In addition — something [13] more horrible — when he wants to kill troubled consciences with excessive sorrow, he knows how to transform himself into the figure of Christ so accurately and perfectly that it is impossible for a person in temptation to notice this. Not knowing this, many are driven to the point of despair and commit suicide. For they have been so demented by the devil that they have been convinced that it is most certainly true that they are being tempted and accused, not by the devil but by Christ Himself.

This happened in the year 1527 to the pathetic Dr. Krause, in Halle, who said: "I have denied Christ. Therefore He is now standing in the presence of the Father and accusing me." Taken captive by the tricks of the devil, he had become so convinced of this notion that he would not permit it to be driven out of him by any exhortation or comfort or any divine promises. Thus he despaired and committed suicide most miserably.[14] This was a sheer lie, a bewitchment of the devil, and a fanatical definition of an alien Christ, about which Scripture knows nothing at all. It depicts Christ, not as a judge or a tempter or an accuser but as the Reconciler, the Mediator, the Comforter, the Savior, and the Throne of grace. But being bewitched by the devil, he could not see this then. In opposition to Scripture, therefore, he defined this as the most certain truth: "Christ is accusing you before the Father. He is not standing

---

[13] The Weimar text has *qnod*, which obviously should be *quod*.

[14] On the suicide of Dr. Johannes Krause see the account in Luther's letter to Justus Jonas, December 10, 1527, W, *Briefe*, IV, p. 294.

for you; He is standing against you. Therefore you are damned." This temptation is not human; it is diabolical. And this bewitcher impresses it most powerfully on the heart of a person in temptation. So far as we, who have another belief, are concerned, it is a bitter and obvious lie and a trick of Satan; but so far as those who have been bewitched this way are concerned, it is a truth so certain that nothing is more certain.

Therefore since the devil, who has a thousand dangerous tricks,[15] is able to impress such an obvious and shameful lie on the heart that you would swear a thousand times that it is the most certain truth, one must not be proud but must proceed with fear and humility; and one must call upon Christ our Lord not to permit us to be led into temptation (Matt. 6:13). Smug men, who, after they have heard the Gospel preached once or twice, suppose that they have received a tithe of the Spirit,[16] are finally brought up short in this way; for they do not fear God or give thanks to Him but imagine that they are able not only to keep and defend the doctrine of true godliness but also to stand up in any struggle against the devil, regardless of how arduous it may be. Such men are tools that are ready for the devil to bewitch and to drive to despair.

On the other hand, you must not say: "I am perfect. I cannot fall." But humble yourself, and be afraid, lest you who are standing today fall tomorrow. I am a doctor of theology, and I have already been preaching Christ and fighting against the devil in his false teachers for a number of years; but I have experienced how much difficulty this business has caused me. For I cannot repel Satan as I would like. Nor can I finally grasp Christ as Scripture propounds Him to me, but the devil often suggests a false Christ to me. Thanks be to God, however, for preserving us in the Word, in faith, and in prayer! We know that one should walk in humility and fear in the sight of God and not presume upon our own wisdom, righteousness, doctrine, and courage. One should rely on the power of Christ. When we are weak, He is strong; and through us weaklings He always conquers and triumphs. To Him be glory forever. Amen.

This bewitchment, then, is nothing other than a dementing by

---

[15] The Latin *mille artifex* as a title for the devil is a translation of the familiar German *Tausendkünstler;* cf. *Luther's Works,* 9, p. 189, note 23.

[16] On this concept of first fruits and tithes cf. *Luther's Works,* 3, p. 265, note 36.

the devil, who inserts into the heart a false opinion, one that is opposed to Christ. A bewitched person is one who is taken captive by this opinion. Thus those who are persuaded that they are justified by the works of the Law or by the works of human tradition are bewitched; for this persuasion is directly contrary to faith and to Christ. Paul uses this odious term "bewitch" as an expression of contempt and spite against the false apostles, who were arguing for the doctrine of the Law and of its works with such vehemence. It is as though he were saying: "Alas, what a satanic bewitchment this is! For the mind is corrupted by spiritual witchcraft as the senses are by the physical sort."

That you do not obey the truth?

At first the Galatians had heard and obeyed the truth. Therefore when he says: "Who has bewitched you?" he means that those who were bewitched by the false apostles had now deserted and defected from the truth which they had previously obeyed. But this sounds much harsher, when he says that they do not believe the truth. For by these words he indicates that they have been bewitched and that he wants to break their spell, but that they refuse to recognize or accept this good deed. For it is sure that Paul did not gain all the Galatians; that is, he did not recall all of them from the error of the false apostles to the truth, but the bewitchment still remained in many of them. This is why he uses the vehement words "Who has bewitched you?" It is as though he were saying: "You have been so demented and taken captive by this bewitchment that you cannot obey the truth"; or as though he were saying: "I am afraid that many of you are done for, and that you will never come back to the truth."

Here you hear another encomium on the righteousness that is of the Law or is one's own: It so bewitches men that they cannot obey the truth. The apostles and the early fathers often mentioned this. Thus 1 John 5:16: "There is a sin which is mortal; I do not say that one is to pray for that"; and Heb. 6:4-6: "It is impossible to restore again to repentance those who have once been enlightened, who have tasted the heavenly gift, and have become partakers of the Holy Spirit, and have tasted the goodness of the Word of God and the powers of the age to come, if they then commit apostasy." At first sight these words sound as though some Novatus had spoken them.[17] But the apostles were forced to speak this way on account of the heretics, although they did not, like the Novatians, deny to the lapsed a return through repentance to the communion of the faithful. Today, too, we must speak this way because of the authors and masters of errors and sects, and we must say that such men never return to the truth. Some do indeed return, but only those who have been taken captive by a milder bewitchment, not the leaders and authors of the bewitchment. These must keep the title that Paul attributes to them here, namely, that they neither hear nor endure the truth but are concerned how to resist the truth and how to evade the arguments and passages of Scripture that are cited against them. For they have been taken captive and are persuaded that they have the most certain truth and the purest understanding of Scripture. Anyone who is persuaded of this does not listen, much less yield, to others. Thus I do not listen to anything at all that is contrary to my doctrine; for I am certain and persuaded through the Spirit of Christ that my doctrine of Christian righteousness is the true and certain one.

Before whose eyes Jesus Christ was publicly portrayed.

It was very harsh when Paul had said that the Galatians were so bewitched that they did not obey the truth. But it is even harsher when he adds that Christ Jesus was portrayed before their eyes in such a way that they could have touched Him with their hands, and that they still did not obey the truth. Thus he convicts them on the basis of their own experience. It is as though he were saying: "You have been so bewitched, deceived, and taken captive by the erroneous opinions of the false apostles that you do not obey the truth. And it was useless when I, with great diligence and effort, portrayed and described Christ Jesus publicly before your eyes as crucified among you."

With these words he is referring to his earlier arguments, in which he had said that Christ is a minister of sin to those who want to be justified by the Law, that such men nullify the grace of God, and that for them Christ died to no purpose. In their presence he had urged these arguments more vigorously and had developed them

---

[17] Luther expressed his difficulties with this text in his preface to the Epistle to the Hebrews in his translation of the New Testament; cf. *Luther's Works*, 35, pp. 394—395, notes 45—46. By "Novatus" Luther means the schismatic and martyr Novatian, who died in 257 or 258.

at greater length, as though some painter had been portraying Christ
Jesus as crucified before their very eyes. Now that he is absent, he
recalls this to their memory when he says: "before whose eyes, etc."
It is as though he were saying: "No painter can depict Christ as
accurately to you with his colors as I have depicted Him with my
preaching. And yet you persist in your bewitchment!"

As crucified among you.

"What did I portray, then? Christ Himself. In what way? In
such a way that He was crucified among you." He is using very
harsh words here. Earlier he had said that those who seek righteousness on the basis of the Law nullify the grace of God, and that
for them Christ died to no purpose. Now he adds that such people
even crucify Christ, who had been living and reigning in them. It is
as though he were saying: "Not only have you nullified the grace
of God; not only has Christ died to no purpose for you. But now
He has been most shamefully crucified among you." The Epistle to
the Hebrews speaks the same way in the sixth chapter (6:6): "They
crucify the Son of God on their own account and hold Him up to
contempt."

It should strike terror into a man just to hear the terms "monk"
or "tonsure" or "cowl" or "monastic rule," no matter how much the
papists adore these abominations and boast that they are the height
of religion and sanctity. Thus before the Gospel was revealed, we
were unable to judge otherwise about them; for we had been reared
in human traditions, which obscured Christ and made Him utterly
useless to us. And now we hear Paul say that those who seek to be
justified by the Law of God are not only the deniers and the murderers but the guiltiest crucifiers of Christ. Now if those who seek
to be justified through the righteousness of the Law and through
its works are crucifiers of Christ, what, I ask you, are those who seek
salvation and eternal life through the filth of human righteousness
and the doctrines of demons (1 Tim. 4:1)?

But who would ever have believed or understood that it is
such a horrible and abominable crime to become a "religious,"
as they call it, that is, to become a Mass priest, a monk, or a nun?
Surely no one. Yet they themselves have taught that monasticism
is a new baptism.[18] Can anything be said that is more horrible than

[18] On the notion of monasticism as a second Baptism and its roots in Jerome
cf. *Luther's Works*, 24, p. 128, note 72.

that the kingdom of the papists is the kingdom of those who spit upon and recrucify *Christ, the Son of God?* [19] Christ, who once was crucified and rose again — Him they crucify in themselves and in the church, that is, in the hearts of the faithful. With their rebukes, slanders, and insults they spit at Him; and with their false opinions they pierce Him through, so that He dies most miserably in them. And in His place they erect a beautiful bewitchment, by which men are so demented that they do not acknowledge Christ as the Justifier, Propitiator, and Savior but think of Him as a minister of sin, an accuser, a judge, and a condemner, who must be placated by our works and merits.

From this opinion there later arose the most wicked and noxious doctrine in the entire papacy: "If you want to serve God, to merit the forgiveness of sins and eternal life, and also to help others to reach salvation, enter a monastery, and vow obedience, chastity, and poverty." Taken captive as they were and inflated by this false opinion of their holiness, the monks imagined that they were the only ones in a state and life of perfection, and that the other Christians led an ordinary life because they did not observe chastity, poverty, obedience, etc., but merely were baptized and observed the Ten Commandments. But over and above what the monks had in common with other Christians they also observed works of supererogation and the counsels of Christ.[20] Therefore they hoped that they would have a merit and a place in heaven among the foremost saints, far above the rest of the Christian rabble.

This was really a monstrous illusion of the devil. With it he had demented nearly all people. And the saintlier someone wanted to appear, the more he was taken captive by this bewitchment, that is, by the noxious notion of his own righteousness. This was why we could not at all see Christ as the Mediator and Savior but simply supposed that He was a severe judge, who had to be placated by our works. This was to blaspheme Christ to the utmost and, as Paul said earlier, to nullify the grace of God, to make Christ die to no purpose and not only be killed by us but shamefully crucified. And this is actually what Christ was referring to on the basis of Daniel: "the desolating sacrilege, standing in the holy place" (Matt.

[19] Where we have italics the original has all capital letters.

[20] Cf. *Luther's Works,* 21, p. 4; and Thomas Aquinas, *Summa Theologica,* I—II, Q. 108, Art. 4.

24:15). Therefore every monk and every self-righteous person who seeks the forgiveness of sins and righteousness by his own works or afflictions is a recrucifier of the Christ who lives and reigns — not, of course, in the person of Christ Himself but in his own heart and in the hearts of others. And whoever enters a monastery with the idea that by the observance of the monastic rule he will be justified is entering a den of robbers who recrucify Christ (Matt. 21:13).

Paul uses very grave and severe words here. He does so in order to frighten the Galatians and recall them from the doctrine of the false apostles. It is as though he were saying: "Consider what you have done. Because you want to be justified through the Law, you have crucified Christ again. And I am showing and depicting this before your eyes so clearly that you can see it and touch it. If righteousness comes through the Law, then Christ is a minister of sin and died to no purpose. If this is true, then it certainly follows that Christ has been crucified again in you."

He adds this phrase "in you" purposely, because Christ in His own person is not crucified any more and does not die any more (Rom. 6:9); but He dies in us when we, having rejected pure doctrine, grace, faith, and the free forgiveness of sins, seek to be justified either through self-chosen works or through works commanded in the Law. Then Christ is crucified in us. As I have said earlier in greater detail, this false and wicked idea of seeking to be justified on the basis of the Law or of works is nothing but the illusion and bewitchment of the devil, by which men are so demented that they do not recognize the blessing of Christ at all. In all their life they do nothing but deny the Lord, who has purchased them with His blood (2 Peter 2:1) and in whose name they were baptized, and even crucify Him again in themselves. Therefore let anyone who is seriously concerned about godliness flee this Babylon as quickly as possible, and let him be horrified at the very hearing of the name of the papacy. For its wickedness and abomination are so great that no one can describe them in words or evaluate them except with spiritual eyes.

Paul emphasizes these two arguments and impresses them on the Galatians very diligently: first, that they have been taken captive and bewitched by the devil in such a way that they do not listen to the truth that is being portrayed most clearly before their eyes; secondly, that they crucify Christ again in themselves. These words seem to be simple and free of all eloquence, but they are so great

that they surpass all human eloquence. Only in the Spirit, therefore, is it comprehensible how great an evil it is to want to be justified through the righteousness of the Law or through one's own
righteousness. As Paul says here, it means being bewitched by the
devil and becoming disobedient to the truth and a recrucifier of
Christ. What a lovely encomium of the righteousness of the Law
or of one's own righteousness!

Therefore the apostle is aflame with the greatest possible zeal;
and he seriously denounces, or rather condemns, the righteousness
of the Law and of works, and he accuses it of the crime of crucifying
the Son of God again. For he intends to indict the notion of one's
own righteousness as vigorously and as sharply as is necessary. It
cannot be denounced and condemned enough — so dangerous a thing
it is, so easy it is for Lucifer to fall on account of it, so irreparable
is the damage caused by it. Therefore he uses such sharp words
against it that he does not spare even the Law of God but refers
to it all, and in such a way that he seems to be condemning it. He
prosecutes it with such sharpness because he is constrained by a very
great urgency. Although the Law is holy, righteous, and good, it
must become, as it were, the mask of a hypocrite who wants to be
justified by works. Now he aims an argument at them that they cannot deny, one based on experience, and says:

2. *Let me ask you only this: Did you receive the Spirit by works of
the Law, or by hearing with faith?*

"If I had nothing else against you," he says, "I would seize upon
your own experience." He speaks these words with an indignant
mind. It is as though he were saying: "All right. Answer me, your
pupil; for you have suddenly become so learned that you are now
my masters and teachers. Did you receive the Spirit from the works
of the Law or from the preaching of the Gospel?" With this argument he so convicts them that they have nothing they can say
against it. For their own obvious and manifest experience was contradicting them and saying that they had received the Spirit, not
from the works of the Law but from the preaching of the Gospel.

Here again I admonish you that Paul is speaking not only about
the Ceremonial Law but about the entire Law. For he is arguing
from a sufficient division.[21] If he were speaking only about the Cere-

---

[21] See p. 138, note 56.

monial Law, there would not be a sufficient division. It is a dilemma consisting of two parts, one of which must necessarily be true and the other false. Thus: "You received the Spirit either from the Law or from the hearing of faith. If it was by the Law, then it was not by the hearing of faith; if it was by the hearing of faith, then it was not by the Law. There can be no middle ground. For whatever is not the Holy Spirit or hearing with faith is clearly the Law." We are dealing here with the issue of justification. But there are only two ways to justification: either the Word of the Gospel or the Law. Therefore the Law is being taken universally here, as something completely diverse and distinct from the Gospel. But it is not only the Ceremonial Law that is distinct from the Gospel; the Decalog, too, is distinct from it. Therefore Paul is dealing here with the Law as a whole.

Accordingly, Paul is arguing from a sufficient division in this way: "Tell me," he says, "did you receive the Holy Spirit through the Law or through the preaching of the Gospel? Now answer. You cannot say 'through the Law,' because as long as you were under the Law and were doing its works, you never received the Holy Spirit. You taught and heard the Law of Moses every Sabbath. But it was not experienced or seen that the Holy Spirit was ever given to anyone, whether teacher or pupil, through the teaching of the Law. Besides, you not only taught and heard the Law; but with great effort and labor you endeavored to carry it out by works. On this basis above all you should have received the Holy Spirit if He had been granted through the Law, since you were not only teachers and pupils of the Law but doers of it as well (James 1:22). Yet you cannot show that this ever happened. But after the Gospel had come, and before you had performed any work or fruit of the Gospel, you immediately received the Holy Spirit, merely by hearing with faith." As Luke testifies in Acts (10:44), when the proclamation of Peter and Paul merely sounded, the Holy Spirit came upon those who heard the Word, and they received various gifts through Him, so that they spoke with new tongues.

"Therefore it is obvious that the Holy Spirit was granted to you solely by your hearing with faith, before you did good works or produced any fruit of the Gospel. On the other hand, even when the Law was performed, it never brought the Holy Spirit — much less when it was merely heard. Therefore not only the hearing of the Law but also the effort of the zeal with which you tried to carry out the Law with your works is useless. Therefore even though some one attempts everything — that is, even though he has zeal for God and bends every effort to be saved through the Law and exercises himself day and night in the righteousness of the Law — still he is laboring and wearing himself out in vain. For those who do not know the righteousness of God and try to establish their own righteousness, as Paul says elsewhere (Rom. 10:3), do not submit to God's righteousness. Again: "Israel, who pursued the righteousness which is based on Law, did not succeed in fulfilling that Law" (Rom. 9:31). Here Paul is speaking of the manifestation of the Spirit in the primitive church. The Holy Spirit descended in a visible form upon believers. By this sign He testified clearly that He was present in the proclamation of the apostles. He also testified that those who heard the Word of faith from the apostles were accounted righteous in the sight of God, for otherwise He would not have descended upon them.

Therefore this powerful argument must be diligently considered. It is repeated often in the Book of Acts, which was written to substantiate this argument. That entire book treats of nothing else than that the Holy Spirit is not given through the Law but is given through the hearing of the Gospel. For when Peter preached, the Holy Spirit immediately fell upon all those who heard the Word. In one day three thousand who heard Peter's proclamation believed and received the gift of the Holy Spirit (Acts 2:41). Thus Cornelius received the Holy Spirit, though not on the basis of the alms he gave; but when Peter had opened his mouth and was still speaking, the Holy Spirit fell upon all those who were listening to the Word with Cornelius (Acts 10:44). These are clear arguments from experience, and divine works that are infallible.

Luke also writes about Paul in the fifteenth chapter of Acts. Here he says that when Paul had been preaching the Gospel together with Barnabas among the Gentiles and had returned to Jerusalem, he attacked the Pharisees and the pupils of the apostles, who insisted on circumcision and the observance of the Law as necessary for salvation. He curbed them in such a way that the entire church was astonished at the narrative recited by him and Barnabas, when it had heard that God had worked so many great signs and miracles through them among the Gentiles. Those who were zealous for the Law were amazed how it was possible that uncircumcised Gentiles, who did not observe the Law and its works and who did not have the righteousness of the Law, could still come to the grace of being justified and of receiving the Holy Spirit, just as the circumcised Jews did. Here Paul and Barnabas cited nothing except their evident experience, which so convinced the others that they could not contradict them. In this way Sergius Paulus, the proconsul (Acts 13:6-12), and all the cities, regions, and kingdoms in which the apostles preached came to believe, without the Law or works, solely by the hearing of faith.

Therefore in the entire Book of Acts, taken as a whole, nothing is discussed except that Jews as well as Gentiles, righteous men as well as sinners, are to be justified solely by faith in Christ Jesus, without Law or works. This is indicated both by the sermons of Peter, Paul, Stephen, Philip, and others, and by the examples of the Gentiles and the Jews. For just as through the Gospel God gave the Holy Spirit to Gentiles who lived without the Law, so He gave the Holy Spirit also to the Jews, not through the Law or through the worship and sacrifices commanded in the Law but solely through the proclamation of faith. If the Law had been able to justify, and if the righteousness of the Law had been necessary for salvation, then certainly the Holy Spirit would not have been granted to the Gentiles, who did not observe the Law. But evident experience testifies that the Spirit was granted to those without the Law; and the apostles, Peter, Paul, Barnabas, and others saw this. Therefore the Law does not justify; but only faith in Christ, which the Gospel proclaims, does so.

All this must be diligently observed because of our opponents, who do not observe what is being discussed in the Acts of the Apostles. I used to read this book, but I did not understand anything at all in it. Therefore when you hear or read the term "Gentiles" in Acts or anywhere else in the Scriptures, you should know that it is not to be taken in the natural sense but must be taken in a theological sense for those who are without the Law and are not under the Law, as the Jews were; thus it was said earlier in the second chapter (Gal. 2:15): "We who are Jews by birth and not Gentile sinners." Therefore for the Gentiles to be justified by faith is nothing else than that men who do not perform the Law and its works, who are not circumcised and who do not perform sacrifices, are justified and receive the Holy Spirit. How? Not through the Law and its works — for they do not have the Law — but gratis and without the intervention of anything else except the hearing of the Gospel.

Thus Cornelius and his friends whom he had called to his house do not do anything, nor do they look at any preceding works; and yet as many as are present receive the Holy Spirit. Peter alone is speaking. They themselves are sitting and not doing anything. They are not thinking about the Law; much less are they keeping it. They are not sacrificing; they are not concerned about undergoing circumcision. They are paying attention only to the words of Peter. By his proclamation he brought the Holy Spirit into their hearts, and visibly at that; for they spoke with tongues and praised God.

But here someone could carp and say: "Who knows whether it really was the Holy Spirit?" Well, let him carp. Surely when the Holy Spirit bears witness in this way, He is not lying but is indicating by this that He regards the Gentiles as righteous and that He justifies them by no other means than solely by the message of the Gospel or by the hearing of faith in Christ.

It is also evident in Acts how much the Jews were amazed at this unheard-of thing. "For the believers from among the circumcised who came with Peter to Caesarea were amazed, because the gift of the Holy Spirit had been poured out even on the Gentiles in the house of Cornelius" (Acts 10:45). Also those who were in Jerusalem criticized Peter for going to uncircumcised men and eating with them (Acts 11:3). But when they had heard the story told by Peter in the sequence in which it had happened with Cornelius, they were amazed, glorified God, and said: "Then to the Gentiles also God has granted salvation" (Acts 11:18).

The statement and report that God was giving salvation also to the Gentiles was not only intolerable at first, but it gave the greatest possible offense to the believing Jews, which they could not easily overcome. For they had this prerogative over all other nations, that they were the people of God. To them belonged the sonship, the glory, the worship, etc. (Rom. 9:4). In addition, they exerted themselves with the greatest effort in the righteousness of the Law; they labored all day long; they bore the burden of the day and the scorching heat (Matt. 20:12). They also had promises about the observance of the Law. Therefore they could not help murmuring against the Gentiles and saying: "Look, the Gentiles are coming suddenly, without any heat or burden. Nevertheless, without labor they have the same righteousness and the same Holy Spirit that we were unable to obtain by labor and through the burden of the day and the scorching heat. Yes, they have labored, but only for one hour; and this labor refreshed them more than it wearied them. Then why did God torture us with the Law if it was of no use for obtaining righteousness? He is now preferring the Gentiles to us, who have been burdened for a long time with the yoke of the Law. For we, who are the people of God, are being vexed all the day long (Ps. 44:22). And they are being made equal with us, they who are not the people of God, do not have the Law, and have never done anything good!"

Therefore this council of the apostles was convoked with the greatest urgency at Jerusalem, in order that the minds of the Jews might be set at ease; for although they believed in Christ, the opinion that the Law of Moses had to be observed was rooted very firmly in their hearts. Then Peter, proceeding from his own experience, opposed himself to them and said (Acts 11:17): "If God gave the same gift to them as He gave to us when we believed in the Lord Jesus Christ, who was I that I could withstand God?" And again (Acts 15:8-10): "God who knows the heart bore witness to them, giving them the Holy Spirit just as He did to us; and He made no distinction between us and them but cleansed their hearts by faith. Now therefore why do you make trial of God by putting a yoke upon the necks of the disciples which neither our fathers nor we have been able to bear?" With these words Peter overturns the entire Law at once. It is as though he were saying: "We do not want to observe the Law, because we cannot. But through the grace of our Lord Jesus Christ we believe that we are saved, just as they are." Thus here Peter relies completely on this argument, that God has granted the same grace to the Gentiles as to the Jews. It is as though he were to say: "My brethren, we do not have to observe the Law. For when I was preaching to Cornelius, I learned through my own experience that without the Law the Holy Spirit was granted to the Gentiles, solely through hearing with faith. Therefore they are by no means to be burdened with the Law, which neither we nor our fathers were able to bear. Accordingly, you, too, should reject this idea, that salvation comes through the Law." And the Jews who believed did this gradually; but the wicked ones, who were even more offended by this proclamation, were finally hardened completely.

Thus in Acts you will find the comments, the experiences, and the sermons of the apostles, as well as examples in support of this argument against the stubborn notion of the righteousness of the Law. For this reason we ought to love this book more and read it more diligently; for it contains very firm testimonies that can comfort and sustain us against the papists, who are our Jews and whose abominations and pretenses we attack and condemn by our doctrine in order that we may make clear the blessings and the glory of Christ. Although they have nothing firm to present against us — for the Jews could argue against the apostles that they had received the Law and their entire system of worship from God — they try to defend their wicked traditions and abominations with no less stubbornness than did the Jews to defend their Law, which they had received from God. Above all, they insist that they are sitting in the place of bishops, and that they have the authority to govern the churches. But they are doing this in order to bring us into slavery and to force us to say that we are justified not by faith alone but by "faith formed by love." [22] But we set against them the Book of Acts, that they may read it and consider the history contained in it. They will discover that the summary and the argument of this book is: We are justified solely by faith in Christ, without works; and the Holy Spirit is granted solely by hearing the message of the Gospel with faith, not by the message of the Law or by the works of the Law.

Therefore we teach as follows: "Man, although you may fast, give alms, honor your parents, obey the magistrate, be subject to the master of the house, etc., you are not justified through this. This message of the Law, 'Honor your parents' (Ex. 20:12), does not justify either when it is heard or when it is performed. Then what does justify? Hearing the voice of the Bridegroom, hearing the proclamation of faith — when this is heard, it justifies. Why? Because it brings the Holy Spirit who justifies."

From this it is sufficiently evident what the distinction is between the Law and the Gospel. The Law never brings the Holy Spirit; therefore it does not justify, because it only teaches what we ought to do. But the Gospel does bring the Holy Spirit, because it teaches what we ought to receive. Therefore the Law and the Gospel are two altogether contrary doctrines. Accordingly, to put righteousness into the Law is simply to conflict with the Gospel. For the Law is a taskmaster; it demands that we work and that we give. In short, it wants to have something from us. The Gospel, on the contrary, does not demand; it grants freely; it commands us to hold out our hands and to receive what is being offered. Now demanding and granting, receiving and offering, are exact opposites and cannot exist together. For that which is granted, I receive; but that which I grant,

---

[22] See p. 88, note 7.

I do not receive but offer to someone else. Therefore if the Gospel is a gift and offers a gift, it does not demand anything. On the other hand, the Law does not grant anything; it makes demands on us, and impossible ones at that.

Here our opponents cite the example of Cornelius against us. Both the Master of the *Sentences* and Erasmus, in his *Diatribe,* discuss him.[23] They say: "As Luke testifies, Cornelius was a good man, righteous, one who feared God, gave many alms to the people, and prayed to God continually. Therefore he merited the forgiveness of sins and the sending of the Holy Spirit 'by congruity.'" I reply: Cornelius was a Gentile — something that our opponents cannot deny, for the words that Peter uses in Acts 10:28 clearly testify to this. "You know," he says, "how unlawful it is for a Jew to visit a Gentile." Therefore he was a Gentile. He was not circumcised, did not observe the Law, and did not even think about the Law, since it did not pertain to him. Yet he is justified and receives the Holy Spirit. And, as I have said, this argument — that the Law neither helps nor contributes to righteousness — is presented throughout the whole Book of Acts.

Let this suffice, then, to defend the doctrine of justification: Cornelius was a Gentile. He was not circumcised and did not observe the Law; therefore he was not justified by the Law; he was justified by hearing with faith. Hence God does justify without the Law. And, as a consequence, the Law does not accomplish anything toward righteousness. For otherwise God would have granted the Holy Spirit only to the Jews, who had the Law and kept it, rather than to the Gentiles, who did not have the Law and certainly did not keep it. But the very opposite happened, for the Holy Spirit was granted to those who did not have the Law. Therefore manifest experience testifies that the Holy Spirit is granted to those who do not keep the Law. Consequently, righteousness does not come from the Law. In this way an answer is provided to the objections of our opponents, who do not understand the true meaning of justification.

Here again our opponents raise an objection and say: "All right, so Cornelius was a Gentile and did not receive the Holy Spirit through the Law. Nevertheless, since the text clearly says that he was a righteous man who feared God, gave alms, etc., it is probable that through

[23] Peter Lombard, *Sententiarum libri quatuor,* Book III, Dist. 25, par. 4, *Patrologia, Series Latina,* CXCII, 810; on Erasmus' use of this reference from Acts 10 cf. Luther, *The Bondage of the Will* (W, XVIII, 739).

all this he merited receiving the Holy Spirit." I reply: Cornelius was a righteous and holy man in accordance with the Old Testament on account of his faith in the coming Christ, just as all the patriarchs, prophets, and devout kings in the Old Testament were righteous, having received the Holy Spirit secretly on account of their faith in the coming Christ. But the sophists do not make a distinction between faith in the coming Christ and faith in the Christ who has already come. Therefore if Cornelius had died before Christ was revealed, he still would not have been damned; for he had the faith of the patriarchs, who were saved solely by faith in the Christ to come (Acts 15:11). Therefore he remained a Gentile, uncircumcised, without the Law. Nevertheless, by faith in the coming Messiah he worshiped the same God as the patriarchs. But because the Messiah had come, it was necessary now that He be shown to him by the apostle Peter, not as One who was still to be expected but as One who had already come.

It is necessary beyond measure to know this doctrine about faith in the Christ to be revealed and in the Christ already revealed — if I may add this admonition in passing. For now that Christ has been revealed, we cannot be saved by faith in the coming Christ; but we are obliged to believe that He has already come, has fulfilled everything, and has abrogated the Law. Therefore it was necessary also that Cornelius be imbued with a new faith, namely, that Christ had already come, although he had previously believed that He was still to come. Thus faith yields to faith, "from faith to faith" (Rom. 1:17).

Therefore the sophists err when they say that Cornelius achieved grace and the sending of the Holy Spirit by attaining a work "of congruity" through the moral and natural deeds of reason. For to be a righteous man and to fear God are attributes, not of a Gentile or a natural man but of a spiritual man, who already has faith. For unless he believed in God and feared God, he would not hope that he would obtain anything from Him by prayer. Therefore Cornelius is first commended by Luke for his righteousness and his fear of God, and only then is he commended for his works and alms. They do not consider this. No, they grab only this little statement, that he gave alms to the poor; and they hold fast to it. For this seems to support them in their idea of the merit of congruity. But first the person or the tree must be commended, then his works or his fruits. Cornelius is a good tree because he is righteous and fears God. Therefore he produces good fruit, gives alms, and calls upon God. And these fruits are pleasing to God on account of faith. This is why the angel commends him for his faith in the coming Christ and transfers him from this faith to the faith in the Christ who had already been disclosed; for he says (Acts 10:5): "Bring one Simon. He will tell you, etc." Therefore just as Cornelius was without the Law before Christ had been revealed, so after Christ was revealed, he did not receive either the Law or circumcision. And just as he did not observe the Law previously, so he did not observe it afterwards either. Consequently, this argument stands very firmly: Cornelius was justified without the Law; therefore the Law does not justify.

In the same way Naaman the Syrian was no doubt a good and devout man and had a correct idea of God. And although he was a Gentile and did not belong to the kingdom of Moses, which was flourishing at that time, still his flesh was purified, the God of Israel was revealed to him, and he received the Holy Spirit. For this [24] is what he says (2 Kings 5:15): "Behold, I know that there is no God in all the earth but in Israel." He does nothing whatever; he does not observe the Law; he is not circumcised. He prays only that as much earth may be given to him as two mules can carry. For he says to the prophet Elisha (2 Kings 5:17-18): "Henceforth your servant will not offer burnt offering or sacrifice to any god but the Lord. In this matter may the Lord pardon your servant: When my master goes into the house of Rimmon to worship there, leaning on my arm, when I bow myself in the house of Rimmon." And the prophet says to him (2 Kings 5:19): "Go in peace." When a Jew hears this, he goes to pieces with rage and says: "Do you mean that the Gentile is to be justified even though he has not observed the Law, and that he is to be compared with us who are circumcised?"

Much earlier, therefore, while the kingdom of Moses was still standing and flourishing, God indicated that He justified men without the Law, just as He certainly justified many kings in Egypt and in Babylon, also Job, and other Oriental peoples. And then Nineveh, that great city, was justified and received from God the promise of salvation that it would not be destroyed. How? Not because it heard and kept the Law, but because it believed the Word of God that Jonah the prophet was preaching. For these are the words of the prophet (Jonah 4:5): "And the people of Nineveh believed God; they proclaimed a fast, and put on sackcloth"; that is, they did penance. Our opponents stoutly leap over this "believed," and yet

---

[24] The Weimar text has *Si*, but we have read *Sic*.

[W, XL, 341, 342]

the whole force of the statement is in this word. You do not read in the prophecy of Jonah: "And the people of Nineveh accepted the Law of Moses, were circumcised, sacrificed, and performed all the works of the Law." No, you read: "Believing, they did penance in sackcloth and ashes."

This happened before Christ appeared, when faith in the coming Christ still prevailed. Therefore if the Gentiles were justified then without the Law and secretly received the Holy Spirit while the regime of the Law was still standing, why should the Law be required for righteousness at the present time, when it has been abrogated, now that Christ has appeared? Thus this is a most powerful argument — an argument drawn from the experience of the Galatians: "Did you receive, etc.?" For they are forced to admit that they had heard nothing about the Holy Spirit before Paul's preaching, but that when he preached the Gospel, they had received the Spirit.

Today we are forced to admit the same thing, since we have been convinced by the testimony of our own conscience, namely, that the Spirit is not given through the Law but is given through hearing with faith. For previously, under the papacy, many have tried with great labor and effort to observe the Law, the statutes or decrees of the fathers, and the traditions of the pope. And some so weakened and damaged their bodies with severe and constant exercises in vigils, fasts, and prayers [25] that finally they were not fit to do anything. Yet all they accomplished by this performance was to torment themselves miserably. They could never arrive at the point of having a tranquil conscience and peace in Christ. On the contrary, they were perpetually in doubt concerning God's will toward them. But now, since the Gospel teaches that the Law and works do not justify, but that faith in Christ does, knowledge, a sure understanding, a joyful conscience, and a true judgment about every way of life and about everything else follow. Now the believer can easily judge what he could not judge before: that the papacy, with all its religious orders and traditions, is wicked. For such great blindness used to prevail in the world that we supposed that the works which men had invented not only without but against the commandment of God were much better than those which a magistrate, the head of a household, a teacher, a child, a servant, etc., did in accordance with God's command.

[25] The Weimar text has *orationem*, but we have read *orationum*.

[W, XL, 342, 343]

Surely we should have learned from the Word of God that the religious orders of the papists, which alone they call holy, are wicked, since there exists no commandment of God or testimony in Sacred Scripture about them; and, on the other hand, that other ways of life, which do have the Word and commandment of God, are holy and are divinely instituted. But at that time we were immersed in such horrible darkness that we could not judge correctly about anything. Now that the light of the Gospel is gleaming, all the ways of life in the world are under our certain and infallible judgment. On the basis of the Word of God we pronounce the sure conviction that the way of life of a servant, which is extremely vile in the sight of the world, is far more acceptable to God than all the orders of monks. For God approves, commends, and adorns the status of servants with His Word, but not that of the monks. Therefore this argument, which is based on experience, should have the greatest validity also among us. For although various people performed many difficult deeds of one sort or another under the papacy, they could never be certain of the will of God toward them but were always in doubt. They could never attain to the knowledge of God, of themselves, and of their vocation; they never felt the testimony of the Spirit in their hearts. But now that the truth of the Gospel is shining, they receive most certain instruction about all these things solely through hearing with faith.

I am not speaking at such great length without reason. It seems to be exceedingly inadequate to say that the Holy Spirit is granted solely through hearing with faith and that nothing at all is demanded of us but that we refrain from all our works and just listen to the Gospel. The human heart neither understands nor believes that such a great prize as the Holy Spirit can be granted solely through hearing with faith; but it thinks this way: "The forgiveness of sins, deliverance from sin and death, the granting of the Holy Spirit, of righteousness, and of eternal life — this is all something important. Therefore you must do something great to obtain these inestimable gifts." The devil approves of this opinion and magnifies it in the heart. Therefore when reason hears: "You cannot do anything to obtain the forgiveness of sins except only to listen to the Word of God," it immediately exclaims: "Oh, no! You are making the forgiveness of sins too meager and contemptible!" Thus the greatness of the gift is responsible for our not accepting it. Because such a great treasure is being offered freely, it is despised.

But we must learn by all means that forgiveness of sins, Christ, and the Holy Spirit are granted — and granted freely — only when we hear with faith. Even our huge sins and demerits do not stand in the way. We must not consider how great the thing is that is being given and how unworthy we are; otherwise the greatness both of the thing and of our unworthiness will frighten us away. But we must bear in mind that it pleases God to grant this inexpressible gift to us freely — to us who are unworthy. As Christ says in Luke 12:32: "Fear not, little flock, for it is your Father's good pleasure to give you [*give*, He says] the kingdom." To whom? To you unworthy ones, who are His little flock. Therefore if I am little and the thing that is being given to me is great — in fact, the greatest there is — I must think that the One who is giving it to me is also great and that He alone is great. If He is offering it and wants to give it, I do not consider my own sin and unworthiness. No, I consider the fatherly will that He who is giving it has toward me. I accept the greatness of the gift with joy; and I am happy and grateful for such an inestimable gift granted to me in my unworthiness, freely and by hearing with faith.

But, as I have said, reason is offended and says: "When you teach men to do nothing at all to obtain such an immense gift except to listen to the Word, this seems to verge on a great contempt for grace and to make men smug, lazy, and sleepy, so that they lose their grip and do not do any good works at all. Therefore it is not good to preach this; nor is it true. Men must be urged to labor, sweat, and exert themselves toward righteousness; then they will obtain this gift." In former times the Pelagians made the same objection to the Christians.[26] But listen to Paul, who says here: "Not by your own labor and sweat or by the works of the Law but by hearing with faith you have received the Holy Spirit." Or listen to Christ Himself, who gives the following answer to Martha when she is deeply concerned and finds it almost unbearable that her sister Mary is sitting at Jesus' feet, listening to His words, and leaving her to serve alone. "Martha," He says (Luke 10:41-42), "you are anxious and troubled about many things; one thing is needful. Mary has chosen the good portion, which shall not be taken away from her." Therefore a man becomes a Christian, not by working but by listening. And so anyone who wants to exert himself toward righteousness

---

[26] Luther may be thinking of a passage like Augustine, *De correptione et gratia*, IV, 6.

must first exert himself in listening to the Gospel. Now when he has heard and accepted this, let him joyfully give thanks to God, and then let him exert himself in good works that are commanded in the Law; thus the Law and works will follow hearing with faith. Then he will be able to walk safely in the light that is Christ; to be certain about choosing and doing works that are not hypocritical but truly good, pleasing to God, and commanded by Him; and to reject all the mummery of self-chosen works.

Our opponents regard faith as a matter altogether inconsequential and of no value. But I am experiencing how difficult and arduous a matter it is. So are all those who seriously embrace it with me. It is easy to say that the Spirit is received solely by hearing with faith; but it is not so easy to hear, accept, believe, and keep as it is to speak of it. Therefore if you hear from me that Christ is the Lamb of God, sacrificed for your sins, see that you really listen to this. Paul purposely calls it "the hearing of faith," not "the Word of faith," although there is not much difference. He means a Word that you believe when you hear it, so that the Word is not only the sound of my voice but is something that is heard by you, penetrates into your heart, and is believed by you. Then it is truly hearing with faith, through which you receive the Holy Spirit; and after He has been received, you will also mortify your flesh.

Godly people experience how willing they are to hold to the Word with a full faith when it has been heard, and how willing they are to eradicate their opinion about the Law and about their own righteousness; but in their flesh they feel a struggle that resists the Spirit with might and main. Reason and the flesh simply want to work together. This notion, "One must be circumcised and observe the Law," cannot be completely banished from us; but it remains in the hearts of all godly people. Therefore there is in godly people a perpetual struggle between the hearing of faith and the works of the Law, because the conscience is always murmuring and thinking that when righteousness, the Holy Spirit, and eternal salvation are promised solely on the basis of hearing with faith, this is too easy a way. But try it in earnest, and experience for yourself how easy it is to listen to the Word of faith! Of course, He who is granting this is great, and He grants great things willingly and unreservedly, without reproach to anyone. But your capacity to understand is limited, and your faith is weak, creating such a struggle for you that you cannot accept the gift when it is offered. Just let your conscience murmur, and let this "one must" keep on recurring. But endure it for a while and hold your ground until you conquer this "one must." Thus, as faith gradually increases, that opinion about the righteousness of the Law will decrease. But this cannot be done without a great conflict.

3. *Are you so foolish? Having begun with the Spirit, are you now being ended with the flesh?*

Now that this argument has been presented, namely, that the Spirit is granted through hearing with faith, not through the works of the Law, Paul begins to exhort the Galatians and to deter them from a twofold danger or loss. He says: "Are you so foolish or senseless that, having begun with the Spirit, you are now being ended with the flesh?" This is the first danger. The second is (v. 4): "Did you experience so many things in vain?" These are rhetorical devices: on the one hand, to deter someone from danger and loss, and, on the other hand, to persuade him on the basis of what is useful, honorable, and easy. Therefore he says: "Having begun with the Spirit." That is: "Your religion was begun and undertaken in a very beautiful manner." Or, as he says later (Gal. 5:7): "You were running well." What is going on? "Now you want to be ended with the flesh. Indeed, now you are being ended with the flesh."

Here Paul is opposing the Spirit and the flesh. By "flesh" he does not mean sexual lust, animal passions, or the sensual appetite, because in this passage he is not discussing sexual lust or other desires of the flesh. No, he is discussing the forgiveness of sins, the justification of the conscience, the attainment of righteousness in the sight of God, and liberation from the Law, sin, and death. And yet he says here that after they have forsaken the Spirit, they are now being ended with the flesh. Thus "flesh" is the very righteousness and wisdom of the flesh and the judgment of reason, which wants to be justified through the Law. Therefore whatever is best and most outstanding in man Paul calls "flesh," namely, the highest wisdom of reason and the very righteousness of the Law.

This passage must be considered because of our slanderers, the papists, who twist it against us and say that under the papacy we began with the Spirit, but that now we have taken wives and are being ended with the flesh.[27] As though celibacy or not having

[27] It will be recalled that even Philip Melanchthon expressed ambivalent feelings about Luther's marriage in 1525.

a wife were a spiritual life, and as though it were no impediment to
the spiritual life if someone is not satisfied with one harlot but has
several! They are insane men who do not understand what the Spirit
or the flesh is. The Spirit is whatever is done in us through the
Spirit; the flesh is whatever is done in us in accordance with the
flesh and apart from the Spirit. Therefore all the duties of Christians
— such as loving one's wife, rearing one's children, governing one's
family, honoring one's parents, obeying the magistrate, etc., which
they regard as secular and fleshly — are fruits of the Spirit. These
blind men do not distinguish between vices and the things that are
good creatures of God.

Paul's statement that the Galatians "have begun with the Spirit"
should also be considered. Therefore he ought to have continued in
the active voice: "You now end with the flesh." He does not do this,
but he says in the passive voice: "You are being ended with the
flesh." [28] Therefore the righteousness of the Law, which Paul calls
"the flesh" here, is so far from justifying that those who defect to it
after receiving the Spirit through the hearing of faith are ended by it;
that is, they are finished and completely destroyed. Therefore those
who teach that the Law should be performed with the purpose that
men might be justified through it are doing the greatest possible
damage to consciences while they claim to be counseling them, and
they condemn them while they claim to be justifying them. Paul is
always looking obliquely at the false apostles. For they were insisting
on the Law. They were saying: "Mere faith in Christ does not take
away sin, placate the wrath of God, or justify. Therefore if you want
to obtain these benefits, you must not only believe in Christ; but
in addition you must observe the Law, be circumcised, keep the
feasts, perform sacrifices, etc. If you do this, you will be free from
sin, the wrath of God, etc." "On the contrary," Paul says, "by this
very action you establish unrighteousness, provoke the wrath of God,
add sin to sin, fall from grace and nullify it, extinguish the Spirit,
and are ended with the flesh along with your disciples." This is the
first danger from which he deters the Galatians, namely, that if they
seek to be justified through the Law, they will lose the Spirit and
will destroy the best sort of beginning by the worst sort of finish.

The second danger or loss is: "Did you experience so many things
in vain?" It is as though he were saying: "Do not consider only how

[28] The Latin version has *consummamini*.

beautifully you began and how miserably you have lost your good beginning and the course you had begun so well; or how you have defected from the first fruits of the Spirit by relapsing into the ministry of sin and death and into the sorrowful and miserable slavery of the Law. But consider also this, that you have suffered many things for the sake of the Gospel and of Christ, namely, the robbery of your possessions, insults and slanders, and danger to both your bodies and your lives. Everything was running along and succeeding beautifully with you. Your doctrine was correct, and your lives were holy; with patience you suffered many evils for the name of Christ. But now both your doctrine and your faith are lost, both your acting and your suffering, both the Spirit and His fruits in you."

From this it is abundantly clear what harm is caused by a righteousness that comes from the Law or is one's own, namely, that those who put their trust in it immediately lose inestimable possessions. It is something truly pathetic for someone so quickly and easily to lose such glory and assurance of conscience in the sight of God, or to undergo so many arduous sufferings and dangers to his possessions, wife, children, body and life, and yet to undergo all this in vain and to no purpose. On the basis of these two topics someone could write an encomium of the righteousness that comes from the Law or from oneself and develop it at great length by dwelling on each item individually. He could tell what Spirit it was with whom they had begun, and the sufferings they had undergone for the sake of Christ — which these were and how great and how many. But no rhetoric can describe these things, for what Paul is discussing here is something enormous: the glory of God; victory over the world, the flesh, and the devil; righteousness; eternal life; and, on the other hand, sin, despair, eternal death, and hell. And yet in a moment we lose these inestimable gifts and acquire these horrible and unceasing evils. The authors of all this are the false teachers, when they transfer us from the truth of the Gospel to erroneous doctrine. They do this not only very easily but also with a great pretext of piety.

If it really is in vain.

This is a correction by means of which Paul softens his earlier rebuke, which had been a little harsh. He does this as an apostle, so as not to terrify the Galatians unduly. He does indeed scold them, but in such a way that he always pours in oil, so as not to drive them to despair.

That is why he says: *"If it really is*[29] in vain."* It is as though he were saying: "Nevertheless, I have not altogether discarded hope for you. But if you want to desert the Spirit and to end with the flesh, that is, to follow the righteousness of the Law as you have begun to do, then you should know that all your glory and confidence in God is empty and that all your sufferings are useless. It is my duty to speak with you a little harshly about this, to present the case vigorously, and to scold you sharply, especially since the importance of the issue demands it; otherwise you may think that it matters not at all or very little if you reject Paul's doctrine and hear or accept another. Still I do not cut off all hope from you, if you will only return to your senses. For children who are sick, weak, and full of sores are not to be rejected but must be cared for and cherished even more diligently than those who are healthy." Thus Paul, as an expert physician, transfers nearly all the blame to the false apostles, the authors of this dreadful disease; and, on the other hand, he treats the Galatians very gently, in order to heal them by this mildness. According to Paul's example, we, too, should scold those who are weak, and cure and bear their disease in such a way that we comfort them meanwhile; for if they are dealt with too harshly by us, they will despair.

5. *Does He who supplies the Spirit to you and works powerful deeds among you do so by works of the Law or by hearing with faith?*

This argument, which is based on the experience of the Galatians, so delights the apostle that, after scolding them and deterring them from a double danger, he now repeats the argument; and he does so with an addition: *"He who* supplies, etc." That is: "Not only have you received the Spirit by hearing with faith, but everything that you have known and done you have by hearing with faith." It is as though he were saying: "It was not enough that God gave you the Spirit once. But the same God has always abundantly supplied and increased the gifts of the Spirit, so that when you have once received the Spirit, He might always grow and be more efficacious in you."

From this it is evident that the Galatians had performed miracles or had at least produced powerful deeds, that is, the fruits of faith

[29] In this paragraph and the next, as previously (cf. p. 200, note 19), we have used italics where the original uses capitals.

which the true disciples of the Gospel usually produce. For the apostle says elsewhere that the kingdom of God does not consist in talk but consists in power (1 Cor. 4:20). Now power means not only to be able to talk about the kingdom of God but also in fact to show that God is efficacious in us through His Spirit. Thus he says of himself earlier, in the second chapter (Gal. 2:8): "He who worked through Peter for the mission to the circumcised worked through me also for the Gentiles."

Therefore when a preacher preaches in such a way that the Word is not frustrated in producing fruit but is efficacious in the hearers — that is, when faith, hope, love, patience, etc., follow — then God supplies the Spirit and performs powerful deeds in the hearers. Similarly, Paul says here that God has supplied the Spirit to the Galatians and has performed powerful deeds among them. It is as though he were saying: "Through my preaching God has not only brought it about that you believed but also that you lived holy lives, produced much fruit of faith, and suffered evil. By the same power of the Spirit you, who used to be covetous, adulterous, angry, impatient, and hostile, have become generous, chaste, gentle, patient, and loving toward your neighbors." Later on, in the fourth chapter (Gal. 4: 14-15), he gives testimony about them that they had received him, Paul, as an angel of God, in fact, as Jesus Christ, and that they loved him so strongly that they would have plucked out their eyes for him.

To love your neighbor so ardently that you are ready to surrender your money, property, eyes, your life, and everything you have for his salvation, and also to bear all adversities patiently — these are certainly powerful deeds of the Spirit. "And these powerful deeds," he says, "you received and had before these false teachers came to you. But you did not receive them from the Law; you received them from God, who supplied and daily increased the Spirit in you in such a way that the Gospel had a very happy course among you as you taught, believed, worked, and bore your adversities. Since you know all this, being convinced also by the witness of your own conscience, how does it happen that you do not produce the same powerful deeds that you produced before? That is, you are not teaching correctly, believing devoutly, living righteously, doing good works, and bearing evil patiently. Finally, who has corrupted you in such a way that you do not feel as loving toward me as you once did? Now you do not receive Paul as an angel of God or as Christ Jesus; you would not be willing to pluck out your eyes and give them to me. How does it happen, I ask you, that you do not yearn for me with such ardor anymore, and that you now prefer those false apostles, who seduce you so miserably?"

This is how it is happening to us today. At the outset of the preaching of the Gospel there were very many to whom our doctrine was appealing and who had a sincere and respectful attitude toward us; and powerful deeds and the fruit of faith followed upon the preaching of the Gospel. What is happening now? Suddenly there arise fanatical spirits, Anabaptists, and Sacramentarians; and in a short time they subvert everything that we had been building for such a long time and with so much sweat. They also make us so odious to those who used to love us dearly and who accepted our doctrine with thanks that now nothing is more offensive to them than our name. But the devil is the author of this wickedness, because in his members he performs powerful deeds that are opposed and hostile to the powerful deeds of the Holy Spirit. "Therefore," says the apostle, "your experience should have taught you, you Galatians, that these wonderful and powerful deeds did not come from the works of the Law. For just as you did not have them before hearing with faith, so you do not have them now that you do have the false apostles ruling among you."

We can say the same thing today to those who boast that they are evangelicals [30] and have been delivered from the tyranny of the pope: "Did you overcome the tyranny of the pope and achieve freedom in Christ through the fanatical spirits or through us, who have preached faith in Christ?" If they are willing to admit the truth here, they will be compelled to say: "Through the preaching of faith, of course." And it is true that at the outset of our preaching the doctrine of faith ran along very smoothly. Indulgences, purgatory, vows, Masses, and similar abominations came tumbling down, taking with them the ruin of the entire papacy. No one could justly condemn us; for the doctrine was pure, strengthening and comforting many consciences that had long been oppressed by human traditions under the papacy, which was a real tyranny and torment of consciences. Therefore many people thanked God that through the Gospel, which we were the first to preach at that time, they were rescued from these snares and from this torment of conscience.

[30] On other abuses of the term "evangelical" cf. *Luther's Works*, 23, pp. 10—11.

But then the sectarians arose. By their denial of the bodily presence of Christ in the Supper, by their profanation of Baptism, by their destruction of images, and by their abrogation of all ceremonies they wanted to overthrow the papacy all at once and thus to tarnish our reputation.[31] Soon our doctrine acquired a bad name, because it was commonly noised about that its proponents did not agree among themselves. This offended many people, turned them away from the truth, and aroused in the papists the hope that because our doctrine was inconsistent with itself, both it and we would soon come to ruin, and that in this way they would recover their strength and regain their original authority and dignity.

The false apostles argued and urged vigorously that the Galatians, who had now been justified by faith in Christ, should be circumcised and observe the Law of Moses if they wanted to be freed from their sins and from the wrath of God, and to obtain the Spirit. Actually, however, by this very means they burdened them with sins even more. For sins are not removed by the Law, nor is the Spirit granted through it; but the Law only produces wrath and arouses terrors. In the very same way today these sectarians wanted to contribute to the welfare of the catholic church and immediately to overthrow the entire papacy, and to bury it by abrogating ceremonies, destroying images, and attacking the sacraments. But by these very means they have not helped the church; they have harmed it. They have not overthrown the papacy; they have strengthened its hold.

But if, in the common consensus with us in which they began, they had taught and diligently urged the doctrine of justification — that is, that we are justified neither by the righteousness of the Law nor by our own righteousness but solely by faith in Christ — then certainly this one doctrine would gradually, as it had begun to do, have overthrown the entire papacy with all its brotherhoods, indulgences, orders, relics, forms of worship, invocation of saints, purgatory, Masses, vigils, vows, and the endless other abominations of that sort. But they have neglected the preaching of faith and of Christian righteousness, and have tried to accomplish this end in another way, with great damage both to sound doctrine and to the churches. It has happened to them somewhat as the German proverb about fishing ahead of the net says, for by trying to catch them

[31] See Luther's discussion of this in *Luther's Works*, 40, pp. 79 ff.

with their hands they have driven away the fish which the net was about to enclose.[32]

Therefore the papacy is collapsing and tumbling down today, not by the tumults of the sectarians but by the proclamation of the doctrine of justification. This doctrine has not only weakened the kingdom of the Antichrist, but until now it has also sustained and defended us against his violence. If we had not had this protection, both the sectarians and we along with them would have perished long ago. Yet they are so far away from acknowledging this blessing that, as the psalmist says (Ps. 109:4), they deny us the love they owe us and attack us with spiteful minds. But the doctrine of justification is this, that we are pronounced righteous and are saved solely by faith in Christ, and without works. If this is the true meaning of justification — as it certainly is, or it will be necessary to get rid of all Scripture — then it immediately follows that we are pronounced righteous neither through monasticism nor through vows nor through Masses nor through any other works. And thus the papacy is overthrown without the abrogation of any external things, without tumult, without any human force, without any attack upon the sacraments — solely by the Spirit. Nor is this victory obtained by us; it is obtained through the Christ whom we preach and confess.

The facts themselves confirm what I am now saying. For at the time when the papacy first began to lean and to fall over, the sectarians did not do anything at all, since they could not do anything. They kept silence. We, on the other hand, taught and urged nothing except this doctrine of justification, which at that time was the only thing threatening the authority of the pope and laying waste his kingdom. But when the sectarians saw that the papacy was leaning and falling over, and that the fish were congregating at the net, they wanted to overthrow and completely destroy the papacy all at once, to deprive us of the glory, and with their own hands to catch all the fish that had congregated at the net. But they were only playing at the work, for they did not catch them; they only drove them away. Thus the sectarians overthrew the papacy by their tumults just as the false apostles achieved righteousness for the Galatians by their doctrine that the Law was to be observed. If they had only taught the doctrine of justification diligently, the images and the other abuses in the church would have fallen over on their

---

[32] Luther quotes the proverb in German: *Fur dem hamen fischen.*

own. But they were motivated by κενοδοξία,[33] for they wanted it
noised about that they had overthrown the papacy themselves. Neglecting the doctrine of justification, therefore, they stirred up those
tumults, by which they nearly crushed us and meanwhile substantiated the papists in their abominations. That is the kind of
success our efforts achieve when we seek our own glory rather
than the glory of God!

Neither the pope nor the devil is afraid of those tumults and of
such outward show. But the doctrine of faith, which proclaims that
Christ alone is the Victor over sin, death, and the devil — this doctrine
is frightening to him. For it destroys his kingdom; and, as I have
said, it sustains and defends us today against all the gates of hell
(Matt. 16:18). If we were not depending on this anchor, we would
be compelled to adore the pope once more; nor would there be
any device or means to resist him. For if I were to join the sectarians,
my conscience would be unsure. They have no authority to oppose
the pope, since they seek their own glory and not the glory of God.
Therefore if I were not equipped with other weapons than theirs,
I would not dare attack the papacy; much less would I dare presume
that I might lay waste the papacy.

But they say: "The pope is the Antichrist!" [34] All right; but against
this Paul sets the fact that he has a ministry of teaching, that the
power to administer the sacraments and to bind and loose resides
with him, and that he has this power by inheritance through the
laying on of hands from the apostles. Therefore he is not deposed
from his seat by these tumults, but rather in this manner, if I say:
"I am willing to kiss your feet, pope, and to acknowledge you as
the supreme pontiff, if you adore my Christ and grant that we have
the forgiveness of sins and eternal life through His death and resurrection and not through the observance of your traditions. If you
yield here, I shall not take away your crown and power. But if
you do not, I shall constantly cry out that you are the Antichrist;
and I shall announce that all your ceremonies and religion are not
only a denial of God but supreme blasphemy and idolatry." The
sectarians do not do this; they only try to take away the crown
and power of the pope by external force. Therefore their effort is

[33] A reference to Phil. 2:3, the only passage of the New Testament where
this noun occurs; the adjective appears in Gal. 5:26.

[34] Cf. *Luther's Works*, 13, p. 417, note 30, on the backgrounds of this
identification.

useless. This needs to be done above all, in order that the ungodliness and the abominations of the pope by which he has deceived the whole world under the pretext of holiness and religion may be exposed. If I do this, I shall see what is left afterwards; for I have taken away the kernel and leave him the husks. They, on the other hand, take away the husks and leave him the kernel.

In short, just as powerful deeds are not performed by the works of the Law, so those external works that the sectarians urge accomplish nothing in the church but tumults, greater confusion, and a barrier to the Spirit. Experience attests to this. For they did not knock the pope down by overturning images and attacking the sacraments. In fact, they made him even haughtier. But he has been and still is being knocked down by the Spirit, that is, by the preaching of faith, which testifies that Christ was delivered for our sins. Here the righteousness and the slavery of the pope's laws must collapse.

Meanwhile, however, I have often made the offer and still make the offer that I am gladly willing to bear the laws of the pope, provided that he leaves them free and does not bind consciences to them so that men think that they are justified for observing them and damned for not observing them.[35] But he does not do this; for if he did not bind consciences to his laws, where would his power be? Therefore he is concerned above all to hold consciences bound and captive by his laws. That is the basis of the statement: "Unless you obey the Roman see, you cannot be saved."[36] That is also the basis of this thunder and lightning in his bulls: "Let anyone who dares resist in bold temerity know that he must bear the wrath of Almighty God."[37] Here he denies salvation to all who do not obey his laws, and he promises eternal life to all who observe them. Thus he drives us into the net of the righteousness of works, as if no one could be justified and saved without observing his laws. In short, not with one word does he mention faith; but he teaches only his own ideas. But if he were to concede that all his laws contribute nothing to righteousness in the sight of God, then I for my part would also concede much to him. But then his kingdom

[35] See also p. 92, note 8.

[36] Cf. p. 87, note 6.

[37] The formula reads: *Qui ausu temerario contraire praesumpserit, ille noverit se incursurum indignationem omnipotentis Dei.*

would collapse on its own. For if the pope were to lose his power to save and to damn, he would be nothing more than a mere idol. In other words, the righteousness of the heart ignores all laws, not only those of the pope but also those of Moses. For true righteousness does not come through the works of the Law; it comes through hearing with faith, which is followed by the powerful deeds and fruits of the Spirit.

6. *Thus Abraham believed God, and it was reckoned to him as righteousness.*

Up to this point Paul has been arguing on the basis of experience. And he vigorously urges this argument that is based on experience. "You have believed," he says, "and having believed, you have done miracles and have performed many outstanding and powerful deeds. You have also suffered evils. All this is the effect and operation, not of the Law but of the Holy Spirit." This the Galatians were obliged to admit, for they could not deny the things that were going on before their eyes and were available to their senses. Hence this argument, based on experience or on its effects in the Galatians themselves, is very strong and clear.

Now Paul adds the example of Abraham and recites testimonies from Scripture. The first is from Gen. 15:6: "Abraham believed, etc." He urges this passage strongly here, just as he does especially in Rom. 4:2. "If Abraham was justified by works," he says, "he has righteousness and something to boast about, but not before God," only before men; for before God he has sin and wrath. But he was justified before God, not because he worked but because he believed. For Scripture says: "Abraham believed, and it was reckoned to him as righteousness." Paul expounds and develops this passage there as magnificently as it deserves (Rom. 4:19-24): "Abraham," he says, "did not weaken in faith when he considered his own body, which was as good as dead, because he was about a hundred years old, or when he considered the barrenness of Sarah's womb. No distrust made him waver concerning the promise of God; but he grew strong in his faith as he gave glory to God, fully convinced that God was able to do what He had promised. That is why his faith was 'reckoned to him as righteousness.' But the words 'it was reckoned to him' were written not only for his sake but also for our sakes."

With these words Paul makes faith in God the supreme worship, the supreme allegiance, the supreme obedience, and the supreme sacrifice. Whoever is an orator, let him develop this topic. He will see that faith is something omnipotent, and that its power is inestimable and infinite; for it attributes glory to God, which is the highest thing that can be attributed to Him. To attribute glory to God is to believe in Him, to regard Him as truthful, wise, righteous, merciful, and almighty, in short, to acknowledge Him as the Author and Donor of every good. Reason does not do this, but faith does. It consummates the Deity; and, if I may put it this way, it is the creator of the Deity, not in the substance of God but in us.[38] For without faith God loses His glory, wisdom, righteousness, truthfulness, mercy, etc., in us; in short, God has none of His majesty or divinity where faith is absent. Nor does God require anything greater of man than that he attribute to Him His glory and His divinity; that is, that he regard Him, not as an idol but as God, who has regard for him, listens to him, shows mercy to him, helps him, etc.[39] When He has obtained this, God retains His divinity sound and unblemished; that is, He has whatever a believing heart is able to attribute to Him. To be able to attribute such glory to God is wisdom beyond wisdom, righteousness beyond righteousness, religion beyond religion, and sacrifice beyond sacrifice. From this it can be understood what great righteousness faith is and, by antithesis, what a great sin unbelief is.

Therefore faith justifies because it renders to God what is due Him; whoever does this is righteous. The laws also define what it means to be righteous in this way: to render to each what is his.[40] For faith speaks as follows: "I believe Thee, God, when Thou dost speak." What does God say? Things that are impossible, untrue, foolish, weak, absurd, abominable, heretical, and diabolical – if you consult reason. For what is more ridiculous, foolish, and impossible than when God says to Abraham that he is to get a son from the body of Sarah, which is barren and already dead?

Thus when God proposes the doctrines of faith, He always proposes things that are simply impossible and absurd – if, that is, you want to follow the judgment of reason. It does indeed seem ridiculous and absurd to reason that in the Lord's Supper the body

[38] On the meaning of such statements as this cf. *Luther's Works*, 13, p. 88, note 21.

[39] Cf. p. 127, note 42.

[40] A quotation from the first section of Book I of the *Institutes* of Justinian; cf. *Luther's Works*, 36, p. 357, note 17.

and the blood of Christ are presented, that Baptism is "the washing of regeneration and renewal in the Holy Spirit" (Titus 3:5), that Christ the Son of God was conceived and carried in the womb of the Virgin, that He was born, that He suffered the most ignominious of deaths on the cross, that He was raised again, that He is now sitting at the right hand of the Father, and that He now has "authority in heaven and on earth" (Matt. 28:18). Paul calls the Gospel of Christ the crucified "the Word of the cross" (1 Cor. 1:18) and "the folly of preaching" (1 Cor. 1:21), which the Jews regarded as offensive and the Greeks as a foolish doctrine. Reason judges this way about all the doctrines of the faith; for it does not understand that the supreme form of worship is to hear the voice of God and to believe, but it supposes that what it chooses on its own and what it does with a so-called good intention [41] and from its own devotion is pleasing to God. When God speaks, reason, therefore, regards His Word as heresy and as the word of the devil; for it seems so absurd. Such is the theology of all the sophists and of the sectarians,[42] who measure the Word of God by reason.

But faith slaughters reason and kills the beast that the whole world and all the creatures cannot kill. Thus Abraham killed it by faith in the Word of God, in which offspring was promised to him from Sarah, who was barren and past childbearing. Reason did not immediately assent to this Word in Abraham. Surely it fought against faith in him and regarded it as something ridiculous, absurd, and impossible that Sarah, who was not only ninety years old now but was also barren by nature, should give birth to a son. Faith certainly had this struggle with reason in Abraham. But faith won the victory in him; it killed and sacrificed God's bitterest and most harmful enemy. Thus all devout people enter with Abraham into the darkness of faith,[43] kill reason, and say: "Reason, you are foolish. You do not understand the things that belong to God (Matt. 16:23). Therefore do not speak against me, but keep quiet. Do not judge; but listen to the Word of God, and believe it." Thus devout people, by their faith, kill a beast that is greater than the world; and so they offer a highly pleasing sacrifice and worship to God.

[41] That is, a good intention would make a neutral work good; it would not make an evil work good. See p. 267, note 70.

[42] The notes from Luther's lecture contain the term *Erasmiani* here, but the editors have generalized the reference.

[43] Cf. p. 113, note 32.

Compared with this sacrifice and worship of the devout, all the religions of all the nations and all the works of all the monks and self-righteous people are absolutely nothing. For by this sacrifice, in the first place, they slay reason, which is the greatest and most invincible enemy of God, because it despises God and denies His wisdom, justice, power, truthfulness, mercy, majesty, and divinity. In the second place, by this same sacrifice they ascribe glory to God; that is, they regard Him as just, good, faithful, truthful, etc., and believe that He can do everything, that all His words are holy, true, living, and powerful. This is the most acceptable allegiance to God. Therefore no greater, better, or more pleasing religion or worship can be found in the world than faith.

On the other hand, the self-righteous, who do not have faith, do many things. They fast; they pray; they lay crosses on themselves. They suppose that in this way they are placating the wrath of God and meriting grace. But they do not give glory to God; that is, they do not regard Him as merciful, truthful, and faithful to His promises. No, they consider Him an angry judge, who must be placated by their works. In this way they despise God, accuse Him of lying in all His promises, and deny Christ and all His blessings. In short, they depose God from His throne and set themselves up in His place. Neglecting and despising the Word of God, they select acts of worship and works that they themselves like. They suppose that God is pleased with these, and they hope to receive a reward from Him for them. Therefore they do not bring death to reason, God's bitterest enemy; they give it life. They deprive God of His majesty and divinity, and they attribute this to their own works.

Therefore faith alone attributes glory to God. Paul testifies to this in the case of Abraham in Rom. 4:20, when he says: "Abraham grew strong in faith as he gave glory to God." And he adds from Gen. 15:6 that this was imputed to him as righteousness. This is not without cause. For Christian righteousness consists in two things, namely, faith in the heart and the imputation of God. Faith is indeed a formal righteousness;[44] but this does not suffice, for after faith there still remain remnants of sin in the flesh. The sacrifice of faith began in Abraham, but it was finally consummated only in death. Therefore the second part of righteousness has to be added, which perfects it in us, namely, divine imputation. Faith does not

[44] Cf. p. 127, note 43.

give enough to God formally, because it is imperfect; in fact, it is barely a little spark of faith, which only begins to attribute divinity to God. We have received the first fruits of the Spirit, but not the tithes.[45] Nor is reason completely killed in this life. Hence lust, wrath, impatience, and other fruits of the flesh and of unbelief still remain in us. Not even the more perfect saints have a full and constant joy in God. But, as Scripture testifies concerning the prophets and the apostles, their feelings change; sometimes they are sad, sometimes joyful. But because of their faith in Christ such faults are not laid to their charge; for otherwise no one could be saved. From these words, "It was imputed to him as righteousness," we conclude, therefore, that righteousness does indeed begin through faith and that through it we have the first fruits of the Spirit. But because faith is weak, it is not perfected without the imputation of God. Hence faith begins righteousness, but imputation perfects it until the day of Christ.

The sophists also dispute about imputation when they discuss the acceptance of a work.[46] But they speak apart from Scripture and contrary to it, for they apply it only to works. They do not consider the uncleanness and the inner diseases of the heart, such as unbelief, doubt, contempt and hate for God; these deadly beasts are the fountain and cause of all evils. They consider only the outward and coarse faults and unrighteousness, which are little streams that proceed from those fountains. Therefore they ascribe acceptance to good works; that is, God accepts works, not because it is owing to them but by "congruity." But we exclude all works and come to grips with the heads of the beast called reason,[47] which is the fountainhead of all evils. It neither fears nor loves nor trusts in God; it smugly despises Him. It is moved neither by His threats nor by His promises. It is not delighted by His words or His deeds. Instead, it murmurs against Him, is angry with Him, judges and hates God. In short, it is "hostile to God" (Rom. 8:7) and does not attribute glory to Him. If this vicious beast — that is, reason — were killed, all outward and coarse sins would be nothing.

Therefore the first thing to be done is that through faith we kill

[45] See p. 196, note 16.

[46] Cf., for example, Thomas Aquinas, *Summa Theologica*, I—I, Q. 48, Art. 5.

[47] From the manuscript of Luther's lecture it is evident that he is thinking here of the Hydra of classical mythology.

unbelief, contempt and hatred of God, and the murmuring against His wrath, His judgment, and all the words and deeds of God; for then we kill reason. It can be killed by nothing else but faith, which believes God and thus attributes His glory to Him. It does this in spite of the fact that He speaks what seems foolish, absurd, and impossible to reason, and in spite of the fact that God depicts Himself otherwise than reason can either judge or grasp, namely, this way: "If you wish to placate Me, do not offer Me your works and merits. But believe in Jesus Christ, My only Son, who was born, who suffered, who was crucified, and who died for your sins. Then I will accept you and pronounce you righteous. And whatever of your sin still remains in you I will not impute to you." If reason is not slaughtered, and if all the religions and forms of worship under heaven that have been thought up by men to obtain righteousness in the sight of God are not condemned, the righteousness of faith cannot stand.

When reason hears this, it is immediately offended and says: "Then are good works nothing? Have I toiled and borne the burden of the day and the scorching heat (Matt. 20:12) for nothing?" This is the source of that revolt of the nations, kings, and princes against the Lord and against His Christ (Ps. 2:1-2). The pope with his monks does not want to give the impression of having erred; much less will he permit himself to be condemned. Likewise the Turk and others.

I have said this in interpretation of the sentence "And it was reckoned to him as righteousness," in order that the students of the Sacred Scriptures may understand how Christian righteousness is to be defined properly and accurately, namely, that it is a trust in the Son of God or a trust of the heart in God through Christ. Here this clause is to be added to provide the differentia for the definition: "which faith is imputed as righteousness for the sake of Christ." For, as I have said, these two things make Christian righteousness perfect: The first is faith in the heart, which is a divinely granted gift and which formally believes in Christ; the second is that God reckons this imperfect faith as perfect righteousness for the sake of Christ, His Son, who suffered for the sins of the world and in whom I begin to believe. On account of this faith in Christ God does not see the sin that still remains in me. For so long as I go on living in the flesh, there is certainly sin in me. But meanwhile Christ protects me under the shadow of His wings and spreads over me the wide heaven of the forgiveness of sins, under which I live in safety. This prevents God from seeing the sins that still cling to my flesh. My flesh distrusts God, is angry with Him, does not rejoice in Him, etc. But God overlooks these sins, and in His sight they are as though they were not sins. This is accomplished by imputation on account of the faith by which I begin to take hold of Christ; and on His account God reckons imperfect righteousness as perfect righteousness and sin as not sin, even though it really is sin.

Thus we live under the curtain of the flesh of Christ (Heb. 10:20). He is our "pillar of cloud by day and pillar of fire by night" (Ex. 13:21), to keep God from seeing our sin. And although we see it and feel remorse of conscience, still we keep running back to Christ, our Mediator and Propitiator, through whom we reach completion and are saved. In Him is everything;[48] in Him we have everything; and He supplies everything in us. On His account God overlooks all sins and wants them to be covered as though they were not sins. He says: "Because you believe in My Son, even though you have sins, they shall be forgiven, until you are completely absolved from them by death."

Let Christians strive to learn completely and perfectly this doctrine of Christian righteousness, which the sophists neither understand nor are able to understand. But let them not suppose that they can learn it thoroughly all at once. Therefore let them make the effort to read Paul often and with the greatest diligence. Let them compare the first with the last; in fact, let them compare Paul as a whole with himself. Then they will find that this is the situation, that Christian righteousness consists in two things: first, in faith, which attributes glory to God; secondly, in God's imputation. For because faith is weak, as I have said, therefore God's imputation has to be added. That is, God does not want to impute the remnant of sin and does not want to punish it or damn us for it. But He wants to cover it and to forgive it, as though it were nothing, not for our sakes or for the sake of our worthiness or works but for the sake of Christ Himself, in whom we believe.

Thus a Christian man is righteous and a sinner at the same time,[49] holy and profane, an enemy of God and a child of God. None of the sophists will admit this paradox, because they do not understand

[48] The text of the Weimar has *ut* here, but we have read *et*.

[49] The Latin phrase, which has since become a technical term, is *simul iustus et peccator*.

the true meaning of justification. This was why they forced men to go on doing good works until they would not feel any sin at all. By this means they drove to the point of insanity many men who tried with all their might to become completely righteous in a formal sense but could not accomplish it. And innumerable persons even among the authors of this wicked dogma were driven into despair at the hour of death, which is what would have happened to me if Christ had not looked at me in mercy and liberated me from this error.

We, on the other hand, teach and comfort an afflicted sinner this way: "Brother, it is impossible for you to become so righteous in this life that your body is as clear and spotless as the sun. You still have spots and wrinkles (Eph. 5:27), and yet you are holy." But you say: "How can I be holy when I have sin and am aware of it?" "That you feel and acknowledge sin — this is good. Thank God, and do not despair. It is one step toward health when a sick man admits and confesses his disease." "But how will I be liberated from sin?" "Run to Christ, the Physician, who heals the contrite of heart and saves sinners. Believe in Him. If you believe, you are righteous, because you attribute to God the glory of being almighty, merciful, truthful, etc. You justify and praise God. In short, you attribute divinity and everything to Him. And the sin that still remains in you is not imputed but is forgiven for the sake of Christ, in whom you believe and who is perfectly righteous in a formal sense. His righteousness is yours; your sin is His."

As I have said, therefore, any Christian is a supreme pontiff, because, first, he offers and slaughters his reason and the mind of the flesh, and, secondly, he attributes to God the glory of being righteous, truthful, patient, kind, and merciful. This is the continuous evening and morning sacrifice in the New Testament. The evening sacrifice is to kill the reason, and the morning sacrifice is to glorify God. Thus a Christian is involved, daily and perpetually, in this double sacrifice and in its practice. No one can adequately proclaim the value and the dignity of Christian sacrifice.

Therefore this is a marvelous definition of Christian righteousness: it is a divine imputation or reckoning as righteousness or to righteousness, for the sake of our faith in Christ or for the sake of Christ. When the sophists hear this definition, they laugh; for they suppose that righteousness is a certain quality that is first infused into the soul and then distributed through all the members. They cannot strip off the thoughts of reason, which declares that righteousness is a right judgment and a right will. Therefore this inestimable gift excels all reason, that without any works God reckons and acknowledges as righteous the man who takes hold by faith of His Son, who was sent into the world, who was born, who suffered, and who was crucified for us.

So far as the words are concerned, this fact is easy, namely, that righteousness is not in us in a formal sense, as Aristotle maintains,[50] but is outside us, solely in the grace of God and in His imputation. In us there is nothing of the form or of the righteousness except that weak faith or the first fruits of faith by which we have begun to take hold of Christ. Meanwhile sin truly remains within us. But the fact itself is not easy or trivial; it is serious and important, because the Christ who is given to us has not done something meager for us and has not been playing. But, as Paul said earlier (Gal. 2:20), He "loved us and gave Himself for us"; and (Gal. 3:13) "He became a curse for us." It is not an idle speculation that Christ was given for my sins and was made accursed for me in order that I might be rescued from eternal death. To take hold of the Son and to believe in Him with the heart as the gift of God causes God to reckon that faith, however imperfect it may be, as perfect righteousness. Here we are in an altogether different world — a world that is outside reason. Here the issue is not what we ought to do or by what sort of works we may merit grace and the forgiveness of sins. No, here we are in a divine theology, where we hear the Gospel that Christ died for us and that when we believe this we are reckoned as righteous, even though sins, and great ones at that, still remain in us.

This is also how Christ defines the righteousness of faith in the Gospel of John. He says (John 16:27): "The Father Himself loves you. Why does He love you? Not because you were Pharisees, irreproachable in the righteousness of the Law, circumcised, doing good works, fasting, etc. But it is because 'I chose you out of the world' (John 15:19). And you have not done anything except that 'you have loved Me and have believed that I came from the Father.' This object, this 'I' sent from the Father into the world, this pleased you. And because you have taken hold of this object, the Father

---

[50] Aristotle's *Nicomachean Ethics*, Book V, seems to be what Luther has in mind.

loves you, and you please Him." Nevertheless, in another passage He calls them evil and tells them to ask for the forgiveness of sins.[51] These two things are diametrically opposed: that a Christian is righteous and beloved by God, and yet that he is a sinner at the same time. For God cannot deny His own nature. That is, He cannot avoid hating sin and sinners; and He does so by necessity, for otherwise He would be unjust and would love sin. Then how can these two contradictory things both be true at the same time, that I am a sinner and deserve divine wrath and hate, and that the Father loves me? Here nothing can intervene except Christ the Mediator. "The Father," He says, "loves you, not because you are deserving of love, but because you have loved Me and have believed that I came from the Father" (John 16:27).

Thus a Christian remains in pure humility. He really and truly feels that there is sin in him and that on this account he is worthy of wrath, the judgment of God, and eternal death. Thus he is humbled in this life. Yet at the same time he remains in a pure and holy pride, by which he turns to Christ. Through Him he strengthens himself against this feeling of divine wrath and judgment; and he believes that he is loved by the Father, not for his own sake but for the sake of Christ, the Beloved.

From this it is clear how faith justifies without works and how the imputation of righteousness is necessary nevertheless. Sins remain in us, and God hates them very much. Because of them it is necessary for us to have the imputation of righteousness, which comes to us on account of Christ, who is given to us and grasped by our faith. Meanwhile, as long as we are alive, we are supported and nourished at the bosom of divine mercy and forbearance, until the body of sin (Rom. 6:6) is abolished and we are raised up as new beings on that Day. Then there will be new heavens and a new earth (Rev. 21:1), in which righteousness will dwell. Under the present heaven meanwhile sin and wicked men dwell, and the godly have sin. Therefore Paul complains in Rom. 7:23 about the sin that still remains in the saints, and yet he says later on (Rom. 8:1) that "there is no condemnation for those who are in Christ Jesus." Who will reconcile those utterly conflicting statements, that the sin in us is not sin, that he who is damnable will not be damned, that he who is rejected

[51] Luther may be thinking of Matt. 7:11 (addressed to the disciples) and of Matt. 6:12.

will not be rejected, that he who is worthy of wrath and eternal death will not receive these punishments? Only the Mediator between God and man, Jesus Christ (1 Tim. 2:5). As Paul says, "there is no condemnation for those who are in Christ Jesus."

7. *So you see that it is men of faith who are the sons of Abraham.*

This is a general statement and the principal argument of Paul against the Jews, that those who believe, not those who are descended from his flesh and blood, are the sons of Abraham. Paul vigorously presses this argument here as well as in the fourth and ninth chapters of Romans. For this was the supreme confidence and boast of the Jews (John 8:33): "We are the offspring and the sons of Abraham. He was circumcised and observed the Law. Therefore if we want to be true sons of Abraham, we must imitate our father." It was truly an outstanding ground of boasting and of confidence to be the offspring of Abraham, for no one can deny that God spoke to the offspring of Abraham and about the offspring of Abraham. But this prerogative was of no benefit to unbelieving Jews. Therefore Paul, especially here, contends vigorously against this argument and deprives the Jews of this supreme confidence. As the chosen instrument of Christ (Acts 9:15) he was able to do this more than anyone else. For if we had had to argue against the Jews from the beginning without Paul, we would probably have accomplished little against them.

Thus Paul battles against the confidence of the Jews, who proudly boasted: "We are the offspring of Abraham." "Fine." "Abraham was circumcised and observed the Law. We do the same thing." "I concede this. Then what? You do not intend to be righteous and to be saved on this account, do you? No! Let us go to the patriarch Abraham himself, and let us see by what means he was justified and saved. Certainly not on account of his outstanding virtues and holy works — not because he forsook his fatherland, his family, and his father's house; not because he accepted circumcision and observed the Law; not because he was ready, at the command of God, to sacrifice his son Isaac, in whom he had the promise of descendants — but because he believed God. Therefore he was not justified by anything else except faith. If you want to be justified by the Law, your father Abraham ought to have been justified by the Law even more. But Abraham could neither be justified nor receive the forgiveness of sins and the Holy Spirit except by faith. Since this is true according to the testimony of Scripture, why do you contend so for the Law and for circumcision, and maintain that you have righteousness and salvation through the Law, when Abraham himself, who was your father, your source, and your head, and in whom you boast, was justified and saved without the Law, by faith alone?" What reply can be made to this argument?

Therefore Paul concludes with the sentence: "It is men of faith who are the sons of Abraham." Descent by blood or physical procreation does not create sons of Abraham in the sight of God. "Of this Abraham," he says, "who is the servant of God and whom God has chosen and justified by faith, no one is regarded as a son in the sight of God on the basis of physical procreation. But in the sight of God sons like him himself, who was the father, must be given to him. But he himself was a father of faith, and he began to be justified and to be pleasing to God, not because he was able to procreate or because he had circumcision and the Law, but because he believed God. Therefore anyone who wants to be a son of Abraham the believer must himself believe. Otherwise he is a son, not of the Abraham who was elected, accepted, and justified, but only of the Abraham who procreated, who is nothing else than a man like another man – conceived, born, and confirmed in sin, without the Holy Spirit, and therefore damned. Such also are the sons who are physically descended from him. They trace nothing back to their father but flesh and blood, sin and death. Therefore they, too, are damned. And so this boast, 'We are the offspring of Abraham,' is vain and futile."

Paul illustrates this argument in Rom. 9 by examples from Scripture, although the Jews evade these. Ishmael and Isaac both were the offspring and natural sons of Abraham. Nevertheless, Ishmael, who was as much the son of Abraham as Isaac was and who should have been the first-born if physical procreation had had any prerogative or if this could have produced sons of Abraham – Ishmael is excluded, and Scripture says (Gen. 21:12): "Through Isaac shall your descendants be named." So also when Esau and Jacob were still in their mother's womb and had done neither good nor evil, it was said (Gen. 25:23): "The elder shall serve the younger." In Mal. 1:2-3 we read: "I have loved Jacob, but I have hated Esau." Therefore it is evident that it is men of faith who are the sons of Abraham.

But here someone may object, as the Jews do and as certain

triflers are doing today, that the vocable "faith" in Hebrew means
"truth," and that therefore it is being misapplied by us;[52] also that
this passage in Gen. 15:6 is speaking about something physical,
namely, about the promise of descendants, and that therefore it
should simply be understood of the faith of Abraham and is misapplied by Paul to our faith in Christ. In a similar way they could
object that the passage which Paul cites from Habakkuk a little
later (Gal. 3:11) speaks about faith in the fulfillment of the complete vision, not merely about the faith in Christ, to which Paul
applies it. Finally they could raise an objection to the entire
eleventh chapter of Hebrews about faith and examples of faith.
Thus today some tyros want to give an impression of great wisdom
by claiming that the Hebrew term means "truth," not "faith," and
that the passage in Genesis which Paul quotes speaks about Abraham's
faith in the promise of descendants, not about faith in Christ. On
this basis they want to prove that Paul's quotations and proofs do
not establish anything. These are vainglorious men; in these matters
they are searching for praise and a reputation for wisdom and
learning where they should do so least of all. But for the sake of
simple people let us reply to their sophistries.

To the first I reply as follows: Faith is nothing else but the truth
of the heart, that is, the right knowledge of the heart about God.
But reason cannot think correctly about God; only faith can do so.
A man thinks correctly about God when he believes God's Word.
But when he wants to measure and to believe God apart from the
Word, with his own reason, he does not have the truth about God
in his heart and therefore cannot think or judge correctly about Him.
Thus when a monk supposes that his cowl, his tonsure, and his
vows please God, that these make him acceptable, and that grace
and eternal life are granted to him for these, he does not have
a true idea about God; he has an idea that is wicked and a lie.
Thus truth is faith itself, which judges correctly about God, namely,
that God does not look at our works and our righteousness, since
we are unclean, but that He wants to be merciful to us, to look at us,
to accept us, to justify us, and to save us if we believe in His Son,
whom He has sent to be the expiation for the sins of the whole world
(1 John 2:2). This is the true idea about God, and it is really
nothing other than faith itself. By my reason I cannot understand

[52] This seems to be directed against Johannes Cochlaeus; cf. *Luther's Works,*
35, p. 187, note 29.

or declare for certain that I am accepted into grace for the sake of Christ, but I hear this announced through the Gospel and take hold of it by faith.

To the second sophistry I reply that Paul is right in citing the passage from Gen. 15 concerning faith in Christ. For all the past promises were contained in the Christ who was to come. In the same way the faith of the patriarchs was contained in Him. Therefore the faith of the patriarchs was the same as ours (Acts 15:10-11; 1 Cor. 10:4). Christ testifies to this in the case of Abraham when He says in John 8:56: "Abraham rejoiced that he was to see My day; he saw it and was glad." Yet the faith of the patriarchs was attached to the Christ who was to come, just as ours is attached to the One who has already come. In his own time Abraham was justified by faith in the Christ who was to come; if he were living today, he would be justified by faith in the Christ now disclosed and present. Thus I said earlier that Cornelius first believed in the Christ who was to come, but that after he had been admonished by Peter, he believed that He had already come.[53] Therefore diverse times do not alter faith or the Holy Spirit or His gifts. For there has always been and still is the same will and idea about Christ in the fathers of the past and in the sons of the present. Thus we also have a Christ who is to come, and we believe in Him just as the fathers in the Old Testament did. For we expect Him to come again on the Last Day with glory, to judge both the living and the dead; and we believe that He has already come for our salvation. Therefore this reference of Paul offends no one but those silly carpers.

Yet for us it is not at all permissible to return to the Christ who is to come, except insofar as we expect Him on the Last Day as our Redeemer, who is to liberate us from all evils. For if we did that, we would believe that Christ has not yet been revealed but is still to be revealed. Thus we would be denying Christ and all His blessings, denying the Holy Spirit, making God a liar, and testifying that He has not yet performed what He has promised — which is what the Jews do.

As I have said, therefore, Paul is right in citing concerning faith in Christ the passage from Genesis which speaks of the faith of Abraham, because Abraham and the other patriarchs were justified by faith in Christ, just as we are — they by faith in the One who was

[53] Cf. p. 210.

to come, we by faith in the Christ who is present. We are now discussing the nature and meaning of justification, which is the same in both, whether Christ has come or is still to come. It is enough, therefore, for Paul to show that the Law does not justify, but that only faith does, whether it be in the Christ who is to come or in the One who is present.

Today Christ is still present to some, but to others He is still to come. To believers He is present and has come; to unbelievers He has not yet come and does not help them. But if they hear His Word and believe, Christ becomes present to them, justifies and saves them.

"Rejecting everything," Paul says, "whether it be reason or the Law or works or the procreation of the patriarchs, you know from this example of Abraham and from the clear testimony of Scripture that it is men of faith who are sons of Abraham, whether they be Jews or Gentiles." For, as he says in Rom. 4:13, Abraham had the promise that he would inherit the world; that is, in his descendants all the families of the earth were to be blessed, and he was to be called "the father of the nations" (Rom. 4:17). And to keep the Jews from misinterpreting the word "nations" concerning themselves only, Scripture guards against this and says not simply "father of nations" but (Rom. 4:17): "I have made you the father of many nations." Therefore Abraham is the father not only of the Jews but also of the Gentiles.

From this it is evident that the sons of Abraham are not his physical sons, since he is not the physical father of the Gentiles, but his sons according to faith, as Paul declares in Rom. 4:17: "I have made you the father of many nations — in the presence of the God in whom you have believed." Therefore Paul sets up two Abrahams, one who procreates and one who believes. Abraham has sons, and he is the father of many nations. Where? In the presence of God, where he believes; not in the presence of the world, where he procreates. Here he is a son of Adam, a sinner, or even more a worker of the righteousness of the Law, who lives according to reason, that is, in a human way. But all this has nothing to do with the believer.

This discussion of the example of Abraham involves at the same time Holy Scripture itself, which says that we are reckoned righteous by faith. Therefore this is a very powerful argument on two counts, both because of the example of Abraham and because of the authority of Scripture.

8. *And the Scripture, foreseeing that God would justify the Gentiles by faith.*

These things pertain to the earlier argument. Paul wants to say this: "You Jews boast excessively about the Law, and you exalt Moses with wonderful praises beyond all bounds because God spoke with him in the bush." Thus the Jews brag against us very superciliously, as I myself have heard them say from time to time: "You Christians have apostles, pope, bishops, etc. But we Jews have patriarchs and prophets. In fact, we have God Himself, who spoke to us in the bush, on Sinai when He gave us the Law, and in the temple. Just produce such a boast and such testimony on your behalf against us!" To this Paul, the apostle to the Gentiles, answers them: "This bragging and boasting of yours does not accomplish anything. For the Scripture preceded it and foresaw a long time before the Law that the Gentiles were not to be justified by the Law but by the blessing of Abraham's progeny, a progeny that was promised to him four hundred and thirty years before the Law was given (as Paul says later in Gal. 3:17). The Law that was given so many years later could not make weak or obsolete this promise of the blessing given to Abraham, but it has remained firm and will remain forever. What can the Jews say to this?"

This argument is very strong, because it is based on a very definite period of time. The promise of a blessing was given to Abraham four hundred and thirty years before the people of Israel received the Law. For to Abraham it was said: "Because you have believed God and given glory to Him, therefore you will be the father of many nations." There, by the promise of God, Abraham is established as the father of many nations; and the inheritance of the world is given to him for his sons before there was a Law. "Then why are you bragging, you Galatians, that you obtain the forgiveness of sins, become sons of God, and receive the inheritance through the Law, which followed the promise by a long interval, namely, by four hundred and thirty years?"

In Baptism there is the promise of salvation (Mark 16:16): "He who believes, etc." If anyone denies here, as the fanatical spirits do today, that righteousness and salvation are granted to an infant as soon as he is baptized; if anyone evades this promise in this way by saying that it becomes valid when a man reaches the use of reason and is able to do good works and to obtain what is set forth in the promise by doing good works; if anyone says that Baptism is not a sign of the will of God toward us but only a mark that distinguishes believers from unbelievers — such a person utterly deprives Baptism of salvation and attributes salvation to works.[54] This is what the false apostles and their disciples did in everything. They preached the Law and its glory to excess, but they neglected and despised the promise given to Abraham four hundred and thirty years before the Law. They refused to recognize that Abraham — of whom they never-theless boasted as the father of their entire nation — was justified by nothing else than by faith alone when he was still uncircumcised and living so many centuries before the Law, as Scripture clearly testifies in Gen. 15:6: "Abraham believed God, etc." Later on, when he had already been reckoned as righteous on account of his faith, Scripture mentions circumcision in Gen. 17:10: "This is My covenant, which you shall keep between Me and you." By this argument Paul con-victs the false apostles vigorously and shows most clearly that Abra-ham was justified by faith, without circumcision and before circum-cision and four hundred and thirty years before the Law. He argues this way also in Rom. 4, namely, that righteousness was imputed to Abraham before circumcision and that he was righteous while he was still uncircumcised, therefore long before the Law.

"Therefore," says Paul, "Scripture well foresaw and anticipated your boasts and bragging about the righteousness of the Law and of works. When? Before circumcision and the Law, because the Law was given four hundred and thirty years after the promise, when Abraham had not only been justified without the Law and before the Law but was also dead and buried. And his righteousness with-out the Law flourished not only until the Law was given, but it will flourish until the end of the world. If the father of the entire Jewish nation was justified without the Law and before the Law, much more are his sons justified in the same way their father was. Therefore righteousness is by faith, not by the Law."

Preached the Gospel beforehand to Abraham, saying: In you shall all the nations be blessed.

"Abraham believed God" and "I have established you as the father" — these very clear and magnificent statements, which com-mend faith very highly and contain promises of spiritual things, the

[54] Apparently Luther is thinking not only of the Anabaptists but of Zwingli as well; cf. *Luther's Works,* 37, p. 141.

Jews not only ignore completely; but they also reason captiously about them and distort them with their foolish and wicked glosses. For they are blind and callous; therefore they do not see that in these passages faith toward God and righteousness in the sight of God are being treated. With the same perversity they evade this outstanding passage about the spiritual blessing (Gen. 12:3): "In you all the nations of the earth shall be blessed." They explain "bless" as "to praise, to wish well, to pronounce glorious." [55] Thus it would mean: "Blessed are you, O Jew, born of the progeny of Abraham. Blessed are you, O foreigner, you who worship the God of the Jews and join them." Therefore they suppose that blessing is nothing but praise and boasting in this world, that a man may boast that he is descended from the lineage and family of Abraham. But this is to distort the statements of Scripture, not to expound them. With the words "Abraham believed" Paul defines and sets before our view an Abraham who is a believer, who is righteous, who has the promise, and who is spiritual, one who is not in error and in the old flesh, one who is born not of Adam but of the Holy Spirit. About this Abraham, renewed by faith and reborn by the Holy Spirit, Scripture speaks and announces that he is to be the father of many nations, and that the Gentiles are to be given to him as an inheritance, when it says: "In you all the nations of the earth shall be blessed."

Paul urges this vigorously, as does Scripture itself when it says (Gen. 15:6): "Abraham believed God, etc." It does not attribute righteousness to Abraham except as a believer. Therefore Scripture speaks about Abraham as he is in the sight of God. In this new argument there is described a new Abraham, separate from the physical bed, marriage, and procreation. He is set forth as he is in the sight of God, that is, believing and justified through faith. To him as a believer Scripture announces: "You will be the father of many nations," and "In you all the nations of the earth shall be blessed." Paul says: "Scripture anticipates and treads underfoot all the bragging and boasting of the Jews about the Law, because the inheritance of the Gentiles was given to Abraham, not through the Law and circumcision but before it, by faith alone."

Therefore it is a vain boast of the Jews when they want to be regarded as blessed because they are the descendants and the sons of Abraham. It is indeed an outstanding prerogative and boast in

[55] Cf. the passage from Nicholas of Lyra cited in *Luther's Works,* 2, p. 264, note 19.

the sight of the world to be a descendant of Abraham (Rom. 9), but in the sight of God this is not the case. Therefore the Jews wickedly distort this passage about the blessing when they explain it as only a physical blessing. Scripture is speaking expressly about a blessing that is spiritual in the sight of God, and it neither can nor should be understood any other way. "In you they shall be blessed." In which "you"? "In you, Abraham the believer, or in your faith, or in the Christ who is to be, who is your descendant and in whom you believe, I say, all the nations of the earth shall be blessed. That is, all the nations shall be your blessed sons, just as you yourself are blessed. As it is written (Gen. 15:5), 'So shall your descendants be.' "

From this it follows that the blessing and the faith of Abraham are the same as ours, that Abraham's Christ is our Christ, and that Christ died for Abraham's sins as well as for ours. John 8:56: "Abraham saw My day and was glad." Therefore everything is the same. Hence permission is not to be granted to the Jews to trifle with this word "blessing" or to distort it. They look at Scripture through a veil (2 Cor. 3:15). Therefore they do not consider what is dealt with in the promises made to the fathers or what is at issue in them. Nevertheless, we must observe this above all, namely, that God speaks with Abraham, not about the Law or about what is to be done but about what is to be believed; that is, God speaks with him about promises that are grasped by faith. What does Abraham do? He believes these promises. What does God do for Abraham the believer? He imputes faith to him as righteousness, and He adds many more promises besides: "I am your shield" (Gen. 15:1); "In you all the nations of the earth shall be blessed" (Gen. 12:3); "You shall be the father of many nations" (Gen. 17:5); "So shall your descendants be" (Gen. 15:5). These are invincible arguments at which no one can carp if the statements of Scripture are considered diligently and seriously.

9. *So then, those who are men of faith are blessed with Abraham who had faith.*

Here the emphasis and whole force is on the words "with Abraham who had faith." For Paul is obviously distinguishing between Abraham and Abraham by making one and the same person into two persons. It is as though he were saying: "There is an Abraham who does works and an Abraham who has faith. We are not concerning ourselves with the Abraham who does works. For if he is justified by works, he has something to boast about, but not in the sight of God. Let that Abraham who begets offspring, who does works, who is circumcised, and who observes the Law apply to the Jews. But another Abraham applies to us, namely, the one who had faith, the one of whom Scripture says that he received the blessing of righteousness through his faith and that he received the promise of the same blessing for all those who believe as he did. Then the world is promised to Abraham, but to the one who has faith. Therefore all the world is to be blessed, that is, is to receive the imputation of righteousness, if it believes as Abraham did."

Now the blessing is nothing else than the promise of the Gospel. And that all the nations are blessed means that all the nations hear the blessing, or that the divine blessing, which is the promise, is preached and spread among all nations through the Gospel. By reason of their spiritual understanding the prophets have drawn from this passage many prophecies, such as Ps. 19:4: "Their voice goes out through all the earth." In short, all the prophecies concerning the kingdom of Christ and concerning the spreading of the Gospel have their origin in this passage: "In you all the nations of the earth shall be blessed." Therefore that the nations are blessed means that righteousness is granted to them, that they are reckoned as righteous, which does not happen except through the Gospel. For Abraham was not justified in any other way than by hearing the Word of promise, of blessing, and of grace. Therefore just as the imputation of righteousness reached Abraham through hearing with faith, so it reached all the nations and still does. For it is the Word of the same God — the Word which was addressed to Abraham first and later to all nations.

To bless, then, is to preach and teach the Word of the Gospel, to confess Christ, and to propagate the knowledge of Him among others. This is the priestly office and the continuing sacrifice of the church in the New Testament — the church which distributes this blessing by preaching, by administering the sacraments, by granting absolution, by giving comfort, and by using the Word of grace that Abraham had and that was his blessing. Since he believed this, he received the blessing. So we, too, are blessed if we believe it. And this blessing is something to boast of, not in the sight of the world but in the sight of God. For we hear that our sins are forgiven and that we have been accepted by God; that God is our Father and that we are His children, with whom He does not want to be wrathful, but whom He wants to liberate from sin, death, and all evil, and to whom He wants to grant righteousness, life, and His kingdom. The prophets preach about this blessing everywhere. They did not look at the promises made to the fathers as frigidly as the ungodly Jews did and as the sophists and sectarians do today; but they read them and stressed them with great diligence, and they drew from this source whatever they prophesied about Christ and His kingdom. Thus the prophecy in Hos. 13:14: "From death I shall redeem them. O death, I shall be your death!" and similar sayings of other prophets all flowed from these promises, in which God promised to the fathers the crushing of the serpent's head (Gen. 3:15) and the blessing of all the nations (Gen. 12:3).

Therefore if the nations are blessed — that is, if they are reckoned as righteous in the sight of God — then sin and death must retreat; and in their place must come righteousness, salvation, and eternal life, not on account of works but on account of faith in Christ. As I have said, the passage in Gen. 12:2, "In you all the nations of the earth shall be blessed," does not speak about a blessing by the mouth, which is to wish someone well and to congratulate him, but about the sort of blessing that belongs to the imputation of righteousness that avails in the sight of God, that redeems from the curse of sin and from everything that follows sin. This blessing is given only through faith, because the text states clearly: "Abraham believed, etc." Hence it is a purely spiritual blessing and the only blessing; although it may be cursed by the world, as it surely is, still it avails in the sight of God. Thus this is a powerful passage, that those who are men of faith possess this promise of the blessing given to the Abraham who had faith. And so Paul anticipates the argument of the Jews, who boast about an Abraham who procreated, worked, and was righteous in the sight of men, not about one who had faith.

Just as the Jews boast only about an Abraham who does works, so the pope sets forth only a Christ who does works or is an example. "Anyone who wants to live a godly life," he says, "must walk as Christ has walked, according to His own statement in John 13:15: 'I have given you an example, that you also should do as I have done to you.'" We do not deny that the example of Christ should be imitated by the godly and that good works must be done, but the pious do not become righteous in the sight of God on this account. Paul is not introducing a discussion of what we ought to do. No, he is discussing how we are to be justified. Here nothing but Christ dying for sins and rising again for our righteousness should be set forth. He must be grasped by faith as a gift, not as an example. Reason does not understand this. Therefore just as the Jews do not imitate the Abraham who had faith but imitate the Abraham who performed works, so the papists and all self-righteous people do not look at and grasp the Christ who justifies but look at and grasp the Christ who performs works; and thus they retreat so much farther from Christ, from righteousness and salvation. But if both groups want to be saved, it is necessary that the former imitate the Abraham who had faith and that the latter take hold of the Christ who justifies and saves — the Christ whom Abraham himself took hold of and through whom he was blessed.

It was certainly an outstanding ground for boasting that Abraham accepted circumcision when God commanded it, that he was provided with brilliant virtues, and that in everything he was obedient to God. Thus it is a laudable and happy thing to imitate the example of Christ in His deeds, to love one's neighbors, to do good to those who deserve evil, to pray for one's enemies, and to bear with patience the ingratitude of those who requite good with evil. But none of this contributes to righteousness in the sight of God. The outstanding good deeds of Abraham did not help him to be pronounced righteous in the sight of God; in the same way imitation of the example of Christ does not make us righteous in the sight of God. For us to be righteous in the sight of God a price far higher than human righteousness or the righteousness of the Law is required. Here we must have Christ to bless and save us, just as Abraham had Him as his Blesser and Savior. How? Not through works but through faith. Therefore the Abraham who had faith is vastly different from the Abraham who did works, and Christ who blesses and redeems is vastly different from Christ the example. Here Paul is dealing with Christ who redeems and Abraham who has faith, not with Christ the example and Abraham who does works. Therefore he adds, with meaning and great emphasis: "Those who are men of faith are blessed with Abraham who had faith." Thus the Abraham who had faith must be separated from the Abraham who did works as far as heaven is separated from earth. The one who has faith is a completely divine man, a son of God, the inheritor of the universe. He is the victor over the world, sin, death, and the devil. Hence he cannot be praised enough. Let us not permit this Abraham who had faith to be hidden in the grave, as he is so far as the Jews are concerned. But let us extol and proclaim him with the highest praises, and let us fill heaven and earth with his name; thus we shall see nothing whatever of the Abraham who does works, so important will the Abraham who has faith be to us. For when we speak about this Abraham who has faith, we are in heaven. But later on, when we do the things that were done by the Abraham who did works, human and earthly things rather than divine and heavenly things (except insofar as they had been divinely granted to him), we live among men on earth. Therefore the Abraham who has faith fills heaven and earth; thus every Christian fills heaven and earth by his faith, so that beyond it he cannot see anything at all.

On the basis of the word "bless" Paul now assembles an argument from contraries,[56] for Scripture is filled with antitheses. It is the mark of an intelligent man to discern the antitheses in Scripture and to be able to interpret Scripture with their help. Thus the word "blessing" here quickly implies its opposite, namely, "curse." For when Scripture says that all nations are blessed in faith or with the Abraham who had faith, it necessarily follows that apart from faith or apart from the Abraham who had faith all are accursed, whether Jews or Gentiles. Since the promise of blessing for all nations was given to Abraham, there is no blessing to be expected anywhere else except in the promise made to Abraham and now broadcast throughout the world by the Gospel. Therefore whatever is outside this blessing is accursed, as Paul clearly teaches when he says:

10. *For all who rely on works of the Law are under a curse.*

Therefore the curse is a kind of flood that swallows up whatever is outside Abraham, that is, outside faith and the promise of the blessing of Abraham. Now if the Law itself, given through Moses by a divine command, subjects those who are under it to a curse, much more will those laws and traditions do so which have been invented by human reason. If anyone, therefore, wants to escape the curse, let him take hold of the promise of the blessing, or the faith of Abraham; otherwise he will remain under the curse. From this passage, "shall be blessed in you," it follows that all nations before, during, and after Abraham are under a curse and are to be under a curse forever, unless they are blessed in the faith of Abraham, to whom the promise of the blessing was given, to be broadcast to his descendants.

[56] Cf. Aristotle, *Prior Analytics,* Book I, chs. 2—3.

It is very useful to know all this; for it serves to comfort consciences, so that we may learn to separate the righteousness of faith very far from the righteousness of the flesh or civic righteousness. Here Paul is dealing, not with a political topic but with a theological and spiritual one, with something in the sight of God. This is said to keep some incompetent person from carping and saying that he is cursing and condemning political laws and those who occupy political office. Jerome labors here, but he says nothing that matters;[57] and the sophists are more speechless than fish. Therefore readers must be warned that in this passage nothing is being discussed that concerns civic laws, customs, or political matters — these are ordinances of God and good things, which Scripture elsewhere approves and commends — but that the spiritual righteousness by which we are justified in the sight of God and are called sons of God in the kingdom of heaven is the topic of discussion here. In short, nothing is set forth here about our physical life. Here Paul is treating of eternal life, where no blessing is to be hoped for or no righteousness is to be sought apart from the promise of the blessing of Abraham, either through the Law or through human traditions or through anything else that can be mentioned in this life. Let civic laws and ordinances remain in their proper order and place, and let the householder and magistrate make laws that are ever so good and fine. Yet none of this will liberate a man from the curse in the sight of God. The kingdom of Babylon, divinely instituted and entrusted to kings, had very good laws; and all the nations were commanded to obey them. Nevertheless, obedience to these laws did not save anyone from the curse of the divine Law. Thus we obey the imperial laws; but we are not righteous in the sight of God on this account, for here we are dealing with another issue.

Not without reason do I urge this distinction; for it is very important to know it, even though only a few observe it or hold to it. Besides, it is easy to mix heavenly and political righteousness. In political righteousness law and works must be looked at; but in spiritual, divine, and heavenly righteousness all law and works must be completely banished from sight, and only the promise and blessing of Abraham must be beheld, which sets forth Christ, the Blesser, the Dispenser of grace, and the Savior. Thus this spiritual righteousness, without the Law or any works, looks only at the grace and

---

[57] Jerome, *Commentarius in Epistolam S. Pauli ad Galatas*, II, *Patrologia, Series Latina*, XXVI, 383—4.

blessing offered and granted through Christ as this was promised to Abraham and believed by him.

Consequently, it is easy to see that this argument is very forceful. For if this blessing is to be hoped for and received through Christ alone, then it necessarily follows by contrariety that it is not received through the Law. Therefore those who are under the Law are not blessed but remain under the curse, because the blessing was given to the Abraham who had faith, before the Law and without the Law. But with the faith with which he believed in the Christ who would give the blessing — with this same faith we believe in the Christ who is present; and thus we are justified by faith, as Abraham was justified by faith. Therefore those who are under the Law are under a curse.

The pope and the bishops cannot endure this. And it is not proper for us to keep silence; for we must confess the truth and say that the papacy is under a curse, that the laws and statutes of the emperor are under a curse, because, according to Paul, whatever is outside the promise and the faith of Abraham is under a curse. When our opponents hear this, they interpret our words perversely, as though we taught that the government is not to be treated with respect or as though we were fomenting rebellion against the emperor, condemning all laws, disrupting and destroying commonwealths, etc. But they are doing us a grave injustice. For we distinguish between a physical and a spiritual blessing, and we say that the emperor is blessed with a physical blessing; for it is a blessing to have a kingdom, laws, civic ordinances, or to have a wife, children, a house, and property. All these are good creatures granted by God. But by this physical blessing, which is temporary and has an end, we are not delivered from the eternal curse. Therefore we do not condemn the laws; nor are we seditious against the emperor. We teach that he is to be obeyed, feared, venerated, and adored — but in a civil manner. But when it comes to our theological doctrine, which deals with righteousness in the sight of God, there we boldly say with Paul that whatever is outside the promise and the faith of Abraham is under a curse and remains under a curse that is heavenly and eternal; here another life after this present one and another blessing after this physical one are to be sought.

In short, we say that all things are good creatures of God. To have a wife, children, and property, or to have laws, political ordinances, and ceremonies — these are divine blessings in their place; that is, they are temporal blessings pertaining to this life. But the self-righteous of all ages — Jews, papists, sectarians, etc. — confuse and mix up these blessings, because they do not distinguish between physical and spiritual blessings. Thus they say: "We have the Law. It is good, holy, and righteous. Therefore we are justified through it." Who is denying that the Law is good, etc.? But, on the other hand, it is also the Law of the curse, of sin, of wrath, and of death. Therefore a distinction must be made here as follows: God has a double blessing, a physical one for this life and a spiritual one for eternal life. Hence we say that it is a blessing to have riches, children, etc., but only at its own level, namely, for this present life. But for eternal life it is not enough to have physical blessings, for ungodly people flourish and abound in these most of all. Nor is it enough to have civic and legal righteousness, for ungodly people flourish very much in this as well. God dispenses these gifts of His freely in the world to both good and bad, just as "He makes His sun rise on the evil and on the good, and sends rain on the just and on the unjust" (Matt. 5:45); for He is generous to everyone. For Him it is a mere trifle to subject the whole created world under the feet of the ungodly. Rom. 8:20 says: "The creation was subjected to futility, not of its own will." Therefore those who have only these physical blessings are not on that account the sons of God, spiritually blessed in the sight of God, as Abraham was. They are under a curse, as Paul says: "All who rely on works of the Law are under a curse."

Paul could have put this into a universal proposition: "Whatever is apart from faith is under a curse." He does not do so; but he selects something which, except for faith, is the best, the greatest, and the loveliest among the physical blessings of the world, namely, the Law of God. "Although this is indeed holy and divinely instituted," he says, "still it does not accomplish anything but to subject all men to a curse and keep them under a curse." If the divine Law subjects men to a curse, much more will lesser laws and blessings do so. To make it properly and clearly understood what he calls being under a curse, Paul proves and declares this by the testimony of Scripture when he says:

For it is written: Cursed be everyone who does not abide by all things written in the book of the Law, and do them.

With this testimony, taken from Deut. 27:26, Paul seeks to prove that all who are under the Law or under the works of the Law are accursed or under the curse, that is, under sin, the wrath of God, eternal death, and all evils. For, as I have said earlier, he is not speaking about a physical or a political curse; he is speaking about a spiritual and eternal one, which must be the curse of eternal death and of hell. This is an amazing kind of proof, because Paul proves the affirmative statement, "All who rely on works of the Law are under a curse," on the basis of this negative statement borrowed from Moses, "Cursed be everyone who does not abide by all things, etc." These two statements, Paul's and Moses', are in complete conflict. Paul's is: "Whoever does the works of the Law is accursed." Moses' is: "Whoever does not do the works of the Law is accursed." How can these be reconciled? Or (what is more) how can the one be proved on the basis of the other? What sort of proof would it be, I ask you, if I sought to prove this statement, "If you observe the commandments of God, you will enter life" (Matt. 19:17), on the basis of the statement, "If you do not observe the Commandments of God, you will enter life"? Would I not be proving one contrary on the basis of another? What a beautiful method of proof! And yet Paul's method of proof here is very similar. No one understands this passage unless he has the correct doctrine of justification. Jerome really sweats over it, but he leaves it unexplained.[58]

Undoubtedly Paul treated this passage at greater length when he was among the Galatians; otherwise the Galatians would not have understood what Paul had in mind, since here he merely touches on it briefly and in passing. But because they had heard this expounded by him before, it was recalled to their memory as soon as they had been reminded. These two statements are not contradictory; they are in complete agreement. We, too, teach the same way: "It is not the hearers of the Law who are righteous before God, but the doers of the Law will be justified" (Rom. 2:13); and, on the other hand, those who do works according to the Law are damned. For the doctrine of justification says: "Whatever is outside the faith of Abraham is accursed"; nevertheless, the justification of the Law "ought to be fulfilled in us" (Rom. 8:4). To a man who is ignorant of the doctrine of faith, these statements seem to be utterly contradictory and to sound no different from these utterly absurd statements: "If you have fulfilled the Law, you have not fulfilled it; if you have not fulfilled it, you have fulfilled it."

[58] Cf. p. 249, note 57.

It must be noted first of all, therefore, what topic Paul is discussing, what he has in mind, and how he looks at Moses. As I have often said, he is discussing a spiritual topic here, one that is apart from the political sphere and from all laws. He is looking at Moses with different eyes from those of the hypocrites and false apostles, and he is expounding the Law in a spiritual way. Hence the whole force is on the term "do." To do the Law is to keep it not only externally but correctly and perfectly. There are two classes of doers of the Law. The first are those who rely on works of the Law; against these Paul contends and battles in this entire epistle. The second are those who are men of faith, about whom we shall speak a little later. Now to rely on the Law or on the works of the Law and to be a man of faith are altogether contrary, just as the devil and God, sin and righteousness, death and life are contrary. Those who rely on the Law are those who want to be justified through the Law; those who are men of faith are those who trust that they are justified solely by mercy. Anyone who says that righteousness is on the basis of faith damns and curses the righteousness of works; on the other hand, anyone who says that righteousness is on the basis of the Law damns and curses the righteousness of faith. Therefore these two are exact contraries. Here Paul is not speaking about the Law and works taken in a metaphysical sense; he is speaking about how they are used and interpreted, namely, that hypocrites want to be justified through the Law and works.

Whoever considers this understands easily that to keep the Law is to do what is commanded in the Law not only in appearance but in the Spirit, that is, truly and perfectly. But where can we find someone who keeps the Law this way? Just let him be produced, and we will praise him! Here our opponents immediately respond: "The doers of the Law will be justified" (Rom. 2:13). All right. But first let us define who these doers are. They call someone a doer of the Law if he performs the works of the Law and thus is justified by these "preceding works." This is not keeping the Law according to Paul, because, as I have said, relying on works and being a man of faith are contraries. Therefore to want to be justified by works of the Law is to deny the righteousness of faith. On this basis, when those who are self-righteous keep the Law, they deny the righteousness of faith and sin against the First, Second, and Third Commandments, and against the entire Law, because God commands that He be worshiped by believing and fearing Him. But they, on the contrary, make works into righteousness, without faith and against faith. Therefore by their very keeping of the Law they act in a manner that is most contrary to the Law, and they sin most seriously and grievously. For they deny the righteousness, the mercy, and the promises of God; they deny Christ, together with all His blessings; and in their heart they establish, not the righteousness of the Law — which they do not understand, much less keep — but a mere figment and idol of the Law. It is inevitable, therefore, that by doing the Law they not only do not keep it, but that they even sin and deny the Divine Majesty in all His promises. Certainly the Law was not given for this!

Therefore they misuse the Law, because they do not understand it. As Paul says in Rom. 10:3: "Being ignorant of the righteousness that comes from God, and seeking to establish their own, they did not submit to God's righteousness." For they are blind, and they do not understand how faith and the promises are to be interpreted. They rush into Scripture without any judgment and take hold of only one part of it, namely, the Law. This they think they fulfill by works. But this is a mere dream, a bewitchment and a delusion of the heart; and the righteousness of the Law which they think they are producing is in fact nothing but idolatry and blasphemy against God. Therefore it is necessary that they remain under the curse.

Thus it is impossible for us to keep the Law in the manner they dream of, much less for us to be justified through it. Evidence for this comes, first, from the Law itself, which has an altogether opposite effect. For it increases sin, works wrath, accuses, terrifies, and condemns. How, then, could it justify? Second, the promise shows the same thing. For it was said to Abraham: "In you shall all the nations be blessed." Hence there is no blessing except in the promise to Abraham; and if you are outside this, you are and remain under the curse. If you are under the curse, you do not fulfill the Law, because you are under sin, the devil, and eternal death, all of which surely accompany the curse. In short, if righteousness came through the Law, then God would be promising in vain and showering His blessing in vain. Since God knew that we could not keep the Law, He foresaw this long before the Law. He took the initiative in coming to Abraham, and He promised the blessing, saying: "In you shall all the nations be blessed." Thus He testified that all the nations would be blessed, not through the Law but through the promise of Abraham. Therefore those who neglect or despise the promise and then grasp hold of the Law in order to be justified through it are under a curse.

Therefore "to do" is first to believe and so, through faith, to keep the Law. For we must receive the Holy Spirit; illumined and renewed by Him, we begin to keep the Law, to love God and our neighbor. But the Holy Spirit is not received through the Law — for "those who are under the Law," says Paul, "are under a curse" — but through hearing with faith, that is, through the promise. We must be blessed solely with Abraham and by his faith in the promise. Therefore it is necessary above all to take refuge in the promise, so that we may hear the sound of blessing, that is, the Gospel. This must be believed. The sound of the promise to Abraham brings Christ; and when He has been grasped by faith, then the Holy Spirit is granted on Christ's account. Then God and our neighbor are loved, good works are performed, and the cross is borne. This is really keeping the Law; otherwise the Law remains permanently unkept. Therefore, clearly and properly defined, "to do" is simply to believe in Jesus Christ, and when the Holy Spirit has been received through faith in Christ, to do the things that are in the Law. Nor can it be any other way, because Scripture says that outside the promise there is no blessing, not even in the Law. Hence it is impossible for us to keep the Law without the promise. The blessing, which is the proclamation about Christ, who was promised to Abraham as the One through whom the world is to be blessed, must be present.

You cannot produce anyone in all the world to whom the title "doer of the Law" applies apart from the promise of the Gospel. "Doer of the Law" is, therefore, a fictitious term, which no one understands unless he is outside and beyond the Law in the blessing and the faith of Abraham. Thus he is a true doer of the Law who receives the Holy Spirit through faith in Christ and then begins to love God and to do good to his neighbor. Hence "to do" includes faith at the same time. Faith takes the doer himself and makes him into a tree, and his deeds become fruit. First there must be a tree, then the fruit. For apples do not make a tree, but a tree makes apples. So faith first makes the person, who afterwards performs works. To keep the Law without faith, therefore, is to make apples without a tree, out of wood or mud, which is not to make apples but to make mere phantasies. But once the tree has been planted, that is, once there is the person or doer who comes into being through faith in Christ, then works follow. For there must be a doer before deeds, not deeds before the doer. So "the doer of the Law is justified"; that is, he is accounted as righteous (Rom. 2:13).

A doer does not get this name on the basis of works that have been performed; he gets it on the basis of works that are to be performed. For Christians do not become righteous by doing righteous works; but once they have been justified by faith in Christ, they do righteous works. In civil life the situation is different; here one becomes a doer on the basis of deeds, just as one becomes a lutenist by often playing the lute, as Aristotle says.[59] But in theology one does not become a doer on the basis of works of the Law; first there must be the doer, and then the deeds follow.

The sophists themselves are obliged to confess, as they also teach, that if a moral work, performed externally, is not done with a sincere heart, a good will, and a true command of reason, it is a pretended work.[60] This is the source of the proverb among the Germans: "The cowl conceals many a rascal." For an ungodly and evil scoundrel can imitate the very works that a godly man does on the basis of faith, as Judas did the same works the other apostles did. Then what is lacking in Judas' works, since he is doing the same things the rest of the apostles do? Here the sophist responds, on the basis of his moral philosophy: "The person, the will, and the dictate of reason are all evil. Judas is an evil man, and he has a perverse heart." Thus they themselves are obliged to admit that in civil and external matters works do not justify unless they involve at the same time an upright heart, attitude, and will. How much more are they obliged to admit this in theology, where there must be, before anything else, the knowledge of God and faith, which purifies the heart! Therefore they go along in works and in the righteousness of the Law, as Judas went along in the works of the apostles; they do not understand what they are saying or what they are saying it about. For the Law was not given in order to justify; it was given in order to work wrath, to disclose sin, to reveal the wrath and judgment of God, and to threaten eternal death. When they read this in Paul, they do not even see it; much less do they understand it. Therefore they are not worthy even of being called hypocrites; but they are masks and ghosts, who have obviously been bewitched, when they dream that they are righteous by works of the Law. For, as I have said, "doer of the Law" as they

[59] Perhaps a reference to Aristotle, *Politics*, Book VIII, ch. 6.
[60] Cf. Thomas Aquinas, *Summa Theologica*, I—II, Q. 109, Art. 4.

GALATIANS — 1535
[W, XL, 403—405]

define "doer of the Law," is a fictitious term, nothing but a monstrosity that does not exist anywhere.

Therefore when Paul proves the passage, "All who rely on works of the Law are under a curse," on the basis of the statement of Moses, "Cursed be everyone, etc.," he is not proving one contrary on the basis of another, as appears at first sight; but he is proving it correctly and very well. For Moses means and states the same thing Paul does when he says: "Cursed be everyone who does not abide, etc." For no one abides by it. Therefore those who rely on works of the Law do not keep the Law; and if they do not keep it, then they are under a curse. But because there are two sorts of doers of the Law, as I have said, true ones and hypocrites, the true ones must be separated from the hypocrites. The true ones are those who through faith are a good tree before they bear fruit and doers before they do works. Moses is speaking about these too. And unless they are of this sort, they are under a curse. Now none of the hypocrites are of this sort, because they have the idea that they want to achieve righteousness by works and to make themselves righteous persons by this means. For this is how they think: "We who are sinners and unrighteous men want to be made righteous. How? On the basis of works." Therefore they act like a foolish architect who would try to make a foundation out of a roof or a tree out of fruit. For when they seek to be justified through works, they try to make the works into the worker, which is the exact opposite of what Moses does; he makes such a worker subject to the curse just as much as Paul does.

In "keeping" the Law, therefore, they not only do not keep it, but they also deny the First Commandment, the promises of God, and the blessing promised to Abraham. They deny faith and try to bless themselves by their own works, that is, to justify themselves, to set themselves free from sin and death, to overcome the devil, and to capture heaven by force [61] — which is to deny God and to set oneself up in place of God. For all these are exclusively works of the Divine Majesty, not of any creature, whether angelic or human. Therefore Paul could easily predict on the basis of the First Commandment that abominations would be established in the church by Antichrist. For those who teach that some other worship is necessary for salvation than the worship set down in the First Commandment —

[61] This may be a reference to Matt. 11:12.

which is fear, trust, and love toward God — are antichrists and are setting themselves up in place of God (2 Thess. 2:4). Hence Christ predicted: "Many will come in My name, saying: 'I am the Christ'" (Matt. 24:5). Thus we today can say, both easily and surely: Whoever seeks righteousness apart from faith and through works denies God and makes himself into God. This is what he thinks: "If I do this work, I shall be righteous. I shall be the victor over sin, death, the devil, the wrath of God, and hell; and I shall attain eternal life." Now what is this, I ask you, but to arrogate to oneself a work that belongs to God alone, and to show that one is God? Therefore it is easy for us to prophesy and to judge with certainty about all those who are outside the faith that they are not only idolaters but idols who deny God and set themselves up in place of God (2 Thess. 2:4). Peter prophesied on this same basis when he said (2 Peter 2:1): "There will be false teachers among you, who will deny the Master who bought them."

In the Old Testament all the prophecies against idolaters flowed from the First Commandment. For all the kings and prophets, together with all the unfaithful people, did nothing else than what the pope and all the hypocrites always do. "By observing this worship," they supposed, "we shall praise and serve God, who brought us out of the land of Egypt." Thus Jeroboam made two golden calves and said (1 Kings 12:28): "Behold your gods, O Israel, who brought you up out of the land of Egypt." He was saying this about the true God, who had done this work. And yet he, together with the entire nation, was an idolater, because they worshiped God contrary to the First Commandment. They paid attention only to the work; when this was done, they thought that they were righteous in the sight of God, which was to deny God Himself, about whom they proclaimed with their mouths that He had brought them up out of the land of Egypt. About such idolaters Paul says (Titus 1:16): "They profess to know God, but they deny Him by their deeds."

Therefore all hypocrites and idolaters try to do the works that properly pertain to the Deity and belong completely and solely to Christ. They do not actually say with their mouths: "I am God; I am Christ." Yet in fact they arrogate to themselves the divinity of Christ and His function. In fact, then, they do say: "I am Christ. I am the Savior — not only my own but for others as well." Thus the monks have taught, and they have persuaded the whole world of this, that they are able to justify not only themselves with their hypocritical sanctity but also others to whom they communicate it, even though it is the proper function of Christ alone to justify the sinner. Thus the pope, by extending his divinity over the whole world, has denied and completely suppressed the work of Christ and His divinity.

It is useful for these things to be taught and considered carefully, for they help one to judge about all Christian doctrine and all human life. They also help to confirm consciences and enable one to understand all prophecies and all Scripture, with judgment about everything. For anyone who properly knows all this can declare for certain that the pope is the Antichrist. He can understand for certain what it means to deny God or to deny Christ; what Christ meant when He said (Matt. 24:5): "Many will come in My name, saying, 'I am the Christ'"; what it means to "oppose God and exalt oneself against every so-called god or object of worship" (2 Thess. 2:4); what it means to "take one's seat in the temple of God, proclaiming oneself to be God" (2 Thess. 2:4); what it means for the abomination to stand in the holy place (Matt. 24:15). All these things have their source in the refusal of this accursed hypocrisy to be justified by a divine blessing and formed by God the Creator. It refuses to be merely passive matter but wants actively to accomplish the things that it should patiently permit God to accomplish in it and should accept from Him. And so it makes itself the creator and the justifier through its own works and spurns the blessing promised and given to Abraham and to his believing children. Thus every hypocrite is the material and the worker at the same time (even though this is contrary to philosophy, since the same thing cannot act upon itself [62]) — the material, because he is a sinner; and the worker, because he puts on a cowl or selects some other work through which he hopes to merit grace and to save both himself and others. Thus he is creature and creator at the same time. Therefore no one can describe in words how horrible and dreadful a thing it is to seek righteousness apart from the blessing, in the Law and in works. For this is the abomination standing in the holy place (Matt. 24:15), which denies God and establishes a creature in the place of the Creator.

Therefore when Moses says: "Cursed be everyone, etc.," he is speaking about those who are doers of the Law. But the doers of

---

[62] Cf. Aristotle, *Physics*, Book VII, ch. 1.

the Law are believers, who, having received the Holy Spirit, fulfill the Law and love God and their neighbor. Thus the "doer of the Law" is not one who becomes a doer on the basis of his deeds; he is one who, having already become a person through faith, then becomes a doer. For in theology those who have been made righteous do righteous things, not as in philosophy, where those who do righteous things are made righteous. Therefore we, being justified by faith, do good works, through which, as 2 Peter 1:10 says, our call and election are confirmed and made more certain day by day. But because we have only the first fruits of the Spirit and do not yet have the tithes,[63] and because remnants of sin remain in us, we do not keep the Law perfectly. But this is not imputed to us who believe in Christ — in Christ, who was promised to Abraham and has blessed us. For meanwhile we are cherished and fed, for the sake of Christ, in the lap of the forbearance of God. We are that wounded man who fell among robbers; whose wounds the Samaritan bound up, pouring on oil and wine; whom he set on his own beast and brought to an inn and took care of; and whom he entrusted to the innkeeper upon departing, with the words: "Take care of him" (Luke 10:30-35). Thus we are cherished meanwhile as in an inn, until the Lord reaches out His hand a second time, as Isaiah says, to deliver us (Is. 10: 10-11).

As I have said, therefore, the statement of Moses, "Cursed be everyone who does not abide by all things, etc.," is not contrary to Paul's declaration that all who rely on works of the Law are under a curse. For Moses demands a doer who keeps the Law perfectly. But where are we to find such a one? Nowhere. Paul admits that he is not such a one, because he says in Rom. 7:15: "I do not do what I want"; and David says: "Enter not into judgment with Thy servant" (Ps. 143:2). Therefore Moses, together with Paul, necessarily drives us to Christ, through whom we become doers of the Law and are accounted guilty of no transgression. How? First, through the forgiveness of sins and the imputation of righteousness, on account of faith in Christ; secondly, through the gift and the Holy Spirit, who creates a new life and new impulses in us, so that we may keep the Law also in a formal sense. Whatever is not kept is forgiven for the sake of Christ. Besides, whatever sin is left is not imputed to us. Thus Moses agrees with Paul and means the same thing when he says: "Cursed be everyone, etc.," because he denies

63 Cf. p. 196, note 16.

that they are keeping the Law when they want to justify themselves on the basis of works; and with Paul he concludes that they are under a curse. Therefore Moses requires true doers, who are men of faith, just as Paul condemns those who are not true doers, that is, who are not men of faith. There is no problem here. Moses was speaking negatively and Paul affirmatively, provided that you define correctly what "doing" means. Thus both are true, namely, that all are under a curse who do not abide by all things, etc., and that those who rely on works of the Law are under a curse. So much for the argument on the basis of contraries: "If the nations are blessed in the Abraham who has faith, it is necessary that they be under a curse."

Since this passage provides the occasion, something must be said about the arguments that are usually put forth by the opponents of our doctrine that we are justified by faith alone. There are many passages in the Scriptures, both in the Old Testament and in the New, about works and rewards; our opponents depend on these and think that by means of these they can successfully overthrow the doctrine of faith, which we teach and maintain. Therefore we have to be equipped, so that we may be able not only to teach those who are on our side but also to reply to the objections of our opponents.

The sophists, as well as anyone else who does not grasp the doctrine of justification, do not know of any other righteousness than civil righteousness or the righteousness of the Law, which are known in some measure even to the heathen. Therefore they snatch the words "do," "work," and the like, from moral philosophy and from the Law, and transfer them to theology, where they act in a way that is not only evil but ungodly. Philosophy and theology must be carefully distinguished. Philosophy also speaks of a good will and of right reason, and the sophists are forced to admit that a work is not morally good unless a good will is present first. And yet they are such stupid asses when they proceed to theology. They want to prescribe a work before the good will, although in philosophy it is necessary for the person to be justified morally before the work. Thus the tree is prior to the fruit, both in essence and in nature. They themselves admit this and teach that in nature being precedes working and that in ethics a good will is required before the work.[64] Only in theology do they reverse this and put a work ahead of right reason.

[64] Cf. p. 256, note 60.

Therefore "doing" is one thing in nature, another in philosophy, and another in theology. In nature the tree must be first, and then the fruit. In moral philosophy doing means a good will and right reason to do well; this is where the philosophers come to a halt. Therefore we say in theology that moral philosophy does not have God as its object and final cause, since Aristotle or a Sadducee or a man who is good in a civic sense calls it right reason and good will if he seeks the common welfare of the state and tranquillity and honesty. A philosopher or a lawyer does not ascend any higher. He does not suppose that through right reason he will obtain the forgiveness of sins and eternal life, as the sophist or the monk does. Therefore a heathen philosopher is much better than such a self-righteous person, because he remains within his limits, having in mind only honesty and tranquillity, and not mixing divine things with human. The sophist does not act this way. He supposes that God pays attention to his good intention and his works. Therefore he mixes human things with divine and pollutes the name of God; these things he obviously draws from moral philosophy, except that he abuses this worse than a heathen does.

Therefore we have to rise higher in theology with the word "doing," so that it becomes altogether new. For just as it becomes something different when it is taken from the natural area into the moral, so it becomes something much more different when it is transferred from philosophy and from the Law into theology. Thus it has a completely new meaning; it does indeed require right reason and a good will, but in a theological sense, not in a moral sense, which means that through the Word of the Gospel I know and believe that God sent His Son into the world to redeem us from sin and death. Here "doing" is a new thing, unknown to reason, to the philosophers, to the legalists, and to all men; for it is a "wisdom hidden in a mystery" (1 Cor. 2:7). In theology, therefore, "doing" necessarily requires faith itself as a precondition. This is how you must answer all the passages of Scripture about works, in which our opponents stress the words "working" and "doing": These are theological terms, not natural or moral ones. If they are natural or moral, they are taken according to their usage. But if they are theological, they include right reason and a good will, which is incomprehensible to human reason, blinded as it is at this point; and another reason must come into being, which is the reason of faith. Therefore "doing" is always understood in theology as doing with faith, so that doing with faith is another sphere and a new realm, so to speak, one that is different from moral doing. When we theologians speak about "doing," therefore, it is necessary that we speak about doing with faith, because in theology we have no right reason and good will except faith.

You have this rule beautifully and clearly stated in Heb. 11, where many and various works of the saints are listed from Holy Scripture, as of David, who killed a lion and a bear, and who killed Goliath. Here a bungling jackass of a sophist looks only at the outward appearance of the work, as a cow looks at a new gate. But this work must be looked at in such a way that first you consider what sort of person David was before he performed this work, namely, that he was the sort whose heart trusted in the Lord God of Israel, as the text clearly states (1 Sam. 17:37): "The Lord who delivered me from the paw of the lion and from the paw of the bear, will deliver me from the hand of this Philistine." Again (1 Sam. 17: 45-47): "You come to me with a sword and with a spear and with a javelin; but I come to you in the name of the Lord of hosts, the God of the armies of Israel, whom you have defied. This day the Lord will deliver you into my hand, and I will strike you down, and cut off your head, because the Lord saves not with sword and spear." Therefore you see that he was righteous and acceptable to God, strong and constant in faith, before he did this work. Accordingly, David's "doing" is neither a natural doing nor a moral doing; it is a doing in faith.

Thus the same epistle says of Abel that by faith he offered up a better sacrifice to God than Cain did (Heb. 11:4). If the sophists come upon this passage as it is written in Genesis (where it is simply described that both Cain and Abel offered up their gifts, and that the Lord had regard for Abel and his offering [Gen. 4:3-4]), they immediately take hold of the words "they offered gifts" and "the Lord had regard for Abel's offering." And they exclaim: "Here you can hear and see that God had regard for offerings; therefore works do justify!" Thus these filthy swine think that righteousness is something moral, since they look only at the mask of the work and not at the heart of the one who is doing the work. And yet in philosophy itself they are obliged to look, not upon the bare work but upon the good will of the one who does the work. But here they simply cling to the words "they offered gifts" and "the Lord had regard for offerings"; they do not see that the text in Genesis explicitly states that the Lord had regard first for Abel because his person was pleasing on account of faith, and only then for his offerings. In theology, therefore, we speak of works, sacrifices, offerings, and gifts that are faithful, that is, that are offered and performed in faith, as the Epistle to the Hebrews explains. "By faith," it says (Heb. 11:4), "Abel offered a more acceptable sacrifice"; "by faith Enoch was taken up" (Heb. 11:5); "by faith Abraham obeyed" (Heb. 11:8). Here, then, you have a rule about how one should reply plainly to the arguments raised by our opponents about works, namely, "This or that man did this work in faith." And thus you nullify all their arguments.

From this it is evident that in theology the work does not amount to anything without faith, but that faith must precede before you can do works. For "without faith it is impossible to please God, but whoever would draw near to God must believe" (Heb. 11:6). Therefore the writer of the Epistle to the Hebrews says that the sacrifice of Abel was better because he believed. But because Cain was an ungodly man and a hypocrite, he performed a work that was moral, or rather one that was reasonable, by which he sought to please God. Therefore the work of Cain was hypocritical and faithless; in it there was no faith in grace but only a presumption about his own righteousness. And so the "doing," the gift, and the offering of Abel are faithful; but those of Cain are faithless. Thus our opponents are forced to concede that in all the works of the saints the faith on account of which the works are pleasing is presupposed. In theology, therefore, there is a new "doing," one that is different from moral "doing."

In addition, we also distinguish faith in this way, that sometimes faith is understood apart from the work and sometimes with the work. For just as a craftsman speaks about his material in different ways and a gardener speaks about a tree as either barren or fruit-bearing, so the Holy Spirit speaks about faith in different ways in Scripture: sometimes, if I may speak this way, about an abstract or an absolute faith and sometimes about a concrete, composite, or incarnate faith. Thus if Christ is looked at on the basis of outward appearance, He seems to be a mere man. And yet Scripture sometimes speaks of Christ as God, and sometimes it speaks of Him as composite and incarnate. Faith is absolute or abstract when Scripture speaks absolutely about justification or about those who are justified, as you see in the Epistle to the Romans and in the Epistle to the Galatians. But when Scripture speaks about rewards and works, then it is speaking about faith as something compound, concrete, or incarnate. We shall recite some examples of this faith, as, for example, "faith working through love" (Gal. 5:6); "To the pure all things are pure" (Titus 1:15); "If you would enter life, keep the Commandments" (Matt. 19:17); "He who does them shall live by them" (Gal. 3:12); "Depart from evil, and do good" (Ps. 37:27).[65] In these and similar passages — which are innumerable in Holy Scripture — where mention is made of "doing," Scripture is always speaking of doing in faith. Thus when it says: "Do this, and you will live," it means: "Take care first that you be faithful, that you have right reason and a good will, that is, faith in Christ. When you have this, you can do works."

It is no wonder, then, if merits and rewards are promised to this incarnate faith, that is, to this working faith, such as the faith of Abel, or to faithful works. And why should Holy Scripture not speak in these different ways about faith when it speaks in different ways about Christ as God and man? That is, sometimes it speaks about His whole Person, sometimes about His two natures separately, either the divine or the human nature. If it speaks about the natures separately, it is speaking of Him absolutely; but if it speaks about the divine nature united with the human in one Person, then it is speaking of Christ as composite and incarnate. In this sense I can truly say: "The Infant lying in the lap of His mother created heaven and earth, and is the Lord of the angels." I am indeed speaking about a man here. But "man" in this proposition is obviously a new word and, as the sophists themselves say, stands for the divinity;[66] that is, this God who became man created all things. Here creation is attributed solely to the divinity, since the humanity does not create. Nevertheless, it is said correctly that "the man created," because the divinity, which alone creates, is incarnate with the humanity, and therefore the humanity participates in the attributes of both predicates. Thus it is said: "This man Jesus led Israel out of Egypt, struck down Pharaoh, and did all the things that belong to God." Here everything is being attributed to the man on account of the divinity.

Therefore when Scripture says (Dan. 4:27): "Redeem your sins by showing mercy" or (Luke 10:28) "Do this, and you will live," it is necessary to see first of all what this "doing" is. For in these

[65] See p. 145, note 64.

[66] Cf. *Luther's Works*, 37, p. 210, on such language.

passages, as I have said, Scripture is speaking about faith in the concrete rather than in the abstract, in a composite sense rather than in a bare or simple sense. Therefore the meaning of the passage, "Do this, and you will live," is "You will live on account of this faithful 'doing'; this 'doing' will give you life solely on account of faith." Thus justification belongs to faith alone, just as creation belongs to the divinity; nevertheless, just as it is true to say about Christ the man that He created all things, so justification is attributed to incarnate faith or to faithful "doing." Therefore one must not think, as the sophists and hypocrites usually do, that works justify absolutely and simply as such, and that merits and rewards are promised to moral works rather than solely to works done in faith.

Therefore let us permit the Holy Spirit to speak, as He does in the Scriptures, either about abstract, bare, and simple faith or about concrete, composite, and incarnate faith. Everything that is attributed to works belongs to faith. For works must not be looked at in a moral sense; they must be looked at in a theological and faithful sense. Therefore in theology let faith always be the divinity of works, diffused throughout the works in the same way that the divinity is throughout the humanity of Christ. Anyone who touches the heat in the heated iron touches the iron; [67] and whoever has touched the skin of Christ has actually touched God. Therefore faith is the "do-all" in works, if I may use this expression.[68] Thus Abraham is called faithful because faith is diffused throughout all of Abraham. When I look at Abraham doing works, therefore, I see nothing of the physical Abraham or of the Abraham who does works, but only Abraham the believer.

I am inculcating these things so diligently in order to set forth the doctrine of faith clearly, so that you may be able to reply correctly and easily to the objections of our opponents, who confuse philosophy and theology and make theological works into moral works. A theological work is a work done in faith; thus a theological man is a man of faith. In like manner, a right reason and a good will are a reason and will in faith. Thus faith is universally the divinity in the work, the person, and the members of the body, as the one and only cause of justification; afterwards this is attributed to the matter on account of the form, to the work on account of

---

[67] On the origins of this image cf. *Luther's Works,* 23, p. 123, note 95.

[68] The term is *fac totum;* see also *Luther's Works,* 3, p. 90, note 7.

the faith. The kingly authority of the divinity is given to Christ the man, not because of His humanity but because of His divinity. For the divinity alone created all things, without the cooperation of the humanity. Nor did the humanity conquer sin and death; but the hook that was concealed under the worm, at which the devil struck, conquered and devoured the devil, who was attempting to devour the worm.[69] Therefore the humanity would not have accomplished anything by itself; but the divinity, joined with the humanity, did it alone, and the humanity did it on account of the divinity. So here faith alone justifies and does everything; nevertheless, it is attributed to works on account of faith.

These words "doing" and "working" are to be taken in three ways: the essential or natural way (although the sophists have invented certain neutral works, which they say are neither good nor bad[70]), the moral way, and the theological way. In essences or natures and in moral matters, as I have said, these words are taken in their usual way. But in theology they become completely new words and acquire a new meaning. Therefore all the hypocrites, who want to be justified on the basis of the Law and have false ideas about God, belong to moral "doing"; against them Paul is disputing here. For they have the sort of "doing" that proceeds from a moral or human right reason and good will. Therefore their work is merely moral or rational, not a faithful or theological work, one that includes faith. When you read in Scripture, therefore, about the patriarchs, prophets, and kings that they worked righteousness, raised the dead, conquered kingdoms, etc., you should remember that these and similar statements are to be explained according to a new and theological grammar, as the eleventh chapter of the Epistle to the Hebrews explains them: "By faith they worked righteousness, by faith they raised the dead, by faith they conquered kings and kingdoms." Thus faith embodies and informs[71] the "doing." And if our opponents are sane, they cannot deny this; nor do they have anything with which to contradict or oppose it. They can, of course, scream that Scripture often speaks about "doing" and "working." And we continually reply that it is speaking about a "doing" that has faith. For reason should first be

---

[69] This patristic metaphor has its roots in Job 41:1. It is elaborated, for example, by Gregory of Nyssa, *Orationes catecheticae*, XXIV, 93, 3, *Patrologia, Series Graeca*, XLV, 65.

[70] Cf. Thomas Aquinas, *Summa Theologica*, I—II, Q. 18, Art. 8.

[71] Cf. the discussion on p. 229.

illumined by faith before it works. Once a true idea and knowledge of God is held as right reason, then the work is incarnated and incorporated into it. In this way whatever is attributed to faith is later attributed also to works, but only on account of the faith.

I wanted to say this at some length about the term "doing," because the passage cited from Moses, "and do them," required it. I also thought that it would be worthwhile to admonish students of theology to distinguish carefully between true "doing" and hypocritical "doing," between moral "doing" and theological "doing." When they do this, they can easily explain all those passages that seem to assert a righteousness of works. As I have said, true "doing" is a doing in faith and a theological doing, which someone who seeks righteousness on the basis of works does not have. Therefore every doer of the Law and every moral saint who wants to be justified through human will and reason is under a curse, because he comes before God in the presumption of his own righteousness. In "keeping" the Law he does not keep it. This is what Paul calls "relying on works of the Law," namely, that the hypocrites keep the Law, and yet in keeping it they do not keep it, because they understand this "doing" according to the moral grammar, which does not apply in theology. They do perform works, but out of their own presumption and without a theological right reason and good will, that is, without the knowledge of God and faith. Therefore they are blind and in error, and they remain under the curse.

11. *Now it is evident that no man is justified before God by the Law; for the righteous shall live by faith.*

Another argument, derived from the testimony of the prophet Habakkuk. It is a very weighty and a clear authority that Paul sets against all the statements about the Law and works. It is as though he were saying: "What need is there of a long debate? Here I am producing a very clear testimony of the prophet, at which no one can carp: 'The righteous shall live by faith.' If by faith, then not by the Law, because the Law is not by faith." And Paul interprets the term "faith" in its exclusive and antithetical sense.

The sophists, ready as they are to evade the Scriptures, carp at this passage as follows: "'The righteous shall live by faith,' that is, by a faith that is active, working, or 'formed' by love. But if it is an unformed faith, it does not justify." [72] They themselves have made

---

[72] Cf. *Luther's Works*, 3, pp. 169—170.

up this gloss, and with it they do injury to this passage. If they were to call "formed" faith the true and theological or, as Paul calls it, the ἀνυπόκριτος faith (1 Tim. 1:5), which God calls faith, then this gloss of theirs would not offend me. For then faith would not be distinguished from love; it would be distinguished from a vain idea of faith, as we also distinguish between a counterfeit faith and a true faith. A counterfeit faith is one that hears about God, Christ, and all the mysteries of the incarnation and redemption, one that also grasps what it hears and can speak beautifully about it; and yet only a mere opinion and a vain hearing remain, which leave nothing in the heart but a hollow sound about the Gospel, concerning which there is a great deal of chatter. In fact, this is no faith at all; for it neither renews nor changes the heart. It does not produce a new man, but it leaves him in his former opinion and way of life. This is a very pernicious faith, and it would be better not to have it. A moral philosopher is better than such a hypocrite with such a faith.

If they were to distinguish between a "formed faith" and a false or counterfeit faith, their distinction would not offend me at all. But they speak of faith formed by love; and they posit a double faith, namely, formed and unformed.[73] This noxious and satanic gloss I cannot help detesting violently. "Although infused faith may be present," they say, "which is a gift of the Holy Spirit, as well as acquired faith, which we ourselves produce by our many acts of believing, nevertheless they are both unformed and must be formed by love." [74] According to their opinion, faith by itself is like a picture or a beautiful thing in the darkness, which is perceived only when light, that is love, reaches it. And so love is the form of faith, and faith is merely the "matter" of love. In this way they prefer love to faith and attribute righteousness, not to faith but to love. For that by virtue of which something is what it is, is the same thing, only more so. Therefore when they do not attribute righteousness to faith except on account of love, they are attributing nothing at all to faith.

In addition, these subverters of the Gospel say that even infused faith, which has not been received by hearing or produced by any actions but has been created in man by the Holy Spirit, can coexist with mortal sin, and that the most wicked men can have it; and there-

73 See p. 88, note 7.

74 On this distinction cf. also *Luther's Works*, 24, p. 321, note 9.

fore, they say, if it is alone, it is vain and completely useless, even if it should perform miracles. Thus they deprive faith of its task and give this to love, so that faith amounts to nothing at all unless the "form," namely, love, is added to it. According to this malignant figment of the sophists, faith, that miserable virtue, would be a sort of unformed chaos, without any work, efficacy, or life, a purely passive material. This is blasphemous and satanic; it calls men away from Christian doctrine, from Christ the Mediator, and from the faith that takes hold of Christ. For if love is the form of faith, then I am immediately obliged to say that love is the most important and the largest part in the Christian religion. And thus I lose Christ, His blood, His wounds, and all His blessings; and I cling to love, so that I love, and I come to a moral kind of "doing," just as the pope, a heathen philosopher, and the Turk do.

But the Holy Spirit knows how to speak and, as the sophists wickedly imagine, could easily have said: "The righteous shall live by a formed faith." But He purposely omits this and simply says: "The righteous shall live by faith." Therefore let the sophists go hang with their wicked and malignant gloss! We want to retain and to extol this faith which God has called faith, that is, a true and certain faith that has no doubts about God or the divine promises or the forgiveness of sins through Christ. Then we can remain safe and sure in Christ, the object of faith, and keep before our eyes the suffering and the blood of the Mediator and all His blessings. Faith alone, which takes hold of Christ, is the only means to keep us from permitting this to be removed from our sight. Therefore this malignant gloss must be repudiated, and this passage must be understood of faith alone. Paul himself shows this when he argues against a formed faith as follows:

12. *But the Law does not rest on faith.*

The sophists say: "The righteous shall live if his faith is formed." Paul, on the other hand, says: "The Law does not rest on faith." But what is the Law? Is it not also a commandment of love? In fact, the Law commands nothing else but love, as the text says (Matt. 22:37): "You shall love the Lord your God with all your heart, etc." Again (Deut. 5:10): "Showing steadfast love to thousands of those who love Me." And again (Matt. 22:40): "On these two commandments depend all the Law and the prophets." Thus if the Law commanding love conflicts with faith, then love is not of faith. In this way Paul clearly refutes the gloss made up by the sophists about a "formed faith," and, putting the Law aside, he speaks only about faith. Once the Law has been put aside, love is also put aside, as well as everything that belongs to the Law; all that is kept is faith, which justifies and makes alive.

Paul is arguing on the basis of a very clear testimony of the prophet that there is simply no one who attains to justification and life in the sight of God except the believer, who attains to righteousness and life on the basis of faith, without the Law or love. The reason: The Law does not rest on faith, that is, the Law is not faith or anything about faith; it does not believe. Nor are the works of the Law faith. Therefore faith is something different from the Law, just as the promise is something different from the Law. But the promise is not grasped by doing; it is grasped only by believing.

As in philosophy, at the first division, substance and accident are distinct,[75] so in theology the promise and the Law are as distinct as heaven and earth. But if the promise and the Law are distinct, then faith and works are distinct also. Hence it is impossible for faith to rest on the Law, because faith rests only on the promise. Therefore it only accepts and knows God, and it consists only in receiving good things from God. But the Law and works consist in doing and in giving to God. Thus Abel the sacrificer gives to God, but Abel the believer receives from God. Therefore from this passage in the prophet Paul draws the very forceful conclusion that the righteous shall live by faith, that is, by faith alone, because the Law does not belong to faith at all. The Law is not the promise, but faith clings to and rests on the promise. Accordingly, just as the Law and the promise are distinct, so are works and faith. Hence the gloss of the sophists, which joins the Law to faith, is false and wicked; in fact, it extinguishes faith and puts the Law in place of faith.

Paul is speaking continually about those who want to keep the Law morally, not theologically. But whatever is said about theological good works is simply attributed to faith alone.

For he who does them shall live by them.

I understand this part of the statement as irony, although it can be expounded in a moral sense, namely, that those who keep the Law morally, that is, without faith, shall live by it; that is, they will

---

75 Cf., for example, Aristotle, *Metaphysics*, Book V, ch. 30.

[W, XL, 425—427]

not be punished but will have physical rewards from it. But I take this passage as a general statement, like that saying of Christ (Luke 10:28): "Do this, and you will live," so that it is a kind of irony or ridicule. "Yes, just go ahead and do it!"[76] Paul wants to show here what the righteousness of the Law and of the Gospel is, exactly and accurately. The righteousness of the Law is to keep the Law, according to the statement: "He who does them, etc." The righteousness of faith is to believe, according to the statement, "The righteous shall live by faith." Therefore the Law requires that we perform something for God. Faith does not require our doing; it requires that we believe the promise of God and accept something from Him. Therefore the function of the Law, at its highest level, is to work, just as that of faith is to assent. Thus the Law provides doing, and faith provides believing; for faith is faith in the promise, and the work is the work of the Law. This is why Paul lingers over the term "doing." To show clearly what the righteousness of the Law and what that of faith is, he contrasts the one with the other, the promise with the Law and faith with works. He says that nothing follows from the Law except doing; but faith is something altogether different, namely, that which clings to the promise.

Therefore these four things must be distinguished perfectly. For just as the Law has its proper task, so the promise has its proper task. Refer doing to the Law, believing to the promise. As widely as the Law and the promise are distinct, so far apart are faith and works — even if you understand "doing works" in a theological sense. For Paul is discussing something else here. He is urging the distinction between doing and believing, so that he may separate love from faith and show that faith alone justifies, because the Law, whether it is done morally or theologically or not at all, contributes nothing whatever to justification. The Law pertains to doing. But faith is not of this sort; it is something completely different — something that is required before the Law is kept, so that when faith is preexistent, a beautiful incarnation can take place.

Therefore faith always justifies and makes alive; and yet it does not remain alone, that is, idle. Not that it does not remain alone on its own level and in its own function, for it always justifies alone. But it is incarnate and becomes man; that is, it neither is nor remains idle or without love. Thus Christ, according to His divinity,

---

[76] Here even the printed version breaks into German: *Ia thue es nur.*

is [77] a divine and eternal essence or nature, without a beginning; but His humanity is a nature created in time. These two natures in Christ are not confused or mixed, and the properties of each must be clearly understood.[78] It is characteristic of the humanity to have a beginning in time, but it is characteristic of the divinity to be eternal and without a beginning. Nevertheless, these two are combined, and the divinity without a beginning is incorporated into the humanity with a beginning. Just as I am obliged to distinguish between the humanity and the divinity, and to say: "The humanity is not the divinity, and yet the man is God," so I make a distinction here and say: "The Law is not faith, and yet faith does works. Faith and works are in agreement concretely or compositely, and yet each has and preserves its own nature and proper function."

Thus you have the reason why Paul puts such stress on this passage, namely, in order to distinguish faith plainly from love. Therefore let the sophists go to the devil with their accursed gloss, and let that expression "faith formed" be damned! You should constantly say that these terms, "faith formed," "unformed," "acquired," etc., are monstrosities of the devil, produced to destroy Christian doctrine and faith, to blaspheme Christ and tread Him underfoot, and to establish the righteousness of works. You should say this, I mean, in order to keep the one true and correct faith — the faith without works. Although works follow faith, yet faith should not be works, and works should not be faith, lest they be confused; but the boundaries and the realms of the Law or works and of faith should be correctly distinguished from one another.

When we believe, therefore, then we live simply on account of Christ, who is without sin, who is also our mercy seat [79] and forgiveness of sins. On the other hand, when we keep the Law, we do indeed perform works; but we do not have righteousness and life. For it belongs to the Law not to justify and give life but to disclose sin and to kill. Of course, the Law says: "He who does them shall live by them." But where is the one who does them? Where is the one who loves God with all his heart, etc., and his neighbor as himself? Therefore there is no one who keeps the Law. And even though he tries his best to keep it, yet in keeping it he does not

[77] The original has *et*, but *est* seems more likely.

[78] A quotation from the dogmatic decree of the Council of Chalcedon of 451.

[79] This appears to be an allusion to the term *propitiatorium* in Heb. 9:5.

keep it; therefore he remains under the curse. Faith, however, does not perform works; it believes in Christ, the Justifier. And so a man does not live because of his doing; he lives because of his believing. Yet a believer does keep the Law; but what he does not keep is forgiven him through the forgiveness of sins for Christ's sake, and what sin there is left is not imputed to him.

When Paul says: "He who does them, etc.," he is comparing the righteousness of the Law and that of faith, as he also does in Romans 10:5 ff. It is as though he were saying: "It would indeed be fine if someone kept the Law. But since no one does so, we must take refuge in Christ, who was put under the Law to redeem those who were under the Law (Gal. 4:4). Believing in Him, we receive the Holy Spirit and begin to keep the Law. Because of our faith in Christ what we do not keep is not imputed to us. But in the life to come believing will cease, and there will be a correct and perfect keeping and loving. For when faith ceases, it will be replaced by glory, by means of which we shall see God as He is (1 John 3:2). There will be a true and perfect knowledge of God, a right reason, and a good will, neither moral nor theological but heavenly, divine, and eternal. Meanwhile we must persevere here in faith that has the forgiveness of sins and the imputation of righteousness through Christ. Therefore no legalist keeps the Law. Since he is without faith, he is under a curse." Thus Paul clearly distinguishes the worker of the Law from the man of faith. He is not speaking here about the believing doer of the Law; he is speaking about the doer of the Law who does not have the forgiveness of sins through Christ but wants to be justified solely through the Law.

It must be carefully noted that Paul calls only those righteous who are justified without the Law, through the promise or through faith in the promise. Keeping the Law, therefore, is something fictitious or a fictitious term, which means nothing apart from faith. Those who rely on works of the Law and want to give the appearance of keeping the Law do not keep it; for he draws the universal conclusion that all who rely on works of the Law are under a curse, under which they would not be if they kept the Law. It is indeed true that he who does these things shall live by them, that is, shall be blessed. But where is this man? Nowhere. That is why I have said that this passage from Moses is to be understood in two ways, politically and theologically. For the Law was given for two uses. The first is to restrain those who are uncivilized and wicked. In this sense the statement, "He who does these things shall live by them," is a political statement. It means: If a man obeys the magistrate outwardly and in the civil realm, he will avoid punishment and death. The civil magistrate has no right to impose punishments upon him or to execute him but permits him to live with impunity. This is the civil use of the Law, which is valid for the restraint of the uncivilized. But Paul is not pressing that use here, but he is discussing this passage theologically. He says: "If a man does these things, etc." It is as though he were saying: "If men could keep the Law, they would be blessed. But where are they? Therefore they are not doers of the Law unless they are first justified before and without the Law, through faith."

Therefore it must be carefully noted that Paul is not speaking here about those who are justified by faith; he is cursing and condemning those who rely on works of the Law. Let us not rave with Jerome, who was so deceived by his precious Origen that he understood almost nothing in Paul; they both regarded him as a political legislator. "Does this mean," Jerome asks, "that all the patriarchs were accursed even though they were circumcised, offered sacrifices, and observed the Law?" [80] Thus he rushes into Paul without any judgment and does not make a distinction between the true doers of the Law who are justified by faith and the doers who rely on works of the Law.

Obviously Paul is not saying anything here against those who are justified by faith and are true doers, because they do not rely on works of the Law; but he is opposing those who not only do not observe the Law but do what is contrary to the Law. For the Law commands that they fear, love, and worship God by faith. But they ignore God; they do not worship and love Him, but they love themselves under the pretext of the name of God. As Scripture says (Rom. 2:24): "My name is blasphemed among the Gentiles on account of you." Therefore they are unrighteous, sacrilegious, and idolatrous men, who sin most gravely especially against the First Commandment. Besides, they have the most violent lusts, wrath, and other great passions. In short, there is nothing good in them, except that outwardly they want to give the appearance of being righteous and keeping the Law.

But we who are justified by faith, as the patriarchs, prophets,

[80] Jerome, *Commentarius in Epistolam S. Pauli ad Galatas*, II, *Patrologia, Series Latina*, XXVI, 384.

and all the saints were, do not rely on works of the Law so far as justification is concerned. To the extent that we are in the flesh and still have remnants of sin in us, we are under the Law (though not under the curse, because for the sake of Christ, in whom we believe, this is [81] imputed to us). The flesh is hostile to the Law of God; and lust not only does not fulfill the Law but even sins against the Law. Indeed, it battles against us and takes us captive into bondage (Rom. 7:23). But if the Law is not fulfilled in the saints, but many things happen contrary to the Law, since they still have lust and the remnants of sin and so much filth still remains, hindering them so that they cannot fear and love God perfectly, cannot call upon Him with sure confidence, and cannot revere His Word enough — if this is so, how much more this is true of a man who is not justified, who is opposed to God, and who with all his heart neglects, despises, and hates the Word and the work of God! You see, then, that Paul is speaking here about those who want to fulfill the Law and to be justified without having received faith, not, as Jerome thinks, about the patriarchs and the saints, who had already been justified by faith.

13. *Christ redeemed us from the curse of the Law, having become a curse for us — for it is written: Cursed be everyone who hangs on a tree.*

Here again Jerome and the sophists who followed him are distressed.[82] They most miserably lacerate this passage, which is filled to overflowing with comfort; and they strive anxiously with what they think is godly zeal not to permit the insult of being called a curse or an execration to come to Christ. Therefore they evade this statement this way: "Paul was not speaking in earnest here." Thus they said, in a way that was as reprehensible as it was wicked, that Scripture, whose passages do not contradict themselves, does contradict itself in Paul. They show this as follows: "The statement from Moses that Paul cites here does not speak about Christ. In addition, the universal expression 'everyone' that Paul has is not added in Moses. Furthermore, Paul omits the phrase 'by God,' which occurs in Moses. In short, it is obvious enough that Moses is speaking about a criminal or a thief who has deserved the cross by his wicked deeds, as Scrip-

[81] We have translated the text as it stands, but it would seem to make more sense with an additional *non*.

[82] Jerome, *Commentarius in Epistolam S. Pauli ad Galatas*, II, *Patrologia, Series Latina*, XXVI, 387—388.

ture testifies clearly in Deut. 21:22-23." Therefore they ask how this sentence can be applied to Christ, that He is accursed by God and hanged on a tree, since He is not a criminal or a thief but righteous and holy. Perhaps this may impress the inexperienced; for they suppose that the sophists are speaking in a way that is not only subtle but also very pious, and that they are defending the honor of Christ and are religiously admonishing all Christians not to suppose wickedly that Christ was a curse. Therefore it must be determined what Paul's intent and meaning are.

Paul guarded his words carefully and spoke precisely. And here again a distinction must be made; Paul's words clearly show this. For he does not say that Christ became a curse on His own account, but that He became a curse "for us." Thus the whole emphasis is on the phrase "for us." For Christ is innocent so far as His own Person is concerned; therefore He should not have been hanged from the tree. But because, according to the Law, every thief should have been hanged, therefore, according to the Law of Moses, Christ Himself should have been hanged; for He bore the person of a sinner and a thief — and not of one but of all sinners and thieves. For we are sinners and thieves, and therefore we are worthy of death and eternal damnation. But Christ took all our sins upon Himself, and for them He died on the cross. Therefore it was appropriate for Him to become a thief and, as Isaiah says (53:12), to be "numbered among the thieves."

And all the prophets saw this, that Christ was to become the greatest thief, murderer, adulterer, robber, desecrator, blasphemer, etc., there has ever been anywhere in the world. He is not acting in His own Person now. Now He is not the Son of God, born of the Virgin. But He is a sinner, who has and bears the sin of Paul, the former blasphemer, persecutor, and assaulter; of Peter, who denied Christ; of David, who was an adulterer and a murderer, and who caused the Gentiles to blaspheme the name of the Lord (Rom. 2:24). In short, He has and bears all the sins of all men in His body — not in the sense that He has committed them but in the sense that He took these sins, committed by us, upon His own body, in order to make satisfaction for them with His own blood. Therefore this general Law of Moses included Him, although He was innocent so far as His own Person was concerned; for it found Him among sinners and thieves. Thus a magistrate regards someone as a criminal and punishes him if he catches him among thieves, even though the man has never committed anything evil or worthy of death. Christ was not only found among sinners; but of His own free will and by the will of the Father He wanted to be an associate of sinners, having assumed the flesh and blood of those who were sinners and thieves and who were immersed in all sorts of sin. Therefore when the Law found Him among thieves, it condemned and executed Him as a thief.

This knowledge of Christ and most delightful comfort, that Christ became a curse for us to set us free from the curse of the Law — of this the sophists deprive us when they segregate Christ from sins and from sinners and set Him forth to us only as an example to be imitated. In this way they make Christ not only useless to us but also a judge and a tyrant who is angry because of our sins and who damns sinners. But just as Christ is wrapped up in our flesh and blood, so we must wrap Him and know Him to be wrapped up in our sins, our curse, our death, and everything evil.

"But it is highly absurd and insulting to call the Son of God a sinner and a curse!" If you want to deny that He is a sinner and a curse, then deny also that He suffered, was crucified, and died. For it is no less absurd to say, as our Creed confesses and prays, that the Son of God was crucified and underwent the torments of sin and death than it is to say that He is a sinner or a curse. But if it is not absurd to confess and believe that Christ was crucified among thieves, then it is not absurd to say as well that He was a curse and a sinner of sinners. Surely these words of Paul are not without purpose: "Christ became a curse for us" and "For our sake God made Christ to be sin, who knew no sin, so that in Him we might become the righteousness of God" (2 Cor. 5:21).

In the same way John the Baptist called Christ "the Lamb of God" (John 1:29). He is, of course, innocent, because He is the Lamb of God without spot or blemish. But because He bears the sins of the world, His innocence is pressed down with the sins and the guilt of the entire world. Whatever sins I, you, and all of us have committed or may commit in the future, they are as much Christ's own as if He Himself had committed them. In short, our sin must be Christ's own sin, or we shall perish eternally. The wicked sophists have obscured this true knowledge of Christ which Paul and the prophets have handed down to us.

Is. 53:6 speaks the same way about Christ. It says: "God has laid on Him the iniquity of us all." These words must not be diluted but must be left in their precise and serious sense. For God is not joking in the words of the prophet; He is speaking seriously and out of great love, namely, that this Lamb of God, Christ, should bear the iniquity of us all. But what does it mean to "bear"? The sophists reply: "To be punished." Good. But why is Christ punished? Is it not because He has sin and bears sin? That Christ has sin is the testimony of the Holy Spirit in the Psalms. Thus in Ps. 40:12 we read: "My iniquities have overtaken Me"; in Ps. 41:4: "I said: 'O Lord, be gracious to Me; heal Me, for I have sinned against Thee!' "; and in Ps. 69:5: "O God, Thou knowest My folly; the wrongs I have done are not hidden from Thee." In these psalms the Holy Spirit is speaking in the Person of Christ and testifying in clear words that He has sinned or has sins. These testimonies of the psalms are not the words of an innocent one; they are the words of the suffering Christ, who undertook to bear the person of all sinners and therefore was made guilty of the sins of the entire world.

Therefore Christ not only was crucified and died, but by divine love sin was laid upon Him. When sin was laid upon Him, the Law came and said: "Let every sinner die! And therefore, Christ, if You want to reply that You are guilty and that You bear the punishment, you must bear the sin and the curse as well." Therefore Paul correctly applies to Christ this general Law from Moses: "Cursed be everyone who hangs on a tree." Christ hung on a tree; therefore Christ is a curse of God.

And this is our highest comfort, to clothe and wrap Christ this way in my sins, your sins, and the sins of the entire world, and in this way to behold Him bearing all our sins. When He is beheld this way, He easily removes all the fanatical opinions of our opponents about justification by works. For the papists dream about a kind of faith "formed by love." Through this they want to remove sins and be justified. This is clearly to unwrap Christ and to unclothe Him from our sins, to make Him innocent, to burden and overwhelm ourselves with our own sins, and to behold them, not in Christ but in ourselves. This is to abolish Christ and make Him useless. For if it is true that we abolish sins by the works of the Law and by love, then Christ does not take them away, but we do. But if He is truly the Lamb of God who takes away the sins of the world, who became a curse for us, and who was wrapped in our sins, it necessarily follows that we cannot be justified and take away sins through love. For God has laid our sins, not upon us but upon Christ, His Son. If they are taken away by Him, then they cannot be taken away by us. All Scripture says this, and we confess and pray the same thing in the Creed when we say: "I believe in Jesus Christ, the Son of God, who suffered, was crucified, and died for us."

This is the most joyous of all doctrines and the one that contains the most comfort. It teaches that we have the indescribable and inestimable mercy and love of God. When the merciful Father saw that we were being oppressed through the Law, that we were being held under a curse, and that we could not be liberated from it by anything, He sent His Son into the world, heaped all the sins of all men upon Him, and said to Him: "Be Peter the denier; Paul the persecutor, blasphemer, and assaulter; David the adulterer; the sinner who ate the apple in Paradise; the thief on the cross. In short, be the person of all men, the one who has committed the sins of all men. And see to it that You pay and make satisfaction for them." Now the Law comes and says: "I find Him a sinner, who takes upon Himself the sins of all men. I do not see any other sins than those in Him. Therefore let Him die on the cross!" And so it attacks Him and kills Him. By this deed the whole world is purged and expiated from all sins, and thus it is set free from death and from every evil. But when sin and death have been abolished by this one man, God does not want to see anything else in the whole world, especially if it were to believe, except sheer cleansing and righteousness. And if any remnants of sin were to remain, still for the sake of Christ, the shining Sun, God would not notice them.

This is how we must magnify the doctrine of Christian righteousness in opposition to the righteousness of the Law and of works, even though there is no voice or eloquence that can properly understand, much less express, its greatness. Therefore the argument that Paul presents here is the most powerful and the highest of all against all the righteousness of the flesh; for it contains this invincible and irrefutable antithesis: If the sins of the entire world are on that one man, Jesus Christ, then they are not on the world. But if they are not on Him, then they are still on the world. Again, if Christ Himself is made guilty of all the sins that we have all committed, then we are absolved from all sins, not through ourselves or through our own works or merits but through Him. But if He is innocent and does not carry our sins, then we carry them and shall die and be damned in them. "But thanks be to God, who gives us the victory through our Lord Jesus Christ! Amen." (1 Cor. 15:57.)

Now let us see how two such extremely contrary things come

together in this Person. Not only my sins and yours, but the sins of the entire world, past, present, and future, attack Him, try to damn Him, and do in fact damn Him. But because in the same Person, who is the highest, the greatest, and the only sinner, there is also eternal and invincible righteousness, therefore these two converge: the highest, the greatest, and the only sin; and the highest, the greatest, and the only righteousness. Here one of them must yield and be conquered, since they come together and collide with such a powerful impact. Thus the sin of the entire world attacks righteousness with the greatest possible impact and fury. What happens? Righteousness is eternal, immortal, and invincible. Sin, too, is a very powerful and cruel tyrant, dominating and ruling over the whole world, capturing and enslaving all men. In short, sin is a great and powerful god who devours the whole human race, all the learned, holy, powerful, wise, and unlearned men. He, I say, attacks Christ and wants to devour Him as he has devoured all the rest. But he does not see that He is a Person of invincible and eternal righteousness. In this duel, therefore, it is necessary for sin to be conquered and killed, and for righteousness to prevail and live. Thus in Christ all sin is conquered, killed, and buried; and righteousness remains the victor and the ruler eternally.

Thus also death, which is the almighty empress of the entire world, killing kings, princes, and all men in general, clashes against life with full force and is about to conquer it and swallow it; and what it attempts, it accomplishes. But because life was immortal, it emerged victorious when it had been conquered, conquering and killing death in turn. About this wondrous duel the church beautifully sings: "It was a great and dreadful strife when death with life contended." [83] The Prince of life, who died, is alive and reigns. Through Christ, therefore, death is conquered and abolished in the whole world, so that now it is nothing but a picture of death. Now that its sting is lost, it can no longer harm believers in Christ, who has become the death of death, as Hosea sings (13:14): "O death, I shall be your death!"

Thus the curse, which is divine wrath against the whole world, has the same conflict with the blessing, that is, with the eternal grace and mercy of God in Christ. Therefore the curse clashes with the blessing and wants to damn it and annihilate it. But it cannot. For

---

[83] On this *mirabile duellum* cf. *Luther the Expositor*, pp. 185—186.

the blessing is divine and eternal, and therefore the curse must yield to it. For if the blessing in Christ could be conquered, then God Himself would be conquered. But this is impossible. Therefore Christ, who is the divine Power, Righteousness, Blessing, Grace, and Life, conquers and destroys these monsters — sin, death, and the curse — without weapons or battle, in His own body and in Himself, as Paul enjoys saying (Col. 2:15): "He disarmed the principalities and powers, triumphing over them in Him." Therefore they can no longer harm the believers.

This circumstance, "in Himself," makes the duel more amazing and outstanding; for it shows that such great things were to be achieved in the one and only Person of Christ — namely, that the curse, sin, and death were to be destroyed, and that the blessing, righteousness, and life were to replace them — and that through Him the whole creation was to be renewed. If you look at this Person, therefore, you see sin, death, the wrath of God, hell, the devil, and all evils conquered and put to death. To the extent that Christ rules by His grace in the hearts of the faithful, there is no sin or death or curse. But where Christ is not known, there these things remain. And so all who do not believe lack this blessing and this victory. "For this," as John says, "is our victory, faith" (1 John 5:4).

This is the chief doctrine of the Christian faith. The sophists have completely obliterated it, and today the fanatics are obscuring it once more. Here you see how necessary it is to believe and confess the doctrine of the divinity of Christ. When Arius denied this, it was necessary also for him to deny the doctrine of redemption. For to conquer the sin of the world, death, the curse, and the wrath of God in Himself — this is the work, not of any creature but of the divine power. Therefore it was necessary that He who was to conquer these in Himself should be true God by nature. For in opposition to this mighty power — sin, death, and the curse — which of itself reigns in the whole world and in the entire creation, it is necessary to set an even higher power, which cannot be found and does not exist apart from the divine power. Therefore to abolish sin, to destroy death, to remove the curse in Himself, to grant righteousness, to bring life to light (2 Tim. 1:10), and to bring the blessing in Himself, that is, to annihilate these things and to create those — all these are works solely of the divine power. Since Scripture attributes all these to Christ, therefore He Himself is Life, Righteousness, and Blessing, that is, God by nature and in essence. Hence those who deny the divinity of Christ lose all Christianity and become Gentiles and Turks through and through.

As I often warn, therefore, the doctrine of justification must be learned diligently. For in it are included all the other doctrines of our faith; and if it is sound, all the others are sound as well. Therefore when we teach that men are justified through Christ and that Christ is the Victor over sin, death, and the eternal curse, we are testifying at the same time that He is God by nature.

From this it is evident enough how horribly blind and wicked the papists were when they taught that these fierce and mighty tyrants — sin, death, and the curse — who swallow up the whole human race, are to be conquered, not by the righteousness of the divine Law (which, even though it is just, good, and holy, cannot do anything but subject one to a curse) but by the righteousness of human works, such as fasts, pilgrimages, rosaries, vows, etc. But, I ask you, who has ever been found who conquered sin, death, etc., if he was equipped with this armor? In Eph. 6:13 ff. Paul describes a far different armor to be used against these savage beasts. By putting us, naked and without the armor of God, up against these invincible and almighty tyrants, these blind men and leaders of the blind (Matt. 15:14) have not only handed us over to them to be devoured but have also made us ten times greater and worse sinners than murderers or harlots. For it belongs exclusively to the divine power to destroy sin and abolish death, to create righteousness and grant life. This divine power they have attributed to our own works, saying: "If you do this or that work, you will conquer sin, death, and the wrath of God." In this way they have made us true God by nature! Here the papists, under the Christian name, have shown themselves to be seven times greater idolaters than the Gentiles. What happens to them is what happens to the sow, which "is washed only to wallow in the mire" (2 Peter 2:22). And, as Christ says (Luke 11:24-26), after a man has fallen from faith, the evil spirit returns to the house from which he was expelled and brings along seven other spirits more evil than himself and dwells there; and the last state of that man becomes worse than the first.

With gratitude and with a sure confidence, therefore, let us accept this doctrine, so sweet and so filled with comfort, which teaches that Christ became a curse for us, that is, a sinner worthy of the wrath of God; that He clothed Himself in our person, laid our sins upon His own shoulders, and said: "I have committed the sins that all men have committed." Therefore He truly became accursed according to the Law, not for Himself but, as Paul says, ὑπὲρ ἡμῶν. For unless He had taken upon Himself my sins, your sins, and the sins of the entire world, the Law would have had no right over Him, since it condemns only sinners and holds only them under a curse. Therefore He could neither have become a curse nor have died, since the cause of the curse and of death is sin, of which He was innocent. But because He took upon Himself our sins, not by compulsion but of His own free will, it was right for Him to bear the punishment and the wrath of God — not for His own Person, which was righteous and invincible and therefore could not become guilty, but for our person.

By this fortunate exchange with us He took upon Himself our sinful person and granted us His innocent and victorious Person. Clothed and dressed in this, we are freed from the curse of the Law, because Christ Himself voluntarily became a curse for us, saying: "For My own Person of humanity and divinity I am blessed, and I am in need of nothing whatever. But I shall empty Myself (Phil. 2:7); I shall assume your clothing and mask; and in this I shall walk about and suffer death, in order to set you free from death." Therefore when, inside our mask, He was carrying the sin of the whole world, He was captured, He suffered, He was crucified, He died; and for us He became a curse. But because He was a divine and eternal Person, it was impossible for death to hold Him. Therefore He arose from death on the third day, and now He lives eternally; nor can sin, death, and our mask be found in Him any longer; but there is sheer righteousness, life, and eternal blessing.

We must look at this image and take hold of it with a firm faith. He who does this has the innocence and the victory of Christ, no matter how great a sinner he is. But this cannot be grasped by loving will; it can be grasped only by reason illumined by faith. Therefore we are justified by faith alone, because faith alone grasps this victory of Christ. To the extent that you believe this, to that extent you have it. If you believe that sin, death, and the curse have been abolished, they have been abolished, because Christ conquered and overcame them in Himself; and He wants us to believe that just as in His Person there is no longer the mask of the sinner or any vestige of death, so this is no longer in our person, since He has done everything for us.

Therefore if sin makes you anxious, and if death terrifies you,

just think that this is an empty specter and an illusion of the devil —
which is what it surely is. For in fact there is no sin any longer,
no curse, no death, and no devil, because Christ has conquered and
abolished all these. Accordingly, the victory of Christ is utterly
certain; the defects lie not in the fact itself, which is completely
true, but in our incredulity. It is difficult for reason to believe such
inestimable blessings. In addition, the devil and the sectarians —
the former with his flaming darts (Eph. 6:16), the latter with their
perverse and wicked doctrine — are bent on this one thing: to obscure
this doctrine and take it away from us. It is above all for this
doctrine, on which we insist so diligently, that we bear the hate and
persecution of Satan and of the world. For Satan feels the power
and the results of this doctrine.

Now that Christ reigns, there is in fact no more sin, death, or
curse — this we confess every day in the Apostles' Creed when we
say: "I believe in the holy church." This is plainly nothing else
than if we were to say: "I believe that there is no sin and no death
in the church. For believers in Christ are not sinners and are not
sentenced to death but are altogether holy and righteous, lords
over sin and death who live eternally." But it is faith alone that
discerns this, because we say: "I believe in the holy church." If you
consult your reason and your eyes, you will judge differently. For
in devout people you will see many things that offend you; you will
see them fall now and again, see them sin, or be weak in faith,
or be troubled by a bad temper, envy, or other evil emotions.
"Therefore the church is not holy." I deny the conclusion that
you draw. If I look at my own person or at that of my neighbor,
the church will never be holy. But if I look at Christ, who is the
Propitiator and Cleanser of the church, then it is completely holy;
for He bore the sins of the entire world.

Therefore where sins are noticed and felt, there they really are
not present. For, according to the theology of Paul, there is no more
sin, no more death, and no more curse in the world, but only in
Christ, who is the Lamb of God that takes away the sins of the
world, and who became a curse in order to set us free from the curse.
On the other hand, according to philosophy and reason, sin, death, etc.,
are not present anywhere except in the world, in the flesh, and in
sinners. For the theology of the sophists is unable to consider sin
any other way except metaphysically, that is: "A quality clings to
a substance or a subject. Therefore just as color clings to a wall,

so sin clings to the world, to the flesh, or to the conscience. Therefore it must be washed away by some opposing motivations, namely, by love." But the true theology teaches that there is no more sin in the world, because Christ, on whom, according to Is. 53:6, the Father has laid the sins of the entire world, has conquered, destroyed, and killed it in His own body. Having died to sin once, He has truly been raised from the dead and will not die any more (Rom. 6:9). Therefore wherever there is faith in Christ, there sin has in fact been abolished, put to death, and buried. But where there is no faith in Christ, there sin remains. And although there are still remnants of sin in the saints because they do not believe perfectly, nevertheless these remnants are dead; for on account of faith in Christ they are not imputed.

Therefore this is an important and powerful argument that Paul is presenting here against the righteousness of works: "Neither the Law nor works redeem from the curse, but only Christ." Therefore I implore you for God's sake to distinguish Christ from the Law and to pay diligent attention to how Paul is speaking and to what he is saying. "It is necessary," he says, "that all who do not keep the Law be under a curse." But no one keeps the Law. Therefore the first proposition is true, namely, that all men are under a curse. Then he adds a second proposition: "Christ has redeemed us from the curse of the Law, having become a curse for us." Therefore the Law and works do not redeem from the curse. On the contrary, they drag us down and subject us to the curse. Therefore love, which, according to the sophists, "informs" faith, not only does not redeem from the curse but forces and wraps us into it even more.

But just as Christ is something different from the Law and from the works of the Law, so the redemption of Christ is altogether different from my merit based on works of the Law; for it had to be Christ Himself who redeemed us from the curse of the Law. Therefore whoever does not take hold of Christ by faith remains under the curse. Not even the sophists are so stupid as to say that Christ is our work or our love, for Christ is something altogether different from a work that we do. No papist, no matter how insane he is, will have the audacity to say that the alms he grants to someone in need or the obedience that a monk yields is a Christ. For Christ is God and man, "conceived by the Holy Spirit, born of the Virgin Mary, etc." Now about Him Paul says that He became a curse for us to redeem us from the curse of the Law. Therefore the Law, works, love, vows, etc., do not redeem; they only wrap one in the curse and make it even heavier. Therefore the more we have performed works, the less able we are to know and to grasp Christ.

But Christ is grasped, not by the Law or by works but by a reason or an intellect that has been illumined by faith. And this grasping of Christ through faith is truly the "speculative life," about which the sophists chatter a great deal without knowing what they are saying.[84] The speculation by which Christ is grasped is not the foolish imagination of the sophists and monks about marvelous things beyond them; it is a theological, faithful, and divine consideration of the serpent hanging from the pole, that is, of Christ hanging on the cross for my sins, for your sins, and for the sins of the entire world (John 3:14-15). Hence it is evident that faith alone justifies. But once we have been justified by faith, we enter the active life. In this way the sophists could have made a correct distinction between the contemplative and the active life, if they had called the former Gospel and the latter Law; that is, if they had taught that the speculative life should be included and directed by the Word of God and that in it nothing else is to be looked at except the Word of the Gospel, but that the active life should be sought from the Law, which does not grasp Christ but exercises itself in works of love toward one's neighbor.

And so this text is clear, that all men, even the apostles or prophets or patriarchs, would have remained under the curse if Christ had not put Himself in opposition to sin, death, the curse of the Law, and the wrath and judgment of God, and if He had not overcome them in His own body; for those savage monsters could not be overcome by any human power. Now Christ is not the Law, He is not a work of the Law, He is not an "elicited act";[85] but He is a divine and human Person who took sin, the condemnation of the Law, and death upon Himself, not for Himself but for us. Therefore the whole emphasis is on the phrase ὑπὲρ ἡμῶν.

Therefore we should not imagine Christ as an innocent and private person who is holy and righteous only for Himself; this is what the sophists and nearly all the fathers, Jerome and others, have done.[86] It is, of course, true that Christ is the purest of persons;

[84] Cf. the discussion in Luther's Works, 3, pp. 275—276.

[85] See p. 128, note 45.

[86] See p. 276, note 82.

but this is not the place to stop. For you do not yet have Christ, even though you know that He is God and man. You truly have Him only when you believe that this altogether pure and innocent Person has been granted to you by the Father as your High Priest and Redeemer, yes, as your Slave. Putting off His innocence and holiness and putting on your sinful person, He bore your sin, death, and curse; He became a sacrifice and a curse for you, in order thus to set you free from the curse of the Law.

You see, then, with what a completely apostolic spirit Paul treats this serious argument about the blessing and the curse, when he not only subjects Christ to the curse but even says that He became a curse. Thus he calls Him "sin" in 2 Cor. 5:21 when he says: "For our sake God made Him to be sin who knew no sin." Although these statements could be correctly expounded by saying that Christ became a "curse," that is, a sacrifice for the curse, or "sin," that is, a sacrifice for sin; nevertheless, it is more pleasing if the precise meaning of the terms is preserved for the sake of greater emphasis. For when a sinner really comes to a knowledge of himself, he feels himself to be a sinner not only concretely or adjectivally but abstractly and substantively. That is, he seems to himself to be not only miserable but misery itself; not only a sinner, and an accursed one, but sin and the curse itself. Thus in Latin, when we want a strong way to say that someone is a criminal, we call him a "crime." [87] It is something awful to bear sin, the wrath of God, the curse, and death. Therefore a man who feels these things in earnest really becomes sin, death, and the curse itself.

Thus Paul treats this topic in a truly apostolic way, because no sophist or legalist or Jew or fanatic or anyone else speaks this way. Who would dare quote this passage from Moses, "Cursed be everyone who hangs on a tree," and apply it to Christ Himself? By the same principle by which Paul applied this sentence, "Cursed be everyone, etc.," to Christ, we can apply not only all of Deut. 27 but all collected curses of the Mosaic Law to Christ. For just as Christ for His own Person is innocent of this general Law, so He is of all others. And just as for us He violated this general Law and was hanged on the tree as a criminal, a blasphemer, a parricide, and a traitor, so He violated all other laws as well. For all the curses of the Law were gathered together in Him, and therefore He bore and sustained

---

[87] The term *scelus* was a vulgar word for "scoundrel."

them in His own body for us. Consequently, He was not only accursed; but He became a curse for us.

This is really the apostolic way to interpret the Scriptures. For without the Holy Spirit a man cannot speak this way; that is, he cannot include the entire Law in one word and gather it all at once in Christ, and, on the other hand, include all the promises of Scripture and say that these are fulfilled in Christ once and for all. Therefore this argument is apostolic and very powerful, based as it is, not on one passage in the Law but on all the laws; and Paul relies heavily on it.

You see here with what diligence Paul read the Scriptures and how carefully he weighed and considered the individual words of this passage (Gen. 22:18): "In you shall all the nations be blessed." First he argues as follows from the term "bless": "If the blessing is to come upon all nations, then all nations are under the curse — even the Jews, who have the Law of Moses." And he quotes evidence from Scripture by which he proves that the Jews, who are under the Law, are under the curse: "Cursed be everyone who does not abide, etc."

Next Paul diligently weighs the words "all nations," on the basis of which he argues as follows: "The blessing pertains not only to the Jews but also to all the nations of the entire world. But if it pertains to all nations, it is impossible for it to come through the Law of Moses, since no nations except the Jews had this. Moreover, although the Jews had the Law, still the blessing did not come to them through it; on the contrary, the more they tried to keep it, the more subject they became to the curse of the Law. Therefore there has to be another righteousness, one that far surpasses the righteousness of the Law; through it the blessing comes not only to the Jews but also to all nations in the whole world."

Finally Paul explains the phrase "in your offspring" as follows: "A certain man was to be born of the offspring of Abraham. I mean Christ, through whom the blessing was to come upon all nations. Since Christ was to bless all nations, whom He found to be accursed, He Himself had to remove the curse from them. But He could not remove it through the Law, because the curse is only increased by this. So what did He do? He attached Himself to those who were accursed, assuming their flesh and blood; and thus He interposed Himself as the Mediator between God and men. He said: 'Although I am flesh and blood and live among those who are accursed, nevertheless I am the blessed One through whom all men are to be blessed.' Thus He joined God and man in one Person. And being joined with us who were accursed, He became a curse for us; and He concealed His blessing in our sin, death, and curse, which condemned and killed Him. But because He was the Son of God, He could not be held by them. He conquered them and triumphed over them. He took along with Him whatever clung to the flesh that He had assumed for our sake. Therefore all who cling to this flesh are blessed and are delivered from the curse."

Undoubtedly Paul treated these things at great length in the presence of the Galatians. For this is the proper task of the apostles: to illuminate the work and the glory of Christ and to strengthen and comfort troubled consciences. For the rest, when those who know no other righteousness than that of the Law fail to hear what one ought to do or ought not to do, but hear only that Christ, the Son of God, has assumed our flesh and joined Himself to the accursed in order to bless all nations this way — they either understand none of this or understand it in a purely physical way. They are preoccupied with other thoughts and with fantastic imaginings. Therefore these things are nothing but riddles to them. Even for us, who have the first fruits of the Spirit (Rom. 8:23), it is impossible to understand and to believe fully, because all this is so contradictory to human reason.

In short, all evils were to flood over us, as they will flood over the wicked eternally. But Christ, who became guilty of all laws, curses, sins, and evils for us, stepped in between; He took upon Himself and abolished all our evils, which were supposed to oppress and torment us eternally. They overwhelmed Him once, for a brief time, and flooded in over His head, as in Ps. 88:7 and 16 the prophet laments in Christ's name when he says: "Thy wrath lies heavy upon Me, and Thou dost overwhelm Me with all Thy waves" and: "Thy wrath has swept over Me; Thy dread assaults destroy Me." Being delivered in this way from these eternal terrors and torments by Christ, we shall enjoy eternal and indescribable peace and joy, provided that we believe this.

These are the adorable mysteries of Scripture, the true cabala,[88]

---

[88] The renewal of contacts between Christians and Jews in the time of humanism had aroused interest in the cabala; Johannes Reuchlin had written a book about it in 1517, *De arte cabbalistica.* Here Luther sets "the true cabala" against this speculative doctrine.

which even Moses disclosed rather obscurely in a few places; which the prophets and apostles knew and handed down from hand to hand to their posterity; and in which, though it was still in the future, the prophets rejoiced more than we do, even though it has now been revealed.

14. *That in Christ Jesus the blessing of Abraham might come upon the Gentiles.*

Paul always has this passage, "In your Offspring," in view, because the blessing promised to Abraham could not come to the nations except through Abraham's Offspring, Christ. How? He Himself had to become a curse, that the promise given to Abraham, "In your Offspring shall all the nations be blessed," might be fulfilled. What is promised here could not happen in any other way than that Jesus Christ should become a curse, join Himself to the accursed nations, remove the curse from them, and bless them with His blessing.

And here you see what the merits of our salvation are, which are "of congruity" and which "of condignity"! As I have reminded you earlier,[89] you should recall that the word of blessing is not empty, as the Jews imagine when they interpret the blessing as a spoken or written greeting; but Paul is dealing here with sin and righteousness, with death and life in the sight of God. Therefore, as we have often said earlier, he is speaking of things that are inestimable and incomprehensible when he says: "That in Christ Jesus the blessing of Abraham might come upon the Gentiles."

You see in addition by what means we receive this blessing. The preparation for it, that is, the merit of congruity and of condignity; the works by which this righteousness is achieved — these are the fact that Christ Jesus became a curse for us. For we are ignorant of God and hostile to Him; we are dead in sins and accursed. Therefore our merit is nothing whatever. For what would an accursed sinner, ignorant of God, dead in sins, and worthy of the wrath and judgment of God, be able to merit? When the pope excommunicated someone, whatever such a person did was a curse. How much more will someone who is accursed before Christ and apart from Christ produce nothing but curses! Therefore the one and only way to avoid the curse is to believe and to say with sure confidence: "Thou, O Christ, art my sin and my curse"; or rather:

[89] Cf. p. 243, note 55.

"I am Thy sin, Thy curse, Thy death, Thy wrath of God, Thy hell. But Thou art my Righteousness, Blessing, Life, Grace of God, and Heaven." For the text clearly states: "Christ became a curse for us." Therefore we are the reason why He became a curse; indeed, we are His curse.

This is a very powerful passage, one that is filled with comfort. Although it does not satisfy the blinded and stubborn Jews, it does satisfy us, who are Christians, who have been baptized, and who have accepted this doctrine. And it draws the powerful conclusion that through the curse, sin, and death of Christ we are blessed, that is, justified and made alive. So long as sin, death, and the curse remain in us, sin damns us, death kills us, and the curse curses us; but when these things are transferred to Christ, what is ours becomes His and what is His becomes ours. Let us learn, therefore, in every temptation to transfer sin, death, the curse, and all the evils that oppress us from ourselves to Christ, and, on the other hand, to transfer righteousness, life, and blessing from Him to us. For He does in fact bear all our evils, because God the Father, as Isaiah says (53:6), "has laid the iniquity of us all on *Him*."[90] And He willingly took them upon Himself. For He was not guilty; but He did this in order to do the Father's will, by which we would be sanctified eternally.

This is the indescribable and infinite mercy of God which Paul would like to spread abroad with an enthusiastic and generous flow of words; but the human heart is too limited to comprehend, much less to describe, the great depths and burning passion of divine love toward us. Indeed, the very greatness of divine mercy produces not only difficulty in believing but incredulity. Not only do I hear that God Almighty, the Creator of all, is good and merciful; but I hear that the Supreme Majesty cared so much for me, a condemned sinner and a child of wrath (Eph. 2:3) and of eternal death, that He did not spare His own Son, but gave Him up into a most shameful death (Rom. 8:32), in order that He might hang in the midst of thieves and become sin and a curse for me, the sinner and accursed one, and in order that I might be made righteous, blessed, and a son and heir of God. Who can adequately proclaim this goodness of God? Not even all the angels. Therefore Holy Scripture

---

[90] Here again we have used italics where the original has capitals; cf. p. 219, note 29.

speaks about other things than a political, philosophical, or even a Mosaic book; it speaks about the indescribable and utterly divine gifts that surpass not only all human and angelic understanding (Phil. 4:7) but everything else as well.

That we might receive the promise of the Spirit through faith.

"The promise of the Spirit" is a Hebraism; it means "the promised Spirit." Now the Spirit is freedom from the Law, from sin, death, the curse, hell, and the wrath and judgment of God. Here our merit of congruity or condignity is nothing; but only the free promise and gift disclosed to Abraham that we might be free from all evil and receive everything good is important. We do not receive this freedom and gift of the Spirit by any other merits than by faith; it alone takes hold of the promise, as Paul says clearly here: "That we might receive the promise of the Spirit, not through works but through faith."

This is a very sweet and truly apostolic doctrine. It announces that what "many prophets and kings desired to see and to hear" (Luke 10:24) has been fulfilled and has now been revealed to us. And such passages as this one were collected from various statements of the prophets, who foresaw long before in the Spirit that through this man Christ everything was to be changed, renewed, and put in order. Hence the Jews, who had the Law of God, nevertheless expected a Christ beyond the Law. None of the prophets or rulers of the people of God established a new Law; but Elijah, Samuel, David, and all the others remained under the Law of Moses. They did not institute a new Decalog or a new kingdom and priesthood, because the transformation of the kingdom and the priesthood, of the Law and of worship, was reserved for that One of whom Moses had prophesied long before (Deut. 18:15): "The Lord your God will raise up for you a prophet like me from among you, from your brethren — *Him* [91] you shall heed"; as though he were saying: "Him alone and no one else!"

The patriarchs understood this very well. For none of them could teach anything greater or more sublime than Moses himself, who laid down the supreme laws about the highest and greatest things, such as the Decalog, especially the First Commandment (Ex. 20:2-3): "I am the Lord your God. You shall have no other

[91] Cf. p. 292, note 90.

gods before Me." "You shall love the Lord your God with all your heart, etc." (Deut. 6:5.) This Law about the love of God includes even the angels. Therefore it is the source of all divine wisdom. And yet another teacher was supposed to come, namely, Christ, who was to teach something far greater and better even than these supreme laws, namely, grace and the forgiveness of sins. Therefore this text is extremely powerful; for in this very brief clause, "that we might receive the promise of the Spirit through faith," Paul expressed everything all at once. And so, since he could not go any farther — because there was nothing greater or sublimer for him to say — he stops here.

I have indicated earlier how to solve the problem of the passages that our opponents produce from Scripture regarding works and reward, namely, that by definition they must always be expounded theologically.[92] Thus if the statement from Dan. 4:24, "redeem your sins by giving alms," is produced, one must immediately consult the grammar — not the moral grammar but the theological grammar. This will show that "redeem" here is a matter not of morality but of faith, that it includes faith. For in Sacred Scripture a work presupposes a good will and a right reason, not in the moral sense but in the theological, which means faith. In this way you can easily stop the mouth of the sophists. For they themselves are forced to grant, as they teach on the basis of Aristotle, that every good work proceeds from choice.[93] If this is true in philosophy, it is much more necessary in theology that a good will and a right reason based on faith should precede a work. And this is the purport of all the imperatives and of all the statements that teach the Law, as the eleventh chapter of the Epistle to the Hebrews clearly explains (11:4): "By faith Abel obtained, etc."

This solution, although very sure, is, of course, inadequate. Nevertheless, it should be the chief argument and the principal resource of Christians in opposition to all the temptations and objections, not only of our opponents but of the devil himself; for they attack our Head, that is, Christ. Moreover, even if the sophists are more clever than I and so overwhelm and entangle me with their arguments in favor of works and against faith that I simply cannot untangle myself — although they cannot actually do this —

[92] See p. 265.

[93] Aristotle, *Nicomachean Ethics*, Book III, ch. 2.

yet I would rather have the honor of believing in Christ alone than of being persuaded by all the passages that they could produce against me in support of the righteousness of works.

Therefore one should simply reply to them as follows: "Here is Christ, and over there are the statements of Scripture about works. But Christ is Lord over Scripture and over all works. He is the Lord of heaven, earth, the Sabbath, the temple, righteousness, life, sin, death, and absolutely everything. Paul, His apostle, proclaims that He became sin and a curse for me. Therefore I hear that I could not be liberated from my sin, death, and curse through any other means than through His death and His blood. Therefore I conclude with all certainty and assurance that not my works but Christ had to conquer my sin, death, and curse. Even on natural grounds reason is obliged to agree and to say that Christ is not my work, that His blood and His death are not a cowl or a tonsure or a fast or a vow, and that in granting me His victory He was not a Carthusian. Therefore if He Himself is the price of my redemption, if He Himself became sin and a curse in order to justify and bless me, I am not put off at all by passages of Scripture, even if you were to produce six hundred in support of the righteousness of works and against the righteousness of faith, and if you were to scream that Scripture contradicts itself. I have the Author and the Lord of Scripture, and I want to stand on His side rather than believe you. Nevertheless, it is impossible for Scripture to contradict itself except at the hands of senseless and stubborn hypocrites; at the hands of those who are godly and understanding it gives testimony to its Lord. Therefore see to it how you can reconcile Scripture, which, as you say, contradicts itself. I for my part shall stay with the Author of Scripture."

Therefore if someone is not sufficiently educated to be able to reconcile or resolve such passages of Scripture about works and is obliged nevertheless to listen to the insistence of our opponents as they vigorously press such passages, let such a person simply reply as follows: "You are stressing the servant, that is, Scripture — and not all of it at that or even its more powerful part, but only a few passages concerning works. I leave this servant to you. I for my part stress the Lord, who is the King of Scripture. He has become my merit and the price of my righteousness and salvation. I hold to Him, I cling to Him, and I leave to you the works that you have never performed anyway." Neither the devil nor any self-righteous person can rob you of this answer or refute it. You are also safe in the sight of God; for your heart is fixed on the object of faith, who is called Christ. He was crucified and accursed, not for Himself but for us, as the text says: γενόμενος ὑπὲρ ἡμῶν κατάρα. Stress this passage; set it against all the statements about works, and say: "Are you listening to this, Satan?" Then he has to yield, because he knows that Christ is his Lord.

15. *To give a human example, brethren: no one annuls even a man's will, or adds to it, once it has been ratified.*

After his principal and most powerful argument Paul adds another, one that is based on the analogy of a man's will; this seems to be a rhetorical argument. Of course, reason could carp at this and say: "Paul, are you transferring human things to the divine realm?" Thus Cicero says about Homer: "He transferred human qualities to the gods rather than divine qualities to us." [94] It is certainly true that these arguments are the weakest of all, when we argue from human things to divine. That is what Scotus usually does. "Man," he says, "can love God above all things. He loves himself above all things. Much more will he love God. For the greater a good thing is, the more lovable it is." From this argument he draws the inference that merely by his natural powers a man is able without difficulty to fulfill the supreme commandment (Deut. 6:5): "You shall love the Lord your God with all your heart, etc." Because, he says, a man is able to love a lesser good above all things and even sells his life, the most cherished good of all, for a miserable and paltry sum, therefore he can certainly do this for God's sake, according to Scotus.[95]

You have often heard from me that civil and domestic ordinances are divine, because God Himself has established and approved them, as He has the sun, the moon, and other creatures. Therefore an argument based on an ordinance of God or on creatures is valid so long as it is used properly. Thus the prophets very often used the analogy of creatures, calling Christ the sun; the church, the moon; and the clergy, stars.[96] There are also innumerable other analogies in the prophets — analogies of trees, thorns, flowers, and fruits of

[94] Cicero, *On the Nature of the Gods,* Book II, ch. 28.

[95] Cf. p. 128, note 45.

[96] Luther is thinking of passages like Mal. 4:2 and Dan. 12:3.

the earth. The New Testament, too, is filled with such analogies. Therefore where there is a divine ordinance in a creature, it is good to base an argument on it and to transfer it to divine matters.

Thus Christ argues from human matters to divine in Matt. 7:11 when He says: "If you, then, who are evil, know how to give good gifts to your children, how much more will your Father who is in heaven give good things to those who ask Him!" So also Paul [97] (Acts 5:29): "One must obey men; much more must one obey God." And Jer. 35:16: "The Rechabites have kept the command which their father gave them. How much more should you have obeyed Me! But you have not obeyed Me." These are divine ordinances, that fathers should give things to their children and that children should obey their fathers. Therefore such arguments are good, since they are based on a divine ordinance. But if arguments are based on human feelings that are depraved, they are evil and have no validity at all. Such is the argument of Scotus: "I love a lesser good; therefore I love a greater good even more." Here I deny the conclusion, because my loving is not a divine ordinance but a demonic depravity. It should indeed be so that when I love myself or some other creature, I love God the Creator more; but it does not happen that way, because self-love is something wicked by which I love myself in opposition to God.

I am saying this to prevent anyone from objecting that an argument from human matters to divine ones is not valid. Now I am not disputing whether this argument is rhetorical or dialectical. All I am saying is that an argument in which one reasons from human matters to divine ones is strong enough so long as we base it on a divine ordinance, as in the present case. For the civil law contains something that is a divine ordinance: that a man's will may not be annulled. So long as the testator is alive, it has not yet been ratified; but once he has died, it may not be altered. Yet this is not spoken de facto, but de jure; that is, what should happen and what may properly be done, because the law states that a will is not to be altered; in fact, the laws command that a last will is to be observed religiously, and a last will is one of the most sacred of human matters.

On the basis of this custom of human wills, then, Paul argues as follows: "How does it happen that men are obeyed, but God is

[97] Luther says "Paul," but Acts puts these words into the mouth of Peter.

disobeyed? Political and civic ordinances are observed religiously; here nothing is altered, nothing added, nothing taken away. Only our theology, to which all the creatures nevertheless bear witness — only it suffers alteration and addition." It is very persuasive when Paul argues this way from the examples and laws of men. That is why he says: "To give a human example." It is as though he were saying: "In wills and in other human business there is a performance, and what the law commands is observed. Why does not the same thing happen even more in the testament of God, which God Himself promised to Abraham and to his offspring?" Therefore this is a sufficiently strong argument, based as it is on a divine ordinance.

16. *Now the promises were made to Abraham and to his offspring. It does not say: And to offsprings, referring to many; but, referring to one: And to your offspring, which is Christ.*

Here Paul uses a new term and calls the promises of God a testament. A testament is nothing else than a promise, except that it has not yet been revealed but is still only signified. Now a testament is not a law; it is a gift. For heirs do not look for laws or for enforcement; they look for an inheritance from a testament. Therefore Paul first explains the terms, and then he applies the analogy and stresses the term "offspring." "To Abraham," he says, "the promises were made; that is, the testament was drawn or ordained for him." Therefore something was promised and granted to him. It was not laws that were handed down to him, but a testament about a spiritual blessing. If, therefore, we observe human testaments or promises, why do we not observe divine ones as well, which are the testament of God, of which a human testament is only an allegory or mask? Again, if we observe the signs, why do we not rather observe the things that are signified? For the testament spoken to Abraham was not human — although it would not be violated even if it were — but divine.

Now the promises were spoken to him, not for all the Jews or for many offspring but for one Offspring, which is Christ. The Jews do not accept this interpretation of Paul's; they imagine that there is a shift of number here and say that a singular is being used for a plural.[98] But we remain with the spirit of the apostle, who does not stress the term "offspring" without purpose; he explains in a truly apostolic way that this Offspring is Christ. Even if the Jews deny

[98] On the "seed" cf. also *Luther's Works*, 2, pp. 259—266; the grammatical device being referred to here is ἐναλλαγή.

this, we have the sufficient and powerful arguments that Paul cited earlier; these they cannot deny, and these arguments support the present one as well. So far the analogy or allegorical picture of the divine ordinance, that is, of a human testament. Now he expounds and applies it.

17. *This is what I mean: the Law, which came four hundred and thirty years afterward, does not annul a covenant previously ratified by God, so as to make the promise void.*

Here the Jews could object: "God was not content with giving the promises to Abraham, but four hundred and thirty years afterward He also promulgated the Law. Having spread abroad His promises, as that which could not justify, God added something better, namely, the Law, so that upon its arrival as a more worthy successor not idle men but the doers of the Law would be justified through it. Therefore the Law that followed the promise abrogated it." The Jews have many evasions of this sort. But Paul refutes this objection clearly and forcefully, saying: "The Law could not abrogate the promises. On the contrary, in fact, the testament that was made and promised to Abraham — 'In your Offspring, etc.' — is the testament of God, ratified before the circumcision of the entire Jewish nation. For the promises that Scripture contained were the letters; to them seals were added later on, namely, circumcision and other ceremonial laws. Therefore the Law that came four hundred and thirty years after the promise did not abolish it; nor would it have taken anything away from the promise if it had come sooner. But now that the Law was given so many centuries after the promise, it does not make it invalid."

But let us permit these two to confront each other; and let us see which is more powerful, that is, whether the promise abolishes the Law or the Law abolishes the promise. If the Law abolishes the promise, then it follows that by our works we make God a liar and make His promise invalid. For if the Law justifies, it liberates from sin and death, and, consequently, so do our works and human powers that keep the Law; then the promise made to Abraham becomes invalid and altogether useless. Then it follows that God is a liar and a babbler. For if one who promises does not want to perform what he has promised but wants to make it invalid, what does this mean but that he is a liar and a babbler? But it is impossible for the Law to make God a liar and for our works to render the promise invalid.

Therefore it must be valid and firm — since God does not promise without purpose — even if we were able to observe and fulfill the Law. And even if we were to concede that all men are as holy as the angels are — which is impossible — and that they do not need the promise at all, even then it must be asserted that the promise is altogether sure and firm; for otherwise God would be found to be a deceiver or a liar who either would promise to no purpose or would not be willing to perform what He has promised. Therefore just as the promise is before the Law, so it is above the Law.

God acted properly in giving the promise such a long time before the Law, lest it be said that righteousness is given through the Law, not through the promise. Moreover, it was intentional that He preceded the Law with the promises; for if He had wanted us to be justified by the Law, He would have given it four hundred and thirty years before the promise or certainly with the promise. But now He is completely silent about the Law at first; He establishes it finally after four hundred and thirty years. Meanwhile, for that entire time, He speaks about His promises. Therefore the blessing and the gift of righteousness came before the Law, through the promise. And therefore the promise is superior to the Law. Thus the Law does not abrogate the promise. But faith in the promise, by which believers were saved even before Christ was revealed, and which is now being preached through the Gospel to all the nations of the universe, destroys the Law, so that it can no longer increase sin or terrify sinners or reduce to despair those who take hold of the promise by faith.

A great emphasis, or rather irony, is concealed in Paul's explicit reference to four hundred and thirty years. It is as though he were saying: "If you understand arithmetic, count on your fingers what the interval is between the giving of the promise and the Law. Certainly there was a promise a long time ago, even while there was no Law (that is, for four hundred and thirty years)." Therefore this is a rather vigorous argument based on a specific interval.

Here Paul is not speaking about the Law in general but only about the written Law. It is as though he were saying: "God could not regard our worship, works, and merits that did not yet exist, because there was as yet no Law that commanded worship, required works, and promised life to those who kept it. 'He who does them' He says 'shall live by them.' Thus if I were to give a field or a house to a man to whom I owed nothing and did so not out of constraint but purely out of good will, and if after twenty or more years had passed since I did him this favor I imposed a law upon him about doing this or that, he could not say that he had merited the favor by his works when he had received it from me so many years before by sheer grace, without my having requested anything of him. In the same way God could not regard works and merits that preceded righteousness, because the promise and the gift of the Holy Spirit came four hundred and thirty years before the Law." This is what Paul stresses in irony.

In the same way we can say: "Our Christianity existed four hundred and thirty years before our monastic life; that is, our sins were expiated by the death of Christ one thousand six hundred years ago, before any monastic order, any penitential canon, or any merit of congruity and condignity had ever been thought up. How, then, would we do satisfaction for our sins now by our works and merits?"

"If, then," he says, "the Jews acquire righteousness through the Law, how did Abraham acquire it? Through the Law? No, because the Law was not yet in existence. If the Law was not yet in existence, then neither works nor merit were either. What was in existence at that time? Nothing but the promise. Therefore the promise justifies, not the Law." Thus Paul gathers powerful arguments based on the analogy of specific times and persons from everywhere, and no sane man can carp against them. Therefore let us fortify our consciences with such arguments, for in our temptations it is marvelously beneficial to meditate on them. They lead us from the Law and from works to the promise and to faith, from wrath to grace, from sin to righteousness, from death to life.

As I often insist, therefore, these two, the Law and the promise, must be very carefully distinguished; for they are as far apart in time, place, person, and all features as heaven and earth, the beginning of the world and its end. They are indeed close together, because they are joined in one man or in one soul. Nevertheless, in attitude and function they should be separated as far as possible, in such a way that the Law has dominion over the flesh, but the promise reigns sweetly in the conscience. If you assign a specific place to each one this way, you walk safely between them, in the promise in heaven and in the Law on earth, in the Spirit of grace and peace in Paradise and in the flesh of works and torment on earth. And then the troubles that the flesh is forced to bear will not be difficult, for the promise is

[W, XL, 469—471]

sweet and delights the heart in a wonderful way. But if you confuse these two and place the Law in your conscience but the promise of freedom in your flesh, the sort of confusion takes place that there was in the papacy. Then you do not know what is Law and what is promise, what is sin and what is righteousness.

If, then, you want to divide the Word of truth rightly (2 Tim. 2:15), you must distinguish the promise from the Law as far as possible, both in your attitude and in your whole life. It is not without purpose that Paul urged this argument so diligently; for he saw that in the church this evil would arise, namely, that the Word of God would be confused, which means that the promise would be mixed with the Law and in this way be completely lost. For when the promise is mixed up with the Law, it becomes Law pure and simple. For this reason you should accustom yourself to distinguish the Law from the promise even in time, so that when the Law comes and accuses your conscience, you say: "Lady Law, you are not coming on time; you are coming too late. Look back four hundred and thirty years; if these were rolled back, you could come. But you are coming too late and tardily; for you have been preceded for four hundred and thirty years by the promise, to which I agree and in which I gently rest. Therefore you have nothing to do with me; I do not hear you. Now I am living after Abraham the believer; or rather, I am living after the revelation of Christ, who has abrogated and abolished you." Thus let Christ always be set forth to the heart as a kind of summary of all the arguments in support of faith and against the righteousness of the flesh, the Law, works, and merits.

Thus far I have recounted nearly all the most powerful arguments that Paul treats in this epistle in support of the doctrine of justification; among these the most important and the most effective is the one he urges most both here and in Romans, the argument about the promise. For no one can deny that the promise is not the Law. Now he takes the words of the promise, "In your Offspring they shall be blessed, etc.," and carefully considers them. Then he treats times and persons, and then the Offspring itself, explaining that this is Christ. Finally he declares, by means of an antithesis, what the Law does, namely, that it consigns one under a curse. And thus he inverts the arguments that the false apostles were using in defense of the righteousness of the Law and turns them against the false apostles themselves. "You are stressing the Law," he says, "as necessary for salvation. Have you not read that it says: 'He who does them shall live by them'? But who does them? Therefore as many as rely on works of the Law are under a curse." Thus where the false apostles want to conclude that righteousness and life are from the Law, Paul turns their words around and concludes that the curse and death are from the Law. Thus he adequately protects and defends the doctrine of Christian righteousness by supporting it on the basis of the promise, in which he shows that the Offspring of Abraham himself is Christ, with His death, resurrection, blessing, and victory over all nations. He refutes the arguments of his opponents on the basis of the words of the Law, by which he says that the Law is so far from justifying that it has exactly the opposite effect, namely, that it consigns men under the curse. Now there follows the conclusion of these arguments.

18. *For if the inheritance is by the Law, it is no longer by promise.*

So also in Rom. 4:14: "If it is the adherents of the Law who are to be the heirs, faith is null, and the promise is void." Nor can it come out any other way; for the distinction is altogether clear, that the Law is not the promise. Natural reason, no matter how blind it is, is still forced to admit that it is one thing to promise and another thing to demand, one thing to grant and another to accept. If a horse could speak, it would be forced to say that it is one thing when a stableboy offers it oats to eat and another thing when the stableboy mounts it and rides it. Therefore the promise and the Law are as far apart from each other as heaven and earth. For the Law demands: "Do this!" The promise grants: "Accept this!"

Therefore Paul concludes as follows: The blessing is given on the basis of the promise; therefore it is not given on the basis of the Law. For the promise says: "In your Offspring they will be blessed." Therefore he who has the Law does not have enough, for he does not yet have the blessing and so remains under the curse. Hence the Law cannot justify, because the blessing has not been added to it. In addition, if the inheritance were by the Law, God would be found to be a liar, and the promise would become void. Likewise, if the Law could obtain the blessing, why would God promise it, saying, "In your Offspring, etc."? Why would He not rather say: "Do this, and you will receive the blessing!" or "By keeping the Law you can merit eternal life"? This is an argument from contraries: The inheritance is given on the basis of the promise; therefore it is not on the basis of the Law.

But God gave it to Abraham by a promise.

This is undeniable, that before there was a Law, God by a promise granted Abraham the blessing or inheritance, that is, the forgiveness of sins, righteousness, salvation, and eternal life, which means that we are the sons and heirs of God and fellow heirs with Christ (Rom. 8:17). For Genesis clearly says (22:18): "In your Offspring shall all the nations be blessed." There the blessing is granted without regard for the Law or works. For before Moses was born or anyone had thought about the Law, God had already taken the initiative and granted the inheritance. "Then why do you boast that you attain righteousness through the Law, when righteousness, life, and salvation were given to Abraham your father without the Law and before the Law, in fact, before there was anyone who could have kept the Law?" Anyone who is not moved by all this is blind and stubborn. I have already set forth the argument about the promise carefully and at length, and so now I am only touching on it in passing.

Up to this point the most important part of this epistle has been set forth. Now there follow the analogies of the custodian and the young heir, the allegory about the two sons of Abraham, Isaac and Ishmael, and finally some commandments about morals. In this latter part of the epistle Paul is speaking rhetorically rather than teaching.

19. *Why, then, the Law?*

When we teach that a man is justified without the Law and works, this question necessarily follows: "If the Law does not justify, why, then, was it given?" Again: "Why does God prod and burden us with the Law if it does not give life? Why is it necessary for us to be strained and vexed so hard by it if these others, who have worked only one hour, are made equal to us, who have borne the burden of the day and the scorching heat (Matt. 20:12)?" For as soon as the grace proclaimed by the Gospel comes, this great murmuring arises, without which the Gospel cannot be proclaimed. The Jews had the opinion that if they observed the Law, they would be justified. Therefore when they heard the Gospel teach that Christ came into the world to save not the righteous but sinners, and that these latter will go into the kingdom of God before them, they became extremely indignant. They complained that for so many centuries they had borne the yoke of the Law with great trouble and labor and had been miserably vexed and oppressed by the tyranny of the Law without any results, in fact, at the greatest inconvenience to themselves; on the other hand, the idolatrous Gentiles had obtained grace without any labor or trouble. Thus our papists murmur today, saying: "What good did it do us to live for twenty, thirty, or forty years in the monastic life; to vow chastity, poverty, and obedience; to read the canonical hours, to say Mass, and to afflict our body with fasts, prayers, and chastisements — if a husband or a wife, a prince, public official, teacher or pupil, a merchant or a servant carrying sacks, or a servant girl sweeping the house are not only equal to us but better and worthier?" [99]

Therefore this is a difficult question. Reason is brought short by it and cannot answer it but is offended by it in the highest degree. Because reason does not know anything except the Law, it necessarily deals with this and supposes that righteousness is attained through it. Accordingly, when it hears this statement of Paul's, novel and unheard-of in the world, that the Law was given on account of transgressions, it judges as follows: "Paul is abolishing the Law, for he is saying that we are not justified through it. Yes, he is a blasphemer against the God who gave the Law; for he says that it was given on account of transgressions. So let us live as the Gentiles do, who do not have the Law! Let us sin and abide in sin, so that grace may abound. 'Let us do evil that good may come' (Rom. 3:8)." This is what happened to the apostle Paul, and the same thing is happening to us today. For when the rabble hear from the Gospel that righteousness comes by the sheer grace of God and by faith alone, without the Law or works, they draw the same conclusion the Jews drew then: "Then let us not do any works!" And they really live up to this.

What, then, are we to do? This evil troubles us severely, but we cannot stop it. When Christ preached, He had to hear that He was a blasphemer and a rebel; that is, that His teaching was seducing men and making them seditious against Caesar. The same thing happened to Paul and to all the apostles. No wonder the world accuses us in a similar way today. All right, let it slander and persecute us! Still we must not keep silence on account of their troubled consciences; but we must speak right out, in order to rescue them from the snares of the devil. Nor should we pay attention to how our doctrine is abused by the vicious and wicked rabble, who cannot be cured

[99] Cf. *Luther's Works*, 21, pp. 281—283.

whether they have the Law or not. On the contrary, we should pay attention to how suffering consciences are to be counseled, lest they perish with the wicked rabble. If we were to keep silence, the consciences that are so inextricably captured and ensnared in laws and human traditions would have no comfort at all.

Therefore when Paul saw that some were opposing his doctrine while others were intent on the freedom of the flesh and became worse because of his doctrine, he comforted himself with this, that he was an apostle of Jesus Christ for the proclamation of faith to the elect of God (2 Tim. 2:10); in the same way we today are doing everything for the sake of the elect, to whom we know our doctrine is beneficial. I am so bitterly opposed to the dogs and swine, some of whom persecute our doctrine while others tread our liberty underfoot, that I am not willing to utter a single sound on their behalf in my whole life. I would rather that these swine of ours, together with those dogs, our opponents, still be subjected to the tyranny of the pope than that the holy name of God be blasphemed on their account.

Therefore the grumbling, "If the Law does not justify, it is nothing," is a fallacious conclusion. For just as the conclusion is not valid if one says: "Money does not justify; therefore it is nothing. The eyes do not justify; therefore I shall pluck them out. The hands do not justify; therefore I shall cut them off" — so this conclusion is not valid: "The Law does not justify; therefore it is nothing." To each thing one must attribute its proper function and use. When we deny that the Law justifies, we are not destroying or condemning it. But to the question, "Why, then, the Law?" we give an answer that is different from the one given by our opponents, who, in their distorted thinking, imagine for the Law a function and use that does not lie in the nature of things.

We are debating against this abuse and this imaginary function of the Law, and we reply with Paul that the Law does not pertain to justification. But by this we are not asserting that the Law is nothing, as they immediately infer: "If the Law does not justify, it was given to no purpose." No. The Law has its proper function and use; but this is not the one that our opponents attribute to it, namely, that of justifying. It does not belong to the Law to be used for justification; therefore we teach that it must be separated from this as far as heaven is from earth. With Paul we say that "the Law is good, if anyone uses it lawfully" (1 Tim. 1:8), that is, if anyone uses the

Law as Law. If I define the Law with a proper definition and keep it in its own function and use, it is a very good thing. But if I transfer it to another use and attribute to it what should not be attributed to it, I distort not only the Law but all theology.

Therefore Paul is arguing here against those vicious hypocrites who say: "Why, then, the Law?" They find altogether intolerable the statement of Paul: "The Law was added because of transgressions." For they suppose that the function of the Law is to justify. And that is the general opinion of human reason in all the sophists and in the whole world about religion and about righteousness that it is achieved by the works of the Law. Reason will not permit this extremely dangerous opinion to be taken away from it by any means at all, because it does not understand the righteousness of faith. Hence the papists babble, not so much foolishly as wickedly: "The church has the Law of God; it has the decrees of the councils and the writings of the holy fathers. If it lives according to these, it is holy." No one will persuade them that by their self-chosen works and their religion they are only provoking the wrath of God, not placating it. No self-righteous people believe this, but they suppose the very opposite. Therefore the presumption of righteousness is the dregs of all the evils and the sin of all the sins of the world. For all other sins and vices can be corrected, or at least prohibited by the punishment of the magistrate. But this sin, each man's personal presumption of his own righteousness, peddles itself as the height of religion and sanctity, because it is impossible for the nonspiritual man to judge rightly about this issue. Therefore this disease is the highest and greatest empire of the devil in the whole universe, truly the head of the serpent (Gen. 3:15) and the snare by which the devil captures all men and holds them captive (1 Tim. 3:7). For by nature all men think that the Law justifies. To the objection, "Why, then, the Law, if it does not justify?" Paul therefore replies as follows: "Not because of justification but

Because of transgressions it was added.

These are distinct matters; therefore their use is distinct also. Hence the uses of these things must not be confused. "A woman shall not wear anything that pertains to a man, nor shall a man put on a woman's garment" (Deut. 22:5). Let the uses of the things remain distinct; otherwise sheer confusion results. The male was not created for spinning; the woman was not created for warfare. Let the proper station and task be attributed to each person: let the preacher and bishop teach; let the prince, etc., rule; let the people obey the magistrate. In this way let every creature serve in its own order and place. Let the sun shine by day, and the moon and stars by night. Let the sea produce fish, the earth produce plants, and the forests produce animals and wood.

In the same way let not the Law usurp for itself an alien function and use, that of justification; but let it leave this solely to grace, to the promise, and to faith. Let the monks fast, pray, and dress differently from the rest of the Christian people. Let them do this, that is, and even more to tame the flesh and put it to death. But let them not attribute to these disciplines the function of justifying in the sight of God, for this is an alien function that does not belong to them. What, then, is the function of the Law? Transgression. Really a lovely function! "The Law," he says, "was added because of transgressions"; that is, the Law was added beyond and after the promises until the offspring would come. Thus in Rom. 5:20: "The Law came in," that is, after the promises of grace and until Christ, who would fulfill the promises.

Here one must know that there is a double use of the Law. One is the civic use. God has ordained civic laws, indeed all laws, to restrain transgressions. Therefore every law was given to hinder sins. Does this mean that when the Law restrains sins, it justifies? Not at all. When I refrain from killing or from committing adultery or from stealing, or when I abstain from other sins, I do not do this voluntarily or from the love of virtue but because I am afraid of the sword and of the executioner. This prevents me, as the ropes or the chains prevent a lion or a bear from ravaging something that comes along. Therefore restraint from sins is not righteousness but rather an indication of unrighteousness. Therefore just as a rope holds a furious and untamed beast and keeps it from attacking whatever it meets, so the Law constrains an insane and furious man lest he commit further sins. This restraint makes it abundantly clear that those who have need of it — as does everyone who is outside Christ — are not righteous but unrighteous and insane, whom it is necessary to tame with the rope and with prison to keep them from sinning. Therefore the Law does not justify.

Thus the first understanding and use of the Law is to restrain the wicked. For the devil reigns in the whole world and drives men to all sorts of shameful deeds. This is why God has ordained magistrates, parents, teachers, laws, shackles, and all civic ordinances, so that, if they cannot do any more, they will at least bind the hands of the devil and keep him from raging at will. Therefore just as ropes and chains are bound upon men who are possessed and in whom the devil is ruling powerfully, to keep them from harming someone, so the whole world, which is possessed by the devil and is being led headlong into every crime, has the magistrate with his ropes and chains, that is, his laws, restraining its hands and feet lest it rush headlong into all sorts of evil. If it does not permit itself to be restrained this way, it will pay with the price of its head. This civic restraint is extremely necessary and was instituted by God, both for the sake of public peace and for the sake of preserving everything, but especially to prevent the course of the Gospel from being hindered by the tumults and seditions of wild men. Paul is not discussing that civic use here; it is indeed very necessary, but it does not justify. For as a possessed person is not free and mentally balanced just because his hands and feet are bound, so when the world is most restrained from external acts of disgrace by the Law, it is not righteous on that account but remains unrighteous. In fact, this very restraint indicates that the world is wicked and insane and that it is driven by its prince, the devil; otherwise there would be no need for it to be kept from sinning by laws.

The other use of the Law is the theological or spiritual one, which serves to increase transgressions. This is the primary purpose of the Law of Moses, that through it sin might grow and be multiplied, especially in the conscience. Paul discusses this magnificently in Rom. 7. Therefore the true function and the chief and proper use of the Law is to reveal to man his sin, blindness, misery, wickedness, ignorance, hate and contempt of God, death, hell, judgment, and the well-deserved wrath of God. Yet this use of the Law is completely unknown to the hypocrites, the sophists in the universities, and to all men who go along in the presumption of the righteousness of the Law or of their own righteousness. To curb and crush this monster and raging beast, that is, the presumption of religion, God is obliged, on Mt. Sinai, to give a new Law with such pomp and with such an awesome spectacle that the entire people is crushed with fear. For since the reason becomes haughty with this human presumption of righteousness and imagines that on account of this it is pleasing to God, therefore God has to send some Hercules, namely, the Law, to attack, subdue, and destroy this monster with full force. Therefore the Law is intent only on this beast, not on any other.

Hence this use of the Law is extremely beneficial and very necessary. For if someone is not a murderer, adulterer, or thief, and abstains from external sins, as that Pharisee did (Luke 18:11), he would swear, being possessed by the devil, that he is a righteous man; therefore he develops the presumption of righteousness and relies on his good works. God cannot soften and humble this man or make him acknowledge his misery and damnation any other way than by the Law. Therefore the proper and absolute use of the Law is to terrify with lightning (as on Mt. Sinai), thunder, and the blare of the trumpet, with a thunderbolt to burn and crush that brute which is called the presumption of righteousness. Hence God says through Jeremiah (23:29): "My Word is a hammer which breaks the rock in pieces." For as long as the presumption of righteousness remains in a man, there remain immense pride, self-trust, smugness, hate of God, contempt of grace and mercy, ignorance of the promises and of Christ. The proclamation of free grace and the forgiveness of sins does not enter his heart and understanding, because that huge rock and solid wall, namely, the presumption of righteousness by which the heart itself is surrounded, prevents this from happening.

Therefore this presumption of righteousness is a huge and a horrible monster. To break and crush it, God needs a large and powerful hammer, that is, the Law, which is the hammer of death, the thunder of hell, and the lightning of divine wrath. To what purpose? To attack the presumption of righteousness, which is a rebellious, stubborn, and stiff-necked beast. And so when the Law accuses and terrifies the conscience — "You must do this or that! You have not done so! Then you are condemned to the wrath of God and to eternal death!" — then the Law is being employed in its proper use and for its proper purpose. Then the heart is crushed to the point of despair. This use and function of the Law is felt by terrified and desperate consciences, who yearn for death or want to inflict death on themselves because of the anguish of conscience.

Therefore the Law is a hammer that crushes rocks, a fire, a wind, and a great and mighty earthquake that overturns mountains. When Elijah could not bear the terrors of the Law that were signified by these events, he wrapped his head in his mantle; and after the storm he had seen was over, there came a still small voice, in which the

Lord was present (1 Kings 19:11-13). But the violence of the fire, the storm, and the earthquake had to come first, before the Lord Himself followed in the still small voice.

The awesome spectacle and the pomp with which God gave the Law on Mt. Sinai symbolize this use of the Law. There was the utmost sanctity in the people of Israel, who had come out of Egypt. "We," they boasted, "are the people of God. We shall do whatever the Lord our God has said." (Ex. 19:8.) In addition, Moses sanctified the people, commanding them to wash their clothing, to stay away from women, and to prepare themselves for three days. There was no one there who was not extremely holy. On the third day Moses led the people out from the camp to the mountain, into the presence of the Lord, so that they could hear His voice. What happens? When the Children of Israel see the horrible spectacle of the mountain smoking and burning, the black clouds, and the lightning flashing in that dense darkness; and when they hear the blare of the trumpet steadily growing louder and longer; and when they hear the thunder and the lightning, they draw back in terror, and, standing far off, they say to Moses: "We shall gladly do everything, just so that the Lord does not speak with us, lest we die by being devoured by this great fire! You teach us, and we shall listen." What good did it do them, I ask you, to be clean, to wear white garments, to stay away from women, to be holy? None whatever. None of them could endure this presence of God in His majesty and glory; but all of them were terrified and crushed by fear, so that they drew back as though they were impelled by the devil. For God is a consuming fire (Heb. 12:29), in whose presence no flesh at all is able to stand.

Therefore the Law has this function, which it had on Mt. Sinai, when it was first given and heard by those who were washed, righteous, purified, and chaste. Yet it brought these saints to a recognition of their misery and to the very point of despair and death. No purity helped them then; but their sense of impurity, unworthiness, sin, judgment, and the wrath of God was so great that they fled from the presence of the Lord and were not able to hear His voice. "What is any flesh," they said, "to hear the voice of the Lord, the living God, and to be able to live? Today we have seen that when God speaks with man, man cannot endure it." Now they are speaking much differently from the way they spoke a little earlier, when they were saying: "We are the holy people of God, whom the Lord has chosen as His very own in preference to all the nations of the world. We shall do everything that the Lord has spoken." This is what finally happens to all self-righteous people who are drunk with the presumption of their own righteousness. They think that when there is no trouble, they are the dearly beloved of God, and that God has regard for their vows, fasts, little prayers, and alms and will grant them a special crown in heaven in exchange for these. But when thunder and lightning come out of the blue, the fire and hammer that smashes rocks, that is, the Law of God that reveals sin and that shows the wrath and judgment of God, they are driven to despair.

I urge you, who are to be the teachers of others, to learn this doctrine of the true and proper use of the Law carefully; for after our time it will be obscured again and will be completely wiped out.[100] Today, while we are still alive and are insistently urging this doctrine, there are nevertheless very few, even among those who want to seem "evangelical" and who acknowledge the Gospel with us, who correctly understand the use of the Law. What do you think will happen when we have been taken away? Right now I am not even speaking about the Anabaptists, the Neo-Arians,[101] and the spirits who blaspheme the Sacrament of the body and blood of Christ; they are all as ignorant of this proper use and function of the Law as the papists are. They have long since defected from the pure doctrine of the Gospel to laws. Therefore they do not teach Christ. They boast and swear that they are intent on nothing except the glory of God and the salvation of the brethren, and that they teach the Word of God purely; but in fact they distort the Word of God and twist it into an alien meaning, so that it is forced to tell them what they themselves imagine. Under the name of Christ, therefore, they teach their own dreams, and under the name of the Gospel nothing but laws and ceremonies. And so they are and remain true to form, that is, monks, performers of works, legalists, and ritualists; all they do is to think up new names and new works.

Therefore it is a matter of no small moment to believe correctly about what the Law is and what its use and function are. Thus it is evident that we do not reject the Law and works, as our opponents falsely accuse us. But we do everything to establish the Law, and we require works. We say that the Law is good and useful, but in

[100] Here again (cf. p. 178, note 94) the printed version of Luther's lectures preserves an echo of his spoken words when he speaks of his forebodings about the future of the doctrine of justification.

[101] On the "Neo-Arians" cf. *Luther's Works,* 1, p. 16, note 28.

[W, XL, 485—487]

its proper use, namely, first, as we have said earlier, to restrain civic transgressions; and secondly, to reveal spiritual transgressions. Therefore the Law is a light that illumines and shows, not the grace of God or righteousness and life but the wrath of God, sin, death, our damnation in the sight of God, and hell. For just as on Mt. Sinai the lightning, the thunder, the dark cloud, the smoking and burning mountain, and the whole horrendous sight did not make the Children of Israel happy or alive but terrified them, made them almost helpless, and disclosed a presence of God speaking from the cloud that they could not bear for all their sanctity and purity, so when the Law is being used correctly, it does nothing but reveal sin, work wrath, accuse, terrify, and reduce the minds of men to the point of despair. And that is as far as the Law goes.

On the other hand, the Gospel is a light that illumines hearts and makes them alive. It discloses what grace and the mercy of God are; what the forgiveness of sins, blessing, righteousness, life, and eternal salvation are; and how we are to attain to these. When we distinguish the Law from the Gospel this way, we attribute to each its proper use and function. You will not find anything about this distinction between the Law and the Gospel in the books of the monks, the canonists, and the recent and ancient theologians. Augustine taught and expressed it to some extent. Jerome and others like him knew nothing at all about it.[102] In other words, for many centuries there has been a remarkable silence about this in all the schools and churches. This situation has produced a very dangerous condition for consciences; for unless the Gospel is clearly distinguished from the Law, Christian doctrine cannot be kept sound. But when this distinction is recognized, the true meaning of justification is recognized. Then it is easy to distinguish faith from works, and Christ from Moses, as well as from the magistrate and all civil laws. For everything apart from Christ is a ministry of death for the punishment of the wicked. Therefore Paul answers the question this way:

The Law was added because of transgressions.

That is, so that transgressions might be increased, recognized, and made more visible. And in fact this is what happens. For when through the Law a man's sin, death, the wrath and judgment of God, and hell are revealed to him, it is impossible for him not to become

---

[102] When Luther contrasted Augustine with Jerome, it was generally to the latter's disadvantage; cf. p. 84, note 3, and *Luther's Works*, 32, p. 189.

impatient, murmur, and hate God and His will. He cannot endure the judgment of God and his own death and damnation, and yet he cannot flee. Then he inevitably falls into hate and blasphemy against God. When there was no trouble, he was a big saint; he worshiped and praised God, genuflected, and gave thanks, as that Pharisee did in Luke (18:11). But now that sin and death have been revealed, he would want God not to exist. In this way the Law produces extreme hate toward God. This means that through the Law sin is not only disclosed and recognized, but that through this disclosure sin is increased, inflated, inflamed, and magnified. This is what Paul is saying in Rom. 7:13: "It was sin, working death in me through what is good, in order that sin might be shown to be sin, and through the commandment might become sinful beyond measure." There he discusses this effect of the Law at some length.

To the question, "If the Law does not justify, what is its purpose?" Paul, therefore, replies: "Although the Law does not justify, it is nevertheless extremely useful and necessary. In the first place, it acts as a civic restraint upon those who are unspiritual and uncivilized. In the second place, it produces in a man the knowledge of himself as a sinner, who is therefore subject to death and worthy of eternal wrath." But what is the value of this effect, this humiliation, this wounding and crushing by the hammer? It has this value, that grace can have access to us. Therefore the Law is a minister and a preparation for grace. For God is the God of the humble, the miserable, the afflicted, the oppressed, the desperate, and of those who have been brought down to nothing at all. And it is the nature of God to exalt the humble, to feed the hungry, to enlighten the blind, to comfort the miserable and afflicted, to justify sinners, to give life to the dead, and to save those who are desperate and damned. For He is the almighty Creator, who makes everything out of nothing. In the performance of this, His natural and proper work,[103] He does not allow Himself to be interfered with by that dangerous pest, the presumption of righteousness, which refuses to be sinful, impure, miserable, and damned but wants to be righteous and holy. Therefore God has to make use of that hammer of His, namely, the Law, to break, bruise, crush, and annihilate this beast with its false confidence, wisdom, righteousness, and power, so that it learns that it has been destroyed and damned by its evil. Then, when the conscience has been terri-

[103] Cf. p. 38, note 21.

fied this way by the Law, there is a place for the doctrine of the Gospel and of grace, which raises it up again and comforts it; it says that Christ did not come into the world to break the bruised reed or to quench the dimly burning wick (Is. 42:3) but to announce the Gospel to the poor, to bind up the brokenhearted, and to proclaim liberty to the captives (Is. 61:1).

But it takes work and labor for someone who has been terrified and bruised by the Law to be able to raise himself up and to say: "Now I have been crushed and troubled enough. The time of the Law has caused me enough misery. Now it is time for grace and for listening to Christ, from whose mouth there come messages of grace. Now it is time to see, not the smoking and burning Mt. Sinai, but Mt. Moriah, where the seat, the temple, and the mercy seat of God are, that is, Christ, who is the King of righteousness and peace. There I shall hear what the Lord is speaking to me; He is speaking peace to His people." In fact, the foolishness of the human heart is so great that in its conflict of conscience, when the Law performs its function and carries out its true use, the heart not only does not take hold of the doctrine of grace, which gives a sure promise and offer of the forgiveness of sins for the sake of Christ, but it actually looks for more laws to help it out. "If I live longer," it says, "I shall improve my life. I shall do this and that. I shall enter a monastery; I shall live frugally and content myself with bread and water; I shall go about barefoot." Unless you do the very opposite here; that is, unless you send Moses and his Law away to the smug and stubborn, and unless you, in your fears and terrors, take hold of Christ, who suffered, was crucified, and died for your sins, your salvation is over and done with.

It follows, therefore, that the Law with its function does contribute to justification — not because it justifies, but because it impels one to the promise of grace and makes it sweet and desirable. Therefore we do not abolish the Law; but we show its true function and use, namely, that it is a most useful servant impelling us to Christ. After the Law has humbled, terrified, and completely crushed you, so that you are on the brink of despair, then see to it that you know how to use the Law correctly; for its function and use is not only to disclose the sin and wrath of God but also to drive us to Christ. None but the Holy Spirit is intent on this use of the Law or preaches the Gospel, because nothing but the Gospel says that God is present with those who are contrite in heart (Is. 57:15). Therefore if you have

been crushed by that hammer, do not use your contrition wrongly
by burdening yourself with even more laws. Listen to Christ when
He says (Matt. 11:28): "Come to Me, all who labor and are heavy
laden, and I will give you rest." When the Law drives you this way,
so that you despair of everything that is your own and seek help and
solace from Christ, then it is being used correctly; and so, through
the Gospel, it serves the cause of justification. This is the best and
most perfect use of the Law.

Here, then, Paul begins to discuss the Law under a new heading
and to define what it is; the occasion for this was his statement that
the Law does not justify. For as soon as reason hears this, it draws
the inference: "Then it is of no use." Therefore it was necessary to
ask, to define correctly, and to reply what the Law is and how it is
to be understood, so that it would not be interpreted more broadly
or more narrowly than it should. For justification, he says, no Law
whatever is necessary. When the debate is about righteousness, life,
and eternal salvation, therefore, the Law must be removed from sight
completely, as though it had never existed or would never exist but
were a mere nothing. For in the issue of justification no one can
adequately remove the Law from sight and look only at the promise.
This is why I said that in our feelings the Law and the promise are
to be separated as far as possible; for in fact they are very close together.

*Till the Offspring should come to whom the promise had been
made.*

Paul does not make the Law permanent; but he says that it was
given and added to the promise because of transgressions, that is, to
restrain them in society but especially to reveal them theologically;
and he says that this was not to be forever but for a certain time.
Here it is necessary to know the predicate, "to what point," [104] that
is, how long the reign or tyranny of the Law was to go on revealing
sin, showing us what we are like and manifesting the wrath of God.
Those who really feel all this would perish instantly if they did not
receive comfort. Unless the days of the Law were shortened, therefore, no one would be saved (Matt. 24:22). And so it is necessary to
predetermine the manner and the time of the Law, beyond which it
is not to prevail. How long, then, is the dominion of the Law to last?
Until the Offspring comes, namely, that Offspring about whom it is

[104] Aristotle, *Categories*, ch. 4.

written: "In your Offspring shall all nations be blessed." Therefore the Law is necessary to the point when the fullness of time (Gal. 4:4) and the Offspring of the blessing comes. Not that the Law itself brings the Offspring or grants righteousness; but in society it restrains and imprisons the untamed, while theologically it denounces, humbles, and terrifies, and drives those who are humble and terrified to long for the Offspring of the blessing.

You may understand the duration of the time of the Law either literally or spiritually. Literally: The Law lasted until Christ. "The Law and the prophets," Christ says, "prophesied until John. From the days of John until now the kingdom of heaven has suffered violence, and men of violence take it by force" (Matt. 11:13, 12). At that time Christ was baptized and began to preach, when in a literal way the Law and the whole Mosaic system of worship came to an end.

In a spiritual sense: The Law must not rule in the conscience any longer than the predetermined time of that Blessed Offspring. Therefore when the Law has disclosed my iniquities to me, has terrified me, and has revealed to me the wrath and judgment of God, so that I begin to blanch and to despair, then the Law has reached the prescribed manner, time, and purpose when it must stop exercising its tyranny, because then it has discharged its function by adequately disclosing the wrath of God and creating terror. Here one must say: "Stop, Law! You have caused enough terror and sorrow. Thou dost overwhelm me with all Thy waves; Thy dread assaults destroy me (Ps. 88:7, 16). O Lord, do not rebuke Thy servant in Thy anger, nor chasten me in Thy wrath (Ps. 6:1)." When these terrors and complaints come, it is the time and the hour of the Blessed Offspring. Then let the Law withdraw; for it was indeed added for the sake of disclosing and increasing transgressions, but only until the point when the Offspring would come. Once He is present, let the Law stop disclosing transgressions and terrifying. Let it surrender its realm to another, that is, to the Blessed Offspring, Christ; He has gracious lips, with which He does not accuse and terrify but speaks better things than the Law, namely, grace, peace, forgiveness of sins, and victory over sin and death.

With the words "till the Offspring should come to whom the promise had been made" Paul indicates, therefore, how long the Law should last, both in a literal and in a spiritual sense. But the spiritual duration of the Law clings very tenaciously to the conscience; therefore a man who is applying the theological use of the Law has great difficulty reaching the end of the Law. Amid the terrors and the feeling of sin the mind cannot achieve the hope that God is merciful and that He wants to forgive sins for the sake of Christ; all it does is to suppose that God is wrathful with sinners and accuses and damns them. Unless there is added a faith that will raise one up again, or unless, in accordance with that saying of Christ about "Where two or three" (Matt. 18:20), there is a brother present who will comfort such a person, oppressed and bruised by the Law, with the Word of God, despair and death are sure to follow. Therefore it is very bad for a man to be alone, especially amid temptations. "Woe to him who is alone when he falls," says Ecclesiastes (4:10), "and has not another to lift him up." Therefore those who established monasticism or the solitary life provided an occasion for despair to innumerable people. If someone separated himself from the company of men for a day or two in order to pray, as we read about Christ that from time to time He withdrew to the mountain alone and spent the night in prayer (Luke 6:12), this would not be dangerous. But it was an invention of the devil when they decided that the solitary life should be permanent. For if a man is alone when he is tempted, he cannot overcome any temptation either of the flesh or of the spirit.

And it was ordained by angels through an intermediary.

This is a slight digression, which Paul does not complete but only touches in passing. Then he goes on. Soon he returns to the topic he had introduced, namely (3:21): "Is the Law, then, against the promises of God?" Now this was the occasion for his digression: There occurred to him a difference between the Law and the Gospel, namely, that the Law which was added to the promises differs from the Gospel not only as to time but also as to author or efficient cause. "For the Law was given through angels (Heb. 2:2); but the Gospel through the Lord Himself." Therefore the message of the Gospel excels the Law, because the Law is the voice of servants, but the Gospel is the voice of the Lord. To reduce the importance of the Law, therefore, and to amplify that of the Gospel, he says that the Law was the doctrine for an extremely short time (since it lasted only until the fulfillment of the promise, that is, until the Blessed Offspring that fulfilled the promise); but the Gospel was forever. Therefore the Law is much inferior to the Gospel, because it was ordained

[W, XL, 494, 495]

through servants, through the angels, while the Gospel was ordained through the Lord Himself. Thus Heb. 1:2 says: "In these last days God has spoken to us by a Son [who is that Blessed Offspring], whom He appointed the Heir of all things, through whom also He created the world." But the Lord speaks much differently from the servants.

In addition, the message of the Law was not only delivered through servants, the angels, but through another servant, who was inferior to the angels, that is, through a man; as he says here, "through the hand of an intermediary," that is, of Moses. Now Christ is not a servant; He is the Lord Himself. He is not the Mediator between God and man according to the Law, as Moses was; but He is the Mediator of a better covenant. As I have said, Paul only touches on this in passing and does not explain it. The Law was delivered through the angels as servants, because on Mt. Sinai Moses and the people heard the speaking God, that is, angels speaking in the person of God. Hence Stephen says in Acts 7:53: "You received the Law as delivered by angels," that is, through angels who delivered it and handed it down, "and you did not keep it." The text of Ex. 3:2 clearly states that an angel appeared to Moses in a flame of fire and spoke with him from the midst of the bush. The Latin text is corrupt here; for it does not have the word "angel," but "Lord." Through an ignorance of the Hebrew language this passage provoked a debate over whether the Lord Himself or an angel spoke to Moses.[105]

Therefore there are two mediators here; one is Moses, and the other is Christ. And here Paul touches on the history in Exodus about the giving of the Law; it says that Moses led the people out of their tents to the meeting with God and gathered them at the base of Mt. Sinai. Here there was a sad and horrible sight: the whole mountain was on fire. When the people saw this, they began to tremble; for they believed that in this violent storm they would soon perish. Because they could not endure the Law as it was being pronounced from Mt. Sinai in all its terror — for the terrifying sound of the Law would have killed the people — they said to Moses (Ex. 20:19): "You step close and hear what the Lord is saying, and then you speak to us." And he says: "I have been the trustee and mediator between God and you." From this it is abundantly clear that Moses was appointed as the mediator between the people and the speaking of the Law.

---

[105] The Douay Version of Ex. 3:2 reflects this: "And the Lord appeared to him in a flame of fire out of the midst of a bush."

You see, therefore, that on the basis of this history Paul wanted to signify this question in a hidden manner: How could the Law justify when the whole people of Israel, who had been made holy, and Moses himself, as the Epistle to the Hebrews says (Heb. 12:21), were terrified and trembled at the sound of the Law? There was nothing here except fear and trembling. What sort of righteousness and holiness is that, not to be able to endure the Law, in fact, not to be able or to want to listen to it but to flee it and to hate it, to hate it more than anything else in the world? Thus the history clearly states that in the very hour in which the people heard the Law nothing was more hateful to them than the Law, and they would have preferred death to hearing the Law. When a man's sin has been disclosed by the rays that the Law shines into his heart, he finds nothing more odious and intolerable than the Law. Then he would rather choose death than endure, even for a brief time, those terrors of the Law. This is a certain sign that the Law does not justify. For if it justified, certainly men would love it, delight in it, and embrace it with a will that would be inclined toward it, not away from it. But where is that will? Nowhere, neither in Moses nor in the entire people; for they all fled in fear and trembling. Whatever one flees, one does not love but dislikes; one does not delight in it but finds it hateful in the highest degree.

Therefore their fleeing shows the infinite hatred of the human heart against the Law and, as a consequence, against God Himself. Even if there were no other argument to prove that righteousness does not come through the Law, this single history, which Paul mentions so briefly with the words "through an intermediary," would be enough. It is as though he were saying: "Do you not remember that your fathers were so unable to listen to the Law that they needed Moses as a mediator? And once he had been appointed, they were so far from loving the Law that by their fearful flight together with their mediator — as the Epistle to the Hebrews testifies (12:21) — they denounced it. If they could have done so, they would have retreated to Egypt, right through the iron mountain. But they were hemmed in and could not escape. Therefore they cry out to Moses (Ex. 20:19): 'You speak to us. For if we listen any longer to the voice of the Lord our God, we shall die.' If, then, they could not listen to the Law, how, I ask you, could they keep it?"

If the people of the Law were compelled to have a mediator, it follows by inevitable logic that the Law did not justify them. What, then, did it do? What Paul says (Rom. 5:20): "Law came in, to increase the trespass." Therefore the Law was a light and a sun, shedding its rays into the hearts of the Children of Israel; thus it frightened them and pounded such wrath and fear of God into them that they despised the Law and its Author, which is a grievous sin. Would you say that people like this are righteous? Certainly not. For those are righteous who hear the Law, embrace it with a good will, and delight in it. But the history of the giving of the Law proves that all the men in the world, no matter how holy — especially since those who had been purified and sanctified could not listen to the Law — are opposed to the Law, are horrified at it, flee from it, and wish that it did not exist. Therefore the Law cannot justify, but it has an altogether opposite effect.

As I have said, Paul only touches on this topic in passing; he does not exhaust it or complete it, for it is too vast. If he had wanted to discuss it at greater length, he would have had to speak about both mediators, Moses and Christ, and would have had to compare them with each other. And so this one topic would have supplied him with plenty of reason for writing a whole new epistle. The history of the giving of the Law in Ex. 19 and 20 would supply enough material to write a large book, even if it were read only in passing and without feeling; nevertheless, it seems very cold, in comparison with other sacred accounts, to those who do not know the true function and use of the Law.

From all this it is evident that if the whole world had been standing at Mt. Sinai as the people of Israel did, it would have been filled with horror and would have fled from the Law. Therefore the whole world is hostile to the Law and hates it bitterly. "But the Law is holy, righteous, and good, and is the uprightness of the will of God" (Rom. 7:12). How, then, can someone be righteous if he not only detests the Law and flees before it but is also an enemy of the God who is the Author of the Law? The flesh cannot act otherwise, as Rom. 8:7 says: "The mind that is set on the flesh is hostile to God; it does not submit to God's Law; indeed, it cannot." Thus it is the height of insanity to hate God and His Law so much that you cannot even listen to it, and then to assert that we are justified by the Law!

Therefore the sophists are blind and do not understand anything of this discussion. They look only at the outward mask of the Law. They imagine that it can be satisfied by civic morality, and that those who keep it externally are righteous in the sight of God. They do not pay attention to its true spiritual effect, which is not to justify consciences and to set them at peace but to increase sin, to cause terror, and to work wrath. Because they ignore this, they conclude that man has a good will and a right reason in relation to the Law of God. But to find out whether this is true, just ask the people of the Law, along with their mediator, who heard the voice of the Law on Sinai. Ask David himself. Whenever in the psalms he complains that he has been cast away from the presence of God, that he is dwelling in hell, and that he is terrified by the greatness of his sin and by the wrath and judgment of God — he does not set sacrifices or even the Law itself against those invincible tyrants, but only the free mercy of God. Therefore the Law does not justify.

If the Law were submissive to my feelings; that is, if it gave approval to my hypocrisy and boasting, my presumption and confidence in my own righteousness; if it were to grant that I could be justified in the sight of God without the mercy of God or faith in Christ, with its help alone, as the whole world naturally believes about the Law; if the Law were to say that God is influenced and overcome by works and that He is obliged to grant a reward for these works, so that I would not need any God but could be my own god, meriting grace by my own works and being able to save myself by my own merits, apart from Christ the Savior — if, I say, the Law were that submissive to me, then it would be joyous, sweet, and precious. That is how exceedingly well reason can flatter itself. But this would last only until such a time as the Law would penetrate to its proper use and function; then it would become evident that reason cannot endure the rays of the Law. Then some Moses would have to come along and become the mediator.

The passage in 2 Cor. 3:7-18 about the veiled face of Moses is pertinent here. On the basis of the account in Ex. 34 Paul shows that the Children of Israel not only lost the true and theological use of the Law but could not even endure it. In the first place, Paul says, this was because they could not look at the purpose of the Law on account of the veil that Moses placed over his face. In addition, they could not look at the unveiled face of Moses because of the brightness of his countenance. Therefore Moses would cover his face with a veil when he was about to speak with them, for without this they could not endure his message. That is, they could not even listen to Moses, their intermediary, unless he in turn employed another intermediary, namely, the veil. How, then, could they listen to the voice of God or of an angel when they could not listen to the voice of Moses, a human being and their own intermediary at that, unless he veiled his face? Therefore unless the Blessed Offspring comes to raise up and comfort the man who has heard the Law, he will certainly be led by his despair into scorn for the Law and into hate and blasphemy against God. From day to day he will grow worse in his lying against God; for the deeper his fear and confusion of conscience goes and the longer it lasts, the more his hate and blasphemy against God will grow.

This history teaches also what the power of the free will is. The people are terrified, and they tremble. Where is the free will now; where is their good will and right reason? What does the free will do here in these men who have been purified and who are holy? It is of no help at all; it darkens the reason and turns the good will away. It neither receives nor greets nor joyfully embraces the Lord, who comes with lightning, thunder, and fire to Mt. Sinai. It cannot listen to the voice of the Lord, but says: "Let not the Lord speak with us, lest we die." We see, therefore, what the power of the free will is in the Children of Israel, who, even when they have been sanctified, neither will nor can listen to a single syllable or letter of the Law. Therefore all those praises of the free will are mere nonsense.[106]

20. *Now an intermediary implies more than one.*

Paul is beginning now to compare the two intermediaries; and he is speaking generally, since the term "intermediary" is a general one. "An intermediary implies more than one." Thus there is no intermediary between God and God; but this term necessarily includes two, one of whom needs intercession and the other not. Therefore an intermediary implies not one but two, and two who disagree with each other. According to this general definition, Moses is an intermediary, because he mediates between the Law and the people, who cannot endure the theological use of the Law. Therefore a new face has to be put on the Law, and its voice has to be changed; that is, the theological message of the Law, or the living Law in experience, has to put on a mask and become tolerable and audible through the human voice of Moses.

Now when the Law has been masked this way, it no longer speaks in its majesty but through the mouth of Moses. Nor does it carry

[106] An echo of Luther's controversy with Erasmus over the freedom of the will.

out its function this way any longer; that is, it does not pound terror into consciences. And so men simply do not understand it now but are made smug, sleepy, and presumptuous hypocrites through it. And yet one or the other has to happen: Either the Law must be separated from its proper use by a veil; but then, as I have said, it creates hypocrites; or it must appear in its proper use without the veil, and then it kills, because the human heart cannot endure the Law in its true use without the veil. If you look at the purpose of the Law without a veil, therefore, you must either take hold of the Blessed Offspring — that is, you must look beyond the purpose of the Law at Christ, who is the fulfillment of the Law and who says: "The Law has frightened you enough. Take heart, My son; your sins are forgiven" (Matt. 9:2) — or you must have Moses with his veil as your intermediary.

This is why Paul says as a general principle: "An intermediary implies more than one." It was impossible for Moses to be the intermediary only of God, because God does not need an intermediary. Nor is he the intermediary only of the people. But between God and the people, who are not in harmony with God, he acts as the mediator. For it is the function of an intermediary to reconcile the offended party with the offending party. Nevertheless, as I have said, Moses is the sort of intermediary who merely changes the sound of the Law and makes it tolerable to hear, not one who provides the strength to keep the Law. In other words, he is an intermediary of the veil, and therefore he does not grant the power of the Law except in the veil. Therefore it is necessary for his disciples to remain hypocrites.

But what do you suppose would have happened if the Law had been given without Moses, either before or after Moses, and there had been no intermediary, but the people had been unable either to flee or to have an intermediary? Either the people would have been crushed with extreme terror and would have expired immediately; or, if they were to be saved, another intermediary would have had to come to intercede between the Law and the people in such a way that the Law would have remained unimpaired in its force, but the people would have come into harmony with the Law. Moses comes into the breach and becomes the intermediary; he makes the mask and puts on the veil, but he cannot remove the terror of the conscience before the Law. Therefore when Moses and his veil have been put away and a man in the hour of death or in a struggle of conscience feels the wrath and judgment of God over the sin that the Law discloses and increases, then, if he is not to despair, there must come another Mediator who will say: "You shall survive, sinner; that is, you will not die, even though the Law and its wrath remain."

That Mediator is Jesus Christ. He does not change the sound of the Law, as Moses did; nor does He cover it with a veil or lead me away from a view of the Law. But He sets Himself against the wrath of the Law and abolishes it; in His own body and by Himself He satisfies the Law. Afterwards He says to me through the Gospel: "Of course, the Law is horrible and wrathful. Do not be afraid, however, or run away; but stand fast. I take your place and make satisfaction to the Law for you." He is a far different Mediator from Moses, who intercedes between a wrathful God and the sinner. Here the intercession of Moses is of no use, for now he has disappeared and has discharged his function with his veil. Here there is a confrontation between a desperate sinner or a dying man and an offended and wrathful God. Therefore another Mediator than Moses must come to make satisfaction to the Law, take away its wrath, and reconcile me, a damned sinner who has been sentenced to eternal death, to the wrathful God.

Paul mentions this Mediator in passing when he says: "An intermediary implies more than one"; for the word "mediator" naturally means one who mediates between an offender and the one who has been offended. We are the offenders; God with His Law is the offended. And the offense is such that God cannot forgive it and we cannot remove it. Therefore there is grave discord between God, who is One in Himself, and us. Nor can God revoke His Law, but He wants it to be observed. And we who have transgressed the Law of God cannot flee from the sight of God. Therefore Christ has stepped into the breach as the Mediator between two utterly different parties separated by an infinite and eternal division, and has reconciled them. How? As Paul says elsewhere (Col. 2:14-15), "He canceled the bond which stood against us with its legal demands; this He set aside, nailing it to the cross. He disarmed the principalities and powers and made a public example of them, triumphing over them in Him." And so He is not the Mediator of one; He is the Mediator of two who were in the utmost disagreement.

This passage is powerful and effective for refuting the righteousness of the Law and for teaching us that in the matter of justification the Law must be removed as far away as possible. The very term "Mediator" serves to confirm the argument that the Law does not justify. Otherwise what need would there be of a Mediator? Since human nature cannot listen to the Law, it is obvious that it is even less able to keep it or to come to terms with the Law. Therefore the Law does not justify.

As I often remind you, almost to the point of excess, this is the true doctrine of the Law, which every Christian should diligently strive to learn. He should know how to define precisely and properly what the Law is — its use, its manner, its power, its time, and its purpose, namely, that it has an effect exactly opposite from that which all men suppose, since by nature this dangerous notion that the Law justifies has been planted into them. Therefore I am afraid that when we die, this doctrine will pass away again; for before the Last Day the world must be filled with horrible darkness and error.[107]

Let anyone who can understand, therefore, understand that in Christian theology and according to its proper description the Law does not justify but has exactly the opposite effect: It discloses us to ourselves; it shows us a wrathful God; it manifests wrath; it terrifies us. It not only reveals sin but causes it to abound, so that where there was a small sin at first, it becomes large through the illumination of the Law; then a man begins to hate the Law, to run away from it, and with a perfect hatred to hate God, the Originator of the Law. As reason itself is forced to admit, this is surely not being righteous through the Law. No, it is sinning against the Law in two ways: first, having a will that is not only so averse to the Law that it cannot listen to it but acts contrary to it; secondly, hating the Law so much that you wish it were abolished, along with God, its Author, who is supremely good.

What greater blasphemy can there be, what more horrible sin, than to hate God, to turn away from His Law and not to be able to listen to it, although it is supremely good and holy? For the record clearly states that the people of Israel refused to listen to the best Law, the holiest and by their nature the most joyful sounds, namely (Ex. 20:2-12): "I am the Lord your God, who brought you out. You shall have no other gods. Showing steadfast love to thousands. Honor your father, that you may live long on the earth." It shows, too, that they needed an intermediary. They could not endure this supreme, perfect, and divine wisdom, this beautiful, wonderful, and sweet teaching. "Let not God speak to us," they say, "lest we die. You speak to us"

[107] Cf. p. 312, note 100.

(Ex. 20:19). This is really an amazing thing, not to be able to listen to your highest and sweetest good, namely, that you have a God who is merciful, who wants to "show steadfast love to thousands" for you. You are not able to listen to that which defends you: "You shall not kill. You shall not commit adultery. You shall not steal." For with these words God surrounds your life, your wife, and your possessions as though with a wall and protects them against all the power and reviling of evil men.

Therefore the Law cannot do anything except that with its light it illumines the conscience for sin, death, judgment, and the hate and wrath of God. Before the Law comes, I am smug and do not worry about sin; when the Law comes, it shows me sin, death, and hell. Surely this is not being justified; it is being sentenced, being made an enemy of God, being condemned to death and hell. Therefore the principal purpose of the Law in theology is to make men not better but worse; that is, it shows them their sin, so that by the recognition of sin they may be humbled, frightened, and worn down, and so may long for grace and for the Blessed Offspring. This is a summary of the argument that Paul, in this digression, based on the word "intermediary."

But God is One.

God has not offended anyone; therefore He does not need any intermediary. But we have offended God; therefore we do need an Intermediary — not that Moses, but Christ, who speaks better things to us. So far the digression; now Paul returns to the point he had begun to make.

21. *Is the Law, then, against the promises of God?*

Earlier Paul said that the Law does not justify. Then let us abolish it! No; for it, too, has its usefulness. What is that? It brings men to a recognition of themselves; it discloses and increases sin. Here immediately another question arises: If the Law merely makes men worse by disclosing their sin to them, it conflicts with the promises of God; for God seems merely to be irritated and offended by the Law, so that He neither observes nor keeps His promises. "We Jews thought the opposite, namely, that through the Law we are kept and held in that outward discipline, so that God may be moved by this to speed the disclosure of the promise, and so that by this discipline we might merit the promise." Paul replies: "No. Quite the contrary, in fact. If you pay attention to the Law, the promise is held back even more." For human reason offends the God who promises when it refuses to listen to His good and holy Law but says: "Let not God speak to us" (Ex. 20:19). Should God keep His promises for those who not only do not accept His Law and discipline but hate it bitterly and run away from it? Here, as I have said, the question immediately arises: Then the Law seems to stand in the way of the promises of God? Paul only touches on this question in passing and goes on; still he does reply to it and says:

Certainly not.

Why? First, because God is not moved to make His promises by our worthiness, merits, or good works; but He promises purely on the basis of His inexhaustible and eternal goodness and mercy. He does not say to Abraham: "Because you have observed the Law, therefore all nations shall be blessed in you." But to one who was uncircumcised, who did not have the Law, and who was still an idolater, as is written in Joshua 24:2, He says: "Go from your country: I will be your Protector" (Gen. 12:1-3); and again: "In your Offspring, etc." (Gen. 22:18). These are completely absolute promises that God promises to Abraham freely, without any condition or any consideration of works or merits, whether preceding or subsequent.

This is chiefly an argument against the Jews, who suppose that the divine promises are being hindered by their sins. God does not delay His promises, Paul says, on account of our sins; nor does He hasten them on account of our righteousness and our merits. He does not consider either one. Therefore even if we were made worse through the Law and hated God more, God would still not be moved by this to defer the promise; for it does not depend on our worthiness and righteousness but on His goodness and mercy. Therefore it is a pure fiction when the Jews say: "The Messiah has not come, because our sins are delaying His coming." As though God would become unjust on account of our sins or a liar on account of our lies! He Himself always remains righteous and truthful, whether we sin or do not sin. Therefore His truth is the only reason for His observing and fulfilling the promise.

Secondly, although the Law discloses and increases sin, it is still not against the promises of God but is, in fact, for them. For in its true and proper work and purpose it humbles a man and prepares him — if he uses the Law correctly — to yearn and seek for grace. For only when a man's sin is disclosed and increased through the Law does he begin to see the wickedness of the human heart and its hostility toward the Law and toward God, the Author of the Law. Then he seriously feels that he not only does not love but hates and blasphemes God, the supremely good, with His most holy Law. Now he is forced to confess that there is nothing good in him at all. When he has been crushed and humbled this way, he acknowledges that he is truly miserable and damned. Therefore when the Law forces a man to acknowledge his evil this way and to confess his sin sincerely, it has performed its function; its time has come to an end, and the time of grace has come, when the Blessed Offspring is to arrive, who will raise up and comfort the man who has been frightened and wounded by the Law.

For this reason, therefore, the Law is not against the promises of God: first, because the promise does not depend on the Law but on the truth of God; secondly, because in its highest and greatest use the Law humbles and by humbling makes men groan, sigh, and seek the hand of the Mediator. It makes His grace and mercy very sweet — as Ps. 109:21 says, "Thy mercy is sweet" — and His gift precious beyond the telling. Thus it makes us ready for Christ. He who has never tasted the bitter will not remember the sweet;[108] hunger is the best cook. As the dry earth thirsts for rain, so the Law makes the troubled heart thirst for Christ. To such hearts Christ tastes sweetest; to them He is joy, comfort, and life. Only then are Christ and His work understood correctly.

Therefore the best use of the Law is to be able to employ it to the point that it produces humility and a thirst for Christ. He Himself requires thirsting souls and attracts them in a most charming manner to Himself when He says (Matt. 11:28): "Come to Me, all who labor and are heavy laden, and I will give you rest." Therefore He gladly soaks and irrigates this dry ground. He does not pour out His waters on ground that is fertile or fat or free of thirst. His blessings are inestimable. Therefore He grants them only to the needy; He preaches good news to the poor (Luke 4:18) and gives water to the thirsty. "If anyone thirst," He says in John 7:37, "let him come to Me." "He heals the brokenhearted" (Ps. 147:3). That is, He comforts and saves those who have been vexed and troubled by the Law. Accordingly, the Law is not against the promises of God.

---

[108] On this proverb see *Luther's Works*, 23, p. 272, note 44.

*For if a Law had been given which could make alive, then right-
eousness would indeed be by the Law.*

With these words Paul indicates that no Law whatever can make
alive but can only kill. Therefore my works, which I do not do
according to the laws of the pope or human traditions but according to the Law of God, do not justify me in the sight of God; they
only establish me as a sinner. They do not placate the wrath of God;
they arouse it. They do not achieve righteousness; they remove it.
They do not make me alive; they slay me. When he says: "If a Law
had been given," therefore, he is teaching with very clear words that
not even the divine Law makes alive, but that it has precisely the
opposite effect. Although these words of Paul are clear enough,
they are altogether obscure and unknown to the papists. For if they
understood them, they would not boast as they do about the free
will, human powers, works of supererogation, and the like. But to
keep from appearing to be obviously wicked pagans who shamefully
deny the words of an apostle of Christ, they always evade such statements of Paul about the Law's — that is, the Decalog's — disclosing
sin and working wrath by setting forth this wicked gloss: "Paul is
speaking about the Ceremonial Law, not about the Moral Law."
But when Paul says: "If a Law had been given," he is speaking
precisely and plainly and not making an exception of any Law.
Therefore the gloss of the sophists is not valid at all. For the ceremonial laws were commanded by God just as much and were observed
just as rigidly as the moral laws; the Jews observed circumcision no
less religiously than they did the Sabbath. Therefore the apostle is
speaking about the entire Law.

These words of Paul are chanted and read in all the churches of
the papacy,[109] and yet the teaching and life in these churches are
the very opposite. Paul simply says that no Law was given to make
alive. The sophists, on the contrary, teach the very opposite and
declare that many, in fact, countless, laws were given to make alive.
Although they do not say this in so many words, that is how they
actually feel. Clear evidence for this comes from monasticism; from
the numberless human laws, traditions, and ceremonies; from the
works and the merits of congruity and condignity; and from the
innumerable other wicked forms of worship they have instituted.
They have suppressed the Gospel and proclaimed only these things

[109] The epistle for the Thirteenth Sunday after Trinity is Gal. 3:15-22.

instead, promising that those who observe such forms of worship will certainly obtain grace, the forgiveness of sins, and eternal life. These statements of mine cannot be denied, for their books still stand as sure witnesses of all this.

We, on the other hand, declare with Paul that no law, whether it is human or divine, justifies or makes alive. Therefore we distinguish the Law from righteousness as sharply as death from life or hell from heaven. We are prompted to declare this by the clear statement of Paul: "The Law was not given in order to justify, make live, or save, but merely in order to condemn, kill, and destroy, contrary to the opinion of all men, who naturally suppose that the Law was given in order to obtain righteousness, life, and salvation."

Such a proper distinction between the function of the Law and that of the Gospel keeps all genuine theology in its correct use. It also establishes us believers in a position as judges over all styles of life and over all the laws and dogmas of men. Finally it provides us with a faculty for testing all the spirits (1 John 4:1). By contrast, because the papists have completely intermingled and confused the doctrine of the Law and that of the Gospel, they have been unable to teach anything certain either about faith or about works or about styles of life or about judging the spirits. And the same thing is happening to the sectarians today.

After these refutations and arguments, therefore, Paul teaches, at some length and with considerable beauty, that if you consider the true and best use of the Law, it is nothing but some sort of discipline toward righteousness. It humbles men and makes them ready for the righteousness of Christ, if it performs its proper function, that is, if it makes them guilty, terrifies them, makes them conscious of sin, wrath, death, and hell. When this has happened, the presumption of their own righteousness and holiness disappears, and Christ, with His blessings, begins to become sweet. Therefore the Law is not against the promises of God; it is for them. Although it does not fulfill the promise and does not grant righteousness, still, in its use and function, it humbles us and thus makes us ready for the grace and blessing of Christ.

"If, therefore," says Paul, "some Law had been given that could grant life — and if this were true, that Law would first have to grant righteousness, since we do not achieve life unless we have righteousness first — then righteousness would truly be on the basis of Law, and there would be life in consequence of this. Again, if there were some monastic order, some style of life, some work, or some way of religion that could achieve the forgiveness of sins, righteousness, and life, then such an order, etc., would truly justify and make alive. But this is contrary to Scripture, which consigns all things to sin, regardless of whether they are under the Law or outside the Law. Therefore it is impossible for any law or any work to exist that could justify and make alive." And therefore Paul says:

22. But the Scripture consigned all things to sin.

Again Paul shows in the clearest of words that the Law does not make alive. And here our opponents, with open eyes and ears, are blind and deaf. "The Scripture," Paul says, "has consigned all things to sin." Where has it done so? Nowhere more powerfully than in its promises, as in Gen. 3:15: "The Seed of the woman shall crush the head of the serpent"; and in Gen. 22:18: "In your Offspring, etc." Thus wherever there is a promise of Christ in the Scriptures, there righteousness, blessing, salvation, and life are promised. By the principle of contraries, therefore, righteousness, blessing, salvation, and life are not present there now. No, sin, a curse, death, the devil, and eternal destruction are there.

In its very promises, therefore, Scripture consigns all men to sin and the curse. This is over and above other explicit passages in the Law, such as the one from Deut. 27:26 that was quoted by Paul earlier (v. 10): "Cursed be everyone who does not abide by all things, etc." In clear terms this passage consigns and subjects to sin and the curse not only those who sin against the Law openly or fail to keep it outwardly but also those who are subject to the Law and bend every effort to keep the Law; such were the Jews, as I said earlier. This passage consigns to sin all the monks, hermits, and Carthusians, with their religious professions and vows, which they imagine to be so holy that if someone dies shortly after promising a vow, he flies directly to heaven. For here you are told very clearly that absolutely everything has been consigned to sin. Therefore neither the vow nor the highest religious profession of the Carthusian is righteousness, but everything is condemned. How? Through this promise of "the Seed of the woman" and similar ones, also through this Law, "Cursed be everyone" and similar ones. Therefore none of the monks or Carthusians or Celestines [110] will crush the head of the serpent; but they will all remain crushed under the head of the serpent, that is, under the power of the devil. But who believes this?

In other words, whatever is outside Christ and the promise — with no exceptions, whether it be the Ceremonial Law or the Moral Law or the Decalog, whether it be divine or human — is consigned to sin. When someone says "all things," he does not except anything. Therefore we conclude with Paul that apart from faith in Christ, all the statesmanship and laws of the Gentiles, no matter how good and necessary, and all forms of worship and religion are subject to sin, death, and eternal damnation unless, as follows next, there is added the promise on the basis of faith in Christ Jesus. A great deal has been said about this earlier.

Therefore the proposition "Faith alone justifies," which our opponents find altogether intolerable, is true; for Paul concludes very forcefully here that the Law does not make alive, because it was not given for that purpose. If the Law neither justifies nor makes alive, then works do not justify either. This is the inference Paul wants to draw when he says that the Law does not make alive, namely, that works do not make alive either. It sounds more forceful to say "The Law does not make alive" than to say "Works do not make alive." If the Law itself does not justify even when it is kept — although it is impossible to keep it — much less will works do so. Therefore faith alone justifies, without works. Paul will not stand for the addition "Faith justifies with works," but he proceeds by negation both in Rom. 3:20 — "No human being will be justified by works of the Law" — and in chapter 2:16 above — "by works of the Law shall no one be justified." And here, too, he says: "The Law was not given to make alive."

That what was promised to faith in Jesus Christ might be given to those who believe.

Earlier Paul said that Scripture has consigned all things to sin. Is this to be forever? No, but only until what was promised has been given. Now the promise is the very inheritance or blessing promised to Abraham, that is, deliverance from the Law, sin, death, and the devil; and the gift of grace, righteousness, salvation, and

110 The Celestines were strict "hermit" Benedictines; the order went out of existence in the eighteenth century.

eternal life. That promise, he says, is not obtained by any merit, Law, or work; but it is given. To whom? To believers. Believers in whom? In Jesus Christ, the Blessed Offspring who redeems believers from sin in order that they may receive the blessing. These words are not obscure; they are very clear. Nevertheless, it takes effort to observe them diligently and to weigh their force and seriousness correctly. For if all things have been consigned to sin, it follows that all the Gentiles are accursed and lack the glory of God, that they are subject to the wrath of God and to the dominion of Satan, and that no one can be delivered from all these by anything except by faith in Christ Jesus. Therefore Paul battles mightily in these words against the fanatical opinions of the sophists and of all self-righteous people about the righteousness of the Law and of works, "that what was promised to faith in Jesus Christ might be given to those who believe."

I have already shown at some length how one should respond to the passages that speak about works and about reward.[111] The discussion does not require us to speak about works now; for the point under consideration here is not works but justification, namely, that it is not obtained through the Law and works but through faith in Christ, since all things are under sin and the curse. Apart from the issue of justification, no one can adequately praise true good works. Who can adequately proclaim the usefulness and the effect of even one work that a Christian does in faith and on the basis of faith? It is more precious than heaven and earth. Therefore the whole world cannot grant a reward in this life equal to the value of one truly good work. Nor does the world have the grace to praise the good works of the pious, much less to reward them; for it does not notice them, or, if it does notice, it regards them, not as good works but as wicked crimes; and it hounds those who perform them from the face of the earth as a most dangerous menace to the human race. So it was that Christ, the Savior of the world, was subjected to the shameful death of the cross in exchange for His great and inestimable blessings. So it was that the apostles, who brought the Word of grace and eternal life to the world, became καθάρματα of the world and the περίψημα of all things (1 Cor. 4:13). A worthy reward for such benefits! But works that are done apart from faith, no matter how holy they seem in appearance, are under sin and

[111] Cf. p. 294, note 92.

the curse. Therefore they are so far removed from making their performers worthy of grace, righteousness, and eternal life that in fact they heap sin upon sin. This is how the pope, "the man of sin and the son of perdition" (2 Thess. 2:3), and all his followers work. All the self-righteous and the heretics who reject faith work this way too.

23. Now before faith came.

Paul continues to declare the usefulness and necessity of the Law. Earlier (v. 19) he said that it was added on account of transgressions. This does not mean that it was the chief purpose of God in giving the Law only to cause death and damnation; as he says also in Rom. 7:13: "Did that which is good bring death to me? By no means!" For the Law is a Word that shows life and drives us toward it. Therefore it was not given only for the sake of death. But this is its chief use and end: to reveal death, in order that the nature and enormity of sin might thus become apparent. It does not reveal death in a way that takes delight in it or that seeks to do nothing but kill us. No, it reveals death in order that men may be terrified and humbled and thus fear God. The text of Ex. 20:20 itself shows this clearly: "Do not fear," it says, "for God has come to prove you, and that the fear of Him may be before your eyes, that you may not sin." Therefore the function of the Law is only to kill, yet in such a way that God may be able to make alive. Thus the Law was not given merely for the sake of death; but because man is proud and supposes that he is wise, righteous, and holy, therefore it is necessary that he be humbled by the Law, in order that this beast, the presumption of righteousness, may be killed, since man cannot live unless it is killed.

Although the Law kills, therefore, God still uses this effect of the Law, this death, for a good use, namely, for life. When God saw that the most widespread pestilence in the whole world, that is, hypocrisy and confidence in one's own saintliness, could not be restrained and crushed in any other way, He decided to kill it by means of the Law. This was not to be permanent; but it had as its purpose that when this pestilence was killed, man would be raised up again and would hear this voice beyond the Law: "Do not fear. I did not give the Law and kill you through it with the intent that you should remain in death, but that you should fear Me and live." A presumption of good works and of righteousness leaves no room

[W, XL, 518, 519]

for the fear of God. But where there is no fear of God, there cannot be a thirst for grace and life. Therefore God must have a mighty hammer to crush the rocks, and a fire burning in the midst of heaven to overthrow the mountains, that is, to crush that stubborn and perverse beast, presumption. When a man has been brought to nothing by this pounding, despairs of his own powers, righteousness, and works, and trembles before God, he will, in his terror, begin to thirst for mercy and the forgiveness of sins.

Before faith came, we were confined under the Law, kept under restraint until faith should be revealed.

This means that before the time of the Gospel and of grace came, it was the function of the Law to keep us confined under it as though we were in prison.

This is a beautiful and most appropriate analogy, which shows what the Law accomplishes and how upright it causes men to be. Therefore it must be carefully weighed. No thief or murderer or criminal who has been captured loves his fetters or the foul prison in which he is held bound. In fact, if he could, he would destroy his prison and his iron shackles and reduce them to ashes. In prison he does indeed refrain from doing evil, not out of good will or out of a love for righteousness but because the prison prevents him. Now that he is locked up, he does not despise and hate his sin and crime — in fact, he heartily laments that he is not free and is unable to commit further crimes — but he hates his prison; and if he could get out, he would return to his former life of crime. Such is the power of the Law and such is righteousness on the basis of the Law that it forces us to be outwardly good so long as it threatens transgressors with penalties and punishment. Then we comply with the Law out of fear of punishment, but we do so unwillingly and with great indignation. What kind of righteousness is that, if you refrain from evil because you are compelled by the threat of punishment? In actual fact, therefore, this righteousness of works is nothing but to love sin, to hate righteousness, to despise God and His Law, and to adore the worst sort of wickedness. As vigorously as a thief loves prison and hates his crime, so readily do we obey the Law, do what it commands, and refrain from what it forbids.

Meanwhile, however, the Law has this benefit: Even though men's hearts may remain as wicked as possible, it restrains thieves, murderers, and public criminals to some extent, at least outwardly and politically. For if such men did not have at least a slight belief that sin is punished in the world by the rack, the gallows, and the sword, and that it is punished after this life by eternal death and hell, then no magistrate, father, or teacher would be able to restrain the madness of these men by any force or by laws and fetters. Wicked people are deterred to some extent by the threats of the Law, which strike terror into their minds, so that they do not rush headlong into all sorts of crime. But meanwhile they would rather that there were no Law, no punishment, no hell, and finally no God. If God did not have a hell and did not punish evil men, everyone would love and praise Him. But because He does punish evil men, and because all men are evil, therefore, to the extent that they are confined under the Law, they cannot avoid hating God and blaspheming Him in the extreme.

In addition, the Law confines men not only politically but also theologically. That is, the Law is also a spiritual prison and a true hell; for when it discloses sin and threatens death and the eternal wrath of God, man can neither run away nor find any comfort. For it does not lie within the power of man to shake off the horrendous terrors that the Law brings on or any other sadness of the heart. This is the source of the sounds of lamentation and complaint from the saints throughout the psalms: "In hell who shall give Thee praise?" (Ps. 6:5). For then a man is confined in a prison from which he cannot escape; and he does not see how he can be delivered from these bonds, that is, set free from these terrors. Thus the Law is a prison both politically and theologically. In the first place, it restrains and confines the wicked politically, so that they are not carried headlong by their passions into all sorts of crime. Secondly, it shows us our sin spiritually, terrifying and humbling us, so that when we have been frightened this way, we acknowledge our misery and our damnation. And this latter is the true and proper use of the Law, even though it is not permanent; for this confining and custody under the Law must not last any longer than until the arrival of faith; and when this comes, this theological prison of the Law comes to an end.

Here again we see that the Law and the Gospel, which are utterly distinct from each other and are separated as more than mutually contradictory, are nevertheless very closely joined in experience. Paul indicates this when he says: "We were confined under the Law, kept under restraint until faith should be revealed." Therefore it is not

enough for us to be confined under the Law; for if nothing else were
to follow, we would be forced to despair and to die in our sins.
But Paul adds that we are confined and restrained under a custodian,
the Law, not forever but until Christ, who is the end of the Law
(Rom. 10:4). Therefore this terror, humiliation, and custody are not
to last forever; they are to last until faith should come. That is, they
are for our salvation and for our benefit, so that we who have been
terrified by the Law may taste the sweetness of grace, the forgiveness
of sins, and deliverance from the Law, sin, and death, which are not
acquired by works but are grasped by faith alone.

Whoever knows how to bring these utterly contradictory things
together amid temptation — that is, whoever knows that when the
Law is most terrifying, then the end of the Law and the beginning
of grace and of future faith are present — such a person uses the
Law correctly. None of the wicked know this art. Cain did not
know it when he was confined in the prison of the Law and experienced the seriousness of his sin. At first he was outside the prison;
that is, he did not feel any of the terror even after he had committed
the murder of his brother; but he made a miserable pretense and
thought that it was unknown to God Himself. "Am I my brother's
keeper?" he says (Gen. 4:9). But when he heard (Gen. 4:10): "What
have you done? The voice of your brother's blood is crying to Me
from the ground," then he began to feel this prison seriously. What
brought this about? He remained confined in the prison; he did not
join the Gospel with the Law, but he said (Gen. 4:13): "My punishment is greater than I can bear." He looked only at the prison,
without considering that his sin was disclosed to him in order that
he might look for grace from God. Therefore he despaired and
denied that he had a God. He did not believe that he was confined
under grace and faith; he believed that he was confined only under
the Law.

These words, "confined and kept under restraint under the Law,"
are not vain or speculative or sophistic; they are true and serious.
The custody or prison signifies the true and spiritual terrors by which
the conscience is so confined that it cannot find a place in the whole
wide world where it can be safe. In fact, as long as these terrors
last, the conscience feels such anxiety that even if heaven and earth
were ten times as large and broad as they are, they would seem
narrower than a mouse's hole. Then a man is simply deprived of
all wisdom, power, righteousness, counsel, and help. For the con-

science is a very delicate thing. Therefore when it is confined in the prison of the Law, it sees no exit opening before it; it sees the narrowness steadily increasing ad infinitum. For then it senses the wrath of God, who is infinite and from whose hand it cannot escape, as the psalm says (139:7): "Whither shall I go from Thy Spirit?"

Therefore just as civic confinement or prison is the affliction of the body by which the prisoner is deprived of the use of his body, so the theological prison is the trouble and anxiety of the spirit by which the prisoner is deprived of peace of conscience and quietness of heart. Yet this is not forever, as the reason supposes when it feels this prison, but "until faith should be revealed." Therefore the heart that has been confined under the Law should be encouraged and comforted this way: "Brother, you have indeed been confined. But you should know that this is not being done so that you will be held in the confinement of this prison forever, for it is written that we are confined until faith should be revealed. Therefore you are being afflicted by this prison, not to do you harm but to re-create you through the Blessed Offspring. You are being killed by the Law in order to be made alive through Christ. Therefore do not despair, as Cain, Saul, and Judas did. They did not get beyond their confinement in this prison, but they remained in the confinement and therefore were driven to despair. You must act differently from them in these terrors of conscience. That is, you must know that it is a benefit to you to be confined and perplexed this way; but you must see to it that you use your confinement correctly, that is, for the sake of the faith to come. For God does not want to trouble you in such a way that you remain in trouble; He does not want to kill you in such a way that you remain in death. 'I have no pleasure,' He says through the prophet, 'in the death of the sinner' (Ezek. 33:11). But He wants to trouble you so that you may be humbled and may acknowledge that you need the mercy of God and the blessing of Christ."

Therefore this custody under the Law should not be forever but should last only until faith. This is also what Psalm 147:11 teaches: "The Lord takes pleasure in those who fear Him," that is, in those who are oppressed by this custody of the Law. But immediately it adds the words "in those who hope in His steadfast love." Therefore these two things, which are in fact so utterly diverse, must be joined together. What is more contradictory than to sense fear and horror before the wrath of God and at the same time to hope in

His steadfast love? The first is hell, the second is heaven; and yet in the heart these must be joined as closely as possible. Speculatively they can be joined together very easily; but practically it is the most difficult thing in the world to join them together, as I have learned very often from my own experience. The papists and the sectarians know absolutely nothing about this. When they read or hear these words of Paul, the words remain utterly obscure and unknown; and when the Law shows them their sin, accusing and terrifying them, they find neither counsel nor aid but despair utterly, as Cain and Saul did.

Since, as has been said, the Law is our tormentor and our prison, it is certain that we do not love it but hate it violently. Therefore anyone who says that he loves the Law is lying and does not know what he is saying. A thief or a robber who loved his prison and his shackles would be insane and out of his mind. But since, as I have said, the Law confines us, it is certain that we are its bitterest enemies. In other words, we love the Law and its righteousness just as much as a murderer loves prison. Then how could we be justified by the Law?

Kept under restraint until faith should be revealed.

Paul is referring to the time of fulfillment, when Christ came. But you should apply it not only to the time but also to feelings; for what happened historically and temporally when Christ came — namely, that He abrogated the Law and brought liberty and eternal life to light — this happens personally and spiritually every day in any Christian, in whom there are found the time of Law and the time of grace in constant alternation. The Christian has a body, in whose members, as Paul says (Rom. 7:23), the Law and sin are at war. By sin I understand not only lust but all of sin, as Paul usually speaks about sin, saying that it not only still clings to a flesh that is Christian and baptized, but that it battles against it and captures it, producing at least a powerful urge, if not actual assent or action. Even though a Christian does not fall into coarse sins like murder, adultery, or theft, he still is not free of impatience, grumbling, hatred, and blasphemy against God — sins that are completely unknown to the human reason. They force him against his will to despise the Law; they force him to flee from the countenance of God; they force him to hate and blaspheme God. For just as sexual desire is powerful in the body of the young man, and just as the ambition to gain glory and possessions is powerful in the mature man, and just as greed is powerful in the old man, so in the saintly man impatience, grumbling, hate, and blasphemy against God are powerful. There are examples of this throughout the Psalms, Job, Jeremiah, and all Scripture. Therefore when Paul describes this spiritual struggle, he uses very emphatic and meaningful terms like "being at war," "fighting back," and "making captive."

In the experience of the Christian, therefore, both are found, the time of Law and the time of grace. The time of Law is when the Law disciplines, vexes, and saddens me, when it brings me to a knowledge of sin and increases this. Then the Law is being employed in its true use, which a Christian experiences constantly as long as he lives. Thus Paul was given "a thorn in the flesh, a messenger of Satan, to harass him" (2 Cor. 12:7). He wished that he could feel, for a single moment, the joy of the conscience, the happiness of the heart, and a foretaste of eternal life. He also wished that he could be rid of the disturbance of the spirit. Therefore he requested that this trial be taken away from him. This did not happen, but he heard from the Lord (2 Cor. 12:9): "Paul, My grace is sufficient for you; for My power is made perfect in weakness." Every Christian experiences the same struggle. There are many hours in which I dispute with God and fight back at Him impatiently. The wrath and judgment of God are displeasing to me. On the other hand, my impatience and grumbling are displeasing to Him. This is the time of Law, under which a Christian always exists according to the flesh. "For the desires of the flesh are always against the Spirit, and the desires of the Spirit are against the flesh; for these are opposed to each other," as chapter five says below (Gal. 5:17).

The time of grace is when the heart is encouraged again by the promise of the free mercy of God and says (Ps. 42:5): "Why are you cast down, O my soul, and why are you disquieted within me? Do you not see anything except Law, sin, terror, sadness, despair, death, hell, and the devil? Are there not also grace, the forgiveness of sins, righteousness, comfort, joy, peace, life, heaven, God, and Christ? Stop troubling me, O my soul. What are Law, sin, and all evils in comparison with these? Hope in God, who did not spare His own Son but gave Him up to the death of the cross for your sins (Rom. 8:32)." This, then, is what it means to be confined under the Law according to the flesh, not forever but until the coming of Christ.

[W, XL, 525—527]

When you are terrified by the Law, therefore, say: "Lady Law, you are not the only thing, and you are not everything! Besides you there is something greater and better, namely, grace, faith, blessing. These do not accuse me; they do not terrify or condemn me. But they comfort me, command me to have hope, and promise me sure victory and salvation in Christ. Therefore there is no reason for me to despair."

Anyone who would know this art well would deserve to be called a theologian. The fanatics of our day, who are always boasting about the Spirit, as well as their disciples, seem to themselves to know it superbly. But I and others like me hardly know the basic elements of this art, and yet we are studious pupils in the school where this art is being taught. It is indeed being taught, but so long as the flesh and sin remain, it cannot be learned thoroughly.

Therefore the Christian is divided this way into two times. To the extent that he is flesh, he is under the Law; to the extent that he is spirit, he is under the Gospel. To his flesh there always cling lust, greed, ambition, pride, etc. So do ignorance and contempt of God, impatience, grumbling, and wrath against God because He obstructs our plans and efforts and because He does not immediately punish the wicked who despise Him. These sins cling to the flesh of the saints. Therefore if you do not look at anything beyond the flesh, you will remain permanently under the time of the Law. But those days have to be shortened, for otherwise no human being would be saved (Matt. 24:22). An end has to be set for the Law, where it will come to a stop. Therefore the time of Law is not forever; but it has an end, which is Christ. But the time of grace is forever; for Christ, having died once for all, will never die again (Rom. 6:9-10). He is eternal; therefore the time of grace is eternal also.

We should not run through such outstanding declarations in Paul so sluggishly, as the papists and the sectarians usually do; for these declarations contain words of life that wonderfully comfort and strengthen afflicted consciences. Those who understand them correctly can judge rightly what faith is and what false and true fear are; they can also judge all their feelings and discern all the spirits. The fear of God is something holy and precious, but it should not be eternal. It must always be present in a Christian, because sin is always present in him. But it must not be alone; for then it is the fear of Cain, Saul, and Judas, that is, a servile and despairing fear. By faith in the Word of grace, therefore, the Christian should conquer fear, turn his eyes away from the time of Law, and gaze at Christ Himself and at the faith to come. Then fear becomes sweet and is mixed with nectar, so that he begins not only to fear God but also to love Him. Otherwise, if a man gazes only at the Law and at sin, to the exclusion of faith, he cannot drive out his fear but will finally despair.

Thus Paul distinguishes beautifully between the time of Law and the time of grace. Let us learn also to distinguish the times of both, not in words but in our feelings, which is the most difficult of all. For although these two are utterly distinct, yet they must be joined completely together in the same heart. Nothing is more closely joined together than fear and trust, Law and Gospel, sin and grace; they are so joined together that each is swallowed up by the other. Therefore there cannot be any mathematical conjunction that is similar to this.

With the passage (v. 19) "Why, then, the Law?" Paul began to treat the Law and the use and abuse of the Law, having found an occasion for this in his argument that believers obtain righteousness on the basis of grace and the promise, not on the basis of the Law. That argument produced the question "Why, then, the Law?" For when reason hears that righteousness or the blessing is obtained on the basis of grace and the promise, it immediately draws the inference "Then the Law is worthless." The matter of the Law must be considered carefully, both as to what and as to how we ought to think about the Law; otherwise we shall either reject it altogether, after the fashion of the fanatical spirits who prompted the peasants' revolt a decade ago by saying that the freedom of the Gospel absolves men from all laws,[112] or we shall attribute to the Law the power to justify. Both groups sin against the Law: those on the right, who want to be justified through the Law, and those on the left, who want to be altogether free of the Law. Therefore we must travel the royal road, so that we neither reject the Law altogether nor attribute more to it than we should.

What I have stated earlier so often about both uses of the Law, the political or Gentile use and the theological use, indicates clearly

---

112 That is, 10 years before the printing of this commentary, i. e., in 1525, the Peasants' War.

that the Law was not laid down for the righteous but, as Paul teaches
elsewhere (1 Tim. 1:9), for the unrighteous. But there are two kinds
of unrighteous men: those who are to be justified and those who
are not to be justified. Those who are not to be justified are restrained
by the civic use of the Law; for they should be bound with the chains
of laws, as wild and untamed beasts are bound with ropes and chains.
This use of the Law never ceases, but Paul is not dealing principally
with it here. Those who are to be justified, on the other hand, are
disciplined by the theological use of the Law for a time; for it does
not last forever, as the civic use does, but it looks forward to the
coming of faith, and when Christ comes, it is finished. From this it
is abundantly clear that all the passages in which Paul treats the
spiritual use of the Law must be understood about those who are
to be justified, not about those who have already been justified.
For, as has been said often enough, these latter are far above and
beyond any Law. Therefore the Law should be imposed upon those
who are to be justified, so that they may be kept in custody under it
until the righteousness of faith comes. This is not because they
obtain righteousness through the Law — for that would be to abuse
the Law, not to use it correctly — but so that when they have been
terrified and humbled by the Law they may take refuge in Christ,
who "is the end of the Law, that everyone who has faith may be
justified" (Rom. 10:4).

Therefore the Law is abused, in the first place, by all the self-
righteous and the hypocrites, who imagine that men are justified
by the Law. For such a use of the Law does not discipline and press
men toward the faith to come; it creates self-satisfied, smug, and
supercilious hypocrites who are puffed up and presumptuous about
their righteousness and about the works of the Law, and thus it
hinders the righteousness of faith. In the second place, the Law is
abused by those who want to excuse Christians from it altogether, as
the sectarians attempted to do and on this basis stimulated the
peasants' revolt. Today there are many even in our own party who
are doing the same thing; having been snatched from the tyranny of
the pope by the teaching of the Gospel, they imagine that Christian
liberty is carnal license to do whatever they please. As Peter says
(1 Peter 2:16), they "use their freedom as a pretext for evil"; and
on their account the name of God and the Gospel of Christ are
being blasphemed everywhere today (Rom. 2:24). Someday they will
receive a punishment worthy of this wickedness of theirs. In the

third place, the Law is abused also by those who, when they feel its terrors, do not understand that these are to last only until Christ. In such men the abuse is a cause for despair, just as in the hypocrites it is a cause for pride and presumption.

The true use of the Law, on the other hand, cannot be measured by any price, namely, when the conscience that has been confined under the Law does not despair, but becomes wise through the Holy Spirit and declares in the midst of its terrors: "All right, I have been confined under the Law, but not eternally. In fact, this confinement will turn out to my benefit. How? If, when I have been confined this way, I sigh and look for the hand of the One who will help me." In this way the Law is like a stimulus that drives the hungry toward Christ, in order that He may fill them with His benefits. Therefore the proper function of the Law is to make us guilty, to humble us, to kill us, to lead us down to hell, and to take everything away from us, but all with the purpose that we may be justified, exalted, made alive, lifted up to heaven, and endowed with all things. Therefore it does not merely kill, but it kills for the sake of life.

24. *So that the Law was our custodian until Christ came.*

When Paul says that "the Law was our custodian until Christ came," he once more joins Law and Gospel together in feeling, even though in themselves they are as far apart as possible. This analogy of the custodian is truly outstanding; therefore it must be considered carefully. Although a schoolmaster is very useful and really necessary for the education and training of boys, show me one boy or pupil who loves his schoolmaster! For example, did the Jews love Moses warmly and willingly do what he commanded? Their love and obedience toward Moses was such, as the history shows, that at times they would have been willing to stone him. Therefore it is impossible for a pupil to love his schoolmaster. For how could he love the one by whom he is being detained in prison, that is, by whom he is being forbidden to do what he would like to do? If he commits something that is against his schoolmaster's orders, he is denounced and scolded by him; what is more, he is forced to embrace and kiss his whip.[113] How wonderful the pupil's righteousness is, that he obeys a threatening and harsh schoolmaster and even kisses his whip! Does he do this willingly and joyfully? When the schoolmaster is absent, he will

---

[113] From other references in Luther it seems that it was customary for a child to have to kiss the whip after he had been punished.

break the whip or throw it into the fire. And if he had authority over the schoolmaster, he would not let himself be beaten by the schoolmaster's whips but would order that the schoolmaster be whipped. Nevertheless, a schoolmaster is extremely necessary for a boy, to instruct and chastise him; for otherwise, without this instruction, good training, and discipline, the boy would come to ruin.

Therefore the schoolmaster gives the boy the impression of being his taskmaster and executioner and of holding him captive in prison. To what end and for how long? So that this severe, hateful authority of the schoolmaster and the slavery of the boy will last forever? No, but for a predetermined time, so that this obedience, prison, and discipline may work for the boy's good and so that in due time he may become the heir and the king. For it is not the father's intention that the son be subject to the schoolmaster forever and be whipped by him, but that through the instruction and discipline of the schoolmaster the son may be made fit for accession to his inheritance.

Thus Paul says that the Law is nothing but a custodian. But he adds "until Christ came." Thus he said above (v. 19): "The Law was added because of transgression, till the Offspring should come"; and (v. 22) "Scripture consigned all things to sin, that what was promised, etc."; and (v. 23) "we were confined under the Law, kept under restraint until faith should be revealed." Therefore the Law is not simply a custodian; it is a custodian "until Christ came." For what kind of custodian would it be who would merely annoy and whip a boy and would teach him nothing? That is the kind of teacher the previous century had, when the schools were a veritable prison and hell, and the teachers were tyrants and executioners. The boys continually suffered floggings; they studied with great effort and untiring diligence; but very few of them ever accomplished anything.[114] The Law is not such a teacher. It not only frightens and annoys, as an unskilled and stupid teacher only whips his pupils and does not teach them anything. But with its whippings it drives us to Christ, just as a good teacher whips, trains, and disciplines his pupils in reading and writing with the purpose of bringing them to a knowledge of the liberal arts and of other good things, so that eventually they may do with pleasure what initially, when they were forced to it by their teacher, they did involuntarily.

[114] The notes of Luther's lectures indicate that he was speaking here of his own experience as a schoolboy. But the printed version has generalized his words.

By means of this fine illustration, therefore, Paul shows the true use of the Law: that it does not justify hypocrites, because they remain outside Christ in their presumptuousness and smugness; on the other hand, if those who have been frightened use the Law as Paul teaches, it does not leave them in death and damnation but drives them to Christ. Those who continue in these terrors and in their faintheartedness and do not take hold of Christ by faith despair utterly. With this allegory of the custodian, therefore, Paul clearly portrays the true use of the Law. For just as the custodian scolds, drives, and troubles his pupils, not with the intention that this custody should last forever, but that it should come to an end when the pupils have been properly educated and trained and that they should then eagerly and freely enjoy their liberty and their inheritance without the constraint of their custodian, so those who are frightened and crushed by the Law should know that these terrors and blows will not be permanent, but that by them they are being prepared for the coming of Christ and the freedom of the Spirit.

That we might be justified by faith.

The Law is a custodian, not until some other lawgiver comes who demands good works, but until Christ comes, the Justifier and Savior, so that we may be justified through faith in Him, not through works. But when a man feels the power of the Law, he neither understands nor believes this. Therefore he usually says: "I have lived damnably.[115] For I have transgressed all the Commandments of God, and therefore I have been sentenced to eternal death. If God were to add a few years or at least a few months to my life, I would want to improve my life and thereafter live in a holy way." Thus a man makes an abuse of the true use of the Law; and, losing sight of Christ, he looks for another lawgiver. For when it is seized by these terrors and anxieties, reason takes it upon itself to promise God that it will fulfill all the works of the entire Law. This was the source of so many sects of monks; this was why so many forms of worship were established; this was why so many works were thought up — to merit grace and the forgiveness of sins. For those who thought up all this experienced the custody of the Law, not until Christ but until a new Law or Christ, the Lawgiver, rather than Christ, the abolisher of the Law, should come.

[115] Cf. p. 5, note 2.

But the true use of the Law is this, that I know that by the Law I am being brought to an acknowledgement of sin and am being humbled, so that I may come to Christ and be justified by faith. But faith is neither a Law nor a work; it is a sure confidence that takes hold of Christ, who "is the end of the Law" (Rom. 10:4). How? Not by abrogating the old Law and passing a new one or by being a judge who needs to be appeased by works, as the papists taught. But He "is the end of the Law, that everyone who has faith may be justified"; that is, everyone who believes in Christ is righteous, and the Law cannot accuse him. This is the true power and the true use of the Law. Therefore the Law is good, holy, useful, and necessary, so long as one uses it in a legitimate way. Its civic use is good and necessary, but its theological use is the most important and the highest. But the Law is abused, first, by hypocrites who attribute to it the power to justify, and, secondly, by men of despair who do not know that the Law is a custodian until Christ comes, that is, that the Law humbles us, not to harm us but to save us. For God wounds in order to heal; He kills in order to make alive.

But, as I have warned earlier, Paul is speaking about those who are to be justified, not about those who have been justified. Therefore when you want to discuss the Law, you must accept the subject matter of the Law, namely, the sinner and wicked person. The Law does not justify him; but it places his sin before his eyes, crushes him, leads him to a knowledge of himself, and shows him hell and the wrath and judgment of God. This is the proper function of the Law. Then there follows the application of this function: the sinner should know that the Law does not disclose sins and humble him to make him despair, but that the Law was instituted by God so that by its accusation and crushing it might drive him to Christ, the Savior and Comforter. When this happens, he is no longer under a custodian. But those who already have faith are not under the Law but are free of it, as Paul shows at once in the words that follow. The Law disciplines only the wicked, who have not yet been justified. This use is extremely necessary; for since the whole world is in the power of sin (1 John 5:19), there is need for this ministry of the Law to reveal sin; for without it no one could come to righteousness, as we have said at great length earlier. But what does the Law do in those who have been justified through Christ? Paul replies in these words, which are a sort of appendix:

25. *But now that faith has come, we are no longer under a custodian.*

That is, we are free from the Law, our prison and our custodian; for after faith has been revealed, it no longer terrifies and troubles us. Paul is speaking here about the faith promulgated through Christ at a specific time. For having assumed human nature, Christ came once for all at one time, abrogated the Law with all its effects, and by His death delivered the entire human race from sin and eternal death. Therefore if you consider Christ and what He has accomplished, there is no Law anymore. Coming at a predetermined time, He truly abolished the entire Law. But now that the Law has been abolished, we are no longer held in custody under its tyranny; but we live securely and happily with Christ, who now reigns sweetly in us by His Spirit. But where the Lord is, there is freedom (2 Cor. 3:17). If we could perfectly take hold of Christ, who has abrogated the Law and reconciled us sinners to the Father by His death, then that custodian would have no jurisdiction whatever over us. But the law in our members is at war with the law of our mind (Rom. 7:23), and it interferes so that we cannot take hold of Christ perfectly. Therefore the defect is not in Christ; it is in us, because we have not yet shed the flesh, to which sin clings as long as we live. So far as we are concerned, then, we are partly free of the Law and partly under the Law. With Paul we serve the Law of God with our mind, but with our flesh we serve the law of sin (Rom. 7:25).

From this it follows that according to our conscience we are completely free of the Law. Therefore this custodian must not rule in our conscience, that is, must not menace it with his terrors, threats, and captivity. No matter how he tries this, the conscience remains unmoved; for it has in view Christ the crucified, who abolished all the claims of the Law upon the conscience, "having canceled the bond which stood against us with its legal demands" (Col. 2:14). Therefore the conscience must be as unaware, in fact, as dead toward the Law as a virgin is toward a man, and vice versa. This does not come by works or by any righteousness of the Law; it comes by faith, which takes hold of Christ. According to our feelings, however, sin still clings to the flesh and continually accuses and troubles the conscience. So long as the flesh remains, there remains the Law, the custodian who continually terrifies and distresses the conscience with his demonstrations of sin and his threats of death. But it is always encouraged by the daily coming of Christ. Just as He once came into the world at a specific time to redeem us from the harsh dominion of our custodian, so He comes to us spiritually every day, causing us to grow in faith and in our knowledge of Him. Thus the conscience takes hold of Christ more perfectly day by day; and day by day the law of flesh and sin, the fear of death, and whatever other evils the Law brings with it are diminishing. For as long as we live in a flesh that is not free of sin, so long the Law keeps coming back and performing its function, more in one person and less in another, not to harm but to save. This discipline of the Law is the daily mortification of the flesh, the reason, and our powers, and the renewal of our mind (2 Cor. 4:16).

Thus we have received the first fruits of the Spirit (Rom. 8:23), and the leaven hidden in the lump; the whole lump has not yet been leavened, but it is beginning to be leavened. If I look at the leaven, I see nothing but the leaven; but if I look at the mass of the lump, there is not merely the leaven anymore. Thus if I look at Christ, I am completely holy and pure, and I know nothing at all about the Law; for Christ is my leaven. But if I look at my flesh, I feel greed, sexual desire, anger, pride, the terror of death, sadness, fear, hate, grumbling, and impatience against God. To the extent that these are present, Christ is absent; or if He is present, He is present weakly. Here there is still need for a custodian to discipline and torment the flesh, that powerful jackass, so that by this discipline sins may be diminished and the way prepared for Christ. For just as Christ came once physically, according to time, abrogating the entire Law, abolishing sin, and destroying death and hell, so He comes to us spiritually without interruption and continually smothers and kills these things in us.

I am saying this in order that you may know how to reply when the objection is raised: "All right, Christ has come into the world and abolished our sins once for all, cleansing us with His blood. Then why should we listen to the Gospel? What need is there of the Sacrament and of absolution?" It is true that if you consider Christ, the Law and sin have really been abolished. But Christ has not yet come to you; or if He has come, there are still remnants of sin in you, and you have not yet been completely leavened. For where there is lust, sadness of heart, fear of death, and the like, there the Law and sin are still present; there Christ is not yet present. For when He comes, He drives out fear and sadness, and brings peace and security to the conscience. To the extent that I take hold of Christ by faith, therefore, to that extent the Law has been abrogated for me. But my flesh, the world, and the devil do not permit faith to be perfect. I would, of course, wish that the little light of my faith that is in my heart might be diffused through my whole body and all its members. But this does not happen; it is not diffused all at once, but it has begun to be diffused. Meanwhile our comfort is that we have the first fruits of the Spirit and have begun to be leavened, but that we shall be completely leavened when this sinful body is destroyed and we arise new with Christ. Amen.

Therefore although "Christ is the same yesterday and today and forever" (Heb. 13:4), and although Adam and all the faithful before Christ had the Gospel and faith, nevertheless Christ came once for all at a set time, and faith came once for all when the apostles preached the Gospel throughout the world. In addition, Christ comes spiritually every day; through the Word of the Gospel faith also comes every day; and when faith is present, our custodian, with his gloomy and grievous task, is also forced to yield. But Christ comes spiritually as we gradually acknowledge and understand more and more what has been granted to us by Him. 2 Peter 3:18 says: "Grow in the grace and knowledge of our Lord and Savior Jesus Christ."

26. *For in Christ Jesus you are all sons of God, through faith.*

As a very good teacher of faith, Paul always has these words on his lips: through faith, in faith, on the basis of faith in Christ Jesus, etc. He does not say: "You are sons of God because you are circumcised, listen to the Law, and keep its works," as the Jews imagined and as the false apostles taught; but "through faith in Christ Jesus." Therefore the Law does not create sons of God; much less do human traditions. The Law cannot beget men into a new nature or a new birth; it brings to view the old birth, by which we were born into the kingdom of the devil. Thus it prepares us for the new birth, which takes place through faith in Christ Jesus, not through the Law, as Paul clearly testifies: "You are all sons of God through faith." It is as though he were saying: "Even though you have been troubled, humbled, and killed by the Law, the Law has not made you righteous. It has not made you sons of God, but faith has. Which faith? Faith in Christ. Therefore faith in Christ, not the Law, creates sons of God." The same thing is written in John 1:12: "To all who believed, He gave power to become children of God."

I leave it to the orators to explain, and expand upon, this topic
of the inestimable grace and glory that we have in Christ Jesus,
namely, that we miserable sinners, by nature children of wrath
(Eph. 2:3), may arrive at this honor, that through faith in Christ
we are made children and heirs of God and fellow heirs with Christ
(Rom. 8:17), lords of heaven and earth. Nevertheless, no tongue,
either of men or of angels (1 Cor. 13:1), could proclaim the glory
of this magnificently enough.

27. *For as many of you as were baptized into Christ have put on
Christ.*

Putting on Christ is understood in two ways: according to the
Law and according to the Gospel. According to the Law (Rom.
13:14), "Put on the Lord Jesus Christ; that is: Imitate the example
and the virtues of Christ. Do and suffer what He did and suffered."
So also 1 Peter 2:21: "Christ suffered for us, leaving us an example,
that we should follow in His steps." In Christ we see the height of
patience, gentleness, and love, and an admirable moderation in all
things. We ought to put on this adornment of Christ, that is, imitate
these virtues of His. In this sense we can imitate other saints as well.

But to put on Christ according to the Gospel is a matter, not of
imitation but of a new birth and a new creation, namely, that I put
on Christ Himself, that is, His innocence, righteousness, wisdom,
power, salvation, life, and Spirit. We were dressed in the leather
garment of Adam, which is a deadly garment and the clothing of
sin.[116] That is, we were all subjected and sold into the slavery of sin;
horrible blindness, ignorance, and a contempt and hatred of God
are present in us. Besides, we are filled with evil lust, uncleanness,
and greed. By propagation from Adam we have acquired this garment, that is, this corrupt and sinful nature, which Paul calls "the
old man." He must be put off with all his activities, so that from
sons of Adam we may be changed into sons of God (Eph. 4:22 and
Col. 3:9). This does not happen by a change of clothing or by any
laws or works; it happens by the rebirth and renewal that takes place
in Baptism, as Paul says: "As many of you as were baptized have
put on Christ." Titus 3:5: [117] "He saved us, in virtue of His own
mercy, by the washing of regeneration." For in those who have

[116] On the mystical interpretation of this garment cf. *Luther's Works*,
2, p. 144, note 21.
[117] The original has "Titus 1."

been baptized a new light and flame arise; new and devout emotions come into being, such as fear and trust in God and hope; and a new will emerges. This is what it means to put on Christ properly, truly, and according to the Gospel.

In Baptism, then, it is not the garment of the righteousness of the Law or of our own works that is given; but Christ becomes our garment. But He is not the Law, not a lawgiver, not a work; He is the divine and inestimable gift that the Father has given to us to be our Justifier, Lifegiver, and Redeemer. To put on Christ according to the Gospel, therefore, is to put on, not the Law or works but an inestimable gift, namely, the forgiveness of sins, righteousness, peace, comfort, joy in the Holy Spirit, salvation, life, and Christ Himself.

This passage must be studied carefully, in opposition to the fanatical spirits who minimize the majesty of Baptism and speak wickedly about it. Paul, by contrast, adorns Baptism with magnificent titles when he calls it "the washing of regeneration and renewal in the Holy Spirit" (Titus 3:5). And here he says that all who have been baptized have put on Christ. Now, as I have said, Paul is speaking about a "putting on," not by imitation but by birth. He does not say: "Through Baptism you have received a token by which you have been enlisted in the number of the Christians"; this is what the sectarians imagine when they make of Baptism merely a token, that is, a small and empty sign.[118] But he says: "As many of you as have been baptized have put on Christ." That is: "You have been snatched beyond the Law into a new birth that took place in Baptism. Therefore you are no longer under the Law, but you have been dressed in a new garment, that is, in the righteousness of Christ." Therefore Paul teaches that Baptism is not a sign but the garment of Christ, in fact, that Christ Himself is our garment. Hence Baptism is a very powerful and effective thing. For when we have put on Christ, the garment of our righteousness and salvation, then we also put on Christ, the garment of imitation.

28. *There is neither Jew nor Greek, there is neither slave nor free, there is neither male nor female.*

Here many other titles could be added of offices that have been divinely ordained. For example: "There is neither magistrate nor

---

[118] Cf. p. 242, note 54.

subject, neither professor nor listener, neither teacher nor pupil, neither lady nor servant." For in Christ Jesus all social stations, even those that were divinely ordained, are nothing. Male, female, slave, free, Jew, Gentile, king, subject — these are, of course, good creatures of God. But in Christ, that is, in the matter of salvation, they amount to nothing, for all their wisdom, righteousness, devotion, and authority.

With the words "there is neither Jew," then, Paul vigorously abolishes the Law. For here, where a new man comes into existence in Baptism and where Christ is put on, there is neither Jew nor Greek. Now he is not speaking of the Jew in a metaphysical sense, according to his essence; but by "Jew" he means someone who is a disciple of Moses, who is subject to the laws, who has circumcision, and who observes the form of worship commanded in the Law. Where Christ is put on, he says, there is no Jew any longer, no circumcision, no temple worship, no laws that the Jews keep. For Christ has abolished throughout the world whatever laws there are in Moses. Therefore the conscience that believes in Christ should be so sure that the Law with its terrors and threats has been abrogated that it simply does not know whether Moses or the Law or the Jew ever existed, for Christ and Moses are utterly incompatible. Moses comes with the Law and various works and forms of worship; but Christ, granting grace and righteousness, comes absolutely without the Law or any demands of works. John 1:17: "The Law was given through Moses; grace and truth came through Jesus Christ."

With the next words, "nor Greek," Paul also rejects and condemns the wisdom and righteousness of the Gentiles. Among the Gentiles there were many great and outstanding men, such as Xenophon, Themistocles, Marcus Fabius, Atilius Regulus, Cicero, Pomponius Atticus, and many others.[119] Endowed as they were with excellent, in fact, heroic virtues, they administered their commonwealths very well and accomplished many brilliant things for the welfare of the commonwealth. And yet, with all their wisdom, power, honorable deeds, outstanding virtues, laws, righteousness, worship, and religion — for we must not imagine that the Gentiles were simply despisers of honesty and religion, but all the nations scattered all over the world had their own laws, worship, and religion, without which the human race cannot be governed — with all these adornments, I say, they amounted to nothing in the sight of God. Therefore whatever be-

---

[119] Cf. p. 123, note 40.

longs to domestic, political, and divine justice, such as the justice of the Law, with the highest obedience, performance of the Law, and sanctity — none of this amounts to anything in the sight of God. Then what does? The garment of Christ, which we put on in Baptism.

Thus no matter how diligently a slave performs his duty, obeys his master, and serves faithfully; or if a free man directs and governs either the commonwealth or his private affairs in a praiseworthy way; or whatever a male does as a male, getting married, administering his household well, obeying the magistrate, maintaining honest and decent relations with others; or if a lady lives chastely, obeys her husband, takes good care of the house, and teaches her children well — these truly magnificent and outstanding gifts and works do not avail anything toward righteousness in the sight of God. In other words, whatever laws, ceremonies, forms of worship, righteousness, and works there are in the whole world, even those of the Jews, who were the first to have a kingdom and a priesthood that was divinely instituted and ordained, together with its laws, devotion, and forms of worship — nevertheless none of these can take away sins or deliver from death or save.

"Therefore, O Galatians, your false apostles are seducing you when they teach that the Law is necessary for salvation. In this way they are snatching you from the great glory of your new birth and sonship and are calling you back to your old birth and to the miserable slavery of the Law. From sons of God who are free they are making you slaves of the Law, so long as they seek to distinguish among persons on the basis of the Law." There is, of course, a distinction among persons in the Law and in the sight of the world; and there must be one there, but not in the sight of God, where all men are equal. "All have sinned and fall short of the glory of God" (Rom. 3:23). In the presence of God, therefore, let Jews and Gentiles and all the world keep silence (Hab. 2:20). Of course, God has various ordinances, laws, styles of life, and forms of worship in the world; but these do not achieve anything to merit grace or attain eternal life. As many as are justified, therefore, are justified, not on account of their observance of human or divine Law but on account of Christ, who has abrogated all laws [120] everywhere. The Gospel sets Him forth to us as the only One who placated the wrath of God by His own blood, as the Savior; without faith in Him, the Jews will not be saved through

120 The Weimar text has *legis,* but we have read *leges.*

the Law, nor the monk through his religious order, nor the Gentile through his wisdom, nor the magistrate through political righteousness, nor the householder through domestic righteousness, nor the servant and maid through obedience.

For you are all one in Christ Jesus.

These are magnificent and very glorious words. In the world and according to the flesh there is a very great difference and inequality among persons, and this must be observed very carefully. For if a woman wanted to be a man, if a son wanted to be a father, if a pupil wanted to be a teacher, if a servant wanted to be a master, if a subject wanted to be a magistrate — there would be a disturbance and confusion of all social stations and of everything. In Christ, on the other hand, where there is no Law, there is no distinction among persons at all. There is neither Jew nor Greek, but all are one; for there is one body, one Spirit, one hope of the calling of all, one and the same Gospel, one faith, one Baptism, one God and Father of all, one Christ, the Lord of all (Eph. 4:4-6). The same Christ whom Peter, Paul, and all the saints have, we have too — you and I and all believers; and all baptized infants have the same one also. Here the conscience knows nothing about the Law but looks only at Christ. This is why Paul always makes it a practice to add the words "in Christ Jesus"; if Christ is lost sight of, everything is over.

The fanatical spirits today speak about faith in Christ in the manner of the sophists. They imagine that faith is a quality that clings to the heart apart from Christ. This is a dangerous error. Christ should be set forth in such a way that apart from Him you see nothing at all and that you believe that nothing is nearer and closer to you than He. For He is not sitting idle in heaven but is completely present with us, active and living in us as chapter two says (2:20): "It is no longer I who live, but Christ who lives in me," and here: "You have put on Christ." Therefore faith is a constant gaze [121] that looks at nothing except Christ, the Victor over sin and death and the Dispenser of righteousness, salvation, and eternal life. In his epistles, therefore, Paul sets forth and urges Jesus Christ in almost every verse. He sets Him forth through the Word, since Christ cannot be set forth any other way than through the Word and cannot be grasped any other way than through faith.

[121] The Weimar text has *intutus,* but we have read *intuitus.*

This is beautifully shown by the story of the bronze serpent, which is a figure of Christ (John 3:14). The Jews, who were being bitten by the fiery serpents, were commanded by Moses to do nothing but look at that bronze serpent with a fixed gaze. Those who did so were healed merely by their fixed gaze at the serpent. But the others, who did not listen to Moses, looked at their wounds rather than at the serpent and died. Thus if I am to gain comfort in a struggle of conscience or in the agony of death, I must take hold of nothing except Christ alone by faith, and I must say: "I believe in Jesus Christ, the Son of God, who suffered, was crucified, and died for me. In His wounds and death I see my sin; and in His resurrection I see victory over sin, death, and the devil, and my righteousness and life. I neither hear nor see anything but Him." This is the true faith of Christ and in Christ, through which we become members of His body, of His flesh and of His bones (Eph. 5:30). Therefore in Him we live and move and have our being (Acts 17:28). Hence the speculation of the sectarians is vain when they imagine that Christ is present in us "spiritually," that is, speculatively, but is present really in heaven.[122] Christ and faith must be completely joined. We must simply take our place in heaven; and Christ must be, live, and work in us. But He lives and works in us, not speculatively but really, with presence and with power.

29. *And if you are Christ's, then you are Abraham's offspring, heirs according to promise.*

In a short statement Paul here transfers all the glory of Lebanon to the desert; that is, he makes all the Gentiles the offspring of Abraham and transfers to the Gentiles the fatherhood and the blessing promised to Abraham. Scripture had predicted long before that this would happen when it said (Gen. 22:18): "In your Offspring shall all the nations be blessed." Because we Gentiles believe and because by faith we receive the blessing of the Offspring of Abraham, therefor Scripture calls us sons of Abraham and hence heirs. And so we are all one in Christ, who is the Offspring of Abraham. Hence the promise, "In your Offspring, etc.," applies also to us Gentiles; and the Christ who is promised here is ours also. Of course, the promise was given only to the Jews, not to the Gentiles, as Ps. 147:19-20 states: "He declares His word to Jacob. He has not dealt thus with any other

---

[122] See, for example, *Luther's Works*, 37, pp. 232—234.

nation." Nevertheless, what was promised comes to us through faith, by which alone the promise of God is received. Although it was not promised to us, it was promised about us; for we were named in the promise, "In your Offspring, etc." The promise shows clearly that Abraham was to be the father not only of the Jewish nation but of many nations, the heir not of one kingdom but of the entire world (Rom. 4:13). Thus the glory of the whole kingdom of Christ has been transferred to us. Therefore all laws are completely abrogated in the heart and conscience of the Christian, even though they still remain outwardly in the flesh. About this I have spoken at great length earlier.

CHAPTER FOUR

1. *I mean that the heir, as long as he is a child, is no better than a slave, though he is the owner of all the estate;*

2. *but he is under guardians and trustees until the date set by the father.*

You see how ardently and astutely Paul tries to call the Galatians back, and how he presents his case with powerful arguments based on experience, on the example of Abraham, on the Scriptures, on chronology, and on analogy. He does this so much that often he appears to be repeating a case he has already concluded. Earlier he seemed to have finished the discussion of justification when he concluded that men are justified in the sight of God by faith alone. But because this political illustration about the young heir occurs to him afterwards, he cites it too, in the hope of perhaps convincing the unletterd Galatians by this means. Thus by a kind of divine cunning he lies in wait for them and tries to catch them, as he says elsewhere (2 Cor. 12:16): "I was crafty and got the better of you by guile." For ordinary people are caught more easily by analogies and illustrations than by difficult and subtle discussions; they would rather look at a well-drawn picture than a well-written book. Therefore after the analogy of the human testament and about the prison and the custodian he also cites this very familiar one about the heir, in order to convince them. For teaching it is useful to be able to produce many analogies and illustrations; not only Paul but also the prophets and Christ used them. Later, toward the very end of the epistle, he will become rhetorical.

"You see," he says, "even in civil law, that although the heir is the owner of the entire estate of his father, he is still a slave. Of course, he has the promise and the blessing of his inheritance. Nevertheless, before the time of emancipation,[1] as the lawyers call it,

[1] "*Emancipatio* is the release of a *filius* or *filia familias* from family ties and the *patria potestas* by a voluntary renunciation of the *pater familias*. The *emancipatus* became hereby a person *sui iuris* and, if male, a *pater familias* even though he had not yet a family of his own." Adolf Berger, "Emancipatio," in M. Cary et al. (edd.), *The Oxford Classical Dictionary* (Oxford, 1949), p. 313.

has arrived, he is held and subjected to guardians and trustees, just as a pupil is to a custodian. They do not entrust the administration or control of his goods to him, but they force him to serve. He lives and eats on his own property as though he were a slave. Therefore he is no different from a slave so long as the time of his imprisonment and captivity lasts, that is, so long as he is under his taskmasters and superintendents. This subjection and captivity is actually for his own good; otherwise he would dissipate his goods foolishly. Still his captivity is not permanent; but it is finished at a definite date, which his father has set."

3. *So with us; when we were children, we were slaves to the elements of this world.*

So it was with us when we were children. We were indeed heirs, having the promise of a future inheritance to be granted through Abraham's Offspring, Christ, who was to bless all nations. But because the time had not yet fully come, Moses, our guardian, manager, and custodian, came and held us confined and captive, to prevent us from taking the upper hand and gaining control and possession of our inheritance. Meanwhile, however, just as an heir is nourished by the hope of his coming freedom, so Moses nourished us with hope in the promise to be revealed in due time, namely, when Christ came. Before His coming it was the time of the Law; when He came, this was finished, and the time of grace is at hand.

Now the time of the Law is finished in two ways: first, through the coming of Christ into the flesh at a time set by the Father. For Christ became man in time just once, "born of the virgin, born under the Law, to redeem those who were under the Law" (Gal. 4:4-5). "He entered once for all into the Holy Place, taking His own blood, thus securing an eternal redemption" (Heb. 9:12). Secondly, that same Christ who once came in time comes to us in spirit every day and every hour. With His own blood, to be sure, He redeemed and sanctified all men just once. But because we are not yet perfectly pure but remnants of sin still cling to our flesh and the flesh wars against the spirit, therefore He comes spiritually every day; day by day He completes the time set by the Father more and more, abrogating and abolishing the Law.

Thus He came in spirit to the patriarchs every day before He came once and for all at a specified time. They had Christ in spirit; they believed in Him as One who was to be revealed, as we believe in Him as One who has been revealed; and they were saved through Him just as we are, in accordance with the statement (Heb. 13:8): "Jesus Christ is the same yesterday and today and forever." Yesterday, before the time of His coming in the flesh; today, when He has been revealed in time; now and forever He is the same Christ. Through one and the same Jesus Christ, therefore, all believers, past, present, and future, are delivered from the Law, justified, and saved.

Therefore Paul says: "So with us; when we were children, we were slaves to the elements of this world"; that is, the Law was dominant over us and oppressed us with harsh slavery as serfs and captives. In the first place, it was a political restraint upon uncivilized and carnal men to keep them from rushing headlong into all sorts of crimes. The Law threatens transgressors with punishment; and if they were not afraid of this, they would do nothing but commit evil. Those who are restrained by the Law this way are dominated by the Law. In the second place, the Law accused, terrified, killed, and condemned us before God spiritually or theologically. This was the chief dominion of the Law over us. Therefore just as an heir who is subject to guardians is whipped and forced to obey their rules and to carry out their orders carefully, so consciences before Christ are oppressed by the harsh tyranny of the Law; that is, they are accused, terrified, and condemned by the Law. Now this dominion, or rather tyranny, of the Law is not permanent but is supposed to last only until the time of grace. Therefore the function of the Law is indeed to denounce and to increase sin, but for the purpose of righteousness; and to kill, but for the purpose of life. For the Law is a custodian until Christ comes.

Therefore just as guardians treat a young heir harshly, lording it over him and giving him orders, and just as he is compelled to be subject to them, so the Law accuses, humbles, and enslaves us, so that we are slaves to sin, death, and the wrath of God, which is surely the most miserable and terrible form of slavery. But just as the domination of the guardians and the subjection [2] and slavery of the young heir are not permanent but last only until the date set by the father, when he no longer needs the protection of trustees and is no longer subject to them but can enjoy his inheritance from his father as he pleases, so the Law dominates us, and we are forced to be slaves and captives under its dominion, but not permanently. For an additional phrase is appended: "until the date set by the

[2] The Weimar text has *subiecto,* but we have read *subiectio* instead.

father." And the Christ who was promised came and redeemed us who were being oppressed by the tyranny of the Law.

On the other hand, Christ did not come for the smug hypocrites and the openly wicked despisers; nor did He come for the despairing, who think that there is nothing left but the terrors of the Law which they are experiencing. He was not given for such people, and He is useless to both groups. But He is useful to those who have been troubled and terrified by the Law for a time; for they do not despair amid the grave terrors caused by the Law, but they confidently draw near to Christ, the throne of grace,[3] who has redeemed them from the curse of the Law by being made a curse for them; and here they obtain mercy and find grace.

Therefore the emphasis lies on the phrase "we were slaves," as though he were saying: "Our conscience was subject to the Law, which exercised its tyranny over us with all its might. It whipped us as a tyrant whips his captive slave. It held us confined and captive; that is, it made us fearful, sad, pale, and desperate, by threatening us with eternal death and damnation." This theological slavery is very harsh — not permanently, however, but as long as it lasts, as long as we are children, that is, until Christ comes. So long as He is absent, we are slaves, confined under the Law, lacking grace, faith, and all the gifts of the Holy Spirit. But after Christ comes, the imprisonment and slavery of the Law come to an end.

To the elements of this world.

Some have thought that Paul is speaking here of the physical elements: fire, air, water, and earth.[4] But Paul has his own special way of speaking. He is referring here to the Law of God itself, which he calls "the elements of this world" by the figure of depreciation.[5] His words sound violently heretical. Elsewhere, too, Paul often speaks in a very condescending way about the Law. He calls it "the letter that kills" or "the ministry of death and damnation" or "the power of sin." He deliberately chooses these loathsome names,

---

[3] An allusion to the identification of Christ as ἱλαστήριον in Rom. 3:25.

[4] Jerome reports that "some regard these [elements] as the angels that preside over the four elements of the world, namely, earth, water, fire, and air." *Commentarius in Epistolam S. Pauli ad Galatas*, II, *Patrologia, Series Latina*, XXVI, 397.

[5] The Latin *tapinosis*, derived from the Greek, was the technical term for rhetorical depreciation: cf. Aristotle, *Rhetorica ad Alexandrum*, ch. 36.

which show the power and function of the Law clearly and accurately, in order to frighten us away from the Law in the matter of justification. For when it is used at its very best, the Law is unable to do anything but make the conscience guilty, increase sin, and threaten with death and eternal damnation.

Paul calls the Law "elements of this world," that is, the outward letter and traditions set down in some book. For even though the Law restrains from evil and drives to good works in society, such an observance of it does not deliver from sin, does not justify, and does not lead to heaven but leaves one in the world. For I do not obtain eternal life for avoiding murder, adultery, and stealing. These outward virtues and this honest way of life are not the kingdom of Christ or heavenly righteousness. They are the righteousness of the flesh and of the world, which not only self-righteous people like the Pharisee in Luke (18:11) but even heathen have. Some people produce this righteousness of the world to avoid the penalties of the Law; others, to be hailed by men as reliable, righteous, and patient. Therefore it should be called a deception and hypocrisy rather than righteousness.

In its highest use and force, then, the Law cannot do anything but accuse, frighten, condemn, and kill. Now where terror and a sense of sin, death, and the wrath of God are present, there is certainly no righteousness, nothing heavenly, and no God, but only the things of the world. The world is nothing but the dregs of sin, death, the wrath of God, hell, and all the evils that the terrified and the sad experience but that the smug and the contemptuous do not experience. Even in its best use, therefore, the Law can only produce a knowledge of sin and the terror of death. Sin, death, and the other evils are things of the world. It follows, then, that the Law does not produce anything life-giving or saving or heavenly or divine, but only things of the world. This is why Paul correctly calls it "the elements of this world."

Although Paul calls the entire Law "elements of the world," as can be seen clearly from what has already been said, nevertheless he is speaking with such contempt especially about the ceremonial laws. Even if these are very helpful, he says that they apply only to certain external matters, such as food, drink, clothing, prescribed places, set times, the temple, festivals, washings, sacrifices, and the like, which are purely of this world and were prescribed by God for use in this present life, not as a means of justifying and saving in the sight of God. By the term "elements of the world," therefore, he rejects and condemns all the righteousness of the Law, which was based on those outward ceremonies, ordained and divinely prescribed for a set time; he uses an extremely contemptuous name and calls it "the elements of the world." Thus the imperial laws are elements of the world; for they deal with matters of the world, that is, with matters that pertain to this present life, such as money, possessions, inheritances, murders, adulteries, robberies, and the like, with which the Second Table of the Decalog also deals. Elsewhere (1 Tim. 4:1) Paul calls the decretals and papal laws forbidding marriage and food "doctrines of demons"; these are elements of the world, except that they issue wicked commands that are contrary to the Word of God and faith.

Therefore the Law of Moses produces nothing that goes beyond the things of the world; that is, it merely shows both politically and theologically the evils that there are in the world. With its terrors it merely drives the conscience to thirst and yearn for the promise of God and to look at Christ. But for this the Holy Spirit is necessary, to say to the heart: "After the Law has performed its function in you, it is not the will of God that you merely be terrified and killed, but that you recognize your misery and your lost condition through the Law and then do not despair but believe in Christ, who is 'the end of the Law, that everyone who has faith may be justified' (Rom. 10:4)." Clearly there is nothing of the world being granted here; but everything of the world comes to an end here, and so do all the laws, while that which is divine begins. So long as we are under the elements of the world, therefore — that is, under the Law, which says nothing about Christ but merely discloses and increases sin and causes wrath — we are slaves, subject to the Law, even though we have the promise of the blessing to come. The Law does indeed say (Deut. 6:5): "You shall love the Lord your God," but it is unable to supply the means by which I do this or acquire Christ.

I am not saying this with the intention that the Law should be held in contempt. Paul does not intend this either, but that it should be held in esteem. But because Paul is dealing here with the issue of justification — a discussion of justification is something vastly different from a discussion of the Law — necessity demanded that he speak of the Law as something very contemptible. When we are dealing with this argument, we cannot speak of it in sufficiently vile and odious terms either. For here the conscience should consider and know nothing except Christ alone. Therefore we should make every effort that in the question of justification we reject the Law from view as far as possible and embrace nothing except the promise of Christ. This is easy enough to say; but in the midst of trial, when the conscience is contending with God, it is extremely difficult to be able to accomplish this. It is especially difficult when the Law is terrifying and accusing you, showing you your sin, and threatening you with the wrath of God and with death, to act as though there had never been any Law or sin but only Christ and sheer grace and redemption. It is difficult also, when you feel the terror of the Law, to say nevertheless: "Law, I shall not listen to you, because you have an evil voice. Besides, the time has now fully come. Therefore I am free. I shall no longer endure your domination." Then one can see that the most difficult thing of all is to distinguish the Law from grace; that it is simply a divine and heavenly gift to be able in this situation to believe in hope against hope (Rom. 4:18); and that this proposition of Paul's is eminently true, that we are justified by faith alone.

From this you should learn, therefore, to speak most contemptuously about the Law in the matter of justification, following the example of the apostle, who calls the Law "the elements of the world," "traditions that kill," "the power of sin," and the like. If you permit the Law to dominate in your conscience instead of grace, then when the time comes for you to conquer sin and death in the sight of God, the Law is nothing but the dregs of all evils, heresies, and blasphemies; for all it does is to increase sin, accuse, frighten, threaten with death, and disclose God as a wrathful Judge who damns sinners. If you are wise, therefore, you will put Moses, that lisper and stammerer, far away with his Law; and you will not let his terrors and threats affect you in any way at all. Here he should be as suspect to you as an excommunicated and condemned heretic, worse than the pope and the devil, and therefore not to be listened to at all.

Apart from the matter of justification, on the other hand, we, like Paul, should think reverently of the Law. We should endow it with the highest praises and call it holy, righteous, good, spiritual, divine, etc. Apart from our conscience we should make a god of it; but in our conscience it is truly a devil, for in the slightest trial it cannot encourage or comfort the conscience but does the very opposite, frightening and saddening it and depriving it of confidence in righteousness, of life, and of everything good. This is why Paul calls the Law "weak and beggarly elements" later on (Gal. 4:9). Therefore let us not permit it to dominate our conscience in any way, especially since it cost Christ so much to remove the tyranny of the Law from the conscience. For this was why "He became a curse for us, to redeem us from the curse of the Law" (Gal. 3:13). Therefore let the godly person learn that the Law and Christ are mutually contradictory and altogether incompatible. When Christ is present, the Law must not rule in any way but must retreat from the conscience and yield the bed to Christ alone, since this is too narrow to hold them both (Is. 28:20). Let Him rule alone in righteousness, safety, happiness, and life, so that the conscience may happily fall asleep in Christ, without any awareness of Law, sin, or death.

Paul uses this figure of speech, "elements of the world," purposely; as I have said, he greatly diminishes the authority and glory of the Law by this means, in order to arouse us. For when an attentive reader of Paul hears the apostle call the Law "the ministry of death" and "the letter that kills," he immediately thinks: "Why does he attribute such odious and, in the judgment of reason, even blasphemous names to the Law, which is a divine teaching revealed from heaven?" To such a person, who is concerned and puzzled about the reason for these names, Paul responds that the Law is both holy, righteous, good, etc., and the ministry of sin and death, but that it looks different to different people. Before Christ it is holy, after Christ it is death. When Christ comes, therefore, we must know nothing whatever about the Law, except to the extent that it has dominion over the flesh, which it constrains and oppresses. Until we die, the Law and the flesh, for which the dominion of the Law is hard to bear, will be in conflict.

Paul is the only one to use this phraseology, when he calls the Law of God "elements of the world" or "weak and beggarly elements" or "the power of sin" or "the letter that kills." The other apostles did not speak this way about the Law. Therefore let every student of Christian theology carefully observe this way of speaking that Paul has. Christ calls him "a chosen instrument" (Acts 9:15). Therefore He gave him a most excellent way of speaking and a unique phraseology, different from that of the other apostles, so that he, as the chosen instrument, may faithfully lay the foundations of the doctrine of justification and set it down clearly.

4. *But when the time had fully come, God sent forth His Son, born of woman, born under the Law,*

5. *to redeem those who were under the Law.*

That is: "After the time of the Law had been completed, and Christ was now revealed and had delivered us from the Law, and the promise had been spread abroad to all nations, etc."

Note carefully how Paul defines Christ here. Christ, he says, is the Son of God and of the woman. He was born under the Law on account of us sinners, to redeem us who were under the Law. In these words Paul has included both the Person and the work of Christ. The Person is made up of the divine and the human nature. He indicates this clearly when he says: "God sent forth His Son, born of woman." Therefore Christ is true God and true man. Paul describes His work in these words: "Born under the Law, to redeem those who were under the Law."

It seems that Paul insults the Virgin, the mother of the Son of God, by calling her simply "woman." This bothered some of the ancient fathers, who would have preferred that he use the title "virgin" here rather than "woman." [6] But in this epistle Paul is dealing with the most important and sublime subject matter: the Gospel, faith, Christian righteousness, the definition of the Person of Christ, the meaning of His work, what He undertook and accomplished on our behalf, and what blessings He brought to us miserable sinners. The magnitude of this awesome subject matter was the reason why he did not consider the matter of virginity. It was enough for him to proclaim the inestimable and infinite mercy of God, that God saw fit to have His Son born of the female sex; therefore he mentions, not the worthiness of this sex but merely the sex itself. By mentioning the sex he indicates that Christ Himself was made a true man by birth from the female sex. It is as though he were to say: "He was born, not of a male and a female but merely of the female sex." When he merely mentions the female sex, therefore, his phrase "born of woman" is the same as though he were saying "born of a virgin."

Furthermore, this passage testifies that when the time of the Law was completed, Christ did not establish a new Law to follow the old Law of Moses but abrogated it and redeemed those who were being oppressed by it. Therefore it is a very wicked error when the monks

---

[6] Cf. Jerome, *Commentarius in Epistolam S. Pauli ad Galatas,* II, *Patrologia, Series Latina,* XXVI, 398.

and sophists portray Christ as a new lawgiver after Moses, not un-
like the error of the Turks, who proclaim that their Mohammed is
the new lawgiver after Christ. Those who portray Christ this way
do Him a supreme injury. He did not come to abrogate the old Law
with the purpose of establishing a new one; but, as Paul says here,
He was sent into the world by the Father to redeem those who were
being held captive under the Law. These words portray Christ truly
and accurately. They do not ascribe to Him the work of establishing
a new Law; they ascribe to Him the work of redeeming those who
were under the Law. Christ Himself says in John 8:15: "I judge no
one"; and elsewhere (John 12:47): "I did not come to judge the world
but to save the world." That is: "I did not come to promulgate a law
and to judge men according to it, as Moses and other lawgivers did.
I am performing a more sublime and a better function. I judge and
condemn the Law. The Law kills you, and I kill it in turn; and so
through death I abolish death."

We adults, who are imbued with the noxious doctrine of the
papists, which we absorbed into our very bones and marrow, acquired an opinion of Christ altogether different from the one that
Paul sets forth here. No matter how much we declared with our
mouths that Christ had redeemed us from the tyranny and slavery
of the Law, actually we felt in our hearts that He was a lawgiver,
a tyrant, and a judge more fearful than Moses himself. Even today,
in the great light of the truth, we cannot completely banish this
wicked opinion from our minds. So stubbornly do things to which
we have been accustomed since youth cling to us! You young people,
who are still unspoiled [7] and have never been infected by this wicked
notion, have less difficulty in teaching purely about Christ than we
adults have in banishing these blasphemous illusions about Him from
our minds. Yet you have not altogether escaped the wiles of the devil.
For even if you have not yet been imbued with this wicked idea of
Christ as a lawgiver, you still have the same source [8] of this idea in
you, namely, the flesh, the reason, and the wickedness of our nature,
which cannot think of Christ in any other way than as a lawgiver.
Therefore you must contend with all your might, in order that you
may learn to acknowledge and regard Christ as Paul portrays Him
in this passage. But if, in addition to the wickedness of our nature,

[7] The rather obscure original reads *testae adhuc recentes;* see also p. 178,
note 94.

[8] "Source" is a slightly free rendering of *materialia.*

there come wicked teachers – of whom the world is full today, both the old and the new variety – they lend support to the wickedness of our nature; and the evil is doubled. For when wicked instruction is applied to a nature that is already corrupted in itself, it is impossible not to develop a false Christ. As I have said, reason invents him on its own; and then bad instruction makes him grow and impresses him on our minds so strongly that he cannot be eliminated without great labor and effort.

It is extremely important, therefore, to keep in view and always to consider this statement, so delightful and full of comfort, as well as others like it which define Christ properly and accurately; for then throughout our life, in every danger, in the confession of our faith in the presence of tyrants, and in the hour of death, we can declare with a sure and steady confidence: "Law, you have no jurisdiction over me; therefore you are accusing and condemning me in vain. For I believe in Jesus Christ, the Son of God, whom the Father sent into the world to redeem us miserable sinners who are oppressed by the tyranny of the Law. He poured out His life and spent it lavishly for me. When I feel your terrors and threats, O Law, I immerse my conscience in the wounds, the blood, the death, the resurrection, and the victory of Christ. Beyond Him I do not want to see or hear anything at all."

This faith is our victory (1 John 5:4); with it we conquer the terrors of the Law, of sin, death, and every evil, though not without a great struggle. Those who are truly devout and are vexed by severe trials every day really sweat over this. They often get the idea that Christ intends to rebuke us, that He intends to demand of us an account of how we have spent our lives, that He intends to accuse and condemn us. They cannot be sure that He was sent by the Father to redeem us who were oppressed by the tyranny of the Law. The reason is this: the saints have not yet shed the flesh completely, and it conflicts with the Spirit. Therefore the terrors of the Law, the fear of death, and other sad specters keep coming back to hinder faith, so that one does not take hold of the blessing of Christ, who has redeemed us from the slavery of the Law, with as much certainty as one should.

But in what manner or way has Christ redeemed us? The manner was as follows: He was born under the Law. When Christ came, He found us all captive under guardians and trustees, that is, confined and constrained under the Law. What did He do? He Himself is Lord of the Law; therefore the Law has no jurisdiction over Him and cannot accuse Him, because He is the Son of God. He who was not under the Law subjected Himself voluntarily to the Law. The Law did everything to Him that it did to us. It accused us and terrified us. It subjected us to sin, death, and the wrath of God; and it condemned us with its judgment. And it had a right to do all this, for we have all sinned. But Christ "committed no sin, and no guile was found on His lips" (1 Peter 2:22). Therefore he owed nothing to the Law. And yet against Him — so holy, righteous, and blessed — the Law raged as much as it does against us accursed and condemned sinners, and even more fiercely. It accused Him of blasphemy and sedition; it found Him guilty in the sight of God of all the sins of the entire world; finally it so saddened and frightened Him that He sweat blood (Luke 22:44); and eventually it sentenced Him to death, even death on a cross (Phil. 2:8).

This was truly a remarkable duel, when the Law, a creature, came into conflict with the Creator, exceeding its every jurisdiction to vex the Son of God with the same tyranny with which it vexed us, the sons of wrath (Eph. 2:3). Because the Law has sinned so horribly and wickedly against its God, it is summoned to court and accused. Here Christ says: "Lady Law, you empress, you cruel and powerful tyrant over the whole human race, what did I commit that you accused, intimidated, and condemned Me in My innocence?" Here the Law, which once condemned and killed all men, has nothing with which to defend or cleanse itself. Therefore it is condemned and killed in turn, so that it loses its jurisdiction not only over Christ — whom it attacked and killed without any right anyway — but also over all who believe in Him. Here Christ says (Matt. 11:28): "Come to Me, all who labor under the yoke of the Law. I could have overcome the Law by My supreme authority, without any injury to Me; for I am the Lord of the Law, and therefore it has no jurisdiction over Me. But for the sake of you, who were under the Law, I assumed your flesh and subjected Myself to the Law. That is, beyond the call of duty I went down into the same imprisonment, tyranny, and slavery of the Law under which you were serving as captives. I permitted the Law to lord it over Me, its Lord, to terrify Me, to subject Me to sin, death, and the wrath of God — none of which it had any right to do. Therefore I have conquered the Law by a double claim:[9]

[9] Bernard of Clairvaux, *Sermones in cantica*, Sermon XX, *Patrologia, Series Latina*, CLXXXIII, 867; cf. also *Luther's Works*, 22, p. 269, note 50.

first, as the Son of God, the Lord of the Law; secondly, in your person, which is tantamount to your having conquered the Law yourselves."

Paul speaks this way about this remarkable duel throughout his writings. To make the subject more joyful and clear, he usually portrays the Law by personification [10] as some sort of powerful person who condemned and killed Christ. Christ then overcame death and conquered this person in turn, condemning and killing him. Thus in Eph. 2:14-15: "He has slain the hostility in Himself"; and again, in 4:8, on the basis of Ps. 68:18: "When He ascended on high, He led a host of captives." He uses the same personification in the epistles to the Romans, the Corinthians, and the Colossians: [11] "for sin He condemned sin" (Rom. 8:3). By this victory of His, Christ has driven the Law to flight out of our conscience, so that it can no longer confound us in the sight of God or bring us to despair and condemn us. Of course, it does not cease manifesting our sin, accusing, and terrifying; but when the conscience takes hold of this word of the apostle – "Christ has redeemed us from the Law" – it is encouraged by faith and receives comfort. Then, with a kind of holy pride, it insults the Law and says: "I am not threatened by your terrors and threats at all, for you have crucified the Son and God, and crucified Him in a supreme act of injustice. Therefore the sin that you committed against Him is unforgivable. You have lost your jurisdiction, and finally you have been conquered and strangled not only for Christ but even for me as a believer in Him." He has granted us this victory. Therefore the Law has gone out of existence for us permanently, provided that we abide in Christ. Therefore "thanks be to God, who has given us the victory through our Lord Jesus Christ" (1 Cor. 15:57).

This also serves to support the idea that we are justified by faith alone. For when this duel between the Law and Christ was going on, no works or merits of ours intervened. Christ alone remains there; having put on our person, He serves the Law and in supreme innocence suffers all its tyranny. Therefore the Law is guilty of stealing, of sacrilege, and of the murder of the Son of God. It loses its rights and deserves to be damned. Wherever Christ is present or is at least named, it is forced to yield and to flee this name as the devil flees

[10] Cf. p. 162, note 81.

[11] Luther seems to be thinking of passages like Rom. 8:3, perhaps 2 Cor. 5:21, and Col. 2:15.

the cross.[12] Therefore we believers are free of the Law through Christ, who "triumphed over it in Him" (Col. 2:15). This glorious triumph, accomplished for us through Christ, is grasped not by works but by faith alone. Therefore faith alone justifies.

And so the words "Christ was born under the Law" are very meaningful and should be considered this way; for they indicate that the Son of God, who was born under the Law, did not perform one or another work of the Law or submit to it only in a political way, but that He suffered all the tyranny of the Law. For the Law exercised its full function over Christ; it frightened Him so horribly that He experienced greater anguish than any man has ever experienced. This is amply demonstrated by His bloody sweat, the comfort of the angel, His solemn prayer in the garden (Luke 22:41-44), and finally by that cry of misery on the cross (Matt. 27:46): "My God, My God, why hast Thou forsaken Me?" But He endured these things to redeem us who were under the Law, that is, those who were sorrowful, frightened, and desperate, who were burdened by sins, as for that matter all of us still are. For according to the flesh we still sin against all the commandments of God every day. But Paul commands us to have hope when he says: "God sent forth His Son."

Thus Christ, the divine and human Person, begotten of God in eternity and of the Virgin in time, came not to institute laws but to bear them and abolish them. He did not become a teacher of the Law; He became a disciple obedient to the Law, so that by this obedience of His He might redeem us who were under the Law. All this is completely different from the teaching of the papists, who made Christ a lawgiver, and a severer lawgiver than Moses. Here Paul is teaching the very opposite, namely, that God sent forth His Son under the Law; that is, that He made Him bear the judgment and the curse of the Law, sin, death, etc. Moses, who is an agent of sin, wrath, and death, captured, bound, condemned, and killed Christ; and Christ endured it. Christ acted toward the Law in a passive, not in an active way. Thus He is not a lawgiver and judge in accordance with the Law, but by making Himself a servant of the Law He became our Redeemer from the Law.

When Christ issues commandments in the Gospel and teaches, or rather interprets, the Law, this belongs, not to the doctrine of justification but to the doctrine of good works. Besides, teaching the Law

---

[12] On a related idea see *Luther's Works*, 22, p. 147, note 109.

is not the proper function of Christ on account of which He came into the world; it is an accidental function, just as when He healed the sick, raised the dead, helped the poor,[13] and comforted the afflicted. These are glorious and divine works, of course; but they are not peculiar to Christ. For the prophets taught the Law too, and performed miracles. But Christ is true God and man. In His conflict with the Law He suffered its extreme fierceness and tyranny. By performing and bearing the Law He conquered it in Himself. And then, when He rose from the dead, He condemned the Law, our most hostile enemy, and abolished it, so that it can no longer condemn or kill us. Therefore it is Christ's true and proper function to struggle with the Law, sin, and death of the entire world, and to struggle in such a way that He undergoes them, but, by undergoing them, conquers them and abolishes them in Himself, thus liberating us from the Law and from every evil. Therefore teaching the Law and performing miracles are special benefits of Christ, which were not the chief reason for His coming. For the prophets and especially the apostles did greater miracles than Christ Himself did (John 14:12).

Now since Christ has conquered the Law in His own Person, it necessarily follows that He is God by nature. For except for God no one, neither a man nor an angel, is above the Law. But Christ is above the Law, because He has conquered and strangled it. Therefore He is the Son of God, and God by nature. If you grasp Christ as He is described by Paul here, you will neither go wrong nor be put to shame. Then you will be [14] in a position to judge about all the various styles of life and about the religion and worship of the whole world. But if this true picture of Christ is removed or even obscured, there follows a sure confusion of everything; for the unspiritual man cannot judge about the Law of God. Here the skill of the philosophers, the jurists, and of all men is deficient. For the Law rules man; therefore it judges man, and man does not judge the Law. Only the Christian judges the Law. How? To say that it does not justify. Then what is the purpose of keeping it if it does not justify? The final cause of the obedience of the Law by the righteous is not righteousness in the sight of God, which is received by faith alone, but the peace of the world, gratitude toward God, and a good example by which others are invited to believe the Gospel. The pope confused ceremonial

---

13 The Weimar text has *indignis,* but we have read *indigis.*

14 The Weimar text has *erit,* but we have read *eris.*

matters, moral matters, and faith in such a way that he did not discriminate among them at all, except that eventually he preferred ceremonial matters to moral matters, and moral matters to faith.

So that we might receive adoption as sons.

That is, divine sonship. Paul is embellishing the passage from Gen. 22:18: "In your Offspring, etc." Earlier he had named righteousness, life, the promise of the Spirit, redemption from the Law, the covenant, and the promise as the blessing given to the offspring of Abraham. Here he names sonship and the inheritance of eternal life, for these things flow from the blessing. Once the curse that is sin, death, etc., has been removed by this blessed Offspring, its place is taken by the blessing that is righteousness, life, and everything good. Thus you see that when he wanted to, Paul could spill over with words and speak at length.

But by what merit have we received this righteousness, sonship, and inheritance of eternal life? By none. For what could be merited by men confined under sin, subjected to the curse of the Law, and condemned to eternal death? Therefore we have received all this freely and without deserving it, yet not without merit. What merit was it, then? Not ours, but that of Jesus Christ, the Son of God, who was born under the Law, not for Himself but for us (as Paul said earlier [Gal. 3:13] that He was made a curse for us), and who redeemed us who were under the Law. Therefore we have received this sonship solely by the redemption of Jesus Christ, the Son of God, who is our most abundant and eternal merit, whether of congruity or of condignity. Together with this gift of sonship, moreover, we have also received the Holy Spirit, whom God, through the Word, sends into our hearts, "crying: 'Abba! Father!'" as now follows.

6. *And because you are sons, God has sent the Spirit of His Son into your hearts.*

The Holy Spirit is sent forth in two ways. In the primitive church He was sent forth in a manifest and visible form. Thus He descended upon Christ at the Jordan in the form of a dove (Matt. 3:16), and upon the apostles and other believers in the form of fire (Acts 2:3). This was the first sending forth of the Holy Spirit; it was necessary in the primitive church, which had to be established with visible signs on account of the unbelievers, as Paul testifies. 1 Cor. 14:22: "Tongues are a sign, not for believers but for unbelievers." But later on, when the church had been gathered and confirmed by these signs, it was not necessary for this visible sending forth of the Holy Spirit to continue.

The second sending is that by which the Holy Spirit, through the Word, is sent into the hearts of believers, as is said here: "God has sent the Spirit of His Son into your hearts." This happens without a visible form, namely, when through the spoken Word we receive fire and light, by which we are made new and different, and by which a new judgment, new sensations, and new drives arise in us. This change and new judgment are not the work of human reason or power; they are the gift and accomplishment of the Holy Spirit, who comes with the preached Word, purifies our hearts by faith, and produces spiritual motivation in us. Therefore there is the greatest possible difference between us and the enemies and perverters of the Word. We, by the grace of God, are able to declare and judge with certainty, on the basis of the Word, about the will of God toward us, about all laws and doctrines, about our own lives and those of others. On the other hand, the papists and the fanatical spirits are unable to judge with certainty about anything. The latter distort and pervert the Word; the former persecute and blaspheme it. But without the Word it is impossible to form any sure judgments about anything.

It is not evident, of course, that we have been renewed in our minds and that we have the Holy Spirit. Yet our very ability to judge, our speech, and our confession are evidence enough that the Holy Spirit is in us with His gifts. For formerly we were unable to judge about anything at all. We did not speak and confess that all our deeds are sinful and condemned and that Christ alone is our merit of congruity and condignity, as we now do since the sun of truth has been shining. Therefore it should not affect us if the world, whose works we declare to be evil, judges that we are the most dangerous heretics and insurrectionists, overthrowers of religion and of the public peace, and possessed by the devil, who speaks through us and governs all our actions. In opposition to this perverse judgment of the world let us be satisfied with the testimony of our conscience, by which we know as a certainty that it is a divine gift when we not only believe in Jesus Christ but proclaim and confess Him openly in the presence of the world. As we believe in our heart, so we speak with our lips, according to the statement of the psalm (116:10): "I believed, and so I spoke; but I am greatly afflicted."

We also discipline ourselves in piety and avoid sin as much as we can. If we do sin, it is not deliberate; we sin through ignorance, and we regret it. We can fall, for the devil is lying in wait for us day and night. The remnants of sin also cling to our flesh. So far as the flesh is concerned, then, we are sinners even after we have received the Holy Spirit. Externally there is not much difference between the Christian and another socially upright human being. The works of the Christian are cheap in appearance: He does his duty according to his calling; he rules the commonwealth; he runs the household; he tills the field; he helps, supports, and serves his neighbor. The unspiritual man does not praise these works but thinks of them as common and as nothing, as something that laymen and even heathen do. For the world does not perceive the things of the Spirit of God (1 Cor. 2:14); therefore it forms a distorted judgment of the works of the pious. It not only admires the superstition of the hypocrites and their self-chosen works but takes a religious attitude toward them and supports them with generous gifts. On the other hand, it is so far away from acknowledging that the works of the pious are good — they are, of course, cheap and meager in appearance, but they are good and acceptable to God when they are done in faith, a joyful spirit, obedience, and gratitude toward God — that it denounces and condemns them as the height of wickedness and unrighteousness. Therefore there is nothing that the world believes less than that we have the Holy Spirit. But in a time of tribulation or of the cross and the confession of faith (which is the proper and principal work of believers), when one must either forsake wife, children, property, and life or deny Christ, then it becomes evident that by the power of the Holy Spirit we confess the faith, Christ, and His Word.

Therefore we must not doubt that the Holy Spirit dwells in us; but we must be sure and acknowledge that we are, as Paul says, "a temple of the Holy Spirit" (1 Cor. 6:19). For if someone experiences love toward the Word, and if he enjoys hearing, speaking, thinking, lecturing, and writing about Christ, he should know that this is not a work of human will or reason but a gift of the Holy Spirit. For it is impossible for these things to happen without the Holy Spirit. On the other hand, where there is hate and contempt for the Word, there the devil, "the god of this world" (2 Cor. 4:4), is reigning, blinding the hearts of men and holding them captive, to keep the light of the Gospel of the glory of Christ from shining upon them. This is what we see in the rabble today; they do not care about the Word at all but smugly despise it, as though it did not pertain to them at all.

Those in whom there is some glow and yearning for the Word should acknowledge with gratitude that this feeling has been infused into them by the Holy Spirit. For we are not born with this feeling; nor can we be instructed to acquire it by any laws. It is the right hand of the Most High, pure and simple, that has changed us (Ps. 77:10). Therefore when we are glad to hear the proclamation about Christ, the Son of God, who was made man for us and subjected Himself to the Law to redeem us, then with and through that proclamation God surely sends the Holy Spirit into our hearts. Therefore it is extremely profitable to the pious to know that they have the Holy Spirit.

I am saying this in order to refute the dangerous doctrine of the sophists and the monks, who taught and believed that no one can know for a certainty whether he is in a state of grace, even if he does good works according to his ability and lives a blameless life.[15] This statement, widely accepted and believed, was a principle and practically an article of faith throughout the papacy. With this wicked idea of theirs they utterly ruined the doctrine of faith, overthrew faith, disturbed consciences, abolished Christ from the church, obscured and denied all the blessings and gifts of the Holy Spirit, abrogated the true worship of God, and established idolatry, contempt of God, and blasphemy in the hearts of men. For anyone who has such doubts about the will of God toward him and who does not believe for a certainty that he is in a state of grace cannot believe that he has the forgiveness of sins, that God cares about him, or that he can be saved.

Augustine says correctly and faithfully that anyone can certainly see his own faith if he has it.[16] This is what they deny. "Far be it from me," they say, "that I should believe for a certainty that I am in a state of grace, that I am holy, and that I have the Holy Spirit, even if I do live a holy life and do everything I should." This wicked idea, on which the entire kingdom of the pope rests, is one that you young people should flee and regard with horror as a dangerous plague; for you have not yet been imbued with it. We older ones were reared in it from childhood and imbibed it in such a way that it grew into the very innards of our hearts. Therefore it was not without difficulty that we learned the true faith that we teach. We must by all means believe for a certainty that we are in a state of grace,

15 Cf. the Decrees and Canons of the Council of Trent, Session VI, Canons 13, 15, 16.

16 See, for example, *De Trinitate*, Book XIV, ch. 3.

that we are pleasing to God for the sake of Christ, and that we have the Holy Spirit. "Anyone who does not have the Spirit of Christ does not belong to Him" (Rom. 8:9). In addition, whatever he thinks, says, and works in doubt is sin; "for whatever does not proceed from faith is sin" (Rom. 14:23).

Therefore anyone who exercises a position of authority in the church or in the government should believe for a certainty that his office is pleasing to God. But he would never be able to believe this if he did not have the Holy Spirit. But you say: "I have no doubt that this office is pleasing to God, since it is a divine ordinance. But I do have doubts about my person and whether it is pleasing to Him." Here one must seek the help of theology, which is chiefly concerned with making us certain that not only the office occupied by the person but the person himself is pleasing to God. For it is the person who was baptized, who believes in Christ, who was cleansed of all sins by His blood, who lives in the fellowship of the church, who not only loves the pure doctrine of the Word but takes great pleasure in its propagation and in the growth of the number of believers, and who, on the other hand, hates the pope and the fanatical spirits with their wicked doctrine, in accordance with the statement (Ps. 119:113): "I hate double-minded men, but I love Thy Law."

Therefore we should believe for a certainty that not only our office but also our person is pleasing to God. Whatever our person says, does, or thinks in private is pleasing to God, not indeed on our account but on account of Christ, whom we believe to have been born under the Law for us. Now we are most certain that Christ is pleasing to God and that He is holy. To the extent that Christ is pleasing to God and that we cling to Him, to that extent we, too, are pleasing to God and holy. And although sin still clings to our flesh and we still fall every day, still grace is more abundant and more powerful than sin. For the mercy and the truth of the Lord reign over us forever. Therefore sin is unable to frighten us or to make us doubt the grace of God that is in us. Christ, that mighty giant, has abolished the Law, condemned sin, and destroyed death and every evil. So long as He is at the right hand of God interceding for us, we cannot have any doubts about the grace of God toward us.

In addition, God has also sent the Spirit of His Son into our hearts, as Paul says here. Now Christ is completely certain that in His Spirit He is pleasing to God. Since we have the same Spirit of Christ, we, too, should be certain that we are in a state of grace, on account of

Him who is certain. So much for the internal testimony, by which the heart should believe with complete certainty that it is in a state of grace and that it has the Holy Spirit. But the external signs, as I have said earlier, are these: to enjoy hearing about Christ; to teach, give thanks, praise, and confess Him, even at the cost of property and life; to do one's duty according to one's calling in a manly way, in faith and joy; not to take delight in sin; not to invade someone else's calling but to serve one's own; to help a needy brother, comfort the sorrowful, etc. By these signs we are assured and confirmed a posteriori that we are in a state of grace. The wicked have these signs too, but not in a pure way. From this it is abundantly clear that the pope with his doctrine only disturbs consciences and finally brings them to the brink of despair; for he not only teaches them to be in doubt, but he commands it. Therefore, as the psalm says (5:9), "there is nothing sure in his mouth"; or, as another says (10:7), "under his tongue are mischief and iniquity."

Here we see also how great the weakness of faith is in those who are pious. For if we believed for a certainty that we are in a state of grace, that our sins have been forgiven, that we have the Spirit of Christ, and that we are the sons of God, then we would be truly happy and thankful to God for this inexpressible gift (2 Cor. 9:15). But because we experience the opposite feelings, namely, fear, doubt, sorrow, etc., we do not dare believe this for a certainty. In fact, our conscience supposes that it would be great presumption and pride to arrogate this glory to itself. Therefore this matter is understood correctly only when it is transferred to practice, for without experience it is never learned.

Let everyone accustom himself, therefore, to believe for a certainty that he is in a state of grace and that his person with its works is pleasing to God. But if he senses that he is in doubt, let him exercise his faith, struggle against the doubt, and strive for certainty, so that he can say: "I know that I have been accepted and that I have the Holy Spirit, not on account of my worthiness or virtue but on account of Christ, who subjected Himself to the Law on our account and took away the sins of the world (John 1:29). In Him I believe. If I am a sinner, and if I err, He is righteous and cannot err. Besides, I enjoy hearing, reading, singing, and writing about Him. There is nothing I want more than to make His Gospel known to the world and to convert many people."

These things certainly testify that the Holy Spirit is present. For such things do not come into being in the heart by human powers; nor are they acquired by any exercises or efforts. But they are achieved through Christ. First He justifies us by our knowledge of Him. Then He creates a clean heart (Ps. 51:10), produces new motives, grants the certainty by which we believe that for His sake we are pleasing to the Father, and grants the sure judgment by which we approve the things of which we were formerly ignorant or utterly contemptuous. Therefore we should strive daily to move more and more from uncertainty to certainty; and we should make an effort to wipe out completely that wicked idea which has consumed the entire world, namely, that a man does not know whether he is in a state of grace. For if we are in doubt about our being in a state of grace and about our being pleasing to God for the sake of Christ, we are denying that Christ has redeemed us and completely denying all His benefits. You younger men are able to grasp the doctrine of the Gospel easily and to avoid this dangerous opinion, for you have never been infected by it.

Crying: Abba! Father!

Paul could have said: "God has sent the Spirit of His Son into our hearts, praying: 'Abba! Father!'" But he purposely says "crying," to indicate the trial of the Christian who is still weak and who believes weakly. In Rom. 8:26 he calls this crying "sighs too deep for words." "Likewise," he says, "the Spirit helps us in our weakness; for we do not know how to pray as we should, but the Spirit Himself intercedes for us with sighs too deep for words."

It is a very great comfort when Paul says here that the Spirit of Christ, sent by God into our hearts, cries: "Abba! Father!" and when he says in Rom. 8:26 that He helps us in our weakness and intercedes for us with sighs too deep for words. Anyone who truly believed this would not fall away in any affliction, no matter how great. But many things hinder this faith. In the first place, our heart was born in sin. In the second place, we have the innate evil in us that we are in doubt about the favor of God toward us and cannot believe for a certainty that we are pleasing to God. Besides, "our adversary, the devil, prowls around, issuing terrible roars" (1 Peter 5:8); and he says: "You are a sinner. Therefore God is wrathful with you and will destroy you forever." We have nothing to strengthen and sustain us against these great and unbearable cries except the bare Word, which sets Christ forth as the Victor over sin, death, and every evil. But it is effort and labor to cling firmly to this in the midst of trial and conflict, when Christ does not become visible to any of our senses. We do not see Him, and in the trial our heart does not feel His presence and help. In fact, Christ appears to be wrathful with us and to be deserting us at such a time. Besides, in this trial a man feels the power of sin, the weakness of the flesh, and his doubt; he feels the fiery darts of the devil (Eph. 6:16), the terrors of death, and the wrath and judgment of God. All these things issue powerful and horrible cries against us, so that there appears to be nothing left for us except despair and eternal death.

But in the midst of these terrors of the Law, thunderclaps of sin, tremors of death, and roarings of the devil, Paul says, the Holy Spirit begins to cry in our heart: "Abba! Father!" And His cry vastly exceeds, and breaks through, the powerful and horrible cries of the Law, sin, death, and the devil. It penetrates the clouds and heaven, and it reaches all the way to the ears of God.

With these words, then, Paul wants to indicate the weakness there still is in the pious, as in Rom. 8:26: "The Spirit helps us in our weakness." For because the awareness of the opposite is so strong in us, that is, because we are more aware of the wrath of God than of His favor toward us, therefore the Holy Spirit is sent into our hearts. He does not whisper and does not pray but cries very loudly: "Abba! Father!" and intercedes for us, in accordance with the will of God, with sighs too deep for words. How?

In deep terrors and conflicts of conscience we do indeed take hold of Christ and believe that He is our Savior. But then the Law terrifies us most, and sin disturbs us. In addition, the devil attacks us with all his stratagems and his fiery darts (Eph. 6:16), trying with all his might to snatch Christ away from us and to rob us of all comfort. Then there is nothing to keep us from succumbing and despairing, for then we are the bruised reed and the dimly burning wick (Is. 42:3). Meanwhile, however, the Holy Spirit is helping us in our weakness and interceding for us with sighs too deep for words (Rom. 8:26), and He is bearing witness with our spirit that we are children of God (Rom. 8:16). Thus the mind is strengthened amid these terrors; it sighs to its Savior and High Priest, Jesus Christ; it overcomes the weakness of the flesh, regains its comfort, and says: "Abba! Father!" This sighing, of which we are hardly aware, Paul calls a cry and a sigh too deep for words — a sigh that fills heaven and earth.

He also calls it a cry and a sigh of the Spirit, because when we are weak and tempted, then the Spirit sets up this cry in our heart.

No matter how great and terrible the cries are that the Law, sin, and the devil let loose against us, even though they seem to fill heaven and earth and to overcome the sighs of our hearts completely, still they cannot do us any harm. For the more these enemies press in upon us, accusing and vexing us with their cries, the more do we, sighing, take hold of Christ; with heart and lips we call upon Him, cling to Him, and believe that He was born under the Law for us, in order that He might redeem us from the curse of the Law and destroy sin and death. When we have taken hold of Christ by faith this way, we cry through Him: "Abba! Father!" And this cry of ours far exceeds the cry of the devil.

But we are far from supposing that this sigh which we emit amid the terrors and in our weakness is a cry — so far indeed that we hardly understand that it is even a sigh. For so far as our own awareness is concerned, this faith of ours, which sighs to Christ in temptation, is very weak. That is why we do not hear this cry. We have only the Word. If we take hold of this in the struggle, we breathe a little and sigh. To some extent we are aware of this sigh, but we do not hear the cry. But "He who searches the hearts of men," Paul says (Rom. 8:27), "knows what is the mind of the Spirit." To Him who searches the hearts this sigh, which seems so meager to the flesh, is a loud cry and a sigh too deep for words, in comparison with which the great and horrible roars of the Law, sin, death, the devil, and hell are nothing at all and are inaudible. It is not without purpose, then, that Paul calls this sigh of the pious and afflicted heart the crying and indescribable sighing of the Spirit; for it fills all of heaven and earth and cries so loudly that the angels suppose that they cannot hear anything except this cry.

Within ourselves, however, there is the very opposite feeling. This faint sigh of ours does not seem to penetrate the clouds in such a way that it is the only thing to be heard by God and the angels in heaven. In fact, we suppose, especially as long as the trial continues, that the devil is roaring at us terribly, that heaven is bellowing, that the earth is quaking, that everything is about to collapse, that all the creatures are threatening us with evil, and that hell is opening up in order to swallow us. This feeling is in our hearts; we do not hear these terrible voices or see this frightening face. And this is what Paul says in 2 Cor. 12:9: that the power of Christ is made perfect in our weakness. For then Christ is truly almighty, and then He truly reigns and triumphs in us when we are, so to speak, so "all-weak" [17] that we can scarcely emit a groan. But Paul says that in the ears of God this sigh is a mighty cry that fills all of heaven and earth.

Likewise in Luke 18:1-8, in the parable of the unjust judge, Christ calls this sigh of the pious heart a cry, and a cry that cries to God incessantly day and night. He says: "Hear what the unrighteous judge says. And will not God vindicate His elect, who cry to Him day and night? Will He delay long over them? I tell you, He will vindicate them speedily." Today, amid all the persecution and opposition from the pope, the tyrants, and the fanatical spirits, who attack us from the right and from the left, we cannot do anything but emit such sighs. But these have been our cannon and our instruments of war; with them we have frustrated the plans of our opponents all these years, and we have begun to demolish the kingdom of Antichrist. But they will provoke Christ to hasten the day of His glorious coming, when He will abolish all principalities, powers, and might, and will put all His enemies under His feet. Amen.[18]

Thus in Exodus the Lord says to Moses at the Red Sea (14:15): "Why do you cry to Me?" That was the last thing Moses was doing. He was in extreme anguish; therefore he was trembling and at the point of despair. Not faith but unbelief appeared to be ruling in him. For Israel was so hemmed in by the mountains, by the army of the Egyptians, and by the sea that it could not escape anywhere. Moses did not even dare mumble here. How, then, did he cry? Therefore we must not judge according to the feeling of our heart; we must judge according to the Word of God, which teaches that the Holy Spirit is granted to the afflicted, the terrified, and the despairing in such a way that He encourages and comforts them, so that they do not succumb in their trials and other evils but conquer them, though not without very great fear and effort.

The papists imagined that the saints had the Holy Spirit in such a way that they never experienced or had any temptations.[19] They speak about the Holy Spirit only speculatively, as the fanatical spirits do today. But Paul says that the power of Christ is made perfect in

[17] This is our own coinage as a translation for Luther's coined word *omni-infirmi.*

[18] Cf. Luther's prayer in the preface to the Smalcald Articles, *The Book of Concord,* p. 291.

[19] Cf. *Luther the Expositor,* pp. 75—77.

our weakness (2 Cor. 12:9), and that the Holy Spirit helps us in our weakness and intercedes for us with sighs too deep for words (Rom. 8:26). Therefore we have the greatest need for the aid and comfort of the Holy Spirit, and He is also nearest to us when we are at our weakest and nearest to despair. If someone passes through evil with a courageous and happy spirit, then the Holy Spirit has already performed His work in him. But He really performs His work in those who are thoroughly terrified and who have come near to what the psalm calls "the gates of death" (9:13). Thus I have just said that Moses saw the very presence of death in the water and wherever he turned his gaze. Therefore he was in the deepest anxiety and despair, and undoubtedly he sensed in his heart the loud cry of the devil against him, saying: "This entire people will perish today, for they cannot escape anywhere. You alone are responsible for this great calamity, for you led them out of Egypt." Then there came the cry of the people, who said (Ex. 14:11-12): "Is it because there are no graves in Egypt that you have taken us away to die in the wilderness? It would have been better for us to serve the Egyptians than to die in the wilderness." Then the Holy Spirit was present in Moses, not speculatively but actually; He interceded for him with sighs too deep for words, so that Moses sighed to God and said: "Lord, it was at Thy command that I led the people out. Therefore do Thou help!" This sigh is what He calls "crying."

I have discussed this at some length in order to show what the work of the Holy Spirit is and how He usually carries it out. In temptation we must not on any account decide this matter on the basis of our feeling or of the cry of the Law, sin, and the devil. If we want to follow our feeling here or to believe those cries, we shall decide that we are bereft of all help from the Holy Spirit and that we have been utterly banished from the presence of God. Should we not rather remember, then, that Paul says that the Holy Spirit helps us in our weakness and cries: "Abba! Father!"? That is, He emits what seems to us to be some sort of sob and sigh of the heart; but in the sight of God this is a loud cry and a sigh too deep for words. In every temptation and weakness, therefore, just cling to Christ and sigh! He gives you the Holy Spirit, who cries: "Abba! Father!" Then the Father says: "I do not hear anything in the whole world except this single sigh, which is such a loud cry in My ears that it fills heaven and earth and drowns out all the cries of everything else."

You will notice that Paul does not say that the Spirit intercedes for us in temptation with a long prayer, but that He intercedes with a sigh, and one that is too deep for words. He does not cry loudly and tearfully: "Have mercy on me, O God" (Ps. 51:1); but He merely utters the words of a cry and a sigh, which is "Oh, Father!" This is indeed a very short word, but it includes everything. Not the lips, but the feelings are speaking here, as though one were to say: "Even though I am surrounded by anxieties and seem to be deserted and banished from Thy presence, nevertheless I am a child of God on account of Christ; I am beloved on account of the Beloved." Therefore the term "Father," when spoken meaningfully [20] in the heart, is an eloquence that Demosthenes, Cicero, and the most eloquent men there have ever been in the world cannot attain. For this is a matter that is expressed, not in words but in sighs, which are not articulated in all the words of all the orators; for they are too deep for words.

I have indicated in a variety of ways that the Christian man must believe for a certainty that he is in a state of divine grace, and that he has the cry of the Holy Spirit in his heart, especially when he is performing his proper function, which is to confess or to suffer for confessing. I did this in order that you might utterly repudiate the wicked idea of the entire kingdom of the pope, the teaching that a Christian man must be uncertain about the grace of God toward him. If this opinion stands, then Christ is completely useless. For whoever doubts the grace of God toward him this way must necessarily doubt the promises of God and therefore the will of God, as well as the birth, suffering, death, and resurrection of Christ. There is no greater blasphemy against God than to deny the promises of God and God Himself, Christ, etc. Therefore it was the height not only of insanity but of wickedness when the monks were so zealous in enlisting the youth of both sexes in the monasteries for their religious and, as they called them, "holy" orders, as a sure state of salvation; and then, once they were enlisted, they commanded them to doubt the grace of God. Thus the pope also summoned the whole human race to the obedience of the holy Roman Church as a holy estate in which they would be sure to obtain salvation, and then he commanded those who obeyed his laws to have doubts. In this way the kingdom of Antichrist first boasts and exaggerates the sacredness of its laws, orders, and rules, and it promises the certainty of eternal life to those who observe them; but then, when the miserable beings have been punishing their bodies for a long time in accordance with

[20] This is a slightly free rendering of *formaliter*.

[W, XL, 587—589]

human traditions by keeping vigils, fasting, etc., their reward for all
this is not to know whether or not this obedience of theirs is pleasing
to God. Satan took a horrible delight in the killing of souls by the
papists. Therefore the papacy is a veritable torture chamber of consciences and the very kingdom of the devil.

To prove and support this wicked error of theirs, they used the
statement of Solomon in Eccl. 9:1: "The righteous and the wise and
their deeds are in the hand of God; whether it is love or hate, man
does not know." [21] Some of them applied this statement to the hate
of God in the future, others to that in the present; but neither group
understood Solomon, who in this passage is not saying anything like
what they imagine. Moreover, the chief point of all Scripture is that
we should not doubt but hope, trust, and believe for a certainty that
God is merciful, kind, and patient, that He does not lie and deceive
but is faithful and true. He keeps His promises and has now accomplished what He had promised, handing over His only Son into death
for our sins, so that everyone who believes in the Son should not
perish but have eternal life (John 3:16). Here there can surely be
no doubt whether God has been reconciled and is favorably disposed
toward us, whether the hate and wrath of God have been removed;
for He permits His own Son to die for us sinners. But no matter how
much the whole Gospel sets this forth everywhere or how many times
it teaches it, this one statement of Solomon, misunderstood at that,
was worth more, especially among the devotees and monks of the
stricter sort, than all the promises and comfort of all Scripture, yes,
than Christ Himself. They abused Scripture for their own destruction, and they received a just punishment for despising the Scriptures
and neglecting the Gospel.

It is important for us to know all this. For one thing, the papists
are giving the impression today that they have never done anything
wrong; therefore they must be convicted on the basis of their own
abominations, which they have spread throughout the world, as is
attested by their own books, of which an infinite number on this subject still exist. In addition, we can become sure this way that we
have the pure and true doctrine of the Gospel — an assurance of which
the papacy cannot boast. If everything else were sound there, still
this monster of uncertainty is worse than all the other monsters. And
although it is obvious that the enemies of Christ teach what is un-

[21] See Luther's more extended discussion of this passage in his *Commentary on Ecclesiastes* of 1532 (W, XX, 158).

certain, because they command consciences to be in doubt, still they
are so filled with the madness of Satan that in their smugness they
condemn and kill us who disagree with them, as though we were the
heretics and they were completely certain of their doctrine.

Let us thank God, therefore, that we have been delivered from
this monster of uncertainty and that now we can believe for a certainty that the Holy Spirit is crying and issuing that sigh too deep for
words in our hearts. And this is our foundation: The Gospel commands us to look, not at our own good deeds or perfection but at God
Himself as He promises, and at Christ Himself, the Mediator. By
contrast the pope commands us to look, not at God as He promises,
not at Christ our High Priest, but at our own works and merits. From
the latter course, doubt and despair necessarily follow; but from the
former, certainty and the joy of the Spirit. For I am clinging to God,
who cannot lie. He says: "I am giving My own Son into death, so
that by His blood He might redeem you from sin and death." Here
I cannot have any doubts, unless I want to deny God altogether. And
this is the reason why our theology is certain: it snatches us away
from ourselves and places us outside ourselves, so that we do not depend on our own strength, conscience, experience, person, or works
but depend on that which is outside ourselves, that is, on the promise
and truth of God, which cannot deceive. The pope does not know
this; therefore he and his furies have the wicked notion that no one,
not even those who are righteous and wise, can know whether he is
worthy of love. But if they are righteous and wise, they surely know
that they are loved by God; otherwise they are not righteous and wise.

What is more, this statement of Solomon does not say anything
at all about either the hatred or the favor of God toward men. It is
a political statement, rebuking the ingratitude of men. For the perversity and ingratitude of the world is so great that it often repays
evil to those who have deserved good from it and sometimes even
treats them very rudely; on the other hand, it elevates and honors the
wicked. So David, a holy man and a very good king, was driven out
of his kingdom; the prophets, Christ, and the apostles were killed.
The histories of all nations attest that many men who deserved the
best from their country were driven into exile by their own fellow
citizens, that they had a miserable life there, and that some of them
came to a bitter end in prison. Therefore Solomon is not speaking
here about the conscience as it deals with God, or about the favor
and judgment of God, but about the judgments and wills of men

among themselves, as though he were saying: "There are many right-eous and wise men through whom God does many good things and provides peace for human beings. But these human beings are so far from acknowledging this that they often repay evil to such men in exchange for their great benefactions. Regardless of how much good a man does, therefore, he still does not know whether by this diligence and faithfulness of his he merits hatred or favor from men."

That is what has happened to us in our day. Although we thought that we would find favor with our brethren for preaching the Gospel of peace, life, and eternal salvation to them, we found, instead of favor, the bitterest hatred. There were many who found our doctrine pleasing at first and endorsed it eagerly. We thought that they would be our brethren and friends, who would be joined with us in unani-mous agreement and would plant and propagate this doctrine among others. But now we are experiencing that they are false brethren and our bitterest enemies. They are planting error, distorting and over-throwing what we teach correctly and faithfully, and creating the worst kind of scandal in the churches. Therefore let anyone who does his duty piously and faithfully in whatever area of life he may be, and who receives the ingratitude and hatred of men in return for his good deeds, not torture himself to death on this account; but let him say with Christ (Ps. 109:3-4): "They hate Me without cause. In re-turn for My love they accuse Me, even as I make prayer for them."

With this wicked doctrine, by which he commands men to doubt the favor of God toward them, the pope has removed God and all His promises from the church, has undermined the blessings of Christ, and has abolished the entire Gospel. Then these troubles followed of necessity, because men depended, not on God as He promises but on their own works and merits. When this happens, a man can never be certain about the will of God but is continually forced to waver and finally even to despair. It is impossible ever to decide what God wills and what is pleasing to Him, except in His Word. This Word makes us certain that God cast away all His wrath and hatred toward us when He gave His only Son for our sins. The sacraments, the power of the keys, etc., also make us certain; for if God did not love us, He would never have given us these. Thus we are overwhelmed with endless evidence of the favor of God toward us. Now that the plague of uncertainty, with which the entire church of the pope is infected, is driven away, let us believe for a certainty that God is favorably disposed toward us, that we are pleasing to Him and of concern to

Him on account of Christ, and that we have the Holy Spirit, who intercedes for us with a crying and a sighing too deep for words.

In form this crying and sighing is that amid your trial you do not call God a tyrant, an angry judge, or a tormentor, but a Father — even though the sighing may be so faint that it can hardly be felt. By contrast the other crying is very great and is felt very strongly, when in genuine terror of conscience we call God wicked, cruel, an angry tyrant, and a judge. For then it seems that God has forsaken us and that He wants to banish us to hell. That is how the saints often complain in the psalms (Ps. 31:22, 12): "I am driven far from Thy sight"; "I have become like a broken vessel." This is certainly not a sigh that says: "Father"; it is the roar of hatred for God that cries loudly: "Harsh judge, cruel tormentor!" Now it is time to turn your eyes away from the Law, from works, and from your own feelings and conscience, to lay hold of the Gospel, and to depend solely on the promise of God. Then there is emitted a little sigh, which silences and drowns out that violent roaring; and nothing remains in your heart but the sigh that says: "Abba! Father! However much the Law may accuse me, and sin and death may terrify me, nevertheless Thou, O God, dost promise grace, righteousness, and eternal life through Christ." And so the promise produces the sigh that cries: "Father!"

I have nothing against it when some explain that the one name is Greek and the other Hebrew; that Paul purposely wanted to use both because of the twofold nature of the church as gathered from Gentiles and Jews; and that Gentiles and Jews do indeed call God "Father" in different languages, but the cry of both is the same, since both cry: "Father!" [22]

7. So through God you are no longer a slave but a son.

This is a rhetorical exclamation [23] and a conclusion, as though Paul were saying: "Now that it is established that we have received the Spirit through the hearing of the Word and that we can cry in our hearts: 'Abba! Father!' then it is surely defined in heaven that there is no slavery anymore, but sheer liberty, adoption, and sonship." Who produces it? The sigh. How? Because it is the

[22] Augustine, *Expositio Epistolae ad Galatas*, 31, *Patrologia, Series Latina*, XXXV, 2126—2127.

[23] An *epiphonema* was a rhetorical exclamation; cf. Quintilian, *Institutiones Oratoriae*, VIII, 5, 11.

Father who promises. But He is not a Father to me unless I respond to Him as a son. First the Father offers me grace and fatherhood by means of His promises; all that remains is that I accept it. This happens when I cry out with that sigh and when I respond to His voice with the heart of a son, saying: "Father!" Then Father and son come together, and a marriage is contracted without any ceremony or pomp. That is, nothing comes in the way: no Law, no work is demanded here. For what would a man do in these terrors and in this horrible darkness of trial? There is only the Father here, promising and calling me His son through Christ, who was born under the Law. And I for my part accept, reply with a sigh, and say: "Father!" There is no demand here, but only the sigh of the son, who grows confident in the midst of tribulation and says: "Thou dost promise and dost call me 'son' on account of Christ. I accept and call Thee 'Father.'" This is becoming a son completely without works. But these things cannot be understood without the experience.

Paul is not applying the term "slave" here as he does earlier, in Gal. 3:28, when he says: "There is neither slave nor free." But here he is thinking of the slave of the Law, that is, of the one who is subject to the Law, as he says a little earlier (4:3): "We were slaves to the elements of the world." Therefore to be a slave, according to what Paul says here, means to be sentenced and imprisoned under the Law, under the wrath of God, and under death; it means to acknowledge God, not as God or as Father but as a tormentor, an enemy, a tyrant. This is truly to live in slavery and in a Babylonian captivity, and to be cruelly tormented in it. For the more someone performs works under the Law, the more he is oppressed by its slavery. That slavery, he says, has ended; it does not strain and oppress us any longer. Paul speaks in the concrete: "You are no longer a slave." But the meaning is clearer if we restate it in the abstract this way: There is no slavery in Christ, but only sonship; for when faith comes, the slavery ends, as he also says earlier, in Gal. 3:25.

Here Paul shows clearly that no terror, wrath, disturbance, or death — that is, no function or jurisdiction of the Law — is to be permitted into the Christian conscience. Much less are the monsters and sacrileges of human traditions to be permitted. For in the matter of justification I must be ignorant of the divine Law and not permit it to rule in any way over my conscience. Much less shall I permit my conscience to be dominated by the filth of the pope, regardless of how much he may "roar like a lion" (Rev. 10:3) and threaten that I shall incur the indignation of Almighty God. Here I must say: "Law, your obedience will not penetrate to the throne where Christ, my Lord, is sitting. Here I will not listen to you. (Much less, Antichrist, will I listen to your monstrous teachings!) For I am a free man and a son, who does not have to be subject to any slavery or any Law of slavery." Therefore do not let Moses — much less the pope — enter the bridegroom's chamber to lie there, that is, to reign over the conscience which Christ has delivered from the Law to make it free of any slavery. Let the slaves remain in the valley with the ass, and let Isaac ascend the mountain along with Abraham, his father.[24] That is, let the Law have its dominion over the flesh and the old self; let this be under the Law; let this permit the burden to be laid upon it; let this permit itself to be disciplined and vexed by the Law; let the Law prescribe to this what it should do and accomplish, and how it should deal with other men. But let the Law not pollute the chamber in which Christ alone should take His rest and sleep; that is, let it not disturb the conscience, which should live only with Christ, its Bridegroom, in the realm of freedom and sonship.

"If you cry: 'Abba! Father!'" he says, "then certainly you are no longer slaves; then you are free men and sons. Therefore you are without the Law, without sin, and without death; that is, you are saved and have nothing more of anything evil." Therefore sonship brings with it the eternal kingdom and all the inheritance of heaven. How great the measure and the glory of this gift is, the human mind cannot even conceive in this life; much less can it express this. Meanwhile we see this dimly (1 Cor. 13:12). We have this faint sigh and this tiny faith, which depends only on hearing the sound of the voice of Christ as He promises. According to sense, therefore, this is only the center of the circle; but in fact it is a very large and infinite sphere. What a Christian has is in fact something very large and infinite, but according to his view and sense it is very small and finite. Therefore we must not measure this by human reason and sense; we must measure it by another circle, that is, by the promise of God; just as He is infinite, so His promise is infinite, even though meanwhile it is enclosed in these

24 Cf. p. 116, note 34.

[W, XL, 596—598]

narrow limits and in what I might call the Word of the center. Now we see the center; eventually we shall see the circumference as well. Therefore there is nothing left that is in a position to accuse, terrify, and bind the conscience. There is no slavery any longer; there is only sonship, which brings us not only freedom from the Law, sin, and death but also the inheritance of eternal life, as now follows.

If a son, then an heir through Christ.

Whoever is a son must be an heir as well. For merely by being born he deserves to be an heir. No work and no merit brings him the inheritance, but only his birth. Thus he obtains the inheritance in a purely passive, not in an active way; that is, just his being born, not his producing or working or worrying, makes him an heir. He does not do anything toward his being born but merely lets it happen. Therefore we come to these eternal goods — the forgiveness of sins, righteousness, the glory of the resurrection, and eternal life — not actively but passively. Nothing whatever interferes here; faith alone takes hold of the offered promise. Therefore just as in society a son becomes an heir merely by being born, so here faith alone makes men sons of God, born of the Word, which is the divine womb in which we are conceived, carried, born, reared, etc. By this birth and this patience or passivity which makes us Christians we also become sons and heirs. But being heirs, we are free of death and the devil, and we have righteousness and eternal life. This comes to us in a purely passive way; for we do not do anything, but we let ourselves be made and formed as a new creation through faith in the Word.

Now it transcends all the capacity of the human mind when he says "heirs," not of some very wealthy and powerful king, not of the emperor, not of the world, but of Almighty God, the Creator of all. Therefore this inheritance of ours is, as Paul says elsewhere (2 Cor. 9:15), "inexpressible." If someone could believe with a certain and constant faith, and could understand the magnitude of it all, that he is the son and heir of God, he could regard all the power and wealth of all the kingdoms of the world as filth and refuse in comparison with his heavenly inheritance. Whatever the world has that is sublime and glorious would make him sick. And the greater the pomp and glory of the world is, the more detestable it would be to him. In other words, whatever the world admires and exalts most, that is foul and worthless in his eyes. For what is the whole world with its power, wealth, and glory in comparison with God, whose heir and son he is? He also desires anxiously to depart with Paul and to be with Christ (Phil. 1:23). Nothing more delightful could happen to him than a premature death, which he would embrace as the most joyous peace; for he would know that it is the end of all his evils and that through it he comes into his inheritance. In fact, a man who believed this completely would not go on living very long but would soon be consumed by his overwhelming joy.

But the law in our members at war with the law of our mind (Rom. 7:23) does not permit faith to be perfect. This is why we need the aid and comfort of the Holy Spirit, who, in our anxiety, intercedes for us with a sigh too deep for words (Rom. 8:26), as was said earlier. Sin still clings to the flesh, continually disturbing the conscience and hindering faith, so that we cannot joyfully see and desire the eternal wealth granted to us by God through Christ. When he experiences this conflict of the flesh against the Spirit, Paul himself exclaims (Rom. 7:24): "Wretched man that I am! Who will deliver me from this body of death?" He accuses his "body," which he really should have loved, and gives it a very ugly name, calling it his "death," as though he were saying: "My body afflicts and harasses me more than death itself." Even in his case this interrupted the joy of the Spirit. He did not always have pleasant and happy thoughts about his future inheritance in heaven, but over and over he experienced sadness of the spirit and fear.

From this it is evident how difficult a thing faith is; it is not learned and grasped as easily and quickly as those sated and scornful spirits imagine who immediately exhaust everything contained in the Scriptures.[25] The weakness and struggle of the flesh with the spirit in the saints is ample testimony how weak their faith still is. For a perfect faith would soon bring a perfect contempt and scorn for this present life. If we could grasp and believe for a certainty that God is our Father and that we are His sons and heirs, the world would immediately seem vile to us, with everything that it regards as precious, such as righteousness, wisdom, kingdoms, power, crowns, gold, glory, riches, pleasure, and the like. We would not be so concerned about food. We would not attach our hearts so firmly to physical things that their presence would give us confidence and

[25] See a similar statement of 1530 in *Luther's Works*, 14, p. 7.

their removal would produce dejection and even despair. But we would do everything with complete love, humility, and patience. Of course, the heretics boast of these things; but in fact there is nothing more cruel, proud, and impatient than they are. But now, as long as our flesh is powerful, our faith weak, and our spirit infirm, we act in the opposite way. Therefore Paul says correctly that in this life we have only the first fruits of the Spirit (Rom. 8:23) and that we shall have the tithes later.

Through Christ.

Paul always has Christ on his lips and cannot forget Him. For he foresaw that in the world, even among those who claimed to be Christians, nothing would be less well known than Christ and His Gospel. Therefore he continually inculcates Him and presents Him to our view. Whenever he speaks about grace, righteousness, the promise, sonship, and the inheritance, he always makes a practice of adding "in" or "through" Christ, at the same time taking a sidelong look at the Law, as though he were saying: "We do not obtain these things through the Law and its works, much less through our own abilities or the works of human tradition, but through Christ alone."

8. *Formerly, when you did not know God, you were in bondage to beings that by nature are no gods;*

9. *but now that you have come to know God, or rather to be known by God, how can you turn back again to the weak and beggarly elements, whose slaves you want to be once more?*

This is the conclusion of Paul's argument. From here until the end of the epistle he will not argue very much but will set forth commandments about morality. But first he scolds the Galatians in great indignation for having let this divine and heavenly doctrine be stolen from their hearts so quickly and easily; it is as though he were saying: "You have teachers who want to lead you back into the slavery of the Law. I did not do this, but by my doctrine I 'called you out of darkness into the marvelous light' (1 Peter 2:9); I set you free from slavery and established you in the liberty of the sons of God. I did not proclaim the works of the Law and the merits of men to you; I proclaimed righteousness and the free gift of heavenly and eternal possessions through Christ. Since this is how things are,

why do you forsake the light and return so easily to the darkness?
Why do you permit yourselves to be dragged down with such ease
from grace to the Law and from liberty to slavery?"

Here we see again, as I have warned earlier, that it is very easy
to fall from faith. The example of the Galatians attests to this; so
does the example of the Sacramentarians, the Anabaptists, and others
today. With great zeal and diligence we inculcate, urge, and empha-
size the teaching of the faith by speaking, reading, and writing; we
distinguish the Gospel from the Law in a very pure way. And yet
we accomplish very little. The fault is the devil's, who is wondrously
skilled at seducing people; and there is nothing he finds more intolerable than the true knowledge of grace and faith in Christ. To remove
Christ from the gaze and from the heart, he produces other specters,
by which he gradually leads men from faith and the knowledge of
grace to the discussion of the Law. When he has achieved this,
Christ has been removed. It is not without purpose, therefore, when
Paul inculcates Christ in almost every verse; nor when he sets forth
the teaching of faith so purely, attributing righteousness solely to it,
and detracts from the Law, showing that it has exactly the opposite
effect, namely, that it works wrath and increases sin. He would
want to persuade us not to let Christ be torn out of our hearts by
any means. Let not the bride send the Groom away from her
embrace, but let her always cling to Him; for as long as He is
present, there is no danger, but only the sighing (Rom. 8:26),
Fatherhood, sonship, and the inheritance.

But why does Paul say that the Galatians are "turning back to
the weak and beggarly elements," that is, to the Law, when they
never had the Law, since they were Gentiles (even though, as we
shall say later, he writes this also to Jews)? Or why does he not
rather speak this way: "Once, when you did not know God, you
were in bondage to beings that by nature are no gods. But now
that you know God, why do you forsake the true God and turn
back again to the worship of idols?" Is defecting from the promise
to the Law and from faith to works the same for Paul as serving
gods that by nature are no gods? I reply: Whoever falls from the
doctrine of justification is ignorant of God and is an idolater. Therefore it is all the same whether he then returns to the Law or to the
worship of idols; it is all the same whether he is called a monk or
a Turk or a Jew or an Anabaptist. For once this doctrine is undermined, nothing more remains but sheer error, hypocrisy, wickedness,

and idolatry, regardless of how great the sanctity that appears on the outside.

The reason is this: God does not want to be known except through Christ; nor, according to John 1:18, can He be known any other way. Christ is the Offspring promised to Abraham; on Him God founded all His promises. Therefore Christ alone is the means, the life, and the mirror through which we see God and know His will.

Through Christ God announces His favor and mercy to us. In Christ we see that God is not a wrathful taskmaster and judge but a gracious and kind Father, who blesses us, that is, who delivers us from the Law, sin, death, and every evil, and endows us with righteousness and eternal life through Christ. This is a sure knowledge of God and a true divine conviction, which does not deceive us but portrays God Himself in a specific form, apart from which there is no God.

Whoever surrenders this knowledge must necessarily develop this notion: "I shall undertake this form of worship; I shall join this religious order; I shall select this or that work. And so I shall serve God. There is no doubt that God will regard and accept these works and will grant me eternal life for them. For He is merciful and kind, granting every good even to those who are unworthy and ungrateful; much more will He grant me His grace and eternal life for so many great deeds and merits!" This is the height of wisdom, righteousness, and religion about which reason is able to judge; it is common to all the heathen, the papists, the Jews, the Mohammedans, and the sectarians. They cannot rise higher than that Pharisee in Luke (18:11-12). They do not know the righteousness of faith or Christian righteousness. The unspiritual man does not understand the things that belong to God (1 Cor. 2:14); also "no one understands, no one seeks God" (Rom. 3:11). Therefore there is no difference at all between a papist, a Jew, a Turk, or a sectarian. Their persons, locations, rituals, religions, works, and forms of worship are, of course, diverse; but they all have the same reason, the same heart, the same opinion and idea. The Turk thinks the very same as the Carthusian, namely, "If I do this or that, I have a God who is favorably disposed toward me; if I do not, I have a God who is wrathful." There is no middle ground between human working and the knowledge of Christ; if this knowledge is obscured, it does not matter whether you become a monk or a heathen afterwards.

Therefore it is completely insane when the papists and the Turks do battle against each other about religion and the worship of God; each contends that he has the true religion and worship of God. In fact, even the monks are not in agreement among themselves; one wants to be regarded as holier than another merely because of some foolish outward ceremonies, when in their hearts the opinions of them all are more alike than eggs. For this is what they all think: "If I do this work, God will have mercy on me; if I do not, He will be wrathful." Therefore every man who falls away from the knowledge of Christ necessarily rushes into idolatry; for he must invent a form for God that does not exist anywhere, as the Carthusian trusts that because of his observance of his monastic rule, and the Turk that because of his observance of the Koran, he pleases God and will receive from Him the reward for his labor.

A God of this kind, who forgives sins and justifies in this manner, cannot be found anywhere. Therefore it is all a vain imagination and a dream, the invention of an idol in the heart. For nowhere has God promised that He intends to justify men and save them on account of religious orders, observances, and forms of worship that have been thought up and established by men. In fact, as all Scripture attests, nothing is more abominable to God than such self-chosen works and forms of worship; He even overthrows kingdoms and empires on account of such things. Therefore all those who trust in their own ability and righteousness are serving a god who by nature is no god but is a god only in their opinion. For He who is true God by nature speaks this way: "I am not pleased with any righteousness, wisdom, or religious observance except the one by which the Father is glorified through the Son. Whoever takes hold of this Son and of Me or of My promise in Him through faith — to him I am God, to him I am Father; him I accept, justify, and save. All the rest remain under wrath, because they worship him who by nature is no god."

Whoever defects from this doctrine will necessarily fall into an ignorance of God and an ignorance of the righteousness, wisdom, and proper worship of God. He will be an idolater, remaining under the Law, sin, death, and the rule of the devil; and everything he does will be lost and condemned. Therefore when an Anabaptist imagines that he is pleasing to God if he is rebaptized; if he forsakes his house, wife, and children; if he mortifies his flesh; and if he endures many discomforts or even death itself, there is not even a tiny bit of the knowledge of Christ in him. Having excluded Christ, he is the captive of his own dreams about works, about forsaking everything, and about self-mortification. In spirit or in heart he is no different from a Turk, a Jew, or a papist, except so far as the outward appearance, ritual, or work that he chooses for himself is concerned. Thus all the monks have the same trust in works, even though they differ so far as their garb and other externals are concerned.

Thus there are many others today who want to be counted as evangelical theologians and who, so far as their words are concerned, do teach that men are delivered from their sins by the death of Christ. Meanwhile, however, they insult Christ most grievously by distorting and overthrowing His Word in a villainous and wicked manner. In addition, they teach faith in a way that attributes more to love than to faith; for they imagine that God regards and accepts us on account of the love with which we love God and our neighbor after we have already been reconciled. If this is true, then we have no need whatever of Christ. In this way they serve, not the true God but an idol of their own heart — an idol which they have made up for themselves. For the true God does not regard or accept us on account of our love, virtue, or newness of life (Rom. 6:4); He does so on account of Christ. But they raise the objection: "Yet He commands that we love Him with all our heart." All right, but it does not follow: "God has commanded; therefore we do so." If we loved God with all our heart, etc., then, of course, we would be justified and would live on account of that obedience, according to the statement (Lev. 18:5): "By doing this a man shall live." But the Gospel says: "You are not doing this; therefore you shall not live on account of it." For the statement, "You shall love the Lord," requires perfect obedience, perfect fear, trust, and love toward God. In the corruption of their nature men neither do nor can produce this. Therefore the Law, "You shall love the Lord," does not justify but accuses and damns all men, in accordance with the statement (Rom. 4:15): "The Law brings wrath." But "Christ is the end of the Law, that everyone who has faith may be justified" (Rom. 10:4).

Thus a Jew who observes the Law with the intention of making himself pleasing to God through this obedience is not worshiping the God of his fathers; on the contrary, he is an idolater, adoring a dream and an idol of his own heart that does not exist anywhere. For the God of his fathers, whom he claims to be worshiping, promised

Abraham an Offspring who was to bless all nations. Thus God is known and the blessing is granted, not through the Law but through the Gospel of Christ.

"Formerly, when you did not know God, you were in bondage" — although Paul addresses these words, strictly speaking, to the Galatians, who were Gentiles, nevertheless with the same words he reprimands the Jews; for although they rejected idols outwardly, inwardly they adored them even more than the Gentiles did, as he says of them in Rom. 2:22: "You who abhor idols, do you commit sacrilege?" The Gentiles were not the people of God, and they did not have the Word; therefore their idolatry was overt. But the Jews who were idolaters embellished their wicked worship with the name and the Word of God, as all the self-righteous usually do; and with this appearance of piety they impressed many people. Therefore the saintlier and the more spiritual the idolatry is in appearance, the more damage it does.

But how can these two contradictory statements that Paul makes be harmonized: "You did not know God" and "You worshiped God"? I reply: By nature all men have the general knowledge that there is a God, according to the statement in Rom. 1:19-20: "To the extent that God can be known, He is known to them. For His invisible nature, etc." Besides, the forms of worship and the religions that have been and remained among all nations are abundant evidence that at some time all men have had a general knowledge of God. Whether this was on the basis of nature or from the tradition of their parents, I am not discussing at the moment.[26]

But here again someone may raise the objection: "If all men know God, why does Paul say that before the proclamation of the Gospel the Galatians did not know God?" I reply: There is a twofold knowledge of God: the general and the particular. All men have the general knowledge, namely, that God is, that He has created heaven and earth, that He is just, that He punishes the wicked, etc. But what God thinks of us, what He wants to give and to do to deliver us from sin and death and to save us — which is the particular and the true knowledge of God — this men do not know. Thus it can happen that someone's face may be familiar to me but I do not really know him, because I do not know what he has in his mind. So it is that men know naturally that there is a God, but they do

---

[26] Luther had occasion to ponder this question again in his exposition of Genesis; see, for example, *Luther's Works*, 2, pp. 211—212.

not know what He wants and what He does not want. For it is written (Rom. 3:11): "No one understands God"; and elsewhere (John 1:18): "No one has ever seen God," that is, no one knows what the will of God is. Now what good does it do you to know that God exists if you do not know what His will is toward you? Here different people imagine different things. The Jews imagine that it is the will of God that they should worship God according to the commandment of the Law of Moses; the Turks, that they should observe the Koran; the monk, that he should do what he has learned to do. But all of them are deceived and, as Paul says in Rom. 1:21, "become futile in their thinking"; not knowing what is pleasing to God and what is displeasing to Him, they adore the imaginations of their own heart as though these were true God by nature, when by nature these are nothing at all.

Paul indicates this when he says: "When you did not know God, that is, when you did not know what the will of God is, you were in bondage to beings that by nature are no gods; that is, you were in bondage to the dreams and imaginations of your own hearts, by which you made up the idea that God is to be worshiped with this or that ritual." From the acceptance of this major premise, "There is a God," there came all the idolatry of men, which would have been unknown in the world without the knowledge of the Deity. But because men had this natural knowledge about God, they conceived vain and wicked thoughts about God apart from and contrary to the Word; they embraced these as the very truth, and on the basis of these they imagined God otherwise than He is by nature. Thus a monk imagines a God who forgives sins and grants grace and eternal life because of the observance of his rule. That God does not exist anywhere. Therefore the monk neither serves nor worships the true God; he serves and worships one who by nature is no god, namely, a figment and idol of his own heart, his own false and empty notion about God, which he supposes to be the surest truth. But even reason itself is obliged to admit that a human opinion is not God. Therefore whoever wants to worship God or serve Him without the Word is serving, not the true God but, as Paul says, "one who by nature is no god."

Therefore it does not make much difference whether you call the "elements" here the Law of Moses or some of the traditions of the Gentiles, even though Paul is speaking specifically and chiefly about the "elements" of Moses. For someone who falls away from grace into the Law is no better off in his fall than someone apart from grace who falls into idolatry. Apart from Christ there is nothing but sheer idolatry, an idol and a false fiction about God, whether it is called the Law of Moses or the law of the pope or the Koran of the Turk. And so he says with a certain wonder:

9. *But now that you have come to know God.*

It is as though he were saying: "It really strikes me as amazing that you who know God on the basis of the proclamation of faith now fall away so suddenly from the true knowledge of the will of God. For I thought that you held to this knowledge with such certainty and firmness that I had almost no fear that you would be overthrown with such ease. Yet now, because of the agitation of the false apostles, you have been turned back again to the weak and beggarly elements, whose slaves you want to be once more. But on the basis of my proclamation you came to regard it as the will of God that He wants to bless all nations, not through circumcision or the observance of the Law but through the Christ promised to Abraham. Those who believe in Him are blessed with Abraham, who had faith (Gal. 3:9); they are sons and heirs of God. This, I say, is how you came to know God."

Or rather to be known by God.

This is a rhetorical correction.[27] Paul corrects his first sentence ("now that you have come to know God") or rather inverts it this way: "or rather to be known by God." For he was afraid that they might lose God altogether. It is as though he were saying: "Alas, the situation has now come to the point that you do not even know God correctly, because you are returning from grace to the Law. Nevertheless, God still knows you." As a matter of fact, our knowing is more passive than active; that is, it is more a matter of being known than of knowing. Our "activity" is to permit God to do His work in us; He gives the Word, and when we take hold of this by the faith that God gives, we are born as sons of God. Therefore the statement, "You have come to be known by God," means "You have been visited by the Word; you have been granted faith and the Holy Spirit, by whom you have been renewed." Therefore even with the words "You have come to be known by God" he is disparaging the righteousness of the Law and denying that we obtain

---

[27] The Latin term is *castigatio rethorica.*

a knowledge of God because of the worthiness of our works. "For no one knows the Father except the Son and anyone to whom the Son chooses to reveal Him" (Matt. 11:27). And again (Is. 53:11): "By His knowledge shall He make many to be accounted righteous, for He shall bear their iniquities." Therefore our knowledge about God is purely passive.

Thus Paul is deeply amazed that those who already know God through the Gospel have been seduced by the false apostles and turn back again so quickly to the weak and beggarly elements. In the same way I would regard it as surprising if our church — which has, by the grace of God, been beautifully established in pure doctrine and sound faith — were to be subverted by some sermon or other from a fanatic and thus were to refuse to acknowledge me as its teacher any longer. And this is what will happen someday — if not during our lifetime, then after we have died. Then many who want to be masters will arise; under the pretext of piety they will teach perverse doctrines, and in a short while they will subvert everything that we have built up over a long period of time and with great effort. We are no better than the apostles, who during their lifetimes witnessed the doleful sight of the overthrow of the churches that they had planted by their ministry. Therefore it is not surprising if we are forced to witness the same evil today in the churches where the sectarians are in control; and after we are dead, they will take over other churches as well and will infect and overthrow them with their poison. Nevertheless, Christ will continue to reign to the end of the world, but in a wondrous way, as He did under the papacy.

Now Paul speaks very insultingly about the Law when he calls it "elements," as he did earlier, at the beginning of the fourth chapter (v. 3), and not simply "elements" but "weak and beggarly elements." Is it not blasphemy to use such names for the Law of God? In its proper use the Law ought to support the promises and grace. If it conflicts with these, it is no longer the holy Law of God; then it is a false and diabolical doctrine that only produces despair, and therefore must be repudiated and excommunicated. When he calls the Law "weak and beggarly elements," therefore, he is speaking of the Law as it is used by proud and presumptuous hypocrites, who seek to be justified through it, not of the Law understood spiritually, which effects wrath. For in its proper use, as we have said so often, the Law restrains the wicked but terrifies and humbles the proud. On this score it is not only a powerful and rich element but omnipotent and extremely wealthy, in fact, an invincible omnipotence and wealth. For if you were to compare the Law with the conscience, then it is the conscience that is "weak and beggarly," while the Law is extremely powerful and rich, having more power and riches than all of heaven and earth could contain; therefore even one iota or dot (Matt. 5:18) of the Law could kill the whole human race, as the history of the giving of the Law in Ex. 19 and 20 testifies. So delicate a thing is the conscience that it trembles and turns pale even for a very minor sin. Now this is the true and theological use of the Law, but Paul is not discussing that here.

But Paul is discussing the hypocrites who abuse the Law, that is, who have fallen away from grace or who have not yet come to grace and strive for justification through the Law, straining and wearying themselves day and night in the works of the Law. Thus Paul testifies of the Jews in Rom. 10:2-3: "I bear them witness that they have a zeal for God, that they labor day and night. But this is not enlightened, for they are ignorant of the righteousness that comes from God." Such people are confident that they can be so strengthened and enriched by the Law that they will be able to set their own strength and riches of righteousness, which they have from the Law, against the wrath and judgment of God, and that thus they will be able to appease God and be saved. It is in this connection that you would be right in calling the Law "weak and beggarly elements," that is, something that cannot help and has neither aid nor counsel.

Anyone who wanted to grow rhetorical here could develop these words further actively, passively, and neutrally.[28] Actively: the Law is a weak and beggarly element because it makes men weaker and more beggarly. Passively: because it does not have of itself the power and ability to grant or confer righteousness. And neutrally: of itself it is weakness and poverty, which afflict and trouble the weak and the poor more and more all the time. Trying to be justified through the Law, therefore, is as though someone who is already weak and sick were to ask for some even greater trouble that would kill him completely but meanwhile were to say that he intends to cure his disease by this very means; or as though someone suffering from epilepsy were to catch the plague in addition; or as though a leper were to come to another leper, or a beggar

[28] Cf. Cicero, Orator, 46, 155.

to another beggar, with the aim of giving him assistance and making him rich. As the proverb says, one of these is milking a billy goat and the other is holding the sieve! [29]

This is a lovely depreciation,[30] by which Paul wants to indicate that those who seek to be justified through the Law receive the benefit of becoming weaker and more beggarly day by day. On their own they are already weak and beggarly, that is, they are "by nature children of wrath" (Eph. 2:3), sentenced to death and to eternal damnation; and now they take hold of something that is sheer weakness and beggarhood in order to become strong and rich. Therefore everyone who falls away from the promise to the Law, from faith to works, is doing nothing but imposing an unbearable yoke upon himself in his weak and beggarly condition (Acts 15:10). By doing this he becomes ten times as weak and beggarly, until he finally despairs, unless Christ comes and sets him free.

The same thing is shown by the Gospel story (Mark 5:25-26) about the woman who had suffered from a flow of blood for twelve years and had suffered much under many physicians, on whom she had spent all that she had; but she could not be cured by them but grew worse with longer care. Therefore those who perform the works of the Law with the intention of being justified through them not only do not become righteous but become twice as unrighteous; that is, as I have said, through the Law they become weaker, more beggarly, and incapable of any good work. I have experienced this both in myself and in many others. Under the papacy I saw many of the monks who performed many great works with burning zeal in order to acquire righteousness and salvation; and yet there was nobody in the world more impatient, weaker, and more miserable than they, and nothing more unbelieving, fearful, and desperate than they. Political officials, who were involved in the most important and difficult issues, were not as impatient and as womanishly weak, or as superstitious, unbelieving, and fearful as such self-righteous men.

Therefore anyone who seeks righteousness through the Law does nothing by his repeated actions but acquire the habit [31] of this

---

[29] From a German proverb corresponding to the "moron jokes" of twentieth-century America.

[30] Cf. p. 362, note 5.

[31] Luther uses the Greek word ἕξις here, from Aristotle, *Nicomachean Ethics*, Book I, ch. 8.

first action, which is that God in His wrath and awe is to be appeased by works. On the basis of this opinion he begins to do works. Yet he can never find enough works to make his conscience peaceful; but he keeps looking for more, and even in the ones he does perform he finds sin. Therefore his conscience can never become sure, but he must continually doubt and think this way: "You have not sacrificed correctly; you have not prayed correctly; you have omitted something; you have committed this or that sin." Then the heart trembles and continually finds itself loaded down with wagonloads of sins that increase infinitely, so that it deviates further and further from righteousness, until finally it acquires the habit of despair. Many who have been driven to such despair cried out miserably in the agony of death: "Miserable man that I am! I have not observed the rules of my monastic order. Where shall I flee from the countenance of Christ, the wrathful Judge? If only I had been a swineherd or the most ordinary of men!" Thus at the end of his life a monk is weaker, more beggarly, more unbelieving, and more fearful than he was at the beginning, when he joined the order. The reason is that he endeavored to strengthen himself by means of weakness and to enrich himself by means of poverty. The Law or human traditions or the rule of his monastic order were supposed to heal and enrich him in his illness and poverty, but he became weaker and more beggarly than the tax collectors and harlots. For such people do not have that miserable habit of works on which to depend but are extremely aware of their sins and yet can say with the tax collector (Luke 18:13): "God, be merciful to me a sinner!" On the other hand, a monk who has been trained in the weak and beggarly elements has acquired this habit: "If you observe the monastic rule, you will be saved." He has been so crazed and captivated by this false idea that on account of it he is incapable of grasping grace or even of remembering grace. Therefore neither past nor present works are enough for him, regardless of their quantity and quality; but he continually looks at and looks for ever-different ones, by which he attempts to appease the wrath of God and to justify himself, until in the end he is forced to despair. Therefore he who falls away from faith and follows the Law is like the dog in Aesop, which snapped at the shadow and lost the meat.[32]

Therefore it is impossible for men who want to provide for

[32] A favorite fable of Luther's; cf. *Luther's Works*, 13, p. 396.

their salvation through the Law, as all men are inclined to do by nature, ever to be set at peace. In fact, they only pile laws upon laws, by which they torture themselves and others and make their consciences so miserable that many of them die before their time because of excessive anguish of heart. For one law always produces ten more, until they grow into infinity. This is shown by the innumerable *Summae* that collect and expound such laws, and especially by that diabolical one entitled "the Angelic." [33]

In other words, anyone who strives to be justified by the Law is trying something that he can never achieve. Here one can apply, as I see that the fathers did, the sayings of learned and wise men about a useless work, such as "rolling a rock" or "dipping water with a sieve." [34] I think that by such tales and parables the fathers wanted to commend to their pupils the distinction between the Law and the Gospel, to indicate that those who forsake grace may indeed tire and wear themselves out with difficult and troublesome labor, but that they accomplish a useless work. Therefore such men are correctly said to be "rolling a rock," that is, to be sweating foolishly, as the poets tell about Sisyphus: each time he rolled the rock from the bottom of the mountain to the top, it would roll right back again. [35] And "dipping water with a sieve" means wearing oneself out with an inexhaustible and a useless labor; thus the poets tell that the daughters of Danaus in the underworld carried water in cracked jars to a container with a hole in it. [36]

I wish that you students of Sacred Scripture would equip yourselves with such parables, in order to retain the distinction between Law and Gospel better, namely, that trying to be justified by the Law is like counting money out of an empty purse, eating and drinking from an empty dish and cup, looking for strength and riches where there is nothing but weakness and poverty, laying a burden upon someone who is already oppressed to the point of

[33] The *Summa angelica* is not, as the Weimar editors suggest, the *Summa* of Thomas Aquinas, despite his title *Doctor angelicus,* but the *Summa de casibus conscientiae* of Angelo Carletti di Chivasso (1411—95); cf. *Luther's Works,* 2, p. 314, note 83.

[34] This saying, which Luther cites as *cribro aquam haurire* (apparently because of the myth of the Danaides [see note 36 below]), was originally *imbrem in cribrum gerere,* as, for example, in Plautus, *Pseudolus,* I, 1, 100.

[35] On Sisyphus cf. Homer, *Odyssey,* XI, 593 ff.

[36] See Horace, *Carmina,* III, XI, 23 ff.

collapse, trying to spend a hundred gold pieces and not having even a pittance, taking clothing away from a naked man, imposing even greater weakness and poverty upon someone who is sick and needy, etc.

Now who would ever have believed that the Galatians, who had learned a pure and sure doctrine from this great apostle and teacher, could be led away from it so suddenly and be completely overthrown by the false apostles? It is not without reason that I remind you so often how easy apostasy from the truth of the Gospel is, for even devout people do not consider enough how precious and how necessary a treasure the true knowledge of Christ is. Therefore they do not work with as much care and diligence as they should to attain and keep it sure and firm. Besides, a majority of those who hear the Word are not disciplined by a cross; and they do not struggle with sin, death, and the devil. But they live smugly without any conflict. Because such people are not armed with the Word of God against the wiles of the devil, they are not disciplined or put to the test by temptations; therefore they never experience the application and the power of the Word either. To be sure, they follow present-day theologians and are persuaded by their words that they believe correctly in the matter of justification; but when these have departed, and when wolves come in sheep's clothing (Matt. 7:15), the same thing will happen to these men that happened to the Galatians, namely, they will be seduced and overthrown quickly and easily.

Now Paul has his own peculiar phraseology, which the rest of the apostles did not use. For none of them except Paul gave such names to the Law, calling it a "weak and beggarly element," that is, worse than useless for justification. And if Paul had not done it first, I would not have dared use such a name for the Law but would have regarded it as the height of blasphemy. But I have spoken about this at length earlier, pointing out to what extent the Law is weak and beggarly and to what extent it is very powerful and rich.

If the Law of God is weak and useless for justification, much more are the laws of the pope weak and useless for justification. I do not intend to reject and condemn his laws altogether; for I say that many of them are useful for external discipline, to keep everything orderly in the churches and to prevent quarrels and hatred, just as the imperial laws are useful for the administration of the commonwealth. But the pope is not content with this commendation and application of his laws, but he demands that we believe that we are justified and receive salvation by their observance. This we deny. And with the same confidence and assurance with which Paul spoke out against the Law of God we declare — in opposition to the decrees, traditions, and laws of the pope — that they are not only weak, beggarly, and useless elements so far as righteousness is concerned but also damnable, accursed, and demonic; for they blaspheme grace, overthrow the Gospel, destroy faith, and abolish Christ.

To the extent that the pope requires the observance of these laws for salvation, he is Antichrist and the vicar of Satan. And all those who support him and accept these abominations and blasphemies of his, or observe them with the intention of meriting the forgiveness of sins through them, are slaves of Antichrist and of the devil. Now for many centuries the entire papal church has been teaching and observing these things as something necessary for salvation. Hence the pope "takes his seat in the temple of God, proclaiming himself to be God; he opposes and exalts himself against every so-called god or object of worship" (2 Thess. 2:4). For men have feared and revered the laws and ordinances of the pope more than the Word and the ordinances of God. Therefore he became lord of heaven, earth, and hell; and he wore a triple crown.[37] Therefore the cardinals and bishops, his creatures, became the kings and princes of the world. And so, if he did not burden consciences with his laws, he would not retain his tremendous power, eminence, and wealth for long; but his whole kingdom would quickly come to ruin.

The topic that Paul is treating here is extremely important and worthy of the most careful consideration, namely, that falling away from the grace of God is the same as losing all knowledge of the truth. Therefore those who fall away from grace do not know their own sin or the Law they follow or themselves or anything else at all. They want to be teachers of the Law, Paul says, but they do not understand what they are saying or what they are saying it about. For without the knowledge of grace, that is, of

---

[37] The tiara had originally been a double crown, presumably to symbolize the sovereignty of the pope over both church and state; but in the fifteenth century it became a triple crown, and this was taken to symbolize his control (cf. Matt. 16:19) over earth, heaven, and hell (or, more technically, purgatory).

the Gospel of Christ, it is impossible for a man to think that the Law is a weak and beggarly element, useless for righteousness. In fact, he supposes the very opposite about the Law, namely, not only that it is necessary for salvation, but that it strengthens the weak and enriches the beggarly, that is, that those who keep it merit righteousness and eternal salvation. If this opinion stands, the promise of God is denied and Christ is removed, while lies, wickedness, and idolatry are established. The pope, along with all his bishops, schools, and his entire synagog, has taught that his laws are necessary for righteousness. Thus he was a teacher of weak and beggarly elements, by which he made the church of Christ all over the world very ill and very poor; that is, by obscuring Christ and by covering over and burying His Gospel he has burdened and miserably afflicted the church with his wicked laws. And so if you want to observe the laws of the pope without any offense to conscience, you should observe them without any presumption of righteousness; for this is granted through Christ alone.

Whose slaves you want to be once more?

Paul adds this to show that he is speaking about those who are proud and presumptuous, as I have already shown earlier. For elsewhere he calls the Law holy, good, etc. For example, in 1 Tim. 1:8: "We know that the Law is good, if anyone uses it lawfully," that is, politically, for restraining the wicked; and theologically, for terrifying and bruising the proud. But anyone who uses the Law to obtain righteousness in the sight of God does not know what he is saying or what he is saying it about; and he makes the good Law dangerous and damnable for him.

Therefore Paul denounces the Galatians for wanting to be slaves once more, and he condemns their slavery. For if someone wants to be a slave to the Law, then the Law becomes weakness and beggardom for him who is already weak and beggarly. Then two sick beggars get together, neither of whom is in a position to help the other. One strong man can support ten weak men, but this does not mean that ten weak men can support one strong man. A patient man can uphold many men, indeed an entire kingdom; an impatient man cannot uphold even one man. Being strong men, we would be very glad to support the Law, but in its power and richness, that is, to the extent that it has dominion over the body. In this sense, I say, we would be willing to observe all the laws promulgated by the pope and the jurists; for then we would be serving the laws only according to our body and its members, not according to our conscience. But the pope demands that his laws be observed with this idea in mind: "If you keep them, you are righteous; if you do not, you are damned." Then the Law is a weak and beggarly element. And where there is such enslavement of the conscience, there cannot be anything but weakness and beggardom. Therefore the whole emphasis is on the word "to be slaves." Paul is emphasizing it so that the conscience may not be a slave, captive to the Law, but may be free, not the slave of the Law but its master; for the Law is dead to it and it to the Law, as was said at great length in chapter two above (v. 19).

10. *You observe days, and months, and seasons, and years!*

With these words Paul shows clearly what the false apostles were teaching, namely, the observance of days, months, seasons, and years. Nearly all the theologians interpret this passage to refer to the astrological days of the Chaldeans: The Gentiles observed certain set days and months for carrying on their affairs and predicting the events of their lives, and the Galatians were doing the same thing at the prompting of the false apostles.[38] Augustine, whom the later interpreters followed, expounded these words of Paul as a reference to that Gentile practice, although later on he also interprets them as a reference to the days, months, etc., of the Jews.[39] There is a discussion of this rather troublesome problem in the *Decrees*.[40]

But Paul is instructing the conscience. Therefore he is speaking, not about the Gentile practice of observing days, etc., something that pertains only to the body, but about the Law of God and the observance of days, months, etc., according to the Law of Moses. In other words, he is speaking about religious days, months, and seasons, which the Galatians were observing, on the basis of instruction by the false apostles, as a means of obtaining justification. For Moses had commanded the Jews to observe religiously the

[38] On Luther's attitude toward astrology see also *Luther's Works*, 1, pp. 44 to 45.

[39] Augustine, *Expositio Epistolae ad Galatas*, 34, *Patrologia, Series Latina*, XXXV, 2129.

[40] Various opinions from Augustine, Jerome, and other sources are compiled in Thomas Aquinas, *Summa Theologica*, I—II, Q. 103, Art. 4.

Sabbath, the new moon, the first and the seventh month, three set seasons or festivals — namely, Passover, the Feast of Weeks, and the Feast of Booths — the Sabbatical Year, and the Year of Jubilee.[41] Now the Galatians had been forced by the false apostles to observe these same rites as something necessary for righteousness. This is why he says that they have lost grace and Christian liberty, and have turned back to the slavery of the weak and beggarly elements. They had been persuaded by the false apostles that these laws had to be observed; that when they were observed, they granted righteousness; but that when they were neglected, they brought damnation. But Paul does not permit consciences to be bound by the Mosaic Law in any way, but everywhere he sets them free from the Law. "Now I, Paul," he says later on, in chapter five (v. 2), "say to you that if you receive circumcision, Christ will be of no advantage to you." In Col. 2:16 he says: "Let no one pass judgment on you in questions of food and drink or with regard to a festival or a new moon or a Sabbath." Thus Christ says (Luke 17:20): "The kingdom of God does not come by observance." Much less should consciences be burdened and ensnared by human traditions.

Here someone may say: "If the Galatians sinned in observing days and seasons, why is it not sinful for you to do the same?" I reply: We observe the Lord's Day, Christmas, Easter, and similar holidays in a way that is completely free. We do not burden consciences with these observances; nor do we teach, as did the false apostles and as do the papists, that they are necessary for justification or that we can make satisfaction for our sins through them. But their purpose is that everything be done in the church in an orderly way and without confusion, so that external harmony may not be disturbed; for in the spirit we have another kind of harmony. Thus it happened once that Victor, the Roman pontiff, excommunicated all the churches of Asia for no other reason than that they celebrated Easter at another time than the Church of Rome observed it. Irenaeus rebukes this action of Victor's, and it was surely worthy of rebuke.[42] For it was the utmost madness to hand the churches of the East over to the devil on account of such a trifle. Therefore this knowledge about the observance of

---

[41] Of these observances the new moon is not explicitly prescribed in the Law of Moses, though it appears to be presupposed in passages like Num. 28:1-10. On the three set seasons cf. Lev. 23.

[42] Cf. Eusebius, *Ecclesiastical History,* Book V, chs. 23—24.

days and seasons was rare, even among great men. Jerome did not have it, and Augustine would not have understood it if he had not been troubled and provoked by the Pelagians.[43]

Most of all, however, we observe such holidays to preserve the ministry of the Word, so that the people may gather on certain days and at certain seasons to hear the Word, to learn to know God, to have Communion, to pray together for every need, and to thank God for His spiritual and temporal blessings. And I believe that this was the chief reason why the fathers instituted the Lord's Day, Easter, Pentecost, etc.

11. *I am afraid I have labored over you in vain.*

With these words Paul testifies that he was deeply troubled by the fall of the Galatians. He would like to scold them more severely, but he is afraid that too severe a scolding would not correct them but would irritate them even more and alienate them from him. As he writes, therefore, he changes and softens his words and transfers practically all the blame to himself, saying: "I am afraid I have labored over you in vain." That is: "It distresses me that I have preached the Gospel among you with such great care and faithfulness, but without results." Therefore he handles them with extreme gentleness and with true fatherly care; at the same time he rebukes them quite sharply, but implicitly. For when he says that he has labored in vain, that is, that he has preached the Gospel among them without results, he is implying either that they are stubbornly unbelieving or that they have fallen away from the teaching of faith. In either case, whether they were unbelieving or have fallen away from the teaching of faith, they are still sinners, wicked, unrighteous, and damned; as such, it is vain for them to obey the Law or to observe days, months, etc. This is a kind of implicit excommunication, because by these words he indicates that they are separated from Christ unless they return to the sound teaching. Nevertheless, he does not pass sentence explicitly. For he felt that he would accomplish nothing by scolding them more harshly; therefore he mutes his pen and addresses them very sweetly, saying:

12. *Become as I am, for I also have become as you are.*

This passage is not intended for instruction but is filled with feelings which should be expressed by rhetoric. Thus far Paul has been

[43] Cf. p. 313, note 102.

instructing them; and in the course of the instruction he has been prompted by his great indignation about things to lose his temper over the Galatians and to denounce them with rather harsh words, calling them foolish, bewitched, unbelievers of the truth, crucifiers of Christ, etc. Now that he has completed the more forceful part of his epistle, he begins to feel that he has handled the Galatians too severely. Being concerned that by his harshness he may have done more harm than good, he tells them that this severe rebuke proceeded from a fatherly and truly apostolic spirit. He becomes amazingly rhetorical and overflows with sweet and gentle words, so that if he had offended anyone with his sharp denunciation, as he had undoubtedly offended many, the gentleness of his language would set things right again.

He also teaches by his example that pastors and bishops should take a fatherly and motherly attitude, not toward the ravenous wolves (Matt. 7:15) but toward the miserable, misled, and erring sheep, patiently bearing their weakness and fall and handling them with the utmost gentleness. Nor can they be called back to the right way by any other means, for a more severe rebuke is more likely to anger them than to bring them back to their senses.

And let me add this admonition in passing: It is the nature and the result of sound doctrine that when it is taught and learned well, it unites the minds of men in supreme harmony. But where men neglect the faithful doctrine and embrace errors, that harmony of mind is disrupted. As soon as brethren or pupils are deceived by fanatical spirits and fall away from the doctrine of justification, they immediately begin to persecute the pious with bitter hatred, even though previously they loved them dearly.

We are experiencing this today in our false brethren, the Sacramentarians and the Anabaptists. When the evangelical cause was just beginning, they enjoyed listening to us or at least reading our writings; they recognized the gift of the Holy Spirit in us, and they revered us on account of it. Some of them even lived as part of our family and behaved very modestly in our midst. But when they left us and were subverted by the fanatical spirits, no one was more hostile to our doctrine and to our name than they. They hate the papists too, but not as viciously as they hate us. Therefore I often wonder greatly how such a bitter and vicious hatred could have come so suddenly into the hearts of those who had embraced us with such love. For we did not offend them even in the slightest way; nor did we give them a reason for persecuting us with such hatred. In fact, they are obliged to admit that our principal aim was to illumine the blessing and the glory of Christ and to teach the truth of the Gospel purely, now that God has revealed it through us to an ungrateful world in these last days. Then why do they hate us so bitterly? There is no other reason than that they have been listening to new teachers. Infected by their poison, they are so inflamed against us that they fume and rage with an implacable hatred.

But it appears to me that this is the fate of the apostles and of all faithful teachers, as the apostles testify in all their epistles that their disciples and hearers rewarded them by becoming infected with the wicked opinions of fanatics and turning against them. There were a few among the Galatians who remained constant in the doctrine of Paul. All the others, being misled by the false apostles, no longer acknowledged Paul as their teacher; in fact, nothing was more loathsome to them than the name and the teaching of Paul. And I am afraid that he did not succeed in calling very many of them back with this writing. If a similar situation were to befall us — that is, if in our absence our church were to be overthrown by fanatics and we were to write, not one but many epistles to this place — we would accomplish little or nothing. Except for a few of the firmer ones our followers would treat us no differently from the way we are being treated today by those who have been misled by the sectarians; they would sooner worship the pope than heed our warnings or approve our doctrine. No one will persuade them that, having lost Christ, they are now once more in bondage to the weak and beggarly elements and to beings that by nature are no gods. Nothing is more intolerable to them than to hear that their teachers are perverters of the Gospel of Christ and disturbers of consciences and churches. "The Lutherans," they say, "are the only ones who do not have any sense; who do not preach Christ; who do not have the Holy Spirit, the gift of prophecy, and the authentic interpretation of Scripture. Our theologians are not inferior to them in any way; in fact, in many respects they excel them, because they follow the Spirit and teach spiritual things. They, by contrast, have not yet attained to the true theology; but clinging to the letter, they teach nothing but the catechism, faith, love, and the like." [44]

Therefore, as I often say, a fall from faith is as grave as it is easy,

[44] See, for example, *Luther's Works*, 40, pp. 54 ff.

all the way from the heights of heaven to the depths of hell. It is not a human fall, like that into murder or adultery; it is a satanic fall. For those who fall this way cannot be easily healed; but if they persist stubbornly in their error, their last state becomes worse than the first. As Christ says (Luke 11:24-26), "when an unclean spirit that has been cast out of its house returns, it does not enter it alone but brings along seven other spirits more evil than itself, and they dwell there."

Therefore Paul was told by the Spirit to avoid doing more harm than good to the minds of the Galatians by his sharp rebuke and by his pious zeal in calling them foolish, etc. This was a danger especially because he knew that the false apostles were active among them, and that they would put the worst construction on this rebuke, which came from a fatherly concern, and would exclaim: "Now Paul, whom some of you praise so much, is betraying the real spirit in which he acts. In your presence he wanted to give the impression of being your father; but when he is absent, his letters show that he is a tyrant." Therefore he was so overwhelmed with a faithful concern and a fatherly anxiety that he simply did not know what or how to write to them. For it is extremely dangerous to plead your cause in writing with those who are far away when they have already begun to hate you and have been persuaded by others that your cause is not a good one. Therefore he says a little later in his consternation (Gal. 4:20): "I am perplexed about you"; that is, "I do not know what to do with you."

Become as I am, for I also have become as you are.

These words should not be understood as pertaining to doctrine, but they should by all means be understood as pertaining to attitudes. Therefore the meaning of this passage is not "Become as I am; that is, think about doctrine just as I do." No, it is "Take the same attitude toward me that I take toward you." It is as though he were saying: "Perhaps I have rebuked you too harshly. But forgive me my harshness. Do not judge my heart on the basis of my words, but judge my words on the basis of the attitude of my heart. My words seem hard, and the rod seems severe; but my heart is gentle and fatherly. Therefore, my Galatians, accept my rebuke in the sense in which it was intended. For the issue demanded that I give the appearance of being harsh with you."

Our rebukes are harsh too, and our pen is vigorous. But our heart is certainly not bitter or envious or vindictive against our opponents. On the contrary, there is in us a godly agitation and sorrow of spirit. I do not hate papists and other erring spirits in such a way that I invoke evil upon them or wish that they would perish. No, I would wish that they would return to the way and be saved together with us.

A teacher punishes his pupil, not to do him harm but to do him good. Of course, the rod is harsh; but the discipline is extremely necessary for the boy, and the intention of the punisher is friendly and sincere. Thus a father punishes his son, not to ruin him but to improve him. The whippings are harsh and painful for the boy, of course. "For the moment all discipline seems painful rather than pleasant; later it yields the peaceful fruit of righteousness to those who have been trained by it" (Heb. 12:11). But the father's attitude is upright and sincere. If he did not love his son, he would not punish him; he would send him away, despair of his being saved, and let him perish. When he punishes him, this is a sign of his fatherly feeling for his son and is for the son's own good. "You should regard my rebuke this way also. Then you will not judge it to be harsh; you will consider it beneficial. Take the same attitude toward me that I take toward you. I have a friendly heart toward you; I require the same of you."

Thus Paul speaks soothingly to the Galatians and emphasizes his soothing, in order to soften and heal the minds he had irritated with his bitter rebuke. Still he does not retract his rebuke. He admits that it was harsh and sharp; "but necessity," he says, "forced me to rebuke you quite harshly. I am softening my rebuke, however, by reminding you that it came from a very kind and gentle heart. A physician gives a sick man a very bitter medicine, not because he wants to harm the sick man, but because he wants to help him this way. Therefore if something bitter is given to the sick man, this should be blamed, not on the physician but on the medicine and on the sickness. You should think the same way about my harsh denunciation."

Brethren, I beseech you, you did me no wrong.

Is it "beseeching" according to Paul when he calls the Galatians bewitched, disobedient to the truth, and crucifiers of Christ? I would sooner call this an insult. But he interprets it, not as an insult but as beseeching; and in fact this is what it is, as though he were saying: "True, I have rebuked you a little harshly. But take it in the proper way. Then you will understand that my rebuke was not a rebuke but was a beseeching." Thus if a father whips his son, it is the same as though he were saying to him: "My son, I beseech you to behave yourself." It is a punishment in its appearance; but if you look at the father's heart, it is a gentle request.

You did me no wrong.

It is as though Paul were saying: "Why should I be angry with you or disparage you with a sorrow of spirit, since you have done me no wrong?" "Then why are you calling us perverters, deserters of your doctrine, insane, bewitched, etc.? This is abundant evidence that we have offended you." "No, you have not offended me; you have offended yourselves. Therefore I am as distressed as I am, not on my own account but on your account. Do not think, therefore, that my rebuke proceeds from an angry heart or from anger or from any other hurt. For I call God as my witness that you have done me no injury whatever but have in fact done many favors for me."

By soothing the Galatians this way Paul prepares their minds to bear the fatherly rebukes with filial feeling. This is like tempering absinthe or bitter medicine with honey and sugar to make it sweet again. Thus when parents have given their children a sound thrashing, they soothe them by offering them cookies, cakes, pears, apples, and such little presents, by which the children recognize that the parents meant it for their good, even though the punishment was severe.

13. *You know that it was because of weakness of the flesh that I preached the Gospel to you at first;*

14. *and though my condition was a trial to you, you did not scorn or despise me, but received me as an angel of God, as Christ Jesus.*

Paul is explaining what favors he had received from the Galatians. "The first favor," he says, "which I regard as the greatest of them all, was this: When I first began to preach the Gospel among you and did so because of weakness of the flesh and great trials, this cross of mine did not offend you. But you were so good, sweet, generous, and loving toward me that you not only were not offended by the weakness of my flesh, my trials, and my danger, which were almost the end of me, but you attended me with the greatest love and received me as an angel of God or even as Christ Jesus."

This is surely a great commendation of the Galatians, that they accepted the Gospel from a man as despised and afflicted as Paul was. He preached the Gospel among them despite the rage and fury of both Jews and Gentiles; for everyone who was powerful, wise, learned, or religious hated, persecuted, and spat upon Paul, stepped all over him and slandered him. The Galatians were not offended by any of this. Banishing the sight of his weakness, trial, and peril from their eyes, they not only listened to Paul in his need, shame, misery, and affliction, and acknowledged that they were his pupils; they even received him and listened to him as an angel of God, in fact, as Christ Jesus. This is outstanding praise and credit for the Galatians. Surely he did not give such praise to any of the others to whom he wrote as he gave here to the Galatians.

Jerome and certain other of the ancient fathers explain this weakness of the flesh in Paul as either a disease of the body or a temptation of sexual desire.[45] Those good fathers were living when the church was enjoying temporal success, free of any cross or persecution. At that time the bishops began to increase and prosper in wealth, public esteem, and glory in the world; and many of them tyrannized the people in their charge, as the history of the church testifies. Few of them did their duty, and those who wanted to give the appearance of doing it neglected the teaching of the Gospel and preached their own commandments. Now when knowledge, training, and the pure interpretation of the Word are not present among pastors and bishops, they cannot avoid being smug; for they are not being disciplined by the trials, the cross, and the persecutions that inevitably follow the pure preaching of the Word. Therefore it was impossible for Paul to find understanding among them. By the grace of God, however, we have the pure teaching of faith, which we also freely confess. Therefore we are compelled to bear the bitter hatred and persecution of the devil and the world. If we were not being disciplined by the power and the wiles of tyrants and heretics, as well as by terrors of heart and the flaming darts of Satan (Eph. 6:16), Paul would be as obscure and unknown to us as he was to the whole world in past centuries and still is today to our opponents, the papists and the fanatics. Therefore it is the gift of prophecy and our own effort, together with inward and outward trials, that opens to us the meaning of Paul and of all the Scriptures.

By "weakness of the flesh" Paul does not mean disease or sexual

[45] Jerome, *Commentarius in Epistolam S. Pauli ad Galatas*, II, *Patrologia, Series Latina*, XXVI, 406.

desire; he means the suffering or affliction that he bore in his body, as contrasted with strength or power. But lest we appear to be doing injury to these words, let us listen to Paul himself. In 2 Cor. 12:9-10 he says: "I will all the more gladly boast of my weaknesses, that the power of Christ may rest upon me. For the sake of Christ, then, I am content with weaknesses, insults, hardships, persecutions, and calamities; for when I am weak, then I am strong." And in chapter eleven (vv. 23-25) he writes: "With far greater labors, far more imprisonments, with countless beatings, and often near death. Five times I have received at the hands of the Jews the forty lashes less one. Three times I have been beaten with rods; once I was stoned. Three times I have been shipwrecked, etc." These sufferings, which he bore in his body, are what he calls "weakness of the flesh," not the poor health of his body. It is as though he were to say: "When I preached the Gospel among you, I was overwhelmed by various afflictions and troubles. From every side I was threatened by the plots and attacks of Jews, Gentiles, and false brethren. I was troubled by hunger and by a lack of everything. I was the κάθαρμα of the world and the περίψημα of all things (1 Cor. 4:13)." He mentions this weakness of his frequently, as in 1 Cor. 4; in 2 Cor. 4, 6, 11, 12; and elsewhere.

Therefore it is clear enough that Paul calls "weaknesses of the flesh" the afflictions that not only he but the other apostles suffered. Although they were weak in the flesh, they were strong in spirit; for the power of Christ dwelt in them, and it continually ruled and triumphed through them. Paul himself testifies to this in 2 Cor. 12:10 in the words: "When I am weak, then I am strong"; again (v. 9): "I will all the more gladly boast of my weaknesses, that the power of Christ may rest upon me"; and in chapter two (v. 14) he says: "Thanks be to God, who in Christ always leads us in triumph." It is as though he were saying: "Regardless of how cruelly the devil, the unbelieving Jews, and the heathen rage against us, we continue unconquered by all their insults. Whether they like it or not, our doctrine prevails and triumphs." Such was the power and courage of the spirit in the apostles, with which he here contrasts the weakness and slavery of their flesh.

This weakness of the flesh in the pious is extremely offensive to reason. Therefore Christ Himself says (Matt. 11:6): "Blessed is he who takes no offense at Me"; and Paul says in 1 Cor. 1:23: "We preach Christ crucified, a stumbling block to Jews and folly to Gentiles." Therefore it is something great that you acknowledge as Lord of all and Savior of the world One about whom you hear that He was the most miserable of all, the least of men, "scorned by men, and despised by the people" (Ps. 22:6) — in other words, despised by all and finally condemned to death on the cross by His own people, especially by those among them who were the best, the wisest, and the saintliest. It is, I say, something great not to be dissuaded by these huge offenses, to be able to despise all of them, and to make this Christ, who was shamefully spat upon, scourged, and crucified, more than the riches of all the wealthy, more than the power of all the mighty, more than the wisdom of all the learned, more than the crowns of all the kings, more than the religion of all the saintly.

Thus it was something great that the Galatians were not scandalized by the offensive weakness and ugly form of the cross which they saw in Paul but received him as an angel or as Christ Jesus. Just as Christ says that His disciples continued with Him in His trials (Luke 22:28), so Paul says that the Galatians did not despise the trial that he bore in his flesh. He has good reason to praise them as extravagantly as he does.

Now the apostles, and especially Paul, experienced not only the outward trials we have just discussed but also inward and spiritual ones, as Christ did in the garden. Such was the trial of which he complains in 2 Cor. 12:7, a σκόλοψ in the flesh, a messenger of Satan, to harass him. It is impossible for anyone afflicted with these profound trials to be troubled by sexual desire. I am reminding you of this in passing because the papists, upon seeing the Latin translation "stimulus in the flesh," interpreted it as the stimulus of sexual desire.[46] But the Greek word is σκόλοψ, which means a very sharp stake or thorn; therefore it was a spiritual trial. It does not matter that he adds the word "flesh," saying: "A thorn was given me in the flesh." He purposely calls it a thorn in the flesh; for the Galatians and others with whom Paul had contact often saw him moved by great sadness, trembling, terrified, and crushed by an unspeakable sorrow and grief.

Therefore the apostles had not only physical but also spiritual trials. Paul testifies to this about himself in 2 Cor. 7:5, where he speaks of "fighting without and fear within." In the last chapter of Acts (28:15) Luke says that after Paul had struggled for a long time in a stormy sea and was sad in spirit, he was restored and took courage upon seeing the brethren who came from Rome to meet him at the

[46] The Latin of 2 Cor. 12:7 has *stimulus carnis.*

Forum of Appius and Three Taverns. And in Phil. 2:27 he confesses that God had mercy on him when He cured Epaphroditus, who was ill and near to death, lest Paul should have sorrow upon sorrow. In addition to their outward physical trials, therefore, the apostles also suffered sorrow of the spirit.

But why does Paul say that the Galatians did not scorn him? Surely they did scorn him, for they defected from his Gospel! Paul expounds himself: "When I first preached the Gospel to you," he says, "you did not do what most other people did, who were so offended by my weakness and by the trials I had in my flesh that they scorned me and spat upon me." Human reason is easily offended by the ugly shape of the cross. It regards as insane those who try to comfort, help, and care for others, or who boast about their great riches, righteousness, power, and victory over sin, death, and every evil, and about their happiness, salvation, and eternal life — when meanwhile these same people are needy, weak, sorrowful, and despised, and are mistreated and killed as enemies of the state and of religion, not only by the rabble but by people of quality in both the political and the ecclesiastical realm. Whoever kills them thinks he is offering service to God (John 16:2). And so when they promise eternal blessings to others while they themselves are perishing so miserably in the sight of the world, they are ridiculed and forced to hear (Luke 4:23): "Physician, heal yourself!" This is the source of the complaints throughout the Psalms (Ps. 22:6, 11): "I am a worm, and no man. Be not far from me; for trouble is near, and there is none to help."

Therefore it is really a magnificent commendation of the Galatians that they were not offended by Paul's weakness and trial but received him as an angel of God, indeed as Christ Jesus. It is, of course, a great and outstanding virtue to listen to an apostle. But it is a greater virtue, and truly a heroic one,[47] to listen to one who was as miserable, weak, and contemptible as Paul here admits that he was among the Galatians, and to receive such a one as an angel from heaven or to hold him in such esteem as though he were Christ Jesus, without being offended by his great weakness and his cross. In these words, therefore, he greatly praises the virtue of the Galatians, saying that it will be with him forever and is so gratifying to him that he wants everyone to know about it.

Meanwhile, however, as he praises their kindness and goodness

[47] An echo of the phrase used in canonization proceedings, "a virtue more than heroic."

so extravagantly, he indicates by a gentle hint how much they had loved him before the false apostles came along; and at the same time he exhorts them to receive him as their apostle with the same love and reverence as before. From this it is quite evident that the false apostles seemed to have greater authority among the Galatians than Paul himself had. This prompted the Galatians to prefer them greatly to Paul, whom they had previously not only loved warmly but received as an angel of God.

15. *What has become of the blessedness you felt?*

It is as though Paul were to say: "How blessed you were thought to be! How praised and blessed you were then!" There is a similar expression in the canticle of Mary (Luke 1:48): "All generations will call me blessed," that is, will bless me. The words "What has become of the blessedness you felt?" are emphatic, as though he were to say: "You were not only blessed but altogether blessed and commended."

In this way Paul tries to temper and sweeten the bitter drink, that is, the sharp rebuke; for he is afraid that the Galatians can be offended by it, especially because he knows that the false apostles will slander it and put the worst construction on it. For it is the virtue and the nature of those vipers to impugn words that proceed from a godly and open heart, and to twist them around shrewdly and deceitfully into the very opposite meaning from that in which they were spoken. They are marvelous masters at this art, surpassing the genius and skill of all the orators. For they are driven by a wicked spirit which so deranges them that they are inflamed against godly people with a satanic poison and cannot interpret their words and writings in any other than a malicious way. They act just like spiders, which suck poison out of the finest and most beautiful flowers through no fault of the flowers but only of their own.[48] Therefore with his honeyed and soothing words he wants to prevent the false apostles from having an opportunity to slander him and twist his words in a captious way, as follows: "Paul is treating you in an inhuman manner, calling you insane, bewitched, and disobedient to the truth. This is a definite sign that he is not interested in your salvation but regards you as damned and rejected by Christ."

[48] This saying is traced to 1573 by Thomas Draxe, *Bibliotheca scholastica instructissima* (1633); but obviously it is much older, for Luther seems to be citing it in a proverbial form. Cf. H. L. Mencken (ed.), *A New Dictionary of Quotations* (New York, 1942), p. 92.

*For I bear you witness that, if possible, you would have plucked
out your eyes and given them to me.*

Paul is praising the Galatians beyond all measure. "Not only," he
says, "did you treat me with the utmost humanity and reverence,
receiving me as an angel of God; but if circumstances or necessity
had demanded, you would have plucked out your eyes and given
them to me, yes, given up your lives for me." And surely the Galatians did give up their lives for him. For when they accepted and
supported Paul, whom the world regarded as the most dangerous,
accursed, and damnable of all, they earned for themselves, as the
partisans and defenders of Paul, the displeasure and the hatred of
both Gentiles and Jews. So today the name of Luther is completely
contemptible to the world. Whoever praises me sins more gravely than
any idolater, blasphemer, perjurer, fornicator, adulterer, murderer, or
thief. Therefore the Galatians must really have been well founded
in the doctrine and faith of Christ, because they accepted and supported Paul, who was despised by the world, at such peril to themselves. Otherwise they would not have taken on themselves the burden of the hostility of all men.

16. *Have I, then, become your enemy by telling you the truth?*

Here Paul shows the reason why he is speaking so soothingly to
the Galatians; he suspects that they regard him as hostile to them
because he has rebuked them so harshly. "I beg you," he says, "to
separate these reproaches from my doctrine. Then you will find that
I have been doing this, not in order to reproach you but in order to
teach you the truth. My epistle is harsh, I admit. But with this harshness I am intent upon calling you back to the truth of the Gospel, from
which you have been removed, and keeping you there. Therefore
you should apply this harshness and this bitter drink, not to your
persons but to the disease. Do not regard me as your enemy because
I have scolded you severely, but regard me as your father. For if
I did not love you intensely as my own children and know that I was
very dear to you, I would not scold you so severely.

"It is a friend's responsibility, if his friend is in the wrong, to admonish him freely; and the one who has been admonished does not
become angry with his friend because of the friendly admonition and
statement of the truth but is grateful to him and shows it. In the
world, of course, it is extremely common that the truth arouses hatred

and that someone who tells the truth is regarded as an enemy. This does not happen among friends, much less among Christians. Since I scolded you purely out of love, in order to keep you in the truth, you should not be angry with me or forsake the truth because of my fatherly rebuke; nor should you suspect that I am your enemy." All this is said by Paul to support the statement (v. 12): "Become as I am. You did me no wrong."

17. *They make much of you, but for no good purpose.*

Now Paul attacks the flattery of the false apostles. For Satan usually makes an impression on simple people through his servants by wonderful tricks and wiles, as Paul says in Rom. 16:18, "by fair and flattering words." First they swear by all that is holy that they are intent upon nothing but advancing the glory of God. They say that they are prompted by the Spirit to teach the sure truth when they see that the miserable people are being neglected and are not being taught the Word correctly by someone else; thus they propose to deliver the elect from errors and to bring them to the true light and to the knowledge of the truth. In addition, they promise sure salvation to those who accept their teaching. With this pretext of piety and in such sheep's clothing (Matt. 7:15) ravenous wolves do great damage to the churches unless watchful and faithful shepherds resist them.

In this passage Paul is anticipating a possible objection;[49] for the Galatians could say: "Why do you inveigh so bitterly against our teachers for flattering us? After all, they do this out of a divine zeal and pure love. Surely this should not offend you!" "They do indeed flatter you," he says, "but for no good purpose." Thus we today are forced to hear from the Sacramentarians that by our stubbornness we are splitting the love and harmony of the churches, because we reject their doctrine of the Lord's Supper. It would be more appropriate, they say, if we shut our eyes just a little, especially since the only danger involved here is that because of this one doctrine we may arouse such discord and controversy in the church; for, after all, they do not disagree with us on any article of Christian doctrine except the one doctrine of the Lord's Supper.[50] To this I reply: "A curse

[49] An *occupatio* was a rhetorical device by which one anticipated the objections to be raised by one's opponent and answered them before he had an opportunity to raise them; cf. Cicero, *De Oratore*, III, 53, 205.

[50] For a fuller explanation of this cf. *Luther's Works*, 37, pp. 163—165.

upon any love and harmony whose preservation would make it necessary to jeopardize the Word of God!"

Thus the false apostles pretended that they loved the Galatians deeply and that they were moved by a divine sort of zeal toward them. Now zeal is an angry love or, so to speak, a godly envy. In 1 Kings 19:14 Elijah says: "I have been very zealous for the Lord." In this sense a husband is zealous for his wife, a father for his son, a brother for his brother; that is, he loves him deeply, but in such a way that he hates his faults and tries to correct them. Such was the zeal the false apostles pretended to have for the Galatians. Paul concedes that they do burn with an extreme love for the Galatians, that they make much of them and are concerned for them, but for no good purpose. Simple people are deceived by this show and pretense, when impostors affect a burning love and concern for others. Therefore Paul warns us here to make a distinction between good and evil zeal. The good zeal is, of course, praiseworthy, but not the evil. "I make much of you too," Paul says, "as much as they do. Now judge which zeal is better, mine or theirs; which is good and faithful, and which is evil and carnal. Therefore do not be so easily impressed by their zeal"; for

They want to shut you out, that you may make much of them.

It is as though he were saying: "They do indeed burn for you with extreme zeal and love, but their purpose is that you may make much of them in return and shut me out. If their zeal were faithful and sincere, they would permit you to love us along with them. But they hate our teaching; therefore they want it to be completely wiped out among you and their own teaching to be circulated. To accomplish this more smoothly, they are trying to alienate you from us by this flattery and to arouse your hostility, so that you may hate us as well as our teaching and may attach your zeal and effort to them, love only them, and accept their teaching." Thus he makes the false apostles suspect to the Galatians by saying that they are lying in wait for them and making an impression on them by means of a beautiful external appearance. In this way Christ warns us, saying (Matt. 7:15): "Beware of false prophets, who come to you in sheep's clothing."

Paul suffered the same trial that we suffer today. He was deeply distressed by the indignity of seeing his fine teaching followed by so many sects, upheavals, disturbances of public life, and revolutions, all of which caused endless trouble and scandal. The Jews accused him of being a pestilent fellow, an agitator among his people throughout the world, and a ringleader of the sect of the Nazarenes (Acts 24:5), as though they were saying: "He is a seditious and blasphemous fellow who preaches a message that not only subverts the Jewish commonwealth, so beautifully established by divine laws, but also abolishes and undermines the Decalog, our religion, our worship, and our priesthood. Throughout the world he is spreading the so-called Gospel, from which endless troubles, seditions, scandals, and sects have arisen." He was obliged to hear the same thing from the Gentiles, who cried out in the city of Philippi that he was disturbing their city and advocating customs which it was not lawful for them to accept (Acts 16:20-21).

Both Jews and Gentiles attributed such disturbances of the public peace — as well as other calamities, famine, war, dissension, and party spirit — to the teaching of Paul and the other apostles; and so they persecuted them as enemies of the public peace and of religion. Nevertheless, the apostles did not desert their ministry on this account but carried it out vigorously, preaching and confessing Christ. For they knew that they had to obey God rather than men (Acts 5:29) and that it was better for the entire universe to be thrown into tumult and contention than for Christ not to be preached or for even one soul to perish.

Meanwhile, however, these offenses could not help causing great sorrow to the apostles; for they really were not made of iron. It moved them deeply that the nation for which Paul was willing to be accursed by Christ (Rom. 9:3) was going to perish with all its splendor. They saw that great upheavals and universal revolutions would follow this doctrine of theirs, and that endless sects were arising while they were still alive — something that was bitterer for them than death, especially for Paul. It was a sad message for Paul when he heard that the Corinthians denied the resurrection of the dead (1 Cor. 15:12), to say nothing of anything else, or when he heard that the churches founded by his ministry were being disturbed, that the Gospel was being overthrown by the false apostles, and that all Asia and other great men besides had turned away from him (2 Tim. 1:15). But he knew that his teaching was not the cause of these scandals and sects. Therefore he did not lose heart and did not forsake his calling but went right ahead; he knew that the Gospel he preached was "the power of God for salvation to everyone who had faith" (Rom. 1:16), regardless of how foolish and offensive a doctrine it seemed to be to Gentiles and

Jews. He knew that those who were not offended by this Word of
the cross were blessed, whether they were preachers or hearers, as
Christ also says (Matt. 11:6): "Blessed is he who takes no offense
at Me." He knew, on the other hand, that those who regarded this
doctrine as foolish and heretical were damned. Confident in his
πληροφορία, therefore, he spoke out with Christ against the Jews and
Gentiles who were irritated and offended by his doctrine (Matt.
15:14): "Let them alone; they are blind guides of the blind."

Today we are forced to listen to the same thing to which Paul and
the other apostles were forced to listen then: that from our Gospel
there have arisen many troubles, sedition, war, party spirit, and endless offenses. Whatever upheaval there is today is blamed on us. But
surely we do not plant heresies and godless dogmas, but we preach
the Gospel message that Christ is our Justifier and Savior. In addition, if our opponents want to be truthful, they are obliged to concede this much to us, that by our doctrine we have not given any
occasion for sedition, upheaval, or war; but we have taught that by
divine commandment the government is to be honored religiously
and revered. Nor are we the originators of offense; but when wicked
people are offended, this is their own fault, not ours. We have the
commandment of God to teach the doctrine of the Gospel without
any regard for offense. Our opponents are irritated by this doctrine
because it condemns their doctrine and their idolatry. Therefore they
produce offenses on their own; in the schools this is called "taking
offense," which neither should nor can be avoided.[51] Christ preached
the Gospel without being hindered by the offense of the Jews. "Let
them alone," He said, "they are blind" (Matt. 15:14). The more the
high priests forbade the apostles to teach in the name of Jesus, the
more they testified that this Jesus, whom they had crucified, was Lord
and Christ (Acts 2:36), and that whoever called upon Him would
be saved (Rom. 10:13); "for there is no other name under heaven
given among men by which we must be saved" (Acts 4:12).

With the same confidence we today proclaim Christ, without paying heed to the cries of the wicked papists and of all our opponents,
who complain that our teaching is seditious and blasphemous because
it disturbs the status quo, overthrows religion, plants heresy, and, in
short, is the source of every evil. When Christ and the apostles

51 Thomas Aquinas distinguishes between *scandalum activum* (offense that
is given) and *scandalum passivum* (offense that is taken); *Summa Theologica*,
II—II, Q. 43, Art. 2.

preached, the same complaints were raised by the wicked Jews; soon
after this the Romans came and, in accordance with their prophecy,
destroyed both their holy place and their nation (John 11:48). Therefore let the enemies of the Gospel today beware lest they themselves
be overwhelmed by the very evils they are predicting. They exaggerate the offense caused by the marriage of priests or by our eating
meat on Friday.[52] But when they mislead and destroy innumerable
souls by their wicked doctrine, when they offend the weak by their
evil example, when they blaspheme and condemn the Gospel of the
glory of the great God, when they persecute and slay those who support sound doctrine — all this is not offensive to them but is an obedience and a worship that is most pleasing to God! Therefore let us
"let them alone, for they are blind leaders of the blind" (Matt. 15:14).
"Let the evildoer still do evil, and the filthy still be filthy" (Rev.
22:11). But because we believe, we shall speak (2 Cor. 4:13), as we
sigh, enduring the persecutions of our opponents, until Christ our
High Priest and King comes from heaven — which we hope will be
soon — and, as a righteous Judge, inflicts vengeance on those who do
not obey His Gospel (2 Thess. 1:8). Amen.

The offenses cited by the wicked do not affect the pious at all.
For they know that the devil bitterly hates this teaching of salvation
and that he distorts it with endless offenses in order to eradicate it
completely. Previously, when human traditions were taught in the
churches, the devil did not rage so. "When the strong man, fully
armed, guarded his own palace, his goods were in peace; but when
one stronger than he assailed him and overcame or bound him and
broke up his house, he began to rage and scream furiously" (Luke
11:21-22). This is a sure indication that the doctrine we set forth is
divine. Otherwise Behemoth would sleep and hide under the shadows
in the reeds and mud (Job 40:21-22); but now that he prowls around
like a roaring lion (1 Peter 5:8) and stirs up so many disturbances,
this is a sign that he feels the power of our preaching.

Nevertheless, when Paul says: "They make much of you, but for
no good purpose," he indicates in passing who were the originators
of the sectarianism, namely, those zealous spirits who have always
overthrown true doctrine and disturbed the public peace. Driven by
a foolish zeal, they imagine that they have some special sanctity,
modesty, patience, and learning. Therefore they are confident that

[52] Cf. p. 216, note 27.

they can contribute to the salvation of all men, that they can teach doctrines that are more sublime and salutary, and that they can establish better forms of worship and ceremonies than other theologians, whom they despise, whose authority they minimize, and whose good teachings they corrupt. Not only in Galatia but wherever Paul and the other apostles had preached, men who were driven by such foolish zeal stirred up sects, which were then followed by endless offenses and great upheavals. For, as Christ says (John 8:44), the devil is a liar and a murderer. Therefore he not only makes a habit of troubling consciences with the false teaching of his servants but also of arousing sedition, war, etc.

Today Germany has many such zealots. They affect great piety, modesty, learning, patience, etc.; but in fact they are ravenous wolves (Matt. 7:15) and are intent upon nothing in their hypocrisy but to put us in the shade and shut us out completely, so that the people will revere them alone and preach only their doctrine. Here it is inevitable that sectarianism, controversy, conflict, and sedition should follow. But what shall we do? We cannot forbid this any more than Paul could. Nevertheless, he did win some, who heeded these warnings of his. Thus I hope that by our warnings, too, some will be called back from the errors of the sectarians.

18. *For a good purpose it is always good to be made much of, and not only when I am present with you.*

It is as though Paul were to say: "I praised you for being so zealous for me and for loving me so dearly when I preached the Gospel among you in the weakness of my flesh. Now that I am absent, you should treat me with the same love and zeal, as though I had never gone away. For even though I am absent in body, you still have my teaching, which you should still observe, since through it you have received the Holy Spirit; and you should think that Paul is always present as long as you have his teaching. Therefore I do not criticize your zeal; I praise it. Yet I praise it only if it is the zeal of God or of the Spirit, not the zeal of the flesh. The zeal of the Spirit, which is zealous for something good, is always good; but the zeal of the flesh is not." And so he lauds the zeal of the Galatians in order to soothe their minds and make them patient of his scolding. It is as though he were saying: "Put a good construction on my rebuke, for it comes from a spirit that is neither evil nor angry but is sorrowful and deeply concerned for you."

This is a rhetorical example of how a faithful shepherd should be concerned for his sheep and should make every possible effort, so that by scolding, soothing, and asking he may keep them in sound doctrine and win them away from those who would mislead them.

19. *My little children, with whom I am again in travail until Christ be formed in you!*

This also belongs to the rhetoric by which Paul punishes the spirit of the Galatians with gentle and soothing words; endearingly he calls them his little children. All the words are chosen to appeal to the emotions and gain favor.

"With whom I am again in travail." This is an allegory. The apostles — like all teachers, though in a special way — acted in the place of parents; just as the latter give birth to the form of the body, so the former to the form of the mind. Now the form of the Christian mind is faith, the trust of the heart, which takes hold of Christ, clings only to Him and to nothing else besides. A heart that is equipped with such confidence has the true form of Christ, which is provided by the ministry of the Word. 1 Cor. 4:15: "I became your father through the Gospel," namely, in the Spirit, so that you might know Christ and believe in Him; 2 Cor. 3:3: "You are a letter from Christ delivered by us, written not with ink but with the Spirit of the living God." For the Word proceeds from the mouth of the apostle and reaches the heart of the hearer; there the Holy Spirit is present and impresses that Word on the heart, so that it is heard. In this way every preacher is a parent, who produces and forms the true shape of the Christian mind through the ministry of the Word.

At the same time Paul attacks the false apostles in passing, as though he were to say: "Through the Gospel I truly became your father. But those corrupters and distorters came and established a new image in your heart, not that of Christ but that of Moses, so that your confidence no longer rests on Christ but on the works of the Law. This is an alien and completely diabolical form, not the true form or the form of Christ."

Paul does not say: "I am again in travail with you until my form be formed in you." No, he says: "until Christ be formed in you." That is: "I am laboring in order that you may acquire the form and likeness of Christ again, not that of Paul." With these words he rebukes the false apostles again; for they abolished the form of

Christ in the minds of the believers and made up another form, namely, their own. "They desire to have you circumcised," he says in Gal. 6:13, "that they may glory in your flesh."

The apostle also speaks of this form of Christ in Col. 3:10: "Put on the new nature, which is being renewed in knowledge after the image of its Creator." Therefore Paul wants to restore the image of God or of Christ in the Galatians. It had been deformed or distorted by the false apostles, and it consists in this, that they feel, think, and want exactly what God does, whose thought and will it is that we obtain the forgiveness of sins and eternal life through Jesus Christ, His Son, whom He sent into the world to be the expiation for our sins and for those of the whole world (1 John 2:2), so that through the Son we might acknowledge Him as our Father, who has been placated and is kindly disposed toward us. Those who believe this are like God; that is, they think of God altogether as He feels in His heart, and they have the same form in their mind that God or Christ has. This, according to Paul, is to "be renewed in the spirit of your minds and to put on the new nature, created after the likeness of God" (Eph. 4:23-24).

Therefore Paul says that he is in travail again with the Galatians, but in such a way that the form of the children is not the form of the apostle and that the sons do not bear the image of Paul or of Cephas (1 Cor. 1:12) but that of another father, namely, Christ. "He is the One," he says, "whom I want to form in you, so that in everything you feel as Christ Himself feels. In short, I am in travail with you; that is, I am laboring anxiously again to call you back to your original faith, which you lost when you were deceived by the cleverness of the false apostles and fell back into the Law and works. Therefore a new and difficult labor has been laid upon me, to lead you back from the Law to faith in Christ." This is what he calls "being in travail."

20. *I could wish to be present with you now and to change my tone.*

These are purely apostolic concerns. It is commonly said that a letter is a dead messenger, because it cannot give any more than it has. No letter is written so carefully that nothing is lacking in it. Circumstances vary; so do the elements of time, place, person, custom, and attitude, none of which a letter can express. Therefore it affects the reader in various ways; sometimes it makes him sad and sometimes happy, depending on how the reader feels. But the living voice, on the other hand, is able to interpret, soften, and correct whatever has been said in a rather harsh or intemperate way. Therefore Paul wishes that he could be present, so that he could modify and change his tone as he saw that the circumstances and attitudes required. Thus if he saw that some of them were excessively disturbed, he could moderate his speech to keep from saddening them too much; but if he saw that they were excessively elated, he could rebuke them more harshly, to keep them from becoming too smug and eventually contemptuous.

Therefore the apostle is at a loss to determine how to deal with them at a distance by mail. It is as though he were to say: "If my letter is a little harsh, I am afraid that I may offend more of you with it than I correct; if it is a little gentle, it may accomplish nothing among the hard and unfeeling ones, because dead letters and syllables give only what they have. On the other hand, a living voice is a queen in comparison with a letter; for it can add and subtract, and it can adjust itself to all the forms and qualities of attitude, time, place, and person. In other words, I would like to convert you by letter, that is, call you back from the Law to faith in Christ. But I am afraid that I shall not accomplish this with a dead letter. If I were present with you, however, I could change my tone, scolding the stubborn and soothing the weak, as the circumstances of each require."

For I am perplexed about you.

That is: "I am so distraught in my mind that I do not know what and how to deal with you in a letter from far away." Truly apostolic feelings are being described here. He does not miss anything; he scolds the Galatians, beseeches them, soothes them, commends their faith with wonderful words, and as a genuine orator presents his case with great care and faith — all in order to call them back to the truth of the Gospel and to win them away from the false apostles. His words are not cold; they are ardent and hot. Therefore they should be carefully considered.

21. *Tell me, you who desire to be under law, do you not hear the Law?*

Paul wanted to close the epistle here. He did not want to write any more. No, he wanted to be present in person and to speak with the Galatians. But while he is anxious in his mind about this matter, he introduces this allegory at this point; it probably occurred to him here. The common people are deeply moved by allegories and parables; therefore Christ also used them often. They are like pictures of a sort, which show things to simple people as though before their very eyes and for this reason have a profound effect on the mind, especially of an uneducated person. First he strikes the ears of the Galatians with words and writing; then with this allegory he beautifully portrays the same thing to their eyes.

Now Paul was a very fine craftsman at presenting allegories; for he made a practice of applying them to the teaching of faith, to grace, and to Christ, not to the Law and to works, as Origen and Jerome did. These men deserve to be criticized, because they made awkward and inept allegories out of the simplest statements of Scripture, in which allegories have no place. Therefore it is unfortunate and may even be dangerous to imitate them in the treatment of allegories; for unless someone has a perfect knowledge of Christian doctrine, he will not be successful at presenting allegories.

But why does Paul use the name "Law" for Genesis, from which he cites the history of Ishmael and Isaac, when that book is not a book of law, and especially when the passage he quotes contains no law but only the simple narrative about the two sons of Abraham? In Jewish fashion Paul usually calls the first book of Moses "Law." Even though it has no law except that which deals with circumcision, but chiefly teaches faith and testifies that the patriarchs were pleasing to God on account of their faith, still the Jews called Genesis together with the other books of Moses "Law" because of that one law of circumcision. Paul, who was himself a Jew, did the same thing. And Christ included not only the books of Moses under the name "Law" but even the psalms. John 15:25: "It is to fulfill the Word that is written in their Law (Ps. 35:19), 'They hated Me without a cause.'"

22. *For it is written that Abraham had two sons, one by a slave and one by a free woman.*

23. *But the son of the slave was born according to the flesh, the son of the free woman through promise.*

It is as though Paul were saying: "You have forsaken grace, faith, and Christ; and you have defected to the Law, wanting to be under it and to gain wisdom from it. Therefore I shall discuss the Law with you. I ask you to look at it carefully. You will find that Abraham had two sons, Ishmael by Hagar and Isaac by Sarah.

Both were true sons of Abraham. Ishmael was the true son of
Abraham no less than Isaac was; for both were born of the same
father, the same flesh, the same seed. Then what was the difference
between them?" The difference, Paul says, is not that one mother
was a free woman and the other a slave — although this does contribute to the allegory — but that Ishmael, who was born of the slave,
was born according to the flesh, that is, apart from the promise and
the Word of God, while Isaac was not only born of the free woman
but also in accordance with a promise. "So what? Still Isaac was
born of the seed of Abraham, just as Ishmael was." "I grant this.
Both were sons of the same father. And yet there is a difference.
Even though Isaac was born of the flesh, this was preceded by God's
promising and naming him." No one but Paul has ever observed this
difference, which he gathered this way on the basis of the text of
Genesis.

When Hagar conceived and gave birth to Ishmael, there was no
voice or Word of God that predicted this; but with Sarah's permission Abraham went in to Hagar the slave, whom Sarah, because
she was barren, gave him as his wife, as Genesis testifies. For Sarah
had heard that by the promise of God Abraham was to have an offspring of his own body, and she hoped to become the mother of this
offspring. But when she had been waiting anxiously for many years
after the promise and saw that the realization of the promise was
being postponed, she thought that she had been disappointed of
her hope. Therefore the saintly woman gave in to the honor of her
husband and resigned her right to another, that is, to the slave.
Yet she did not permit her husband to marry another wife outside
their home; but she gave him her slave in marriage, so that she
might obtain children by the slave. For this is what the narrative
in Gen. 16:1-2 says: "Sarai, Abram's wife, bore him no children. She
had an Egyptian maid whose name was Hagar; and Sarai said to
Abram: 'Behold now, the Lord has prevented me from bearing children; go in to my maid; it may be that I shall obtain children by her.'"

It was an act of great humility for Sarai to demean herself this
way and to bear this trial of faith with such equanimity. She thought
to herself: "God is not a liar. What He has promised to my husband
He will certainly perform. But perhaps God does not want me to be
the mother of this offspring. I shall not envy Hagar this honor.
Let my lord go in to her; perhaps I can obtain children by her."
Therefore Ishmael was born without the Word, solely at the request

of Sarah herself. Here there was no Word of God that commanded or promised Abraham a son; but everything happened by chance, as Sarah's words indicate: "It may be," she says, "that I shall obtain children by her." Since there was no statement from God that preceded, as there was when Sarah gave birth to Isaac, but only the statement of Sarah, it is abundantly clear that Ishmael was Abraham's son only according to the flesh and without the Word; therefore he was expected and born by chance, like any other child.

Paul noticed this. And in Rom. 9:7 he carefully sets forth this argument, which he repeats here as part of the allegory; and he comes to the powerful conclusion that not all the sons of Abraham are sons of God. For Abraham has sons of two kinds: those who are born jointly of him and of the Word or promise of God, as Isaac was; and those who are born of him without the Word of God, as Ishmael was. With this argument, which is like Christ's argument in Matt. 3:9 and John 8:37, Paul stops the mouths of the proud Jews, who boast that they are the offspring and children of Abraham. It is as though he were to say: "It does not follow: 'I am the genuine offspring of Abraham; therefore I am a child of God. Esau was a genuine child; therefore he was an heir.' No, those who want to be sons of Abraham must be children of promise over and above their physical birth, and they must believe. In the last analysis, those who have the promise and believe are the true sons of Abraham and, consequently, of God."

But because Ishmael was not promised to Abraham by God, he was a son only according to the flesh, not according to the promise. Therefore he was expected and born by chance, like other children. For no mother knows whether she is going to have a child; or if she senses that she is pregnant, she still does not know whether it will be a boy or a girl. But Isaac was named definitely in Gen. 17:19. "Sarah your wife," the angel said to Abraham, "shall bear you a son, and you shall call his name Isaac." Here both the son and the mother are explicitly named. Thus for the humility with which Sarah yielded her right and suffered the contempt of Hagar (Gen. 16:4) God granted her the honor of being the mother of the promised son.

24. *Now this is an allegory.*

Allegories do not provide solid proofs in theology; but, like pictures, they adorn and illustrate a subject.[53] For if Paul had not

[53] See *Luther the Expositor,* p. 89.

proved the righteousness of faith against the righteousness of works by more substantial arguments, he would not have accomplished anything with this allegory. But because he has already fortified his case with more solid arguments — based on experience, on the case of Abraham, on the evidence of Scripture, and on analogy [54] — now, at the end of the argument, he adds an allegory as a kind of ornament. For it is very fine, once the foundation has been properly laid and the case has been firmly established, to add some kind of allegory. Just as a picture is an ornament for a house that has already been constructed, so an allegory is a kind of illumination of an oration or of a case that has already been established on other grounds.

> *These women are two covenants. One is from Mt. Sinai, bearing children for slavery; she is Hagar.*

25. *Now Hagar is Mt. Sinai in Arabia.*

Abraham is a type [55] of God, who has two sons, that is, two nations, represented by Ishmael and Isaac. They were born of Hagar and of Sarah, who signify the two covenants, the old and the new. The old covenant is from Mt. Sinai, bearing children for slavery; she is Hagar. For the same mountain that the Jews call Sinai — a name it seems to have because of its thickets and brambles — the Arabs call "Hagar" in their language, as not only Paul but also Ptolemy and the scholia of the Greeks indicate.[56] In the same way other mountains receive different names among various nations. Thus the mountain that Moses calls Hermon is called "Sirion" by the Sidonians and "Senir" by the Amorites.[57]

Now it is quite fitting that Mt. Sinai has the same name in Arabic as the slave woman, and I imagine that this similarity of names gave Paul the idea and opportunity to pursue this allegory. Therefore just as Hagar the slave truly gave birth to a son for Abraham, not an heir but a slave, so Sinai, the allegorical Hagar, truly gave birth to a son for God, namely, a physical people. And just as Ishmael was a true son of Abraham, so the people of Israel have

[54] Apparently this is intended as a rough outline of the epistle up to this point. The first two chapters deal with experience; Abraham is discussed in ch. 3:1-9; the testimonies of Scripture are in ch. 3:10-22; the analogies in chs. 3:23—4:7.

[55] The word translated as "type" is *figura*.

[56] See also *Luther's Works*, 2, p. 108, on Ptolemy.

[57] On Luther's use of etymologies see also *Luther's Works*, 22, pp. 421—422.

the true God as their Father, who gave them His Law and supplied them with His oracles, with a religion, a form of worship, and a temple, as Ps. 147:19 says: "He declares His Word to Jacob." Nevertheless, this was the difference: Ishmael was born of the slave according to the flesh, that is, without a promise; therefore he could not be the heir. Thus the mystical Hagar, that is, Mt. Sinai, on which the Law was given and the old covenant established, gave birth to a people for God, the great Abraham, yet without a promise, that is, a physical and enslaved people, not an heir of God. For the Law did not have promises added to it about Christ and His blessings, about deliverance from the curse of the Law, sin, and death, and about the free gift of the forgiveness of sins, righteousness, and eternal life. But the Law says (Lev. 18:5): "By doing this a man shall live."

Therefore the promises of the Law are conditional. They do not promise life freely; they promise it to those who keep the Law. Therefore they leave consciences in doubt, because no one keeps the Law. But the promises of the new covenant do not have any condition attached; they do not demand anything of us; they do not depend on our worthiness as a condition. Instead, they bring and grant us the forgiveness of sins, grace, righteousness, and eternal life freely, for Christ's sake. This has been treated by us at greater length elsewhere.

Therefore the Law or the old covenant contains only physical promises, to which some such condition as this is always attached: "If you will hear My voice" (Ps. 95:7); "If you will keep My covenant" (Ex. 19:5); "If you walk in My ways, you will be My people" (Deut. 28:9). The Jews did not pay attention to this; but they took hold of these conditional promises and made them absolute and unconditional, which they thought that God could never revoke but had to keep. And so when they heard the prophets — who were able to distinguish properly between the physical promises of the Law and the spiritual promises about Christ and His kingdom — predict that the city of Jerusalem, the temple, the kingdom, and the priesthood would be laid waste, they persecuted and killed them as heretics and blasphemers against God; for they did not see the condition that was attached: "If you keep My commandments, it will be well with you."

Therefore Hagar the slave gave birth to nothing but a slave. And so even though Ishmael was a genuine son of Abraham, he was not an heir but remained a slave. What was lacking? The promise and blessing of the Word. Thus the Law given on Mt. Sinai, which the Arabs call "Hagar," gives birth to nothing but slaves; for there was no promise of Christ added to the Law. "And so if you forsake the promise and faith and turn back again to the Law and works, O Galatians, you will remain slaves forever. That is, you will never be free of sin and death; but you will remain under the curse of the Law. For Hagar does not give birth to a child of promise or an heir; that is, the Law does not justify, does not grant sonship and an inheritance but rather hinders it and works wrath."

She corresponds to the present Jerusalem, for she is in slavery with her children.

This is a marvelous allegory. Just as Paul made Sinai into Hagar earlier, so now he would like to make Jerusalem into Sarah; but he neither dares nor is able to do so. Instead, he is compelled to associate Jerusalem with Mt. Sinai; for he says that it applies to Hagar, since Mt. Hagar reaches all the way to Jerusalem. It is, of course, true that there are continuous mountains all the way from Arabia Petraea to Kadesh-barnea in Judea. Therefore he says: "The present Jerusalem, that is, the earthly and temporal one, is not Sarah but belongs to Hagar; for in it the reign of Hagar is exercised. In it there is the Law that gives birth into slavery. There are the worship, the temple, the kingdom, the priesthood; and whatever was ordained on Sinai on the basis of the Law as its source, that is carried on in Jerusalem. Therefore I connect it with Sinai and include them both in the same term, namely, Sinai or Hagar."

I for my part would not have had the courage to handle this allegory in this manner. I would rather have said that Jerusalem is Sarah, or the new covenant, especially since it was there that the preaching of the Gospel began, the Holy Spirit was granted, and the people of the New Testament came into being. And I would have thought that I had constructed a very apt allegory. Therefore not everyone has the skill to play around with allegories. For a pretty external appearance will impress a person in such a way that he will go astray, as here all of us would have thought it appropriate to say that Sinai is Hagar and Jerusalem is Sarah. Now Paul does indeed make Sarah into Jerusalem — yet not the physical Jerusalem, which he simply attaches to Hagar, but the spiritual and heavenly Jerusalem, where the Law does not rule and the physical people are not enslaved with their children, as they are in Jerusalem, but where the promise rules and the spiritual people are free.

To bring about the complete abolition of the Law and of the reign established on Hagar, the earthly Jerusalem with all its ornaments, the temple, its form of worship, etc., was horribly laid waste, with the permission of God. Although the new covenant began there and went out from there into the whole world, it still pertains to Hagar; that is, it is the commonwealth of the Law, of the form of worship, and of the priesthood established by Moses. In other words, it was born of Hagar the slave, and therefore it is in slavery together with its children. That is, it remains in the works of the Law and never attains to the freedom of the Spirit; it remains forever under the Law, under sin and an evil conscience, under the wrath and judgment of God, under the sentence of death and of hell. Of course, it does have the freedom of the flesh; it has a physical realm, magistrates, wealth, possessions, etc. But we are speaking about the freedom of the Spirit, where we are dead to the Law, sin, and death, and where we live and reign as free men in grace, the forgiveness of sins, righteousness, and eternal life. The earthly Jerusalem cannot achieve these things; therefore it remains with Hagar.

26. But the Jerusalem above is free, and she is our mother.

The earthly Jerusalem, says Paul, which is down below and has the authority of the Law, is Hagar and is in slavery with its children; that is, it is not set free from the Law, sin, and death. But the Jerusalem that is above, that is to say, the spiritual Jerusalem, is Sarah, although Paul does not use the proper noun "Sarah" but refers to her with the adjective "free." She is truly lordly and free; and she is our mother, giving birth, not into slavery, as Hagar does, but into freedom. Now the heavenly Jerusalem above is the church, that is, believers scattered throughout the world, who have the same Gospel, the same faith in Christ, the same Holy Spirit, and the same sacraments.

Therefore you must not interpret "above" anagogically, as the sophists do, applying it to what they call the church triumphant in heaven; you must apply it to the church militant on earth.[58] This is not strange, for the godly are said to have their being in heaven. Phil. 3:20: "Our πολίτευμα is in heaven," not in a local sense; but to

[58] This allegory of Jerusalem was used by the medieval exegetes as a classic instance of the "spiritual sense" of Scripture.

the extent that a Christian believes, to that extent he is in heaven; and to the extent that he does his duty in faith, to that extent he is doing it in heaven. Eph. 1:3: "who has blessed us in Christ with every spiritual blessing in the heavenly places." Therefore the spiritual and heavenly blessing must be distinguished from the earthly blessing, which is to have a good government and household, to have children, peace, wealth, food, and other physical advantages. But the heavenly blessing is to be set free from the Law, sin, and death; to be justified and made alive; to have a gracious God; to have a confident heart, a joyful conscience, and spiritual comfort; to have a knowledge of Christ, the gift of prophecy, and the revelation of the Scriptures; to have the gifts of the Holy Spirit; to rejoice in God, etc. — these are the heavenly blessings of the church of Christ.

Therefore the Jerusalem that is above, that is, the heavenly Jerusalem, is the church here in time. It is not, by anagoge, our fatherland in the life to come or the church triumphant, as the idle and unlettered monks and scholastic doctors imagined. They taught that there are four senses of Scripture — the literal, the tropological, the allegorical, and the anagogical — and by means of these they misinterpreted almost every word of Scripture.[59] Thus, according to them, Jerusalem literally signified the city of that name; tropologically, a pure conscience; allegorically, the church militant; and anagogically, our heavenly fatherland or the church triumphant. With these awkward and foolish fables they tore Scripture apart into many meanings and robbed themselves of the ability to give sure instruction to human consciences. But Paul says here that the old, earthly Jerusalem pertains to Hagar; that she is in slavery with her children; that she has been abolished; and that a new and heavenly Jerusalem, which is lordly and free, has been divinely established, not in heaven but on earth, to be the mother of us all, of whom we have been born and are being born every day. Therefore it is necessary that this mother of ours, like the birth she gives, be on earth among men; yet she gives birth in the Spirit, by the ministry of the Word and of the sacraments, not physically.

I say this to keep us from being led astray by our thoughts into heaven. We should know that Paul is contrasting the Jerusalem that is above with the earthly Jerusalem, not spatially but spiritually. Spiritual things are distinct from physical or earthly things. Spiritual

[59] Cf. *Luther's Works*, 1, p. 87, note 10.

things are "above"; earthly things are "below." Thus the Jerusalem that is above is distinguished from the physical and temporal Jerusalem that is below, as I have said, not spatially but spiritually. For the spiritual Jerusalem, which began in the physical Jerusalem, has no prescribed location, as the one in Judea does; but it is scattered throughout the world and can be in Babylonia, Turkey, Tartary, Scythia, India, Italy, or Germany, on the islands of the sea, on mountains, in valleys, and everywhere in the world where there are men who have the Gospel and believe in Christ.

Therefore Sarah, or Jerusalem, our free mother, is the church, the bride of Christ who gives birth to all. She goes on giving birth to children without interruption until the end of the world, as long as she exercises the ministry of the Word, that is, as long as she preaches and propagates the Gospel; for this is what it means for her to give birth. Now she teaches the Gospel in such a way that we are set free from the curse of the Law, from sin, death, and other evils, not through the Law and works but through Christ. Therefore the Jerusalem that is above, that is, the church, is not subject to the Law and works; but she is free and is a mother without Law, sin, or death. And as the mother is, so are the children to whom she gives birth.

Therefore this allegory teaches in a beautiful way that the church should not do anything but preach the Gospel correctly and purely and thus give birth to children. In this way we are all fathers and children to one another, for we are born of one another. I was born of others through the Gospel, and now I am a father to still others, who will be fathers to still others; and so this giving birth will endure until the end of the world. But I am speaking, not about Hagar's giving birth, who gives birth to slaves through the Law, but about free Sarah's, who gives birth to heirs without the Law, without works or their own efforts. That Isaac is the heir and Ishmael is not, even though both are genuine sons of Abraham, takes place through the Word of promise, specifically (Gen. 17:19): "Sarah your wife shall bear you a son, and you shall call his name Isaac." Sarah understood this very well, and therefore she said (Gen. 21:10): "Cast out this slave woman with her son" — words that Paul quotes below (v. 30). Therefore just as Isaac has the inheritance from his father solely on the basis of the promise and of his birth, without the Law or works, so we are born as heirs by Sarah, the free woman, that is, by the church. She teaches, cherishes, and carries us in her womb, her bosom, and her arms; she shapes and perfects us to the form of Christ, until we grow into perfect manhood (Eph. 4:13). Thus everything happens through the ministry of the Word. It is the duty of a free woman to go on giving birth to children endlessly, that is, to sons who know that they are justified by faith, not by the Law.

27. *For it is written: Rejoice, O barren one that dost not bear; break forth and shout, thou who art not in travail; for the desolate hath more children than she who hath a husband.*

Paul quotes this passage, which is completely allegorical, from the prophet Isaiah. It is written, he says, that the mother of many children, who has a husband, must grow sick and perish, while the barren one, who does not bear, must have very many children. Hannah sings the same way in her canticle, from which Isaiah took this prophecy (1 Sam. 2:4-5): "The bows of the mighty are broken, but the feeble gird on strength. Those who were full have hired themselves out for bread, but those who were hungry have ceased to hunger. The barren has borne seven, but she who has many children is forlorn." It is an amazing thing, she says: the one who was prolific will be barren, and the one who was barren will be prolific. Those who were mighty, satisfied, alive, righteous, blessed, rich, and glorious will be feeble, hungry, sentenced to death, sinful, condemned, poor, and shameful; and, on the other hand, the feeble and the hungry will be mighty and satisfied.

With this allegory from the prophet Isaiah, Paul shows the difference between Hagar and Sarah, that is, between the synagog and the church, or between the Law and the Gospel. It is as though he were saying: "The Law, the husband of a prolific woman, that is, of the synagog, gives birth to very many children." For men of every age, not only the ignorant but those who are the wisest and best — in other words, the whole human race with the exception of the children of the free woman — do not see or recognize any other righteousness, not to say any more excellent righteousness, than that of the Law. (Now under the term "Law" I am including all laws, both human and divine.) Therefore if they follow the Law and perform its outward works, they think they are righteous. All such men are slaves, not free men, because they are sons of Hagar, who gives birth into slavery. If they are slaves, they do not share in the inheritance but are cast out of the house. "The slaves do not continue in the house forever" (John 8:35); in fact, they have now been thrown out of the kingdom of grace and freedom. "He who does not believe is condemned already" (John 3:18). Therefore they remain under the curse of the Law, under sin, death, and the power of the devil, under the wrath and judgment of God.

Now if even the Moral Law of God, the Decalog, gives birth only to slaves — that is, does not justify but only terrifies, accuses, condemns, and brings consciences to the point of despair — how, I ask you, could the laws of the pope or human traditions justify? Therefore anyone who teaches or urges either the Law of God or human traditions as something necessary for righteousness in the sight of God does nothing other than give birth to slaves. And yet such theologians are regarded as the best; they earn the applause of the world and are the most prolific mothers, that is, have an infinite number of disciples. Since reason does not understand what faith and true godliness are, it neglects and despises them. Naturally, it is impressed by superstition and hypocrisy, that is, by the righteousness of works, which is so brilliant and successful that it is the mighty empress of the universe. Therefore those who teach the righteousness of works on the basis of the Law give birth to many sons, but all of these are slaves who will be thrown out of the house and condemned.

Sarah, the free woman, on the other hand, that is, the true church, seems to be barren; for the Gospel, the Word of the cross, which the church preaches, is not as brilliant as is the teaching about the Law and works, and therefore it has few pupils who cling to it. Besides, it has the reputation of forbidding good works, making men idle and faint, stirring up heresies and sedition, and being the cause of every evil. Therefore it does not seem to have any success or prosperity; but everything seems to be filled with barrenness, waste, and despair. Hence the wicked are fully persuaded that the church will soon perish along with its doctrine. The Jews were altogether sure that the church established by the apostles would soon be deserted. To it they gave the hateful name "sect"; for so they spoke to Paul in Acts 28:22: "With regard to this sect we know that everywhere it is spoken against." Similarly today, how often, I ask you, have our opponents rejoiced in a false hope that we would surely be crushed at this or that time? Christ and the apostles were crushed; but when they were dead, the teaching of the Gospel was spread more widely than when they were alive. Thus our opponents can crush us, but "the Word of the Lord will abide forever" (1 Peter 1:25). Regardless of how barren and deserted the church of Christ seems, therefore, or of how much it is said to teach heretical and seditious doctrine, it alone gives birth to children and heirs, through the ministry of the Word.

Therefore the prophet grants that the church is engaged in a conflict; otherwise he would not urge it to rejoice. He grants that in the eyes of the world it is barren; otherwise he would not call it a barren and desolate one that does not bear. But he says that it is prolific in the eyes of God. Therefore he tells it to rejoice. It is as though he were to say: "Desolate and barren, you do not have the Law as your husband; therefore you do not have children either. But rejoice. For even though you are deprived of the husband Law, like a virgin of marriageable age who has been deserted (he does not want to call her a widow), who would have a husband if he had not deserted her or had not been killed — you, I say, who are desolate and deserted by the husband Law and are not subject to marriage with the Law, will be the mother of an infinite number of children." Therefore the people or the church of the new covenant is completely without Law so far as its conscience is concerned. In the eyes of the world, therefore, it seems to be deserted. But even though it appears barren, without Law or works, yet in the eyes of God it is very prolific, giving birth to an endless number of children, and free ones at that. How? Not through the husband Law but through the Word and the Spirit of Christ, given through the Gospel, it conceives, bears, and rears its children.

With this allegory, then, Paul shows the distinction between the Law and the Gospel very clearly: first, when he calls Hagar the old covenant and Sarah the new; next, when he calls the former a slave and the latter a free woman; finally, when he says that the one who has a husband and is prolific will grow ill and will be cast out of the house with her children, but that the one who is barren and desolate will become prolific and will produce an infinite number of children, all of whom will be heirs. These are the essential differences between the people of faith and the people of the Law. The people of faith does not have the Law as its husband; it is not in slavery; it was not born of the present Jerusalem as its mother. But it has the promise; it is free; and it is born of Sarah, the free woman.

Therefore Paul separates the spiritual people of the new covenant from the Law when he says that this people is not the child of Hagar, who had a husband, but of Sarah, the free woman, who does not know the Law. In this way he sets the people of faith far above and beyond the Law. But if it is above and beyond the Law, then it is justified, not by the Law and works but solely by its spiritual birth, that is, by faith. For spiritual birth is nothing other than faith. Now just as the people of grace neither has the Law nor can have it, so the people of the Law neither has grace nor can have it; for it is impossible for Law and grace to exist together. Either we must be justified by faith and lose the righteousness of the Law, or we must be justified by the Law and lose grace and the righteousness of faith. It is a bitter and tragic loss when we keep the Law and lose grace. On the other hand, it is a fortunate and saving loss when we keep grace and lose the Law.

Seeing that Paul set this forth with the greatest care, we are very careful to show the difference between the Law and the Gospel clearly. This is very easy so far as the words themselves are concerned. For who does not see that Hagar is not Sarah and that Sarah is not Hagar, or that Ishmael neither is nor has what Isaac is and has? This can be determined easily. But in profound terrors and in the agony of death, when the conscience struggles with the judgment of God, to be able to say with firm confidence: "The Law does not apply to me at all, because my mother is Sarah, who gives birth, not to slaves but to free children and heirs" — this is the most difficult thing there is.

With this quotation from Isaiah, Paul proved that Sarah is the true mother, who gives birth to free children and heirs; and, on the other hand, that Hagar does indeed give birth to many children, but that they are slaves, who must be cast out of the house. Besides, since this passage speaks about the abrogation of the Law and about Christian liberty, it must be considered carefully. For just as it is our highest and most important doctrine to know that we are justified and saved through Christ, so, by antithesis, it is very important to have the correct understanding of the abrogation of the Law. The knowledge that the Law has been abrogated is of great value for confirming our teaching about faith and for providing a sure comfort for consciences, especially in their deep anxiety.

I have said several times before, and I repeat now — for this is a thing that cannot be emphasized enough — that the Christian who

by faith takes hold of the benefits of Christ has no Law at all but
is free of it. This passage in Isaiah about the free mother who gives
birth to free children teaches the same thing, namely, that for those
who believe in Christ the entire Law, with all its terrors and troubles,
has been abrogated. Therefore it is a truly outstanding and comforting passage, urging that the barren and desolate one rejoice,
even though, according to the Law, she should rather be ridiculed
or pitied. For according to the Law barren women were accursed.[60]
But the Holy Spirit reverses this sentence and pronounces the barren
one praiseworthy and blessed, but the prolific one who has children
He pronounces accursed. Regardless of how desolate and barren
Sarah, that is, the church, may appear to be in the eyes of the world
because she does not have Law and works, she is, according to the
testimony of the prophet, the prolific mother of an infinite number
of children in the eyes of God. By contrast, regardless of how great
and abundant the fertility and bearing may be under Hagar, there
are no children left; for the children of the slave woman are cast
out of the house together with their mother, and they do not receive
the inheritance with the children of the free woman, as Paul says
below (v. 30).

Since, therefore, we are children of the free woman, the Law,
our old husband (Rom. 7:1-6), has been abolished; as long as it had
dominion over us, it was impossible for us to give birth in the Spirit
to children who knew grace, but they remained slaves. When the
Law has dominion, men are not idle. They work hard, and they
bear the burden of the day and the scorching heat (Matt. 20:12).
They bear and give birth to many children, but both the parents and
the children are illegitimate and do not belong to a free mother.
Therefore they are eventually cast out of the inheritance with Ishmael;
they die and are damned. Hence it is impossible for men to be
justified and saved through the Law. There is, of course, much labor
and birth in the Law; but none of this grants the inheritance. Therefore the Law, with all its children, must be cast out that is, cursed
be any doctrine, life, or religion that strives to achieve righteousness
in the sight of God by means of the Law or works.

When Thomas and other scholastics speak about the abrogation
of the Law, they say that after Christ the civil and ceremonial laws
are fatal, and that therefore they have now been abrogated, but not

---

[60] Luther is thinking of passages like Gen. 16:2; Gen. 28:18; 1 Sam. 1:5;
Luke 1:25.

the moral laws.[61] These men do not know what they are saying. When you want to speak about the abrogation of the Law, discuss chiefly the Law in the proper sense of the word — the Law in the spiritual sense. Include the entire Law, without distinguishing between the civil, the ceremonial, and the moral. For when Paul says that through Christ we have been set free from the curse of the Law (Gal. 3:13), he is certainly speaking about the entire Law, and especially about the Moral Law. It alone actually accuses, curses, and condemns consciences; but the other two kinds do not. Therefore we say that the Law of the Decalog has no right to accuse and terrify the conscience in which Christ reigns through grace, for Christ has made this right obsolete.

This does not mean that the conscience does not feel the terrors of the Law at all. Of course it feels them. But it means that the conscience cannot be condemned and brought to the point of despair by such things. For "there is now no condemnation for those who are in Christ Jesus" (Rom. 8:1); again: "If the Son makes you free, you will be free indeed" (John 8:36). Regardless of how terrified the Christian is by the Law and how much he acknowledges his sin, he does not despair; for he believes in Christ, into whom he has been baptized and through whom he has the forgiveness of sins. Now if our sin has been forgiven through Christ Himself, the Lord of the Law — and forgiven by His having given Himself for it — the Law, that slave, no longer has a right to accuse and condemn us because of our sin; for this has been forgiven, and we have become free by the deliverance of the Son. Therefore the entire Law has been abrogated for believers in Christ.

"But I have not done anything good and am not doing anything now!" Here you neither can nor must do anything. Merely listen to this joyful message, which the Spirit is bringing to you through the prophet: "Rejoice, O barren one that dost not bear!" It is as though He were saying: "Why are you so sorrowful when you have no reason to be sorrowful?" "But I am barren and desolate." "Regardless of how much you are that way, since you have no righteousness on the basis of Law, Christ is still your Righteousness. He became a curse for *you;*[62] He has redeemed you from the curse of the Law (Gal.

---

[61] On the distinction of moral, ceremonial, and judicial precepts cf. Thomas Aquinas, *Summa Theologica,* I—II, Q. 99; on the abrogation of the Law, ibid., Q. 103, Art. 4.

[62] We have used italics where the original has all capitals.

3:13). If you believe in Him, the Law is dead for you. As much as Christ is greater than the Law, that much better is the righteousness you have than the righteousness of the Law. Moreover, you are not barren either, because you have more children than she who has a husband."

A second kind of abrogation of the Law, an outward one, is that the political laws of Moses do not apply to us at all. Therefore we should not restore them to the courthouse or chain ourselves to them in some superstitious way, as some men who were ignorant of this liberty did several years ago.[63] Nevertheless, although the Gospel does not subject us to the civil laws of Moses, it does not completely set us free from obedience to all political laws; but in this bodily life it subjects us to the laws of the state in which we live, and it commands everyone to obey his magistrate and his laws, "not only to avoid God's wrath but also for the sake of conscience" (1 Peter 2:13-14; Rom. 13:5). Nor would it be a sin if the emperor used some of the civil laws of Moses; in fact, it would be a good idea if he did. Therefore the sophists are in error when they imagine that after Christ the civil laws of Moses are fatal to us.

We are not bound by the ceremonies of Moses either, much less by those of the pope. But because this life in the body cannot be completely without ceremonies and rituals, since there must be some sort of discipline, the Gospel permits ordinances to be established in the church regarding festivals, prescribed times, prescribed places, etc., so that the people may know on what day, at what time, and in what place they should gather to hear the Word of God. It permits the appointment of certain lessons, just as in school, especially for the sake of children and uneducated people, so that they can be taught more easily. But it permits such things to be established with the purpose that all things in the church should be done decently and in order (1 Cor. 14:40), not that those who observe such ordinances should merit the forgiveness of sins. Besides, they can be omitted without sinning, so long as this is done without offending the weak. Nor is it true that after Christ has been revealed, the ceremonies of Moses are fatal; otherwise Christians would sin when they observe the festivals of Easter and Pentecost, which the ancient church established on the basis of the example of the Law of Moses, although in a far different manner and for a different purpose.

But here Paul is speaking principally about the abrogation of the

[63] On this view of Moses cf. *Luther's Works,* 35, pp. 161—174.

Moral Law, and this should be considered carefully. He is arguing against the righteousness of the Law in order to establish the righteousness of faith, and he concludes: "If grace alone or faith in Christ justifies, then the entire Law has been completely abrogated." He supports this by the testimony of Isaiah, which invites the barren and desolate church to rejoice. She seems not to have any children of her own or any hope of having children. That is, she does not have disciples and does not receive any applause, because she preaches the Word of the cross about Christ the crucified, in opposition to all the wisdom of the flesh. "But, O barren one," says the prophet, "do not let any of this bother or disturb you. Rather exult and rejoice, for the desolate has more children than she who has a husband. That is, the one who has a husband and many children will grow ill. But you, the barren and desolate one, will abound with children."

Paul calls the church barren because her children are not born by means of the Law or works or any human efforts of powers but in the Holy Spirit through the Word of faith. This is purely a matter of being born, not of doing any works. Those who are prolific, on the other hand, labor and strain greatly in travail; this is purely a matter of doing works, not of giving birth. But those who try to achieve the status of sons and heirs by the righteousness of the Law or by their own righteousness are slaves, who will never receive the inheritance even though they work themselves to death with their great effort; for they are trying, contrary to the will of God, to achieve by their own works what God wants to grant to believers by sheer grace for Christ's sake. Believers do good works; but they do not become sons and heirs through this, for this has been granted to them by their birth. Now that they have become sons for Christ's sake, they glorify God with their good deeds and help their neighbor.

28. *Now we, brethren, like Isaac, are children of promise.*

That is to say: "We are not sons according to the flesh, like Ishmael. Nor are we like Israel, which also boasted of being the offspring of Abraham and the people of God but heard Christ say in John 8:39-40: 'If you were Abraham's children, you would not seek to kill Me, a man who has told you the truth'; and again (cf. John 8:42-44): 'If God were your Father, you would love Me and recognize My voice. Brothers born and reared in the same house recognize one another's voices, but you are of your father the devil.' We are not such children as they, who remain slaves and will be cast out of the house. We, like Isaac, are children of promise, that is, of grace and faith, born of the promise alone." This matter was discussed at sufficient length earlier, in chapter three (v. 8): "In your Offspring shall all the nations be blessed." Therefore we are pronounced righteous, not on the basis of the Law or of works or of our own righteousness but on the basis of pure grace. Paul insisted on the promise so vigorously and stressed it so often because he saw how necessary it is. So much about the allegory, to which he attached the passage from Isaiah as a kind of interpretation. Now he applies the story of Ishmael and Isaac for our instruction and comfort.

29. *But as at that time he who was born according to the flesh persecuted him who was born according to the Spirit, so it is now.*

This passage contains some very powerful comfort. All those who have been born and live in Christ, and who boast of their birth and inheritance from God, will have Ishmael as their persecutor. We are learning this today from our own experience. We see that everything is filled with tumults, persecutions, sects, and offenses. If we did not fortify our minds with this comfort from Paul and others like it, and if we did not hold fast to the doctrine of justification, we would not be able to bear the power and the wiles of Satan. For who would not be affected by the horrible persecutions from our opponents, or by the sects and endless offenses that the fanatical spirits are arousing today? It is especially saddening when we are forced to hear that before the Gospel came everything was tranquil and peaceful, but that since its discovery everything is in an uproar, and the whole world is in tumult and revolution.[64] When the nonspiritual man (1 Cor. 2:14) hears this, he is immediately offended and comes to the conclusion that the disobedience of subjects toward their magistrates; sedition, war, pestilence, hunger; the overthrow of states, regions, and kingdoms; sectarianism, scandals, and endless similar evils have all arisen from this teaching.

We must strengthen and support ourselves against this great offense with this sweet comfort, that in the world the godly must bear the name and reputation of being seditious, schismatic, and troublemakers. This is why our opponents think that they have a most righteous cause — in fact, that they are offering service to God (John 16:2) when they hate, persecute, and kill us. It cannot be otherwise, therefore, than that Ishmael will persecute Isaac; but Isaac does not per-

[64] See also *Luther's Works*, 12, pp. 6 ff., on this accusation.

secute Ishmael in turn. If someone does not want to endure persecution from Ishmael, let him not claim that he is a Christian.

But, I ask our opponents, who so magnify and exaggerate these
evils today, what were the good things that followed the preaching
of Christ and the apostles? The destruction of the Jewish kingdom,
the fall of the Roman Empire, and the upheaval of the whole world!
This was not the fault of the Gospel, which Christ and the apostles
preached for the salvation, not the destruction, of men. But, as Ps. 2
says, it was the guilt of the nations and peoples, of the kings and
princes, who were possessed by the devil and refused to listen to the
Word of grace, peace, life, and eternal salvation but despised and
condemned it as a dogma dangerous to both church and state. Long
before, the Holy Spirit, speaking through David, foretold this when
He said: "Why do the nations conspire, etc.?"

Such a tumult and disturbance is being seen and heard today as
well, and our opponents assign the blame to our teaching. But the
doctrine of peace is not arousing these troubles. It is the "nations,
peoples, kings, and rulers," as Ps. 2 says, who "conspire, plot, set
themselves, and take counsel," not against us, as they suppose, or
against our doctrine, which they accuse of being wrong and seditious,
but "against the Lord and against His Christ." Therefore all their
counsels and efforts are and will be in vain. "He who sits in the
heavens laughs; the Lord has them in derision." Let them shout as
long as they please that these troubles have been stirred up by us.
The psalm still comforts us and says that they are responsible for
these troubles. They do not believe this; much less do they believe
that they are raising a tumult, plotting, and taking counsel against
the Lord and against His Christ. In fact, they think they are taking
a stand on the Lord's side and are defending His glory, and that by
persecuting us they are offering service to God (John 16:2). But the
psalm does not lie, and the final outcome of the affair will prove this.
We for our part are not doing anything but suffering, while our conscience bears witness to us in the Holy Spirit. After all, the doctrine
on account of which such tumults and offenses are being stirred up
is not ours; it is Christ's. We cannot deny the doctrine or forsake its
defense; for Christ says (Mark 8:38): "Whoever is ashamed of Me
and of My words in this adulterous and sinful generation, of him
will the Son of Man also be ashamed."

Therefore anyone who wants to proclaim Christ and to confess
that He is our righteousness will immediately be forced to hear that

he is a "pestilent fellow" (Acts 24:5) who is stirring up everything. "These men who have turned the world upside down," the Jews said about Paul and Silas, "have come here also, and they are acting against the decrees of Caesar" (Acts 17:6-7). And in Acts 24:5: "We have found this man a pestilent fellow, an agitator among all the Jews throughout the world, and a ringleader of the sect of the Nazarenes." In a similar way the Gentiles complain in Acts 16:20: "These men are disturbing our city." Thus they are accusing me today of creating an uproar in the papacy and in the Roman Empire. If I kept silence, all the goods that the strong armed man possesses would be in peace (Luke 11:21); and the pope would not persecute me anymore. But then the Gospel of Christ would be obscured. On the other hand, if I speak out, the pope will be disturbed and overthrown. And so one must either lose the pope, who is temporal, or Christ, who is eternal, and eternal life with Him. But one should choose the lesser of two evils. Rather let the earthly and mortal pope be overthrown than the One who is heavenly and eternal!

When Christ foresaw in the spirit that a great disturbance and revolution in the world would follow His preaching, He comforted Himself this way (Luke 12:49): "I came to cast fire upon the earth; and would that it were already kindled!" Thus we see today that because of the persecution and blasphemy of our opponents and the contempt and ingratitude of the world many evils follow upon the preaching of the Gospel. This bothers us so much that we often think, according to the flesh, that it would have been better if the teaching of godliness had never been circulated and peace had been preserved than that the public peace should be disturbed as it has been since it was made public. But according to the Spirit, we courageously declare with Christ: "I came to cast fire upon the earth; and would that it were already kindled!" Once this fire has been kindled, great upheavals immediately arise. For it is not some king or emperor but the god of this world (2 Cor. 4:4) who is provoked; and he is a powerful spirit and the lord of the whole world. This great adversary is attacked by the weak Word that preaches Christ crucified. Feeling its divine power, Behemoth stirs up all his limbs, shakes his tail, and "makes the deep boil like a pot" (Job 41:31). This is the source of the tumult and uproar in the world.

Therefore we are not impressed when our opponents are offended and shout that no good will come of the preaching of the Gospel. They are blind, faithless, and stubborn; therefore it is impossible for them to see any of the benefits and results of the Gospel. On the other hand, we who believe see the enormous and innumerable benefits and results of the Gospel, even though outwardly and temporarily we are oppressed by many evils, despised, despoiled, slandered, condemned, the περίψημα of all things (1 Cor. 4:4), put to death, and inwardly crushed by the consciousness of our sin and vexed by demons. For we are alive in Christ, in whom and through whom we are kings and lords over sin, death, the flesh, the world, hell, and every evil; through Him we tread underfoot that dragon and basilisk [65] who is the king of sin and death. How? In faith. For our blessing has not yet been revealed. But meanwhile we await it in patience and yet already possess it certainly through faith.

Therefore the doctrine of justification must be learned diligently; it alone can strengthen us against those endless offenses and comfort us in all trials and persecutions. For we see that it cannot be otherwise than that the world should be offended by the teaching of godliness and continually cry that nothing good will come of it. "The unspiritual man does not perceive the gifts of the Spirit of God" (1 Cor. 2:14). All he sees are the outward troubles, the upheavals, revolutions, slaughters, sects, etc. He is offended by the sight of all this, becomes blind, and falls into contempt and blasphemy of the Word.

We, on the other hand, should feel comforted, because our opponents are not accusing and condemning us for manifest crimes like adultery, murder, robbery, etc., but for our teaching. Now what is it that we teach? That Christ, the Son of God, redeemed us from our sins and from eternal death by His death on the cross. Therefore they are attacking, not our lives but our teaching. And this is not ours; it is Christ's. Therefore it is Christ's fault that they attack us; and the sin for which our opponents persecute us was committed, not by us but by Christ. But let them see to it whether they will evict Christ from heaven for this sin, if God please, of being our only Justifier and Savior, and whether they will condemn Him as a heretic and revolutionary! We shall commend this cause of His to Him; and we shall watch and see, happy and secure, who will win, Christ or they. According to the flesh, of course, we are sorry that they, our Ishmaelites, hate and persecute us so furiously. But according to the spirit, we boast of our afflictions, both because we know that we are not bearing them on account of our sins but are bearing them on account

[65] The basilisk or cockatrice was a mythical reptile hatched by a serpent from a cock's egg; cf. Pliny, *Natural History*, VIII, 21, 33.

of Christ, whose goodness and glory we illuminate, and because Paul fortifies us here and says that Ishmael must taunt and persecute Isaac.

The passage from Gen. 21 about Ishmael's persecuting Isaac is interpreted by the Jews to mean that Ishmael was forcing Isaac to commit idolatry. I do not disapprove of their interpretation.[66] Still I do not believe that the idolatry was as crass as the Jews imagine, namely, that Ishmael fashioned images out of mud in a heathen way and forced Isaac to worship these. Abraham would never have stood for this. I think that Ishmael was a saintly man in outward appearance, like Cain, who also persecuted his brother and finally killed him, not because of something physical but chiefly because he saw that God preferred his brother to him (Gen. 4:4-5). Therefore Ishmael was devoted to his religion, offering sacrifices and being busy with good works. He made fun of his brother Isaac and wanted to seem superior to him on two counts, both because of worship and religion and because of his civic dominance and his inheritance. He seemed to have the right to claim this, for he thought that since he was the first-born, both the priesthood and the kingship belonged to him by divine right. Therefore he persecuted Isaac spiritually on account of religion and physically on account of the inheritance.

Whenever the teaching of the Gospel flourishes in the church, there is always this persecution, that the sons according to the flesh persecute the sons according to the promise. Today we endure persecution from our Ishmaelites, the papists and the fanatical spirits, for this one reason, that we teach that righteousness comes through the promise, not through works. The papists persecute us because we do not worship their idols; that is, we do not preach that the righteousness, the works, and the forms of worship invented and instituted by men avail to obtain grace and the forgiveness of sins. They also try to cast us out of the house. That is, they boast that they are the church, the sons of God, and the people of God, and that the inheritance belongs to them. On the other hand, they excommunicate us as heretics and revolutionaries; and if they can, they kill us as an act of service to God (John 16:2). As much as they can, therefore, they cast us completely out of this life and out of that which is to come. The fanatical spirits, for their part, hate us bitterly for attacking and rejecting their errors and heresies, the innovations they are planting in the church. These men, and especially the Anabaptists,

---

[66] Luther translated Gen. 21:9: . . . *dasz er ein Spötter war.*

regard us as much worse than the papists; therefore they hate us more bitterly than they hate them.[67]

As soon as the Word of God appears, the devil becomes angry; and in his anger he employs every power and wile to persecute it and wipe it out completely. Therefore it cannot be otherwise than that he should stir up endless sects and offenses, persecution and slaughter. For he is the father of lies and a murderer (John 8:44); he plants his lies in the world through false teachers, and he murders men through tyrants. Thus he occupies both realms, the spiritual and the temporal: the former through the lies of wicked teachers — to say nothing of how he continually urges everyone individually to heresies and ungodly opinions with his flaming darts (Eph. 6:16) — and the latter through the tyrants' sword. And so on both sides the father of lies and of murder stirs up spiritual and physical persecution against the children of the free woman. The spiritual persecution, by which the fanatics attack us today, is the more vexing and unbearable, because of the offenses with which the devil distorts our teaching; for we are forced to hear that the sects of the Anabaptists and of the Sacramentarians and all other evils have arisen from our teaching.[68] The physical persecution, when the tyrants lie in ambush for our possessions and our bodies, is much more bearable, because it is due, not to our sins but to our confession of the Word of God. Therefore let us learn from the very name of the devil as "father of lies and murderer" — which Christ ascribes to him in John 8:44 — that as long as the Gospel flourishes and Christ reigns, it is necessary for such sects of perdition to arise and for everything to be filled with the raging of murderers who persecute the truth. Anyone who does not know this will be very easily offended; he will forsake the true God and true faith and will return to his old god and to his old faith.

Therefore Paul is fortifying the godly here, so that they are not offended by those persecutions, sects, and scandals. He says: "As at that time he who was born according to the flesh etc."; as though he were to say: "If we are sons born according to the spirit, we must certainly expect persecution from our brother who was born according to the flesh. That is, it is not only the obviously wicked enemies who will persecute us. But even those who were our dear friends at

[67] See also *Luther's Works*, 23, pp. 187—188.

[68] On the relation of Luther's Reformation to the rise of other movements cf. *Luther's Works*, 21, p. 257, note 26.

first, with whom we lived as a family in the same house, who received the teaching of the Gospel from us — they eventually become our bitterest enemies, who persecute us ruthlessly because they are our brethren according to the flesh, who must persecute their brethren born according to the spirit." So Christ complains about Judas in Ps. 41:9: "Even My bosom friend, in whom I trusted, who ate of My bread, has lifted his heel against Me." But our comfort is that we have not given our Ishmaelites any reason to persecute us. The papists persecute us on account of our godly teaching; if we recanted this, they would stop persecuting us immediately. Similarly, if we were to approve the wicked errors of the fanatics, they would applaud us. But because we detest the ungodliness of both parties, they cannot do anything but hate and persecute us bitterly.

But it is not only Paul who fortifies us against this persecution and these offenses, as I have said; but Christ Himself comforts us very sweetly in John 15:19. "If you were of the world," He says, "the world would love its own; but because you are not of the world, but I chose you out of the world, therefore the world hates you." It is as though He were to say: "I am the cause of all the persecutions that you bear; and if you are killed, the responsibility for your death will be Mine. For if you did not preach My Word and confess Me, the world would not persecute you. Nevertheless, you are being treated properly. A servant is not greater than his master (John 13:16). If they persecuted Me, they will persecute you also, because of My name."

With these words Christ transfers all the guilt to Himself and sets us free from every fear, as though He were to say: "The reason why the world persecutes you with violence and with craft is not you yourselves but My name, which you preach and confess. But be of good cheer; I have overcome the world (John 16:33)." We are sustained by this confidence; and we have no doubt that Christ is powerful enough not only to sustain us but to conquer all the power of the oppressors and the wiles of the heretics. He gave ample evidence of this in the case of the Jews and the Romans, whose fierceness and persecution He once bore. He had to bear the wiles of the heretics also; but in time all of them were overthrown and destroyed, and He remained the King and the Victor. Regardless of how much the papists rage today or of how the sectarians distort and corrupt the Gospel of Christ, Christ will remain King forever, and the Word of the Lord will stand forever (1 Peter 1:25); and all

His enemies will be annihilated. In addition, it is very comforting that the persecution of Isaac by Ishmael will not last forever but will continue only for a short time, at the end of which the sentence will be pronounced, as follows:

30. *But what does the Scripture say? Cast out the slave and her son; for the son of the slave shall not inherit with the son of the free woman.*

This statement of Sarah's was certainly distressing to Abraham. Undoubtedly when he heard it, his fatherly feeling for his son Ishmael was aroused; for he had been born of his body. Scripture testifies to this in Gen. 21:11-12 when it says: "The thing was very displeasing to Abraham on account of his son." But God confirmed the sentence pronounced by Sarah and said to Abraham: "Be not displeased because of the lad and because of your slave woman. Whatever Sarah says to you, do as she tells you; for through Isaac shall your descendants be named."

Here the Ishmaelites hear a sentence pronounced against them that overthrows the Jews, the Greeks, the Romans, etc., who persecuted the church of Christ. It will also overthrow the papists and all other self-righteous people, whoever they may be, who boast today that they are the people of God and the church; they hope that they will surely receive the inheritance, and they judge that we who depend on the promise of God are not only barren and desolate but heretics who have been cast out of the church and cannot be sons and heirs. But God turns this judgment of theirs upside down and pronounces the sentence on them that because they are sons of the slave woman and persecute the sons of the free woman, they are to be cast out of the house and are not to share the inheritance with the sons of the promise, to whom, as sons of the free woman, the promise belongs exclusively. This sentence is legitimate, and it is irrevocable; for "Scripture cannot be broken" (John 10:35). Therefore it will most certainly happen that our Ishmaelites will not only lose the authority they have in both church and state but eternal life as well. For Scripture has foretold that the sons of the slave woman are to be cast out of the house, that is, out of the kingdom of grace, because they cannot inherit with the sons of the free woman.

Now it should be noted that the Holy Spirit insults the people of the Law and of works here by calling them "sons of the slave woman." It is as though He were to say: "Why do you boast about

the righteousness of the Law and of works and brag that on its
account you are the people and the children of God? If you do not
know whence you have your birth, I will tell you. You were born
as slaves and of a slave woman. What sort of slaves? Of the Law,
sin, death, and eternal damnation. A slave is not an heir but is
cast out of the house." Therefore the pope, with all his regime and
whatever other self-righteous people there are, regardless of how
saintly they may be in appearance, who trust they will obtain grace
and salvation through laws human or divine — all of them are sons
of the slave woman who will not inherit with the sons of the free
woman but will be cast out of the house. And I am not speaking
now about the ungodly monks, who worshiped their belly as god
(Phil. 3:19) and committed horrible sins that I would just as soon
not mention, but about the best of them, to whom I and many others
belonged, who lived holy lives and tried with might and main to
appease the wrath of God and to merit the forgiveness of sins and
eternal life by the observances of their religious order. These men
must now hear the sentence that the sons of the slave woman are
to be cast out of the house together with the slave woman, their
mother.

When they are carefully considered, such sentences provide us
with certainty and reassurance regarding the doctrine and the righteousness of faith, in opposition to the doctrine and the righteousness
of works. The world embraces and praises the latter, and it despises
and condemns the former. This, of course, is disturbing and offensive
to timid souls, who, even when they see the wickedness and the
unspeakable crimes of the papists publicly exposed, cannot be easily
persuaded that the whole multitude bearing the name and title of
"the church" are in error and that only a few believe correctly about
the doctrine of faith. If the papacy still had the sanctity and austerity
of life that it had at the time of fathers like Jerome, Ambrose,
Augustine, and others, when the clergy did not yet have an evil
reputation for simony, extravagance, pleasures, wealth, adultery,
sodomy, and countless other sins but lived in accordance with the
canons and decrees of the fathers, outwardly religious and holy, and
even practiced celibacy — what, I ask you, would we have been able
to do against the papacy?

Celibacy, which the clergy observed rigorously at the time of
the fathers, is a remarkable thing in the eyes of the world, a thing
that makes a man into an angel. Hence Paul calls it "religion of

angels" in Col. 2:18, and the papists sing about virgins: "He led an angelic life in the flesh, for he lived beyond the flesh." [69] And the so-called "contemplative life," to which the clergy were very devoted then at the cost of all their civic and domestic responsibilities, also presents an impressive front of sanctity. Therefore if the outward appearance of the ancient papacy were still standing, we would accomplish very little against it with our doctrine about faith, especially because we are accomplishing very little against it now, when that primitive reputation for piety and strict discipline has vanished and when all that is evident in the papacy are the dregs and bilge of every vice.

But even if the religion and discipline of the papacy stood now as it did once, we would still have to follow the example of Paul, who attacked the false apostles despite their holy and virtuous fronts, and battle against the self-righteousness of the papal kingdom, saying: "Regardless of how celibate a life you lead or how you conduct yourselves in humility and the religion of angels or how you wear out your bodies with frequent discipline, you are slaves of the Law, of sin, and of the devil; and you will be cast out of the house, because you seek righteousness and salvation through your own works, not through Christ."

Therefore we should pay attention not so much to the sinful lives of the papists as to their wicked doctrine and their hypocrisy, and this is what we chiefly attack. Let us suppose that the religion and the discipline of the ancient papacy were flourishing now and were being observed with the same rigor with which the hermits, Jerome, Augustine, Gregory, Bernard, Francis, Dominic, and many others observed it. We would still have to say: "If you have nothing to set against the wrath and judgment of God except your sanctity and the chastity of your lives, you are clearly sons of the slave woman, who must be cast out of the kingdom of heaven and condemned." Satan does not defend the wicked lives of the papists either — which the more wholesome among them also despise — but he fights to defend and preserve their hypocrisy and work-righteousness. Here he cites the authority of the councils and the examples of the holy fathers, whom he declares to have been the founders of the holy orders and statutes. Therefore we are fighting today, not against the obvious wickedness and vice of the papacy but against its fictitious saints, who think that they lead an angelic life when they observe

[69] The Latin is *Angelicam vitam duxerat in carne, dum praeter carnem vixerat.*

not only the commandments of God but also the counsels of Christ and works that are not required or works of supererogation. We say that this is a waste of time and effort, unless they have grasped that "one thing" which Christ says is the only thing "needful" and, like Mary, have chosen the good portion, which cannot be taken away from them (Luke 10:42).

That is what Bernard did. He was a man so pious, holy, and chaste that I think he deserves to be put ahead of all other monks. Once, when he was gravely ill and despaired of his life, he did not place his trust in the celibacy that he had observed so chastely, or in the good works and acts of piety that he had performed in such quantity; but he put all these far from sight and took hold of the blessing of Christ by faith, saying: "I have lived damnably. But Thou, O Lord Jesus Christ, hast a double right to the kingdom of heaven: first, because Thou art the Son of God; secondly, because Thou hast won it by Thy passion and death. The first Thou dost keep for Thyself by Thy birthright; the latter Thou dost grant to me by the right, not of works but of grace." [70] He did not set his monkery or his angelic life against the wrath and judgment of God but took hold of the one thing that is needful and thus was saved. I believe that Jerome, Gregory, and many other fathers and hermits were saved the same way. There is no doubt that in the Old Testament also many kings of Israel and other idolaters were saved in a similar way, casting away their vain trust in idols at the hour of their death and taking hold of the promise of God regarding the future Offspring of Abraham, the Christ, who was to bless all nations. And if any of the papists are to be saved today, they must depend, not on their own good works and merits but solely on the mercy of God offered to us in Christ; and they must say with Paul (Phil. 3:9): "I do not have a righteousness of my own, based on Law, but that which is through faith in Christ."

31. *So, brethren, we are not children of the slave but of the free woman.*

Here Paul concludes the allegory. "We are not," he says, "children of the slave." That is: We are not under the Law, which gives birth into slavery, which terrifies, accuses, and leads to despair. But we are free of it through Christ; therefore it cannot terrify and condemn us, as we have pointed out in detail earlier. Moreover,

[70] Cf. p. 370, note 9.

regardless of how much the children of the slave woman persecute us for a time, our comfort is still that they will finally be thrown into the outer darkness (Matt. 8:12) and be forced to leave to us the inheritance that belongs to us as children of the free woman.

As we have heard, Paul found in the words "children of the free woman and of the slave" a wonderful opportunity to argue in support of the doctrine of justification. And he deliberately took hold of this word "free" and urged and developed it also in what follows. From it he took the occasion to discuss Christian liberty, the knowledge of which is extremely necessary. For the pope has completely destroyed it and has subjected the church to a miserable and bitter slavery by means of human traditions and ceremonies. The liberty that has been granted to us through Christ is today our chief defense against the tyranny of the pope. Therefore the doctrine of Christian liberty must be carefully considered, both to support the doctrine of justification and to encourage and comfort our consciences against the many disturbances and offenses which, as our opponents claim, have arisen from the Gospel. Now Christian liberty is a completely spiritual matter. The unspiritual man does not understand it (1 Cor. 2:14). In fact, even those who have the first fruits of the Spirit (Rom. 8:23) and who can discourse about it at great length have difficulty keeping it in their hearts. To reason it appears to be a matter of little importance. Therefore unless the Spirit magnifies it and adds weight to it, it will be despised.

Index

By WALTER A. HANSEN

[463]

Christian(s) 5, 10, 11, 23, 26, 35, 45, 81, 97, 100, 120, 124, 130, 133, 134, 139, 157, 159, 163, 170, 171, 172, 178, 188, 200, 214, 217, 232, 233, 241, 248, 256, 277, 290 fn., 294, 326, 334, 340, 341, 342, 343, 344, 358, 373, 376, 380, 391, 392, 394, 424, 440, 445, 447, 448, 451
remains in pure humility 235
wisdom of 6
Christianity 26, 85, 91, 106, 114, 118, 189, 283, 301
chief doctrine of 139
true meaning of 126, 131, 136
Christmas 411
Church(es) 10, 15, 19, 20, 22, 23, 24, 25, 26, 31, 46, 50, 51, 52, 53, 57, 58, 63, 65, 66, 67, 68, 69, 71, 75, 76, 77, 78, 79, 81, 86, 87, 88, 89, 93, 99, 100, 101, 105, 106, 108, 109, 113, 115, 117, 120, 125, 136, 140, 145, 152, 174, 186, 187, 188, 200, 208, 222, 245, 257, 281, 285, 296, 302, 313, 330, 375, 377, 378, 402, 407, 409, 414, 418, 424, 426, 428, 441, 442, 443, 444, 446, 451, 454, 457, 458, 461
abuses in 223
ancient 448
barren and desolate 449
Christian 45
militant 439, 440
of pope 388
of Rome 24, 411

papal 408
primitive 204, 374
Roman 385
triumphant 429, 440
twofold nature of 389
Church year 106 fn.
Cicero 44 fn., 123, 296, 354, 385, 403 fn., 424 fn.
Cilicia 78
Circumcision 7, 52, 53, 59, 60, 61, 68, 78, 79, 81, 82, 83, 84, 85, 86, 87, 89, 91, 92, 95, 101, 102, 104, 105, 111, 112, 120, 121, 122, 123, 138, 145, 152, 181, 204, 206, 211, 236, 237, 242, 243, 247, 299, 330, 354, 401, 411, 433
Citizen 141
Clergy 46, 296, 458, 459
special 106 fn.
Clothing 96, 170, 171, 284, 311, 363, 407
of sin 352
sheep's 407, 424, 425
Cochlaeus, Johannes 238 fn.
Cockatrice 453 fn.
Coena Domini, bull 45 fn.
Coffin 157
Colossians 30, 371
Comfort 7, 24, 32, 35, 42, 48, 64, 108, 109, 113, 153, 161, 162, 167, 195, 276, 278, 279, 280, 283, 292, 306, 316, 329, 337, 341, 351, 353, 357, 369, 371, 372, 380, 381, 384, 386, 393, 440, 450, 456, 461
of conscience 5, 52, 445
Commentarius in Epistolam S. Pauli ad Galatas, by Jerome 24 fn., 47 fn., 61 fn., 68 fn., 69 fn., 74 fn.,

77 fn., 84 fn., 92 fn., 103 fn., 107 fn., 249 fn., 275 fn., 276 fn., 362 fn., 367 fn., 418 fn.
Commentary on Ecclesiastes, by Luther 386 fn.
Communion 412
Condemnation 58, 235, 236, 447
of sins 133
Condignity 124, 125, 126, 127, 131, 134, 135, 175, 176, 181, 183, 291, 293, 301, 330, 374, 375
Confessio Bohemica 70 fn.
Confession 154, 182 fn.
Confusion 48
of conscience 323
satanic and infernal 117
Confutation of the Augsburg Confession 137 fn.
Congruity 124, 125, 126, 127, 130, 131, 134, 135, 172, 173, 175, 176, 181, 182, 183, 209, 219, 230, 291, 293, 301, 330, 374, 375
Connotation 144
Conscience(s) 8, 9, 11, 20, 26, 29, 30, 35, 37, 38, 45, 51, 52, 54, 55, 60, 63, 67, 72, 76, 85, 86, 89, 91, 92, 109, 110, 113, 114, 115, 116, 117, 118, 120, 133, 134, 138, 139, 140, 148, 150, 151, 152, 158, 162, 164, 180, 182, 215, 218, 220, 221, 224, 225, 249, 259, 286, 301, 302, 309, 313, 314, 317, 318, 322, 327, 338, 341, 342, 345, 349,

350, 354, 356, 358,
361, 362, 363, 364,
365, 366, 369, 371,
375, 377, 379, 386,
387, 389, 390, 391,
392, 393, 403, 405,
406, 408, 409, 411,
414, 429, 437, 443,
444, 445, 447, 448,
461
afflictions and terrors
of 5, 161
anguish of 310
comfort of 5, 52
conflict(s) of 10, 72,
166, 315, 381
confusion of 323
damage to 217
enslavement of 410
evil 439
free 82, 97
freedom of 90, 93
joyful 27, 212, 440
justification of 216
justified 159
peace of 28, 31, 149,
339
quiet 26, 27
remorse of 70, 232
sting and remorse of
33
struggle(s) of 36, 324,
357
suffering 306
terrified 5
timid 32
troubled 39, 44, 133,
195, 290, 305
Conscientia 10 fn.
Consciousness of sin 10
Consolation 25, 32, 37,
39, 54, 64, 77, 96,
133
Consul 95
Contrition 154, 182 fn.
Controversy, Luther's
with Erasmus 323 fn.
Conversion 75, 171
Converts 110
Cook 128, 329
Cookies 417
Corinth 23, 63
Corinthians 24, 371, 426

Cornelius 204, 205, 206,
207, 209, 210, 211,
239
Corpus Catholicorum
57 fn.
Couch 157, 158, 163
Council of Chalcedon
273 fn.
Covetousness 40
Cow 191, 192, 194, 263
Cowl(s) 29, 85, 91, 92,
175, 185, 199, 238,
259, 295
conceals many a rascal
256
Craftsman 264
Creator 13, 22, 31, 32,
66, 107, 128, 259,
292, 297, 314, 392,
431
Creed 31, 278, 280
Cretans 188
Crete 81
Cribro aquam haurire
406 fn.
Crucifixion 165
Cruciger, Caspar ix
Custodian 304, 338, 345,
346, 347, 348, 349,
350, 351, 359, 360,
361
Cyprian, St. 66

Damascus 62, 74, 75, 77,
78, 125
Damnation 48, 94, 147,
151, 277, 310, 313,
314, 333, 335, 337,
347, 362, 363, 404,
411, 458
Danaides 406 fn.
Danaus, daughters of 406
Daniel 200
David 95, 108, 109, 133,
260, 263, 277, 280,
293, 322, 387, 451
Days 411
astrological 410
observance of 410, 412
religious 410
De arte cabbalistica, by
Johannes Reuchlin
290 fn.

De correptione et gratia,
by St. Augustine
214 fn.
De doctrina Christiana,
by St. Augustine
92 fn.
De lana caprina 106 fn.
De Oratore, by Cicero
424 fn.
De Trinitate, by St. Augustine 377 fn.
Deacceptare 131 fn.
Death 8, 9, 10, 13, 14,
21, 22, 27, 28, 30,
31, 32, 35, 36, 37,
39, 46, 48, 49, 55,
60, 64, 65, 72, 91,
109, 113, 125, 126,
127, 134, 137, 138,
139, 141, 147, 148,
149, 150, 151, 153,
156, 157, 159, 160,
161, 163, 164, 165,
166, 167, 168, 170,
175, 177, 178, 213,
224, 229, 233, 237,
246, 247, 251, 253,
257, 258, 262, 267,
275, 278, 280, 281,
282, 283, 284, 285,
286, 287, 288, 290,
291, 293, 295, 299,
308, 309, 311, 313,
314, 317, 318, 320,
324, 327, 331, 332,
333, 335, 338, 339,
341, 347, 355, 356,
361, 365, 366, 368,
370, 371, 372, 373,
380, 382, 386, 388,
389, 390, 391, 392,
396, 397, 399, 404,
407, 419, 420, 421,
426, 437, 438, 439,
440, 441, 442, 443,
449, 456, 458
agony of 357, 405, 445
danger of 5
eternal 5, 10, 11, 26,
29, 36, 42, 77, 88,
146, 152, 179, 218,
235, 236, 252, 254,
256, 292, 310, 325,

INDEX TO SCRIPTURE PASSAGES

3:8 — 21
4:4-6 — 356
4:8 — 155, 371
4:11 — 19
4:13 — 442
4:22 — 167, 352
4:23-24 — 431
5:27 — 233
5:30 — 168, 357
6:12 — 51
6:13 ff. — 283
6:16 — 65, 285, 381, 418, 455

Philippians

1:23 — 393
2:3 — 224
2:7 — 284
2:8 — 171, 175, 370
2:15 — 24
2:27 — 421
3:5-6 — 68
3:8 — 41
3:8-9 — 154
3:9 — 460
3:19 — 458
3:20 — 439
4:7 — 293

Colossians

1:2 — 101
1:13 — 14, 42
2:3 — 30
2:9 — 30
2:14 — 38, 349
2:14-15 — 161, 325
2:15 — 9, 282, 371, 372
2:16 — 411
3:9 — 352
3:10 — 431

1 Thessalonians

1:5 — 179
5:17 — 51

2 Thessalonians

1:8 — 428
2:3 — 335
2:4 — 24, 25, 180, 258, 259, 408

1 Timothy

1:5 — 147, 269
1:6 — 131
1:8 — 180, 306, 409
1:9 — 344
2:5 — 236
3:7 — 307
4:1 — 80, 140, 152, 199, 364

2 Timothy

1:10 — 282
1:15 — 426
2:10 — 306
2:15 — 302
2:25 ff. — 6
4:2 — 186

Titus

1:5 — 81
1:5 ff. — 17
1:12 — 188
1:15 — 265
1:16 — 258
3:5 — 228, 352, 353

Hebrews

1:2 — 319
2:2 — 318
6:4-6 — 197
6:6 — 199
7:25 — 11
9:5 — 273
9:12 — 132, 360
10:20 — 232
11 — 263, 267
11:4 — 263, 264, 294
11:5 — 264
11:6 — 264
11:8 — 264
12:11 — 416
12:21 — 320
12:29 — 311
13:4 — 351
13:8 — 361

James

1:22 — 203
1:23-24 — 65
2:19 — 168

1 Peter

1:25 — 54, 66, 444, 456
2:9 — 394
2:10 — 101
2:13-14 — 448
2:16 — 344
2:21 — 165, 352
2:22 — 189, 370
2:24 — 126
5:4 — 24
5:8 — 3, 46, 193, 380, 428

2 Peter

1:4 — 100
1:9 — 71
1:10 — 260
2:1 — 135, 201, 258
2:22 — 283
3:16 — 169
3:18 — 351

1 John

2:2 — 238, 431
3:2 — 274
3:9 — 8
4:1 — 331
4:4 — 193
5:4 — 31, 282, 369
5:4-5 — 162
5:16 — 197
5:19 — 40, 348

Revelation

2:9 — 52
10:3 — 391
12:9 — 192
21:1 — 235
22:11 — 428

APOCRYPHA

Ecclesiasticus

18:7 — 3
37:22-23 — 64

Prayer of Manasses

9 — 36